TimeOut

Stockholm

timeout.com/stockholm

Published by Time Out Guides Ltd, a wholly owned subsidiary of Time Out Group Ltd.
Time Out and the Time Out logo are trademarks of Time Out Group Ltd.

© Time Out Group Ltd 2005
Previous edition 2003

10 9 8 7 6 5 4 3 2 1

This edition first published in Great Britain in 2005 by Ebury
Ebury is a division of The Random House Group Ltd,
20 Vauxhall Bridge Road, London SW1V 2SA

Random House Australia Pty Limited, 20 Alfred Street, Milsons Point, Sydney, New South Wales 2061, Australia
Random House New Zealand Limited, 18 Poland Road, Glenfield, Auckland 10, New Zealand
Random House South Africa (Pty) Limited, Endulini, 5A Jubilee Road, Parktown 2193, South Africa

Random House UK Limited Reg. No. 954009

Distributed in USA by Publishers Group West
1700 Fourth Street, Berkeley, California 94710

Distributed in Canada by Penguin Canada Ltd
10 Alcorn Avenue, Toronto, Ontario, Canada M4V 3B2

For further distribution details, see www.timeout.com

ISBN 1-904978-28-2

A CIP catalogue record for this book is available from the British Library

Colour reprographics by Icon, Crowne House, 56-58 Southwark Street, London SE1 1UN

Printed and bound by Cayfosa-Quebecor, Ctra. De Caldes, KM 3 08 130 Sta, Perpètua de Mogoda, Barcelona, Spain

Time Out Guides Limited
Universal House
251 Tottenham Court Road
London W1T 7AB
Tel + 44 (0)20 7813 3000
Fax + 44 (0)20 7813 6001
Email guides@timeout.com
www.timeout.com

Editorial

Editor Ismay Atkins
Consultant Editor Chad Henderson
Deputy Editors Dominic Earle, Christi Daugherty
Listings Checker Victoria Hesselius
Proofreaders Angela Jameson Potts, Adam Barnes
Indexer Cathy Heath

Editorial/Managing Director Peter Fiennes
Series Editor Ruth Jarvis
Deputy Series Editor Lesley McCave
Business Manager Gareth Garner
Guides Co-ordinator Anna Norman/Holly Pick
Accountants Sarah Bostock, Abdus Sadique

Design

Art Director Mandy Martin
Deputy Art Director Scott Moore
Senior Designer Tracey Ridgewell
Designer Oliver Knight
Junior Designer Chrissy Mouncey
Digital Imaging Dan Conway
Ad Make-up Charlotte Blythe

Picture Desk

Picture Editor Jael Marschner
Deputy Picture Editor Tracey Kerrigan
Picture Researcher Ivy Lahon

Advertising

Sales Director Mark Phillips
International Sales Manager Ross Canadé
International Sales Executive James Tuson
Advertising Sales (Stockholm) Arenholm
Advertising Assistant Lucy Butler

Marketing

Marketing Director, Guides Mandy Martinez
US Publicity & Marketing Associate Rosella Albanese

Production

Production Director Mark Lamond
Production Controller Samantha Furniss

Time Out Group

Chairman Tony Elliott
Managing Director Mike Hardwick
Group Financial Director Richard Waterlow
Group Commercial Director Lesley Gill
Group Marketing Director Christine Cort
Group General Manager Nichola Coulthard
Group Circulation Director Jim Heinemann
Group Art Director John Oakey
Online Managing Director David Pepper
Group Production Director Steve Proctor
Group IT Director Simon Chappell

Contributors

Features in this guide were written and researched by:
Introduction Ismay Atkins. **History** James Savage (*Stockholm syndrome*, *Exodus* Chad Henderson). **Stockholm Today** James Savage. **Architecture** Tanis Bestland Malminen. **Design** David Bartal. **Where to Stay** Stephen Whitlock. **Sightseeing: Introduction** Chad Henderson, Victoria Hesselius. **Gamla Stan** Chad Henderson (*A walk in Gamla Stan* Maria Lindberg Howard, Roger Howard). **Norrmalm & Vasastaden** Chad Henderson (*Concrete calamity* Tanis Bestland Malminen). **Djurgården & Skeppsholmen** Chad Henderson (*Vasa: the acid test* Elizabeth Dacey). **Södermalm & Långholmen** Elizabeth Dacey (*SoFo* Anders Modig). **Östermalm & Gärdet** Christine Demsteader. **Kungsholmen** Christine Demsteader (*Peace man?* Chad Henderson, Christi Daugherty). **Further Afield** Michele Jiménez (*Dead famous* Elizabeth Dacey). **Restaurants** Amy Brown, Ivar Ekman. **Bars** Jonas Leijonhufvud (*Up in smoke* Christi Daugherty). **Cafés** Christine Demsteader. **Shops & Services** Stephen Whitlock (*Fashion & Fashion accessories* Kicki Norman; *Pure glass* Anders Modig; *Booze rules* Chad Henderson). **Festivals & Events** Amy Brown. **Children** Lisa Del Papa. **Clubs** Kristoffer Poppius. **Film** Anna Boreson, Mark Standley. **Galleries** Frida Cornell (*A developing scene* Anders Modig). **Gay & Lesbian** Stephen Whitlock. **Music** Rock, Pop & Jazz Kristoffer Poppius. *Classical Music & Opera* Tobias Niélsen. **Theatre & Dance** Sanna Björling (*Anarchy in August* Claudia Martin). **Trips Out of Town** Jenny Egeland (*Island dreams*, *Islands at war* James Savage; *Way up north* Chad Henderson). **Directory** Victoria Hesselius (*Vocabulary* Claudia Martin; *Further Reference* Claudia Martin, Ismay Atkins, Chad Henderson). **Additional listings checking** Anna-Lena Jönsson.

The Editor would like to thank Sylvie Kjellin at Stockholm Information Service, Cathy Phillips, Ros Atkins, Sara Northey, Dominic Thomas, Carina Blomqvist of the Stockholm Police, Åsa Karlsson at Nordic Light Hotel, Marie Holhammar at Hotel Rival, Sofie Janeck at Hotell Diplomat, Vibeke Stadling at Hotel Birger Jarl, Desiré Kjellberg at First Hotell Reisen and Jesper Tengblad at SL.

Maps JS Graphics (john@jsgraphics.co.uk).

Photography by Matthew Lea, except: pages 10, 13 AKG; page 16 Bridgeman Art Library; pages 19, 26, 185, 270, 272 Corbis; page 21 Scanpix, Camerapress; page 23 www.imagebank.sweden.se (c) Olof Holdar/Stockholm Visitors Board; pages 24, 242 Alamy; pages 60, 227 Images of Sweden; page 68 Stockholms Stadsmuseum; pages 78, 79 Copyright National Museum; pages 83, 184 Elan Fleisher; page 121 Wolfgang Kleinschmidt; pages 182, 186 Swedish National Tourist Board; page 197 Nordisk Film; page 204 Elisabeth Ohlson Wallin; page 237 Peter Strom, page 268 Magnus Uggla, Nordic Photos. The following images were provided by the featured establishment/artist: pages 36, 39, 40, 105, 217, 236, 238.

Contents

Introduction

We expect you've heard the scare stories about Stockholm's bitter climate and the extortionate price of beer. (Neither of which we can wholeheartedly deny, though we would venture so far as to say that, in more general terms, Stockholm is no more expensive than London or Paris, and the winters may be bitter but the summers are sensationally sweet.) These two minus points out of the way, you are in for a treat.

Perched on 14 islands at the point where Lake Mälaren empties into the Baltic Sea, Stockholm is a breathtaking beauty. Twinkling, panoramic vistas greet you around every corner; the waters are so clear and unpolluted that there are swimming spots dotted around the city and fishermen haul in their catch just off Drottninggatan, the equivalent of London's Oxford Street. In addition to the city's ample natural beauty, Stockholmers are so obsessed with designer living that everything from the airport to the park bench – and, since we're on the subject, the Swedes themselves – seems to be good-looking.

In short, Stockholm is positively generous on the eye. But it is also a city of substance. Culture pangs can be sated at over 100 art galleries and 70 museums – impressive stats when you consider that its population is roughly one seventh the size of London's – among them the newly reopened Moderna Museet (Modern Art Museum) and the world-class Vasamuseet.

Considered something of a barometer of cool by people who like to measure such things, Stockholm is a voguish, forward-thinking city, whose inhabitants seem determined to keep their finger right on the pulse, in spite of its out-of-the-way Nordic location. Just clock the number of glossy Swedish (and pan-Nordic) lifestyle mags lining the shelves at the city's newsagents, or the calculated cool clothing sported by young Stockholmers.

Yet, despite being a terribly trendy, high-tech kind of place, Stockholm (and Sweden in general) is simultaneously a hotbed of time-honoured traditions. The result is a curious merger: cutting-edge technology and design meet fervently celebrated folk traditions (such as maypole dancing at Midsummer and crayfish parties under a full moon in August), along with what amounts to an entire seasonal culinary code.

Sweden has evolved from a nation with minimal restaurant culture into a little-known hotspot for foodies. This is particularly true of the capital; 21st-century Stockholm is brimming with fine eateries using Swedish ingredients in new and exciting ways, and in – you guessed it – stylish settings.

Stockholm is an unusually tranquil capital, and you are unlikely to feel remotely flustered there. In fact, it is hard to imagine a more manageable city. English is spoken by nigh on everyone; the public transport system is clean and efficient; there are restaurants, galleries and museums around every corner; navigation couldn't conceivably be much simpler, since Stockholm is naturally portioned up into small islands; and, famously, the city is made up of one third green space and one third water, which leaves you with only one third urbanity to contend with.

If this all sounds excessively rosy, you only have to add what everyone knows about Sweden's strong sense of social equality, sturdy welfare state and long tradition of neutrality before you begin to realise that Stockholm is quite possibly the nicest capital city in the world. Just don't ask us to buy you a beer.

ABOUT TIME OUT CITY GUIDES

Time Out Stockholm is one of an expanding series of travel guides produced by the people behind London and New York's successful listings magazines. Our guides are all written and updated by resident experts who have striven to provide you with all the most up-to-date information you'll need to explore the city, whether you're a local or first-time visitor.

THE LOWDOWN ON THE LISTINGS

Above all, we've tried to make this book as useful as possible. Websites, telephone numbers, transport information, opening times, admission prices and credit card details are all included in our listings. And, as far as possible, we've given details of facilities, services and events, all checked and correct at the time we went to press. However, owners and managers can

five-digit postcode (which is written before the name of the city, for example 111 30 Stockholm), and we've provided these codes for organisations or venues you might need to write to, such as hotels. For all places listed in the city centre we also give a map reference, which indicates the page and square on which the venue will be found on our **street maps** at the back of the book (starting on page 303).

TELEPHONE NUMBERS

The area code for Stockholm is 08, but you don't need to use it when phoning from within the city. Throughout the guide we've listed all phone numbers as you need to dial them from within Stockholm. If you're calling Stockholm from abroad, you must first dial 46 (the code for Sweden) then 8 then the number. For more details of phone codes and charges, *see p288*.

ESSENTIAL INFORMATION

For all the practical information you might need for visiting the city – including visa and customs information, disabled access, emergency telephone numbers, a list of useful websites and the lowdown on the local transport network – turn to the **Directory** chapter at the back of this guide. It starts on page 274.

MAPS

We've included a series of fully indexed colour maps to the city at the back of this guide – they start on page 302 – and, where possible, we've printed a grid reference against all venues that appear on the maps. A map of the Tunnelbana metro system is on page 320.

LET US KNOW WHAT YOU THINK

We hope you enjoy *Time Out Stockholm*, and we'd like to know what you think of it. We welcome tips for places that you consider we should include in future editions and take notice of your criticism of our choices. You can email us on guides@timeout.com.

There is an online version of this book, along with guides to over 45 other international cities, at **www.timeout.com**.

change their arrangements at any time. Before you go out of your way, we'd strongly advise you to call and check opening times, dates of exhibitions and other particulars. While every effort has been made to ensure the accuracy of the information contained in this guide, the publishers cannot accept responsibility for any errors it may contain.

PRICES AND PAYMENT

We have noted where shops, hotels, restaurants, museums and the like accept the following credit cards: American Express (**AmEx**), Diners Club (**DC**), MasterCard (**MC**) and Visa (**V**). Some may also accept other credit cards (including JCB or Carte Blanche).

The prices we've supplied should be treated as guidelines, not gospel. If they vary wildly from those we've quoted, please write and let us know. We aim to give the best and most up-to-date advice, so we always want to know if you've been badly treated or overcharged.

THE LIE OF THE LAND

The centre of Stockholm is small and easy to get around on foot, but we've also given details of the nearest T-bana (metro) station and bus routes for everywhere included in the guide. The city centre is made up of clearly defined islands and neighbourhoods – in our **Sightseeing** chapters we've concentrated on 12 main areas (for an introduction to central Stockholm, *see p60*). Postal addresses in Stockholm include a

What Londoners take when they go out.

Time Out
London

EVERY WEEK

In Context

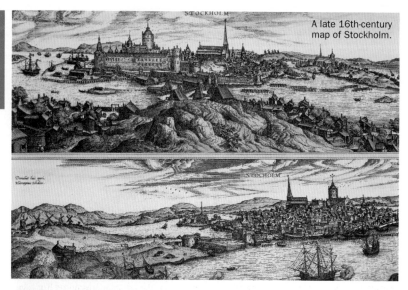

A late 16th-century map of Stockholm.

History

From war-hungry Vikings to the ultimate welfare state.

EARLY BEGINNINGS

The city of Stockholm wasn't founded until the early 1250s but the region that surrounds the city, geographically defined by Lake Mälaren, has been a hotbed of human activity for several millennia.

The earliest evidence of human habitation in Sweden is of nomadic reindeer hunters from continental Europe, who appear to have followed the receding glaciers north into Scandinavia at the end of the last Ice Age in approximately 11,000 BC. By about 7,500 BC Mesolithic hunter-gatherers had migrated to the coastal areas of central and northern Sweden. Between 4,000 and 2,800 BC, villages dotted the southern half of the country, their inhabitants eking out a living as farmers. Sweden's inhabitants began establishing trading links with the wider world during the Bronze Age (1,500 to 500 BC). They had access to abundant supplies of fur and amber, which they traded for raw metals, weapons and decorative objects.

Shortly after the birth of Christ, Scandinavia was 'discovered' by the classical world, the historians of the Roman Empire writing about its geographical location and the fact that its populace was well armed and well equipped with ships. Between AD 550 and 1,000 two main rival groups emerged in Sweden – the Svear, who were based in the Lake Mälaren region, and the Götar, who controlled a swathe of territory to the west and south. (Although the Svear eventually defeated and assimilated the Götar, the geographical terms Svealand and Götaland are still in use today.) Sverige, Sweden's modern name in Swedish, comes from *Svea rike* – the Svea kingdom.

The Viking culture emerged in various parts of Scandinavia in the early ninth century. The word 'Viking' is thought to come from the *viks* (Old Norse for 'inlets') in which they harboured their long ships. The 'Thing', an assembly of powerful men who advised the ruler, was at the centre of Viking politics. Vikings were committed pagans, devoutly worshipping the gods of Norse mythology. Odin was the supreme deity, the god of war and founder of art and culture. Human sacrifice was an important aspect of Viking worship; every nine years nine people were offered to the gods at Uppsala's temple.

There is evidence that the Lake Mälaren Vikings were among the first to set sail in search of new lands. They were probably motivated by rapid population growth at home, as well as persistent domestic unrest. By the mid ninth century they had reached both the Black and Caspian Seas, where they launched attacks on Byzantium and north-east Iran. While often still violent, the Vikings of Sweden were somewhat more business-minded than those of Denmark and Norway, and they successfully developed lucrative trading contacts with Byzantium.

Taken as a group, the Vikings effectively dominated the political and economic life of the whole of Europe until the mid 11th century. Remnants of their civilisation have been uncovered at a number of sites not far from Stockholm's city limits, most notably at Birka, a town founded in about AD 700 that was Sweden's leading trading centre in the early tenth century. Gamla Uppsala is even older than Birka, with some of its royal graves dating back to the sixth century. Stockholm's Historiska Museet has an excellent exhibition introducing visitors to a wealth of information and artefacts that cast light on Viking culture.

CENTURIES OF BLOODY STRUGGLE

The Swedes were among the last Europeans to abandon paganism. In spite of the efforts of a number of crusading monks and priests, and the baptism of King Olof Skötkonung in 1008 (and all his successors after him), many Swedes stubbornly remained true to the old gods until the end of the 11th century. Finally, by the middle of the 12th century, Uppsala had fully shed its bloody pagan history and Sweden's archbishopric was established there. The first Swedish archbishop appointed, in 1164, was an English monk called Stephen.

From the end of the Viking period in the mid 11th century, Swedish history was characterised for several centuries by one deadly power struggle after the other. While there was always one king or another in place, power and influence remained spread widely among an array of local chiefs and noblemen. King Erik Jedvardsson (1156-60), a century after his death, was chosen to become Sweden's patron saint (thanks to the crusade he undertook to christianise Finland). His memory is kept alive today in place names such as St Eriksplan and St Eriksgatan; his remains are entombed at Uppsala Cathedral.

Another big name of the medieval period is Birger Jarl. *Jarl* indicates that he was one of the king's chief administrators. When King Erik Eriksson was deposed in 1229, Birger Jarl was well placed to assume power quickly. He is remembered for two main accomplishments: the long and turbulent process he initiated to centralise political power in Sweden, and the founding of the city of Stockholm. In 1247-51 he made significant progress towards achieving his first goal by using German money and soldiers to successfully defeat a rebellion led by noblemen in the area around Lake Mälaren. Shortly after his victory he offered good trading terms to German merchants, especially those from Lübeck, which led to Sweden's long-lasting and strong ties to the Hanseatic League.

The 13th-century Swedish kingdom consisted of the area around Lake Mälaren, the Stockholm and Åland archipelagos, and the Gulf of Finland all the way to Viborg (now part of Russia). The sea level had dropped in Stockholm's archipelago to such an extent that it was only possible to pass from the Baltic Sea into Lake Mälaren via a narrow channel now known as Norrström, just north of Gamla Stan. This passage became a vital trade route and a key defensive position – both in the middle of the waterways that held Sweden together and blocking any foreign attacks against the Swedish heartland. It is for this reason that in 1252 Birger Jarl chose precisely that spot to erect a mighty fortress, Tre Kronor (on the site of the present-day Kungliga Slottet), thereby founding a settlement that would grow to become the city of Stockholm.

> **'The new Tre Kroner fortress quickly mushroomed into one of Sweden's most important trading centres.'**

Archaeological evidence suggests that there had already been a trading post and a small fortification at this location for some time, but Birger Jarl was the first Swedish leader to fully recognise the island's strategic significance. In the summer of 1252 he wrote two letters in which the name 'Stockholm' was mentioned for the first time. The origin of the name is unclear, but one of the most convincing suggestions is that it comes from the fact that logs (*stockar*) were used to build up the small island (*holme*) upon which the fortress was built. The city was to be besieged many times in the succeeding centuries, by both rebellious peasants and foreign armies, because anyone who wanted to control Sweden knew they had to win over Stockholm's castle.

The new fortress quickly mushroomed into one of Sweden's most important trading centres, where iron products, fur and grain from inland Sweden could be traded with salt from Lüneburg in Germany, cloth from Flanders and wine from Germany, France and Spain. Ships from Lübeck and other Hanseatic towns traded enthusiastically with the expatriate Germans who were setting up copper and iron-ore mines in Bergslagen and Dalarna, north of Mälaren.

Birger Jarl's son Magnus rose to power in 1275, after a nasty power struggle with his brothers. Magnus cracked down on the raucous nobility and in so doing became one of the most powerful kings in Swedish history. One of his key contributions to Swedish society was his decree that declined the nobility of its right to collect taxes and make other financial or material demands upon the lower classes in rural society (known as *våldgästning*). This is credited with preventing feudalism from taking root in Sweden. To tighten his hold on power, he decreed that certain key groups of society should have tax-free status, mainly those who were in the service of the Church or the state (particularly knights in the king's service).

Magnus Ladulås was a keen supporter of the new city of Stockholm and eager to promote its growth. Among many measures, he donated land north of the city, in what is today the area around the Central Station, to monasteries. Stockholm seems to have been well established as a town by about 1300, and a few decades later it had grown to be the most important town in the country (although it was not considered as the capital until at least 1436). The city centre sprouted several churches and monasteries, including that of St Nicholas, now known as Storkyrkan, and the church in the monastery of the Order of St Francis (founded in 1270), now Riddarholmskyrkan.

> **'By the 15th century the Kalmar Union encompassed Norway, Sweden, Finland, Iceland and Greenland, making it the largest kingdom in Europe.'**

After Magnus's death in 1290, power shifted to a faction of nobles led by Torgil Knutsson. In 1302 Magnus's son Birger reached adulthood and assumed the throne. His brothers Erik and Valdemar made it very difficult for him to rule effectively, however: they wanted to split the kingdom three ways rather than rule it alone. After they murdered Knutsson, Birger was forced to do as his brothers demanded, but in 1317 he had them arrested, thrown in prison and starved to death. The nobility, horrified by his bout of fratricide, promptly deposed him, forcing him to flee the country.

The nobility then set out to find a new king. They settled on Magnus, the child of a Swedish duke and, at the age of three, already king of

Norway. Upon reaching adulthood Magnus assumed the throne and set about making some important changes to the Swedish social order. He abolished *träldom*, a form of slavery, in 1335, and established Sweden's first national legal code in 1350. His dual kingdom was huge – after the signing of the treaty of Novgorod in 1323 Finland had officially become part of the Swedish realm – but the vast majority of his subjects lived in abject poverty. In the mid 14th century his kingdom was hit by the bubonic plague and approximately a third of his subjects were wiped out. Sweden's nobility fell on hard times – there were too few workers to support the lifestyles to which they had become accustomed. Seeing that Sweden was weak, Hanseatic merchants seized their chance to push Swedish traders off the best Baltic trade routes.

By the mid 1300s King Magnus was in serious trouble, and it was about this time that the construction of a thick ring wall around Stockholm was initiated. Long-running disputes about the then Danish provinces of Skåne and Blekinge resulted in devastating Danish attacks on Swedish targets. In the early 1360s Sweden's nobility lost all patience with Magnus and enlisted the help of Duke Albrecht of Mecklenburg (1364-88) to unseat him. The ring wall not yet complete, Albrecht and his forces quickly conquered Stockholm and assumed nominal control over the kingdom, but the nobles held the real power and divided up the country between themselves.

THE KALMAR UNION AND DISSENT

Upon the death in 1386 of Bo Jonsson Grip – chief of Sweden's ruling nobles – the nobility turned to Margaret, daughter of Danish King Valdemar and wife of Magnus's son King Håkon of Norway. Since the deaths of her father and husband she had already been made regent in both Denmark and Norway for her son Olof. Though Olof died in 1387, she retained her hold on power in the three kingdoms. In 1389 she was proclaimed ruler of Sweden and in return she confirmed all the privileges of the Swedish nobility. When they asked her to choose a king she nominated 14-year-old Erik VII of Pomerania; he was elected to the post in 1397. As he was already king of Norway and Denmark, Scandinavia now had just one ruler. However, Margaret was the real power behind the throne and remained so until her death in 1412.

In 1397 she formalised a Nordic alliance called the Kalmar Union, whose purpose was to limit both the commercial and political influence of the Hanseatic League. By the start of the 15th century the union encompassed Norway, Sweden, Finland, Iceland and the immensity of Greenland, making it the largest

King Gustav Vasa. *See p14.*

kingdom in Europe. The union was threatened many times over the next 125 years by Swedish rebellion against Danish forces.

Christopher of Bavaria ruled the union from 1439 to 1448, after being elected by the nobility. Upon his death, the noble families of Norway, Sweden and Denmark could not agree on a single candidate to fill the kingships. Sweden's nationalists, led by the Sture family, seized this opportunity to attempt to free Sweden from the union. This led to vicious fighting with Sweden's unionist faction, which was led by the Oxenstierna family. Finally, in 1470, the nationalists had the upper hand and Sten Sture the Elder (1471-97, 1501-3) was appointed the 'Guardian of the Realm'. A year later the Battle of Brunkeberg broke out in the middle of modern Stockholm, resulting in the decimation of the unionist forces. The St George and the Dragon statue in Storkyrkan was donated by Sture to commemorate the victory.

THE GROWTH OF STOCKHOLM

Aside from his crucial military victories, Sten Sture the Elder is remembered for the many technological, cultural and educational steps forward that Sweden made under his leadership. He established Sweden's first university in Uppsala in 1477, and in 1483 Sweden's first printing press was set up. Decorative arts became more sophisticated, as shown by the many fine German- and Dutch-style paintings that adorn Swedish churches of this period. The city continued to grow throughout the 15th century, and by the early 16th century Stockholm had between 6,000 and 7,000 inhabitants, most of them living in present-day Gamla Stan.

Poorer people, such as fishermen and artisans, had begun to build shacks to the north of the city centre, as well as on Södermalm. By Swedish standards it was a large town – the country's largest, in fact – but by continental standards it was tiny. By 1500 Bremen and Hamburg both had about 20,000 inhabitants, while Lübeck had 25,000 and Paris more than 100,000. The *Parhelion Painting* in Storkyrkan (*pictured on p68*) gives an idea of how the city looked around this time; it depicts an unusual light phenomemon seen in 1535.

From the start, the population of Stockholm was a mix of people from different parts of Sweden and other areas of Europe. The largest 'foreign' contingent – between 10 and 20 per cent of the population – was made up of Finns, largely a result of the fact that between the mid 12th and early 19th centuries Finland was a Swedish province. The Germans comprised a smaller, but much more powerful, proportion; since the city had been founded with Hanseatic support, wealthy German merchants had been living in Stockholm from its beginnings. By the 1580s at least 12 per cent of the city's population was of German extraction.

In fact, many German historians regarded Stockholm as a German town in the period before the anti-German rebellion of 1434. Germans continued to dominate Stockholm's city council until 1471, when a decision was made at a national level that Germans would be banned from participating in city politics. Dutch, Scottish, French, English, Italian, Danish, Russian and Polish merchants and traders also became increasingly significant in Stockholm during the 15th century.

By the late 15th century, most Swedes thought the Kalmar Union was a thing of the past, but the alliance was still popular in Denmark and Sweden's rulers had to deal with numerous Danish attacks. When Christian II assumed the Danish throne in 1513, the unionist movement rejoiced, thinking it had now finally found a leader who would be able to crush the Swedish nationalists. Sure enough, Christian attacked Sweden and killed the then ruler Sten Sture the Younger (1512-20). After Sture's death, Christian gathered leading members of the Swedish nobility together at Tre Kronor castle under the guise of granting them amnesty for their opposition to the union. After three days of feasting and celebrating, he locked the doors to the castle and arrested his guests.

Around 90 men were sentenced to death and taken to Stortorget, outside the castle, where they were decapitated or hanged one by one. The event came to be known as the Stockholm Bloodbath, while Christian II came to be known (in Sweden, at least) as Christian the Tyrant.

Following the bloodbath, Sture's followers were endlessly persecuted by King Christian of Denmark – which proved to be a mistake, since it provoked widespread opposition to Danish rule and finally resulted in the complete breakdown of the union in 1521-3. Sweden then became a totally independent country under the strong leadership of Gustav Eriksson, who was crowned King Gustav Vasa (1523-60).

REFORMATION AND EMPIRE

Under Gustav Vasa's long leadership Sweden was changed in two fundamental ways: it was unified under a strong hereditary monarch and it became a Protestant country. Never a particularly religious man, Gustav Vasa's Reformation had much more to do with politics and economics than it did with theology. He was an ambitious king, but cash-strapped, so the handover of Church lands to the Crown and the subordination of the Church, a rival power base, suited his purposes perfectly. Shortly after taking power, he set out on a propaganda campaign in which he stressed the negative role the Church's leadership had played in the past – in particular, Archbishop Gustav Trolle's support for King Christian II in the lead-up to the Stockholm Bloodbath. In the end, he got his way and the Lutheran faith was established as the state religion.

The Reformation led to the state-sanctioned destruction of scores of Swedish monasteries, convents and churches, their riches going directly to an increasingly wealthy and powerful king. Gustav Vasa even had plans to tear down Storkyrkan because he felt it was situated too close to the royal residence at Tre Kronor castle, thereby complicating its defence. But public opinion was strongly opposed to the outright destruction of Stockholm's spiritual heart, so the king relented and decided only to move one of the church's walls slightly. (Gustav Vasa's son Johan was more interested in both architecture and religion than his father, and in the 1580s he had a number of Stockholm's demolished churches rebuilt.)

His larder full and his domestic goals largely accomplished, Gustav Vasa launched a campaign to weaken Russia, Poland and Denmark and thereby make Sweden the dominant Baltic power, beginning with a modestly successful war against Russia in 1555-7. After his death in 1560, his sons, King Erik XIV, King Johan III and King Karl IX, took up the quest. Gustav Vasa (along with his sons) is seen as the monarch who was most responsible for turning Sweden into a nation. He created a modern army, navy and civil service. He and his sons imported men of learning to fill their royal court and introduced the Renaissance style of architecture, painting and sculpture to Swedish high society.

In 1570-95 Sweden fought another war against Russia, with some success. But Denmark was harder to beat – in spite of the break-up of the Kalmar Union, it had remained the most powerful country in the region, as Sweden learned to its cost in the expensive wars of 1563-70 and 1611-13. It was during the reign of Gustav Vasa's grandson, Gustav II Adolf (1611-32), that Sweden began to make some significant progress in its efforts to expand around the Baltic Sea, helped largely by that king's extensive reforms of the armed forces and civil service. By 1617 Sweden had pushed Russia back from the Baltic coastline, and in 1621 it succeeded in taking Riga from Poland.

'By the end of the 17th century Sweden had become the most powerful nation in northern Europe.'

The Thirty Years War, which started in Germany in 1618, finally turned the tide decisively in Sweden's favour in its rivalry with Denmark. After suffering a devastating defeat at the hands of the Swedes in the battle of Lutter-am-Barenburg in 1626, Denmark was forced to pull out of the war. In 1630 Sweden officially entered the war on the side of the Protestants. The resulting peace treaty of 1648 gave Sweden new provinces in northern Germany, and by 1658 a severely weakened Denmark had been forced to surrender parts of Norway plus all Danish provinces east of Öresund to Sweden. As a result, by the end of the 17th century Sweden had become the most powerful nation in northern Europe.

Gustav II Adolf and his chancellor Axel Oxenstierna were eager to develop Stockholm and make it the political and administrative centre of the growing Swedish empire. They issued numerous regulations that strengthened Stockholm's position as a centre of foreign trade, and also founded Sweden's Supreme Court in the city. In 1626 they reorganised the national assembly into four estates – nobility, clergy, burghers and farmers – and based it in Stockholm. The capital's medieval wall was torn down in this period so that the city could expand to the north and south. The old wooden buildings that dominated Södermalm and Norrmalm were razed and replaced by new, straight streets lined with stone buildings.

After Gustav II Adolf's death his young daughter Christina became queen, with Oxenstierna as regent until 1644. In 1654 Christina converted to Catholicism, renounced the throne and moved to Rome, where she lived out her life building up one of the finest art and book collections in Europe. She left the throne to Karl X Gustav (1654-60), who is remembered best for his invasion and defeat of Denmark in 1657, thereby creating the largest Swedish empire ever. He was succeeded by his son, Karl XI (1660-97), who in 1682 pronounced himself to be Sweden's first absolute monarch, answerable only to God.

Stockholm's population grew rapidly during Sweden's age of empire; by the 1670s it had between 50,000 and 55,000 citizens. Literacy had now become important, leading to the establishment of many grammar schools, and creativity flourished under the likes of George

Stiernhielm (1598-1672), the father of modern Swedish poetry. Architecturally this was the age of the Tessins, who completed the fabulous Drottningholms Slott in 1686. It was truly a golden age for Swedish history, in military, cultural, economic and social terms.

AN EMPIRE IN DECLINE AND A CITY IN FLUX

It was during the reign of Karl XII (1697-1718) – who assumed the throne at the tender age of 15 – that Sweden lost her empire. Between 1700 and 1721 Sweden fought the Great Northern War against a number of opponents, notably the defensive alliance of Saxony-Poland, Russia and Denmark. The young king fought valiantly

Exodus

In 1833, Swedish poet and bishop Esaias Tegnér attributed Sweden's population boom to 'the peace, the vaccination and the potatoes'. Meaning, apparently, that thanks for the rarity of war, to mandatory smallpox vaccinations and to widespread cultivation of the vitamin-rich potato, Swedes were living longer and healthier lives. The boom was indeed dramatic: from 1810 to 1850 the Swedish population grew from 2.4 to 3.5 million. Sweden, however, then largely undeveloped and agrarian, could not support such rapid growth, and in the 1840s small groups of dissatisfied Swedes began emigrating to North America. When a devastating famine struck in the 1860s, Swedes left by the hundreds of thousands. By 1910 more than one million Swedes were living across the Atlantic – a startling number considering the population of Sweden in 1900 was only five million.

The early Swedish emigrants to North America were primarily families from rural areas fleeing poverty, oppression and religious persecution. In his classic novel The Emigrants (Utvandrarna), the first of a four-part series, Vilhelm Moberg describes what such a journey in 1850 would have been like. His characters Karl Oskar and Kristina, after losing one of their children to starvation, travel from southern Sweden to Gothenburg by horse and carriage, then from there to New York aboard a sailing ship – a horrific, ten-week-long voyage – and finally over land to Minnesota.

Later emigrants could travel to the US in as little as two to three weeks, via Gothenburg and Liverpool, due to the emergence of

railroads and steamships in the latter half of the 19th century. These emigrants, encouraged by advertisements in newspapers and letters from friends and family, both promising wonders such as 'cornfields that look like forests', had perhaps unrealistically high hopes for their new home. Although the majority established farms in states such as Illinois, Minnesota and Wisconsin, on the 160 acres of land given out by the US Homestead Act of 1862, many others settled in cities, working in construction or as maids. In 1900, for instance, more Swedes were living in Chicago than in Gothenburg, the second largest city in Sweden.

As a result of Sweden's mass emigration, approximately five million Americans today have some degree of Swedish ancestry. Not satisfied with this number alone, certain genealogy-loving Swedes take pleasure in proving their country's international influence. One researcher has demonstrated that actress Julia Roberts has roots in Sweden, as her great-grandmother emigrated to the US as a child in the 1880s from the county of Värmland. It is relatively easy for Americans to search for Swedish ancestors, as the Swedish church kept comprehensive lists of all who emigrated. Though only 50,000 Swedes emigrated from Stockholm during this period of mass emigration, cruise ships arrive in Stockholm every summer, loaded with Americans eager to get in touch with the Swede within. For more information about emigration or Swedish-American genealogy, contact the **Swedish Emigrant Institute** (www.swemi.nu/eng) located in Växjö in southern Sweden.

against the odds to hold on to all of Sweden's far-flung possessions, but suffered a terrible loss to Russia's Peter the Great at the Battle of Poltava in 1709. His bravery in battle is still revered in Sweden's far-right circles to this day. He was finally killed in Norway by a sniper's bullet in 1718. Since he had no heir, the period after Karl's death was marked by a weakening of the monarchy (the end of absolutism) and the rise of the aristocracy. In 1719 the role of the monarch was reduced to that of nominal head of state; it was the chancellor who exercised real power, with the support of shifting aristocratic factions. With the government dominated by cabals of squabbling noblemen, the economy was left to stagnate, and political and social reforms were slow in coming.

By the end of the Great Northern War in 1721, Sweden had lost parts of Pomerania in Germany, as well as its strongholds in modern-day Estonia, Latvia, north-west Russia and Finland. Sweden made disastrous attempts to reconquer at least some of these territories by fighting wars with Russia in 1741-3 and 1788-90. Participation in the Seven Years War (1756-63) resulted in the loss of Swedish territory to Prussia. It was clear that Sweden was no longer a great power in Europe, but it took a very long time for the country's political and military establishment to accept the fact.

This was also a trying time for the citizens of Stockholm – on top of coping with their country's political and military difficulties, the city was repeatedly ravaged by fire and disease. In 1697 the city was devastated by a fire that completely destroyed Tre Kronor, the royal palace and pride of Stockholm. In 1710 plague swept through the city and in just a few

months killed approximately 20,000 people, about a third of the population. Later in the century the city suffered three more devastating fires, which resulted in a municipal ban on wood as a building material for new houses. Over the course of the 18th century the population of the city stayed static at about 70,000 inhabitants; it would probably have declined had there not been a fresh supply of men and women from the countryside every year. Unsanitary conditions, overcrowding, cold and disease all contributed to the fact that Stockholm's death rate was among the highest of all European cities.

But there was a brighter side. In the decades leading up to 1754, Stockholm buzzed with the building of the new Kungliga Slottet to replace Tre Kronor. The construction work was a huge stimulus for the city's artisans, and for Stockholm's economy overall. Foreign painters, furniture makers and craftsmen initially came to work temporarily on the palace, but many decided to stay permanently, opening small businesses and teaching their trades to others. They made a good living, as many noblemen and burghers were quick to order paintings, furniture and wallpaper similar to those in the new royal palace. New industries also began to grow up in Stockholm, such as textile manufacturing, and the city's foreign trade was developing rapidly – not only with Europe but also with the Far East and the Americas.

Many of Stockholm's burghers used their increasing wealth to build larger and larger houses, especially along Skeppsbron in Gamla Stan. New residential neighbourhoods sprang up on Södermalm and Norrmalm, and many of the old houses on Gamla Stan were renovated.

Fire destroys the royal palace, Tre Kronor, in 1697.

SCIENTIFIC, CULTURAL AND INTELLECTUAL PROGRESS

The 18th century was also an age of scientific and intellectual advance in Stockholm, and throughout Sweden. Key figures included the famous botanist Carl von Linné (aka Linnaeus; 1707-78); Anders Celsius (1701-44), inventor of the centigrade temperature scale; and mystical philosopher Emanuel Swedenborg (1688-1772). Sweden's best-loved poet, Carl Michael Bellman (1740-95), did much to encourage Swedish nationalism. Free religious groups also began to form and to challenge the iron-fisted monopoly of the state church; Jews were allowed to settle in Sweden in 1744, and in 1781 Catholics were permitted to establish a church in Stockholm for the first time since the Reformation.

> **'Gustav III was initially popular because he built hospitals, allowed freedom of worship and lessened economic controls.'**

The monarchy regained some of its old power under Gustav III (1771-92). Seeing that the Riksdag (Parliament) was divided, the king seized the opportunity to force through a new constitution that would make the nobility share power with the Crown. Gustav III was initially popular with his subjects because he built hospitals, allowed freedom of worship and lessened economic controls. He was also a man of culture who imported French opera, theatre and literature to Sweden, and in 1782 he founded Stockholm's first opera house, the Kungliga Operan. During his reign, several newspapers were established, and political and cultural debate flourished. The nobility were not so happy with his increasingly tyrannical behaviour, however, especially after the start of the French Revolution. In 1792 an assassin shot Gustav III at a masked ball at the Kungliga Operan; he died two weeks later.

In 1805 Gustav III's successor, Gustav IV Adolf (1792-1809), was drawn into the Napoleonic Wars on the British side. This resulted in a number of gains and losses; most significantly, Sweden lost Finland to Russia and gained Norway from Denmark. All this upheaval resulted in political changes, notably the constitution of 1809, which established a system whereby a liberal monarchy would be responsible to an elected Riksdag.

The union with Norway was established in 1814, and was formalised in the 1815 Act of Union. The settlement took account of the Norwegian desire for self-government, declaring Norway a separate nation from Sweden. However, king Karl XIII (1908-1818) was now sovereign over Norway. The tension between the Swedish desire to strengthen the union, and the Norwegian wish for further autonomy, was set to increase over the century that followed.

Following the death of Karl XIII in 1818, one of Napoleon's generals, Jean-Baptiste Bernadotte, was invited to assume the Swedish throne. He accepted the offer and took the name Karl XIV Johan (1818-44). In spite of the fact that he spoke no Swedish and had never even visited Scandinavia prior to accepting the kingship, Sweden prospered under his rule. He was a strong liberalising influence, both socially and economically. In 1832 he presided over the opening of the Göta Canal, an important transportation corridor that still links Stockholm to Sweden's west coast.

His successor, Oscar I (1844-59), gave women inheritance rights equal to those of their brothers in 1845, passed an Education Act (1842) and a Poor Care law (1855), and then reformed the restrictive craftsmen's guilds. The reign of his son, Karl XV (1859-72), is remembered for introducing a very limited franchise, and reforming the Riksdag in 1866 – the old four estates were replaced with a dual-chamber representative parliament along continental lines. This act marked the beginning of the end for the monarch's role in the country's politics – all Sweden's kings since then have been little more than figureheads.

INDUSTRIALISATION, POPULATION EXPLOSION AND EMIGRATION

Industrialisation arrived late to Sweden, and the mechanisation of what little industry did exist (mining, forestry and the like) was half-hearted – hardly what you would call a revolution. Meanwhile, the rural population had grown steadily through the first half of the 19th century. There was neither enough land, nor jobs in the cities, to support everyone. The poor got used to going hungry, but in 1867-8 the situation became critical when a terrible famine broke out. As a result, over one million Swedes emigrated to North America between 1860 and 1910 – a cataclysmic event for a country whose population in 1860 was only four million (*see p15* **Exodus**).

In the 1860s, Sweden's first railway lines finally opened reliable communications between Stockholm and the country's southern regions; by 1871 the railway to the north was complete. The railways were a boon for nascent industry. The two most notable Swedish manufactured products were to become its high-quality, efficiently made steel and its safety matches (a Swedish invention). By the late 19th century a number of large industries had been established in Stockholm; for example, a shoe factory on Södermalm, a huge Bolinders factory on Kungsholmen producing steam engines, cast-iron stoves, and other household items. In 1876, Lars Magnus Ericsson opened his Ericsson telephone company in Stockholm, and soon the city had more phones per capita than any other city in Europe (a trend that has continued to this day).

By 1900 almost one in four Swedes lived in a city, and industrialisation (based primarily on timber, precision machinery and hardware) was finally in full swing. Stockholm's factories attracted workers from all over the country, causing the capital's population to balloon from 100,000 in 1856 to 300,000 in 1900. Conditions in many factories were appalling, and trade unions emerged to fight for the rights of workers. The unions formed a confederation in 1898 but found it difficult to make progress under harsh laws on picketing.

> **'More buildings were constructed in the 1880s than during the previous seven decades.'**

Living conditions in the city were nearly as bad as working conditions. In response to Stockholm's growing housing crisis, the city planners – led by Claes Albert Lindhagen – put forward a proposal in 1866 to build wide boulevards and esplanades similar to those in Paris, which would create some green space within the city as well as allowing traffic to move freely. The plan resulted in the construction of some of the city's key arteries, such as Birger Jarlsgatan, Ringvägen, Karlavägen and, perhaps most impressive of all, Strandvägen. In just one decade, the 1880s, Stockholm's population increased by 46 per cent – which is why more buildings were constructed in the 1880s than during the previous seven decades. Neighbourhoods such as Östermalm, Vasastaden, Kungsholmen, Hornstull and Skanstull were created at this time.

The late 19th century also saw the arrival of Stockholm's first continental-style hotels, cafés, restaurants, shopping galleries and department stores, to serve the city's upper classes and the beginnings of a tourist industry. Classic hotels and restaurants such as the Grand Hôtel, Berns and Hasselbacken were either opened or entirely remodelled, and many new theatres were built. International exhibitions promoting industry and art were held in Stockholm in 1866 and 1897.

During the same period Swedish dramatist August Strindberg (*see p236* **Anarchy in August**) achieved critical success across Europe, and folk historian Artur Hazelius founded the Nordiska Museet and open-air museum Skansen to preserve Sweden's rich cultural heritage. The Academy of Stockholm (now the University of Stockholm) was founded in 1878, and in 1896 Alfred Nobel donated his fortune to fund the Nobel Prizes.

NEUTRALITY AND SOCIAL DEMOCRACY

In 1901 the Swedish government introduced conscription in reaction to rising militarism in Europe and, more specifically, because of its fears about a potential conflict with Russia. Then in 1905 the union between Sweden and Norway finally dissolved. Norway acquired its own monarchy and took full control of its own affairs, and the Swedish state assumed its current shape.

At the outbreak of World War I Sweden declared itself neutral, in spite of its German sympathies. The British demanded that Sweden enforce a blockade against Germany. When Sweden refused to co-operate, the British blacklisted Swedish goods and interfered with Swedish commercial shipping as much as they could, going so far as to seize ships' cargoes. The economy suffered dramatically and inflation shot through the roof. The British tactics led to rationing, as well as severe food shortages. Demonstrations broke out in 1917-18, partly inspired by the Russian Revolution. The demonstrators focused on food shortages and demands for democratic reforms, particularly the extension of voting rights to women.

The privations of the war helped social democracy make its breakthrough. By the end of the war the party had been active for some time – its first member had been elected to the Riksdag in 1902 – though very much on the margins. After the Russian Revolution, the Social Democrats presented a less drastic alternative to communism in Sweden, and they gained popularity. In 1920 Hjalmar Branting became Sweden's first Social Democratic prime minister. Reforms quickly followed: Sweden introduced voting rights for women; the state-controlled alcohol-selling system was established; and the working day was limited to eight hours.

The Social Democrats' dominance of political affairs began in earnest in the 1930s. From 1932, the party enjoyed an unbroken 40 years in power. This made it possible to take the first steps towards building the notion of a People's Home (Folkhemmet), in which higher taxes would finance a decent standard of living for all. The first components of the welfare system were unemployment benefits, paid holidays, family allowances and increased old-age pensions. The Social Democrats also managed to talk the country's trade unions and major employers into meeting at Saltsjöbaden in 1938 to come to an agreement about how to regulate labour disputes, such as strikes and lock-outs. Known as the Saltsjöbaden Agreement, it marked the start of what was to become Sweden's hallmark corporative capitalism.

At the outbreak of World War II there was little sympathy in Sweden for the Germans – unlike in 1914. Sweden declared neutrality but was in a difficult position. Germany was allied with Finland against the Soviet Union, and the relationship between Sweden and Finland was traditionally close – with Russia the age-old enemy. But when the Soviets invaded Finland in 1939, Sweden was only drawn in to a certain degree, providing weapons, volunteers and refuge to the Finns, but refusing to send regular troops. Sweden's position became even more uncomfortable in 1940, when Germany invaded Denmark and Norway, thus isolating Sweden and compelling it to supply the Nazis with iron ore and to allow them to transport their troops across Swedish territory and in Swedish waters. In 1942 the Swedish navy fought an undeclared war against Soviet submarines.

On the other hand, western Allied airmen were rescued in Sweden and often sent back to Britain, and Danish and Norwegian armed resistance groups were organised on Swedish soil in 1942-3. Jewish lives were also saved, notably by Swedish businessman Raoul Wallenberg, who managed to prevent about 100,000 Hungarian Jews from being deported by the SS. After the Soviet conquest of Budapest in January 1945, Wallenberg was arrested as a suspected spy and disappeared. For years, rumours flew about whether or not he had died in a Moscow prison in 1947; Soviet documents unearthed in 1989 indicated this was what had most likely happened.

The main goal for the Swedish government during the war was not strict neutrality but rather to avoid Sweden being dragged into the war – this was accomplished at high diplomatic and moral cost. Rather than suffering as it had in World War I, Sweden weathered relatively well, since it was now less dependent on foreign imports.

During the first emergence of the Cold War, in 1948-9, Sweden tried to form a defensive alliance with Denmark and Norway, but her plans failed partly because the other two countries wanted close links with the Western allies. When the Danes and Norwegians became members of NATO in 1949, Sweden remained outside. One semi-official reason given for this was Sweden not wanting to leave her friend Finland too isolated and at risk of being pressed by the Soviet Union. But in recent years it has emerged that Sweden was, in fact, in secret co-operation with NATO from as far back as the early 1950s.

FROM THE THIRD WAY TO THE EUROPEAN HIGHWAY

After the end of World War II, a large-scale transformation of Stockholm's city centre began, despite the fact that Stockholm was one of the few European capitals to survive the war unscathed. Once the rebuilding process on the Continent was in full swing, with American-style skyscrapers rising from the ashes of all the bombed-out cities, Sweden felt left out. The city government began to tear down many of its decaying old buildings and construct anew (*see p77* **Concrete calamity?**).

As more and more people moved to Stockholm in the post-war period (the capital's population more than doubled in the 20th century), the city once again developed a severe housing crisis. Stockholm's Tunnelbana metro system was inaugurated in 1950 and several new suburbs were built along it, to the south and north-west.

Under the leadership of Tage Erlander (1946-69), the Social Democrats introduced models for industrial bargaining and full employment that were successful in spurring the economy. At the same time, the country created a national health service and a disability benefits system, improved the quality of its schools and instituted free university education. Sweden established itself as a leading industrial country and was proud of its 'Third Way', a blending of corporative capitalism with a cradle-to-grave social safety net for all.

Olof Palme, assassinated in 1986. *See p20.*

Stockholm syndrome

Shortly after 10am on 23 August 1973, a man wearing a wig, glasses and brown make-up walked into the Kreditbanken at Norrmalmstorg 2. He pulled a sub-machine gun from his jacket, fired a round into the ceiling and shouted, 'Get down to the floor! The party starts.' Thus began a six-day conflict that would become one of the most notorious crimes in Swedish history, and result in a new term that would go on to be used worldwide to describe the unusual behaviour of hostages: 'Stockholm syndrome'.

After botching the robbery early on by shooting a police officer in the hand during an initial confrontation, the robber retreated to a vault, taking three female bank tellers with him as hostages. The robber demanded that the police bring three million kronor to the bank, as well as Clark Olofsson, one of Sweden's best-known criminals, who was serving time for bank robbery and attempted murder of a police officer at the time.

When Olofsson arrived on the scene from Kalmar Prison, Norrmalmstorg looked like a war zone: police in bulletproof vests crouching behind cars, reporters everywhere and sharpshooters in Berzelii Park taking cover behind overturned café tables.

The police sent in Olofsson in the hope that he would stabilise the situation. Olsson remained inside the vault with the hostages, while Olofsson patrolled the bank hall, talked with police officers outside and cleaned out the cash from the tills. On one of these rounds, he found bank employee Sven Säfström, who then was forced to join the other hostages in the vault. Day one turned to day two, and the authorities refused to give into Olsson's demand that he, Olofsson and two hostages be allowed to leave with the money. On day three, the police locked all six people inside the vault.

Having decided that Olsson was not as ruthless as they first thought, police began drilling holes into the roof of the vault to prepare to gas him out. Nearly four days after the vault had been sealed, tear gas was pumped inside and Olsson immediately surrendered. The media coverage of the Norrmalmstorg drama was unprecedented; the event shocked and captivated the nation.

Most of all, though, the Swedish people were surprised by the way the hostages ended up sympathising with their kidnapper – what would come to be known as 'Stockholm syndrome'. The hostages came to view the

---

In 1953 Swedish diplomat Dag Hammarskjöld was appointed secretary-general of the United Nations. A controversial figure who tried to use his position to broker peace in the conflicts of the period, he became a thorn in the side of the superpowers. He died in 1961 in a mysterious plane crash over northern Rhodesia while on a mission to try to solve the Congo crisis. News of his death caused profound sadness across Sweden as he personified the Swedes' perception of themselves as the world's conscience.

Sweden's booming post-war economy produced a great demand for labour that the national workforce could not meet. From about 1950, Sweden began to import skilled labour, primarily from the Nordic countries but also from Italy, Greece and Yugoslavia. This immigration continued unrestricted until the mid 1960s, reaching its peak in 1969-70, when more than 75,000 immigrants were entering Sweden each year. Thereafter numbers fell significantly, although Sweden continued to welcome political refugees, primarily from Latin America (in the 1970s), the Middle East, Asia and Africa (in the 1980s) and the Balkans (in the 1990s). By the mid

1990s, more than one million people – 11 per cent of Sweden's population – were foreign-born.

In the 1970s international economic pressures began to put the squeeze on Sweden's social goals, and it was under Prime Minister Olof Palme's leadership (1982-6) that the Third Way first began to falter. Palme spent a lot of time and energy on building up Sweden's international image, while Sweden's high-tax economy was sliding into stagnation. When an unknown assailant murdered Palme on a Stockholm street in 1986 it created a national trauma.

The end of the Cold War in the late 1980s led to a serious re-evaluation of Sweden's position in international politics. The early 1990s saw the Social Democrats replaced by a centre-right coalition. This coincided with an economic crisis; long-term economic stagnation and budgetary problems led to a massive devaluation of the krona. A programme of austerity measures was then implemented, but it wasn't enough. Sweden suffered its worst recession since the 1930s and unemployment soared to a record 14 per cent. In 1994 the Social Democrats were returned to power.

police, or rather police intervention, as the real threat. One hostage even called the prime minister on the vault telephone in an effort to persuade him to let the hostages leave with Olsson and Olofsson. When the prime minister mentioned that Olsson had shot a police officer, the hostage responded, 'But the police drew their guns first'. It is also reported that hostage Kristin Ehnemark subsequently became friends with Clark Olofsson. Olsson spent eight years in jail and today he lives in Thailand, where he runs a small grocery store. Olofsson, who was found not guilty on appeal to all charges relating to the robbery, continued his life of crime and is currently serving a 14-year sentence in Denmark for drug smuggling.

It wasn't, however, until the kidnap of US newspaper heiress Patty Hearst in 1974 by the Symbionese Liberation Army that the term 'Stockholm syndrome' became internationally known. After her ransom was paid, Hearst shocked the nation by joining forces with her captors and helping to rob banks.

The Stockholm bank hall where the Olsson robbery took place is now an art gallery (Galleri Gunnar Olsson, Norrmalmstorg, 210 777, www.olsson gallery.com).

With both its economy and national confidence severely shaken, Sweden voted (by a very narrow margin) to join the EU, its membership taking effect on 1 January 1995.

Since then, the economy has improved considerably, with both unemployment and inflation falling greatly, particularly during the IT boom of the 1990s. The bursting of the IT bubble in the new millennium seemed to threaten this renewed prosperity, but the industry has picked itself up and Sweden's IT companies remain important contributors to the economy.

Sweden's relationship with the EU remained controversial, with many on the Left fearing that closer co-operation with other European countries threatened to undermine the basic tenets of the welfare state. These arguments were given a good airing in the referendum in 2003 on the euro. Despite support for membership from almost all the major parties, voters chose to stay outside the single currency zone. After the vote, prime minister, Göran Persson, declared that Sweden would not hold another referendum on the issue for at least ten years.

The referendum came just two days after the murder of Anna Lindh, the popular foreign minister, in a Stockholm department store. The killing came as a huge shock to Swedes, who prided themselves on their peaceful, open society. There was much speculation about the extent to which the 'No' vote was influenced by Lindh's death. Another result of Lindh's murder was that Sweden now lacked an obvious successor to Göran Persson. Lindh had been viewed as the 'Crown Princess' of Social Democracy, and her death created a gap that was hard to fill. For many commentators, the euro vote illustrated the difficulties Sweden faces in trying to maintain its generous welfare state in the 21st century.

For most of the past decade, the Left's hold on power has looked secure, with the Social Democrats supported by Miljöpartiet (Greens) and Vänsterpartiet (Left Party). In 2004, however, the traditionally fractious centre-right has started to look more united, and at the time of going to press the four main right-wing parties were planning to launch a joint manifesto for the 2006 election.

Key events

800-1050 The Viking age.
1008 King Olof Skötkonung is the first Swedish king to convert to Christianity.
1150s First invasion of Finland, which later becomes an integrated part of Sweden.
1252 Birger Jarl, Sweden's de facto ruler, founds Stockholm and starts to build Tre Kronor fortress.
1275 Magnus Ladulås becomes king and starts to develop Stockholm.
1350 The Black Death wipes out as much as one third of Sweden's population.
1397 The Kalmar Union is formed by Denmark–Norway and Sweden–Finland, ruled by Queen Margaret in Copenhagen. For the next 125 years there are numerous Swedish rebellions against the union.
1477 Sweden's first university is established in Uppsala.
1520 The Stockholm Bloodbath. Between 80 and 100 political opponents of the Danish king, Christian II, are beheaded on Stortorget.
1523 Gustav Vasa defeats the Danes and is elected king. A long line of Swedish–Danish wars begins.
1524-5 Parliament confiscates Church property, and the Lutheran Reformation unfolds.
1544 Parliament makes the monarchy hereditary.
Early 1500s Stockholm's population is between 6,000 and 7,000.
1628-41 Stockholm's medieval city wall is torn down so that the city can expand.
1630-48 Sweden participates in the Thirty Years War on the side of the Protestants.
1630-50s Planning regulations mean that Stockholm expands on to Södermalm and Norrmalm with straight streets and stone houses.
1686 Drottningholms Slott is completed to designs by Nicodemus Tessins the Elder and Younger.
1700-21 The Great Northern War, during which Sweden fights an alliance of Denmark, Russia and Poland–Saxony, and loses much of her territory.
1719 A new constitution transfers power from the king to Parliament, and the Age of Liberty begins.
1740 The poet Carl Michael Bellman is born; his work encourages Swedish nationalism.
1754 Kungliga Slottet is completed to designs by Nicodemus Tessin the Younger.

1781 Catholics are allowed to establish a church in Stockholm for the first time since the Reformation.
1792 King Gustav III, who had restored the absolute power of the monarchy, is shot; the power of parliament is subsequently restored.
1814 Sweden forces Norway into a union, which is to last until 1905.
1860s The first railway line gives Stockholm increased contact with the rest of the country. Widespread emigration to the US begins.
1872 August Strindberg writes his first major play, *Master Olof*.
1878 The Academy of Stockholm is founded, today the University of Stockholm.
1891 Artur Hazelius opens the folk museum Skansen, as part of a revival of Swedish culture.
1897 A large international exhibition is held on Djurgården.
1900 Stockholm's population reaches 300,000 after tripling in size during the previous 50 years.
1902 Extensive demonstrations for universal suffrage take place.
1907 Men are given the right to vote.
1914-18 Sweden remains neutral during World War I.
1917-18 Stockholm sees political riots inspired by the Russian Revolution.
1921 Women are given the right to vote.
1930s The first steps are taken towards the creation of the welfare state.
1939-45 Sweden remains neutral during World War II.
1950-70 Large parts of the city centre are rebuilt and many historic buildings are lost. The first underground train line is opened.
1955 Compulsory national health insurance is initiated.
1973 The Norrmalmstorg bank robbery turned hostage-taking, which led to the birth of the term 'Stockholm Syndrome'.
1974 The monarchy loses all political power.
1986 Prime Minister Olof Palme is shot dead.
Early 1990s The *krona* is devalued. Sweden is gripped by recession and unemployment soars to 14 per cent.
1995 Sweden joins the European Union.
2000 The Church is separated from the state.
September 2002 In the general election the Social Democrats form a coalition government with the Left Party and the Greens.
September 2003 Foreign Minister Anna Lindh is fatally stabbed in NK department store.

The king and queen of Sweden.

Stockholm Today

Swedes like to do things their way, but Europe is presenting fresh challenges.

As Sweden's population ticked past the nine million mark in August 2004, it was a significant reminder of one of the things that sets it apart from many of its European neighbours. For, although Sweden covers an area the size of California, its population is smaller than that of London. Even so, being a small player in an age of globalisation has done little to dampen the Swedes' enthusiasm for doing things their own way. Indeed, voters' rejection of the European single currency in a referendum in 2003 was a signal that the Swedish model of high taxes and big government still has widespread support.

Though often seen as a liberal, democratic and progressive society from the outside, Sweden harbours plenty of paradoxes. It is a thriving western democracy, yet has been ruled by one party – the Social Democrats – for 65 of the last 74 years. Liberal attitudes towards social issues such as gay marriage and gender equality seem to be juxtaposed by widespread disapproval of 'soft' drugs and draconian restrictions on the sale of alcohol. On top of all this, most Swedes remain committed supporters of the royal family, yet repeatedly elect a party that (in theory, at least) wants to abolish the monarchy.

SOCIAL ISSUES

Sweden prides itself on leading Europe in questions of equality, both racial and sexual. In many ways, men and women are more equal in Sweden than in any other country on earth. Women make up 45 per cent of the Swedish parliament (*Riksdag*) – the second highest proportion in any national parliament in the world (the first is Rwanda). Still, as in the rest of the world, men in Sweden still earn more than women, and female representation on the boards of Sweden's large companies struggles to get above ten per cent.

At the top of the tree, Sweden is still waiting for its first woman prime minister – a possibility made more distant by the murder of Anna Lindh, the popular foreign minister (and widely tipped successor to current premier

Göran Persson), who was stabbed to death in a Stockholm department store in September 2003.

Nevertheless, Sweden's reputation as a beacon of equality is well earned, and it continues to lead the world in areas such as paternity leave (*pappaledighet*), to which all fathers have been entitled for the past 30 years. This right has been increased in the last couple of years, and now fathers are obliged to stay alone with their child for two of their first 16 months in order for their remaining leave to be transferred to the mother. Concern that fathers are still not pulling their weight (and scheduling their leave to coincide with summer and sporting events, such as the football World Cup) means that there is pressure to enforce this rule further by forcing parents to split parental leave evenly. Needless to say, this bold idea has attracted controversy.

Sweden has also taken a lead in gay marriage, being one of the first countries in the world to introduce same-sex registered partnerships. These confer almost all the same rights as marriage, and as far as most people are concerned that is what they are. Now the battle has moved on to the church, with polls showing that six out of ten Swedes back the idea of gay weddings in church. The Church of Sweden, a Lutheran church, has tentatively started considering the idea.

As elsewhere in Europe, immigration is a controversial topic in Sweden. However, it is less of a contentious issue now than it was at the 2002 elections, when anti-immigration parties in some parts of the country won a number of council seats. Of the 1.8 million inhabitants of the County of Stockholm, around 20 per cent were born outside Sweden. When ten new, mainly Eastern European countries joined the European Union in early 2004, Sweden was the only existing member state not to impose special restrictions on immigration. A proposal from the government to impose such restrictions was voted down by a clear majority in the Riksdag.

Still, if all this sounds exceedingly liberal, a visit to a Systembolaget liquor store will show another side of Sweden. These shops are the only places in the country, apart from pubs and restaurants, that are allowed to sell alcohol. They are owned and run by the government (and, as if to cement that relationship, the current head of Systembolaget is married to Prime Minister Göran Persson), and their purpose is to keep alcohol consumption down. 'Systemet', as it is known, remains popular with most Swedes. Surprising perhaps, but strong folk memories of endemic alcohol abuse in the early 20th century mean that many people remain suspicious of their fellow country men's ability to drink sensibly without some

Flags come out for Swedish **National Day**.

help from the state.For more on alcohol law in Sweden, *see p177* **Booze rules**.

The imperative to preserve this restrictive alcohol policy is one reason for continuing scepticism towards the European Union. Sweden was late to join, and since then has distinguished itself as one of the union's 'awkward squad'. As well as rejecting the single currency, it kept strict controls on alcohol brought in from other EU countries until it was forced to relax them in January 2004. Even now political parties, including the Christian Democrats, argue that Sweden should defy the EU, fearing that the Nordic temperament still can't handle its booze.

MONEY MATTERS

Recent years have seen the Swedish economy steady its nerve. The bursting of the IT bubble hit Stockholm hard – it contains more IT and telecoms firms than any other area of Scandinavia – but the information boom left an impressive legacy in terms of knowledge and infrastructure, which is helping to strengthen Swedish business. Sweden consistently tops world rankings for measures such as broadband penetration and 'e-readiness', and continues to pull in plenty of foreign investors, attracted by international companies such as Volvo and Ericsson. Now the buzz that once surrounded IT has, to some extent, transferred to biotechnology, with Swedish (or part-Swedish) companies standing by to help commercialise the fruits of Sweden's knowledge economy.

It is often seen as a paradox that Sweden is home to some of the largest corporations in the world, yet also has some of the western world's highest taxes. In fact, taxes on companies are relatively low, although personal taxes can be high, particularly if you are well off. Still, that hasn't stopped Sweden from producing the richest man in the world, IKEA owner Ingvar Kamprad (who has recently overtaken Bill Gates).

One of the latest wheezes to extract more cash from Stockholm's citizens is a so-called congestion charge, which will be introduced in 2005 for a trial period. The idea is being pushed by Mayor Annika Billström and her fellow Social Democrats in the national government. The charges will be levied on cars driving into Stockholm during peak periods, with the aim of cutting congestion, improving the environment and (cynics would say, most importantly) raising money for the council and central government coffers. Still, it remains to be seen whether the idea can win over the voters; polls consistently show a small majority to be opposed to the charges.

FRIENDSHIPS AND RIVALRIES

Capital cities often enjoy a tense relationship with the provinces, and Stockholm is no exception. In Sweden, the differences are exacerbated by the sheer contrasts between isolated regions in the north of Sweden and the buzzing metropolis of one and a half million people. Predictably, money is often at the heart of regional disagreements.

Recent proposals from the government to redistribute more of Sweden's wealth from rich areas such as Stockholm to remote areas with high unemployment have met with squeals of protest from city councillors and taxpayers alike. However, as most tax in Sweden is set by local councils and relatively little by central government, many people argue more redistribution by way of this 'Robin Hood tax' (so-called because it 'robs' from the rich regions to give to the poor) is the only way to avoid massive inequality between regions.

Rivalry also exists between Stockholm and Sweden's second and third cities, Gothenburg and Malmö. The rivalry is partly provoked by Stockholm's dominance of national political and economic life (perhaps unavoidable given that Stockholm's population is twice as large as that of Gothenburg). There is also an element of class conflict at play, with residents of traditionally working-class Gothenburg viewing Stockholmers as stiff and effete, and Stockholmers having a tendency

to consolidate this by looking down their noses at their compatriots on the west coast.

Malmö, in the far south, was until recently a country cousin chiefly distinguished in the eyes of Stockholmers by its impenetrable accent. However, the opening in 2000 of a bridge linking the city to Danish capital Copenhagen breathed new life into Malmö's economy. It is now a major centre for the biotechnology and IT industries, and Stockholmers can no longer dismiss the city as lightly as they have in the past.

While competition between Swedish regions often remains unspoken, the (usually) friendly rivalries with other Nordic countries are more apparent. Relationships with Norway and Finland are coloured by the centuries-long domination of both countries by Sweden.

Sweden and Norway have something of a big brother-little brother complex. The two countries were in a Swedish-dominated political

Enough already

Sometimes, one word can open up a window into a nation's soul. In Sweden that word is *lagom*. Directly translated it means 'just enough' or 'sufficient', but such blunt translations cannot do justice to the true importance of this word. *Lagom* sums up Swedish ideas of fairness, equality and modesty – the values on which Lutheran, social democratic Sweden is built.

The word's origins are disputed – some say it means 'in accordance with the law', but the more colourful explanation is that it derives from *laget om*, meaning 'around the team'. According to this theory, Viking warriors sharing a cup of mead would take a *lagom* amount before passing it on – enough to satisfy themselves, but leaving enough for everyone else.

In modern Sweden, the idea endures that 'just enough' is perfect, and Swedes take a firm line against excess. Ostentatious displays of wealth are frowned upon, and rugged individualism takes second place to the needs of the society as a whole. IKEA owner Ingvar Kamprad has cultivated a reputation for frugality, and was long held up as an example that a good Swede doesn't flash his money about, no matter how rich he is. However, the revelation in the press that Kamprad owns a string of luxury homes around the world left some Swedes feeling genuinely let down. One country house is *lagom*, so why would any Swede want three?

union until 1905, which has left Swedes feeling a twinge of jealousy at Norway's oil wealth, but also amusement at Norwegians' forays across the border to buy pornography (which is more strictly controlled in Norway) and alcohol, which is even more expensive in Norway than in Sweden. The relationship is also affected by tensions over neutral Sweden's conduct during World War II. The feeling that Swedes turned the other cheek to the Nazi occupation of Norway has left some bitter wounds.

Sweden's relations with Finland and Denmark tend to be more relaxed, although Denmark is still viewed as something of a den of iniquity by some Swedes, thanks to the perception that it takes a relaxed attitude to sex, drugs and alcohol. Despite slight jealousy over the success of Nokia, Sweden's large Finnish population helps Sweden and Finland to enjoy a friendly relationship.

CONSTANCY AND CHANGE

The monarchy continues to command affection from most Swedes. Although plenty of republicans can be found in most political parties, they tend to keep pretty quiet in the knowledge that they have little popular support.

The current king, Carl XVI Gustaf, has a purely ceremonial role, after the 1974 constitution stripped him of formal political power. Nonetheless, he still has the power to create controversy, as was demonstrated when he commended the Sultan of Brunei for his 'enormous closeness to his people'. What would in other countries have passed off as a casual diplomatic pleasantry created a storm in politically correct Sweden, where the king was accused of ignoring the lack of democracy in Brunei.

Despite the occasional royal faux pas, 27-year-old Crown Princess Victoria can look forward to inheriting a secure throne. And while she and the rest of the royal family have had to endure the usual invasions of privacy – Swedish newspapers show the same ferocious interest in royalty as their counterparts in other countries – the private lives of the Swedish royals are rarely discussed as matters of constitutional importance.

While the monarchy stays constant, many other Swedish norms – social, political and economic – are being challenged. Pressure from Europe and the international economy has led to questions being asked about how much of the social democratic state will be left behind for future generations. Combine this with a newly unified centre-right opposition, and Social Democrats must wonder whether they will be in a position to dominate this century as comprehensively as they did the last.

A nation mourns the death of **Anna Lindh**. See p23.

Riddarhuset. *See p29.*

Architecture

Neutrality and conservative planning have helped preserve Stockholm – but to the detriment of daring architecture?

Saved by Sweden's steady wartime neutrality from the kind of widespread destruction suffered by its European neighbours, Stockholm has been able to preserve many – if not all – of its oldest buildings. As a result, today the city's streets are lined with beautiful structures that span almost every architectural period since the city was founded in 1252.

The city's historical heart, **Gamla Stan** (the Old Town), has a fairy-tale feel, with its maze of narrow cobblestone alleys and brightly painted low-rise buildings. But, while Stockholm's oldest buildings may be the most immediately engaging, each period of the city's expansion and development has led to noteworthy and compelling buildings that, aside from being aesthetically pleasing, also reveal a great deal about Swedish culture and society – from the ancient churches of Nordic Christianity though the Renaissance and baroque, to Kafkaesque high-rises in some of the city's suburbs.

To find out more about the development of the city visit **Stockholms Stadsmuseum**

(City Museum; *see p94*), where a selection of milieux and periods are explored.

13TH-CENTURY BEGINNINGS

In 1252 Birger Jarl began constructing **Tre Kronor** castle (only the foundation and the renovated northern wing remain), on the site of several earlier wooden fortresses, in the part of Gamla Stan where the Royal Palace now stands; a town quickly sprang up within its ring wall. The Medeltidsmuseet (underneath the parliament building) and Museet Tre Kronor (underneath the Royal Palace) give indications of what Stockholm was like during this period.

Riddarholmskyrkan, on Riddarholmen, was begun in the late 13th century and is one of the first Gothic buildings constructed in Sweden (though much of it has been rebuilt

▶ Many of the buildings mentioned here are described in more detail in the **Sightseeing** chapters.

Suburban, 12th-century **Solna Kyrka** is one of Stockholm's oldest buildings.

since then; the oldest section is the north aisle). **Storkyrkan** in Gamla Stan was founded in 1306, but gained its present shape in the late 1400s and underwent a baroque makeover in the 1730s. Even older than these buildings are the suburban churches of **Bromma Kyrka** and **Solna Kyrka**, erected in the 1100s even before the official founding of Stockholm.

Birger Jarl's town on Gamla Stan grew steadily. By the 15th century it had developed the maze of narrow lanes that define it to this day. Looking at a map you can see that the lane structure is almost that of a wheel, with spokes radiating out from the centre. Stockholm suffered from a number of devastating fires in its early centuries, and the wheel structure allowed townspeople to rapidly reach the shore for water. Without it the medieval town would probably not have survived to see the 21st century.

In the late 15th century the Church was still the key protagonist in Sweden's architectural development, as it had been since the end of the Viking period, but in the 16th century the balance of power began to change. By 1523 King Gustav Vasa had united Sweden and he was determined to turn it into a modern nation state and hereditary monarchy. He knew that success depended on limiting the influence of the Church and intimidating potential rivals, and that architecture had a role to play.

By the mid 1500s Stockholm had become Sweden's most important town, so the king centralised his power base at Tre Kronor, making it the permanent royal residence. He imported foreign architects and craftsmen to build a series of defensive castles at strategic locations across his realm to ward off Danish attacks. In the late 1500s he commissioned these architects and craftsmen to convert Tre Kronor into a classical Italian Renaissance palace fit for a king of his stature. Unfortunately, Tre Kronor and all its splendour burned to the ground in 1697 – only the northern wing has been saved.

RENAISSANCE STYLES

During the 17th century three different Renaissance styles came to be widely popular, as the aristocracy began to build townhouses in the capital to be able to spend more time at court. The castles in **Vadstena** and **Kalmar** (both a few hours' drive south of Stockholm) are the best remaining examples of the early classicism that defined Tre Kronor. The second style to become popular, German-Dutch Renaissance, appeared in the 1620s – you can recognise it by its highly decorated gables adorned with imaginative ornamental forms. Gamla Stan contains a number of fine examples, including Christian Julius Döteber's **Petersenska Huset** at Munkbron 11-13, as well as **Grillska Huset** and **Schantzska Huset** on Stortorget.

Dutch Palladianism was the third Renaissance style to be all the rage; it is characterised by columns that stretch across at least two storeys. The best example in Stockholm is the palace of **Riddarhuset** (1674), designed by the man who is considered Sweden's first professional architect, Simon de la Vallée. His son Jean was responsible for the building's distinctive *säteri* roof (a roof with a small vertical rise halfway up) – the first of many buildings to be crowned with this entirely Swedish architectural invention. Jean (1620-96) became one of the leading architects of the Carolinian period, along with a German architect named Nicodemus Tessin (1615-81). The Swedish royal court hired Tessin as court architect in 1646. In 1661, he become Stockholm's first official city architect.

SWEDISH BAROQUE AND THE TESSINS

By the mid 17th century Sweden was a great power and King Karl XI wanted to construct grand buildings that would show off his wealth and status. He sent Tessin and Jean de la Vallée to Italy and France for new ideas, and they came back with baroque. Most of the buildings constructed in Stockholm between 1650 and 1730 reflected one of three baroque styles: French, Roman or 'Swedish' (a French-Roman hybrid). The French style is the most fanciful, often created by linking a group of structures together under an imposing copper roof. In creating **Bondeska Palatset** (1662-73) at Riddarhustorget 8, Tessin and de la Vallée worked together, carefully copying French examples. The grand palaces of Rome were clearly the inspiration for de la Vallée's designs for **Oxenstiernska Palatset** (1653) at Storkyrkobrinken 2. Greatly admired, this palace inspired the faintly Roman look of the new **Kungliga Slottet** built shortly thereafter.

The greatest example of truly Swedish baroque is Tessin's **Drottningholms Slott** – where the royal family now lives – just to the west of Stockholm, a World Heritage Site often referred to as Sweden's mini-Versailles. The palace is a majestic blend of Roman and French styles crowned with a *säteri* roof. Church builders latched onto the baroque style too. **Tyska Kyrkan** on Gamla Stan received a lovely baroque makeover in 1638-42, while **Katarina Kyrka** on Södermalm (1656-95), designed by de la Vallée, is a breathtaking example of an entirely baroque construction.

After his father's death, Nicodemus Tessin the Younger (1654-1728) put the finishing touches to **Drottningholms Slott**, his father's masterwork, and designed the impressive gardens. Following the fire at Tre Kronor palace, King Karl XII chose Tessin the Younger to draw up plans for a new palace on the site; he is also well known for his work at the Amalienborg Palace in Copenhagen and the Louvre in Paris. When he died, his son Carl Gustav Tessin (1695-1770) became superintendent of all the royal palaces and it was under his leadership that the new **Kungliga Slottet** (Royal Palace) was completed in 1754.

ROCOCO AND BEYOND

By the end of the 1720s Sweden's upper classes had tired of the ostentation of baroque styles; they wanted more simplicity and rationality in their homes. As if on cue, Carl Gustav Tessin and Carl Hårleman introduced French rococo architecture to Sweden. The style quickly took hold, and many of Stockholm's most beautiful buildings have its standard features: rounded window frames, a low foundation and a mansard roof (four-sided with a double slope on all sides). Hårleman's **Observatoriet** (Observatory; 1748-53) at Observatoriekullen gives a good sense of the simplicity of the style, while Erik Palmstedt's **Börsen** (1773-6) – the former Stock Exchange, now the **Nobelmuseet** – on Stortorget, and the 1727-9 exterior and interior remodelling of **Ulriksdals Slott** in Solna by

Don't miss **Architecture**

The beginnings of a city
Around **Gamla Stan** (*see pp62-72*), the Old Town, plus **Riddarholmskyrkan** (*see p72*) on Riddarholmen.

Art nouveau
Centralbadet (*see p171*), **Kungliga Dramatiska Teatern** (*see p234*), and **Hotels Esplanade** and **Diplomat** (for both, *see p56*).

Uncompromising modernism
Sergels Torg, Hötorgshusen and lower **Norrmalm** (*see pp73-9*).

Postmodernism
Globen (*see p229*), the world's largest spherical building.

The works of Gunnar Asplund
Sweden's most famous architect designed **Stadsbiblioteket** (*see p79*), **Skogskyrkogården** (*see p108*) and **Skandia** cinema (*see p200*).

National Romanticism
Rådhuset (*see p102*).

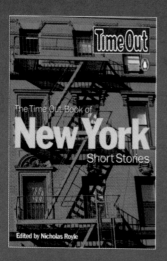
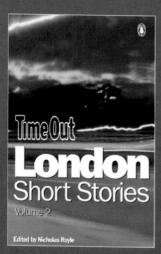
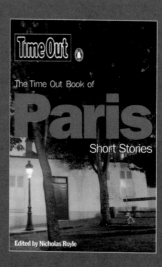

Kina Slott at Drottningholm.

Hårleman and Göran Josuae Adelcrantz give a sense of how elegant Swedish rococo could be.

Mid to late 18th-century architecture in Stockholm is characterised by a light-heartedness not seen in earlier periods. For example, Carl Fredrik Adelcrantz was commissioned to erect **Kina Slott** (Chinese Pavilion) in Drottningholm's park as an exotic gift from King Adolf Fredrik to his queen. Soon after its unveiling in 1763 the fanciful pseudo-Asian pavilion became a popular rural retreat for members of the royal family. Fredrik Magnus Piper's design of **Hagaparken** illustrates the ideals of King Gustav III's reign (1771-92) – it is also the foremost example of an English park in Sweden. It contains many buildings of interest, including the peculiar Pavilion, the sublime Ekotemplet, the playful Koppartälten and the dainty Haga Slott.

As the 18th century reached its end, a more austere classicism came to rule the day again. In 1793 the lakefront side of **Karlbergs Slott** in north-west Stockholm (home of the Swedish military academy) underwent renovation in neo-classical style under the guidance of Louis Jean Desprez and Carl Christopher Gjörwell. Fredrik Blom based his plans for **Rosendals Slott** – a pleasure palace for King Karl XIV Johan on Djurgården – on the tenets of French classicism.

The building, finished in 1827, is easily distinguishable by its light imperial style and delicately ornamented façade.

By the 1830s Swedish architects had tired of all this restraint and turned back to the 'romance' of the Italian and French Renaissance for inspiration, resulting in a revival in the building of highly ornamental exteriors. The National Museum (1846-66), designed by the German architect Friedrich August Stüler, is a prime example of Italian Renaissance, while Adolf Wilhelm Edelsvärd's **Central Station** (1867-71) was clearly inspired by the French Renaissance. Later in the century many architects became fascinated by Sweden's medieval architecture. Fredrik Blom was one of the first; his medieval-inspired **Kastellet** (citadel), a key landmark when approaching the city by sea, was erected in 1846-8. Stockholm's **Synagogan** (Synagogue; 1870) by Fredrik Wilhelm Scholander is a one-of-a-kind house of worship in ancient Eastern style.

In the mid 1800s glass and cast iron became cheaper and more accessible, inspiring architects to create spacious rooms with abundant natural light and to mix styles. Architects also began to work for companies and cities rather than for the royal court or wealthy individuals. New factories, office buildings, hospitals, schools and prisons went up at lightning speed. The monumental **Konradsberg Sjukhus** (1855-75) that Albert Törnqvist built at Gjörwellsgatan 16 offers an insight into the principles of healthcare at the time: its many windows give the building a bright and airy interior, while its strict form and clean lines suggest order and hygiene.

Architect Aron Johansson constructed the bold, baroque-inspired **Riksdagshuset** (Parliament) in 1892-1905. In so doing he raised the ire of the young architects of the nascent National Romantic movement. They argued passionately that its busy exterior was entirely inappropriate – altogether too showy and pretentious for a country whose architectural tradition had always been (in their romantic view, at least) centred on simplicity.

ROMANTICISM AND ART NOUVEAU

In the late 19th century, nationalism was on the rise across Europe. Sweden's National Romantic style emerged in response to the confidence generated by the country's rapidly expanding industrial might. Rather than looking for inspiration abroad, Swedish architects rediscovered their country's own rich architectural tradition. The Scandinavian Renaissance style that had been popular in the 17th century was the main focus. In the 1880s the long-neglected area of Gamla Stan (and its unique 17th-century portals, in particular) began to attract the attention of architects such as Isak Gustav Clason (1856-1930). Curious about medieval building techniques, he designed a new building at Österlånggatan 14 (1888-9) that quite successfully mimicked the look of the medieval originals that surround it.

Clason's enormous **Nordiska Museet** is a fine example of the National Romantic style, with its cupolas, towers and richly adorned portal. When it opened in 1907 it was hailed as a masterpiece, 'the likes of which have not been created since the days of the great Tessin'. The grand indoor market, **Östermalms Saluhall** (1888), is another of Clason's creations. His work

Art goes underground

Think being in transit is a waste of valuable sightseeing time? Not in Stockholm. The city's metro system claims to be the longest art exhibition in the world, stretching a whopping 110 kilometres (68 miles). At present about 90 of the 100 stations contain works of art, but every year the exhibition is updated with new works, both temporary and permanent.

As unlikely as it may sound, many consider the art housed within the Stockholm metro to be the most significant investment in art in Sweden since the end of World War II. Since the 1950s, about 140 artists have worked to create a multitude of paintings, sculptures, ceramic works, engravings, installations and fanciful architectural features. Many more have shown their work as part of temporary exhibitions.

The metro art project started shortly before Stockholm's metro system was inaugurated in 1950, when a group of artists began lobbying politicians on the benefits of art in an underground environment. They argued that art would make the metro inspirational rather than just a dreary means of transport, and that the presence of art would reduce vandalism, creating a soothing environment.

Eventually the artists, led by Siri Derkert and Vera Nilsson, won the support of the city council and a competition was held to collect proposals from artists interested in working on the metro stations. The results of that first competition can be seen on the platforms of the green and red lines of **T-Centralen** station, which include works by Derkert and Nilsson; look for their engravings and stone mosaics on the pillars.

As the metro expanded, more competitions were held to select artists to decorate the stations. A number of well-known Swedish artists and craftsmen participated, and many of them were given the opportunity to design whole stations single-handedly. Some of the

metro art is striking, such as the blue-and-white painted ceiling of the cave-like blue line platform of **T-Centralen** station, while other art is more subtle, such as the patterns from the medieval fabrics decorating the cement floor and walls of **Gamla Stan** station. The ceiling of **Hörtorget** station (*pictured*) glows from the light of twisting neon tubes buzzing in five shades of white, while the grotto of **Kungsträdgården** station is dimly lit by neon gas lamps shining on reproductions of statues of Riddarhuset. Siri Derkert's **Östermalm** station contains political art considered quite radical when first unveiled. Further afield, you'll find Anders Åberg's **Solna Centrum** station, a radical 1970s work focused on environmental issues. Based on Japanese ideas of yin and yang, Takashi Naraha's work at **Vreten** station adds an international touch to the collection.

SL (Stockholm Transport) produces a free pamphlet called 'Art in the Stockholm Metro', that you can pick up from the SL Centre at T-Centralen station. It includes listings of all the metro stations and details of the art on display. Free guided tours are also available.

on **Timmermansorden** (1927), at Eriksbergsparken 1, marks the end of the National Romantic movement.

A drive to preserve Sweden's architectural heritage began at about the same time. In 1891 Artur Hazelius opened **Skansen**, an open-air museum that displays an authentic collection of traditional buildings from all over Sweden. It includes a neighbourhood from the 1700s filled with apartments and small workshops. The National Romantic architects visited the park frequently for inspiration.

Art nouveau (known as *Jugendstil* in Sweden) came briefly into fashion with National Romanticism, but its influence is easier to see in privately owned apartment buildings than in public works of the time. Fredrik Liljekvist's **Kungliga Dramatiska Teatern** (Royal Dramatic Theatre; 1901-8), with its exquisitely sculpted white marble exterior, bright gold detailing and magnificent approach ramp, and **Centralbadet** (1902-5), a huge art nouveau bathhouse built by Wilhelm Klemming, are the two major exceptions. Ferdinand Boberg's **Thielska Galleriet** (1904-5) on Djurgården offers another example of art nouveau influence.

National Romanticism reached its peak in the 1910s. Architects had now turned for inspiration to the time of the 16th-century Vasa kings, and were designing buildings with clean façades displaying little if any decor, and steep roofs. The best example of this style is Stockholm's **Rådhuset** (Courthouse; 1908-15), designed by Carl Westman to look like the Renaissance classicist Vadstena castle.

At the turn of the 20th century Stockholm's city architect Per Olof Hallman (1869-1941) developed ground-breaking residential neighbourhoods. He is best remembered for the artistic flair that he brought to urban planning and for integrating new residential complexes within the surrounding natural environment. Fine examples of his work can be seen in Östermalm in **Lärkstaden** (around Friggagatan and Baldersgatan), **Danderydsgatan** and **Diplomatstaden** (around Dag Hammarskjölds Väg), and in Vasastaden in **Rödabergsområdet** (Falugatan and around).

Ragnar Östberg (1866-1945) is one of the best-known architects of this period. His most famous creation is Stockholm's **Stadshuset** (City Hall; 1923), which was influenced by both Gothic and Italian Renaissance styles. He also designed Östermalms **Läroverket** (now a secondary school called Östra Real; 1906-10) and **Patent och Registreringsverket** (1911-21), the patent and licensing authority's building on Valhallavägen in Östermalm.

During the 1910s classicism slowly became fashionable yet again, and by the 1920s it was

Postmodern **Globen**. *See p35.*

in full swing. The construction of the Stadshuset and the Gothenburg Exhibition of 1923 were the start of a period of international acclaim for Swedish architecture – a heady time, since no one had paid much attention to Swedish architects since Tessin the Younger.

Swedish classicism of the 1920s was known as 'Swedish Grace' because it charmed everyone with its lightness, simplicity and elegance – especially compared with the bombastic works that were constructed in other parts of the world at the time. The best example of Swedish Grace in Stockholm is the **Stadsbiblioteket** (1920-28) built by Gunnar Asplund, who would go on to become the most influential Swedish architect of the 20th century. The interior design of the **Skandia** cinema (1923) on Drottninggggatan is another of his greatly admired works from this period.

MODERNISM AND FUNCTIONALISM

As the leading architect of the Stockholm Exhibition in 1930, Asplund is credited as the man who introduced modernism to Sweden in the form of functionalism (*funkis*). It was a radical approach to architecture that rejected tradition and focused on utilitarianism, rationality, economics and health. After the fair a building boom ensued and scores of sober, pale-coloured *funkis* apartment buildings

The offices of **White**, leaders in Swedish architecture. *See p35.*

sprouted up in a variety of patterns across the city. The best examples can be seen in the Gärdet area of Stockholm, particularly around **Tessinparken** (1932-7), north of Östermalm.

While many tried, Asplund is considered to be the only Swedish architect who fully succeeded in humanising the strict utilitarian underpinnings of functionalism. His most famous functionalist work in the Stockholm area can be seen at **Skogskyrkogården** (Woodland Cemetery; 1914-40), one of the few works of 20th-century architecture selected for UNESCO's World Heritage List (*see p109* **Dead famous**). A collaboration with the architect Sigurd Lewerentz, the Skogskyrkogården project took 26 years to complete and thus provides a good overview of Swedish architecture from the National Romantic period to mature functionalism. Asplund mainly focused on designing the cemetery's buildings; of particular note are the sunny Skogskapellet (chapel; 1918) and the imposing Skogskrematoriet (crematorium; 1934-40). The latter is recognised as one of the most noteworthy buildings of the 20th century.

In the early 1950s many Swedes felt a little left out – across Europe bombed-out cities were being rebuilt in a modernist style, and tall, proud, American-style skyscrapers were popping up all over. And yet there was Stockholm with its embarrassingly old city centre dominated by crumbling, tiny houses. In an effort to modernise, the area to the north

of Gamla Stan, known as the old Klara district, was brutally demolished (with the thankful exception of 16th-century St Clara Kyrka) and later replaced with **Sergels Torg** (1960), Peter Celsing's shiny **Kulturhuset** (1968-73) and an assortment of nondescript office buildings. The city's first skyscrapers were also built nearby: **Hötorgshusen** (1952-6), the five towers that line Sveavägen from Sergels Torg to Hötorget. For more on the history of lower Norrmalm's destruction, *see p77* **Concrete calamity?**.

It was also in the 1950s that Swedish architects tired of traditional functionalism and its strict reliance on straight lines. They began to design buildings in unusual geometric patterns – with a star-shaped foundation, for example, rather than a square or rectangular one. They also reconsidered how buildings should be grouped in relation to one another. These ideas are represented in the acclaimed suburban neighbourhood of **Vällingby**, the first of Sweden's many A-B-C neighbourhoods. A for *arbete* (work), B for *bostad* (home) and C for *centrum* (shopping centre) – an attempt to decentralise the city that ultimately failed.

In the 1960s and '70s Stockholm and many other Swedish cities suffered an acute housing shortage. The government pledged to build a million new homes in ten years (1964-74). Sweden's builders erected new apartment buildings faster than any other country in the world. The most characteristic '**Million Programme**' buildings in Stockholm are in Brandbergen, Hallonbergen, Hallunda and Tensta-Rinkeby.

The 1970s were a tumultuous period for Swedish architecture, and significant ideological shifts took place before the decade was out. This is well illustrated by writer Olof Hultin's comparison of two buildings designed by the firm Coordinator Arkitekter just a decade apart: **Garnisonen** (1965-71) at Karlavägen 100 and **Salénhuset** (1975-8) at Norrlandsgatan 15. Strictly functionalist Garnisonen stands out like a sore thumb, but there isn't anything particularly interesting about it. In designing Salénhuset, however, the firm broke the structure down into its component parts and used a variety of materials to create a building with its own personality that still broadly fits in.

Probably the most visible postmodern building in Stockholm is the indoor arena of **Globen** (1989), the world's largest spherical structure, whose 'geometrical precision has a curiously disruptive effect on the scale of the townscape', as Hultin has written. Another good example of postmodernism is Ricardo Bofill's **Båge** (1992), a colossal residential development on Söder in the shape of a semicircle. Part of the same housing development, Henning Larsen's stubby apartment towerblock at **Medborgarplatsen** was controversial from the moment he submitted the blueprints. It ended up half the height it was meant to be, which has thrown the look of the whole neighbourhood out of kilter.

From 1995 to '98 Spanish architect Rafael Moneo worked on the **Moderna Museet** and **Arkitekturmuseet** on Skeppsholmen, both of which are admired for their boxy interiors. Despite the substantial size of the maze-like complex, Moneo won the praise of Stockholmers for designing it in such a way that it did not overwhelm the historical look and feel of Skeppsholmen.

NEW KIDS ON THE BLOCK

The most significant public building erected in Stockholm recently is **Arken**, by Lise-Lott Söderlund, the new headquarters for the postal service, just north of central Stockholm, in Solna. 'The Ark' does indeed look like a large ship run aground. Glass dominates the imposing structure, with blonde wood and rainbow colours adding highlights.

The architecture firm that has really made its mark on Stockholm in recent years is White (www.white.se), an employee-owned 'idea factory'. Its architects designed the landmark, prism-inspired **Kista Science Tower** by Jan O Larsson, Scandinavia's tallest office building at 160 metres (525 feet); glassy and classy **Clarion**, Stockholm's largest hotel, perched above

Söderleden at the southern end of Södermalm; award-winning **Katsan** (White's own office block at Skanstullsbron); luxurious seaside residences at **Gåshaga Pirar** on Lidingö island; and **Innanhavet** at Hammarby Sjöstad.

Numerous architecture firms and building companies have participated in the construction of **Hammarby Sjöstad** (www.hammarby sjostad.se), a new neighbourhood just south-east of the city centre that, when finished, will comprise 9,000 apartments. The development is unique in that it was built according to an eco-cycle model that ensures a fully integrated system of organic recycling. The neighbourhood is a pleasure to visit, but the high prices have made it difficult to sell the largest, most luxurious homes.

LOOKING TO THE FUTURE

Construction recently began on large new housing developments in the nearby southern suburbs of **Liljeholmen** and **Årsta**, and the city is considering grand plans to transform **Värtahamnen**, an old industrial harbour area just north-east of the centre, into a new neighbourhood as well. Soon new housing will be sprouting up along the northern shores of Kungsholmen too, on land that was previously zoned for industry. There are plans to redevelop the area north of Vasastaden between Stockholm University and Solna's Karolinska University Hospital – covering over the traffic arteries and train tracks to build a labyrinth of offices, laboratories and residential buildings on top.

Perhaps most daring of all, **Solna** recently approved a massive redevelopment of its centre that will cover over Frösundaleden (a busy traffic artery), expanding the shopping centre, freshening up Råsunda Stadion (Sweden's national football stadium), and erecting new residential and commercial buildings, including two controversial skyscrapers.

For visitors who have come to Stockholm hoping to see the work of some of Sweden's most internationally famous contemporary architects – such as Thomas Sandell, Gert Wingårdh and Anders Wilhelmson – the disappointment will be considerable. Other than Arlanda airport's spectacularly unconventional air-traffic control tower (2001), designed by Wingårdh, there is surprisingly little cutting-edge architecture to be seen in Stockholm. Sadly, most world-renowned contemporary Swedish architects are best known for what they have built outside Stockholm. So far their proposals for the Swedish capital – which tend to include skyscrapers, anathema to the city's planners and to many citizens as well – have been roundly and repeatedly rejected. Will their perseverance pay off? Only time will tell.

Sofia Löfstedt's '**Slapstick**' at Svensk Form. *See p38.*

Design

Always functional, but increasingly fun.

Simplicity, graceful forms and functionality are the three pillars of contemporary Swedish design, which has been characterised by a penchant for the sober and rational, and an aversion to over-decoration, for over a century. But globally minded young Swedish designers have started to break new ground and rebel against the traditionally rigid definitions of 'good taste'.

Influenced by their more flamboyant counterparts in Belgium, Holland, the UK and Italy, this new wave of designers can see no reason why Swedish design can't be fun, witty and bold. At the same time, the Swedish design scene is also moving beyond its traditional strongholds of furniture, glassware (*see p160* **Pure glass**) and industrial products, and into the brave new world of fashion (*see p39* **Fashion with flair**), something the Swedes have traditionally left to other nationalities.

Still, fans of the traditional clean lines and minimalism of Nordic style need not worry. The quintessentially 'Swedish look' is based upon a broad historical and philosophical foundation and is, therefore, not immediately threatened by more flamboyant fleeting trends.

HISTORICAL ROOTS

Though modern Swedish design dates back roughly 100 years, its aesthetic roots can be traced further back. The highly influential **Gustavian style**, which came about during the reign of King Gustav III in the 18th century, marked a move away from elaborate baroque to a more classical, restrained elegance characterised by white wood and simple curves. Then, in the late 1800s, the Swedish elite was first exposed to **German art nouveau**, a new style that dramatically changed the way well-to-do Swedes thought about their homes. It marked a further shift towards organic forms and sinewy curves, inspired by nature, and led to even less fancy and more ergonomic furniture and household accessories.

The paintings of late 19th-century artist **Carl Larsson** (1853-1919) played a significant role in the development of Swedish interior design. In 1899 he created a widely reproduced series of watercolours called *Ett Hem* ('A Home'), featuring the simple furniture and pale-coloured textiles created by his wife Karin, who was inspired by local design traditions, the English Arts and Crafts movement and art nouveau trends on the Continent. In Larsson's paintings, it is easy to recognise the rural wooden floors and rectangular woven rag rugs that are still common in nearly every Swedish home. The striped patterns on the simple white-painted chairs are also strikingly similar to those sold today by Swedish interior decorating monolith IKEA, which seems to be rapidly taking over the refurbishment of the world's homes with nearly 200 branches worldwide.

In an essay entitled *Beauty for All* ('Skönhet för Alla'; 1899) inspired by the Larssons' aesthetics, Swedish social critic Ellen Key defined the democratic ideals embodied in the Larssons' rustic home: 'Not until nothing ugly can be bought, when the beautiful is as cheap as the ugly, only then can beauty for all become a reality.' These democratic principles, as well as those expressed by Gregor Paulsson in 1919 in his book *More Beautiful Things for Everyday Use*, still inform Swedish society and influence new design.

> **'Some speculate that Sweden was especially receptive to functionalism – and later to minimalist severity – because of sober Swedish Lutheranism.'**

Many of the classics of Swedish design came out during the creatively fertile 1930s, as modernism blossomed throughout northern Europe. The movement made its breakthrough in Sweden at the Stockholm Exhibition in 1930, organised by influential Swedish architect **Gunnar Asplund** (1885-1940), and the Swedish offshoot came to be known as functionalism. Some speculate that Sweden was especially receptive to the gospel of functionalism – and later to minimalist severity – because of sober Swedish Lutheranism, as well as a national penchant for social engineering.

The fresh air, natural light and access to greenery extolled by Asplund's functionalism quickly became the defining characteristics of Swedish home design and urban planning. During the next two decades, as news of the practical and beautiful designs coming out of the Nordic region spread to other parts of Europe, as well as North America, the reputation of Scandinavian style became firmly established. For more on Asplund's architecture, *see pp33-45.*

FOUNDING FATHERS

The demi gods of Swedish furniture design – Carl Malmsten and Bruno Mathsson – both flourished during the dynamic pre-war period.

Carl Malmsten (1888-1972) sought forms that some described as 'rural rococo', and aspired to a craft-oriented and functional approach to furniture design. The company he founded 60 years ago – **Carl Malmsten Inredning** (*see p173*) – is still in the same family. His counterpart **Bruno Mathsson** (1907-88) is famous for his groundbreaking work with bentwood. Mathsson's light and simple modernistic designs can be seen in Stockholm at **Studio B3**'s permanent showroom (Barnhusgatan 3, Norrmalm, 411 89 07, www.scandinaviandesign.com/b3, closed July).

A third giant of the pre-war design era was modernist architect and designer **Josef Frank** (1885-1967), an Austrian exile in Sweden, who created elegant furniture and vibrant floral textiles. Frank was so ahead of his time that his brilliant patterns look like they could have been created yesterday, and are still very popular. Frank's colourful fabrics can be seen at **Svenskt Tenn** (*see p175*), the design emporium on Sveavägen in Östermalm.

The term 'Scandinavian design' was coined in the 1950s when the exhibition 'Design in Scandinavia' toured northern America, and Nordic design, with its clean lines, high-level functionality and accessibility, became the most internationally influential design movement of the time. The latter half of the 20th century inevitably brought some variance from the founding facets of Swedish design, with designers responding to the times and experimenting. For instance, in the 1960s an 'anti-functional' movement took root as Swedish designers looked to their Italian counterparts for inspiration. Free from the rules of functionalism, they began to produce chairs, lamps and sofas in all sizes, shapes and colours, and in a variety of new and unusual materials, notably plastic.

During the economic boom of the 1980s, eclecticism and postmodernism took over as designers such as **Jonas Bohlin** (born 1953) and **Mats Theselius** (born 1956) began creating 'work of art' furniture in limited editions for sale to collectors. Bohlin's breakthrough came in 1980 with 'Concrete', a chair made out of – you guessed it – concrete.

A kind of neo-functionalist minimalism had taken over by the 1990s. Suddenly every bar and restaurant in the city, it seemed, was painted white, with unobtrusive furniture and almost no decoration on the walls or tables. This Scandinavian ultra-simplicity quickly spread to the rest of the world, in no small part due to the praise it earned from international style magazines such as *Wallpaper**.

DesignTorget

DesignTorget: your first stop for emerging Swedish design. *See p39.*

THE NEW GENERATION

In the new millennium, a fresh generation of creators, inspired by everything from Japanese cartoons and street art to hip hop, are bringing a playful and often witty twist to the local design scene. For example, at the 2004 **Stockholm Furniture Fair** (*see p187*), textile designers **Helen Högberg** and **Johanna Lindgren** impressed with their 'Piece of Cake' exhibit featuring lamps appearing to grow out of the carpet. **Sofia Löfstedt**, another impressive young designer showed similarly creative visual

experimentation with her wrinkled-looking stripey rug called 'Slapstick', which looks as if someone has just tripped over it.

Another key event in the Swedish design calendar is the four-year-old **Future Design Days** (www.futuredesigndays.com), a cutting-edge international design festival held in November; in 2004 it shifted from the west coast, and is now held in Stockholm. The festival takes the stance that all design should have a purpose, and is therefore all-pervasive. Previous guests at the festival have included **Christian von Koenigsegg** (www.koenigsegg.com), founder of the Swedish company bearing his name that makes the fastest street-legal cars in the world (sleekly designed, with oodles of sex appeal); **Ulrika Hydman-Vallien**, the inspiring glassware designer who makes colourful vases that radiate personality (for more on Swedish glass, *see p160* **Pure glass**); and **Jonas Blanking**, who created the innovative hard-shelled, high-tech Boblbee urban backpack (www.boblbee.com) that has been marketed around the world.

DESIGN AROUND TOWN

Many of these young designers' cool creations – ranging from ceramics and jewellery to wine carriers and axes – can be found in Stockholm's five **DesignTorget** (*see p169*) stores, the largest of which is located in Kulturhuset at Sergels Torg. Other upscale design outlets include the **NK** department store (*see p153*), **R.O.O.M** (*see p175*) and **Asplund** (*see p173*).

If money's no issue, head for high-profile **Svenskt Tenn** (*see p175*). Founded by Estrid

Fashion with flair

While Swedish furniture, glassware and industrial design enjoy a solid reputation abroad for quality and elegance, Swedish fashion remains an unknown quantity in most parts of the world. The lone exception is **H&M** (*see p156*), the clothing retail giant that currently operates more than 1,000 stores in 20 different countries. H&M may still have the monopoly but there is currently something of a buzz surrounding new Swedish fashion design, and H&M is having to make way for emerging designers with creative cuts.

Two hot names are **Filippa K**, whose collection has gone on sale in London's Selfridges, and **Johan Lindeberg**. The creative director and co-founder of Filippa K is London-born Swede Filippa Knutsson. Although she grew up in the UK, most of Filippa K's women's clothing designs have a strong Scandinavian influence in their sophisticated simplicity. Johan Lindeberg, meanwhile, is fast becoming a fashion icon in the US with his upmarket J Lindeberg (*see p159*) men's clothing and sportswear brands. Another Swede who has made a splash internationally is **Efva Attling** (*see p165*), whose silver and gold jewellery designs are favoured by the likes of Jennifer Aniston and Madonna.

When it comes to streetwear, two stand-out brands are **Acne** (*see p159*) and **Whyred**, both of which major in men's clothing. For children's fashions, the place to go is pricey but high-quality **Polarn & Pyret** (*see p161*), with its trademark coloured stripes.

In addition to these commercial brands, there are a whole slew of independents worth investigating. Some of those making original statements include rock 'n' roll designer **Ylva Liljefors**; **Marina Kereklidou** for her Gwen Stefani-style outfits; **Nakkna** for minimalist svelte; **Patrick Söderstam** for radical, oversized menswear popular in Japan;

and **Sara von Ehrenheim** for luxurious apparel in fish skin and other unusual materials. For up-and-coming Swedish fashion design, it is worth taking a stroll around the streets of SoFo (*see p94*), which is rich in independent designer boutiques.

For further information on Swedish fashion, call the 25-year-old **Swedish Fashion Council** (Drottninggatan 81A, 411 17 44, www.moderadet.com). Stockholm no longer holds an annual fashion fair, but **Copenhagen Vision** is the leading showcase for Nordic fashion design.

Filippa K.

Ericson (1894-1981), it celebrated its 80th anniversary in 2004 by demonstrating that it's still as relevant as ever. Famed for its work with pewter (its name means 'Swedish Pewter'), Svenskt Tenn hosted an 80th anniversary exhibition exploring the new possibilities of the once-humble alloy. Ten of Sweden's most famous female designers and craftspeople – well-known ceramicists, textile artists and jewellers – were asked to create new objects, such as kettles, miniature sculptures, lamps, floor screens and vases, using pewter; the results are eye-opening. Pictured right are the works of Annika Jarring (*top*) and Signe Persson-Melin (*bottom*).

Alternatively, take a design safari around **SoFo** (*see p94*), on the hip south side of town. SoFo comprises the area south of Folkungagatan and east of Götgatan on Södermalm – hence, SoFo – and is full of cute cafés and postage-stamp-sized fashion and design boutiques, often started by recent graduates of Beckmans School of Design.

If that sounds a little too bijou, then do as many locals do and hop on the free shuttle bus from Regeringsgatan 13 to **IKEA**'s gigantic warehouse store at Kungens Kurva (*see p174*). IKEA's products, though mass-produced and restricted at times by the flat-packing system, are design-savvy, and well-known designers work on its collections. Beware: this mega home-furnishing palace is so vast that once you enter, you may never find your way out.

A good place to get a sense of Swedish design through the years is the **National Museum** (*see p76*), which has a permanent exhibition on Scandinavian design from 1900 to 2000. It is also home to an impressive collection of applied art, design and industrial design from the 14th century to the present day, featuring ceramics, textiles, glass, precious and non-precious metals, and furniture.

For the contemporary scene, pay a visit to **Svensk Form** (Swedish Society of Crafts and Design; Holmamiralens väg 2, Skeppsholmen) – located just around the corner from the recently reopened Moderna Museet – which hosts cutting-edge exhibitions of products ranging from plastic household items and ceramic ovens through to maternity clothes. Established by Nils Månsson Mandelgren in 1845, Svensk Form claims to be the oldest organisation of its kind in the world. Its magazine, *Form*, has been published since 1932, and since 1983 the society has presented the annual Utmärkt Svensk Form awards to the creators of the best-designed new Swedish products of the year.

There has never been a better time to see Swedish design, as 2005 has been designated a **Year of Design** (www.mer designs.com) in Sweden by the government. The goal is not necessarily to surpass Italy in product design or Paris in fashion. Instead, this being Sweden, the focus is on making good design accessible to everyone and functionality will be at the heart of the displays. Virtually every museum or large public institution in the country will have a particular design focus, be it woodwork, handicrafts, art, architecture, advertising, fashion or industrial design.

As part of Sweden's 'Year of Design', a major exhibition, **Inspired 2050** (www.inspired 2050.com), will take place at Kulturhuset (*see p234*), looking ahead at how people might be living, working, eating, loving, shopping and travelling 50 years from now. While the key characteristics of 20th-century Swedish design – simplicity, democracy and functionality – are showing no signs of decline, even in the current experimental climate, only time will tell if they will still be gospel 50 years from now.

Where to Stay

Where to Stay **42**

Where to Stay

Whether you like to sleep afloat, surrounded by antiques or in sleek, designer surroundings you'll find your bed right here.

Berns Hotel. *See p45.*

The Stockholm hotel scene is rather like Swedish society – not so much at the upper levels, not so much at the lower levels, but a large, comfortable middle class. More surprisingly, until recently the capital's hotels tended to be boringly conservative, which is a little odd given that the Swedes are known for sleek, inventive design. But thankfully that seems to be changing. Newer hotels, such as the **Nordic Light** (*see p47*), **Clarion** (*see p53*) and **Rival** (*see p55*), have added colour to the capital, blending a cool Scandinavian aesthetic with the latest hotel comforts.

Where you choose to stay isn't as crucial as it is in less compact cities – here you are rarely more than a walk or a short hop on the Tunnelbana away from your hotel. If you want historic surroundings, opt for Gamla Stan (if you can afford it). For flamboyant nightlife, try somewhere close to Stureplan in Östermalm. For streetwise shopping and a more alternative feel, go to Södermalm. Several hotels in Norrmalm are minutes from the Arlanda Express terminal at Central Station, for easy access to the airport.

The hotel scene in Stockholm is remarkably varied in style: you can stay in a suite in a hotel overlooking the Royal Palace, a cell in a converted prison or in the cabin of a boat once owned by Cary Grant's wife. Interiors can be starkly minimalist, crammed with nautical antiques or tastefully appointed with Gustavian-style antiques.

In 2003 Sweden's Hotel & Restaurant Association introduced a long-awaited official hotel rating system (one to five stars). Many hotels display their rating on a plaque that's reminiscent of the Swedish flag: a yellow H on a blue background. Only seven hotels won full five-star status. One of these is 40 kilometres (25 miles) from Stockholm in **Sigtuna** (Sigtuna Stadshotell), and five are in the city: the **First Hotel Reisen** (*see p43*), the **Grand** (*see p45*), the **Hilton** (*see p53*), the **Sheraton** (*see p49*) and the **Victory** (*see p44*).

Hotel standards are high in Stockholm, and wherever you stay staff will almost certainly speak excellent English. Breakfast is typically a buffet of cereals, fruit, cold cuts, fish, cheese, hot dishes, crispbread, juice, tea and coffee. Swedes value the quality of beds and bedding (some hotels even have a pillow menu). Cultural note: in Sweden double beds tend to come with two single duvets rather than one double-sized one.

Although Stockholm is not a cheap city, it has plenty of youth hostels, and several of them are on boats (*see p48* **Beds on boats**). These aren't scuzzy pads suitable only for students and backpackers, but clean lodgings ideal for families. You don't have to sleep in a dorm with a bunch of strangers – many of them are more like cheap hotels, offering single and double rooms – although you may have to buy (usually cheap) membership if you're not a member of a recognised hostelling association, and you'll pay extra for bedlinen, towels and breakfast.

PRICES AND RESERVATIONS
Because Stockholm is a business hub (seven out of ten visitors are here on business) hotel rates are higher during the week and can drop by as much as half at the weekend. So it's often possible to stay in deluxe surroundings for much less than you'd expect. Always ask about packages and special deals (you may have to book two nights to get a discounted rate). Summer rates, especially in July when Swedes take the month off, are also cheaper.

We've divided the hotels by area and then according to the average price of a weekday double room. The categories are: **deluxe** (from 2,300kr per room); **expensive** (1,900kr-2,300kr per room); **moderate** (800kr-1,900kr per room); and **budget** (under 800kr per room), which also includes youth hostels. Breakfast is included in the price unless stated otherwise.

Because of the volume of business travellers hotels can get booked up, especially during major trade fairs, so it's a good idea to book ahead. The tourist office produces a free hotel brochure and runs a very good reservations service: book online (www.stockholmtown.com), by phone (789 24 56), by email (hotels@ stoinfo.se) or in person at the Hotellcentralen office (*see p288*) on the concourse of Central Station. If you visit the office in person, there's a 50kr fee for a hotel, or 20kr for a hostel (same-day hostel bookings only). Alternatively, you could try Destination Stockholm (663 00 80, www.destination-stockholm.com), which offers hotel and sightseeing packages off-season.

CHAIN HOTELS
When you're hotel hunting, don't ignore the chain option. Most have more of a corporate ambience, but you can expect high standards and service. The following chains have websites available in English: **Choice Hotels Scandinavia** (www.choicehotels.se), **First Hotels** (www.firsthotels.com), **Radisson SAS**

(www.radisson.com), **Rica City Hotels** (www.rica.se) and **Scandic Hotels** (www.scandic-hotels.com), Sweden's largest hotel chain, now part of the Hilton group, which has hotels in the centre and the suburbs.

B&B AGENCIES
One of the cheapest ways to stay in Stockholm is in a private home. The following agencies can arrange a room in a private home for you usually in the range of 200kr-500kr per person: **Stockholm Guesthouse** (www.stockholm guesthouse.com); **Bed and Breakfast Service Stockholm** (www.bedbreakfast.a.se); and **Gästrummet** (www.gastrummet.com).

Gamla Stan

Deluxe

First Hotel Reisen
Skeppsbron 12, 111 30 Stockholm (22 32 60/fax 20 15 59/www.firsthotels.com). T-bana Gamla Stan/ bus 2, 43, 55, 59, 76. **Rates** *Mon-Thur, Sun* single 1,899kr-2,999kr; double 2,649kr-3,299kr; suite 3,999kr-4,999kr. *Fri, Sat* single 1,258kr-2,198kr; double 1,498kr-2,188kr; suite 2,598kr-3,498kr. **Credit** AmEx, DC, MC, V. **Map** p305 H8.

The best Hotels

For watery views
Grand Hôtel (*see p45*), **Hotell Diplomat** (*see p56*), **Hotel Esplanade** (*see p56*), **Hotel J** (*see p58*) and **Radisson SAS Strand Hotel** (*see p47*).

For designer living
The **Hotel Birger Jarl** (*see p51*), **Nordic Light Hotel** (*see p47*) or the **Hotel Rival** (*see p53*).

For cineastes
Hotel Rival (*see p53*).

For budget value
Hotel Tre Små Rum, **Långholmen Hotel & Youth Hostel** or **Zinkensdamm Vandrarhem & Hotel** (for all, *see p56*).

For historic ambience
Clas på Hörnet (*see p51*) or **Victory Hotel** (*see p44*).

For absolute peace and quiet
Hotel J (*see p58*) or **Villa Källhagen** (*see p57*).

Hotel Amaranten.
See p58.

This 17th-century former coffeehouse, once frequented by sailors in search of a caffeine fix, became a hotel in 1819 and is now run by the First Hotel chain, which fully exploits its waterside location. Each of the 144 rooms has some sort of a water view, either directly (from one of the superior rooms) or indirectly via the use of mirrors. There's a sauna in the vaulted cellar, while deluxe rooms have either a sauna or jacuzzi en suite. A good restaurant adjoins the lobby, but sadly, the decor is unexciting – despite occupying such a historic building, the five-star Reisen hasn't shaken off a certain chain-hotel feel. The fantastic location and views do much to appease.
Bar. Business centre. Concierge. Disabled-adapted rooms. Internet (dataport, high-speed, shared terminal). No-smoking rooms. Parking (395kr/day). Pool (indoor). Restaurant. Room service. Sauna. TV (pay movies/VCR).

Lady Hamilton Hotel

Storkyrkobrinken 5, 111 28 Stockholm (50 64 01 00/fax 50 64 01 10/www.lady-hamilton.se). T-bana Gamla Stan/bus 3, 43, 53, 55, 59. **Rates** *Mon-Thur* single 1,790kr-2,190kr; double 2,290kr-2,590kr; triple 2,490kr. *Fri-Sun* single 950kr-1,250kr; double 1,550kr-1,950kr; triple 1,850kr. **Credit** AmEx, DC, MC, V. **Map** p305 H7.
One of three small hotels owned by the Bengtsson family – the others are the Lord Nelson and the Victory (for both, *see below*) – this is probably the nicest of the trio. As the hotels' names suggest, all have some connection with the one-eyed, one-armed British naval hero and other nautical goings-on. A

ship's figurehead and a portrait of Nelson's mistress dominate the lobby at the four-star Lady Hamilton, but the rest of this warren-like building (dating from 1470) is stuffed with antiques. The 34 rooms are each named after a regional wildflower, and there are also four apartments for rent. The beds are fantastically expensive Swedish-made Hästens. The mix of colourful painted cupboards, wall paintings, grandfather clocks and old-fashioned fabrics is charming, if you like that sort of thing. A 14th-century well in the basement is now a plunge pool for the sauna.
Bar. Business centre. Internet (dataport, high-speed, shared terminal). No-smoking rooms. Parking (375kr/day). Restaurant. Room service. Sauna. TV (pay movies).

Victory Hotel

Lilla Nygatan 5, 111 28 Stockholm (50 64 00 00/ fax 50 64 00 10/www.victory-hotel.se). T-bana Gamla Stan/bus 3, 43, 53, 55, 59. **Rates** *Mon-Thur* single 1,990kr-2,190kr; double 2,490kr-2,990kr; suite 3,990kr-5,990kr. *Fri-Sun* single 1,150kr-1,450kr; double 1,750kr-2,350kr; suite 2,750kr-4,550kr. **Credit** AmEx, DC, MC, V. **Map** p305 J7.
Named after Admiral Lord Nelson's flagship, the characterful Victory is the five-star flagship of this three-hotel chain. Inside its crowded walls, you can hardly move for the colourful figureheads, brass instruments, carved whalebone and model boats. A letter dated 1801 from Nelson to Lady Hamilton complaining of seasickness (who knew?) is proudly displayed in the lobby. The 45 rooms, including 22 doubles and four suites, are named after Swedish sea captains. Downstairs are the sauna, meeting rooms and the Leijontornet restaurant, where part of a medieval city tower was unearthed in the 1980s. A hoard of 18,000 silver coins (Sweden's largest silver discovery) was dug up here in 1937. The hotel also has four apartments for periods of two weeks or longer.
Bar. Business centre. Internet (dataport, high-speed, shared terminals). No-smoking rooms. Parking (375kr/day). Pool (indoor). Restaurant. Room service. Sauna. TV (pay movies).

Expensive

Lord Nelson Hotel

Västerlånggatan 22, 111 29 Stockholm (50 64 01 20/fax 506 401 30/www.lord-nelson.se). T-bana Gamla Stan/bus 3, 43, 53, 55, 59. **Rates** *Mon-Thur* single 1,690kr-1,990kr; double 1,990kr-2,290kr. *Fri-Sun* single 850kr-1,050kr; double 1,450kr-1,550kr. **Credit** AmEx, DC, MC, V. **Map** p305 J7.
The smallest (and cheapest) of the Bengtsson family's hotels, the three-star Nelson must also be Sweden's narrowest hotel, only 5m (16ft) wide. On Gamla Stan's tourist strip, this tall, 17th-century building with its glass-and-brass entrance is pretty ship-shape itself. Add in the long mahogany reception desk, the portraits of Nelson, the names of the floors (Gun Deck, Quarter Deck and so on) and assorted naval antiques and you could be forgiven for thinking you were sailing the ocean blue. The 29 recently refurbished rooms

are pleasant but, as on a ship, quite snug – 18 are singles. There's no restaurant, but a snack bar in the lobby serves breakfast and light meals.

Business centre. Internet (dataport, high-speed, shared terminals). No-smoking rooms. Parking (375kr/day). Room service. Sauna. TV (pay movies).

Rica City Hotel Gamla Stan

Lilla Nygatan 25, 111 28 Stockholm (723 72 50/fax 723 72 59/www.rica.se). T-bana Gamla Stan/bus 2, 3, 53, 55. **Rates** *Mon-Thur, Sun* single 1,695kr-1,895kr; double 1,945kr. *Fri, Sat* single 1,050-1,150kr; double 1,590kr. **Credit** AmEx, DC, MC, V. **Map** p305 J7.

Just down the street from the Lord Nelson, this 51-room hotel in a 17th-century building is steps from the waterfront, but none of the rooms has a view. For 65 years it was owned by the Salvation Army, which used it as a hostel until it was purchased by a Norwegian hotel chain in 1998 and transformed into a first-class property. Rooms are elegant, in an understated way, but they aren't very large. If you want to steep yourself in the Old Town, and if location matters more than space, this is the place.

No-smoking rooms. Internet (dataport). Sauna. TV (pay movies).

Norrmalm

Deluxe

Berns Hotel

Näckströmsgatan 8, 111 47 Stockholm (56 63 22 00/fax 56 63 22 01/www.berns.se). T-bana Kungsträdgården or Östermalmstorg/bus 2, 47, 62, *69, 76.* **Rates** single 2,150kr; double 2,500kr-4,000kr; suite 4,700kr-6,400kr. **Credit** AmEx, DC, MC, V. **Map** p305 G8.

This boutique hotel is fantastically located near Kungsträdgården, the shops of Hamngatan and the boats of Nybroviken, and is popular with visiting pop stars and business executives. The hotel adjoins Berns Salonger, a complex combining pulsing bars and restaurants with dramatic historic decor. Don't expect Scandinavian stereotypes here: the simply designed 65 rooms are quite masculine, with cherry wood and marble in rich, dark colours. Some have nifty cylindrical consoles containing the TV, CD-player and minibar. Top-floor rooms have big windows overlooking Berzelii Park. If you really want to push the boat out, consider one of the airy top-floor suites, such as the Parkview, whose private patio overlooks the Dramatan Theatre and the boats of Nybroviken, or the Clock Suite, situated behind the distinctive Berns clock, with a private sauna. Service is first-class, and guests also get to use some of the facilities at Berns' sister hotel, the peerless Grand (*see below*).

Air-conditioning. Bars (7). Business centre. Concierge. Internet (dataport, high speed, shared terminal). No-smoking rooms. Parking (375kr/day). Restaurant. Room service. TV (pay movies/VCR).

Grand Hôtel

Södra Blasieholmshamnen 8, PO Box 16424, 103 27 Stockholm (679 35 00/fax 611 86 86/www.grand hotel.se). T-bana Kungsträdgården/bus 2, 55, 59, 62, 65. **Rates** single 2,300kr-2,900kr; double 3,500kr-4,400kr; suite 5,500kr-22,200kr. **Credit** AmEx, DC, MC, V. **Map** p305 G8.

Columbus Hotell. *See p55.*

As well as visiting royals and rock stars, this sumptuous five-star is where you'll find Nobel Prize winners, who traditionally stay here after the awards ceremony. Built right on the waterfront in 1874 it has splendid views of the royal palace. Each of the 304 rooms is decorated differently, but it's the suites that have the real wow factor (one even has its own tower; but then at 13,200kr you might expect it). Public areas are decorated in a rather heavy classical style, but it has all the facilities you would expect from a world-class hotel. There are two restaurants: Verandan, which serves a traditional smörgåsbord, and the renowned Franska Matsalen (*see p114*). Even if you're not staying here, pop into the Cadier Bar for a Martini with a view. The raspberry jellies in bowls scattered around the hotel are very moreish.
Bar. Business centre. Concierge. Disabled-adapted rooms. Gym. Internet (dataport, high-speed, shared terminal). No-smoking rooms/floor. Parking (375kr/day). Restaurants (2). Room service. Sauna. TV (pay movies/VCR).

Nordic Light Hotel

Vasaplan, PO Box 884, 101 37 Stockholm (50 56 30 00/fax 50 56 30 60/www.nordichotels.se). T-bana T-Centralen/bus 1, 47, 53, 59, 69. **Rates** *Mon-Thur, Sun* single 2,500kr; double 2,700kr-2,900kr. *Sat, Sun* single 1,290kr; double 1,590kr. **Credit** AmEx, DC, MC, V. **Map** p305 G6.

The dour office block exterior here belies a haven of Nordic cool, where suave, black-clad staff whisk by with tremendous efficiency and show impressive attention to detail. The Nordic Light is not just stylish, but it's stylish in a very Scandinavian way: white walls, wooden floors, absurdly comfortable beds, hearty breakfasts and, the icing on the cake, a 'Light Manager' to oversee the hotel lighting. It follows then that sophisticated lighting effects are employed throughout the hotel, with pretty patterns projected on to the walls of the 175 bedrooms and a chandelier that slowly changes colour in the airy bar-restaurant. The wine cellar has one of Scandinavia's largest collections of North American wines. The Light's sibling and near neighbour, the Nordic Sea (*see p48*), is larger and cheaper, and because both hotels attract business travellers there are enticing weekend deals. If you're feeling mushy, ask about the Nordic Love package. The hotel's location in the city centre steps from the Arlanda Express means it's only 20 minutes from hotel check-out to airport check-in.
Bar. Business centre. Disabled-adapted rooms. Gym. Internet (dataport, high-speed, shared terminals). No-smoking rooms. Parking (225kr/day). Restaurant. Room service. Sauna. Spa. TV (pay movies).

Radisson SAS Strand Hotel

Nybrokajen 9, PO Box 16396, 103 27 Stockholm (50 66 40 00/fax 50 66 40 01/www.radissonsas.com). T-bana Kungsträdgården or Östermalmstorg/bus 2, 47, 62, 69, 76. **Rates** *Mon-Thur, Sun* single 1,950kr; double 2,400kr; suite 3,000-6,500kr. *Fri, Sat* single 1,490kr; double 1,695kr; suite 3,000kr-6,500kr. **Breakfast** 165kr. **Credit** AmEx, DC, MC, V. **Map** p305 G8.

This is an excellent business hotel with a little something extra: knock-out views of the boats and ferries moored along Nybrokajen and Strandvägen (superior rooms only). Built in 1912 for the Stockholm Olympics, the hotel has undergone many renovations since then and now all the 152 rooms are tastefully furnished in classic Swedish style. The large, comfortable lobby has sofas and armchairs you can sink right into and a wall full of books to borrow. A real splurge is the Tower Suite, a two-floor apartment with a rooftop terrace, dining room, sitting room and a spiral staircase leading up to the bedroom.
Bar. Disabled adapted rooms. Gym/pool/spa (Sturebadet). No-smoking rooms. Restaurant. Room service. Sauna. Telephone. Sauna. TV (pay movies).

Scandic Hotel Sergel Plaza

Brunkebergstorgs 9, PO Box 16411, 103 27 Stockholm (51 72 63 00/fax 51 72 63 11/www.scandic-hotels.com/sergelplaza). T-bana T-Centralen/bus 43, 47, 52, 56, 65. **Rates** *Mon-Thur, Sun* single 1,700kr-2,900kr; double 2,200kr-3,200kr; suite 5,000kr. *Fri, Sat* single/double 1,250kr-1,750kr; suite 5,000kr. **Credit** AmEx, DC, MC, V. **Map** p305 E7.

Location is this hotel's main allure: it's slap bang in the concrete heart of the city, a credit card's throw from the main shopping streets of Hamngatan and Drottninggatan. The 403 rooms are brightly furnished, though the lobby is a mishmash of styles that takes in red leather sofas, faux-Greek statues and gilt-edged mirrors. There's a Swedish smörgåsbord in the restaurant, but this place is so popular with Japanese tourists that a Japanese breakfast is also served. Families are made to feel welcome, with surprises for children at check-in.
Bars (2). Business centre. Disabled-adapted rooms. Internet (dataports). No-smoking rooms. Parking (250kr/day). Restaurant. Room service. TV (pay movies).

Expensive

Adlon

Vasagatan 42, 112 20 Stockholm (402 65 00/fax 20 86 10/www.adlon.se). T-bana T-Centralan/bus 3, 47, 59, 62, 69. **Rates** *Mon-Thur, Sun* single 1,295kr-1,795kr; double 1,895kr-2,295kr; suite 1,995kr-2,495kr. *Fri, Sat* single 795kr-995kr; double 1,150kr-1,550kr; suite 1,750kr. *Last wk June-mid Aug* weekend prices apply all week. **Credit** AmEx, DC, MC, V. **Map** p305 F6.

Originally opened in 1944 in a late 19th-century building, the Adlon is a family-run hotel close to Central Station on the main thoroughfare of Vasagatan. Unusually, more than 60 of its 83 subtly decorated rooms are singles, so it attracts a large proportion of solo travellers. You'll get a friendly welcome here, but it's worth mentioning that the bedrooms are generally very small. Request one of the recently renovated rooms on the first floor.
Business services. Internet (dataport, high-speed, shared terminal). No-smoking rooms. Parking (250kr/day). TV (pay movies).

Nordic Sea Hotel

Vasaplan, PO Box 884, 101 37 Stockholm (50 56 30 00/fax 50 56 30 60/www.nordichotels.se). T-bana T-Centralen/bus 1, 47, 53, 59, 69. **Rates** *Mon-Thur, Sun single 2,000kr; double 2,200kr. Fri, Sat single 1,090kr, double 1,390kr.* **Credit** *AmEx, DC, MC, V.* **Map** *p305 G6.*

The first thing you notice when you enter the Nordic Sea is water: a 9,000-litre aquarium dominates the lobby and a window opens on to the ultra-chilly Icebar (*see p137*), where the drinks are served in sub-zero conditions. With 367 rooms, and a jaunty blue-and-white colour scheme throughout, the Nordic Sea Hotel is larger and more affordable than the Nordic Light (*see p47*), but (ice or no ice) is not nearly as cool. Still, if you're looking for a fully functional room right next to Central Station, you could do a hell of a lot worse.

Bars (2). Business centre. Disabled-adapted rooms. Internet (dataport, high-speed, shared terminal). No-smoking rooms. Parking (225kr/day). Restaurant. Room service. Sauna. TV (pay movies/VCR).

Beds on boats

Given that Stockholm is built on 14 islands, it makes perfect sense that some hotels ride the waves in the city centre. They have the advantage of uniqueness, but the disadvantages of small cabins and portholes that don't always afford the best views. Still, the gentle rocking is soothing, and they can be affordable, memorable alternatives.

Af Chapman

Flaggmansvägen 8, Skeppsholmen, 111 49 Stockholm (463 22 66/fax 611 71 55/www.stfchapman.com). T-bana Kungsträdgården/bus 2, 55, 62, 65, 76. **Rates** *Members 140kr-210kr; children 85kr. Non-members 185kr-255kr; children 110kr. Annual membership 285kr; 110kr under-25s; free under-15s.* **Credit** *AmEx, MC, V.* **Map** *p306 J9.*

Before we tell you that this is probably the most beautiful youth hostel in the world, we should tell you that it's expected to be closed for renovation for much of 2005. Still, if you get here when it's open, you'll find that this three-masted schooner off Skeppsholmen is a treasured Stockholm landmark. Dating back to 1888, it was once a training ship for the Swedish Navy, but has been a youth hostel since 1949. It holds 138 bunks (in two- to ten-bed cabins), along with shower and toilet facilities. It's not recommended for the claustrophobic or the very tall, but a building back on shore has 155 more beds and additional facilities (shop, internet, kitchen, playroom, reception and pool tables).

Bar. Disabled-adapted rooms. Internet (shared terminal). No-smoking rooms. Parking (30kr/day). Restaurant. TV room.

Den Röda Båten Mälaren

Södermälarstrand, kajplats 6, Södermalm, 117 20 Stockholm (644 43 85/fax 641 37 33/www.theredboat.com). T-bana Slussen/bus 2, 3, 43, 55, 76. **Rates** *Hostel (per person) dormitory 195kr; single 430kr; double 490kr; triple/quad 230kr. Hotel single 675kr-785kr; double 915kr-1,200kr.* **Credit** *MC, V.* **Map** *p314 K7.*

It's hard to miss this cosy waterside hotel, since it's painted bright red. This old Göta Canal steamer, built in 1914, carried lumber until 1950 and was on the verge of being destroyed in the 1960s before a German boat enthusiast turned it into a youth hostel. It has 100 hostel beds in one-, two-, three-, four- and ten-person cabins. Furnishings are rather shabby, but there's a charm to the place.

Bar (summer only). No smoking. Restaurant. TV room.

Gustaf af Klint

Stadsgårdskajen 153, Södermalm, 116 45 Stockholm (640 40 77/78/fax 640 64 16/ www.gustafafklint.se). T-bana Slussen/bus 2,

Sheraton Stockholm Hotel & Towers

Tegelbacken 6, PO Box 195, 101 23 Stockholm (412 34 00/fax 412 34 09/www.sheraton.com/ stockholm). T-bana T-Centralen/bus 3, 43, 59, 62. **Rates** *Mon-Thur, Sun single/double 1,695kr-2,900kr, suite 4,400kr-8,800kr. Fri, Sat single/ double 1,290kr-2,900kr, suite 4,400kr-8,800kr.* **Credit** AmEx, DC, MC, V. **Map** p305 H6.

The Sheraton is just what you expect it to be: a large, brightly decorated international hotel with friendly, efficient service that attracts business travellers and American tourists. Inside you could be in any city, but outside you're neatly placed between the Central Station and Gamla Stan. There's a small champagne-and-cigars bar, Die Ecke, a German restaurant and a clubby lounge, the Liberty Kitchen, for small meals, and there's also a small casino just off the lobby. Opt for an executive room if you want an Old Town view. *Bar. Business centre. Concierge. Disabled-adapted rooms. Gym. Internet (dataport, high-speed, shared terminal). No-smoking rooms. Parking (260kr/day). Restaurants (2). Room service. Sauna.*

3, 43, 55, 76. **Rates** *Hostel* (per person) dormitory 130kr; double 180kr; quad 160kr. *Hotel* single 410kr; double 680kr; triple 900kr; quad 1100kr. **Credit** MC, V. **Map** p314 K8.

This is one of the city's most popular youth hostels, moored steps away from Slussen, near the popular nightclub boat *Patricia*. There are spectacular views from the onboard café but, alas, not from the tiny rooms or dorms. It offers both hotel and youth hostel accommodation, but don't expect much. The furnishings are a bit run-down but the price is right if you're on a tight budget. *Internet (shared terminal). No-smoking rooms. Parking (125kr/day). Restaurant. TV room.*

LogInn Hotel

Södermälarstrand, Kajplats 16, Södermalm (442 44 20/fax 442 44 21/www.loginn.se). T-bana Slussen/bus 2, 3, 43, 55, 76. **Rates** *Mon-Thur, Sun single 695kr-895kr; double 895kr-1,195kr; triple 1,095kr; family 1,395kr. Fri, Sat single 595kr-795kr; double 695kr-895kr; triple 795kr; family 1,195kr.* **Credit** MC, V. **Map** p314 K7.

Opened in 2002, this boat hotel on the edge of Södermalm has 24 cabins offering everything from bunk beds to family rooms. Originally built in 1928, the boat has had a fairly eventful history, serving as a cargo ship in the 1930s, a dive shop in the West Indies in the late '70s and a floating casino in the '80s. Its newest owners have created clean, comfortable rooms, all with private bathrooms with showers. *No smoking. Restaurant. TV room.*

Mälardrottningen

Riddarholmen, 111 28 Stockholm (54 51 87 80/fax 24 36 76/www.malardrottningen. se). T-bana Gamla Stan/bus 3, 53. **Rates** *Mon-Thur, Sun single 1,100kr-2,150kr; double 1,200kr-2,000kr. Sat, Sun single 915kr-2,200kr; double 1,030kr-2,200kr.* **Credit** AmEx, DC, MC, V. **Map** p305 J6.

Once a luxury yacht owned by the heiress Barbara Hutton (ex-Mrs Cary Grant), this is now the classiest of Stockholm's hotel boats and is popular with visiting businessmen. It sits regally on its own perch at Riddarholmen, near Gamla Stan. The 60 cabins are elegant and well equipped, but opt for a double even if you're travelling solo – the extra space is worth the price difference. During the cooler months you'll appreciate the onboard sauna. *Pictured left and below.* *Bar/Café (during summer only). Internet (dataport). No-smoking rooms. Restaurant. Room service. Sauna. TV (pay movies/satellite).*

BERNS HOTEL

Berns Hotel. Tel: +46(0)8 566 322 00. Fax: +46(0)8 566 322 01. frontoffice@berns.se
Näckströmsgatan 8. SE-111 47 Stockholm, Sweden. www.berns.se

Berns, the China Theatre and Grand Hôtel Stockholm are part of Grand Hôtel Holdings

Moderate

Freys Hotel

Bryggargatan 12, PO Box 594, 101 31 Stockholm
(506 213 00/fax 506 213 13/www.freyshotel.se).
T-bana T-Centralen/bus 1, 47, 53, 59, 65. **Rates**
Mon-Thur, Sun single 1,790kr; double 1,895kr. Fri,
Sat single, double from 1,290kr. **Credit** AmEx, DC,
MC, V. **Map** p305 G6.

The Freys Hotel is a likeable, idiosyncratic place,
with 118 cheerfully decorated rooms and a lobby
liberally adorned with dozens of paintings of cats.
The location, down a car-free street close to Central
Station and the shops on Drottninggatan, is convenient if a little drab. Still, you can always cheer
yourself up by visiting the adjoining continental-
style bar, which serves up Stockholm's largest
menu of Belgian beer.

Bar. Disabled-adapted rooms. Internet (dataport,
shared terminal). Restaurant. Sauna. TV (pay movies).

Hotel Bentleys

Drottninggatan 77, 111 60 Stockholm (14 13 95/
fax 21 24 92/www.bentleys.nu). T-bana Hötorget/
bus 1, 47, 52, 56, 65. **Rates** *Mon-Thur, Sun single*
899kr-1,299kr; double 1,199kr-1,499kr; suite 1,699kr.
Fri, Sat single 649kr-949kr; double 799-1,049kr;
suite 1,299kr. *Mid June-mid Aug* weekend prices
apply all wk. **Credit** AmEx, MC, V. **Map** p305 F6.

Like its near-neighbour, the Queen's, Bentleys is a
privately owned hotel in a converted townhouse,
with a beautiful marble staircase and old-fashioned
cage lift. The 60 rooms are simple but clean and
pleasant. From the stained-glass panels in the front
door to the art nouveau patterns on the hallway ceiling, there's real charm to be found here. Staff are welcoming and prices are great given the central
location. Choose one of the rooms situated on the
higher floors with views down over the inner courtyard to make sure that you're not disturbed by the
street noise from Drottninggatan. Bentleys is a
no-smoking hotel, and you'll be fined 500kr if you
break that rule.

Sauna. TV (pay movies/TV room).

Queen's Hotel

Drottninggatan 71A, 111 36 Stockholm (24 94 60/
fax 21 76 20/www.queenshotel.se). T-bana Hötorget/
bus 1, 47, 52, 53, 69. **Rates** single 750kr-1,390kr;
double 795kr-1,490kr. **Credit** AmEx, DC, MC, V.
Map p305 F6.

On the main pedestrian street in the heart of the
shopping district, this hotel is a good bet if you like
hustle, bustle and a convenient location. Family-
owned, it has 32 clean, plain rooms (some en suite).
Only one room has a bathtub. Most of the doubles
are large enough to accommodate an extra bed or
sofa bed. The furniture in the public lounge and TV
room is rather haphazard, but a large piano beckons
in the corner for any guest with the urge to strike up
a tune or two.

Internet (dataport, shared terminal). No-smoking
rooms. TV.

Budget/youth hostels

City Backpackers Inn

Upplandsgatan 2A, 111 23 Stockholm (20 69 20/
fax 10 04 64/www.citybackpackers.se). T-bana
T-Centralen or Hötorget/bus 1, 47, 53, 65, 69.
Rates 180kr-245kr per person; 6-bed apartment
1,500kr. **Credit** MC, V. **Map** p304 F5.

Located in a 19th-century building on Norra
Bantorget square, this 82-bed hostel is convenient,
a ten-minute walk from Central Station, and near
Hötorget and the shopping district. There are two-,
four-, six- and eight-bed rooms, as well as an apartment with a private kitchen, shower and toilet, sleeping up to seven. Facilities include a comfy lounge
with a TV, books and games, kitchen, laundry, free
internet access and – this is Sweden after all –
sauna. There's no curfew. Breakfast not provided.

Internet (shared terminals, high-speed). No-smoking
rooms. Sauna. TV (TV room).

Vasastaden

Expensive

Hotel Birger Jarl

Tulegatan 8, PO Box 190 16, 104 32 Stockholm
(674 18 00/fax 673 73 66/www.birgerjarl.se).
T-bana Rådmansgatan/bus 2, 42, 43, 52. **Rates**
Mon-Thur, Sun single 1,720kr-2,450kr; double
2,035kr-2,381kr; suite 2,940kr-4,700kr. *Fri, Sat & all*
wk in summer single 1,040kr-1,575kr; double 1,250kr-
1,845kr; suite 2,850kr-4,600kr. **Credit** AmEx, DC,
MC, V. **Map** p309 D6.

The Birger Jarl is a design-savvy business hotel –
16 of its 235 rooms are one-offs by some of Sweden's
most idiosyncratic designers, and the rest have been
designed in more conventional (but still very attractive) series of 15 or 20 rooms. Five other rooms have
been given a feng shui makeover. Fans of genuine
retro should check themselves into the Retro Room,
which looks just as it did in 1974, having accident-
ally been overlooked during the hotel's renovation.
The small gym has views over Norrmalm's rooftops
– use it to work up an appetite so you can do justice
to the lavish buffet breakfast. At press time, the
bathrooms were awaiting refurbishment to bring
them up to date with the rest of the hotel. The quiet
location in fairly residential Vasastaden won't suit
everyone, but it's only a short walk from the action.

Bar. Business centre. Disabled-adapted rooms. Gym.
Internet (high-speed, shared terminals). No-smoking
rooms. Parking (195kr/day). Restaurant. Room
service. Sauna. TV (pay movies).

Moderate

Clas på Hörnet

Surbrunnsgatan 20, 113 48 Stockholm (16 51 30/
fax 612 53 15/www.claspahornet.com). T-bana
Tekniska Högskolan/bus 2, 4, 42, 53, 72. **Rates**
Mid Aug-June *Mon-Thur, Sun* single 1,245kr;

Hotel Rival. *See p55.*

double 1,745kr; suite 2,395kr. *Fri, Sat, all wk June-mid Aug* single 795kr; double 1,095kr; suite 1,995kr. **Credit** AmEx, DC, MC, V. **Map** p309 C6.

First opened as an inn in 1731, Clas på Hörnet is an old-fashioned oasis of peace, quiet and antiques on a tree-lined street a short walk from Stureplan and Odenplan. It has only ten rooms (most with four-poster beds), freshened up in 2003 with new carpets and bathrooms, as well as an elegant restaurant serving excellent Swedish food, and a small courtyard with a bar serving food and drinks alfresco. Many guests come from Scandinavian countries, attracted by the historic atmosphere and the late 18th-century Gustavian furnishings, which have been overseen by the Stockholms Stadsmuseum (*see p92*).

Bar. Business centre. Disabled-adapted rooms. Internet (dataport). No-smoking rooms. Parking (220kr/day). Restaurant. Room service. TV (pay movies).

Hotell August Strindberg

Tegnérgatan 38, 113 59 Stockholm (32 50 06/fax 20 90 85/www.hotellstrindberg.se). T-bana Hötorget/bus 1, 47, 53, 65, 69. **Rates** *Sun-Thur* single 825kr-1,225kr; double 1,225kr-1,475kr. *Fri, Sat* single 625kr-825kr; double 825kr-925kr. **Credit** MC, V. **Map** p309 E5.

Near a small park containing a startling nude statue of Swedish dramatist August Strindberg, who once lived down the road, is this welcoming name-sake hotel. In 2004 it expanded to 27 rooms and opened a new lobby (decorated, of course, with a mural of Strindberg, cleverly made from the first three chapters of one of his books). Rooms are simple and restrained, but pleasant, and there's a tranquil courtyard garden with a few tables and a trickling birdbath. All in all, a fine choice in a quiet, central neighbourhood.

Disabled-adapted room. No-smoking rooms. Internet (dataport). TV.

Hotel Gustav Vasa

Västmannagatan 61, 113 25 Stockholm (34 38 01/ fax 30 73 72/www.hotel.wineasy.se/gustav.vasa). T-bana Odenplan/bus 2, 4, 40, 47, 53. **Rates** single 595kr-995kr; double 795kr-1,260kr; family 1,390kr-1,700kr. *Mid-June to mid-August* single 395kr-595kr; double 695kr-795kr; family 1,260kr-1,590kr. **Credit** AmEx, DC, MC, V. **Map** p308 D4.

At Odenplan, facing the majestic Gustav Vasa church, this hotel is a quiet, old-fashioned place. The 37 good-value rooms (some with shared bathroom, all non-smoking) are clean and comfortable, if a bit small and stuffy. The family rooms are big enough for four or five people. An excellent breakfast is served in the sunny breakfast room. Convenient for buses to Arlanda airport.

Business centre. Internet (shared terminals). No-smoking rooms (all). Parking (125kr/day). Room service (breakfast only). TV.

Hotel Oden

Karlbergsvägen 24, PO Box 6246, 102 34 Stockholm (457 97 00/fax 457 97 10/www.hoteloden.se). T-bana Odenplan/bus 2, 4, 40, 42, 47. **Rates** *Mon-Thur, Sun* single 1,095kr-1,700kr; double

1,290kr- 1,700kr. *Fri, Sat, all wk in June, July, Aug* single 770kr-1,230kr; double 950kr-1,230kr. **Credit** AmEx, DC, MC, V. **Map** p308 D4.

This nondescript hotel is really only notable for its low prices. For budget travellers looking to save money on meals, doubles have a fridge and stove (no frying allowed). There's a basic solarium, sauna and exercise room in the basement.

Business centre. Gym. No-smoking rooms. Internet (shared terminal). Parking (110kr/day). Sauna. TV.

Budget/youth hostels

Hostel Bed & Breakfast

Rehnsgatan 21, 113 57 Stockholm (15 28 38/ fax 612 62 56/www.hostelbedandbreakfast.com). T-bana Rådmansgatan/bus 2, 4, 42, 43, 52. **Rates** dormitory 190kr per person; four-bed room 210kr per person; single 375kr; double 500kr. **Credit** MC, V. **Map** p309 D6.

This is your basic youth hostel, centrally located, handy and cheap. There are 36 beds in two-, four-, eight- and ten-bed rooms, plus a summer-only annexe that sleeps 40 in one dormitory (mostly used for school trips). All showers and toilets are shared, it's open all year and it has a kitchen and laundry room. Be warned that it's a basement hostel, so don't expect a room with a window, let alone a view. Do expect a free breakfast, however.

Internet (shared terminal). No smoking. TV room (VCR).

Vanadis Hotell och Bad

Sveavägen 142, 113 46 Stockholm (30 12 11/ fax 31 23 91/www.vanadishotel.com). T-bana Odenplan or Rådmansgatan/bus 2, 4, 40, 52, 70. **Rates** single/double 495kr-595kr. **Credit** AmEx, DC, MC, V. **Map** p309 C5.

The Vanadis is best described as a swimming pool with a hotel attached. It's a peculiarity, to be sure: 53 tiny rooms, each equipped with just a bed, desk, mirror and fan (no wardrobe and, in cheaper rooms, no window), adjoining a large open-air public pool (May-September) adorned with murals of toucans and potted palms, and with a stall selling Lebanese cocktails, all in a park in the city centre. Guests can swim for free in the pool (*see p191*) and the adjacent aquatic amusement park. Breakfast is served at the poolside café. Rooms are small, but so are prices, and the rooms and shared bathrooms are scrupulously clean. The hotel is in the process of building 14 rooms with en suite. Best for families with small children or budget travellers who might fancy a splash.

No-smoking rooms. Pool (outdoor). Restaurant.

Djurgården

Moderate

Scandic Hasselbacken

Hazeliusbacken 20, 100 55 Stockholm (51 73 43 00/ fax 51 73 43 11/www.scandic-hotels.se). Bus 44, 47.

Rates *Mon-Thur, Sun* single/double 1,690kr; suite 2,995kr. *Fri, Sat* single/double 1,390kr; suite 2,995kr. **Credit** AmEx, DC, MC, V. **Map** p306 J11.

The elegant 112-room Scandic Hasselbacken (part of one of Scandinavia's largest hotel chains) was built in 1925, although there was a tavern on this hill as early as the 1740s. The Djurgården setting is sublime: flanked by trees, with a small garden full of peonies, overlooking the fairground rides of Gröna Lund (*see p84*). Its 122 comfortable, typically Svandinavian rooms are unfussy in style, with hardwood floors. It's a popular wedding venue, and the terrace and elegant Restaurang Hasselbacken are busy all weekend. Djurgården is Stockholm's greenest island, dotted with museums and millionaires' homes. Note that there's no Tunnelbana, access is by bus, tram or a small ferry from Slussen. But the Hasselbacken does put you just a short walk from the Vasamuseet (*see p86*) and Skansen (*see p85*), Stockholm's most popular tourist attractions.

Bars (2). Business centre. Disabled-adapted rooms. Internet (dataport, shared terminal). No-smoking rooms. Parking (150kr/day). Restaurants (2). Room service. Sauna. TV (pay movies/VCR).

Södermalm

Deluxe

Clarion Hotel Stockholm

Ringvägen 98, PO Box 20025, 104 60 Stockholm (462 10 00/fax 462 10 99/www.clarionstockholm.com). T-bana Skanstull/bus 3, 4, 55, 74. **Rates** *Mon-Thur, Sun* single 1,095kr-1,795kr; double 1,795kr-3,695kr. *Fri, Sat* single 1,095kr; double 1,495kr. **Credit** AmEx, DC, MC, V. **Map** p314 N8.

In 2003, the Clarion chain opened Stockholm's biggest hotel: a gleaming 532-room property on the southern edge of Södermalm. Yet, despite its size, it is surprisingly classy. Bedrooms are airy and stylish, in Scandinavian fashion, with brightly coloured blankets enlivening crisp white linens and cool white walls. Bathrooms are smart, the lobby is flooded with light and staff are attentive. Because it's primarily a business hotel, room rates plummet in summer and on weekends. For tourists, the main drawback is the location: it's on the opposite side of town from Arlanda airport and a bit of a schlep from the city centre (but then nowhere is that far in compact Stockholm). The lounge bar, Upstairs, which has spectacular views towards Globen.

Bars (2). Business centre. Concierge. Disabled-adapted rooms. Gym. Internet (high-speed, wireless). No-smoking rooms. Parking (270kr/day). Pool. Restaurants (2). Room service. Sauna. TV (pay movies).

Hilton Stockholm Slussen

Guldgränd 8, PO Box 15270, 104 65 Stockholm (51 73 53 00/fax 51 73 53 11/www.hilton.com). T-bana Slussen/bus 2, 3, 43, 53, 76. **Rates** *Mon-Thur, Sun* single 1,450kr-2,490kr; double 2,650kr-2,690kr; suite 3,450kr-4,200kr. *Fri, Sat* single

1,295kr-1,700kr; double 1,495kr-1,900kr; suite 3,450kr-4,200kr. **Credit** AmEx, DC, MC, V. **Map** p314 K7.

Once a Scandic Hotel, this place reopened as Sweden's first Hilton in 2002 and, despite its five-star rating, there's something faintly depressing about its lack of personality. Still, it has what you expect from a high-quality chain: a white marble lobby, two executive floors with their own reception area, bar and breakfast room, plus the added bonus of sweeping views towards Gamla Stan. If you can't justify the cost of an executive double room you can still enjoy the same panorama from the Ekens bar and restaurant, the outdoor terrace, or the smaller lobby bar which is called, appropriately, Views. *Bars (2). Business centre. Concierge. Disabled-adapted rooms. Gym. Internet (dataport). No-smoking rooms. Parking (350kr/day). Pool. Restaurants (2). Room service. Sauna. Spa (beauty treatments and massage). TV (pay movies/VCR/DVD).*

Hotel Rival

Mariatorget 3, PO box 17525, 118 91 Stockholm (545 789 00/fax 545 789 24/www.rival.se). T-bana Mariatorget/bus 4, 43, 55, 66, 74. **Credit** AmEx, DC, MC, V. **Rates** *Mon-Thur, Sun* single 1,990kr-2,550kr; double 2,290kr-2,990kr; suite 3,290kr-5,790kr. *Fri, Sat* single 1,190kr-1,640kr; double 1,340kr-2,690kr; suite 2,990kr-5,790kr. **Map** p314 K6.

The Rival is the most vibrant new addition to the Stockholm hotel scene. It opened in 2003 in the heart of hip Södermalm, created from the best parts of a 1930s hotel that once stood here, combined with high-tech comforts, such as flatscreen TVs, DVD players and Sony PlayStations in every room. The old cocktail bar and plush red-velvet cinema are art deco treasures. Keeping to a cinematic theme, stills from Swedish films hang over every bed, so you can spend the night with Greta Garbo or, perhaps, gaze up at *ABBA: The Movie*. The latter comes as no surprise, since Benny Andersson of ABBA co-owns the hotel. All credit to him, he's done a fine job. His team took a characterful cinema/hotel complex and have made it into an attractive hub within a seriously up-and-coming area. The small rooms are comfortable and stylish, while the large rooms have great views over Södermalm's rooftops. Weekend rates can be excellent (they include breakfast, which weekday rates do not). Check out the next-door Rival café and bakery, which sells some of the city's best bread, and the Rival cinema (*see p199*). *Bar (2). Business centre. Disabled-adapted rooms. Internet (dataport, high-speed, wireless). No-smoking rooms. Parking (340kr/day). Restaurant. Room service. TV (music/DVD/video library).*

Moderate

Columbus Hotell

Tjärhovsgatan 11, 116 21 Stockholm (50 31 12 00/fax 50 31 12 01/www.columbus.se). T-bana Medborgarplatsen/bus 2, 3, 53, 59, 76. **Rates** *Mon-Thur, Sun* single 1,250kr; double 1,550kr;

suite 2,295kr-2,495kr. *Fri, Sat and all wk in mid June-mid Aug* single 950kr; double 1,250kr; suite 1,995kr-2,295kr. **Credit** AmEx, DC, MC, V. **Map** p315 L9.

This 18th-century building on a quiet street a short walk from busy Medborgarplatsen has a colourful history. It's been a brewery, a poor house for beggars and thieves, and a hospital during the 1834 cholera epidemic. In 1976 it became a hostel and then gradually evolved into a charming three-storey hotel, carefully restored with its original polished-wood floors and tasteful Gustavian furnishings. Romantics prefer Room 120 overlooking the pretty Katarina church, though many of the 69 rooms have lovely park views. There are two price categories, and even the cheap rooms, with shared bathrooms, are comfortable. The courtyard is a pleasant place for breakfast or a drink, and there's a guests-only wine cellar. *Bar. Internet (Web TV). No-smoking. Parking (150kr/day). TV (pay movies).*

Ersta Konferens & Hotell

Erstagatan 1K, PO Box 4619, 116 91 Stockholm (714 61 00/fax 714 93 27/www.ersta.se). Bus 2, 3, 53, 66, 76. **Rates** *Mon-Thur, Sun* single 625kr-1,075kr; double 860kr-1,420kr. *Fri, Sat* single 775kr; double 1,120kr. **Credit** MC, V. **Map** p315 L10.

This 22-room hotel is a quiet oasis perched at the tip of Södermalm, where tour buses deposit their riders for one of Stockholm's most phenomenal views. Constructed for the Deacons' Society in 1850, the building is in a square amid beautifully landscaped gardens and across from Ersta Café, overlooking the city. Many of the bright rooms have a view of the water. There are small guest kitchens on each floor, and when the weather's good you can eat breakfast in the garden. There's also a bookshop, church and museum on the premises, as well as a hospital, hospice and senior citizens' home in the building across the street – all vestiges of the deacons' good works. *Business centre. Disabled-adapted rooms. Internet (dataport). No smoking rooms. TV (in some rooms).*

Hotell Anno 1647

Mariagränd 3, 116 46 Stockholm (442 16 80/fax 442 16 47/www.anno1647.se). T-bana Slussen/bus 2, 3, 43, 53, 59. **Rates** *Mon-Thur, Sun* single 885kr-1,795kr; double 995kr-2,045kr; suite 2,995kr; family 1,995kr. *Fri, Sat* single 595kr-1,395kr; double 795kr-1,595kr; suite 1,995kr; family 1,395kr. **Credit** AmEx, DC, MC, V. **Map** p314 K8.

As its name suggests, this is an old building dating back to 1647, and the interior tries earnestly to stay in synch with the historic exterior. The 42 rooms (including one family room sleeping up to six) are a little faded, but the traditional decor (a little heavy on the chintz) somehow makes this forgivable. Besides, the location is terrific: it's hidden down a cul de sac at Slussen, just off Söder's most fashionable shopping street Götgatan, with the cobbled alleys of the Old Town just minutes away. On the other side of the building is Restaurant 1647. *Bar. Internet (dataport, some rooms high-speed). Parking (130kr/day). Restaurant. Room service. TV (pay movies).*

Budget/youth hostels

Hotel Tre Små Rum

Högbergsgatan 81, 118 54 Stockholm (641 23 71/fax 642 88 08/www.tresmarum.se). T-bana Mariatorget/bus 4, 43, 55, 66, 74. **Rates** 695kr. **Credit** AmEx, MC, V. **Map** p314 L6.

This tiny, likeable hotel in Söder had three small rooms (hence the name) when it opened in 1993 but now there are seven (six doubles and one single), sharing three shower rooms. Clean and simple, with pale yellow walls, limestone floors and furniture provided by the Grand Hôtel, it's ideal for budget travellers who plan to spend most of their time out and about. The only communal room is the breakfast room – you can help yourself to pastries, muesli, fruit, bread and drinks. It's run by the very friendly Jakob and Christian, and is just a few minutes' walk from Mariatorget T-bana station.

Internet (shared terminal). No-smoking rooms. TV.

Zinkensdamm Vandrarhem & Hotell

Zinkens Väg 20, 117 41 Stockholm (hotel 616 81 10/hostel 616 81 00/fax 616 81 20/www.zinkensdamm.com). T-bana Hornstull or Zinkensdamm/bus 4, 40, 66, 74. **Rates** *Hostel* bed in corridor 175kr-220kr over-15s; 85kr-110kr 3-15s; single 440kr-485kr; double 470kr-750kr; 3-bed room 615kr-900kr; 4-bed room 700kr-1,060kr. *Hotel Mon-Thur, Sun* single 1,195kr; double 1,495kr. *Fri, Sat and all wk end June-mid Aug* single 855kr; double 1,155kr. **Credit** AmEx, DC, MC, V. **Map** p313 L4.

This youth hostel and family-friendly hotel is tucked away in peaceful Tantolunden park, a few minutes' walk from busy Hornsgatan. Nearby are lots of *koloniträdgårdar* – lovely little allotment gardens with charming wooden houses where Stockholmers cultivate a bit of countryside in the city. The yellow wooden hostel has a large courtyard and a small pub where guests congregate. All the (non-smoking) rooms are clean, and the bedding and furnishings in good shape. The reasonable prices also include a buffet breakfast.

Bar. Internet (dataport). No-smoking rooms (all). Parking (95kr/day). Sauna. TV room.

Långholmen

Budget/youth hostels

Långholmen Hotel & Youth Hostel

Långholmsmuren 20, PO Box 9116, 102 72 Stockholm (720 85 00/fax 720 85 75/www.langholmen.com). T-bana Hornstull/bus 4, 40, 66. **Rates** *Hostel* adult 195kr-240kr, 100kr-125kr 3-15s; 2-bed room 495kr-675kr; 3-bed room 735kr-870kr; 4-bed room 780kr-960kr. *Hotel* Mon-Thur, Sun single 995-1,195kr; double 1,495kr. *Fri, Sat* single 695kr-855kr; double 1,155kr. **Credit** AmEx, DC, MC, V. **Map** p313 K2.

A former Crown Prison has been converted into a far-from-grim property on this small, green island west of Södermalm. Despite some ghoulishly humorous

touches (such as clocks in reception showing the time at Sing-Sing, Alcatraz and other famous penitentiaries), Långholmen is no gimmick, but a surprisingly pleasant and affordable place to stay. Run as a hotel in winter and youth hostel in summer, it has a pub (winter only), a café (summer only, in the former exercise yard) and a 17th-century Wärdshus serving Swedish cuisine. The yellow 19th-century building is still quite jail-like, with cells (yes, that's where you sleep) arranged around a light-filled central atrium. It is a ten-minute walk from Hornstull T-bana station. There's a prison museum on site (*see p95*). All in all, one of Stockholm's most interesting places to stay.

Bar. Business centre. Disabled-adapted rooms. Internet (wireless, high-speed). No-smoking rooms. Parking (free). Restaurant. Room service. TV (some rooms).

Östermalm

Deluxe

Hotell Diplomat

Strandvägen 7C, 104 40 Stockholm (459 68 00/fax 459 68 20/www.diplomathotel.com). T-bana Östermalmstorg/bus 47, 62, 69, 76. **Rates** *Mon-Thur, Sun* single 1,995kr; double 2,595kr-2,895kr; suite 3,395kr-6,490kr. *Fri, Sat* single 1,095kr-1,295kr; double 1,495kr-1,795kr. **Credit** AmEx, DC, MC, V. **Map** p306 G9.

One of Stockholm's best-preserved art nouveau buildings, the six-storey Diplomat, built in 1911, occupies a fortuitous site on glamorous Strandvägen, and rooms at the front have stunning water views. Formerly an apartment building, it was turned into a hotel in the 1960s and is still family-run. Although the 128 rooms are gradually being renovated in a modern Swedish style, the hotel still oozes old-fashioned charm, with its antique cage lift, spiral staircase and intricate stained-glass windows. More modern are the serene first-floor lounge and the light-flooded T-Bar restaurant on the ground floor, which serves excellent brunch and afternoon tea. Lottery winners should head for the Stockholm Suite with its domed ceiling covered in murals. Boats to the archipelago leave from the quay outside. A Stockholm classic.

Bars (2). Business centre. Internet (dataport, high-speed). No-smoking rooms. Parking (290kr/day). Restaurant. Room service. Sauna. TV (satellite/pay movies).

Expensive

Hotel Esplanade

Strandvägen 7A, 114 56 Stockholm (663 07 40/fax 662 59 92/www.hotelesplanade.se). T-bana Östermalmstorg/bus 47, 62, 69, 76. **Rates** *Mon-Thur, Sun* single 1,595kr; double 1,995kr-2,295kr. *Fri, Sat* single 1,095kr; double 1,695kr. **Credit** AmEx, DC, MC, V. **Map** p306 G9.

The Esplanade is next door to the Diplomat, and has the same staggering water views and four-star rating. However, it's cosier and more old-fashioned

Hotel Bentleys. *See p51.*

than its sleeker, more fashionable neighbour. It's also more anxious to play up the fact that it's family-owned. It has kept some of the building's lovely original 1910 art nouveau interiors. All 34 rooms are different, and even if some of them are a little frumpy, it's hard not to love this place.
Internet (dataport, shared terminal). No smoking rooms. Room service (breakfast only). Sauna. TV.

Hotell Kung Carl
Birger Jarlsgatan 21, PO Box 1776, 111 87 Stockholm (463 50 00/fax 463 50 50/www.rica.se). T-bana Hötorget or Östermalmstorg/bus 1, 2, 55, 56. **Rates** *Mon-Thur, Sun* single 1,650kr-1,895kr; double 1,875kr-2,145kr; suite 5,500kr. *Fri, Sat* single 1,250kr-1,500kr; double 1,250kr-1,500kr; suite 5,500kr. **Credit** AmEx, DC, MC, V. **Map** p305 F8.
The Kung Carl has glamorous neighbours – the Versace store flanks the entrance and it's close to affluent Östermalm, home to some of the poshest shops in Stockholm. The hotel is far from fashionable in style, but handily located and characterful. Each of the 112 rooms is uniquely decorated, and there's an oddly shaped central atrium with a small bar and, adjoining it, a pleasant restaurant.
Bar. Disabled-adapted rooms. Internet (web TV, keyboards in all rooms). No-smoking rooms. Parking (220kr/day). Restaurant. Room Service. TV (pay movies, music).

Lydmar Hotel
Sturegatan 10, 114 36 Stockholm (56 61 13 00/fax 56 61 13 01/www.lydmar.se). T-bana Östermalmstorg/bus 1, 2, 55, 56, 62. **Rates** *Mon-Thur, Sun* single 1,900kr; double 2,250kr-2,500kr; suite 4,950kr. *Fri, Sat* single 1,280kr; double 1,520kr-1,790kr; suite 4,100kr. **Credit** AmEx, DC, MC, V. **Map** p305 E8.

The Lydmar is the kind of place favoured by people whose priority is, above all, coolness. The 62 rooms are categorised from S to XXL, and decorated with flair (anything from minimalist to opulent), but we sometimes feel that it is at the expense of common sense: in all-black room 702, only a curtain separates the toilet from the bedroom, while in all-white room 701 the toilet is behind a clear plastic screen. Other rooms are orange (402), purple (423) or black and white with leather cushions (410). It's conveniently close to Stureplan, the hub of Stockholm nightlife, and tends to attract people who stay up late and are happy to find a gig under way in the hotel lobby. The Lydmar has the air of a nightclub with rooms attached – corridors are a little gloomy, and the smell of stale cigarette smoke lingers in the lobby, which doubles as the bar – but when it's this trendy many visitors don't seem to mind.
Bar. Disabled-adapted rooms. Gym (Sturebadet). Internet (wireless, shared terminal). No smoking rooms. Restaurants (2). Room service. TV (pay movies/DVD).

Gärdet

Deluxe

Villa Källhagen
Djurgårdsbrunnsvägen 10, 115 27 Stockholm (665 03 00/fax 665 03 99/www.kallhagen.se). Bus 69. **Rates** *Mon-Thur, Sun* single 1,700kr-2,400kr; double 1,900kr-2,700kr; suite 3,000kr. *Fri, Sat* single 950kr-1,300kr; double 1,100kr-1,600kr; suite 2,000kr. *All wk in summer* single 1,100kr-1,300kr; double 1,300kr-1,600kr; suite 2,000kr. **Credit** AmEx, DC, MC, V. **Map** p307 F13.

Villa Källhagen is a tranquil waterside retreat surrounded by rolling parkland, yet is just a short bus ride from Östermalm. The original Red Cottage inn, dating from 1810, is now in the garden behind the new hotel, which was built in 1990. The sunny rooms feature the best of Scandinavian design, with bright fabrics, and light fittings designed by Josef Frank of Svenskt Tenn (see p175) fame, although the lobby and café could do with sprucing up. Suites have separate sitting rooms and small patios. An excellent restaurant (see p131) serves classic Swedish food with continental influences. With just 20 rooms, you'll need to book well in advance.

Bar. Business centre. Disabled-adapted rooms. Internet (dataport). No-smoking rooms. Parking (free). Restaurants (2). Room service. Sauna. TV (free movies).

Kungsholmen

Expensive

Hotel Amaranten

Kungsholmsgatan 31, 104 20 Stockholm. (692 52 00/fax 652 62 48/www.firsthotel.com). T-bana Rådhuset/bus 1, 40, 52, 56. **Rates** Mon-Thur, Sun single 1,599; double 1,999kr-2,499kr; suite 3,999kr. *Fri, Sat* single 898kr; double 1,148kr-1,348kr; suite 3,999kr. **Credit** AmEx, DC, MC, V. **Map** p304 G4.

The Amaranten has recently emerged as a newly cool hotel on Kungsholmen. Thanks to its swish new decor and its location around the corner from Scheelegatan, one of the city's busiest restaurant rows, this hotel has become something of a hub of activity. The expansive lobby-bar-restaurant has been refurbished, with leather seats in rich, chocolate hues, walnut floors, low-level lighting and a fake fire flickering on a plasma screen. The luxury does not quite carry through upstairs, though, as rooms are more basic. The small, IKEA-look standard rooms are, however, very good value for weekend-breakers. The larger suites feel more dated but, at the time of writing, were awaiting a makeover. If working out is not your style, bypass the gym for the pool and sauna area. The hotel is an easy five-minute walk across the Klara Sjö from Central Station.

Bar. Business centre. Disabled-adapted rooms. Gym. Internet (dataport, high-speed, shared terminal). No-smoking rooms. Parking (260kr). Pool. Restaurants (2). Room service. Sauna. TV (pay movies).

Further afield

Expensive

Hotel J

Ellensviksvägen 1, 131 28 Nacka Strand (601 30 00/fax 601 30 09/www.hotelj.com). Boat from Nybrokajen or Slussen/T-bana to Slussen then bus 404, 443. **Rates** Mon-Fri single 1,195kr-2,795kr; double 1,395kr-3,195kr; suite 3,195kr. *Sat, Sun* single 950kr-2,500kr; double 950kr-3,300kr; suite 2,900kr-3,195kr. **Credit** AmEx, DC, MC, V.

A 20-minute bus, boat or taxi ride from the city, this hotel is beautifully situated on the coast. Named after the J boats of the America's Cup, it feels very New England boathouse. A 1912 summer house and two modern extensions house 44 rooms (numbers 216 and 218 are probably the best). Rooms in the old building are smaller (with shower, no bath) and without balconies. Full of business types during the week, the J is popular at weekends with Stockholmers taking a break from the city. You can rent mini-catamarans and the hotel has its own motorboat. Restaurant J on the quayside has a reputation for poor service but the views ensure that it stays busy.

Bar. Business centre. Disabled-adapted rooms. Internet (dataport, high-speed). No-smoking rooms. Parking (70kr/day). Restaurants (2). Room service. TV (pay movies).

Moderate

Hasseludden Konferens & Yasuragi

Hamndalsvägen 6, 132 81 Saltsjö-Boo (747 61 00/ fax 747 61 01/www.hasseludden.com). Boat from Strömkajen/bus 444 to Orminge Centrum then bus 417 to Hamndalsvägen then 5-10 mins walk. **Rates** (per person) Mon-Thur 1,600kr-1,900kr; suite 2,500kr. *Fri-Sun* 1,800kr-2,100kr; suite 2,500kr. Yasuragi Package *Mon-Thur* 1,490-1,750kr; suite 2,350kr. *Sat-Sun* 1,295kr-1,650kr, suite 2,350kr. **Credit** AmEx, DC, MC, V.

For something unusual, try Hasseludden, Sweden's only Japanese spa, or *yasuragi*, where you can ease travel-weary muscles with a traditional Japanese bath, a swim, or a soak in a steaming outdoor jacuzzi overlooking the sea. Guests are pampered with a *yukata* (robe), swimsuit and slippers. Refresh yourself at the fruit and juice buffet, and try a session of *qi gong*, *do in* or Zen meditation – or go to the sushi school. All 162 sparsely furnished rooms and suites have calm water views. The hotel is a 30-minute boat ride from central Stockholm, so you can always make a day trip out here for the spa (see p172).

Business centre. Internet (dataport). No-smoking rooms. Parking (free). Pool (indoor, jacuzzi outside). Restaurant. Room service. Spa. TV (pay movies).

Camping

Camping is a pleasant and cheap option – but only during Sweden's short-lived summer. Stockholm's most central campsite is **Östermalms Citycamping** (Fiskartorpsvägen 2, 10 29 03), at the Östermalm sports ground behind Stockholms Stadion. Near woodlands, it's got 179 camping spaces, and is open from the end of June to mid August. There's also a site for campervans on **Långholmen** (669 18 90, open late June-late Aug). The tourist office (see p288) produces a guide to campsites in Stockholm and the archipelago. To camp in Sweden, you need a validated **Camping Card**, which you can buy (90kr) at any campsite.

Sightseeing

Introduction

Welcome to the world's most manageable capital.

The tourist office claims that Stockholm has one of the highest numbers of museums in the world for a city of its size and, with 70-odd museums drawing nine million visitors annually, it's easy to see their point. But the city isn't resting on its laurels. In 2004, the island of Skeppsholmen was transformed into a museum lover's paradise, with free entrance to three newly renovated, state-run museums – Moderna Museet, Arkitekturmuseet and Östasiatiska Museet. In reality, though, the most impressive sight of all is Stockholm itself; comprised of 14 islands, centred around medieval Gamla Stan, it guarantees one breathtaking vista after another.

The city breaks down into quickly recognisable, well-defined areas. There's no lurching from one overlapping neighbourhood to another, never quite knowing where you are. This is mainly because most of the city's districts are on self-contained islands.

Stockholm is also very compact; it's never more than a couple of metro stops from one sight to another – though often the best, and most pleasant, way to get around is to walk. It takes about 30 minutes to cross the city, from Norrmalm to Södermalm, but many places are only a few minutes' walk apart.

If you'd prefer to take public transport, the Tunnelbana metro system is fast, clean and efficient, as are the numerous buses that criss-cross the capital. In addition there are ferries between Södermalm, Djurgården and Norrmalm, though not all year round. *See pp276-279* **Getting Around** for detailed information on all the public transport options.

One of your first stops should be the **Stockholm Information Service** (*see p289*), the excellent tourist office located in Norrmalm.

Guided tours

Authorised Guides of Stockholm

50 82 85 08/www.guidestockholm.com.
This association has been around for 50 years and all its guides must complete lengthy training. Individual or group guided tours are given to most of the key sights in Stockholm.

City Sightseeing & Stockholm Sightseeing

58 71 40 20/www.citysightseeing.com/ www.stockholmsightseeing.com.

Vocabulary

It is handy to know the following Swedish words, as they often form part of addresses.

bro bridge; **gamla** old; **gata** street; **gård** farm; **hamn** harbour; **kyrka** church; **lilla** little; **norr** north; **öst** east; **sjö** lake; **slott** palace/castle; **söder** south; **strand** beach; **stora** big; **torg** square/ marketplace; **väg** road; **väst** west.

Tours by bus and foot (City Sightseeing) or boat (Stockholm Sightseeing). The Stockholm Panorama bus tour (1.5hrs, 200kr) is very popular, but the boat tours are probably the most attractive way to see the city. These include the Royal Canal Tour (1hr, 110kr) around Djurgården, and the Under the Bridges Tour (2hrs, 160kr). Tours run all year round (no boat tours from January to March), but are most frequent from May to September. For more information, visit the City Sightseeing ticket booth on Gustav Adolfs Torg by the opera house, or the Stockholm Sightseeing booth on Strömkajen in front of the Grand Hôtel. Walking tours also run several times a day from the end of June to the end of August (1hr, 80kr), departing from Mynttorget. The same company now offers horse and carriage tours of Gamla Stan (June-mid Aug). The carriage takes up to 18 people and costs 90kr per person.

Hot-air balloon flights

Unlike most capital cities, Stockholm allows hot-air balloons to fly over its centre. The season is May to September, and flights are generally in the early evening. Book at least two weeks in advance, and note that bad weather can result in cancellations. Try Scandinavia Balloons (55 64 04 65, www.balloons-sweden.se, 1,695kr per person for 1hr flight) or City Ballong (34 54 64, www.cityballong.se, 1,795kr for 1-1.5hr flight and champagne picnic on the ground afterwards).

RIB Sightseeing

20 22 60/www.ribsightseeing.se.
This company gives speedboat tours of Stockholm and the archipelago at speeds up to 45 knots. Waterproof gear and lifejackets are provided. The 90-minute tours (295kr per person) take you to Djurgården and further out to Waxholm and Fjäderholmarna. Tours run from May to the beginning of September.

Svea Viking

53 25 72 00/www.sveaviking.se.
Boat tours on this replica Viking boat (the world's largest) leave from Gamla Stan's eastern shore to tour Stockholm and the archipelago. Tours run from May to September, and some offer Viking food.

Tourist cards

If you're planning on doing a lot of sightseeing while in town, consider buying a **Stockholm Card** (Stockholmskortet). It provides free admission to more than 70 museums and attractions, plus free travel on the Tunnelbana, city buses, trains and sightseeing boats (but not the city or archipelago ferries), and free street parking at official parking spots. Available for 24, 48 or 72 hours (the time starts from its first use), it costs 260kr, 390kr or 540kr for adults; 100kr, 140kr or 190kr for 7-17s. In the Sightseeing chapters, **Free with SC** indicates which museums provide free entry for Stockholm Card holders.

The less useful **SL Tourist Card** also provides free travel, free admission to Kaknästornet and Gröna Lund, plus 50 per cent off Skansen, but no other discounts. It costs 80kr for 24 hours, 150kr for 72 hours (45kr and 90kr for children). You can purchase both cards at the **Tourist Information Centre** and **Hotellcentralen** (for both, *see p289*), and also at **SL information centres** (*see p273*).

Don't miss Stockholm

Cliffs of Söder
Take in the splendid city views from Monteliusvägen (*see p90*) and Fjällgatan. (*see p91*).

Kungliga Slottet
The striking Royal Palace in the heart of the Old Town. *See p63.*

Moderna Museet
The revamped Modern Art Museum is one of three free museums on the beautiful maritime island of Skeppsholmen. *See p89.*

Skansen
An open-air cultural and historical tour of Sweden. And bears, too. *See p85.*

Stadshuset
Stockholm's iconic tower, and setting for the Nobel Prize banquet. *See p104.*

Take a guided boat tour
The best way to get a feeling for the capital's islands and waterways. *See above.*

Vasamuseet
A world-class museum featuring a perfectly preserved 300-year-old warship. *See p86.*

Sightseeing

Gamla Stan & Riddarholmen

Point zero on the tourist trail: the royal palace and the charming, narrow streets of Old Town.

Gamla Stan

Map p305

The entire island of Gamla Stan, surrounded by the currents of Lake Mälaren and the Baltic Sea, has been designated a cultural landmark by the city of Stockholm. All buildings, land development, signs, lampposts, windows and paint colours are strictly regulated according to period-specific standards. For the lucky 2,800 people who live here, this translates into centuries-old buildings draped in ivy and quiet squares echoing with the sound of water pumps. Those seeking the more contemporary pleasures of waffle cones, street performers and plastic Viking helmets can explore the island's main drag, **Västerlånggatan**, and the central square of **Stortorget**.

Before Stockholm stretched out into the countryside, the whole city was once limited to this small island, referred to historically as 'the city between the bridges'. Some clever people built a fortress on the island's north-eastern shore around the 11th century, which enabled them to control the trade and traffic into Lake Mälaren, but there's no record of an actual city on Gamla Stan – which means 'the Old Town' – until Birger Jarl's famous letter of 1252, which mentioned the name 'Stockholm' for the first time. The island city grew into a horrible mess of winding streets and ramshackle houses until most of the western half burned down in 1625. The city planners finally crafted a few right angles (today the streets surrounding Stora Nygatan and Lilla Nygatan) and tore down the crumbling defensive wall around the island to make room for waterfront properties for the city council. The island was home to the Swedish monarchy for hundreds of years, and the immense and splendid **Kungliga Slottet** (Royal Palace) is still the main sight.

Nowadays, walking around Gamla Stan's charming tangle of narrow streets and alleyways lined with yellow, orange and red buildings is like taking an open-air history lesson. It can get very crowded, but you can avoid the bus-tour clusters by keeping off the main drags or ducking down side streets. The best approach is just to wander at will, soaking up the atmosphere.

Kungliga Slottet

The **Kungliga Slottet** (*see p63*) sits on a hill at the highest point in Gamla Stan, where the old fortress of Tre Kronor once stood, which was almost completely destroyed – except for the north wing – by a fire in 1697. Royal architect Nicodemus Tessin the Younger designed the new palace with an Italianate exterior and a French interior with Swedish influences; it was completed in 1754.

The low, yellowy-brown building is imposing rather than pretty; its monolithic northern façade looms menacingly as you approach Gamla Stan over the bridges from Norrmalm. The square central building around an open courtyard is flanked by two wings extending to the west and two more to the east – rather as if the palace were stretching out its front and hind legs. Between its eastern wings lie the gardens of Logården and between the curved western wings is an outer courtyard; the ticket/ information office and gift shop are in the south-western curve.

The southern façade with its triumphal central arch is the most attractive, along **Slottsbacken**, the hill that leads up from Skeppsbron and the water to the back of **Storkyrkan** (*see p70*). This large space was kept open to make it easier to defend the palace. The obelisk in front of the church, designed by Louis Jean Desprez, was put up in 1799 as a memorial to Gustav III's war against Russia in 1788-90.

Although the palace is the official residence of the royal family, they actually live on the island of Drottningholm (itself well worth a visit, *see pp244-53*), so visitors are welcome to explore its sumptuous **Royal Apartments** (Representationsvåningarna) and museums. The **Museet Tre Kronor** explores the history of the palace, while the **Skattkammaren** (Treasury), **Livrustkammaren** (Royal Armoury) and **Gustav III's Antikmuseum** (Museum of Antiquities) show off its prized possessions. A good deal, if you plan on seeing

most of the palace, is to buy the combined ticket (rather than individual tickets for each attraction), which provides admission to everything except the Livrustkammaren. But the limited opening hours and sheer size of the place mean that you'll probably have to visit a couple of times if you want to see it all.

Another royal museum, the **Kungliga Myntkabinettet** (*see below*) is located at the bottom of Slottsbacken, opposite the entrance to the Royal Armoury. The **Högvakten** (Royal Guard; 402 63 17, www.hogvakten.mil.se) has been stationed at the palace since 1523, and is a popular tourist attraction. The guard changes posts every day in summer but less frequently in winter (June-Aug 12.15pm Mon-Sat, 1.15pm Sun, Sept-May 12.15pm Wed, Sat, 1.15pm Sun), to the sound of a marching brass band. Around 20 soldiers dressed in blue uniforms with silver spiked helmets walk with stiff legs and straight faces in the palace's outer western courtyard. The ceremony can be good free entertainment depending on the size of the crowd and the weather. The whole thing lasts about 35 minutes and schedules are listed in newspapers *Svenska Dagbladet* and *Dagens Nyheter*. For a guaranteed good view of the guard and band, catch them on their parade route from the Armémuseum (*see p97*), from where they leave about 30 minutes before the change.

Kungliga Myntkabinettet

Slottsbacken 6 (51 95 53 04/www.myntkabinettet.se). T-bana Gamla Stan/bus 2, 43, 55, 59, 76. **Open** 10am-4pm daily. **Admission** 45kr; 35kr concessions; 12kr 7-17s; free under-7s. Free Sun. **Free with SC**. **Credit** MC, V. **Map** p305 H8.

The Royal Coin Cabinet, a museum of rare coins and monetary history, is surprisingly large, filling three floors in a building directly south of the palace. The darkened ground floor displays numerous coins in different contexts, from the first coin made in Greece in 625 BC to what is claimed to be the world's biggest coin, weighing a hefty 19.7kg (43lb). The first and second floors house displays on hoards and treasures, savings banks and medals. The museum is cleverly designed, with motion-triggered sounds and lights, multimedia displays and a special exhibition and playroom for kids. Nevertheless, unless you are especially fond of the filthy lucre or an economist, it's probably best to save this museum for a Sunday when admission is free.

Kungliga Slottet

Bordered by Slottsbacken, Skeppsbron, Lejonbacken & Högvaktsterrassen (402 61 30/www.royalcourt.se). T-bana Gamla Stan/bus 2, 43, 55, 59, 76. **Open** *Representationsvåningarna, Museet Tre Kronor & Skattkammaren* Mid May-Aug 10am-4pm daily. Sept-early Jan, Feb-mid May noon-3pm Tue-Sun. Closed 3wks Jan. *Gustav III's Antikmuseum* Mid May-Aug 10am-4pm daily. Closed Sept-mid May.

Sightseeing

A walk in Gamla Stan

Although you can walk across the island of Gamla Stan in 15 minutes, you could easily spend a day exploring its cobblestone streets, historic buildings and quiet – and not-so-quiet – squares. Gamla Stan, previously known as Stadsholmen (Island City), has changed dramatically during its history. This walk takes you through the oldest part, though the buildings here represent nearly all periods, from the 13th to the 20th century.

Start at the northern end of Västerlånggatan, at the corner of Myntgatan.
As you walk south on Västerlånggatan, you are heading into the heart of Stockholm's earliest history. At the time of its founding in the mid 1200s, the new city was confined to this small island, with defensive walls erected along Västerlånggatan and Österlånggatan. Västerlånggatan still has its winding medieval section, but in the last century it has become the area's busiest shopping street. Many of the large, cast-iron shop windows you see here were built from the 1860s to 1880s and are modelled after those found in Paris.

Make two short stops on Västerlånggatan, at Nos.14 and 29.
Just to the right of the portal at Västerlånggatan 14 you'll find medieval **Stenbastugränd** (the street sign is missing), a street dating from 1440. Looking down this narrow lane to the left you will see an old red building with corbel supports, which are projecting pieces of stone used to support weight in medieval buildings. Further south at Västerlånggatan 29 is **Jacob Sauer House**, another medieval building; its architectural mix is typical of Gamla Stan but this example is one of the clearest. The ground floor was reconstructed in the 1880s, whereas the middle façade maintains its 1300s appearance, with its brick herringbone pattern, recesses and pointed arches; the highest floors are from the 1600s.

Continue on Västerlånggatan, turn left on Kåkbrinken and stop at the corner of Prästgatan.
The name Kåkbrinken dates from 1477 – *kåk* means 'pillory' and *brink* means 'steep hill' – referring to the fact that this hill once led up to the city's pillory at Stortorget. Traffic has always been a problem on these narrow streets, and to protect the buildings from damage by horses, carts and other traffic, a cannon, an iron grate and a Viking rune stone were strategically placed on the corners. The rune stone reads,

'Torsten and Frögunn had this stone erected over their son…'. The remainder of the stone is missing so his fate is unknown. In medieval times, Prästgatan (meaning Priest Street) ran just inside the first city wall.

Continue along Kåkbrinken to Stortorget.
To the medieval inhabitants of Stockholm, Stortorget was the central meeting place, the main market and the courthouse. On the north side of the square was the town hall (now the Nobelmuseet; *see p69*), where new laws and regulations were read to the public twice a year from an upstairs window. Penalties ranged from fines and flogging to death by hanging or beheading. As a man's honour was of the utmost importance, some of the most common disputes dealt with at the city council were for personal insults. Stortorget is also the site of the infamous Stockholm Bloodbath in 1520 (*see p67*).

Take Svartmangatan south from Stortorget, and stop in front of Nos.11-13.
Svartmangatan (Black Man Street) is one of Stockholm's oldest streets, and once led to the Dominican monastery. The monks were called 'black brothers' or 'black men' because of their large black robes. You will pass the remains of their monastery, but first stop at Svartmangatan Nos.11-13. In the 1880s this was a meeting place for promoters of social democratic ideals, which had spread from the continent to Sweden. Many people thought these idealistic men were subversives out to overthrow the government, and they were closely watched by the police from across the street. Among them was Hjalmar Branting, who in 1889 formed the Social Democratic Labour Party and later became prime minister. The plaque over the door commemorates the Swedish Metalworkers' Union, one of the many trade unions started here.

Continue along Svartmangatan to the corner of Kindstugatan.
Saint Gertrude's is the official name of what is commonly referred to as **Tyska Kyrkan** (German Church; *see p70*). In medieval times this was the guild house of the city's German merchants, and in the 1570s it was converted into a church; the building took its present form in the 1630s and after a fire in 1878 the spire was reconstructed. Note its frightening gargoyles. In the 1700s the rounded rococo style of the buildings at this intersection made it one of the few turning areas for traffic.

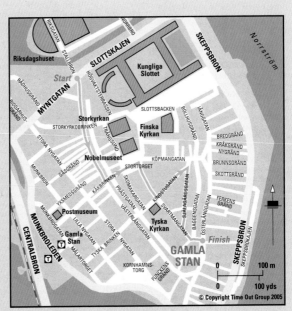

Turn left on Kindstugatan and stop at the Fimmelstången bar at Kindstugatan 14.
Kindstugatan's name is probably a misrepresentation of the old word *kindhäst*, which means 'box on the ear'. This now tranquil street was once the scene of some infamous fights. One of them began at the Fimmelstången tavern, where the renowned poet Lasse 'Lucidor' Johansson was killed in 1674. After a long drinking session with his friends, Lucidor refused to answer a final toast from his companion. A fight broke out and he was subsequently stabbed to death. Lucidor was a brilliant linguist who earned his living writing poems on commission. In 1689, 15 years after his death, his poems were published in the book *Helicons Blomster* (*The Flowers of Helicon*). In June 2004 a first edition of the book was sold for over £3,000 at Christie's in London.

Continue on Kindstugatan to Brända Tomten, the square with the tree, turn right and stop at Själagårdsgatan 13.
Started in the 1420s, **Själagården** was a combined hospital, poorhouse and old people's home run by Storkyrkan. In 1527, when Sweden became a Protestant country, King Gustav Vasa seized the Catholic church's gold and silver, and converted the building into a printing house to help spread the new religious teachings. Over the centuries the building has also been used as a school and a warehouse. In 1935 a functionalistic building was erected on the site above the old medieval cellar, and today it is once again a senior citizens' home operated by Storkyrkan.

Continue on Själagårdsgatan to Tyska Brunnsplan, and turn left on Svartmangatan.

Follow Svartmangatan as it becomes Södra Benickebrinken. Stop at No.4.
The Black Friars' monastery was once located in this area. King Magnus Eriksson and Queen Blanka donated this piece of land to the Dominican monastery in 1336. The monks offered faith-healing and shelter for travellers, but after the Reformation in 1527 the monastery was torn down. All that's left is a small cellar, hidden behind this black iron door. It's occasionally open to the public.

Walk down Södra Benickebrinken to Österlånggatan and stop outside restaurant Den Gyldene Freden at No.51.
Österlånggatan, running north from busy Järntorget, marks the eastern section of the first city wall. The Restaurant **Den Gyldene Freden** (*see p114*) opened on this street in 1722 and soon became one of the most popular taverns in town. It was nearly closed in 1919 but famous Swedish artist Anders Zorn bought the building and had the restaurant completely renovated. When Zorn passed away he bequeathed the building to the Swedish Academy and in 1922 the restaurant reopened to the delight of many Stockholmers. It's famed for its traditional, yet creative Swedish dishes, and its dimly lit, historic interior will transport you to another time.

Admission *Combination ticket* 110kr; 65kr concessions. *Individual tickets* 70kr; 35kr 7-18s; free under-7s. **Free with SC**. **Credit** AmEx, DC, MC, V. **Map** p305 H8.

Representationsvåningarna
Entrance in western courtyard.

The Royal Apartments occupy two floors of the palace and are entered by a grand staircase in the western wing. King Adolf Fredrik and Queen Lovisa Ulrika moved into the new palace in 1754, after five decades of construction and delays following the 1697 fire. The apartments are still used for official ceremonies, although over the years the function of individual rooms has changed repeatedly, from bedroom to audience chamber to roped-off curiosity. The furnishings, tapestries and paintings range in style from ornate rococo to more reserved neo-classical Gustavian. Since it's the stories behind the rooms and decorations that make the palace especially interesting – such as Gustav III's invitation to aristocrats to watch him wake up in the morning – taking a guided tour is highly recommended. Banquets are held several times a year in Karl XI's Gallery in the **State Apartments** on the second floor. This long hall seats up to 150 guests and was modelled after the Hall of Mirrors in Versailles. The ballroom at the end of the gallery is often used as a salon during banquets, with the king and queen standing in the entrance to greet guests. Heads of state stay in the **Guest Apartments** during their visits to the capital, and for this reason parts or all of the palace may be occasionally closed. Downstairs in the Bernadotte Apartments, portraits of the current dynasty's ancestors hang in the **Bernadotte Gallery**, including a large portrait of the former French marshal Karl XIV Johan who became king in 1818. Medals and orders of various kinds are awarded in the **Apartments of the Orders of Chivalry**, and paintings of coats of arms decorate its walls. Until 1975, the monarch opened parliament each year in the impressive **Hall of State**, and directly across from this lies the **Royal Chapel** with pew ends made in the 1690s for the Tre Kronor castle. Services are held every Sunday and all are welcome to attend.

Museet Tre Kronor
Entrance on Lejonbacken.

A boardwalk built through the palace cellars, along with several models, enables visitors to see how war, fire and wealth have shaped the palace seen today. An old well from the former courtyard, a 13th-century defensive wall and the arched brick ceilings are evidence of how the palace was built up around the fortress that was once there. Panels describe life within the castle, archaeological discoveries and building techniques. After the fire of 1697, rumours flew about architect Tessin the Younger's involvement in the fire, since he had hated the castle's former tower and produced his plans for the new palace rather quickly. Walking through the old cellars and peering down into excavations provide the main entertainment, as the exhibits are more informative than dazzling.

Gustav III's Antikmuseum
Entrance on Lejonbacken.

This museum of Roman statues and busts, in two halls in the north-east wing of the palace, has been laid out to look exactly as it did in the 1790s when King Gustav III returned from Italy with the collection, which includes *Apollo and His Nine Muses* and the sleeping *Endymion*. The repairs and additions made to the statues at the time have been left intact, as well as the odd combinations of pieces, such as table legs on fountains. It's worth a look if you have the combined ticket, or an interest in Roman art. Nothing is labelled, in accordance with the period, so take the 20-minute tour (in English) or borrow a pamphlet.

Skattkammaren
Entrance on Slottsbacken.

If you're a fan of jewel-encrusted crowns and gaudy gold, the small Treasury in the basement of the palace is worth a peek. The regalia of past Swedish royal families sparkles behind glass, with orbs, sceptres and crowns in adults' and children's sizes. The museum also contains Gustav Vasa's etched sword of state from 1541, the coronation cloak of Oscar II and the ornate silver baptismal font of Karl XI.

Livrustkammaren
Entrance on Slottsbacken (51 95 55 44/www.lsh.se/ livrustkammaren). T-bana Gamla Stan/bus 2, 43, 55, 62, 76. **Open** *June-Aug* 10am-5pm daily. *Sept-May* 11am-5pm Tue, Wed, Fri-Sun; 11am-8pm Thur. **Admission** 65kr; 50kr concessions; 20kr 7-18s; free under-7s. **Free with SC**. **Credit** AmEx, DC, MC, V. **Map** p305 H8.

The Royal Armoury is one of the palace's best museums – don't miss it. Sweden's oldest museum, founded in 1633, it is stuffed with armour, weapons and clothes from the 16th century onwards, and is

Kungliga Slottet. *See p63.*

housed in the palace's former cellars, which were used for potatoes and firewood. With wonderfully descriptive texts, the museum's first room shows what a bloody and dangerous business being a king once was. It contains the masked costume King Gustav III wore when he was assassinated in 1792, and the stuffed body of Streiff, the horse that Gustav II Adolf was riding when he was killed in battle in 1632. Don't overlook the glass jar preserving the stomach contents of one of the conspirators to Gustav III's murder. Other rooms display splendid mounted knights, suits of armour, swords and muskets. Two rooms of clothes and toys – including a miniature carriage and suit of armour – describe the lost childhoods and early responsibilities of the royal children. The ceremonial coaches of the nobility lie beneath the main floor, in another dimly lit hall. Guided tours in English are no longer given, but audio guides in English are provided.

Other sights

There are plenty of other sights on Gamla Stan apart from the Royal Palace. At the top of Slottsbacken stands the imposing yellow bulk of Stockholm's de facto cathedral, **Storkyrkan** (*see p70*), scene of royal weddings and coronations. Trångsund, the street at the front of the church, leads down to Gamla Stan's main square, **Stortorget**. A former marketplace, it's surrounded by handsome, colourful 18th-century buildings, some containing cafés: the two next door to each other at the western end of the square, **Chokladkoppen** and **Kaffekoppen** (for both, *see p144*), are the best.

The large white building is the former Stock Exchange, designed by Erik Lallerstedt (not to be confused with one of Sweden's most famous chefs by the same name); it now houses the high-tech **Nobelmuseet** (*see p69*), telling the history of the esteemed Nobel Prizes. Lallerstedt also designed the 1778 well in the centre of the square. Due to the land rising, the well dried up in the 19th century and was moved to Brunkebergstorg in Norrmalm, but it was then moved back again in the 20th century.

The notorious **Stockholm Bloodbath** – in which more than 80 noblemen, priests and burghers were hanged or decapitated at the command of the Danish king, Christian II – occurred in Stortorget in 1520. You can see a cannonball in the façade of the building at Stortorget 7, on the corner with Skomakargatan. It is said to have been fired at Christian II at the time of the Bloodbath, but in fact was placed much later, as a joke, probably in 1795 by a furniture dealer named Grevesmühl. Every time the building has been restored the ball has been removed and then carefully replaced.

Round the corner from Stortorget is the **Cornelis Vreeswijkmuseet** (Trångsund 8, 667 73 65, www.cornelis.nu, open mid June-mid Aug noon-4pm Wed-Sun, mid Aug-mid June noon-4pm Sat, Sun, 20kr). The museum is devoted to Cornelis Vreeswijk, a radical folk singer of ballads and blues in the mid 1960s. Displaying his photos, letters and boots, the museum is mainly of interest to fans of his music and the Dutch (he was born in Holland).

Gamla Stan's main thoroughfares of **Västerlånggatan**, **Österlånggatan**, **Stora Nygatan** and **Lilla Nygatan** run north-south along the island. Crowded Västerlånggatan acts

Walking on water

During the Middle Ages, generally regarded as the period from around 1050 to the 1520s (from the introduction of Christianity to Gustav Vasa's rise to power and the Reformation), Stockholm grew from a relatively uninhabited group of islands controlled by local noblemen to the capital city of a unified nation. It all sounds rather grand, but for the inhabitants of medieval Stockholm it was most certainly a bumpy ride.

When the city wasn't fighting off foreign invasions, caught up in civil wars or enduring trade boycotts, it had frequent and devastating fires to deal with, streets filled with muck and unwelcome visits of bubonic plague. Still, it wasn't all bad; on Sundays residents could enjoy a quiet – though mandatory – moment in the splendour of **Storkyrkan** (*see p70*), and once a month one of the town's charities offered free baths.

In early medieval Stockholm most of the houses in the city were made of wood with sod roofs, although these were later replaced with two- to three-storey brick buildings in an effort to curb the threat of fire. Dwellings were a cramped combination of home, business and farm, with pigs in the cellar and tradesmen and merchants dealing with the public from wide, ground-floor openings facing the street (check out Prästgatan and Köpmangatan for the best-preserved medieval buildings). The streets themselves – filled with cows, beggars and the contents of emptied chamber pots – were bridged with wooden logs and later laid with cobblestones. The Swedes even used a kind of pre-ABBA platform-shoe attachment that allowed them to walk above the filth (on display at Stockholms Medeltidsmuseum; *see p72*).

Despite the unsanitary conditions, medieval Stockholmers actually made good use of their rubbish by using it to expand the island. It is estimated that roughly two thirds of present-

day Gamla Stan is built on what was formerly water – though the land has been steadily rising, which has also contributed more land mass. Around the time of the city's founding, in the mid 1200s, the water level reached just below the city walls that stood near present-day Västerlånggatan and Österlånggatan. Since city law allowed residents with waterfront property to extend their land outwards, many homeowners did just that, using trash and other waste as landfill. In fact, many of Stockholm's

as a giant sluice, gently persuading tourists to part with their cash its many small shops. The parallel street – narrow, curving **Prästgatan** – is a quiet alternative to the hubbub and far more atmospheric, giving you a much better idea of life in the crowded medieval city. Located on Österlånggatan, where the shops are less touristy than those on Västerlånggatan, is the new **Ice Gallery** (Österlånggatan 41, 790 55 00, www.ice-gallery.com, open 11am-5pm daily),

affiliated with the well-known Ice Hotel in northern Sweden. Here you can walk inside a re-created ice suite from the hotel, complete with ice bed, walls, furniture and sculptures. At the southern end of Västerlånggatan is **Mårten Trotzigs Gränd**, the city's narrowest street at only 90 centimetres (three feet) wide. A bit further south is **Järntorget**, where you can sit outdoors and enjoy the cakes and pastries of Sundbergs Konditori (*see p144*).

archaeological finds, such as the hundreds of pairs of leather shoes unearthed on Helgeandsholmen, come from areas that were previously underwater. To prevent the buildings from sinking, in the 1970s the government subsidised the ground reinforcement of all buildings in Gamla Stan built on landfill. The history of the city's beginnings certainly puts a new slant on the tourist office's catchphrase for Stockholm: 'beauty on water'.

Those residents without waterfront property, or any property at all, had the most difficult time in medieval Stockholm. Though fines were the most common form of punishment for lawbreakers, thieves could expect to be chained and whipped at the pillory that once stood at Stortorget. Particularly unlucky criminals or repeat offenders had one or both of their ears cut off and were sometimes nailed to the pillory, or even worse, were hanged or buried alive. The person who had to do all the whipping, cutting and hanging was the town executioner, usually a former criminal himself, who lived in an area of town aptly known as Hell (the present-day northern tip of Prästgatan). All new executioners were required to kill their predecessors, but there was one perk to the job: they received their salaries tax-free.

Gamla Stan is today considered one of the best-preserved medieval cities in northern Europe, though countless renovations have left it with a wide variety of architectural styles. To see medieval Stockholm in all its glory, you should head underground, as many of the island's restaurants, shops and attractions contain beautiful medieval vaulted cellars.

Pictured: 'Sun Dogs' by Jacob Elbfas (a 1636 copy of the lost original from 1535), the oldest known depiction of Stockholm.

There are only five hotels on Gamla Stan; two of them – the Victory Hotel and Rica City Hotel Gamla Stan (for both, *see p44*) – are on Lilla Nygatan, as is the surprisingly interesting **Postmuseum** (*see p70*). On nearby Stora Nygatan you can visit **Forum för Levande Historia** (The Living History Forum; 723 87 50, www.levande historia.se, closed Fri), a new government exhibition centre and library on human rights, prejudice and genocide.

The island's churches include the **Tyska Kyrkan** (German Church; *see p70*) and the **Finska Kyrkan** (Finnish Church) – proof of Sweden's long connections with its European neighbours. The latter is housed in a 1640s building opposite the Kungliga Slottet; originally a ball games court for the palace, it has been the religious centre of the Finnish community since 1725. Down the hill from the Finnish Church is the Swedish Institute's excellent bookshop **Sweden Bookshop** (Slottsbacken 10, 453 78 80, www.swedenbookshop.com).

Gamla Stan also contains a number of beautiful palaces, former homes of the aristocracy. On the island's north-western tip on Riddarhustorget is **Bondeska Palatset**, designed by Tessin the Elder and the seat of the Supreme Court since 1949, and the lovely **Riddarhuset** (723 39 90, www.riddarhuset.se). The latter is a superb example of Dutch Palladianism, with a typically Swedish *säteri* roof (a roof with a small vertical rise halfway up), completed in 1674. The nobility governed from here until parliamentary reforms in 1866 knocked them down a notch or two. They still own the place, though, and will let you visit during the lunch hour (11.30am-12.30pm Mon-Fri, admission 40kr) to admire their coats of arms (more than 2,000), signet collection and early 17th-century chair with ivory engravings. Another way to see inside is to attend a concert by the **Stockholm Sinfonietta** (*see p220*).

Nobelmuseet

Börshuset, Stortorget (23 25 06/www.nobel.se/nobel museum). T-bana Gamla Stan/bus 2, 3, 43, 53, 55, 59, 76. **Open** *Mid May-mid Sept* 10am-6pm Mon, Wed-Sun; 10am-8pm Tue. *Mid Sept-mid May* 11am-8pm Tue; 11am-5pm Wed-Sun. **Guided tours** (in English) *Mid May-mid Sept* 11am, 2pm, 4pm Mon, Wed-Sun; 11am, 2pm, 4pm, 5pm Tue. *Mid Sept-mid May* 11am, 4pm Tue-Sun. **Admission** 50kr; 40kr concessions; 20kr 7-18s; 100kr family ticket; free under-7s. **Free with SC**. **Credit** AmEx, MC, V. **Map** p305 J7.

The Nobel Museum opened in 2001 to commemorate the centenary of the Nobel Prizes. Although the museum is not that large, its two theatres showing short films about the laureates, television clips about the prizes and a computer room with an 'e-museum' bombard you with enough information to keep you entertained for a while. You can also listen to acceptance speeches over the years in audio booths, including that of Martin Luther King in 1964. A track on the ceiling moves 758 white placards (one for each prizewinner) around the main hall, each with a description and photo. Alfred Nobel's books, lab equipment and two packs of dynamite are displayed in a side room, along with his death mask and a copy of his one-page will, which called for the creation of the prizes. An exhibit on the Nobel banquet includes a glassed-in table setting and videos of the event. *See also 104* **Peace man?**.

Postmuseum

Lilla Nygatan 6 (781 17 55/www.postmuseum.
posten.se). T-bana Gamla Stan/bus 3, 53. **Open**
May-Aug 11am-4pm Tue-Sun. *Sept-Apr* 11am-4pm
Tue, Thur-Sun; 11am-7pm Wed. **Admission** 50kr;
40kr concessions; 25kr 13-18s; free under-13s.
Free with SC. Credit MC, V. **Map** p305 J7.
Life-size scenes depicting more than 360 years of the
Swedish postal service make the main exhibit of this
museum unexpectedly enjoyable. A mounted postal
carrier, a farm boy running with the mail and a postal
train wagon, among other tableaux, illustrate the
effect of the postal service on people's lives over the
centuries. From 1720 until 1869, the city's only post
office was housed on this spot. The museum opened
in 1906, underwent extensive renovations in 1999
and now occupies the entire building. The second
floor houses an exhibit on stamps and stamp printing, as well as temporary exhibits that are often
worth a look. Lilla Posten downstairs includes a
miniature post office for children and the gift shop
sells stationery, pens and, of course, stamps.

Storkyrkan

Storkyrkobrinken, Trångsund 1 (723 30 10/
www.sthdomkyrko.com). T-bana Gamla Stan/bus 2,
3, 43, 53, 55, 59, 76. **Open** *June-Aug* 9am-6pm
daily. *Sept-May* 9am-4pm daily. **Admission** 20kr;
free under-16s. Free Sept-May. **Map** p305 H7.
Dating from the mid 13th century, 'the Great Church'
is the oldest congregational church in Stockholm and
the site of past coronations and royal weddings. A
huge brick church with a rectangular plan, it's been
extended and rebuilt numerous times. Between 1736
and 1742, its exterior was renovated from medieval

Birger Jarl statue. *See p71.*

to baroque to match the neighbouring palace, and in
1743 the tower was raised to its current height of 66m
(216ft). In the early 1900s, the red bricks of the church
were exposed to achieve a medieval appearance.
Inside, the style is primarily Gothic with baroque
additions – such as the extravagant golden booths
designed for the royal family by the palace architect
Tessin the Younger. The main attraction is Bernt
Notke's intricately carved wooden statue, *St George
and the Dragon*, which is decorated with authentic
elk antlers. The statue symbolises Sten Sture's victory over the Danes in a battle in 1471, and was given
to the church by Sture himself in 1489. (A bronze copy
of the statue can also be found in Köpmantorget, not
far from the church.) Don't miss the famous *Parhelion
Painting*, which shows an unusual light phenomenon
– six sparkling halos – that appeared over Stockholm
on 20 April 1535. It's one of the oldest depictions of
the capital, though the painting is a 1630s copy of the
earlier original. During the summer, theology students give guided tours (in Swedish) of the church's
tower (2pm & 3pm, 30kr), which involves climbing
200 steps on narrow wooden staircases for an amazing view of the black roofs of Gamla Stan. Call 723 30
00 to organise a guided tour in English.

Tyska Kyrkan

Svartmangatan 16A (411 11 88/www.svenska
kyrkan.se/stockholmskyrkor). T-bana Gamla Stan/bus
3, 53. **Open** *May-mid Sept* noon-4pm daily. *Mid*
Sept-Apr noon-4pm Sat, Sun. **Admission** free.
Map p305 J8.
At the height of the Hanseatic League, when
Stockholm had strong trade links with Germany,
many German merchants settled in this area of
Gamla Stan. They originally worshipped at the
monastery on what is now Riddarholmen, but moved
to St Gertrude's guildhouse after its expansion in the
1580s. Baroque renovations in 1638-42 gave the
German Church its present appearance; its tower was
rebuilt after a fire in 1878. Nicodemus Tessin the
Elder designed the royal pews, and Jost Henner created the richly decorated ornaments and figures on
the portal. The church is best viewed from Tyska
Brinken, where the tower rises up 96m (315ft) from
the narrow street. About 2,000 Swedes of German
origin belong to the congregation, and services are
held in German at 11am on Sundays. At the church's
summer concerts you can listen to a replica of a 17th-
century organ, which was constructed for the church
in 2004 at a cost of ten million kronor.

Riddarholmen

Map p305

Separated from Gamla Stan by several lanes
of traffic and a narrow canal, the tiny island
of Riddarholmen is a quiet sanctuary of
cobblestone streets, 17th-century palaces
and spectacular watery views. Most of the
buildings now house government offices, and
no one actually lives permanently on the island.

Riddarholmen, as viewed from Stadshuset.

The main attraction is the medieval brick church, **Riddarholmskyrkan** (*see p71*), which was built in the late 13th century as a monastery for Franciscan monks. In 1527, following the Reformation, the monks were kicked off the island; the church is now the burial site of Swedish monarchs. Riddarholmen was originally called 'Grey Friars' Island' after the colour of the monks' clothing. In the 17th century, Sweden's Age of Greatness, Gustav II Adolf rewarded noblemen who served in the Thirty Years' War with palaces on the island – this is when Riddarholmen received its current name, 'the Island of Knights'.

Next to the church is **Birger Jarls Torg**, the site of an 1854 statue of Stockholm's founder, Birger Jarl, dressed in a helmet and chainmail. Beneath the stones of the square lie the graves from the former church cemetery. The huge white **Wrangelska Palatset** stands to the west of the statue. Constructed as a nobleman's residence in the mid 17th century, it was extensively rebuilt a few decades later by Tessin the Elder, under its new owner, Field Marshal Carl Gustaf Wrangel. The palace became the home of the royal family for several years after the Tre Kronor fire of 1697. In 1792 the murderer of Gustav III was kept in dungeons here during his trial.

On the other side of the square is the well-preserved and pink-coloured **Stenbockska Palatset**, built in the 1640s by state councillor Fredrik Stenbock, and extended and renovated in succeeding centuries. The palaces of Riddarholmen are today used by the Swedish courts and government authorities and are seldom open to the public, but taking a walk around them is highly recommended.

Down by the water on **Evert Taubes Terrass**, you'll find one of the best views in Stockholm, looking out across the choppy water of Riddarfjärden and towards the northern and southern shores of Lake Mälaren. The terrace is named after the much-loved Swedish poet and troubadour Evert Taube (who died in 1976) and there's a bronze sculpture of him, lute in hand, near the water. It's also a prime spot to celebrate the arrival of spring on **Walpurgis Night** (*see p182*), with a bonfire by the water and communal singing. Swedish author and dramatist **August Strinberg** was born here in 1849 in an apartment above the steamboat commission's office, where his father sold tickets for steamboat excursions. At the time, Riddarholmen was a busy port for unloading and selling goods. Although Strindberg's building has long since been torn down, a plaque in Swedish on a nearby wall commemorates the site, and two steamboats docked on the western shore still provide pre-booked tours for groups. For more on Sweden's most famous playwright, *see p236*. An outdoor café is open in the summer, and there's also a restaurant and hotel on the permanently anchored luxury yacht *Mälardrottningen* (*see p49* **Beds on boats**).

North along the waterfront, on Norra Riddarholmshamnen, is the distinctive circular **Birger Jarls Torn**. The only remnant of the defensive fortifications built by Gustav Vasa around 1530 (along with part of the Wrangelska Palatset), it was given its name in the 19th century when it was mistakenly thought to have been built under Birger Jarl 600 years earlier. It's not open to the public.

Riddarholmskyrkan

Birger Jarls Torg (Royal Palace 402 61 30/www.royal court.se). T-bana Gamla Stan/bus 3, 53. **Open** *Mid May-Aug* 10am-4pm daily. *Early-mid Sept* noon-3pm Tue-Sun. *Mid-end Sept* noon-3pm Sat, Sun. Closed Oct-mid May. Tours in English five times a day May-Aug. **Admission** 20kr; 10kr concessions, 7-18s; free under-7s. **Free with SC. No credit cards. Map** p305 J7.

The black, lattice-work spire of Riddarholmskyrkan is one of Stockholm's most distinctive sights, visible from all over the city. Construction on the church started in the late 13th century as a monastery for Franciscan monks. The church's benefactor, King Magnus Ladulås, is buried in the church along with 16 other monarchs, including Gustav III, Gustav II Adolf and, the last to be buried here in 1950, Gustav V. Since the 17th century, only two Swedish monarchs have not been buried here. Additions have been made to the church over time, in part to make room for more graves, since an estimated 500-1,000 people are buried in its floors and vaults – the floor consists almost entirely of grave-covering stone slabs. The southern wall was moved back in the 15th century, the tower was added in the late 16th century, and work began in 1838 on the current cast-iron spire after lightning struck the original. Colourful plaques of the Serafim order, which are awarded to Swedish nobility and visiting heads of state, decorate the walls of the church. The helpful tour guides describe the history of the church, burial ceremonies and what the monarchs look like now in their coffins – whether you want to hear it or not.

Helgeandsholmen

Map p305

This tiny oval-shaped island is connected to Norrmalm and Gamla Stan by two bridges: a pedestrian one at the western end, which connects to Norrmalm's shopping street, Drottninggatan, and a car/pedestrian bridge at the eastern end. The **Riksdagshuset** (Parliament Building; see below) dominates the western half of the island. Walking north, the new parliament building is to your left and the old one to your right, joined by two stone arches. The older section, completed in 1905, was designed by Aron Johansson, with two chambers for a bicameral parliament, baroque motifs and a grand staircase. At the same time he also designed a curved stone building across the street for the Bank of Sweden. After the country changed to a unicameral system in 1971, the bank moved out, the roof was flattened and the parliament's new glass-fronted debating chamber built on top.

This being Sweden, it's a pretty open system of government. There's a very detailed website (in Swedish and English), a new information centre (Storkyrkobrinken 7, www.riksdagen.se) and the parliament building is open for guided tours year round (for information call 786 48 62). You can also visit the public gallery when parliament is in session and listen to debates.

Beneath the lawns at the other end of the island, the **Stockholms Medeltidsmuseum** (see below) provides a fascinating insight into life in medieval Stockholm.

An ambitious two-year engineering project was initiated in 2004 on Helgeandsholmen. The parliament buildings sit on 15,000 wooden piles that are submerged in groundwater and therefore protected from rot. However, fluctuations in the water level – this is the point where Lake Mälaren empties into the sea – and the fact that the land is rising by around 40 centimetres every 100 years, have placed the piles in danger. A new lock and 650 concrete pillars below ground are to create a shield, locating the buildings within the more stable waters of Lake Mälaren.

Riksdagshuset

Riksgatan 3A (786 40 00/www.riksdagen.se). T-bana Kungsträdgården/bus 43, 62. **Open** (guided tours only) *End June-Aug* 11am, 3pm (Swedish), 12.30pm, 2pm (Swedish & English) Mon-Fri. *Sept-end June* noon (Swedish), 1.30pm (Swedish & English) Sat, Sun. **Admission** free. **Map** p305 H7.

Free 50-minute guided tours (meet at Riksgatan 2) of the Riksdagshuset are given in Swedish, English and German. The guides are exceptionally well informed and the tour is interesting – if you don't mind a little education. You'll see the modern semicircular main chamber; at the front is a large tapestry, *Memory of a Landscape* by Elisabet Hasselberg Olsson, woven in 200 shades of grey. Beneath the chamber lies the former bank hall, now a lobby for the parliamentarians. In the old building, where the tour begins and ends, visitors are shown the grand former main entrance with its marble columns and busts of prime ministers, as well as the old dual chambers (now used as meeting rooms). For security reasons, all visitors should be ready to give proof of their identity.

Stockholms Medeltidsmuseum

Strömparterren, Norrbro (508 31 790/www.medel tidsmuseet.stockholm.se). T-bana Gamla Stan/bus 43, 62, 65. **Open** *July-Aug* 11am-4pm Mon, Fri-Sun; 11am-6pm Tue-Thur. *Sept-June* 11am-4pm Tue, Thur-Sun; 11am-6pm Wed. **Guided tours** *English* July, Aug 2pm daily. *Swedish* 1pm daily (not Mon, Sept-June). **Admission** 40kr; 20kr concessions; 5kr 7-17s; free under-7s. **Free with SC**. **Credit** AmEx, MC, V. **Map** p305 H7.

During an excavation of Helgeandsholmen in the late 1970s for the construction of a new parking garage for MPs, archaeologists discovered thousands of artefacts from medieval Stockholm. So, instead of the garage, parliament decided to build this underground museum, containing more than 850 medieval objects, a hidden passage to the castle and a 14th-century cemetery wall. Dimly lit, with spooky sound effects, it's an atmospheric place. The old harbour has been re-created, with a quayside, warehouses and fishing huts smelling of tar, to show the living standards and building techniques of the time. There's also a 20m-long (66ft) wooden ship from the 1520s (discovered off Riddarholmen in 1930) next to the exhibit about archaeology with uncovered skeletons.

Norrmalm & Vasastaden

The city's commercial pulse.

August Strindberg immortalised in **Tegnérlunden**. *See p79.*

Norrmalm

Map p304 & p305

The focus of much indiscriminate bulldozing in the 1960s, Norrmalm – also known as the City – suffered considerable blows to its aesthetic make-up. Visitors shouldn't come expecting any quaint medieval streets then, but Norrmalm certainly is essential viewing – it is Stockholm's modern downtown and its commercial centre, packed with shopping centres, office blocks, restaurants, nightclubs, most of the city's larger and finer hotels, and some key museums and sights.

In Stockholm's early years, city government discouraged construction on Norrmalm out of fear that an enemy attacking Gamla Stan would take shelter in the buildings. It seems the area has always been under threat from something – even in the early 16th century Gustav Vasa tore down many of Norrmalm's structures. By 1602, though, the district had grown to the extent that it was declared a separate city, and it operated as such for three decades. When its competition

with Stockholm became absurd, Norrmalm lost its independence, and by 1637 it was a Stockholm neighbourhood.

Most visitors to Stockholm arrive in Norrmalm, zoomed in on the Arlanda Express to its terminal next to **Central Station** on busy Vasagatan, or by bus to its northern neighbour **Cityterminalen**. They link up to **T-Centralen**, the main Tunnelbana station, where all three lines of the metro network converge. Stepping out from Central Station, you immediately see the kind of functionalist concrete and steel buildings that dominate the area. Behind them peeks the brick tower of the late 16th-century **St Clara Kyrka** (*see p78*), one of the area's oldest churches.

Those wanting to head straight into the heart of the shopping district should take **Klarabergsgatan** from Central Station, which ends at Sergels Torg. To see the water and the more picturesque areas of Norrmalm, head south on the eastern side of Vasagatan. Swing round the corner when you reach the **Sheraton**

Stockholm Hotel & Towers (*see p49*) and walk one block up Jakobsgatan (to avoid the horrible tangle of highways and viaducts). The nearby **Konstakademien** (Royal Academy of Art, www.konstakademien.se) on parallel Fredsgatan, at No.12, occupies a renovated palace designed by Tessin the Elder in the 1670s. The academy was founded by King Gustav III in 1773 and moved into its current premises in 1780. In 1978 it was separated from the Royal University College of Fine Arts, which is today on Skeppsholmen. The academy's terrace bar (*see p137*) is very popular in summer, as is the restaurant **Fredsgatan 12** (*see p115*), with high-profile chef Markus Aujalay at the helm. The academy's art exhibitions are closed in the summer.

Many of Sweden's government departments are nearby, such as the two buildings – one light orange and the other red – called **Rosenbad**, which house the offices of the prime minister. A stone walkway and bicycle path follow the northern shore of **Norrström** – from Rosenbad to the tip of the Blasieholmen peninsula. East on Fredsgatan is **Gustav Adolfs Torg**, named after King Gustav II Adolf, who greatly expanded the city in the early 17th century; an equestrian statue of the king stands in the centre of the square. Not far

away there are Mediterranean antiquities in the **Medelhavsmuseet** and dance costumes in the **Dansmuseet** (for both, *see p76*).

On the square's eastern flank is the grand **Kungliga Operan** (*see p237*), styled after the Royal Palace in the late 19th century, with a splendid chandelier-strewn gold foyer 28 metres (92 feet) long. The original opera building, where King Gustav III was assassinated in 1792, looked exactly like **Arvfurstens Palats**, the building across from it, which was constructed in the 1780s and now is used by the Ministry for Foreign Affairs. The opera house contains a trio of restaurants, varying in splendour and price; the fanciest, and one of Sweden's best, is **Operakällaren** (*see p117*). From the front of the opera house you get a beautiful view across the water towards the Kungliga Slottet; behind it is the earthy red Gothic structure of **St Jacobs Kyrka** (*see p78*).

The long rectangular park of **Kungsträdgården** (King's Garden) stretches north from here. This is a popular venue for open-air events and fairs. Originally a vegetable garden for the royal castle in the 15th century, the park later developed into a pleasure garden and opened to the public in the 18th century. A century later the French-born King Karl XIV Johan tore out the trees, erected a statue of his

Gustaf Vasa Kyrka: Vasastaden's domed beauty. *See p80.*

adoptive father, Karl XIII, and converted the garden into a field for military exercises. After his death it was quietly turned back into a park. The statue of Karl XII – his finger pointing east to his old battlegrounds in Russia – was added in 1868 near the water.

Two tree-lined avenues shade the restaurants and glassed-in cafés along the park's western and eastern edges, although the now-sickly trees are currently being replaced with five-metre-high (16-foot-high) versions, which should be in place by 2006. At the top end of the park, in front of a shallow pool with three fountains, is the touristy Friday's American Bar, while Volvo's newest and oldest cars are displayed in a showroom nearby. At the **Systembolagets Museet** (*see p79*), hidden away in a basement, you can learn all about Sweden's peculiar attitude to alcohol, should you be so inclined; in winter there's skating on the park's ice rink.

The crowded thoroughfare of **Hamngatan** crosses the top of the park. At No.27 is **Sverige Huset**, which will once again be home to the main tourist information centre when renovations to the building are complete in February 2005. Bang opposite is **NK**, Sweden's first and most exclusive department store. For cheaper shops try the **Gallerian** mall (for both, *see p153*) just up the street, which is looking much more spritely after extensive renovation.

A couple of blocks west along from NK is **Sergels Torg**. This two-level area of glass, concrete and underground shops was built after the bulldozer extravaganza of the 1960s (*see p77* **Concrete calamity**). The sunken modernistic square of black and white triangles is a popular spot for political demonstrations; the rather grubby, tall glass tower surrounded by fountains in the middle of the traffic island was designed by sculptor Edvin Öhrström in 1972.

After decades of debate, Sergels Torg is finally due to get get a touch-up – though perhaps not on the scale that some would wish. After much discussion about completely redoing it, all that is to happen now is the addition of a new escalator to the underground and a remodelled T-Centralen ticket hall. The changes won't win any prizes but maybe, given the square's past, this kind of cautious development is exactly what it needs.

Architect Peter Celsing was responsible for **Kulturhuset** (*see p234*), the seven-storey structure that stands behind Sergels Torg like a great glass wall, which he built in the early 1970s. Today it's home to Sweden's only comic book library, **Serieteket**, while next door is one of Stockholm's biggest theatres, **Stadsteatern** (*see p234*). You can play chess on the ground floor or take the escalators up to one of the three art

Gustav Adolfs Torg. *See p74.*

galleries on the floors above. There's a library, an internet café and a branch of **DesignTorget** (*see p169*). The top floor **Café Panorama** (*see p145*) has a great view of the square below.

Several main streets converge on Sergels Torg, including Klarabergsgatan and Sveavägen. The block-long, windowless **Åhléns** department store (*see p153*) occupies the north-west corner of the former, and is one of scores of shopping options. The packed pedestrian street of **Drottninggatan** is lined with shops from its start at the water's edge all the way north to Tegnérgatan.

North from Sergels Torg five glass office buildings stand in a row towards the open space of Hötorget; built in the 1950s, they're city landmarks – whether people want them to be or not. **Hötorget** is home to the **PUB** department store (*see p153*) and an outdoor market selling fruit, flowers and a bit of everything. The indoor, international food hall, **Hötorgshallen** (*see p175*), bustles beneath the **Filmstaden Sergel** (*see p200*). On another side stands the **Konserthuset** (*see p220*). Stockholm's main concert hall is apparently a prime example of Swedish neo-classical style, but to the untrained eye, the 1926 building looks suspiciously like a bright blue box with ten grey pillars attached to it.

Ivar Tengbom modelled the hall on the temples of ancient Greece, and the artworks inside depict figures and scenes from Greek mythology. Tengbom's son, Anders, renovated the building in 1972 to improve the acoustics. Einar Forseth (who also decorated the Golden Hall at the Stadshuset) created the floor mosaics in the entrance hall and main foyer, and Carl Milles sculpted the bronze statue of Orpheus near the front steps. There are guided tours (50kr) on Saturdays when there is a concert, but it's more fun to attend a performance.

Further north on Drottninggatan, **Centralbadet** (*see p171*) is a lovely, art nouveau bathhouse built in 1905, with café tables in its pretty front courtyard. Nearby, **Dansens Hus** (*see p237*) is the capital's main venue for modern dance and, just to the east, on Sveavägen, stands classical **Adolf Fredriks Kyrka**. It has a Greek cross plan and a beautifully painted ceiling; assassinated prime minister Olof Palme is buried in the cemetery here. On the corner of Drottninggatan and Tengnérgatan is the building in which August Strindberg spent the last four years of his life. His apartment is now the **Strindbergsmuseet** (*see p79*) – a must for fans of Sweden's greatest author. On Drottninggatan near the museum a few of Strindberg's famous quotes have been printed on the street in Swedish.

Down at the southern tip of Norrmalm the **Blasieholmen** peninsula pokes out into the water towards Skeppsholmen. At the end of this spur of land stands the imposing limestone façade of Sweden's largest art museum, the **National Museum** (*see below*). North along the waterfront, on Strömkajen, in front of Sweden's only five-star hotel (**Grand Hôtel**, *see p45*), is the boarding point for sightseeing boats and ferries to the archipelago.

Another wharf for ferries (to Djurgården and Slussen) is on the other side of the peninsula at the small harbour of **Nybroviken**. Overlooking the green lawns of Berzelii Park is **Berns Salonger**, a legendary entertainment venue since the 1860s. It is still a nightlife favourite, and its magnificent salons, gilded and topped with crystal chandeliers, now house one of Stockholm's largest restaurants (*see p115*) and numerous bars (*see p135*). The adjoining boutique hotel (*see p45*) is a fine choice.

Dansmuseet

Gustav Adolfs Torg 22-4 (441 76 50/www.dance museum.com). T-bana Kungsträdgården/bus 2, 3, 43, 59, 62, 65. Open June-Aug 11am-4pm Mon-Fri; noon-4pm Sat, Sun. Sept-May 11am-4pm Tue-Fri;

noon-4pm Sat, Sun. **Admission** 50kr; 30kr concessions; free under-12s. **Free with SC**. **Credit** AmEx, MC, V. **Map** p305 G7.

The Dance Museum in the sombre, pillared main hall of a former bank displays costumes from Swedish and Russian ballets, paintings and sketches related to dance, and traditional masks and costumes from Africa, Thailand, China, Japan and Tibet. Standing near the entrance to the exhibit hall is a bronze bust of the museum's founder, Rolf de Maré, who managed the Swedish Ballet in Paris between 1920 and 1925, and opened the museum in the French capital in 1933, the world's first museum dedicated to dance. When the museum closed in the 1940s, the contents relating to Swedish and non-European dance were relocated to Stockholm. The small collection will appeal primarily to those interested in, for example, the development of the tutu.

Medelhavsmuseet

Fredsgatan 2 (51 95 53 80/www.medelhavs museet.se). T-bana Kungsträdgården/bus 3, 43, 62, 65. Open 11am-8pm Tue, Wed; 11am-4pm Thur, Fri; noon-5pm Sat, Sun. Admission 50kr; free under-20s. Free with SC. Map p305 G7.

Artefacts from Greece, Rome, Egypt and Cyprus are housed in the Museum of Mediterranean Antiquities, in a building that was a field marshal's palace in the 1640s. The marble columns and beautiful glass ceiling were designed to look like a Renaissance palazzo. Displayed in the main hall are Roman busts and statues, as well as 18th-century cork models of Roman buildings. A side room features the largest collection of Cypriot excavation finds outside Cyprus, while another room contains medical instruments from 300AD. One floor below are mummies and a six-ton Egyptian basalt sarcophagus. The Gold Room, a vault holding ancient wreaths of gold, is open between 12.30pm and 1pm or 2.30pm and 3pm. The museum is worth a visit once you've seen the city's major attractions. The second-floor café provides an excellent view of Gustav Adolfs Torg.

National Museum

Södra Blasieholmshamnen (51 95 43 00/www.nat ionalmuseum.se). T-bana Kungsträdgården/bus 2, 55, 59, 62, 65, 76. Open June-Aug 11am-8pm Tue; 11am-5pm Wed-Sun. Sept-May 11am-8pm Tue, Thur; 11am-5pm Wed, Fri-Sun. Admission 75kr (60kr Wed); 60kr concessions; free under-16s. Free with SC. Credit AmEx, MC, V. Map p305 H8.

Paintings, sculptures, drawings and decorative arts, dating from the Middle Ages to the present, are displayed here, in Sweden's largest art museum. The National Museum is not as impressive as some of Europe's big art museums, but there are works by the likes of Rembrandt, Rubens, Goya and Degas, and substantial collections of 17th-century Dutch, 18th-century French and 18th- and 19th-century Swedish art (including *Lady with the Veil* by Alexander Roslin; *pictured on p79*). The building, designed in 1866 to look like a northern Italian

Concrete calamity?

In 1974 legendary Swedish journalist Jan Olof Olsson recounted what has become a well-known anecdote: 'This summer an American tourist apparently asked if it was the Russians or the Germans who destroyed Stockholm. We could proudly inform him that we destroyed it all by ourselves.' The destruction he refers to is particularly evident in lower Norrmalm, where historic buildings were torn down in the 1960s in a sadly misjudged attempt to modernise.

It all started innocently enough. Sweden emerged from World War II with a distinct advantage over its war-torn neighours, and Stockholm's politicians soon found they had ample money to create the modern commercial centre they'd longed for. The first phase of the 'renewal' programme was launched and five tall grey office towers were constructed in a line in lower Norrmalm (Hötorgshusen, 1952-6; *pictured*), replacing buildings dating back to the 1600s.

For the politicians of the time, newer meant better, and once it started moving, the wrecking ball continued to swing. Old buildings were demolished and replaced with spacious glass-and-concrete palaces filled with offices and shops along broad, traffic-friendly streets.

From the 1950s until the early 1970s central Stockholm was overrun by bulldozers, cranes and scaffolding. Craters appeared where lively neighbourhoods once stood. Lower Norrmalm's Klara district was hardest hit – **St Clara Kyrka** (*see p78*),

a 16th-century church, was the only historic structure left standing.

During the 1960s, though, Stockholmers began to question the wisdom of the rampant destruction. And by 1971, they'd had enough. Widespread disillusionment led to a week-long protest against plans to cut down 13 elm trees in Kungsträdgården to make way for an underground station. The sheer size of the protest convinced the tree cutters to back down.

That marked the beginning of the end of the 'renewal' destruction. The last major building to be constructed in lower Norrmalm was Peter Celsing's **Kulturhuset** (*see p75*), in 1974. A year later the city cancelled plans for further modernisation. Old buildings would not only be spared, they would now be protected.

To this day the old Klara district is missed by those who knew and loved it, and the controversy surrounding its destruction has never ended. Although Kulturhuset is a well-loved institution, opinions are more divided over Sergels Torg. To some, the square provides an otherwise village-like city with an urban edge, but for others the square's dark underground corridors represent a colossal failure. Most Stockholmers agree, however, that most of the modernist buildings in lower Norrmalm are bland disappointments.

In the end, the Norrmalm renewal experience left Stockholmers with a deeply suspicious attitude towards all proposals for development. And understandably so.

The magnificent **National Museum** in pole position on the water. *See p76.*

Renaissance palace, is grand and awe-inspiring. The central staircase is adorned with colourful frescoes by Carl Larsson, including two large and wonderful works at the top: *Gustav Vasa's Entry into Stockholm 1523* and *Midwinter Sacrifice*. Due to the enormous size of the collection, temporary exhibitions are arranged throughout the year based around historical and national perspectives. Guided tours are available in English in summer. The permanent exhibition on the first floor, 'Design 19002000', showcases 20th-century Scandinavian design, including porcelain, glassware and chairs made of every material known to man. The **Atrium** café/restaurant (*see p145*) is a lovely spot for lunch.

St Clara Kyrka

Klara Östra Kyrkogata 7 (723 30 31/www.st hdomkyrko.com). T-bana T-Centralen/bus 47, 52, 56, 59. **Open** 10am-5pm Mon-Fri; 10am-7pm Sat. **Admission** free. **Map** p305 G6.

The copper spire of this brick 16th-century church across from Central Station rises from a cluster of dull, box-like 1960s buildings. St Clara Kyrka was one of many churches built in the late 16th century during the reign of Johan III, who had a Catholic wife and a love of architecture. He decided to build here in the 1570s since it was the site of a former convent torn down in the Reformation. Dutch architect Willem Boy designed the church, and Carl Hårleman – who also completed the interior of the Kungliga Slottet (*see p63*) – redesigned its roof and spire after a fire in the

mid 18th century. Inside the sunlit church the ceiling is painted with biblical scenes. The congregation gives out meals to the homeless, so the graveyard and nearby steps are often occupied by homeless people. Classical concerts are held at midday. The church's information centre (723 30 28) offers a free map of all the churches in Stockholm and daily listings for church concerts around the city.

St Jacobs Kyrka

Västra Trädgårdsgatan 2 (723 30 38/ www.sthdom kyrko.com). T-bana Kungsträdgården/bus 2, 43, 55, 59, 65. **Open** 24hrs daily. **Admission** free. **Map** p305 G7.

This red church overlooking Kungsträdgården was commissioned in 1588 by King Johan III. The project was abandoned four years later when Johan died, but was resumed in 1630 and completed in 1643. The church is named after the patron saint of pilgrims, who is depicted in the sandstone sculpture above the southern entrance carrying a walking staff. The church underwent several interior renovations in the 19th century, including the addition of five stained-glass panels behind the altar, depicting scenes from the New Testament. Sunday services are held in English at 6pm courtesy of the International Church of Stockholm. Renovations on its façade are set to be completed by the end of 2004.

Strindbergsmuseet

Drottninggatan 85 (411 53 54/www.strindberg smuseet.se). T-bana Rådmansgatan/bus 52, 69.

Open *June-Aug* noon-4pm Tue-Sun. *Sept-May* noon-7pm Tue; noon-4pm Wed-Sun. **Admission** 40kr; 25kr concessions; free under-14s. **Free with SC**. No credit cards. Map p309 E6.

August Strindberg moved into an apartment in the Blå Tornet (Blue Tower) in 1908; it was his last home and is now a museum. Much of it is taken up with temporary exhibits on Strindberg as a writer, dramatist, photographer and painter, but his tiny apartment is the main reason for visiting. An air of reverence dominates: you have to put white slippers on over your shoes to protect the floor, and his bedroom, study and sitting room (no kitchen – a family upstairs sent down food) are preserved as they were at the time of his death, his pens still neatly lined up in rows on his writing desk. It's an atmospheric and moving place: you can imagine the ailing playwright standing on the balcony to greet a torchlit procession of well-wishers on his last birthday, 22 January 1912. He died a few months later on 14 May. *See also p236* **Anarchy in August**.

Systembolagets Museet

Kungsträdgårdsgatan 14 (789 36 42/tours 50 33 27 44/www.systembolaget.se/TjansterEvenemang/Bolags museet). T-bana Kungsträdgården/bus 46, 55, 59, 62, 76. **Open** (guided tours only) *May-Sept* 2pm Wed (in English). Closed Oct-Apr. **Admission** 20kr. No credit cards. Map p305 G8.

Tucked into the basement of Systembolaget's headquarters (from where the state-owned company conducts its monopoly of alcohol sales), this museum presents the history of... well, of itself, really, and of alcohol sales in Sweden. The guided tour – the only way you can see the museum – walks you through some reconstructed sections of stores, from a 1907 pub with a worn wooden counter to a self-service boutique from 1991. The real story told here is how Systembolaget has tried to discourage alcohol consumption – with ration books, blacklists, anti-alcohol marketing campaigns and high taxes. Partly as a result of cheaper prices in neighbouring countries and EU membership, Swedish consumption of alcohol has increased rapidly in recent years – making this mission all the more complicated. Guided tours in English are given during the summer on Wednesdays at 2pm. For more on how to purchase alcohol in Stockholm, *see p177* **Booze rules**.

Vasastaden

Map p308 & p309

Much of the area of Vasastaden (commonly known as Vasastan), which lies north of Norrmalm, was built toward the end of the 1800s to accommodate Stockholm's rapidly growing population. Aside from its main thoroughfares of Sveavägen, Odengatan and St Eriksgatan, the area has remained primarily residential, although it does have a number of worthwhile sights, several beautiful parks and a sprinkling of restaurants, bars and hotels.

The street blocks can be rather long, so you might want to jump on the T-bana.

In southern Vasastaden lies the small, rectangular park of **Tegnérlunden**. At one end a man-made stream flows out of a gazebo; at the other there's a statue of a beefy, naked August Strindberg sitting on a rock. The **Strindbergsmuseet** (*see above*) is on the corner of Drottninggatan, and further east on Tegnérgatan you'll find an array of pubs, restaurants and antique shops. Turn left on broad, tree-lined **Sveavägen** – designed like a Parisian boulevard – and walk two blocks north.

The south-east corner of the hillside park, **Observatorielunden**, is dominated by the grand **Handelshögskolan** (Stockholm School of Economics), designed by Ivar Tengbom, architect of the Konserthuset. Up the steep steps on top of the hill is the **Observatorie Museet** (*see p80*), overlooking a skateboard park. Standing at the park's north-east corner, Gunnar Asplund's bright orange **Stadsbiblioteket** (Stockholm Public Library), is one of Sweden's best known architectural works, instantly identifiable by its round central building. Several blocks north

A Roslin at the **National Museum**. *See p76.*

on Sveavägen is the kid-friendly, indoor water adventure park, **Vilda Vanadis** (*see p191*), in the quiet, hilly park of Vanadislunden.

If you head west from the library along busy Odengatan, you'll reach the triangle-shaped **Odenplan** square, bordered by the beautiful baroque **Gustaf Vasa Kyrka** (*see below*) and surrounded by the rumble of passing buses. Several budget hotels are located in this area.

Two blocks further west is the green retreat of **Vasaparken**, popular with energetic dogs and those who love its outdoor summer cafés. A section of this park will soon be renamed in honour of **Astrid Lindgren**, the author of the *Pippi Longstocking* children's book series, who died in 2002. She lived across the street. The small **Judiska Museet** (*see below*) – the only Jewish museum in Scandinavia – is nearby, and at the end of the park there's the bustling intersection of St Eriksplan.

The neighbourhood of Birkastan, west of St Eriksplan, was originally built in the early 20th century for the working classes, but the charming cafés and restaurants around **Rörstrandsgatan** are becoming increasingly fashionable. If you take St Eriksgatan south, you'll end up on Kungsholmen; if you head north, you'll arrive at the **Vin & Sprithistoriska Museet** (*see below*).

Gustaf Vasa Kyrka

Odenplan (50 88 86 00/www.gustafvasa.nu). T-bana Odenplan/bus 2, 4, 40, 42, 47, 53. **Open** usually 11am-7pm daily. **Admission** free (concerts & activities cost around 100kr). **Map** p308 D4.

The striking 60m-high (200ft) dome of Gustaf Vasa Kyrka rises far above Odenplan and its decidedly less impressive neighbouring buildings. This white church in the Italian baroque style is, without doubt, Vasastaden's most beautiful building. Completed in 1906, Gustaf Vasa Kyrka stands on a triangular island near the intersection of two busy streets. The spectacular 1731 altarpiece is Sweden's largest baroque sculpture, originally created for the Uppsala cathedral. It depicts Jesus on the cross in front of a relief of Jerusalem. The ceiling frescoes in the dome, by Vicke Andrén, show scenes from the New Testament.

Judiska Museet

Hälsingegatan 2 (31 01 43/www.judiska-museet.a.se). T-bana Odenplan/bus 4, 42, 47, 53, 72. **Open** noon-4pm Mon-Fri, Sun. **Admission** 50kr; 20kr-40kr concessions; free under-12s. *Guided tours* 1.30pm Wed, Sun. **Free with SC. Credit** AmEx. **Map** p308 D4.

Across the street from Vasaparken, this small museum contains religious objects and an exhibit on the Holocaust. A Torah, an 18th-century menorah and a variety of *yarmulkes* (skullcaps) are displayed, as well as a wooden Mizrach plaque from the first synagogue in Stockholm, dating from 1795. The museum's temporary exhibitions can be very good – 2004 saw an excellent exhibition on Raoul Wallenberg.

Leksaksland

Hagagränd 2 (30 34 03/www.leksaksland.se). T-bana Odenplan/bus 4, 42, 46, 52, 72. **Open** 11am-4pm Wed-Sun. **Admission** 50kr; 30kr 2-17 yrs. **No credit cards. Map** p309 C5.

Although this museum has changed its name once again – from the Toy Palace to the Land of Toys – its collection of toys from the past 50 years remains consistently entertaining. The toy-obsessed couple who run the museum have arranged nearly all of the toys in mini-vignettes, ranging from historical events to the 'Jungle Mission', in which dozens of grimacing Action Man dolls engage in hand-to-hand combat. Train sets, Smurf villages, dolls and doll's houses all appear, as well as *Star Wars*, *Harry Potter* and *Lord of the Rings* action figures.

Observatorie Museet

Drottninggatan 120 (54 54 83 90/www.observatoriet.kva.se). T-bana Rådmansgatan/ bus 40, 52, 53, 69. **Open** (guided tours only) *Apr-mid June, mid Aug-Oct* noon, 1pm, 2pm Sun. *Oct-Mar* 6-9pm Tue; noon, 1pm, 2pm Sun. (15 June-15 Aug groups or pre-booked tours only). **Admission** 50kr; 25kr 7-18s; free under-7s. **Free with SC. No credit cards. Map** p309 D6.

The Royal Swedish Academy of Sciences built this hill-top observatory in the late 1740s. Now a museum, it's open for guided tours (pre-book for English) of the observation rooms and the 18th-century instruments of Pehr Wargentin, an astronomer and statistician who lived and worked here for 30 years. The guide describes how scientists tried to solve the problems of their day, from calculating the distances between planets to determining longitude at sea. A narrow staircase leads to the dome, where you get a wonderful, unobstructed view of Stockholm. This is one of the city's lesser-known museums, but is well worth a visit. On Tuesday evenings between October and March, you can stargaze through the museum's early 20th-century telescope.

Vin & Sprithistoriska Museet

Dalagatan 100 (744 70 70/www.vinsprit historiska.se). Bus 2, 3, 40, 65, 70. **Open** *Oct-Dec, March-May* 10am-9pm Tue-Thur; 10am-4pm Fri; noon-4pm Sat, Sun. *Jan-Feb, June-Sept* 10am-5pm Tue; 10am-4pm Wed-Fri; noon-4pm Sat, Sun. Guided tours in English *June-Aug* 2pm Wed. **Admission** 40kr; 30kr concessions; free under-12s. **Free with SC. Credit** MC, V. **Map** p308 B3.

Between the 1920s and 1960s, all the imported wine and alcohol consumed in Sweden was processed through this warehouse, now the Historical Museum of Wines and Spirits. A path takes you past re-created environments from Sweden's history of alcohol production and consumption – a home distillery from the 1830s and a wine merchant's store from the early 1900s. You can press buttons to activate some of the machinery and pump a 'spice organ' to test your sense of smell. The excellent free audio tour in English brings the exhibits to life – it's just a shame that this unique museum isn't nearer the centre. Call ahead to book a schnapps or wine tasting.

Djurgården & Skeppsholmen

Essential museums and green oases.

Djurgården

Map p306 & p307

For many Stockholmers the long, green island of Djurgården (pronounced 'your-gore-den') is the city's closest and best substitute for the natural beauty of Sweden's open landscapes. Although people are constantly suggesting that the open area of Gärdet to the north be developed to solve Stockholm's housing shortage, the oasis of Djurgården is clearly off-limits.

Many of Stockholm's, if not Sweden's, best museums and attractions are here, including the world-class **Vasamuseet** (*see p86*), the open-air **Skansen** (*see p85*) museum and **Gröna Lund** amusement park (*see p83*). All are on the island's western half and draw hundreds of thousands of visitors each year. Walking and cycling paths and quiet roads wind through the leafy trees of the rest of the island, which is part of Ekoparken,

the National City Park. Closed to traffic (except for buses and residents) at the weekend, its acres of undeveloped land are a much-loved green retreat from the rest of the city.

Swedish monarchs have owned the island since it was acquired by King Karl Knutsson in 1452. First developed for agriculture, it later became the private hunting grounds of royalty. King Karl XI established a series of manned gates in the 1680s to protect the park from wolves, bears and poverty-stricken peasants looking for food. The Stockholm Exhibition was held here in 1897; many of its buildings and structures are still standing, including the **Djurgårdsbron**, the bridge connecting the island to Östermalm, decorated with four statues of Norse gods, including Thor, the hammer-wielding god of thunder. A branch of the royal court continues to administer the island and uses all the rents and fees it collects for Djurgården's preservation.

Vasa: the acid test

Stockholm's most prized treasure, the *Vasa* warship, is under siege. While she has never been fired upon, nor discharged a single cannon shot, the ship has been silently at war since her untimely sinking on her maiden voyage in 1628. The brackish, previously polluted water in which the *Vasa* was submerged for over three centuries created an inhospitable environment for micro-organisms, staving off attacks from pestilent shipworms and bacteria that might otherwise have destroyed her. But once the *Vasa* was raised to the surface her wood became exposed to a different kind of assailant: sulphuric acid. The ample deposits of sulphur in her oak beams – ironically a by-product of the pollutants from the same raw sewage that helped preserve her for her salvage in 1961 – are oxidising and causing her to slowly disintegrate.

This chemical stowaway first revealed itself after the unusually humid summer of 2000.

The conversion of sulphur into sulphuric acid speeded up during this period, when the museum's climate control system – essential to her preservation – could not handle the rainy weather. But the accelerated attack turned out to be a blessing in disguise, as it exposed the problem, as well a sneaky saboteur: deposits of iron compound from bolts in the beams that act as a catalyst for the conversion of elemental sulphur into wood-dissolving sulphuric acid.

A mammoth effort is under way to come to the *Vasa*'s defence. The initial response was relatively simple and involved treating the wood twice a year with bicarbonate in an attempt to neutralise the acid. To curb further oxidation, the ideal storage temperature of the *Vasa* would be a chilly 10°C (50°F) – rather impractical for a museum. The museum is determined to keep her on public display and, in order to maintain her at the

---

Crossing to the island from Strandvägen, over Djurgårdsbron – where you can rent bicycles, paddleboats and canoes – you'll see the magnificent **Nordiska Museet** (*see p84*) directly in front of you. This city landmark was designed in the style of a Nordic Renaissance palace and holds historical and cultural objects from all over Scandinavia. The path to the right of the bridge leads to **Junibacken** (*see p189*), a children's fantasy land with a train ride through the stories of Astrid Lindgren's books.

Further on lies the don't-miss **Vasamuseet** (*see p86*), home of the vast warship *Vasa*, which sank just off the island of Beckholmen on her maiden voyage in 1628. The ship remained lost on the seabed for three centuries until she was discovered in the 1950s; research continues into ways to prevent her timber from deteriorating (*see above Vasa: the acid test*). Fittingly, the purpose-built museum – one of the most popular in Scandinavia – occupies the site of the former naval dockyard. If you're only going to visit one museum in Stockholm – and there are plenty – make it this one.

The area near the waterfront, **Galärparken**, popular with picnickers and sunbathers, was used by royalty in the 18th century to stage fights between lions and bears. The lions were kept near what is now the Nordiska Museet, hence the name Lejonslätten ('Lions' Den'). East of the Vasamuseet stands the triangular memorial to the 852 people who died when the Estonia ferry sunk in the Baltic en route from Tallinn to Stockholm in 1994.

Djurgårdsvägen, the main route into and around the island, passes by the vast Nordiska Museet, the western entrance to **Skansen** and the quaint, old-fashioned **Biologiska Museet** (*see p84*), devoted to Scandinavian wildlife. Further south, the beautiful **Liljevalchs Konsthall** (*see p203*) stands on the corner of Djurgården's most developed area. It was set up by an unspecified donation of 500,000 kronor in the will of the enormously rich industrialist Carl Fredrik Liljevalch. After the artist Prince Eugen persuaded the state to donate the land, the gallery opened in 1916, with sculptures by Carl Milles over the door and on top of the tall black pillar nearby. It's now one of the best exhibition spaces in Sweden, with contemporary shows that change every three months. Next to the building is the lovely café **Blå Porten** (*see p147*), named after the 19th-century gate near Djurgårdsbron.

Next door the fascinating **Aquaria Vattenmuseum** (*see p84*) sits on the water next to the depot for the island's old-fashioned trams. Its waterfront café has a spectacular view towards Skeppsholmen. Squeals, laughter and live music can be heard coming from the summer-only **Gröna Lund** amusement park (*see p84*), one block to the south. There are several hamburger and pizza places here, as well as the 1920s Hasselbacken restaurant on the hill across the street, next to the **Cirkus** concert/theatre venue (*see p215*).

East of Gröna Lund, **Djurgårdsstaden** is the island's only real residential area. Most

more comfortable temperature of 18-20°C (64-68°F), the ventilation and climate control systems had to be upgraded in 2005. Other measures include the eventual replacement of all iron bolts and a new cradle to support the ship – expensive but necessary.

As a result of a competition, research teams worldwide are taking up *Vasa*'s cause. Each team is looking for a way to halt the warship's disintegration and to preserve her timber. The plight of the *Vasa* may yet find the cure for all waterlogged wooden archaeological discoveries, and the research is expected to benefit marine archaeology the world over.

In a worst case scenario extreme measures may require her to be dismantled and reassembled. However, the museum is fully committed to keeping her on permanent display at all costs, so expect the *Vasa* warship to continue her struggle in public.

For a review of **Vasamuseet**, *see p86*.

of the houses and cottages along this district's narrow streets were built between the mid 1700s and the early 1800s as housing for shipyard workers. About 200 people live here today and the apartments are much sought after. This residential area is often overlooked by tourists, which makes a walk through its well-preserved, historic streets all the more charming. Whipping posts like the one in the district's tiny square, Skampålens Torg, once stood in public places around the city.

Continuing along Djurgårdsvägen, you soon arrive at the main entrance to **Skansen** (*see p85*). Stockholm's number one attraction with 1.4 million visitors a year, it's a mix of open-air history museum, amusement park and zoo, covering almost the entire width of Djurgården – you shouldn't leave Stockholm without seeing it. It includes the **Skansen Akvariet** (*see p86*), which houses monkeys, crocodiles and bats, but you'll have to pay a separate entrance fee to see it.

The 47 bus route ends at the cove of Ryssviken, from where you can walk south to the palatial mansion of **Prins Eugens Waldemarsudde** (*see p84*), which has amazing views of the water, or walk north for about ten minutes to the café at **Rosendals Trädgård** (*see p147*), a great spot for lunch. Nearby is **Rosendals Slott** (*see p85*), the summer retreat of Karl XIV Johan, the French marshal elected as Sweden's crown prince in 1810 and later crowned king.

To explore further east, be prepared to walk, cycle or drive. To reach the eastern half of Djurgården by bus, you'll need to plan ahead and take line 69 from the northern side of Djurgårdsbron. The bus takes you to the south-eastern tip of the island where a Nordic art collection is displayed at swanky **Thielska Galleriet** (*see p86*) and waterfront cafés at Blockhusudden look out on the **Fjäderholmarna** islands. The southern shore of this area of Djurgården is lined with the homes and estates of the extremely wealthy.

Most of eastern Djurgården is a nature reserve with a marsh, old oak trees and paths for horses, bikes and hikers. The narrow canal, **Djurgårdsbrunnskanalen**, which opened in 1834, is a pleasant place for a stroll, lined with trees and ending with a small footbridge near the sea. Enthusiasts of contemporary art should be sure to check out the upbeat café and exhibits at **Magasin 3 Projekt** (661 54 80, www.magasin3.com, closed Nov-end May), the summer exhibition space of **Magasin 3 Stockholm Konsthall** (*see p206*), just north of the Djurgårdsbrunn bridge.

Transport note: there's no Tunnelbana station on or near Djurgården. Bus 44 runs along Djurgårdsvägen as far as Skansen; bus 47, which passes by Central Station, goes further to Ryssviken, as does the historic tram line 7 (660 77 00, daily June to August, weekends only the rest of the year, departing from Norrmalmstorg). Alternatively, catch the Djurgårdsfärjan ferry, run by Waxholmsbolaget (614 64 50) from Slussen (free with an SL card), which stops at a jetty near Gröna Lund and then on Skeppsholmen. Between May and August an alternative route stops at the Vasamuseet and at Nybroplan on Norrmalm.

Aquaria Vattenmuseum

Falkenbergsgatan 2 (660 49 40/tours 660 90 89/ www.aquaria.se). Bus 44, 47/tram 7/ferry from Slussen or Nybroviken. **Open** *Mid June-mid Aug* 10am-6pm daily. *Mid Aug-mid June* 10am-4.30pm Tue-Sat. **Admission** 65kr; 55kr concessions; 35kr 6-15s; free under-6s. **Free with SC. Credit** AmEx, DC, MC, V. **Map** p306 J11.

A waterfall cascades over the entrance of this unusual aquarium next to the *Vasa*. In the intriguing rainforest exhibit, you can go eyeball to eyeball with 1.5m-long (5ft) catfish, then step into a realistic jungle, with dripping plants, chirping insects and rain showers every ten minutes. Elsewhere, sharks and tropical fish swim in a long aquarium, and a mountain waterfall splashes down into a pool of trout. Environmental concerns are highlighted; a sign next to an open manhole encourages you to climb down for a 'sewer adventure', where you see the effects of pollution and acid rain. Outside, there's an exhibit on the Baltic Sea. The water views from the café make it a good pit stop.

Biologiska Museet

Lejonslätten (442 82 15/tours 442 82 70/www. biologiskamuseet.com). Bus 44, 47/tram 7/ferry from Slussen or Nybroviken. **Open** *Apr-Oct* 11am-4pm daily. **Admission** 30kr; 10kr 6-15s; free under-6s. **Free with SC. Credit** AmEx, DC, MC, V. **Map** p306 H11.

Before or after you see the live animals at Skansen's zoo, see the stuffed versions at this small museum devoted to Scandinavian wildlife. The A-frame building styled after a medieval Norwegian church was designed by Agi Lindegren, the architect of Gustaf Vasa Kyrka (*see p80*). Except for replacing a few of its stuffed animals, the museum has remained unchanged since it opened in 1893. On the ground floor old-fashioned dioramas depict a valley in east Greenland and an Arctic cave. Check out the box containing a *'skvader'* – a fantasy hybrid of a hare and a grouse. The double spiral staircase leads to the first floor, where a fabulous 360° diorama wraps around a wooden viewing platform. In this incredibly lifelike display, animals of the coast and forest are shown behind trees, in the water and on cliffs. Artist Bruno Liljefors (whose depictions of nature hang in the National Museet) painted the detailed backdrop. Another platform on the second floor gives a better view of the birds and their nests.

Gröna Lund

Lilla Allmänna Gränd 9 (58 75 01 00/www.grona lund.com). Bus 44, 47/tram 7/ferry from Slussen or Nybroviken. **Open** *End Apr-mid Sept* 11am/noon/3pm/ 5pm-11pm/midnight (call to confirm). **Admission** 60kr; 30kr concessions; 40kr 4-12s; free under-4s. **Free with SC. Credit** AmEx, DC, MC, V. **Map** p306 J11.

Perched on the edge of Djurgården, with great views across the water, Gröna Lund ('the Green Grove') is Sweden's oldest amusement park. Built in 1883 and owned by the same family ever since, its historic buildings and well-preserved rides retain an old-world charm. You can even travel here by boat the way people did more than 100 years ago. Among the older favourites are carousels, bumper cars, Ferris wheels and a Fun House, while the newer fairground thrills come from two rollercoasters intertwined, and the free-fall 'power tower', Europe's highest at (gulp) 80m (264ft). Four of the tower's twelve seats were modified in 2004 to tilt forward 15-17 degrees, creating a new and even more horrifying ride, the free-fall 'tilt'. You can buy multi-ride booklets or pay for each ride separately. Stick around for an evening pop concert, held about once a week. For more info on children's activities at the park, *see p189.*

Nordiska Museet

Djurgårdsvägen 6-16 (51 95 60 00/24-hr recorded info 457 06 60/www.nordiskamuseet.se). Bus 44, 47/tram 7/ferry from Slussen or Nybroplan. **Open** *July, Aug* 10am-5pm daily. *Sept-June* 10am-5pm Tue-Sun. **Admission** 60kr; free under-18s. **Free with SC. Credit** AmEx, MC. **Map** p306 G11.

The Nordiska Museet, Sweden's national museum of cultural history, was the brainchild of Artur Hazelius, who also created Skansen. Everything about the place is big: the building itself, designed by Isak Clason and completed in 1907, is massive, though only a quarter of the originally intended size. On entering the aptly named Great Hall visitors are greeted by Carl Milles' colossal pink statue of a seated Gustav Vasa. (In his forehead is a chunk of oak from a tree planted by the king himself, so legend has it.) The museum's collection of artefacts is immense. Permanent exhibitions include the fashion and folk costumes, recreated table settings from the 16th to the 20th centuries, the Sami people, and Swedish traditions, manners and customs. There are also marvellously detailed doll's houses and a collection of doom-laden paintings and photos by Strindberg that do nothing to dispel his madman image. The Textile Gallery features 500 textiles, hidden from sunlight in birch cabinets, dating from the 1600s onwards. The museum is quite old-fashioned in presentation, but no less fascinating for that. Lekstugan, the play area aimed at kids aged 4 to 12, is always popular.

Prins Eugens Waldemarsudde

Prins Eugens Väg 6 (54 58 37 00/www.waldemar sudde.com). Bus 47/tram 7/ferry from Slussen or Norrmalmstorg. **Open** 11am-5pm Tue, Wed, Fri, Sat; 11am-8pm Thur. **Admission** 75kr; 55kr concessions; free under-18s. **Credit** AmEx, DC, MC, V. **Map** p307 K13.

This beautiful waterfront property, comprising a grand three-storey mansion and an art gallery, was owned by Prince Eugen from 1899 until his death in 1947. The prince, a well-known Swedish landscape painter and the brother of King Gustav V, moved into the mansion upon its completion in 1904. The house's architect, Ferdinand Boberg, later designed the NK department store (*see p152*). The light, simply decorated rooms on the ground floor are furnished as the prince left them. Temporary art exhibitions, featuring the likes of Anders Zorn, Ernst Josephson, Isaac Grünewald and Carl Larsson, as well as the prince's wonderful landscape paintings, are displayed upstairs and in the gallery next door. The gallery was built in 1913 when Prince Eugen ran out of display space for his art collection. The prince himself designed the classical white flowerpots for sale in the gift shop. The mansion and artwork are impressive, but the grounds and views are even more so. Sculptures by Auguste Rodin and Carl Milles adorn the park, which is a great spot to relax, and a path leads on to an 18th-century windmill. You can fill up on fresh waffles at the nearby Ektorpet cottage.

Rosendals Slott

Rosendalsvägen (402 61 30/www.royalcourt.se). Bus 44, 47, 69. **Open** (by guided tour only) *June-Aug.* noon, 1pm, 2pm, 3pm Tue-Sun. **Admission** 50kr; 25kr concessions; free under-7s. **Free with SC. No credit cards. Map** p307 H14.

King Karl XIV Johan's summer retreat, this light yellow building with grey pillars is designed in the Empire style, its wall paintings and decorative scheme reflecting the king's military background. The cotton fabric around the dining room is pleated to resemble an officer's tent, and the frieze in the Red Salon shows the Norse god Odin's victory over the frost giants. The fable of Eros and Psyche is told on the beautifully painted domed ceiling in the Lantern Room. The palace was designed by Fredrik Blom, who also created the Historiska Museet (*see p98*) and Skeppsholm church; it was prefabricated in Norrmalm then shipped out to Djurgården in pieces. Karl Johan always remained a Frenchman at heart: he never ate Swedish food and sometimes forced his less fragrant guests to wash their hands in cologne. The 45-minute tour offered in summer is the only way to see the inside of the palace.

Skansen

Djurgårdsslätten 49-51 (442 80 00/www.skansen.se). Bus 44, 47/tram 7/ferry from Slussen or Nybroviken. **Open** *Oct-Apr* 10am-4pm daily. *May* 10am-8pm daily. *June-Aug* 10am-10pm daily. *Sept* 10am-5pm daily. **Admission** 30kr-80kr; 20kr-30kr 6-15s. **Free with SC. Credit** AmEx, DC, MC, V. **Map** p307 H-J12.

Founded in 1891 by Artur Hazelius, also responsible for the Nordiska Museet (*see p84*), Skansen is a one-stop cultural tour of Sweden. The 150-plus traditional buildings – homes, shops, churches, barns and workshops – are organised as a miniature Sweden, with buildings from the north of the country at the north, those from the middle in the middle, and so on. Most of the structures, situated along paths lined with elm, oak and maple trees, date from the 18th and 19th centuries. The striking 14th-century Norwegian storage hut that overlooks Djurgårdsbrunnsviken is the oldest; newest are the small garden cottages from the 1920s. Most complete is the 1850s quarter, with

Skansen: an open-air tour of Sweden.

cobblestone streets and artisans' workshops, including a baker, glass-blower and potter. Watch them work, then buy the proceeds. Nearly all of the buildings are original and were moved here whole or piece by piece from all over Sweden. Skansen's staff – dressed in folk costumes – spin wool, tend fires and perform other traditional tasks inside some of the buildings (Oct-Apr 11am-3pm; May-Sept 11am-5pm). A new building is being constructed in the town quarter, a replica of an ironmonger's shop from the coastal town of Hudiksvall to the north, and is due to open in spring 2005.

Animals from all over Scandinavia, including brown bears, moose and wolves, are kept along the northern cliff in natural habitats (with the exception of the reindeer's wooden shed and sawdust floor – part of the Sami exhibit, which is slated for remodelling). There's also a petting zoo with goats, hedgehogs and kittens, and an aquarium/zoo, Skansen Akvariet (*see below*), near the southern entrance. An old-fashioned marketplace sits at the centre of the park, and folk-dancing demonstrations – with lots of foot-stamping and fiddle-playing – take place in summer on the Tingsvallen stage.

Hunger pangs can be satisfied at a variety of eating places; the cafeteria-style Restaurang Solliden serves classic Swedish dishes and has a wonderful view of Djurgården and southern Stockholm. The 19th-century Gubbhyllan building to the left of the main entrance houses a Tobacco and Match Museum – it was a Swede who invented the safety match – and an old-fashioned café that serves simple dishes. Skansen is a popular destination on Sweden's national holidays since most of them, including Midsummer and Lucia, are celebrated here in traditional style – for more information, *see pp182-7*. The Christmas market is a big draw too. Don't miss the shop (*see p178*) by the main gate, which is packed with traditional arts and crafts. In the summer on Tuesdays, be sure to stick around for 'Allsång på Skansen', a singalong concert on the Solliden stage that is broadcast nationally at 8pm.

Skansen Akvariet

Djurgårdsslätten 49-51 (660 10 82/www.skansen-akvariet.se). Bus 44, 47/tram 7/ferry from Slussen or Nybroviken. **Open** *Jan-Apr, Sept-Dec* 10am-4pm Mon-Fri; 10am-5pm Sat, Sun. *May* 10am-5pm Mon-Fri; 10am-6pm Sat, Sun. *June* 10am-6pm Mon-Fri; 10am-7pm Sat, Sun. *July* 10am-8pm daily. *1-14 Aug* 10am-7pm daily. *15-31 Aug* 10am-6pm Mon-Fri; 10am-7pm Sat, Sun. **Admission** (plus admission to Skansen; *see above*) 65kr; 35kr 6-15s. **Free with SC**. **Credit** AmEx, DC, MC, V. **Map** p307 J12.
Some of the smallest monkeys you've ever seen are on show in this zoo and aquarium inside Skansen. Bright orange tamarins and pygmy marmosets hang from trees behind glass, and you can walk up the steps of a giant tree house where more than three dozen striped lemurs hop around while chewing on fresh vegetables. The less friendly-looking baboons crawl around a steep hill in another exhibit, complete with a crashed jungle jeep hanging from a branch. You can even pet a boa constrictor and a tarantula.

Prins Eugens Waldemarsudde. *See p84.*

There's lots to see – snakes, a nocturnal room full of bats, and two crocodiles (though they may be sold to a US zoo with more space, due to new laws on animal welfare). If you don't want to pay the separate entrance fee, you can glimpse the baboons and lemurs from outside.

Thielska Galleriet

Sjötullsbacken 6 (662 58 84/www.thielska-galleriet.se). Bus 69. **Open** noon-4pm Mon-Sat; 1-4pm Sun. **Admission** 50kr; 30kr concessions. **No credit cards**.
Wealthy banker and art collector Ernest Thiel built this palatial waterside home on the eastern tip of Djurgården in the early 1900s. The eclectically styled building, with influences from the Italian Renaissance and the Orient, was designed by Ferdinand Boberg, who built Prins Eugens Waldemarsudde (*see p84*) at roughly the same time. Thiel lost most of his fortune after World War I, and the state acquired the property in 1924. Two years later this museum opened, displaying his collection of turn-of-the-20th-century Nordic art, including works by Carl Larsson, Bruno Liljefors and Edvard Munch (a close friend of Thiel). Although works by many of these artists – valued at 24 million kroner – were stolen in the middle of the night on 20 June 2000, a crime that remains unsolved, there are still plenty of paintings to see. Thiel's bathroom has been turned into a small, basic café and the urn containing his ashes lies beneath a statue by Auguste Rodin in the park. If you haven't seen enough Scandinavian art at the National Museet, perhaps this gallery will satisfy you.

Vasamuseet

Galärvarvsvägen 14 (51 95 48 00/Museifartygen 51 95 48 91/www.vasamuseet.se). Bus 44, 47. **Open** *Late Aug-early June* 10am-5pm Mon, Tue, Thur-Sun; 10am-8pm Wed. *Early June-late Aug* 9.30am-7pm daily. **Admission** 70kr; 40kr concessions; 10kr 7-15s; free under-7s. **Free with SC**. **Credit** AmEx, DC, MC, V. **Map** p306 H10.

Nordiska Museet: a vast building for a vast collection of cultural artefacts. *See p84.*

Entering the Vasa Museum for the first time is a jaw-dropping experience, as your eyes adjust to the gloom and you realise the monstrous size of the *Vasa* – the largest and best-preserved ship of its kind in the world. Built in the 1620s when Sweden was at war with Poland, the *Vasa* had two gun decks and 64 cannons, making it the mightiest ship in the fleet. Unfortunately, the gun decks and heavy cannon made the ship top-heavy. During a stability test, in which 30 men ran back and forth across the deck, she nearly toppled over. Still, the king needed his ship and the maiden voyage went ahead. But only a few minutes after the *Vasa* set sail from near present-day Slussen on 10 August 1628, she began to list to one side. The gun ports filled with water and the ship sank after a voyage of only 1,300m (1,400yds). Of the 150 people on board as many as 50 died – the number would have been much higher if the ship had reached Älvsnabben in the archipelago, where 300 soldiers were waiting to board, before it went down. The reason the *Vasa* was so well preserved for her recovery in 1961 – 95% of the ship is original – is because the Baltic Sea is insufficiently saline to contain the tiny shipworm, which destroys wood in saltier seas.

Head first for the theatre to watch a short film about the *Vasa* and her discovery by amateur naval historian Anders Franzén, who spent five years searching for her with a home-made sampler device. On your own or with a tour (there are several daily in English) you can walk around the exterior of the 69m-long (225ft) warship and view the upper deck and keel from six different levels. The ornate stern is covered with sculptures intended to express the glory of the Swedish king and frighten enemies. No one's allowed on board, but you can walk through a re-creation of one of the gun decks. Although the ship is obviously the main attraction, the museum has expanded over the years to include exhibits on 17th-century life and shipbuilding. A new perma-

nent exhibit, opened in 2004, has life-size models of crew members constructed on the basis of skeletons found in the sunken ship. Down by the keel, computers enable you to experiment with the design of ships and test their seaworthiness.

The museum's restaurant has a dockside view of Skeppsholmen, and its gift shop is stocked with everything the *Vasa* enthusiast might need.

Museifartygen

Open *June, mid Aug-end Aug* noon-5pm daily. *July-mid Aug* noon-7pm daily.

The entrance fee to the Vasamuseet also lets you on to two ships docked nearby: the lightship *Finngrundet* (1903), which was anchored in the ice-free part of Sweden's Gulf of Bothnia before lightships were replaced by lighthouses; and the *St Erik* (1915), which was Sweden's first ice-breaker, used to keep the archipelago channels clear. The torpedo boat *T121 Spica* (611 31 60, www.t121spica.se/uk), built in 1966, is also docked here in summer, and guided tours (by donation) are given by former crew members.

Skeppsholmen

Map p306

Once an important naval base and shipyard, the small island of Skeppsholmen is now primarily known for its museums and cultural institutions, many housed in ex-naval buildings. It's also a pleasant place for an amble, either along the tree-lined western shore with views of Gamla Stan, or along the wooden boardwalk of the eastern shore, where private and historic boats are docked.

Crossing the narrow bridge from Blasieholmen, you'll see the **Östasiatiska Museet** (*see p89*) on the hill to your left, housed in a long yellow building designed by Kungliga Slottet architect Nicodemus Tessin

Smells like modern art

The 1998 grand reopening of Stockholm's Moderna Museet featured an exhibition entitled 'Wounds: between Democracy and Redemption in Contemporary Art' in which, among other things, horse carcasses were hung on the wall with hooks. The stench of blood, circling flies and public outcry that arose as a result seems now to have foreshadowed the museum's dark days to come. Given the government's 450-million-kronor expenditure on the construction of the museum, designed by renowned Spanish architect Rafael Moneo, the public had perhaps expected more than maze-like exhibition halls decorated with horse meat, and stuffed golden retrievers in the foyer.

In 1996 a British director, David Elliot, had been hired to elevate the Moderna Museet to the internationally acclaimed status it held in previous decades. Now the flies may as well have been circling around him. Amid controversy surrounding his private sponsorship scheme with Sony (several board members resigned over the imbroglio), and the museum's budget deficit, Elliot resigned in April 2001.

Meanwhile, the museum was found to be rotting from the inside out. Mould-sniffing dogs were called in to confirm what curators had suspected: construction problems had allowed dampness to creep in. The Moderna Museet and Arkitekturmuseet were forced to close in January 2002 for two years, as they were once again renovated.

Yet, in what could have been the bleakest period of the museum's history, a saviour emerged. Swede Lars Nittve, fresh from his victories as director of the tremendously successful Tate Modern in London, was appointed the new director of the Moderna Museet in November 2001. Under the name Moderna Museet c/o, the museum spread out its collection of modern art in spaces across the city and throughout Sweden. The travelling art exhibits were so successful that Sweden's Ministry of Culture designated the Moderna Museet as museum of the year for 2003 – quite an achievement for a museum in exile.

February 2004 saw the (second) reopening of both the Moderna Museet and Arkitekturmuseet – at 164 million kronor over budget and with free admission. Prime Minister Göran Persson, who officiated at the reopening ceremony, said, 'We will not like everything we see here. But I like the thought that I do not like everything I see, it's a good starting point.' True, we may not all appreciate the finer points of a short black-and-white film about a glass of milk exploding, but who can argue against the new espresso bar near the main entrance and sunshine streaming in through the newly enhanced skylights? And this time around, there's not even a whiff of dead animal in the air. The only poor creature to be seen here is Rauschenberg's *Monogram*, a car tyre wrapped around a stuffed goat – all mercifully sealed behind glass.

For a review of **Moderna Museet**, *see p89.*

the Younger in 1700. The round, white, empire-style **Skeppsholmskyrkan** – officially known as Karl Johans Kyrka – stands nearby; designed for the navy by Fredrik Blom, it was completed in 1842 but has now been deconsecrated. To your right is the three-masted schooner **Af Chapman** (*see p48*), now a youth hostel.

Behind the church stands the much talked about **Moderna Museet** (*see below*), occupying an earth-toned building designed by Spanish architect Rafael Moneo and completed in 1998; the adjoining **Arkitekturmuseet** (*see below*) is housed in a former naval drill hall. Both museums were closed in 2002 due to problems with damp and were reopened at the beginning of 2004, following renovations costing in the region of 334 million kroner.

A new exhibition space for photography, **Fotografins Hus** (*see p205*), has opened on the north-east corner of Skeppsholmen in a long, white hall where the navy previously manufactured mines and torpedoes. The annual **Stockholm Jazz Festival** (*see p185*) is held further south on the eastern shore, near *Stockholmsbriggen* (Östra Brobänken, 54 50 24 10, www.stockholmsbriggen.se, open noon-5pm Sun, 20kr), a two-masted wooden ship currently being built according to a mid 19th-century design. On the corner of Skeppsholmen are the **Kungliga Konsthögskolan** (Royal University College of Fine Arts), housed in beautifully restored 18th-century naval barracks, and the headquarters of the Swedish Society of Crafts and Design, **Svensk Form**.

South of Skeppsholmen, and connected to it by a bridge, the tiny granite island of **Kastellholmen** is named after a castle built here in the 1660s. The castle blew up in 1845 after an accident in a cartridge-manufacturing laboratory. A year later, Fredrik Blom designed a new, medieval-style castle with two red towers, one tall and one squat (not open to the public); the castle's cannons are fired on Sweden's national day on 6 June, as well as on the birthdays of the king, queen and crown princess.

Arkitekturmuseet

Exercisplan, Skeppsholmen (58 72 70 00/ www.arkitekturmuseet.se). Bus 65. **Open** 10am-8pm Tue, Wed; 10am-6pm Thur-Sun. **Admission** free. **Credit** AmEx, DC, MC, V. **Map** p306 H9.

The newly renovated Museum of Architecture, in a long hall connected to Moderna Museet (*see below*), could just as easily be the Museum of Swedish Cleanliness: there's not a scuff on its light wood floors, not a mark on its white walls. Displayed on rectangular tables are models of some of Sweden's most famous buildings and architectural projects, including Stockholm's Stadshuset (City Hall), the Royal Palace and the five office buildings at Hötorget. Other models depict Swedish dwellings from 1,000 years

ago to the present, and famous buildings outside Sweden. There's a glassed-in craft and play room for children at one end of the hall, and at the other a spacious room for temporary exhibitions on subjects such as urban planning and national styles. Definitely worth a look for the finely detailed models and the free audio guides, but only architecture enthusiasts will want to spend hours here.

Moderna Museet

Skeppsholmen (51 95 52 00/www.modernamuseet.se). Bus 65/ferry from Slussen. **Open** *Museum* 10am-8pm Tue, Wed; 10am-6pm Thur-Sun. *Photograph library* noon-4pm Tue-Fri. **Admission** free. **Credit** AmEx, MC, V. **Map** p306 H9.

When it opened in 1958, Moderna Museet soon gained a reputation as one of the world's most groundbreaking contemporary art venues. Housed originally in an old, disused naval exercise building, the museum's heyday came in the 1960s and '70s when it introduced Andy Warhol, Jean Tinguely, Robert Rauschenberg, Niki de Saint Phalle and many more to an astonished Swedish audience. The construction of Moneo's new museum building was completed in 1998, but it closed four years later due to structural problems, including widespread mould infestation (*see p88* **Smells like modern art**). The museum reopened in 2004 with a brighter interior, a more open floor plan, an espresso bar and – most importantly – no mould. Its collection of 20th-century art, featuring works by greats such as Picasso, Dali, Pollock and de Chirico, is arranged in reverse chronological order into three areas on the main floor. The terrace of the museum's self-service restaurant offers beautiful views towards Östermalm. There are also two new programmes: 'The 1st at Moderna', which provides a new exhibition on the first of every month, and 'Moderna by Night' (6pm-midnight Fridays), an after-hours event that combines entertainment, food and drink. Although admission to the museum is free, temporary exhibitions charge for admission.

Östasiatiska Museet

Tyghusplan, Skeppsholmen (51 95 57 50/www.mfea.se). Bus 65. **Open** 11am-8pm Tue; 11am-5pm Wed-Sun. **Admission** free. **Credit** AmEx, MC, V. **Map** p306 H9.

After a two-year closure due to renovations, the Museum of Far Eastern Antiquities reopened in September 2004 with free admission. A new permanent exhibition presents prehistoric artefacts unearthed in the 1920s in a Chinese village by the museum's founder, Johan Gunnar Andersson. The exhibits, displayed in a dimly lit room echoing with sounds and voices, include tools and pottery 3,000 to 4,000 years old, descriptions of burial traditions, and the symbols, as well as patterns, of prehistoric earthenware. There are plans to extend the museum into the southern half of the building in 2005, where the museum's fine collection of stoneware and porcelain from the Tang, Song, Ming and Qing dynasties will be displayed. The redesigned gift shop sells Japanese tea sets, books on Asian art, religions and design, calligraphy materials and a variety of Buddha figurines.

Sightseeing

Södermalm & Långholmen

Stockholm's boho heartland and a neighbouring ex-prison island retreat.

Södermalm

Map p313, p314 & p315

Södermalm, fondly known as Söder, is Stockholm's most vibrant and bohemian district. While it's better known for its bars, clubs and restaurants than its museums, in terms of sightseeing no place in Stockholm holds a candle to the impressive views from Söder's northern heights. Once exclusively working-class, the grunge movement of Söder now attracts students and executives alike, and while things are generally more affordable on Söder, the popularity of the area is beginning to bite into the bargain-hunter's opportunities. The district's main focal points are Slussen and Medborgarplatsen, connected by busy Götgatan which runs up the middle of the island.

The first place you'll arrive at from Gamla Stan is the transport interchange of **Slussen** – a busy Tunnelbana and bus station surrounded by a complex clover intersection. Pleasure boats manoeuvre inside the lock (*slussen*) that connects Lake Mälaren to the Baltic Sea. While Slussen is not the most attractive introduction to Söder's charms, it does contain two of the island's main sights: the **Stockholms Stadsmuseum** (*see p92*), where you can learn about the city's history since it was founded in 1252, and **Katarinahissen** (*see p92*), the lift which elevates you to one of the best views in the capital. You can make a meal (or drink) of the view at **Eriks Gondolen** restaurant (*see 127*).

Splendid panoramic views across the water to the city centre are also available from the cliffs along the island's northern edge, particularly on **Monteliusvägen** and **Fjällgatan**. The former rises above Söder Mälarstrand, along which a string of pleasure and commercial boats are moored, including some boat hotels (*see p48* **Beds on boats**); the latter, to the east of Slussen, is a parade of 18th-century houses.

Head south from Slussen along Götgatan, past some fashionable boutiques and classic Söder mainstays – including late-night beer hall **Kvarnen** (*see p139*) – to **Medborgarplatsen**, where there's a small galleria, an indoor farmers' market and two cinema complexes. This large

square has recently undergone a renaissance, adding expansive outdoor seating to stylish restaurants facing Medborgarhuset. Built in 1939, the building houses a library, swimming pool, gym and cultural centre **Mondo** (*see p216*). A memorial to assassinated Swedish Foreign Minister **Anna Lindh**, who gave her last speech on the steps of Medborgarhuset, was inaugurated near the steps on 10 September 2004, the first anniversary of her death. Across the street, the minaret of the city's mosque (**Stockholmsmoskén**; *see p93*), which opened in 2000, rises over the **Björns Trädgard** park, which was being revamped as this book went to press.

Further south lies the quirkily trendy shopping area newly dubbed as **SoFo**, standing for the grid of streets south of Folkungatan, which have a high concentration of independent artists and designers (*see p94* **SoFo**).

Although the residents of Södermalm are today as well off as other Stockholmers, the district is traditionally associated with the working class. Functionalist apartment buildings have replaced nearly all the small wooden houses that once covered the island. However, if you walk west up Bastugatan from Slussen, you pass a charming neighbourhood on adjoining **Lilla Skinnarviksgränd**, with its few remaining 17th- and 18th-century wooden houses. Continue along to the cliffside boardwalk of **Monteliusvägen** for a spectacular view of the bay of Riddarfjärden and **Skinnarviksberget**, Stockholm's highest point at 53 metres (174 feet).

South of here, crossing the busy thoroughfare of Hornsgatan, is **Mariatorget**, a pleasant square that is home to the newly stylish **Rival** complex, which comprises hotel (*see p55*), restaurant (*see p125*), café and cinema (*see p199*), with original art deco features. A block east of Mariatorget is **Maria Magdalena Kyrka** (*see p92*), the oldest church on Söder.

Heading east from Götgatan, walk up Urvädersgränd past the rarely open **Bellmanhuset** (*see p91*), former home of 18th-century balladeer Carl Michael Bellman, to **Mosebacketorg**. This busy cobblestone square

Busy **Medborgarplatsen**. *See p90.*

has been Söder's entertainment centre since the mid 19th century, and is bordered by two of Stockholm's most popular and lively nightlife venues, **Södra Teatern** (*see p216*) and the adjoining **Mosebacke Etablissement** (*see p216*). Together they'll cover all your nightlife needs, from clubbing to drinking, cutting-edge performance to live music; in summer Mosebacke's outdoor terrace provides a fantastic view of Stockholm's harbour. Further south is the landmark **Katarina Kyrka** (*see p92*), masterfully restored in the 1990s to its original baroque splendour, as well as a preserved early 18th-century neighbourhood on **Mäster Mikaels Gata**, which was named after the city's first paid executioner. **Mäster Mikaels Gata** and **Fjällgatan** were connected before the hill was blasted away at the turn of the 20th century to create main road **Renstiernas Gata**.

Södermalm is an expansive district and taking the T-bana or the bus is recommended for those on a time budget. Devotees of old-fashioned forms of transport should visit **Spårvägsmuseet** (*see p92*) in the eastern reaches of the island, near nothing but residential apartments. For those more inclined to seeing the district on foot, Södermalm has some excellent walking paths.

The wide street of Ringvägen curves around the southern border of Södermalm, passing through a shopping centre at Götgatan. The island's biggest and best park, **Tantolunden**, sits near the south-western shore, while the large red-brick church of **Högalidskyrkan**, designed by Ivar Tengbom in the National Romantic style and completed in 1923, stands on a hill to the north. Its octagonal twin towers are a striking landmark visible from many parts of the city.

Towards the western end of Hornsgatan is the residential neighbourhood of **Hornstull**; though widely considered to be up-and-coming, this area holds little sightseeing interest. There is, however, a new indoor and outdoor arty market, **Street** (*see p176*), which has revived the badlands of Hornstulls Strand, selling second-hand clothes, handicrafts and art. Also on Hornstulls Strand is the small local **Kvartersbion** cinema (*see p199*). Residents of Hornstull are proud of their arty, left-leaning neighbourhood; some even sport T-shirts reading 'People's Republic of Hornstull'.

South of Södermalm is another of the city's best-known landmarks, the huge white sphere of sports arena **Globen** (*see p230*).

Bellmanhuset

Urvädersgränd 3 (640 22 29/www.bellmanhuset.se). *T-bana Slussen/bus 2, 3, 53, 59, 76.* **Open** (guided tours only) *Dec-Oct* 1pm 1st Sun of the mth. *Nov* 1pm 2nd Sun of mth. **Admission** 60kr. **No credit cards. Map** p314 K8.

This small house just off Götgatan is the only remaining home of legendary Swedish songwriter Carl Michael Bellman. During his tenancy, between 1770 and 1774, he wrote much of his *Fredmans Epistlar*, a book of 82 songs about Stockholm's drunks and prostitutes that parodies the letters of the apostle Paul in the New Testament. If the monthly tour (in Swedish) fits your sightseeing schedule and you are a Bellman enthusiast, it can be quite entertaining. You will hear about Bellman's life and the history of the building, as well as a troubadour or choir performing his songs.

KA Almgren Sideväveri Museum

Repslagargatan 15 (642 56 16/www.kasiden.se). *T-bana Slussen/bus 2, 3, 43, 53, 55, 59, 76.* **Open** *Jan-Midsummer* 9am-5pm Mon-Thur; 10am-4pm Fri; 11am-3pm Sat. *Midsummer-Dec* 2-5pm Mon-Thur; 9am-5pm Fri; 10am-2pm Sat. **Admission** 55kr-65kr. **Free with SC. No credit cards. Map** p314 L7.

Knut August Almgren stole the technology for this former silk-weaving factory in the late 1820s. While recovering from tuberculosis in France, he posed as a German-speaking Frenchman and gained access to factories where the innovative Jacquard looms with their punch-card system were being used. He took notes, smuggled machinery out of the country and opened a factory in Sweden in 1833. The factory here closed in 1974, but was reopened as a working

Sightseeing

museum in 1991 by a fifth-generation Almgren. It reproduces silk fabrics for stately homes around Scandinavia, including the Chinese Pavilion at Drottningholms Slott. As we went to press this fun, ramshackle factory museum was closed for renovation, expansion and improvements to accessibility; it is expected to reopen for group tours only in summer 2005, then to open fully in September 2005. An additional floor will house an exhibition on the history of silk weaving in Sweden, along with a collection of silk portraits, landscapes and fabrics. You can watch its 160-year-old looms in action on the lower floor producing 2m (6.5ft) of fabric per day. Silk scarves and other handwoven fabrics are on sale in the gift shop.

Katarina Kyrka

Högbergsgatan 15 (743 68 00/www.svkyrkan katarina.com). T-bana Medborgarplatsen or Slussen/ bus 2, 3, 43, 53, 55, 59, 76. **Open** 11am-5pm Mon-Fri; 10am-5pm Sat, Sun. **Admission** free. **Map** p315 L8.
As Södermalm's population grew, it was agreed in the mid 17th century to split Maria Magdalena parish and build a new church. Katarina Kyrka, completed in 1695, was designed by Jean de la Vallé in baroque style with a central plan. A huge fire in 1723 destroyed the church's cupola and half the buildings in the parish. A more recent fire in 1990 burned down all but the church's walls and side vaults. Architect Ove Hildemark reconstructed the church (based on photos and drawings) using 17th-century building techniques. The yellow church with flat white pillars now looks much as it did before, but with a distinctly modern interior. Many victims of the Stockholm Bloodbath of 1520 were buried in the church's large cemetery. Organ music is played at noon on Tuesdays and Thursdays.

Katarinahissen

Stadsgården 6 (642 47 86). T-bana Slussen/ bus 2, 3, 43, 53, 55, 59, 76. **Open** 7.30am-10pm Mon-Sat; 10am-10pm Sun. **Price** 5kr; free under-7s. **Free with SC. No credit cards. Map** p314 K8.
The 38m-tall (125ft) black steel Katarina Lift stands beside the busy intersection at Slussen. Its observation platform and walkway gives pedestrians access to the Katarinaberget district and Mosebacketorg, a favourite Söder square, and it also serves as an entrance to Eriks Gondolen restaurant (*see p127*), housed beneath the walkway. But the main function of the lift is to provide tourists with a stunning view of the bay of Riddarfjärden, Gamla Stan and Djurgården (particularly good at sunset). The original 1883 steam lift was demolished in 1933 and rebuilt two years later – this time running on electricity. If you're thrifty (and fit), you can also reach the platform by climbing the wooden hillside staircase or by walking up Götgatan and turning left on to Urvädersgränd.

Maria Magdalena Kyrka

St Paulsgatan 10 (462 29 40/www.maria magdalena.se). T-bana Slussen/bus 2, 3, 43, 53, 55, 59, 76. **Open** 11am-5pm Mon, Tue, Thur-Sun; 11am-8pm Wed. **Admission** free. **Map** p314 K7.

During his church-destroying spree after the Reformation in 1527, Gustav Vasa tore down the chapel that had stood on this site since the 1300s. His son, Johan III, methodically rebuilt most of the churches in the late 1500s. Construction on this yellowish-orange church with white corners began in 1580, but was not completed for about 40 years. It's Söder's oldest church, though dwarfed by Söder's three most prominent churches – Katarina, Vitaberg and Högalid – and the first in Stockholm to be built with a central plan rather than a cross plan. Tessin the Elder designed the transept in the late 17th century and his son, the Younger, created the French-inspired stonework of the entrance portal in 1716, giving the exterior an overall baroque appearance. The church's rococo interior – with its depiction of Maria Magdalena on the golden pulpit and Carl Fredrik Adelcrantz's elaborate organ screen – was created after a fire in 1759. Several of the cemetery's graves were moved when Hornsgatan was built in 1900. Burial residents include several of Sweden's eminent poets, including beloved troubadour Evert Taube. Stop by for the organ music on Thursdays at 12.15pm.

Spårvägsmuseet

Tegelviksgatan 22 (462 55 31/www.sparvagsmuseet. sl.se). Bus 2, 3, 53, 55, 66. **Open** 10am-5pm Mon-Fri; 11am-4pm Sat, Sun. **Admission** 30kr; 15kr concessions and 7-15s; free under-7s. **Free with SC. Credit** AmEx, MC, V. **Map** p315 M11.
What the Transport Museum lacks in descriptive texts and focused exhibits, it makes up for in quantity – more than 60 vehicles are stored in this former bus station in eastern Söder. Rows of carriages, trams and buses from the late 1800s to the present cover the development of Stockholm's public transport system. For 1kr you can stand in a tramcar from the 1960s and pretend to drive as a grainy film of city streets flashes in front of you. Children can try on a ticket collector's uniform and, in summer, ride a miniature Tunnelbana train (7kr). There's also a café and a shop selling transport-related paraphernalia, including an excellent selection of Brio trains. The museum's nostalgic, forlorn feel makes it perfect for a rainy day visit. Borrow a guidebook in English from the cashier since most of the exhibits are labelled in Swedish.

Stockholms Stadsmuseum

Ryssgården (50 83 16 20/www.stadsmuseum. stockholm.se). T-bana Slussen/bus 2, 3, 43, 53, 55, 59, 76. **Open** 11am-5pm Tue, Wed, Fri-Sun; 11am-7pm Thur. **Admission** 60kr; 50kr concessions; free under-18s. **Free with SC. Credit** AmEx, DC, MC, V. **Map** p314 K8.
Nicodemus Tessin the Elder, who also made additions to Tyska Kyrkan and Riddarholmskyrkan, designed this building in the 1670s. After a fire in 1680, the renovations were supervised by his son, Tessin the Younger – architect of the Royal Palace. Renovations in 2003 spruced up the entrance and the peaceful courtyard tucked below bustling

Södermalmstorg at Slussen, where you can sit and enjoy goodies from the café, which is decorated with fixings from an early 20th-century bakery. The temporary exhibitions on the ground floor are free. A series of rooms on the floor above cover Stockholm's development from 1252 to the present day. One room contains an intricate model of the city's layout in the 1650s; another re-creates the atmosphere and sounds of an 18th-century pub. The government's solution to the 1960s housing shortage – the 'Million Programme' – is the focus of the exhibition on the second floor. The third floor takes you through the realistic models of a Stockholm factory from 1897, plus a city registrar's office and school room from the same period. Don't miss peeking into the two reconstructed flats from the 1940s; one of these tiny rooms housed a family, plus additional lodgers. On the ground floor, Torget, a children's play area, re-creates a city market square and is open at weekends. This is Söder's best museum and a great place to learn about the city.

Stockholmsmoskén
Kapellgränd 10 (50 91 09 00). T-bana Medborgarplatsen/bus 55, 59, 66. **Open** 24hrs. **Prayers** 6 times daily; call for details. **Admission** free. **Map** p315 L8.

The conversion of Katarinastation, a former power station built in 1903, into Stockholm's first mosque led to heated architectural debates. Prior to its inauguration in 2000, Stockholm's Muslim community worshipped in cellars and other cramped spaces, jokingly claiming to be Sweden's biggest underground movement. Ferdinand Boberg, the architect behind Rosenbad (*see p74*), Prins Eugens Waldemarsudde

(*see p84*) and the NK department store (*see p153*), designed Katarinastation. Inspired by Andalusian Moorish architecture, he decorated the lofty main hall in mosaic brick, with floor-to-ceiling vaulted windows. Today, enormous chandeliers and wall-to-wall carpeting clash with the early 20th-century industrial feel. Fittingly, the original structure faces Mecca. As long as shoes are removed and women covered up (robes provided), visitors may view the prayer hall and lecture hall. Before you leave take a look at the massive copper doors embedded with numerous mundane objects by the process of blast-moulding.

Långholmen

Map p313

Just off the north-west tip of Södermalm lies the long, narrow island of **Långholmen** (Long Island). For 250 years this beautiful green island, almost a mile long, was home to a prison, in operation from 1724 to 1975. Thanks largely to the jail, Långholmen has remained undeveloped and, as a result, is something of a green retreat, complete with tree-shaded paths, cliffs dotted with nest-like nooks and two sandy beaches. Today, the remaining part of the **prison** is run as a very pleasant budget hotel/hostel (*see p56*), café, conference centre and prison museum (**Långholmens Fängelsemusuem**; *see p94*).

You can walk to the island across **Långholmsbron** (which provides closest access to the former prison from Hornstull), or via **Pålsundsbron** to the east, near a

Långholmen prison's old exercise yard, now a delightful café.

shipyard dating back to the 1680s. To get to the middle of the island, walk across the enormous **Västerbron** bridge (worth crossing to take in the view of the city) and take the stairs down.

A walking/cycling path leads from the south of the island to the cliffs and beach in the north. **Bellmanmuseet** (*see below*) and the former prison complex lie behind the beach – one of the most popular swimming posts in the city. For outdoor swimming without the hordes, head east to **Klippbadet**, a tiny, sandy cove. To the west of the prison stands **Karlshäll**, the previous residence of the prison warden, now a conference centre and restaurant. Curving back around to the south, take in the grace of the lovingly cared-for wooden sailboats lining the picture-perfect canal. Prisoners used to walk across a bridge to work at factories on **Reimersholme**, a tiny island. Best known historically for the production of *aquavit*, the island is now residential.

Klippbadet.

SoFo

The SoFo story started in September 2003 when three shopkeepers wanted to increase awareness of an area that had, since the mid 1990s, become something of a second home for savvy shoppers with alternative tastes. The Swenglish name SoFo, short for South of Folkungagatan (an unashamed, not to mention ambitious, twist on London and New York's SoHos), was adopted, and the brainstorming session has resulted in a loose network of independent fashion designers; roughly 60 of the area's 140 shops partake. SoFo is bordered to the west by Götgatan, to the south by Ringvägen and to the east by Renstiernas Gata (though lately, in their rush to be part of the city's new trend centre, a few shops have jumped outside these limits).

Like so many other creative hotspots, such as London's Shoreditch, this traditionally working-class area has climbed many a rung on the gentrification ladder. You'll still see plenty of old-school bohos sporting eclectic vintage styles, but the city's trend-smellers are rapidly moving in. In the last decade the area has also become inundated with ad agencies, architects, computer wizards and freelancers' co-ops.

Fashion highlights on the SoFo shopping round are **Le Shop** (*see p159*) on Nytorgsgatan, **Tjallamalla** (*see p160*) and other vintage and second-hand shops on Bondegatan. On Renstiernas Gata, you will

find **Boutique Sportif** (*see p157*). These shops all have genuinely interesting imports, as well as fresh, young Swedish fashion design. You will also find interior design and tableware with retro undertones, for instance in **Aparat** (*see p173*) on Nytorgsgatan. **125 Kvadrat** (*see p178*), on the corner of Östgötagatan and Kocksgatan, is also worth a gander for arts and crafts. 'SoFo nights' take place on the last Thursday of the month, when shops keep their doors open until 9pm. On these nights, many shops also have some kind of event, like impromptu fashion parades or concerts.

Hardcore alternaholics might argue that an area is not alternative once it has been dubbed just that. Cecilia Steiner of **Le Shop** retorts: 'Of course it would be ridiculous if, say, H&M started calling themselves alternative. But in SoFo we are independent shopkeepers who just sell the clothes that we like. We don't have anybody above us deciding.'

The stores and the people might seem terribly hip on the surface, but underneath much of the appeal of this area seems to come down to good, old-fashioned neighbourly values. 'People here help the old lady up the stairs with her heavy shopping bags. Life becomes a lot nicer when you don't partake in the egotistical social decadence

Bellmanmuseet

Stora Henriksvik, Långholmen (669 69 69/
www.bellman.nu). T-bana Hornstull/bus 4, 40, 66,
74. **Open** *March-mid May, Sept, Oct* noon-4pm Sat,
Sun. *Mid May-mid June* noon-4pm Tue-Sun. *Mid*
June-Aug noon-6pm daily. **Admission** 30kr; free
under-15s. **No credit cards. Map** p313 J2.

The oldest part of this attractive two-storey house
was built in the late 17th century as the toll office for
boats travelling into Stockholm. The ground floor is
divided up between a café and a museum devoted to
celebrated 18th-century troubadour/songwriter Carl
Michael Bellman (1740-1795), who used to sing in the
taverns of the city . In the late 18th century, Bellman
would visit Långholmen to see an opera singer friend
who worked at the prison. Copies of portraits, text in
Bellman's handwriting and a replica of his death
mask and lute are on display. The café staff, if they
aren't too busy, are happy to answer questions in
English. The café and gardens are popular with the
bathers using the beach in front of the house, and
concerts take place here in summer.

Långholmens Fängelsemuseum

Långholmen Hotel, Långholmsmuren 20 (720 85 00/
tour bookings 720 85 81/www.langholmen.com).
T-bana Hornstull/bus 4, 40, 66, 74. **Open** 11am-
4pm daily. **Admission** 25kr; 10kr under-14s.
Credit AmEx, DC, MC, V. **Map** p313 K2.

This small museum describes the history of the
Swedish penal system and life inside Kronohäktet
prison before it was turned into a hotel/hostel. You
can visit a typical cell used between 1845 and 1930,
read about Sweden's last executioner, Anders Gustaf
Dalman, and see a scale model of the guillotine
imported from France and used only once in 1910
(the actual guillotine used is stored at the Nordiska
Museet, though not on display). Visitors can view an
assortment of prison paraphernalia, including the
sinister hoods worn to hide an accused person's identity until sentenced (used until 1935). Nowadays, the
Swedish government tries to avoid incarceration and
a quarter of the 12,000 criminals sentenced each year
are electronically tagged rather than imprisoned.
Guided tours in English need to be pre-booked.

Sightseeing

that goes on around the world,' says
Freppa Glejpner, one of the three wise
thirtysomethings who put SoFo on the map.
Nevertheless, whether you are one of the
meek scheduled to inherit the earth or an
unabashedly self-absorbed materialist, the
shopkeepers of SoFo will welcome you
with open arms. Unless they are carrying
someone's groceries, that is.

Taking its branding one step further,
SoFo is scheduled to have its own website
(www.sofo.se) from autumn 2004.

Östermalm & Gärdet

Where the posh like to play.

Östermalm

Map p305, p306 & p310

This affluent area successfully lives up to its snooty image, with wide boulevards, fancy shops and exclusive nightlife. A playground for the rich, beautiful and, often, famous, Östermalm is a shopper's paradise by day and a clubbing hub by night. The main focus of the action is the busy square of **Stureplan**, at the centre of which stands the concrete rain shelter known as **Svampen** (the mushroom), a regular meeting place for the city's clubbing fraternity. Formerly a rather run-down area, Stureplan was revamped at the end of the 1980s and is now party central for glamour-seeking, fashion-conscious Stockholmers.

Nearby are nightclubs **Spy Bar** (*see p196*) and **Sturecompagniet** (*see p196*); bars **East** (*see p141*), **Halv Trappa plus Gård** (*see p127 & p142*) and **Laroy** (*see p142*); and restaurants **Sturehof** (*see p130*), **PA & Co** (*see p128*) and **Brasserie Godot** (*see p130*). Just north of the square, on Sturegatan, is the hip, music-oriented **Lydmar Hotel** (*see p57*), whose lobby bar (*see p142*) pulses with the young and beautiful. The clubs near here close around 5am at the weekend – later than the capital's other party spots – so you'll often see hordes of clubbers queuing in the small hours, in all weathers, to get into the most fashionable places.

Aside from the nightlife, Stureplan is also the city's most upmarket shopping area. The ultra-posh shopping mall **Sturegallerian** (*see p154*) borders the square; as well as designer boutiques, it also houses the exclusive art nouveau bath house **Sturebadet** (*see p172*). Shopaholics can spend a few happy hours trawling the surrounding streets, notably the lower end of **Birger Jarlsgatan** (which extends from the north of the city all the way to the water of Nybroviken), **Biblioteksgatan**, **Grev Turegatan** and **Mäster Samuelsgatan**. This is where you'll find international designer fashion boutiques, classy jewellery, fancy cosmetics and posh chocolates. But don't expect cutting-edge anything in conventional Östermalm – the upper classes, both young and old, come here to reconfirm their status in that time-honoured way: by spending lots of money.

At the bottom end of Birger Jarlsgatan is **Nybroviken**, where the Cinderella and Strömma Kanalbolaget ferries depart for destinations in Lake Mälaren and the archipelago. Classics by Strindberg and Shakespeare are performed in the ornate white marble building facing Nybroplan square, the **Kungliga Dramatiska Teatern** (*see p98*) – one of Stockholm's leading theatres. Nearby is the idiosyncratic **Hallwylska Museet** museum (*see p98*).

If you walk up Sibyllegatan to the right of the theatre, you'll pass three buildings constructed by royal commission. Bread for the royal army was baked at the Kronobageriet, which today houses the charming and child-friendly **Musikmuseet** (*see p99*). The royal family's horses and cars are still kept in the **Kungliga Hovstallet** (*see p99*), the huge brick building to the right of the bakery. Further up is the unusual **Armémuseum** (*see below*), where the royal arsenal used to be stored. Behind this lies 17th-century **Hedvig Eleonora Kyrka**, the former place of worship for the royal navy, which now holds regular classical music concerts.

To catch a glimpse of the Östermalm upper classes, head to **Östermalmstorg** opposite the church. When the first plans for Östermalm were drawn up back in the 1640s, sailors and craftsmen lived around this square. Nowadays, expensive boutiques sell clothes and home accessories, and the pavements are teeming with mink-clad elderly women walking small dogs. On the corner of the square is **Östermalms Saluhall** (*see p175*), a dark red-brick building constructed in 1888 and the flagship of the city's market halls. You can buy all sorts of gourmet delicacies, from fresh Baltic fish to wild rabbit – but it's pricey, so you could just stroll around the magnificent interior with its swooping ceiling.

Östermalm's main green space is the **Humlegården**, the site of the king's hop gardens back in the 16th century and today a pleasant and very popular park with the **Kungliga Bibliotek** (Royal Library) on its southern bank. Theatre performances are held in the park in summer. Further up Karlavägen, on a hill overlooking the city, looms the tall brick tower of **Engelbrektskyrkan**. Designed by the leading Jugendstil architect Lars Israel Wahlman and opened in 1914, the church has an amazingly high nave – supposedly the tallest in Scandinavia.

For another kind of high life, follow the water's edge from Nybroplan along grand **Strandvägen**, lined with luxurious late 19th-century residences and still among the city's most prestigious addresses. There are also a couple of deluxe hotels (including the **Hotell Diplomat**; *see p56*) and one of Stockholm's most celebrated interior design shops, **Svenskt Tenn** (*see p175*). Until the 1940s sailing boats carrying firewood from the archipelago islands used to dock on the quayside at Strandvägen; some of these vintage boats – with labels by each one – are now docked on its southern edge. At the end of Strandvägen is the bridge leading over to leafy Djurgården, and north from there, on Narvavägen, is the imposing **Historiska Museet** (*see p98*); it's Sweden's largest archaeological museum, with an exceptional collection of Viking artefacts.

Strandvägen is part of an esplanade system mapped out for Östermalm in the late 1800s by city planner Albert Lindhagen. The project was only partially implemented, but includes the broad boulevards of Valhallavägen, Narvavägen and Karlavägen – the latter two radiating out from the fountain and circular pond (added in 1929) at **Karlaplan**. The central section of Karlavägen is dotted with sculptures by various international artists, and at its eastern end – on the site of a former military training ground – are the headquarters of Swedish radio and television. The buildings were designed by Erik Ahnborg and Sune Lindström, who were also responsible for the **Berwaldhallen** concert hall (*see p219*) next door, home of the Swedish Radio Symphony Orchestra and Radio Choir.

Beyond the TV and radio buildings, on the border with Gärdet, is **Diplomatstaden**, a complex of grand mansions that houses most of the city's foreign embassies, including those of the UK and US. The adjacent park next to the water is named after Alfred Nobel, scientist, inventor and founder of the famous prizes (*see p104* **Peace man?**).

Armémuseum

Riddargatan 13 (788 95 60/www.armemuseum.org). T-bana Östermalmstorg/bus 2, 47, 55, 62, 69, 76. **Open** 11am-8pm Tue; 11am-4pm Wed-Sun. **Guided tours** *English* July, Aug noon Tue-Sun. *Swedish* July, Aug 1pm daily; Sept-June 1pm Sat, Sun. **Admission** 60kr; 40kr concessions; 30kr 7-18s; free under-7s. Free June-Aug 4-8pm Tue. **Free with SC.** **Credit** MC, V. **Map** p306 F9.

The story of Sweden at war, rather than its military infrastructure, is the museum's dominant theme, which may seem odd since Sweden has avoided conflict for the last 200 years. But with 1,000 years of history on show, you soon learn that the Swedes were once a bloody and gruesome lot. The Army Museum – housed since 1879 in the former arsenal, an impressive white pile built in the 18th century – reopened in May 2000 after seven years of renovation. Exhibited over three floors, it's not all uniforms and gleaming weaponry. Life-size (and life-like) tableaux, such as a woman scavenging meat from a dead horse and doctors performing an amputation, show the horrific effects of war on both soldiers and civilians. The main exhibition begins on the top floor with the late Viking age and the Thirty Years War, and continues below with the 20th century. The ground floor area houses an artillery exhibit and a restaurant. Nominated for the European Museum of the Year Award in 2001, this is one of Stockholm's most fascinating museums. If you miss the highly recommended guided tour in English, the front desk provides a detailed pamphlet, also in English. The Royal Guard marches off from the museum (summer only) for the changing of the guard (*see p63*) at the Kungliga Slottet.

Hallwylska Museet

Hamngatan 4 (51 95 55 99/www.hallwylska museet.se). T-bana Östermalmstorg/bus 2, 47, 55, 62, 69, 76. **Open** (guided tours only) *English* End June-mid Aug 2pm daily. Mid Aug-end June 1pm Sun. *Swedish* End June-mid Aug 11am, noon, 1pm, 3pm, 4pm daily. Sept-end June noon, 1pm, 2pm, 3pm Tue, Thur-Sun; noon, 1pm, 2pm, 3pm, 6pm Wed. **Admission** 65kr; 30kr 7-18s; free under-7s. **Free with SC**. **Credit** AmEx, MC, V. **Map** p305 F8.
Enter the opulent world of Count and Countess Walther and Wilhelmina von Hallwyl in one of Stockholm's most eccentric and engaging museums. This palatial residence was built as a winter home for the immensely rich couple in 1898. Designed by Isak Gustav Clason (architect of the Nordiska Museet), it was very modern for its time, with electricity, central heating, lifts, bathrooms and phones. The Countess was an avid collector of pretty much everything, from paintings and furniture to silverware and armoury that she picked up on her travels around Europe, the Middle East and Africa. She always planned that the house should become a museum and donated the building and its collections to the Swedish state in 1920. Her vision became a reality in 1938 when the Hallwyl Museum was first opened to the public, eight years after her death. The house has been preserved exactly as it was left, and situated among the objets d'art are personal peculiarities, including a chunk of the Count's beard and a slice of their wedding cake. For the ultimate in upstairs-downstairs existence, and a taste of how the other half used to live, the tour takes you through an assortment of 40 incredibly lavish rooms and is led by extremely well-spoken guides amusingly dressed as butlers and maids.

Historiska Museet

Narvavägen 13-17 (51 95 56 00/www.historiska.se). T-bana Karlaplan/bus 42, 44, 47, 56, 69, 76. **Open** *Mid May-mid Sept* 11am-5pm daily. *Mid Sept-mid May* 11am-5pm Tue, Wed, Fri-Sun; 11am-8pm Thur. **Guided tours** *Summer* usually daily. *Winter* Sat, Sun. **Admission** 60kr; 50kr concessions; 30kr students, over-16s; 140kr family; free under-15s. **Free with SC**. **Credit** AmEx, DC, MC, V. **Map** p306 F10.

Karlaplan. *See p97.*

Objects from the Stone Age to the 16th century are displayed in the Museum of National Antiquities, Sweden's largest archaeological museum. The plain design of this 1940 building – the façade looks like a tall brick wall with a door – gives no indication of the treasures within. To see the best exhibit, enter the darkened hall on the ground floor, where an impressive collection of Viking rune stones, swords, skeletons and jewellery is displayed. Detailed texts (in English) and maps describe the Vikings' economy, class structure, travels and methods of punishment. The remaining displays on the ground floor, covering earlier periods, are rather dull. In the large halls upstairs, you'll find beautiful wooden church altarpieces, textiles and other medieval ecclesiastical artworks. And don't miss the basement, where the circular Guldrummet (Gold Room) displays more than 3,000 artefacts in gold and silver, from the Bronze to the Middle Ages. This collection was made possible by a unique Swedish law, more than 300 years old, which entitles the finders of such treasures to payment equal to their market value. In the foyer there's a copy of an Athenian marble lion statue – check out the Viking graffiti on its side. In 2004 the museum hit the headlines in connection with an installation about suicide bombers by an Israeli-born artist. On a visit to the museum, the Israeli ambassador to Sweden intentionally knocked over a lighting stand into the red pool designed to represent blood, shorting the electricity and causing a huge stir.

Kungliga Dramatiska Teatern

Nybrogatan 2 (tour information 665 61 15 or 665 61 75/www.dramaten.se). T-bana Kungsträdgården or Östermalmstorg/bus 2, 47, 55, 62, 69, 76, 91. **Guided tours** *Swedish* July 5.30-6.30pm Wed, Thur, Sat. *English* July by arrangement.

Sightseeing

Historiska Museet. *See p98.*

Tickets 50kr; 25kr under-18s. **Free with SC**.
Credit mAmEx, DC, MC, V. **Map** p305 F8.
Entrusted with the task of performing the classics, as
well as staging new Swedish and foreign drama, the
Royal Dramatic Theatre, or Dramaten, is Stockholm's
number one theatre. It played host to a pre-Hollywood
Greta Garbo and was a home from home for Ingmar
Bergman, who directed plays here for over four
decades, but has now retired. The lavish structure
was built between 1902 and 1908 in Jugendstil style,
with a white marble façade and gilded bronzework.
Paintings and sculptures by Sweden's most famous
artists decorate the building: Theodor Lundberg
created the golden statues of *Poetry* and *Drama* at the
front; Carl Milles was responsible for the large sculp-
tural group below the raised central section of the
façade; and Carl Larsson painted the foyer ceiling.
The theatre's architect, Fredrik Liljekvist, wanted to
create a grand and imposing structure and added the
domed attic to give the building more prominence. It
worked – it's one of Stockholm's most striking structures, particularly when the setting sun hits the
golden lampposts and statues. The auditorium is
equally stunning. A guided tour (call in advance if
you want it in English) covers the main stage, smaller stages and rehearsal rooms (July tours only take
place if there's a show on). For a wonderful view over
Nybroviken, visit the outdoor café on the second-floor
balcony. *See also p234.*

Kungliga Hovstallet

Väpnargatan 1 (402 60 00/www.royalcourt.se).
T-bana Östermalmstorg/bus 2, 47, 55, 62, 69, 76.
Open (guided tours only; in Swedish) *Mid Aug-mid
Dec & mid Jan-mid May* 2pm Sat, Sun. *End June-mid
Aug* 2pm Mon-Fri. **Tickets** 30kr; 10kr under-10s.
No credit cards. **Map** p306 F9.

The royal family's own horses, carriages and cars
are still taken care of in this late 19th-century striped
brick building designed by architect Fritz Eckert.
The building is so vast that it occupies almost the
entire block next to Dramaten (*see p98*). A collection
of 40 carriages from the 19th and 20th centuries
(some still used for ceremonial occasions) stands in
a long hall above the garage. Inside the garage are
11 cars, including a 1950 Daimler and a 1969
Cadillac Fleetwood. The stalls and riding arena may
be empty if you visit in the summer, as this is when
the horses are 'on vacation'. On a practical note,
plump for decent footwear if you plan to visit as the
odds are you will tread in something undesirable.
This place may be a hit for equestrian enthusiasts,
but otherwise the tour (guide speaks English) is not
particularly thrilling.

Musikmuseet

*Sibyllegatan 2 (51 95 54 90/http://stockholm.music.
museum). T-bana Östermalmstorg/bus 2, 47, 55, 62,
69, 76.* **Open** *June, July* 10am-7pm Tue; 10am-4pm
Wed-Sun. *Aug-May* 11am-7pm Tue; 11am-4pm Wed-
Sun. **Admission** 50kr; 25kr concessions; free under-7s.
Free with SC. **Credit** MC, V. **Map** p305 F8.
Home to around 6,000 musical instruments, this fun,
child-friendly museum echoes with a spontaneous
symphony of noise. The hands-on exhibitions allow
you to play an eclectic selection of instruments, from
the electric guitar to the Swedish cow horn. With its
stucco walls, wood-beamed ceilings and narrow window shutters, the building still looks much like the
Crown Bakery it was from the 1640s to 1958, when
it was supplying bread to the Swedish armed forces.
The Music Museum also has the largest collection of
Swedish folk instruments in the world, plus folk
instruments from Africa, Asia and elsewhere in

Musikmuseet. *See p99.*

Europe. Wannabe rock stars should head downstairs to Lirum where a mocked-up stage allows you to belt out ABBA's greatest hits and engage in some serious air guitar on the big screen. There's a regular programme of weekend concerts (call for a programme), and the upper floor is reserved for temporary exhibitions, always worth a look. *See also p190.*

Gärdet

Map p307 & p311

The whole area to the east of Norrmalm was previously called Ladugårdsgärdet, which roughly translates as 'the field of barns'. As more affluent people moved into the district and the association with cattle became less desirable, the city voted in 1885 to change the name to Östermalm. Today, the residential district north of Valhallavägen and the open field and forests to its south-east are known as **Gärdet**, although the undeveloped grassy area is still officially called **Ladugårdsgärdet**.

Functionalist apartment complexes were built for working people in Gärdet and its northern neighbour, **Hjorthagen**, in the 1930s. The apartments are now mainly inhabited by middle-class residents and students. The stately complexes of the **Försvarshögskolan** (Swedish National Defence College) and the **Kungliga Musikhögskolan** (Royal College of Music) are located next to each other on the northern side of Valhallavägen. Just across Lidingövägen (the main road that heads north-east to the island of Lidingö) stands the historic **Stockholms Stadion** (*see p230*), built for the

1912 Olympic Games. It was designed by architect Torben Grut in National Romantic style to resemble the walls surrounding a medieval city. Its twin brick towers are a striking landmark, and numerous sculptures of athletes dot the complex. Today, it's the home ground of Djurgården IF's football team.

Ladugårdsgärdet is part of **Ekoparken** (58 71 40 41, www.ekoparken.com), the world's first national city park, which also includes Djurgården, Hagaparken, Norra Djurgården and the Fjäderholmarna islands. Mainly open grassland and woods, with a few scattered buildings, this portion of the park stretches for about two and a half kilometres (four miles) to the waters of **Lilla Värtan**, on the other side of which lies the island of **Lidingö** (*see p110*). Stockholmers come here to picnic, jog, ride horses or just get a taste of the countryside.

Nearer Östermalm, along the shoreline, there is also 'Museum Park', a convenient cluster of three museums: the **Sjöhistoriska Museet** (*see p101*), **Etnografiska Museet** (*see below*) and **Tekniska Museet** (*see p101*). Keen sightseers with a lot of stamina could try to visit the lot in one day. Bus 69 passes the museums, along Djurgårdsbrunnsvägen. Alternatively, follow the path next to the water, as the view is stunning.

Further east – and also on the 69 bus route – is the **Kaknästornet** broadcasting tower (*see p101*), rising up from the forest like a giant concrete spear chucked into the ground. Ascend to the observation deck at the top of the tower for a fantastic view right across the city; high-altitude refreshments are available in the tower's restaurant and café.

If you follow Kaknäsvägen, the road that runs past the Kaknäs tower, north-east towards the water you will come to a dirt trail in the forest to your right that winds around the scenic shoreline of **Lilla Värtan**. A 100-year-old pet cemetery with dogs, cats and a circus horse lies to the right of the trail.

Etnografiska Museet

Djurgårdsbrunnsvägen 34 (51 95 50 00/www.etno grafiska.se). Bus 69. **Open** 10am-5pm Mon, Tue, Thur-Sun; 10am-8pm Wed. **Guided tours** (book in advance) *Museum* children 1pm Sun; adults 2pm Sun. *Tea house* 5.30pm Wed. **Admission** 50kr; free under-21s. **Free with SC**. **Credit** MC, V. **Map** p307 F14.
The dimly lit ground floor of the exotic-looking National Museum of Ethnography features masks, musical instruments and religious objects from seven holy cities (Auroville, Benin, Benares, Jerusalem, Yogyakarta, Beijing and Teotihuacan). The high ceiling of the second floor was specifically created for the Haisla totem pole, which is part of an exhibition on Native American culture. Traveller's Trunk is a collection of artefacts brought home by Swedish explorers, the oldest of which were seized by the

pupils of famous Swedish botanist Carl Linnaeus on their travels with Captain Cook. There's a wide variety of colourful exhibits, beautifully displayed, but more explanations in English wouldn't hurt. When you're tired of feeling thoughtful, beers and teas of the world are served at the museum's mellow Babjan restaurant. In summer, the restaurant lends bamboo mats for sitting outside. You can also reserve a place for a tea ceremony in the authentic Japanese tea house. Situated in the garden, the tea house was a gift from Japan to promote friendship and cultural exchange between the two nations. There's also a small museum shop selling ethnic toys, trinkets and books.

Kaknästornet

Mörka Kroken 28-30 (789 24 35/restaurant 667 21 80). Bus 69. **Open** *Tower* May-Aug 9am-10pm daily. Sept-Apr 10am-9pm daily. *Restaurant* 11.30am-10pm daily. **Admission** 30kr; 15kr 7-15s; free under-7s. **Free with SC. Credit** AmEx, DC, MC, V.

For an utterly spectacular view of Stockholm and its surroundings, visit this 155m-high (510ft) tower – one of Scandinavia's tallest buildings. On a clear day you can see up to 60km (37 miles) from its observation points up on the 30th and 31st floors. Nearer to hand are the island of Djurgården to the south, Gamla Stan and downtown to the west and the beginning of the archipelago to the east. Designed by Bengt Lindroos and Hans Borgström, the rather ugly concrete structure (itself visible from all over the city) was completed in 1967 and still transmits radio and TV broadcasts. On the ground floor, the Stockholm Information Service operates a busy visitor centre and gift shop. Lunch and dinner are served in the restaurant and café on the 28th floor.

Sjöhistoriska Museet

Djurgårdsbrunnsvägen 24 (51 95 49 00/ www.sjohistoriska.nu). Bus 69. **Open** *Apr-mid Feb* 10am-5pm Tue-Sun. *Mid Feb-Apr* 10am-8pm Tue; 10am-5pm Wed-Sun. **Guided tours** *adults* 1pm, 3pm Sat, Sun; *children* 2pm Sat, Sun (English tours must be pre-booked). **Admission** 50kr; 40kr concessions; 20kr 7-16s; free under-7s. Free Mon. **Free with SC. Credit** MC, V. **Map** p307 F13.

Hundreds of model ships – from Viking longboats to sailing ships, oil tankers and submarines – are displayed within the long, curved National Maritime Museum, designed in 1936 by Ragnar Östberg, the architect behind Stockholm's famous Stadshuset (*see p104*). Occupying a suitably watery setting, it's an extensive and thorough survey – as it should be, considering Sweden's long and dramatic maritime history. Two floors of minutely detailed models are grouped in permanent exhibitions on merchant shipping, battleships and ocean liners. Ship figureheads depicting monsters and bare-breasted women decorate the museum walls, and the upper floor displays two ships' cabins from the 1870s and 1970s. But unless you're a nautical or miniatures enthusiast, it can all be a bit too much, and the temporary exhibitions are probably the main reason for coming. In the basement, the children's room Saltkråkan offers ships and a lighthouse to play in and, aside from a short summer break, a kids' workshop is open on Saturdays and Sundays (noon-4pm).

Tekniska Museet

Museivägen 7 (450 56 00/www.tekniskamuseet.se). Bus 69. **Open** 10am-5pm Mon, Tue, Thur, Fri; 10am-8pm Wed; 11am-5pm Sat, Sun. **Guided tours** *Toy Tech* 11am-5pm Sat, Sun. *What If* 2pm Mon-Fri; 1pm, 3pm Sat, Sun. *Mine* 1pm Sun. *Machine Hall* 1pm Sat, Sun. *Robot Shop* 12.30pm, 2.30pm, 3.30pm Sat, Sun. **Admission** 60kr; 40kr concessions; 30kr 6-19s; 120kr family; free under-6s. Free 5-8pm Wed. **Free with SC. Credit** MC, V. **Map** p307 G14.

Inquisitive kids and adults alike can roam for hours at the Museum of Science and Technology, which has exhibits and activities intended to entertain and educate – and they do. This huge house of learning takes the fear out of physics and covers about 18,000sq m (20,000sq yds). Sweden's oldest steam engine, built in 1832, dominates the large Machine Hall, where aeroplanes – including one of Sweden's first commercial aircraft from 1924 – hang from the ceiling above bicycles, engines and cars. Meet Roberta, 60 tons of futuristic humanoid, among an array of androids in the Robotics exhibition (until August 2006). Size up your mobile to the magnitude of past models, and reminisce about the days before text-messaging, in the high-tech exhibition on telephones. You can also take a break in the cafeteria and pick up a *Star Trek* uniform in the gift shop on your way out. The nearby Telemuseum closed down in 2004 and, as this book went to press, there were plans to collate some of its exhibits to form a permanent display, due to open in autumn 2005, at the Tekniska Museet on the history of telecommunications.

Swanky **Sturegallerian**. *See p96.*

Sightseeing

Kungsholmen

Waterside walks, local restaurants and the city's iconic tower.

Map p303 & p304

Most visitors to Kungsholmen ('King's Island') rarely venture further than the majestic **Stadshuset** (City Hall), an architectural gem visible from far and wide, and the sparkling jewel in the city's crown. The city's famous landmark is a must-see on the tourist trail, but this distinctive tower tends to leave the rest of the island somewhat in its shadow. While what lies beyond is a fairly nondescript mix of apartments, shops and offices, Kungsholmen does also have a sprinkling of tranquil parks and some good neighbourhood restaurants, making it a quiet, pleasant alternative to the bustle of nearby Norrmalm and Gamla Stan. The island is within a whisker of a Swedish mile (6.2 miles/10 kilometres) in circumference, and the island's waterside walkways are popular with joggers seeking a run with a view.

Stadshuset. *See p104.*

During the 1640s, craftsmen, labourers and factory owners were lured to Kungsholmen, then mostly fields, by the promise of a ten-year tax break. The island soon became home to all of the smelly, fire-prone and dangerous businesses that nobody else wanted. Unsurprisingly, given the conditions, many residents became ill, and Sweden's first hospital, the Serafimerlasarettet, was built here in the 1750s, and several more soon followed. During the Industrial Revolution, conditions hit an all-time low – its disease-ravaged, starving inhabitants earned Kungsholmen the nickname 'Starvation Island'. The factories finally left the island in the early 1900s, to be replaced by government agencies, offices and apartment buildings.

The quickest way to get to **Stadshuset** (*see p104*) is to walk across Stadshusbron bridge from Norrmalm – though navigating the roads and railway lines leading from Central Station can be a bit of a nightmare. The Stadshuset is on your left – it's gigantic and hard to miss – and the former Serafimerlasarettet hospital on your right. If you continue on down Hantverkargatan, you'll soon reach **Kungsholms Kyrka**, a 17th-century church with a Greek-cross plan and a park-like cemetery. Two blocks further on, a right on to **Scheelegatan** puts you on one of Kungsholmen's major thoroughfares, packed with restaurants and bars.

Further down Scheelegatan, at the corner of Bergsgatan, squats the city's gigantic, majestic **Rådhuset** (courthouse), designed by Carl Westman (1866-1936), a leading architect of the National Romantic School. Completed in 1915, it was designed to look like 16th-century Vadstena castle in southern Sweden, but also has art nouveau touches. There are no guided tours, but you can wander around the public areas, which include a pleasant cloister-like garden with a sundial. **Polishistoriska Museet** (Police History Museum), behind the courthouse, has been closed since December 2003. As this book went to press the museum was set to reopen at the end of 2005 with a collection including items from the Polistekniska Museet in Solna (www.museer. polisen.se), but a location had not been agreed upon. For more information, call 401 90 63.

Continuing west on Bergsgatan, you arrive at **Kronobergsparken**, a pleasant hillside park

Mälarpromenaden.

with Stockholm's oldest Jewish cemetery in its north-west corner. To the north of the island the **Tullmuseet** (Customs Museum; *see p105*), is inside the Customs Office on Alströmergatan. Nearby is one of Stockholm's trendiest interior design shops, **R.O.O.M.** (*see p174*).

Kungsholmen's shops tend to offer a fairly bland retail diet, but there is an increasing number of individual treats of late. Kungsholmen's main shopping streets are **St Eriksgatan** and **Fleminggatan**, at their most plentiful around the Fridhemsplan Tunnelbana station. Music lovers head to the former for its second-hand CD and vinyl shops. If you work up an appetite, stop for coffee and cakes at **Thelins** (*see p150*), an excellent traditional *konditori*. Alternatively, the bright and airy shopping mall **Västermalmsgallerian** (*see p153*), on the corner of St Eriksgatan and Fleminggatan, offers a decent array of Sweden's favourite brand names and a glass-fronted coffee shop.

The huge but oddly elegant double-spanned **Västerbron** bridge (1935) connects Kungsholmen with Södermalm across the expanse of Lake Mälaren. It's heavily trafficked, but if you can face fumes you'll get a spectacular view of Stockholm from the centre of the bridge.

Marieberg, the area on Kungsholmen just to the north of the bridge, once contained military installations and a porcelain factory, but is now the city's newspaper district. Two of the four Stockholm dailies – *Dagens Nyheter* and *Expressen* – have offices here. The Expressen building, designed by Paul Hedqvist, is prominent, soaring to 82 metres (270 feet); its neon sign is visible for miles at night.

The flat green lawns of adjoining **Rålambshovparken** were created in 1935, at the same time as Västerbron; the sculpture-studded park is popular with runners and picnickers, and there's a small sandy beach just along the shore at Smedsuddsbadet.

Walking and cycling paths line the northern and southern shores of Kungsholmen. For a beautiful view across the water, stroll from the Stadshuset along tree-lined **Mälarpromenaden**. Vintage boats and yachts moor here, and there are a couple of well-placed cafés en route. **Norr Mälarstrand**, the road that runs alongside the promenade, is lined with grand apartment blocks, built in the early 20th century when the factories had finally departed. Look out particularly for No.76, designed by Ragnar Östberg, architect of Stadshuset.

Stadshuset

*Hantverkargatan 1 (50 82 90 59/www.stockholm.se/
stadshuset). T-bana T-Centralen/bus 3, 62.* **Open**
Stadshuset (guided tours only) June-Aug 10am, 11am,
noon, 2pm, 3pm daily; Sept, May 10am, noon, 2pm
daily; Oct-Apr 10am, noon daily. *Tower* Apr 10am-
4.30pm Sat, Sun; May-Sept 10am-4.30pm daily.
Tower closed Oct-Mar. **Admission** Guided tour
50kr; tower 20kr; free under-12s. **Free with SC**.
Credit AmEx, DC, MC, V. **Map** p304 H5.
The City Hall (1923), Stockholm's most prominent
landmark, stands imposingly on the northern shore
of the bay of Riddarfjärden. A massive red-brick
building, it was designed by Ragnar Östberg (1866-
1945) in the National Romantic style, with two inner
courtyards and a 106m (348ft) tower. It's most
famous for hosting the annual Nobel Prize banquet,
held in the Blue Hall on 10 December and attended
by 1,300 guests, after the prizes have been awarded
at the Konserthuset (*see below* **Peace man?**). The
hall – designed to look like an Italian Renaissance
piazza – was meant to be painted blue, but Östberg
liked the way the sun hit the red bricks and changed
his mind. The hall is also the home of an immense
organ, with more than 10,000 pipes and 138 stops.

In the astonishing Golden Hall upstairs, scenes
from Swedish history are depicted on the walls in
18 million mosaic pieces in gold leaf. The artist,
Einar Forseth (1892-1988), covered the northern
wall with a mosaic known as the 'Queen of Lake
Mälaren', representing Stockholm being honoured
from all sides. The beamed ceiling of the Council
Chamber, where the city council meets every
other Monday, resembles the open roof of a Viking
longhouse. The furniture was designed by Carl
Malmsten. The opulent Oval Room, which is part
of the guided tour, is a popular place for Swedish
nuptials. Such is the demand, it's a speedy
marriage merry-go-round as couples tie the knot
in a no-frills 40-second ceremony. The extended
version is three minutes.

Peace man?

Popular myth has it that after Alfred Nobel
invented dynamite he felt so guilty about its
use in warfare that he left most of his fortune
to fund the Nobel Prizes. Reality suggests
otherwise, however – Nobel never actually
expressed remorse about his invention and
continued to develop weapons technology
throughout his life.

Born in Stockholm in 1833, Nobel was
nine years old when his family moved to St
Petersburg, where his father manufactured
naval mines for the tsar. Nobel received a
first-rate education and was fluent in five
languages. During his studies abroad, he
met the inventor of nitroglycerine, Ascanio
Sobrero, and on his return to Russia he and
his father investigated ways to make the
explosive liquid less volatile.

In 1863 Nobel moved to Sweden and
soon began mass-producing nitroglycerine.
After his brother and four others were
killed in an explosion, though, Nobel was
prohibited from experimenting within the
city limits. He eventually discovered that
by mixing nitroglycerine with silica, a stable
paste was formed that could be shaped
into rods. He patented his dynamite in
1867, taking the name from *dunamis*,
the Greek word for power.

Scientist, inventor and industrialist, Nobel
held at the time of his death 355 patents and
owned 90 companies in 20 countries. He had
also written several poems, drafted three
novels and even published his own play. He
may have been inspired to leave his wealth to
a good cause by his long friendship with the
Austrian peace activist Bertha von Suttner, who
wrote the book *Lay Down Your Arms* in 1889.
Expressing not quite the same sentiment,
Nobel believed that one of the best deterrents
to war was the production of weapons so
ghastly that no nation would dare to use them.

When Nobel died alone in his home in
Italy in 1896, his one-page will stated that
his estate should be used for 'prizes to those
who, during the preceding year, shall have
conferred the greatest benefit on mankind'.
Nobel specified the categories of physics,
chemistry, physiology or medicine, literature
and peace. The economics prize was founded
in 1969, when the Swedish National Bank
contributed funds for its creation.

The cash award varies; 2003 Nobel Prize
laureates each received about US$1,000,000.
The Swedish king hands out the prizes at the
Konserthuset (*see p219*) on 10 December,
the anniversary of Nobel's death, followed
by a lavish banquet in Stadshuset's **Blue
Hall**. Sweden and Norway were a political
union when Nobel died, and it is perhaps
for this reason that he chose Norway to award
the peace prize, which it does, on the same
day, in Oslo City Hall.

There is inherent irony in the fact that a
fortune built on weaponry funds the world's
most famous prize for peace. And over the
years the Nobel has certainly had moments
of great controversy. Most of this comes from

You can only visit the interior of the Stadshuset by guided tour, but you can climb the tower independently. Follow a series of winding red-brick slopes then wooden stairs for a fantastic view over Gamla Stan. Three gold crowns – the Tre Kronor, Sweden's heraldic symbol – top the tower. At the edge of the outdoor terrace below the tower, by the waters of Riddarfjärden, are two statues by famous Swedish sculptor Carl Eldh (1873-1954): the female *Dansen* (Dance) and the male *Sången* (Song). For refreshments, a cafeteria-style restaurant, entered from the outdoor courtyard, serves classic Swedish dishes at lunchtime, while the Stadshuskällaren cellar restaurant offers the previous year's menu from the Nobel banquet (cooked fresh, presumably).

Tullmuseet

Alströmergatan 39 (653 05 03/www.tullverket.se/ museum). T-bana Fridhemsplan/bus 1, 3, 4, 57. **Open** 11am-4pm Tue-Sun. **Admission** free. **Map** p303 F2.

The most interesting part of the Customs Museum is its section on smuggling. The oldest exhibits date from the 1920s and 1930s when alcohol was smuggled in from Estonia and Finland due to the alcohol rationing in Sweden at the time. One of the oldest pieces is a pair of XXL knickers dating from the 1920s, with secret pockets to conceal cannisters filled with 96% proof spirit, home-made by a lady caught by Swedish customs (a gurgling noise was heard by customs officers). Among other early methods used to conceal cigarettes and liquor were loaves of bread, teddy bears and sofas. In 1622 a fence and toll (*tull*) booths were built around the edge of Stockholm to raise money for the wars of King Gustav II Adolf, and the museum displays a copy of one of these, as well as an early 20th-century customs office and laboratory. Though a bit off the beaten track, the Customs Museum is free, so take a quick peek if you're in the neighbourhood. As we went to press the museum was adding English text to all its exhibits.

the nomination process. Many people have the right to nominate individuals for the awards, which ensures that the nominees are much more controversial than the winners. Members of state governments can nominate, as can groups associated with previous winners and a relatively long list of other people. Because of this, Adolf Hitler and Slobodan Milosevic have both been nominated. Such outrageous nominations inevitably cause a huge uproar in the media, regardless of the fact that the Nobel committee has little control over who is nominated – they only control the choice of the final prize winner.

In an effort to avoid this bad publicity, and to keep from turning the prize into a competition, the committee does not release the names of nominees. Unfortunately, those who nominate the unlikely candidates – like the right-wing Norwegian parliamentarian who nominated George W Bush and Tony Blair in 2004 – are usually less reticent.

Overall, though, most view the occasional controversial winners and the bogus nominees, as anomalies in an otherwise respectable history of rewarding peace. But it's worth mentioning that, while Henry Kissinger was awarded a Nobel for peace at the end of the Vietnam War, Mahatma Gandhi, nominated several times during his lifetime, never was.

For more information on Nobel, the prizes and previous laureates, visit the **Nobelmuseet** (*see p69*) or visit www.nobel.se.

Sightseeing

Further Afield

A break from the city – within the city.

Haga & around

Rolling green lawns, cool woodlands and 18th-century architecture make **Hagaparken** a popular outdoor destination. One of its biggest draws is the fact that it's within easy reach of the city centre, just north-west of Vasastaden on the western edge of Brunnsviken Bay. The legacy of King Gustav III and architect Fredrik Magnus Piper, this romantic English-style park with wandering paths, scenic views and assorted pavilions forms part of a broader national park in Stockholm, which was christened **Ekoparken** (58 71 40 41, www.eko parken.com) in 1995 by the Swedish parliament. Tagged as the world's first national park within a city, Ekoparken consists of 27 square kilometres (ten square miles) of land and water, cutting a diagonal green swath from the island of Djurgården in the south-east to Ulriksdals Palace in the north-west.

In Haga's northern section, the lush **Fjärilshuset conservatory** (*see p189*) is full of exotic butterflies and tropical rainforest vegetation. To the south, three colourful copper tents form **Koppartälten**. Built as Gustav III's stables and guards' quarters it now houses a restaurant, café and the **Haga Park Museum** (58 71 40 41, free admission), which contains an interesting pictorial history (all text is in Swedish) of the park and its buildings. The 'ruins' of a palace left incomplete after Gustav III's assassination in 1792 are east of the tents. Sweden's current king, Carl XVI Gustaf, was born in nearby **Haga Slott** (171 41 47 00, www.hagaslott.se), a castle now converted into a hotel and conference centre. Other buildings include the waterfront **Gustav III's Paviljong** (402 61 30, www.royalcourt.se), with Pompeii-style interiors by 18th-century interior decorator Louis Masreliéz. It's open for guided tours in summer (June-Aug noon, 1pm, 2pm & 3pm Tue-Sun, 50kr). You can also test the acoustics in the outdoor **Ekotemplet**, originally used as a summer dining room.

The 18th-century obsession with the exotic is evident in the Chinese pagoda and Turkish pavilion in the south of the park. A small island nearby (May 1-3pm Sun, June-Aug 9am-3pm Thur) has been the burial place of Swedish royalty since the 1910s.

On the southern tip of Hagaparken, enjoy a meal or Sunday brunch at **Haga Forum** (Annerovägen 4, 833 48 44, www.vilja gruppen.se/eng/rest/haga), a bus-terminal-turned-modern-restaurant with a terrace overlooking the park and water; information on Ekoparken is also available at Haga Forum. The nearby **Carl Eldhs Ateljémuseum** (*see below*), south of Bellevueparken, contains sculptures by this 20th-century Swedish artist (1873-1954).

Sculptures by other Swedish artists stand in **Norra begravningsplats** (Northern Cemetery), an elaborate 19th-century cemetery to the west across the E4 highway and north of Karolinska Sjukhuset hospital. Alfred Nobel, August Strindberg and Ingrid Bergman lie amid its hedges and landscaped hills.

Bus 3 or 52 will take you to Karolinska Sjukhuset from where you can walk to southern Hagaparken. For northern Haga, take the T-bana to Odenplan then catch bus 515 to the Haga Norra stop. Another way to explore Brunnsviken is by the vintage steamboat operated by **Stockholm Sightseeing/Ekoparken** (587 140 20, www.stockholmsightseeing.com, 80kr). It runs daily from late June to mid-August, with stops at **Stallmästeregården** (a hotel, restaurant and conference centre in the south-west corner of Brunnsviken), Bergianska Trädgården, **Naturhistoriska Riksmuseet** (*see p107*), **Kafé Sjöstugan** (in the north-east corner of the bay), Fjärilshuset and **Haga Slott** (*see above*).

Carl Eldhs Ateljémuseum

Lögebodavägen 10, Bellevueparken (612 65 60). *Bus 515, 40, 46, 52, 73.* **Open** (guided tours only) *Swedish* noon, 1pm, 2pm, 3pm. *English* 1.30pm June-Aug Tue-Sun; May, Sept Sat, Sun. Apr, Oct Sun. Nov-Mar by appointment. **Admission** 50kr; 25kr 7-18s; free under-7s. **No credit cards.** **Map** p309 A5.

Eldh's former studio, built by his friend, architect Ragnar Östberg (better known for designing the iconic Stadshuset), is now a museum containing more than 400 of the artist's works in plaster, clay, bronze and marble. On display are studies and original models of works around town, including the Olympic runners outside Stadion, the male and female figures by the Stadshuset waterfront and the Strindberg statue in Tegnérlunden park. As we went to press, this museum was experiencing financial problems and its future was uncertain; call in advance for an update.

Dead famous

Although the beautifully ornate **Norra begravningsplats** (Northern Cemetery; see p106) houses high-profile figures such as Alfred Nobel, Ingrid Bergman and August Strindberg, the city's most architecturally impressive place of eternal rest is **Skogskyrkogården** (The Woodland Cemetery; 1914-40), which was added to the UNESCO World Heritage Site list in 1994. Bucking the funereal trend of oppressive gloom, it's really a most agreeable cemetery, set in a forested landscape south of the city.

Gunnar Asplund and fellow architect Sigurd Lewerentz designed this cemetery after winning an international competition in 1915. Their design is remarkable for its successful marriage of functionalism and beauty, with chapels and graves merging harmoniously with tall pine trees and grassy open areas, unifying the natural landscape with the human constructions.

The **Skogskapellet** (chapel, 1918; pictured) is admired for its unexpectedly sunny and warm interior, while the gardens, sculptures, lily pond and three chapels comprising the **Skogskrematoriet** (crematorium; 1934-40) made it one of the 20th century's most noteworthy buildings.

Famous graves at Skogskyrkogården include those of Gunnar Asplund himself, as well as the enigmatic superstar Greta Garbo. For an exhibition on the cemetery and its architects, visit the Tallum Pavilion, south of the cemetery. At weekends bus 183 runs within the cemetery.

Swanky though **Norra begravningsplats** is, it isn't deemed exclusive enough for the Swedish royals. Members of the royal family were traditionally buried within the walls and floors of **Riddarholmskyrkan** (see p72), a stone's throw from the royal castle. Since 1910, the royal graveyard (Kungliga Begravningsplatsen) has been located on a small island in Hagaparken, which isn't open to the public.

Other key Stockholm graves include those of assassinated politicians Olof Palme and Anna Lindh, which attract numerous visitors. Palme's grave is in the cemetery at **Adolf Fredriks Kyrka** (see p76) in Norrmalm, not far from where he was gunned down. Lindh's demure marker at **Katarina Kyrka** (see p92) reflects the quiet modesty for which she was respected.

The Vikings left some of Sweden's most conspicuous grave markers. Those interested in Viking heritage should look out for the *gravfält* (grave mounds) dotting the countryside. Most impressively, three burial mounds, raised around AD 500, stand mightily at **Gamla Uppsala** (see pp244-53 **Day Trips**); they are only partially excavated, but appear to contain chieftains.

Skogskyrkogården

Sockenvägen 492, Enskede (508 301 00/508 301 93/kyrkogardsforvaltningen@ stockholm.se). T-bana Skogskyrkogarden/ bus 161. **Admission** free. *Tours 50kr (Swedish only).* **Open** 24hrs daily. *Talum Pavilion 11am-7.30pm Wed; 9am-5pm Thur-Sat; 10am-4pm Sun. Tours May-Aug 5pm Wed, from main entrance on Sockenvägen.*

Sightseeing

Foto Ann Lindberg/lou.b

The world famous museum

Living history, animals, traditions and handicraft

SKANSEN 🦁

www.skansen.se

Kopparlälten. *See p106.*

Sightseeing

Northern Frescati

You'll know you're in Frescati, a cluster of scientific and academic institutions on the eastern shore of Brunnsviken, by the sound of Roslagsvägen, a thoroughfare that cuts through northern Frescati and connects to the E18 to the north. On the west side of the highway (cross under the viaduct) is the Royal Swedish Academy of Sciences, and beyond that, the lovely gardens and conservatories of **Bergianska Trädgården** (*see below*), which borders Brunnsviken. On the east side stands the **Naturhistoriska Riksmuseet** (*see below*), while to the south, in Frescati, lies the sprawling campus of **Stockholm University**, relocated from cramped city quarters to this site in 1970. It is one of Sweden's largest universities with about 35,000 students. From the campus, head east to Ekoparken's **Norra Djurgården** for hiking, horse riding or bird watching, or take a ten-minute walk west to **Brunnsviksbadet**, a local beach, where you can swim or rent canoes.

You can get to northern Frescati on the T-bana to Universitetet, then walk north for about seven minutes. Alternatively, take the Roslagsbanan commuter train, which leaves from Stockholm's Östra station near the Tekniska Högskolan. Get off at Frescati station: the gardens and museum are directly to the west and east, respectively. If you continue on the Roslagsbanan for 15 minutes, you'll reach **Djursholm**, one of Sweden's wealthiest neighbourhoods.

Bergianska Trädgården

Frescati (545 917 00/www.bergianska.se). T-bana Universitetet/bus 40, 540. **Open** *Gardens* 9am-8pm daily. *Edvard Andersons Växthus* 11am-5pm daily. *Victoriahuset* May-Sept 11am-4pm Mon-Fri; 11am-5pm Sat, Sun. Closed Oct-Apr. **Admission** *Gardens* free. *Edvard Andersons Växthus* 40kr. *Victoriahuset* 15kr. Free under-15s. **Free with SC. Credit** MC, V.
Amateur botanists and picnickers will love this idyllic park and botanical garden on a hilly peninsula by Brunnsviken. The Royal Swedish Academy of Sciences, which still conducts research here, moved the garden from Vasastaden to this waterfront area in 1885. Orchids and vines fill Victoriahuset, a small conservatory (1900); its pond contains giant water lilies, measuring up to 2.5m (8ft) across. The more recent Edvard Andersons Växthus, an all-glass conservatory, contains Mediterranean plants and trees in its central room, and flora from Australia, South Africa, California and a rainforest in four corner rooms.

The paths outside curve around the shore and hills, giving you beautiful views of Haga Park across the water, and a chance to check out the 9,000 species of plants growing nearby. There's also a Japanese pond, the Gamla Orangeriet's summer café and the Plantagen nursery and garden supply shop.

Naturhistoriska Riksmuseet

Frescativägen 40 (51 95 40 00/www.nrm.se). T-bana Universitetet/bus 40, 540. **Open** *May, Midsummer-Aug* 10am-7pm Mon-Wed, Fri-Sun; 10am-8pm Thur. *Sept-Apr, June* 10am-7pm Tue, Wed, Fri-Sun; 10am-8pm Thur. **Admission** *Museum* 75kr; 50kr concessions; 50kr 6-18s; free under-6s. *IMAX* 75kr; 50kr 5-18s. *Museum & IMAX* 120kr; 105kr concessions; 80kr 6-18s. **Museum free with SC. Credit** AmEx, MC, V.

Large, dramatic sculptures at Lidingö's **Millesgården**.

Founded in 1739, the National Museum of Natural History is today the largest museum complex in Sweden. More than nine million biological and mineral samples are stored in this monolithic brick building designed in 1907 by Axel Anderberg, architect of the Royal Opera. Beneath the black-shingled roof and light-filled cupola stands an exceptionally well-made tableaux of extinct creatures, prehistoric man and Swedish wildlife. Visitors enter the dinosaur exhibit through a dark volcanic room to find sharp-toothed birds sitting in trees above a skeletal T-Rex and life-like Plateosaurus. The hands-on exhibits about space and the human body include a red Martian landscape, a spaceship's cockpit and a walk-through mouth. Many exhibits are labelled in Swedish only, so borrow a booklet in English from the information desk.

Sweden's only IMAX cinema, the Cosmonova (*see p200*), opened in 1993 and shows movies about the natural world on its huge screen – which also functions as a planetarium. Under-5s are not admitted. The gift shop sells science books, plastic animals and polished rocks. Note: this museum, along with several other state-run museums, is expected to have free admission by January 2005.

Lidingö

Lidingö is an island of suburban tranquillity, just north-east of the city centre, and is largely populated by Stockholm's wealthier classes. The main attraction is **Millesgården** (*see below*), the former home and studio of the sculptor Carl Milles. Lidingö is also the birthplace of Raoul Wallenberg, the World War II Swedish diplomat who disappeared mysteriously in 1945 while in Soviet custody. Sculptures around the island have been erected in his honour.

Understandably, Lidingö is popular with outdoor enthusiasts: there's golf near Sticklinge and at Ekholmsnäs; cycling and jogging paths, which become cross-country ski trails in winter, at Stockby Motionsgård; and one of the nearest downhill ski slopes to Stockholm at the 70-metre high (230-foot) Ekholmsnäsbacken, south of the Hustegafjärden inlet. The beach at Fågelöuddebadet, in Lidingö's north-east corner, has a café and miniature golf course, as do the Breviksbadet outdoor pools in the south.

Millesgården

Heserudsvägen 32 (446 75 90/www.millesgarden.se). T-bana Ropsten then bus 207 or bus 201, 202, 204, 205, 206, 207, 212 to Torsvik then walk. **Open** *Mid May-Aug* 10am-5pm daily. *Sept-mid May* noon-4pm Tue-Fri; 11am-5pm Sat, Sun. **Admission** 75kr; 60kr concessions; 20kr 7-16s; free under-7s. **Free with SC**. **Credit** AmEx, MC, V.
Works by sculptor Carl Milles (1875-1955) are displayed at his home and studio, which he donated to the state in 1936. His bronze statues stand alongside works by other artists on wide stone terraces, and its hilltop setting provides a dramatic backdrop of sky, land and water. The house is decorated with paintings, drawings and antiques purchased by Milles on his travels – he amassed the largest private collection of Greek and Roman statues in Sweden. The studio was not as tranquil as it appears today during three days in 1917, when Milles decided to destroy all his work and start again from scratch. After emigrating to the US in 1931, he became a professor of art in Michigan, where he created more than 70 sculptures – the nudes often had to be fitted with fig leaves. An adjacent exhibition hall, which houses the gift shop, features contemporary and classic modern art.

Eat, Drink, Shop

Restaurants

There's a lot more than just pickled herring these days in Stockholm's smashing smörgåsbord.

Trend is the name of the game on the restaurant scene in Stockholm. This is mainly – if not entirely (the Swedes are renowned for being terribly trend-sensitive all round) – because the city lacks a deep-rooted restaurant culture. Having discovered the joys of fine dining about 20 years ago, Stockholmers have certainly been making up for lost time: restaurant numbers doubled in the 1990s and new places are constantly springing up, vying for the attentions of a new generation of enthusiastic diners.

Without a restaurant tradition to preserve, Swedes tend to latch on feverishly to the latest food fads. Subsequently, Stockholm has a disproportionately large number of expensive and experimental restaurants with designer decor, and not so many time-honoured classics. A few years ago, Asian fusion swept over the restaurant scene (and is still very popular); then came traditional Swedish cooking, known as *husmanskost* (see *p118* **Native nosh**); and lately all the restaurants *du jour* have been focusing on tapas and meat. French and Mediterranean influences are also prevalent, and increasingly more chefs are finding their way back to the classic brasserie in terms of concept and cookery, attracting a wide audience with unpretentious service and menus that cater for most wallets.

Luckily, though, Stockholm's restaurant scene isn't all flightiness – there are also a few well-worn, established places that have done their thing for decades and still do it well (**Pelikan** on Södermalm is one; see *p127*). Traditional Swedish cuisine is well worth seeking out – it is deliciously healthy, with plenty of fresh, locally caught fish, berries and generous use of herbs like dill and parsley.

Stockholm is an increasingly cosmopolitan city, with a selection of Thai, Malaysian, Kurdish, Caribbean, Sichuanese and Lebanese restaurants. They tend to cater to Swedes, so authenticity levels are not as high as cities with larger immigrant communities, but standards are generally high.

The focal point of the restaurant scene is **Stureplan**, but the widespread gentrification of Stockholm in recent years means that good restaurants can be found all over the city. These days you're just as likely to have an expensive dinner in the formerly working-class neighbourhood of **Södermalm** – where the

restaurant scene has metamorphosed recently – as you are in upper-class **Östermalm**. Residential **Kungsholmen** and **Vasastaden** are packed with good neighbourhood restaurants. Given its charm, location and the scores of well-heeled tourists pounding its streets, you would expect **Gamla Stan** to be filled with good restaurants, but it's not. That cute-looking place tucked away in one of the cobbled alleyways is most likely to be a tourist trap serving predictable food.

The best Restaurants

For all that jazz
Glenn Miller Café and Nalen (for both, see *p117*).

For Middle Eastern cuisine
Halv Grek Plus Turk, Phénicia (for both, see *p129*) or Tabbouli (see *p132*).

For going Asian
Ki Mama (see *p121*), Halv Trappa plus Gård (see *p127*), Miyako (see *p127*) or Zense (see *p122*).

For trad Swedish food
Bakfickan (see *p117*), Godthem (see *p124*), Mäster Anders (see *p132*) or Prinsen (see *p130*).

For cheap eats
Chutney (see *p127*), Crêperie Fyra Knop (see *p126*), Yu Love Bibimbap (see *p124*) and Zucchero (see *p126*).

If you win the lottery
Edsbacka Krog (see *p132*), Franska Matsalen (see *p115*), Mistral (see *p113*), Operakällaren (see *p117*) or Pontus in the Green House (see *p113*).

For minimalism, Swedish style
Grill (see *p123*) or Lux (see *p132*).

For when you're sick of minimalism, Swedish style
Cliff Barnes (see *p123*), Glenn Miller Café (see *p117*) and Mäster Anders (see *p132*).

There are a few great restaurants in the Old Town, but for gastronomic exploration, you'd better look elsewhere.

A FEW TIPS

The restaurants of the moment are always packed, so it can sometimes be a battle to find a free table, even on weekdays. For the most popular places, you should book in advance, especially for Fridays and Saturdays. Locals are also driven by pay day, for most the 25th of every month – in the preceding days the restaurants are deserted, only to be filled when pay day comes. Be aware that many of the better restaurants close in July for summer holidays.

Children are welcome everywhere, even in the smartest restaurants, and many places provide high chairs and kids' menus. From 1 June 2005, all restaurants in Sweden will be, by law, smoke-free. For more information on the new law, *see p135* **Up in smoke**.

Many restaurants will have a version of the menu in English, but at the ones that don't, most waiting staff will be happy to translate. For food terms, *see p291* **Vocabulary**.

PRICES, TIMING AND TIPPING

It is expensive to eat out in Stockholm, partly because people tend to go to a restaurant to have a whole new food experience rather than for just a simple well-cooked meal in an informal environment. This, of course, has an effect on the atmosphere, as well as the prices – places can often be more pretentious than cosy. In addition, don't expect restaurants serving Swedish food to be automatically cheaper; local cuisine appears at the upper end of the price scale, alongside French or Italian. If you're looking for a budget meal, your best bet is Indian, Thai or Turkish.

If you're after cheap, fast food on the go, burgers, kebabs, hot dogs and paninis can be bought in most neighbourhoods. More traditional but rarer are the Swedish *strömming* stands (such as the one on Odengatan by the Stadsbiblioteket), which serve delicious fried fish on a piece of bread.

For something fancy at a reasonable price, it's a good idea to have your main meal at lunchtime rather than in the evening. Most Stockholmers eat a proper meal between noon and 1pm, when many restaurants swap their à la carte menu for a fixed-price menu at a considerably lower price – look out for signs offering 'Dagens Lunch' or 'Dagens Rätt'. In the evening, people tend to eat early, around 7-8pm. Most kitchens close around 11pm, even if the restaurant's bar stays open later.

Service is always included in the bill, but it's still quite common to tip up to ten per cent on top. If the food or service is in any way sub-standard, however, it's quite acceptable to leave no tip at all.

Gamla Stan

Contemporary

Mistral

Lilla Nygatan 21 (10 12 24). T-bana Gamla Stan/ bus 3, 53, 59. **Open** 6pm-1am Tue-Fri. **Set menus** 605kr-805kr. **Credit** AmEx, DC, MC, V. **Map** p305 J7.
One of Stockholm's best – and tiniest – restaurants, Mistral offers a thoroughly entertaining and slightly peculiar dining experience. The love child of two young restaurateurs – chef Fredrik Andersson and maître d' Björn Vasseur, both of whom are a constant presence in the open kitchen and 18-seat dining room – Mistral is so personal that it almost feels like someone's home. Fortunately, quite the opposite of down-home cooking, the food is fascinatingly eccentric and always very good. The wine pairings are chosen with care, and even if the bill tends to end on a high note (around 1,500kr per person), the whole experience feels worth it. Given its diminutive size, this is not the place for an intimate tête-à-tête, but rather for a culinary experience of the highest order. Reserve several weeks in advance.

Pontus in the Green House

Österlånggatan 17 (23 85 00/www.pontusfrithiof. com). T-bana Gamla Stan/bus 2, 43, 55, 71, 76. **Open** *Mid Aug-May* 11.30am-3pm, 6-11pm Mon-Fri; 6-11pm Sat. *May-mid Aug* 6-11pm Mon-Fri; 5-11pm Sat. **Main courses** 325kr-450kr. **Set menus** 895kr; 1,200kr. **Credit** AmEx, DC, MC, V. **Map** p305 J8.
If you close a business deal, launch a successful takeover bid or just happen to win the lottery while in Stockholm, this is the place to burn a substantial share of the profits. Upstairs there is a luxury French restaurant of the highest order, where truffles, foie gras, Iranian caviar and other exclusive ingredients are given the full works. You might as well go for the *rustique* tasting menu – a bit steep at 1,200kr *sans* wine, but guaranteed to be a memorable experience. The Greenhouse Bar downstairs is literally and figuratively more down to earth. Here you can get a taste of the kitchen's abilities without emptying your wallet; the menu consists exclusively of starters, most of which share ingredients with the food upstairs, but cost around 100kr. In the summer, only the bar is open for dining.

French/American

Bistro Ruby & Grill Ruby

Österlånggatan 14 (20 60 15/57 76/www.bistro ruby.com). T-bana Gamla Stan/bus 2, 43, 55, 59, 76. **Open** *Restaurant* 5-11pm daily. *Brunch* 1-3pm Sat. *Bar* 5pm-1am daily. Closed 2wks July. **Main courses** *Bistro Ruby* 165kr-263kr. *Grill Ruby* 93kr-395kr. **Credit** AmEx, DC, MC, V. **Map** p305 J8.
These two sister restaurants set out to combine Paris and Texas. Bistro Ruby offers European formality in a classically pleasant environment ideal for a quiet chat. The menu goes from classic French

to more modern Mediterranean influences, and it's all well cooked, tasty and not overworked. Next door, Grill Ruby is noisier and more fun, and it's all about meat – grilled with love and served in huge quantities – so vegetarians should steer clear. With each piece of meat you get a wide choice of tapas, salsas, sauces and other accompaniments. The weekend brunch is recommended.

Brasserie by the Sea

Skeppsbronkajen Tullhus 2 (20 20 95/www.pontus frithiof.com). T-bana Kungsträdgården or Gamla Stan/bus 2, 43, 55, 71, 76. **Open** *Restaurant* noon-3pm, 5-11pm Mon-Fri; 4-11pm Sat, Sun. *Bar* noon-1am Mon-Sat; noon-11pm Sun. **Main courses** 165kr-295kr. **Credit** AmEx, DC, MC, V. **Map** p305 J8.
In the middle of the Skeppsbron quay, in a huge, old customs building, this is a slightly folky establishment with one of Stockholm's best waterfront views (except when there's a cruise ship moored in front). When the sun shines, this is one of the city's most popular places for a beer and a bite to eat. Regrettably, it has a strong expense account ambience, and the French food is decent but priced slightly beyond its station. Owned by the same people as Pontus in the Green House (*see p113*).

Traditional Swedish

Den Gyldene Freden

Österlånggatan 51 (24 97 60/www.gyldenefreden.se). T-bana Gamla Stan/bus 2, 43, 55, 59, 76. **Open** 6-11pm Mon-Fri; 1pm-midnight Sat. **Main courses** 115kr-345kr. **Credit** AmEx, DC, MC, V. **Map** p305 J8.
This first-class restaurant is housed in an 18th-century building owned by the Swedish Academy, and there is something reverently grandiose about the gloomy interior. Since it first opened in 1722, large

sections of Stockholm's cultural elite have dined here – singer-poet Carl Michael Bellman, painter Anders Zorn and singer-composer Evert Taube are all said to have been regular customers. Head chef Ulf Kappen focuses on Swedish ingredients (pike-perch, reindeer, duck) and methods, but does so with creative joy and skill, even if we have noticed some signs of a slight slacking off in the kitchen of late. The menu contains some obvious classics, foremost among them the stuffed pig's trotters, and also offers vegetarian dishes.

Norrmalm

Asian

Buddha Dining & Bar

Biblioteksgatan 9 (54 51 85 00/www.buddha.se). T-bana Östermalmstorg/bus 1, 2, 55, 56. **Open** *Restaurant* 11.30am-11pm Mon-Fri; 1-11pm Sat. *Bar* 11.30am-midnight Mon, Tue, Thur; 11.30-3am Wed; 11.30-4am Fri; 1pm-4am Sat. **Main courses** 159kr-234kr. **Set menus** 395kr; 455kr. **Credit** AmEx, DC, MC, V. **Map** p305 F8.
You can't beat the over-the-top kitsch decor at this restaurant, where interior designer Simon James has transformed a former movie theatre into an oriental oasis – a giant Buddha greets you as you step in. Somehow, the restaurant manages to carry it off, even with walls and ceilings painted deep red, flashing gold Buddhas on the wall and the explosion of oriental pillows and carpets. The sushi here is superbly prepared, as is the dim sum, and dishes make inventive use of Asian flavours and spices. It's open for lunch, too, although the food then is unremarkable continental fare. A welcome alternative to the traditional Swedish fare that dominates this part of town.

Bon Lloc. *See p115.*

Contemporary

Berns Salonger

Berzelii Park (56 63 22 22/www.berns.se). T-bana Kungsträdgården/bus 2, 47, 55, 69, 76. **Open** *Sept-July* 11.30am-3pm Mon, Sun; 11.30am-3pm, 5-11pm Tue-Thur; 11.30am-3pm, 5-11.30pm Fri, Sat. *July-Sept* 11.30am-3pm Mon, Sun; 11.30am-3pm, 5-11pm Tue-Thur; 11.30am-11.30pm Fri; 1-11.30pm Sat. **Main courses** 195kr-315kr. **Credit** AmEx, DC, MC, V. **Map** p305 G8.

Eating here feels a bit like dining in a grand ballroom after most of the wedding party has departed for the reception in the lively disco upstairs, but Sir Terence Conran has done an admirable job at trying to soften and modernise this palatial restaurant and its jaw-dropping decor. The service is perfectly correct, if not particularly warm. The busy kitchen does its best to be industrious and innovative at the same time, producing a crossover cuisine anchored in the Mediterranean. The result is ambitious but the quality is sometimes uneven. The clientele consists mainly of well-dressed tourists and business people from the nearby financial district. The various bars (*see p135*) are always packed, and there's a boutique hotel attached (*see p45*).

Bon Lloc

Regeringsgatan 111 (660 60 60/www.bonlloc.rgsth. com). T-bana Rådmansgatan/bus 2, 42, 43, 44, 52. **Open** *Restaurant* 6-11pm Mon-Sat. *Bar* 5pm-midnight Mon-Sat. Closed July. **Main courses** *Restaurant* 345kr-360kr. *Bar* 125kr-210kr. **Set menus** 545kr-1,150kr. **Credit** AmEx, DC, MC, V. **Map** p309 E7.

Bon Lloc ('Good Place' in Catalan) is definitely the most avant-garde restaurant in town, and is rated by many as Sweden's top restaurant. Chef Mathias Dahlgren has been perfecting his '*estilo nuevo euro*

Latino' cuisine for years and can be credited with kicking off the tapas frenzy that has gripped Stockholm's food scene of late. As you enter this renovated theatre, with its hardwood floors and recessed spotlighting, and take your seat in the stage-like dining area, it's clear that a stellar culinary performance awaits. From the classy brown paper bag of homemade fries that arrives with your pre-dinner drink, to the refresher course of grapefruit sorbet served in a tiny bottle with a straw, it's obvious that Dahlgren and company have a good time in the kitchen. The tapas menu is far superior to its many imitators, and the friendly waiters possess encyclopaedic knowledge of the impressive Spanish wine list. Such quality doesn't come cheap and it's best to reserve your table well in advance.

Franska Matsalen

Grand Hôtel, Blasieholmshamnen 8 (679 35 84/ www.franskamatsalen.com). T-bana Kungsträdgården/ bus 2, 55, 59, 62, 65. **Open** 11.30am-2pm, 6-11pm Mon-Fri; 6-11pm Sat. **Main courses** 225kr-525kr. **Set menus** 625kr-895kr. **Credit** AmEx, DC, MC, V. **Map** p305 G8.

Dining in Stockholm doesn't come any grander than at this classic French dining room in the Grand Hôtel, overlooking the Royal Palace and the harbour. Chef Roland Persson makes good on Franska's promise of world-class French cuisine prepared with the most luxurious of ingredients, but not every dish is worth its exorbitant price tag. A good bet is to go for a set menu, or the always exquisite chateaubriand, and then sit back and enjoy the impeccable service and the muted conversation of the well-to-do clientele. On occasions, guest chefs perform in Franska's open kitchen – always a good show.

Fredsgatan 12

Konstakademien, Fredsgatan 12 (24 80 52/www. fredsgatan12.com). T-bana T-Centralen/bus 3, 53, 59, 62, 65. **Open** *Aug-June* 11.30am-2pm Mon-Fri; 5pm-1am Mon-Sat. **Tapas** 120kr-235kr. **Set menus** 660kr, 990kr. **Credit** AmEx, DC, MC, V. **Map** p305 H7.

Despite all the rave reviews in the press and its award-winning status, we consider F12 to be one of the most overrated restaurants in town. It may be one of Stockholm's most stylish, but trendiness appears sometimes to have trumped good cooking. The menu, divided into five themes, requires extensive explanation, and each dish is presented tapas style, so in order to satisfy an appetite for an average three-course dinner, you need to order at least four to five dishes. True, each dish looks like a miniature food sculpture, but we sometimes feel that the food is prepared with more precision than feeling, and the portions are insultingly small. The clientele are mostly chic young professionals who don't bat an eyelid at the bill before handing over the plastic. The setting, in the Royal Academy of Art (*see p74*), just across the water from the parliament building and Gamla Stan, is spectacular. Our advice? Skip the pricey dinner and head straight for the popular outdoor terrace bar.

BERNS

Berns Restaurant. Tel: +46(0)8 566 322 22. Fax: +46(0)8 566 323 23. restaurant.reservation@berns.se
Berzelii Park. P.O. Box 16340. SE-103 27 Stockholm, Sweden. www.berns.se

Berns, the China Theatre and Grand Hôtel Stockholm are part of Grand Hôtel Holdings

Operakällaren

Kungliga Operan, Karl XIIs Torg (676 58 01/ www.operakallaren.se). T-bana Kungsträdgården/ bus 2, 55, 59, 62, 76. **Open** *Aug-June* 6-10pm daily. **Main courses** 250kr-420kr. **Set menus** 895kr; 1,150kr. **Credit** AmEx, DC, MC, V. **Map** p305 G7.

Operakällaren is without doubt one of Sweden's best restaurants, with the history and setting to match. As the name (Opera Cellar) implies, this restaurant is located in the opera house, which has been open for business since 1787 – although the present building was erected in 1895, from which time the dining room's interior dates. The present restaurant was created in the 1960s by legendary chef Tore Wretman, who more than any other person is responsible for turning the Swedes into foodies. Today you'll find mouthwatering dishes such as black turbot with potato and leek purée, or roast French pigeon with hazelnuts, sweet and sour lentils and vegetable ragout. The desserts here are sublime, particularly the cloudberry gazpacho with almond milk sorbet. This is a luxury establishment on all counts – food, service and wine. And make no mistake, the prices are equally spectacular, with main courses averaging a hard-to-swallow 400kr. Dress to impress.

Restaurangen™

Oxtorgsgatan 14 (22 09 52/www.restaurangentm. com). T-bana Hötorget/bus 1, 43, 52, 56. **Open** *Early Aug-June* 11.30am-2pm, 5pm-1am Mon-Fri; 5pm-1am Sat. (Kitchen closes 11pm). Closed July-early Aug. **Set menus** 275kr; 375kr; 475kr. **Credit** AmEx, DC, MC, V. **Map** p305 F7.

This trend-setting restaurant is not quite as trendy now as when it first opened a few years ago – mainly because tapas-style dining is now popping up everywhere in Stockholm – but its unique dining concept is still drawing a crowd. Chef Melker Andersson, whose creative cooking has brought flair to Restaurangen and its sister establishments Grill (*see p123*) and F12 (*see p115*), dreamed up the ambitious menu, divided into 15 tastes as exhibited in 15 different dishes. Bitter, sour, soy, juniper berry, ginger – each diner creates his or her own rainbow of tastes. Three, five or seven small dishes make up the whole meal, with your choice of a wine (available by the glass) for each course. Restaurangen has unmissable stuff for the adventurous gourmet, but those who prefer cosiness will find it all rather pretentious.

Mediterranean

Glenn Miller Café

Brunnsgatan 21A (10 03 22/www.glennmillercafe. com). T-bana Hötorget/bus 1, 43, 52, 56. **Open** *Restaurant* 5-10.30pm Mon-Sat. *Bar* 5pm-midnight Mon-Thur; 5pm-1am Fri, Sat. **Main courses** 90kr-175kr. **Credit** MC, V. **Map** p305 E7.

This tiny place is a sympathetic bistro for anyone on the lookout for reasonably priced food in a relaxed environment, with jazz performances (*see p215*) some nights as the perfect accompaniment. There are only a few seats and it doesn't take much to pack the place, but the service is personal and the food well cooked. The blackboard lists several starters and main courses, most of them rustic French. Unpretentious restaurants like this are becoming exceedingly hard to find in Stockholm; we hope they don't change a thing.

Traditional Swedish

Bakfickan

Kungliga Operan, Karl XIIs Torg (676 58 09/ www.operakallaren.se). T-bana Kungsträdgården/bus 2, 55, 59, 62, 65. **Open** 11.30am-11.30pm Mon-Fri; noon-11.30pm Sat. **Main courses** 95kr-198kr. **Credit** AmEx, DC, MC, V. **Map** p305 G7.

In the opera house, alongside Operakällaren (*see above*) and Operabaren (*see below*) you'll find Bakfickan (the hip pocket), the little brother of the trio that shares the same giant kitchen. Head here if you've been turned away from the more upscale Opera establishments because you're wearing trainers. Sit at the large counter stretching around the tiny room to eat a late supper of *köttbullar* (meatballs) with a beer, while listening to the opera singers discuss the evening's performance. We're not gone on the salads, but everything else is good-quality traditional Swedish cooking.

Nalen

Regeringsgatan 74 (50 52 92 01/www.nalen.com). T-bana Hötorget/bus 1, 43, 52, 56. **Open** 11.30am-11pm Mon-Fri; 5-11pm Sat. Closed July. **Main courses** 150kr-195kr. **Set menu** 395kr. **Credit** AmEx, DC, MC, V. **Map** p305 E7.

This restaurant – formerly the Grand National – shares space with the old jazz haunt Nalen (*see p215*), which has seen a revival in recent years, and it's worth scouting out even if you're not coming for the entertainment. Nalen offers classic Swedish cuisine with the best of native ingredients, like reindeer, pike-perch and herring, at reasonable prices. The attentive staff anticipate your every need in the sober, sophisticated dining room. The menu even highlights dishes that are safe for those with food allergies, a rare courtesy in Stockholm. The Irish coffee is among the best in town.

Operabaren

Kungliga Operan, Karl XIIs Torg (676 58 08/ www.operakallaren.se). T-bana Kungsträdgården/ bus 2, 55, 59, 62, 65. **Open** Mid Aug-1st wk July 11.30am-3pm, 5pm-1am Mon-Wed; 11.30am-3pm, 5pm-2am Thur, Fri; 12.30pm-2am Sat. **Main courses** 139kr-243kr. **Set menus** 420kr; 495kr; 375kr. **Credit** AmEx, DC, MC, V. **Map** p305 G7.

If you're visiting the opera house but can't stretch to Operakällaren's (*see above*) prices, there is always this place, which is particularly good for Saturday lunch. Sitting in the old leather sofas is like travelling back in time – the white-jacketed waiters seem

Native nosh

Fish

Herring – called **sill** on the west coast and **strömming** in Stockholm – used to be the staple food of the Swedish diet. Today, this little fish is still much loved and always on the menu, in the cheapest lunch restaurant and the poshest luxury establishment. For lunch it's often blackened (*sotare*) and served with mashed potatoes, melted butter and perhaps lingonberry sauce. Don't be put off by the sweet lingonberries: all the savoury traditional foods are served with sweet preserves and sauces – and it tastes great.

Inlagd strömming (pickled herring) is prepared in almost as many different ways as there are Swedes. If you manage to find a traditional Swedish *smörgåsbord* (available in every single restaurant around Christmas), this is what you should start with, before moving on to the meats. A plate of pickled herring and fresh new potatoes with special soured cream (*gräddfil*) will make any Swede foggy-eyed, while **gravad strömming** (pickled herring cured with a mustard sauce) is indispensable for celebrating Midsummer. Served, of course, with some beer and aquavit, a strong liqueur distilled from potato or grain mash and flavoured with caraway seeds (*kalled snaps*).

Red **kräftor** (crayfish) are eaten everywhere when the season starts in August, when there are crayfish parties galore (preferably outside under a full moon). Cooked with huge amounts of dill, they're an unmissable special treat.

Lax (salmon) needs no introduction: just remember that **gravlax** means cured with sugar and salt, not to be confused with the smoked variety. Fish from inland lakes and the Baltic are relatively rare, the most delicious being the **gös** (pike-perch). However, plenty of fish from the west coast lands on the plates of Stockholm's restaurants, and **torsk** (cod), although more and more scarce, is a vital part of Swedish culinary tradition

and is served in many different ways. The most interesting is **lutfisk**, which is only served around Christmas. The cod is salted and air-dried, then soaked in lye, which transforms it into something that looks and tastes nothing like fish. It's served with peas, butter and a béchamel sauce.

Meat

Swedish **köttbullar** (meatballs) are, of course, a speciality, immortalised not least by the Swedish chef in *The Muppet Show*. They're eaten with pickled cucumber, a cream sauce and lingonberries. Bar-restaurant **Kvarnen** (*see p139*) is the right place to go for this most Swedish of dishes.

Pytt i panna is regularly found in most restaurants: it consists of diced and fried meat and potatoes, adorned with a fried egg and pickled beetroots. **Rimmad oxbringa** (lightly salted brisket of beef) is beautifully tender. Anything with '*rimmad*' attached to it means that it is first salted and then boiled.

Kåldolmar (stuffed cabbage rolls) are made Swedish by wrapping cabbage leaves rather than vine leaves around minced pork. The concept was introduced to Sweden when King Karl XII was stranded in Turkey after attempting, and failing, to invade Russia in 1708.

Game, such as **älg** (elk) and **rådjur** (roe deer), are popular in the autumn. They are mainly roasted and served with potatoes, lingonberries and a cream sauce.

Schnapps

Stockholmers use every possible excuse to drink a glass or more of *brännvin* (schnapps). It comes in numerous varieties, highly flavoured with native herbs and spices such as caraway, aniseed, coriander and fennel. The traditional way to drink *brännvin* is to fill the first glass to the brim, the second one halfway. Before downing the glasses, it's customary to sing a *snapsvisa* ('schnapps ditty'). *Skål!*

Eat, Drink, Shop

The Grand Veranda.

For nearly 90 years the Grand Veranda in the front of the hotel have been the natural meeting place in Stockholm. This is a first class restaurant where both traditional Swedish dishes and foreign specialities are on the menu. The smörgåsbord buffet is served all year round.

GRAND HÔTEL
STOCKHOLM – SWEDEN

Grand Hôtel • S. Blasieholmshamnen 8 • P.O. Box 16424, SE-103 27 Stockholm, Sweden
Tel +46 (0)8 679 35 00 • Fax +46 (0)8 611 86 86
info@grandhotel.se • www.grandhotel.se
Grand Hôtel Stockholm, Berns and the China Theatre are part of Grand Hôtel Holdings

Grill. *See p123.*

to have been here since the master carpenters created the magnificent Jugendstil interior. This is the place for excellent Swedish *husmanskost* (*see p118*) and schnapps. The indoor restaurant closes for lunch whenever the weather is warm enough to sit outdoors – it shares an outside dining area with Bakfickan (*see p117*). Don't underestimate the skill of the bartenders; they may look olde worlde, but they make a mean Bellini.

Vasastaden

One of Stockholm's best streets for a spot of spur-of-the-moment dining is **Rörstrandsgatan**, which is lined with restaurants from every corner of the globe. Two good choices are **Paus** (No.18, 34 44 05), and **Norrbacken** (Norrbackagatan 30, 31 25 90); both are ambitious neighbourhood restaurants serving well-prepared, modern Swedish cuisine.

African

Abyssinia
Vanadisvägen 20 (33 08 40). T-bana St Eriksplan/bus 3, 4, 70, 73, 77. **Open** 11am-11pm Mon-Sun. **Main courses** 85kr-165kr. **Credit** MC, V. **Map** p308 C4.
This is one of the best places in Stockholm to try *injera*, the pancake-like bread that serves as the base for most Ethiopian and Eritrean food. The Ethiopian food served at Abyssinia is unpretentious and delicious. You eat with your hands and, if you so wish, you can wash it down with Ethiopian wine. The Abyssinia special, a selection of almost 15 dishes, is well worth trying.

Asian

Ki Mama
Observatoriegatan 13 (33 34 82). T-bana Odenplan/bus 2, 3, 40, 47, 53. **Open** 11.30am-9pm Mon-Fri; 3-9pm Sun. **Main courses** 65kr-95kr. **Credit** MC, V. **Map** p309 D5.
Stockholm's best sushi, hands down. There's a good selection of fish in normal-sized pieces (this is very rare in Sweden, where the sushi tends to be too big to eat in one bite), and reasonable prices. There are some basic but well-prepared Japanese and Korean dishes such as *maguro-don, kari* and *chige*. Rightly popular among locals, for obvious reasons.

Koreana
Luntmakargatan 76 (15 77 08). T-bana Rådmansgatan/bus 2, 4, 42, 43, 52, 72. **Open** 11am-9pm Mon-Fri; 1-9pm Sat. **Main courses** 65kr-140kr. **No credit cards. Map** p309 D6.
This is one of several excellent Asian restaurants on Luntmakargatan. Come here for cheap, fast and authentic Korean food, including *bibimbap* (seasoned vegetables and egg on rice) or *bulgogi* (barbecued beef). The selection of sushi, though good, is more mainstream. Lunchtime is busy and very affordable. For a more upmarket Korean meal, try Arirang (No.65, 673 32 25), which is a few blocks up the street.

Lao Wai
Luntmakargatan 74 (673 78 00). T-bana Rådmansgatan/bus 2, 4, 42, 46, 52, 72. **Open** 11.30am-2pm, 5.30-9pm Tue-Fri; 5.30-9pm Sat. Closed July-mid Aug, 24 Dec-mid Jan. **Main courses** 85kr-175kr. **Credit** AmEx, DC, MC, V. **Map** p309 D6.

Stockholm's best vegetarian restaurant is a bit hidden away, but it's worth seeking out. The base is Chinese, but with influences from several other Asian cuisines. You won't find any meat or animal products; tofu, soya and loads of fresh vegetables take their place. Anyone thinking that veggie restaurants are boring is soon set straight – try the Jian Chang tofu (smoked tofu with shiitake mushrooms, sugar peas and fresh spices). At lunchtime, the menu is reduced to only one option.

Lilla Pakistan

St Eriksgatan 66 (30 56 46/www.lillapakistan.com). T-bana St Eriksplan/bus 3, 4, 70, 72, 77. **Open** 5-10pm Tue-Thur; 5-11pm Fri, Sat. **Main courses** 110kr-285kr. **Credit** AmEx, DC, MC, V. **Map** p308 E3.
Unlike most Indian restaurants in Stockholm, Little Pakistan offers authentic Pakistani and northern Indian dishes. Everything is tasty and well prepared, right down to the *amuse-bouches*. The slightly stuffy staff are aware that their restaurant is no ordinary curry house. Unfortunately, quality comes at a price.

Malaysia

Luntmakargatan 98 (673 56 69). T-bana Rådmansgatan/bus 2, 4, 42, 43, 52, 72. **Open** 10am-10pm Mon-Thur; 10am-11pm Fri; noon-11pm Sat; noon-10pm Sun. Closed 2wks July. **Main courses** 150kr-250kr. **Credit** AmEx, DC, MC, V. **Map** p309 C6.
This restaurant, situated at the end of a row of Asian restaurants on Luntmakargatan (Koreana and Lao Wai are further along the street; for both, *see p121*), is an eye-opener. All the exotic ingredients – kelp, tapioca and curry leaves – are prepared with care

and served with a friendly smile. It's not cheap, but it's worth the expense. There's a very ambitious vegetarian selection.

Narknoi

Odengatan 94 (30 70 70/www.narknoi.nu). T-bana St Eriksplan/bus 3, 4, 47, 53, 65, 72. **Open** 11am-3pm, 5-11pm Mon-Fri; 4-11pm Sat, Sun. **Main courses** 127kr-196kr. **Set menus** 215kr; 255kr. **Credit** AmEx, DC, MC, V. **Map** p308 D4.
A reliable Thai located between Odenplan and St Eriksplan, Narknoi has lime-green walls and is upbeat but not pretentious. The menu has all the compulsory favourites: green curry, lemongrass dishes, noodles. It may seem traditional, but it's not dull – Narknoi knows its stuff without falling into the trap of clichés. The crowd is diverse, and includes locals and visitors.

Zense

Kungstensgatan 9 (20 66 99/www.zense.se). T-bana Rådmansgatan/bus 2, 42, 43, 44, 52. **Open** 11am-1.45pm Mon-Fri; 5-10.30pm Mon-Thur; 5-11.30pm Fri, Sat. **Main courses** 110kr-170kr. **Set menu** 255kr. **Credit** AmEx, DC, MC, V. **Map** p309 D6.
The art of Asian noodles, New York style, is brought to perfection at elegant Zense. Try the delicate plum sauce with spring rolls or the zing of shrimp and egg noodle red curry, bathed in coconut milk. The food is fresh, innovative and satisfying, and is just as outstanding in the dessert stakes: coconut, lime and mango in soups, cookies or sorbets melt on the tongue. The minimalist decor lends a certain Zen-like calm, as do the quietly attentive waiters. Open for lunch and for takeaways in the evenings.

Bistro Sud. *See p124.*

Contemporary

Cliff Barnes

Norrtullsgatan 45 (31 80 70/www.cliff.se). T-bana Odenplan/bus 2, 40, 52, 65, 70. **Open** *Restaurant* 11am-11pm Mon-Fri; 6-11pm Sat. *Bar* 11am-1am Mon-Fri; 6pm-1am Sat. **Main courses** 127kr-185kr. **Credit** AmEx, MC, V. **Map** p308 C4.

If the cool, sleek side of Stockholm starts to get to you, come here to meet regular Swedes being after-work happy, drinking beer (lots of it) and eating good and well-priced food of American inspiration. It's a Margarita pitcher kind of a place, so it gets loud as the nights wears on. The party often starts – and ends – here. Named after JR's rival in *Dallas. See also p137.*

Dining Club

Gästrikegatan 3 (34 15 15/www.diningclub.se). T-bana St Eriksplan/bus 3, 4, 47, 70, 72. **Open** *Restaurant* 5-10.30pm Mon-Sun. **Main courses** 170kr-190kr. **Credit** AmEx, DC, MC, V. **Map** p308 D3.

A smallish restaurant aiming to become the watering hole for Vasastaden's young media elite. The credentials of the owners and staff (most come from Lydmar Hotel; *see p58*) and a few rave reviews have created some hype. The food is indeed good, but not always great, and it tends to be a tad on the expensive side. There's a sleek lounge bar in the basement.

Grill

Drottninggatan 89 (31 45 30/www.grill.se). T-bana Rådmansgatan/bus 40, 47, 52, 65. **Open** *Restaurant* 11.30am-2pm Mon-Sat; 4-11pm Sun. *Bar* 11.30am-1am Mon-Sat; 4pm-midnight Sun. **Main courses** 185kr-340kr. **Credit** AmEx, DC, MC, V. **Map** p309 E6.

This is yet another creation of Melker Andersson, the man behind F12 (*see p115*) and Restaurangen (*see p117*), who has the unusual ability to grasp the basics of both great cooking and efficient marketing. Grill, with its sleek look and its focus on all sorts of grilled meat (*forno al legno*, BBQ, charcoal and rotisserie), leans towards the crowd-pleasing end of the spectrum rather than being gastronomically innovative. The meat-heavy food is good if rather expensive, and guests seem to enjoy themselves.

Rolfs Kök

Tegnérgatan 41 (10 16 96/www.rolfskok.se). T-bana Rådmansgatan/bus 40, 47, 52, 65. **Open** *Restaurant* 11am-11pm Mon-Fri; 5-11.45pm Sat, Sun. *Bar* 11am-1pm Mon-Fri; 5pm-1am Sat, Sun. **Main courses** 155kr-285kr. **Credit** AmEx, DC, MC, V. **Map** p309 E5.

A favourite haunt for nearby publishers and advertising executives, this is a Swedish modern design classic and well worth a visit for both the food and decor. Chairs hang on the grey concrete walls, to be quickly taken down if more diners arrive – on some nights, it all becomes one long table. Solo eaters are lined up at the long bar overlooking the open kitchen. Enjoy fresh fish with tender meat, East Asian ideas combined with southern European

tricks. The creative somersaults usually succeed, though sometimes aim too high. Even so, a visit to Rolfs Kök is always a highly pleasurable experience.

Tranan

Karlbergsvägen 14 (52 72 81 00/30 07 65/www.sture hofgruppen.se). T-bana Odenplan/bus 2, 4, 40, 69, 72. **Open** *Restaurant* 5-11.45pm Mon-Fri; 5-11.45pm Sat. *Bar* 5pm-1am Mon-Sat. **Main courses** 95kr-270kr. **Credit** AmEx, DC, MC, V. **Map** p309 D5.

Formerly a working-class pub, Tranan has drastically changed to reach out to the professionals that now inhabit Vasastaden. This has meant marrying classic Swedish food with French/modern styles, and keeping prices high (although the menu always includes staples below 100kr). This transformation has been managed remarkably well, and Tranan has become something of a modern Stockholm classic. The *isterband* (usually translated as 'lard sausage', but it's actually much tastier than that sounds) is great, as is the *silltallrik* (pickled herring). There's a trendy bar in the basement (*see p138*).

Eastern European

Piastowska

Tegnérgatan 5 (21 25 08). T-bana Rådmansgatan/ bus 2, 42, 43, 52. **Open** 6-11pm Mon-Sat; 11.30am-2pm Tue-Fri. **Main courses** 95kr-195kr. **Credit** MC, V. **Map** p309 D7.

This restaurant gives you a peek into the old Iron Curtain days, when the quite substantial Polish connection in Sweden's history somehow needed hiding. Behind a rather heavy door on the otherwise posh Tegnérgatan lies a re-creation of a Polish family restaurant, with lace tablecloths, photos of Polish soldiers on the walls and heavy but well-prepared Polish food. It's not a restaurant for bright summer evenings, but when the snow is falling, a soup, an entrecôte on a *placek* and Polish beer is just what the soul craves.

Mediterranean

Le Bistro de Wasahof

Dalagatan 46 (32 34 40/www.wasahof.se). T-bana Odenplan or St Eriksplan/bus 4, 40, 47, 53, 72. **Open** *Restaurant* 5-11pm Mon-Sat. *Bar* 5pm-1am Mon-Sat. **Main courses** 81kr-238kr. **Set menus** 285kr-913kr. **Credit** AmEx, DC, MC, V. **Map** p308 D4.

This classic French restaurant near Odenplan acts as a second home to many a writer, actor, singer and well-dressed wannabe. Wasahof is a bar and bistro, and its main contribution to the culinary scene is its seafood – it imports oysters from France and the Swedish west coast. Next door its hipper little sister Musslan (No.46, 34 64 10), meaning 'the clam', serves a younger crowd with the same menu.

Döden i grytan

Norrtullsgatan 61 (32 50 95). T-bana Odenplan/bus 2, 40, 52, 65. **Open** 5pm-midnight Mon-Sat; 5-11pm Sun. **Main courses** 85kr-220kr. **Credit** AmEx, DC, MC, V. **Map** p308 B4.

Eat, Drink, Shop

Don't let the strange biblical name (Death in the Pot) put you off. Nor the location on one of the few dead-end streets in Stockholm that looks like an industrial area of New Jersey – an image reinforced by the restaurant's curtain-covered windows that make this place look like some kind of suspicious social club. No, this isn't a mafia hangout. It's just a welcoming neighbourhood Italian focused on first-class meat – *bistecca* Fiorentina, *salsiccia* in all shapes and sizes, and pasta *all'amatriciana* – with friendly service and great food. The portions are enormous, so don't even think of attempting the full four-course Italian dinner.

Djurgården

Traditional Swedish

Godthem
Rosendalsvägen 9 (661 0722/www.godthem.se). Bus 44, 47. **Open** 11.30am-11pm Mon-Thur; 11.30am-midnight Fri; 12.30pm-midnight Sat; 12.30-11pm Sun. **Main courses** lunch 70kr-155kr; dinner120kr-255kr. **Credit** AmEx, DC, MC, V. **Map** p306 H11.
If you'd like to dine in an idyllic setting reminiscent of an Ingmar Bergman film, you could do worse than Godthem, which, while not always outstanding in the food stakes, offers reliable Swedish *husmanskost*, such as steak served on a plank with *béarnaise* sauce. Sit on the veranda or in the summer garden overlooking Djurgården's canal. Godthem has been in business since 1874, and most regulars seem to find comfort in its plain cooking. The *dagens rätt* (set lunch) makes a particularly good deal, and the inn's Christmas spread (*julbord*) is among the city's most popular.

Wärdshuset Ulla Winbladh
Rosendalsvägen 8 (663 05 71/www.ullawinbladh.se). Bus 44, 47. **Open** 11.30am-10pm Mon; 11.30am-11pm Tue-Fri; 1-11pm Sat; 1-10pm Sun. **Main courses** 195kr-265kr. **Credit** AmEx, DC, MC, V. **Map** p307 H11.
Despite its very picturesque setting, old-fashioned Ulla Winbladh, named after a much beloved friend of Swedish national poet and composer Carl Michael Bellman, does not quite live up to its grande dame reputation. The kitchen seems to cut corners a little too often in serving its traditional Swedish fare, and the service can sometimes verge on arrogant. The safest bet is the classic meatballs or fried *strömming* (Baltic herring), eaten outdoors in summer or in the cosy dining room in winter.

Södermalm

In addition to the restaurants below, there are plenty of cheap fast-food joints in the vicinity of **Medborgarplatsen**. Best of all is the Kurdish hole-in-the-wall **Amida** (Folkungagatan 76), with its enormous, well-prepared portions of grilled meat and couscous.

Asian

Ho's
Hornsgatan 151 (84 44 20/www.restauranghos.com). T-bana Hornstull/bus 4, 40, 66, 74, 77. **Open** 11am-10pm Tue-Thur; 11am-10.30pm Fri; 4-10.30pm Sat; 4-10pm Sun. Closed 2wks Mar. **Main courses** 90kr-235kr. **Credit** AmEx, DC, MC, V. **Map** p313 L3.
Situated off the beaten track in the western end of Södermalm, Ho's has long been a well-kept secret for a small crowd of Chinese and sussed locals. Nowadays Ho's is well known all over town for its personal service and exquisite stir-fries. The menu has the standard selections of chicken, pork, beef, duck, fish and shellfish, plus a few tasty surprises. But in general, it's a no-fuss joint – the deal is straightforward wok-frying with fresh ingredients.

Yu Love Bibimbap
Folkungagatan 74 (644 39 90). **Open** 11.30am-2.30pm, 5-9pm Mon-Fri; 5-9pm Sat. **Main courses** lunch 75kr; dinner 89kr. **Credit** MC, V. **Map** p315 L8.
A cute, brave new restaurant where the Yu family serves only one dish – different varieties of one of Korea's most famous culinary offerings, *bibimbap* (which means, literally, mixed rice). Fortunately, given the narrow choice, the *bibimbap*, whether it's with beef, chicken, shrimp or vegetables, is very good. Seating is at two communal tables, so the small but tastefully decorated space tends to be full.

Contemporary

Bistro Sud
Swedenborgsgatan 8 (640 41 11). T-bana Mariatorget/bus 4, 43, 55, 66, 74. **Open** Food served 5-10pm Mon-Sun. *Bar* 5-11pm Sun, Mon; 5pm-midnight Tue-Thur; 5pm-1am Fri, Sat. **Main courses** 89kr-235kr. **Credit** AmEx, DC, MC, V. **Map** p314 L7.
This is a friendly neighbourhood place for the Mariatorget crowd of well-to-do journalists and

Laid-back SoFo style at **Roxy**.

artists, though some might find service a little over-familiar (the waitresses have a habit of calling all women 'girls'). The menu seems pretentious at first glance – dishes come with 'white bean foam' and 'port syrup', for example – but the food is actually quite straightforward and usually very good, and this is generally a pleasant place to have a bite to eat and rub shoulders in the crowded and relaxed bar.

Folkoperan Bar & Kök

Hornsgatan 72 (84 50 92/www.fbk.se). T-bana Mariatorget/bus 4, 43, 55, 66, 74. **Open** *Restaurant* 4-11pm Tue-Fri; noon-11pm Sat; noon-10pm Sun. *Bar* 4pm-1am Tue-Fri; noon-1am Sat; noon-10pm Sun. **Main courses** 174kr-220kr. **Credit** AmEx, DC, MC, V. **Map** p314 K6.

Apart from the grand entrance next door, it would be easy to forget that this restaurant officially functions as the culinary annexe to the city's alternative opera scene (*see p221*). Most of the clientele come here not for a pre-show drink, but for the restaurant in its own right – there's a bustling bar downstairs, a cosy lounge bar with a good menu upstairs and the main dining room, where ambitious modern food is served at reasonable prices. The T-bone steak is a generous, if slightly roughly handled, piece of meat, served with deep-fried new potatoes, while the poached cod with horseradish is a more subtle and tasty creation. The crowd is dominated by thirtysomethings, and the bars get crowded later on.

Ljunggren

Götgatan 36 (640 75 65). T-bana Slussen/bus 2, 3, 43, 53, 55, 59. **Open** *Restaurant* 11.30am-11pm Mon-Fri; noon-11pm Sat. *Bar* 11.30am-1am Mon-Fri; noon-1am Sat. **Main courses** lunch 80kr-120kr; dinner 135kr-200kr. **Credit** AmEx, DC, MC, V. **Map** p314 L8.

If a restaurant can epitomise 'new Söder' it's Ljunggren, housed in the new, chic Bruno shopping arcade on Götgatan. The ad agency clientele, chummy service, lounge music, communal table, open kitchen and the pan-Asian menu all make one think

of Stureplan seven years ago (or New York 15 years ago) and, as it happens, the same owners ran a restaurant with the same name for the same kind of people near Stureplan a few years ago. The restaurant, which serves food ranging from good to excellent, has become a meeting place for Södermalm's non-Bohemian crowd.

Rival

Mariatorget 3 (545 789 15/www.rival.se). T-bana Mariatorget/bus 4, 43, 55, 66, 74. **Open** *Bistro* noon-11pm Mon-Fri; 5-11pm Sat. **Main courses** *Bistro* 95kr-228kr. *Café* 40kr-80kr. **Credit** AmEx, DC, MC, V. **Map** p314 K7.

This is the house that ABBA built – well, almost. Benny of ABBA fame is one of the three owners of this food and entertainment emporium, which has all the components for a complete date under one roof: eat a fancy dinner, catch a movie, have a late-night cocktail and, if you get lucky, go to bed in one of the high-tech hotel rooms. However, the quality of the food is a bit up and down. After starting out very ambitiously, the owners seem to have decided to keep to a more down-to-earth bistro style, and the tried and tested staples – such as *toast skagen* (shrimp salad on toast), salmon with creamed potatoes or meatballs – are your best bet. For reviews of the cinema and the hotel, *see p199 and p55* respectively.

Roxy

Nytorget (640 96 55/www.roxysofo.se). T-bana Medborgarplatsen/bus 2, 3, 53, 55, 66. **Open** *Restaurant* 5-10pm Tue-Sat. *Bar* 5pm-midnight Tue-Thur, Sun; 5pm-1am Fri, Sat. **Main courses** 110kr-246kr. **Credit** AmEx, DC, MC, V. **Map** p315 M9.

Curiously enough, Nytorget, the summer focal point for the trendy area south of Folkungagatan, has been without an obvious watering hole for a few years. Not any more, though. Roxy, with its stylish but laid-back interior, stylish but laid-back music and stylish but laid-back clientele, is what everyone was waiting for. It has a classy bar, a nice lounge and friendly staff. It is also one of the few non-night-club locales where gay and straight locals meet. The modern, Mediterranean-influenced food is good and reasonably priced, and the menu has a number of small and medium-sized dishes.

Stiernan

Renstiernas Gata 22 (647 97 33/www.stiernan.com). T-bana Medborgarplatsen/bus 2, 3, 53, 71, 76. **Open** *Restaurant* 5-11pm Mon-Sat. *Bar* 5pm-1am Mon-Sat. **Main courses** 195kr-235kr. **Credit** AmEx, DC, MC, V. **Map** p315 M9.

Stiernan might look like just another SoFo bar, albeit a particularly hip and popular one, but there's actually much more to it. Here you find what had, until now, been unheard of in this increasingly fashionable part of Södermalm: a restaurant with a popular bar and top-notch food. Up a short stairway past the crowds is a diminutive eating area where some of Stockholm's friendliest and most professional waiters serve great, occasionally excellent, seasonal food under a Swedish-European banner. Save room for the exquisite desserts.

Mediterranean

Crêperie Fyra Knop

Svartensgatan 4 (640 77 27). T-bana Slussen/bus 2, 3, 43, 55, 59. **Open** 5-11pm Mon-Fri; noon-11pm Sat, Sun. **Main courses** 44kr-74kr. **Credit** AmEx, MC, V. **Map** p314 L8.

Just off Götgatspuckeln (the northern part of Götgatan, where most of the action is), this is a good choice if you're homesick and French, or alternatively if you're just looking for an inexpensive but

romantic meal. The decor is kitsch, complete with old fishing nets and lifebelts, in two dark and cosy little rooms. The savoury and sweet crêpes are delicious and cheap enough that you can go on for a dance at nearby Mosebacke (*see p195*) afterwards.

Lo Scudetto

Åsögatan 163 (640 42 15). T-bana Medborgarplatsen/bus 2, 59, 66, 76, 53. **Open** *Food served* 5-10pm Mon-Sat. *Bar* 5pm-midnight Mon-Sat. Closed 4wks from Midsummer. **Main courses** 95kr-220kr. **Credit** AmEx, MC, V. **Map** p315 M9.

A culinary pioneer at the trendier end of Åsögatan, this local Italian (named after the Italian football league trophy) is not what it seems at first sight. It's rustically styled down, the walls sparsely decorated with portraits of Swedish footballers, with an adjoining hole-in-the-wall bar with a TV always tuned to the local sports station. But don't expect simple sportsman spaghetti here – there's an almost religious relationship with the subtleties of the Italian kitchen, and the bresaola, ravioli and tiramisú are all prepared with a loving and skilful hand. This is one of the city's few Italians in the absolute top class. Reservations are mandatory.

Zucchero

Borgmästargatan 7 (644 22 87). Bus 2, 59, 66, 76, 53. **Open** 11.30am-6pm Mon; 11.30am-9pm Tue-Thur; 11.30am-10pm Fri, Sat; 11.30am-5pm Sun. **Main courses** 100kr-140kr. **Credit** AmEx, DC, MC, V. **Map** p315 L10.

Hidden on the cosy corner of Åsögatan and Borgmästargatan, this café-cum-restaurant is a stylish version of a cheesy 1950s Rome eaterie. The

Zucchero.

crowd is youthful and boisterous, the staff friendly, and the pasta – which is mainly what they serve here – is not altogether fantastic, but a cheap enough reason to come and join the fun.

Middle Eastern

Matkultur
Erstagatan 21 (642 03 53). Bus 2, 3, 53, 66, 76. **Open** *Restaurant* 5-10pm Mon, Tue; 5-11pm Wed-Sat. *Bar* 5pm-midnight Mon-Sat. **Main courses** 130kr-200kr. **Credit** AmEx, DC, MC, V. **Map** p315 L10.
After a stroll on Stockholm's panoramic Fjällgatan, you might end up in this crowded and friendly place. The kitchen is proud of its culinary crossover: Turkish and Lebanese specialities with a hint of Sweden – there's lots of lamb and rice. Prices are moderate, and the customers are young and arty. If you still have strength after a filling dinner, it's also close to the bars on Skånegatan.

Traditional Swedish

Eriks Gondolen
Stadsgården 6 (641 70 90/40/www.eriks.se). T-bana Slussen/bus 2, 3, 43, 53, 76. **Open** *Restaurant* 11.30am-2pm, 5-11pm Mon-Fri; 4-11pm Sat. *Bar* 11.30am-1am Mon-Fri; 4pm-1am Sat. **Main courses** lunch 95kr-175kr; dinner 185kr-295kr. **Set menus** 320kr; 395kr. **Credit** AmEx, DC, MC, V. **Map** p314 K8.
It's hard to imagine a restaurant with a more spectacular view. The name means 'gondola', and the bar is actually suspended over Slussen, underneath the Katarinahissen walkway, overlooking Gamla Stan and the water. As well as the bar, there is an exclusive dining room and a less expensive restaurant (both in the adjoining building, but also with a good view). Enter via the bridge from Mosebacke Torg or take the lift from the waterfront. The menu offers both French and Swedish dishes. This is where locals bring their foreign friends or business associates to impress them.

Pelikan
Blekingegatan 40 (55 60 90 90/www.pelikan.se). T-bana/bus 3, 55, 59, 74. **Open** 11.30am-1am Mon-Fri; 5pm-1am Sat, Sun. **Main courses** 94kr-188kr. **Credit** AmEx, MC, V. **Map** p315 M8.
Not many restaurants feel as genuinely Swedish as this beer hall in southern Södermalm. Its elegant painted ceilings and wood-panelled walls haven't changed since Söder became trendy and restaurants served only *husmanskost*. Classics on offer here include *pytt i panna*, SOS (*smör, ost och sill* – butter, cheese and herring) and meatballs with lingonberries and pickled cucumber. Check the dishes listed on the blackboard to find the real bargains (under 100kr), such as knuckle of pork with root vegetable mash, or fried salted herring with onion sauce. Pairing the food with an ice-cold schnapps is close to compulsory. In the afternoon and early evening the room is dominated by older men in worn

suits drinking beer; later on it gets younger and louder. Staff are of the hearty old-fashioned sort.

Vegetarian

Chutney
Katarina Bangata 19 (640 30 10). T-bana Medborgarplatsen/bus 55, 59, 66. **Open** 11am-10pm Mon-Fri; 2-10pm Sat. **Main courses** 80kr-135kr. **Credit** MC, V. **Map** p315 M8.
Chutney is the local living room for the alternative crowd, complete with handwritten notes advertising 'Waves of Love to Your Inner Child', environmentally conscious art on the walls and vegan food on the plates. The service is friendly, the portions huge and the prices decent. Good for lunch or early dinner after doing the SoFo shopping rounds, with tables on the Katarina Bangata sidewalk for people-watching. More restaurants and bars (including WC, *see p141*) lie just down the street if you're feeling more carnivorous.

Östermalm & Gärdet

Asian

Halv Trappa plus Gård
Lästmakargatan 3 (678 10 50/www.halvtrappa plusgard.se). T-bana Östermalmstorg/bus 1, 2, 55, 56. **Open** *Restaurant* 5-11pm Tue-Sat. *Bar* 5pm-1am Tue; 5pm-3am Wed-Sat. **Set menus** 375kr; 395kr. **Credit** AmEx, DC, MC, V. **Map** p305 F7.
Finally! A Chinese restaurant in Stockholm that doesn't dampen the fire of authentic Sichuanese fare. With elegantly understated decor and knowledgeable staff who know their chilli, you won't find a more sophisticated Chinese restaurant in town. Not every dish makes you reach for the water, but it's all aromatic and infused with classic Sichuanese ingredients like ginger, sesame, peanuts and cinnamon. Forget the desserts and go with one of the finely chosen Chinese teas instead. The lounge upstairs is comfortable and inviting, and the outdoor terrace is a popular summer venue for music and conversation.

Miyako
Kommendörsgatan 23 (662 25 06/www.miyako.se). T-bana Östermalmstorg or Stadion/bus 42, 44, 55, 56, 62. **Open** 5-10pm Mon-Sat. **Main courses** 140kr-240kr. **Set menus** 275kr-490kr. **Credit** AmEx, DC, MC, V. **Map** p310 E9.
You know you're in Stockholm's best Japanese restaurant when you spot Japanese families sitting on tatami mats behind a screen. The shoe-free section of the restaurant has sunken floors so your legs can dangle comfortably as you sit on the large pillows. Relax for hours over a full Japanese meal or sample the sushi as the soothing sound of Asian instrumental music tinkles around you. The friendly staff make the experience even more enjoyable. In addition to Japanese diners, Miyako is always filled with posh locals and families.

Eat, Drink, Shop

Sabai-Soong

Linnégatan 39B (663 12 77/www.sabaisabai.just.nu).
T-bana Östermalmstorg/bus 1, 44, 55, 56, 62. **Open**
Restaurant 11am-11pm Mon-Fri; 3-11pm Sat; 3-10pm
Sun. *Bar* 11am-11pm Mon-Thur; 11am-midnight Fri;
3pm-midnight Sat; 3-10pm Sun. **Main courses**
98kr-189kr. **Credit** AmEx, DC, MC, V. **Map** p310 E9.
Every bit of space at Sabai-Soong, from floor to ceiling, is covered with the likes of stuffed monkeys,
plastic lobsters, coloured lights and beach scene
murals. The Thai food is well prepared and diverse,
and good value for money, the latter not something
easily found in this upmarket neighbourhood. The
children's menu and modest prices explain the abundance of families and young people who keep this
place busy most nights. Staff are brisk and efficient,
and no one waits long for their food.
Other locations: Kammakargatan 44, Norrmalm
(790 09 13).

Contemporary

Babs Kök och Bar

Birger Jarlsgatan 37 (23 61 01). T-bana
Östermalmstorg/bus 1, 2, 55, 56. **Open** *Kitchen*
5-11pm Tue-Sat. *Bar* 5pm-midnight Tue, Wed; 5pm-
1am Thur-Sat. Closed July. **Main courses** 130kr-
170kr. **Credit** AmEx, DC, MC, V. **Map** p309 E7.
You have to walk through the foyer of art-house cinema Zita (*see p200*) to find this down-to-earth bar
and restaurant. Have a drink, eat a simple dish from
the open kitchen, or sip a coffee before the film starts.
It's one of the few places around Stureplan where
it's possible to eat and drink without ending up
broke, and yet there's everything from steak to
ostrich on the menu. Ageing revolutionaries and radical twentysomethings are among the clientele.

Elverket

Linnégatan 69 (661 25 62/www.restaurangel
verket.se). T-bana Karlaplan/bus 42, 44, 56, 62.
Open *Restaurant* 11am-2pm, 6-10pm Mon-Fri; 11am-
4pm, 6-10pm Sat; 11am-4pm, 6-9pm Sun. *Bar* 11am-
midnight Mon-Thur; 11am-1am Fri; 11am-1am Sat;
11am-10pm Sun. **Main courses** lunch 79kr-165kr;
dinner 125kr-205kr. **Credit** AmEx, DC, MC, V.
Map p306 F10.
This busy bar and restaurant is in an old electricity
plant, together with the more experimental stage of
the Dramaten theatre (*see p234*). It's a favourite of
both young suits and black-clad intellectuals. The
atmosphere is friendly – there's a big lounge area
with low sofas where you can relax with a drink. The
food is modern crossover and moderately priced,
with a pre-theatre menu and a selection of tapas. It's
closed for several weeks during the summer, when
the owners retreat to the island of Gotland to run
their restaurant there.

Lydmar Hotel

Sturegatan 10 (56 61 13 00/01/www.lydmar.se).
T-bana Östermalmstorg/bus 1, 2, 42, 55, 56. **Open**
Restaurant 11.30am-2pm, 5-11pm Mon-Fri; 1-11pm

Sat, Sun. *Bar* 11.30am-1am Mon-Thur; 11.30am-2am
Fri; 6pm-2am Sat; 6pm-1am Sun. **Main courses**
lunch 95kr-155kr; dinner 185kr-285kr. **Credit** AmEx,
DC, MC, V. **Map** p305 E8.
This popular watering hole for glitterati, well-paid
consultants and the occasional jazz singer or movie
star is actually a hotel restaurant. Then again, this
is the ever-hip Lydmar Hotel (*see p58*), so perhaps
that's not surprising. Near Stureplan, this is a place
with a pulse. Dining here can sometimes be a bit
loud, with the live jazz or soul music drowning out
conversation, but the modern Swedish food is usually good, sometimes great and always fashionable.
Mains are surprisingly simple; order something as
everyday as a grilled fillet of lamb or beef and it will
arrive perfect and virtually 'naked' – garnishes come
on the side. This is a good place to start an evening
out in Stureplan, or to watch the in-crowd do their
thing. You'll find the same crowd nursing their
hangovers at the popular weekend brunch, which
offers everything from burgers to omelettes and
American pancakes.

PA & Co

Riddargatan 8 (611 08 45/www.sturehofgruppen.se).
T-bana Östermalmstorg/bus 2, 47, 55, 62, 65. **Open**
Restaurant 5-11pm daily. *Bar* 5pm-midnight daily.
Main courses 95kr-250kr. **Credit** AmEx, DC, MC,
V. **Map** p305 F8.
This restaurant – which a few years ago had a much
discussed novel dedicated to it – has long been a
favourite hangout of advertising execs, writers and
journos. And no wonder. The food, Swedish classic
and international fare, is often superb, with a constantly changing menu that pulls off outrageous combinations such as smoked duck with halloumi cheese,
pineapple and curry dressing. With just 38 seats, and
no reservations allowed, tables fill up fast, but the
friendly bartenders make the wait in the bar pleasurable. Once you've got your table, hang on to it for
hours, as many do, soaking up the camaraderie of a
restaurant that feels more like someone's living room.

Riche

Birger Jarlsgatan 4 (54 50 35 60). T-bana
Östermalmstorg/bus 2, 47, 55, 62, 65. **Open**
Kitchen 11.30am-midnight Mon-Fri; noon-midnight
Sat. *Bar* 11.30-1am Mon, Tue; 11.30am-2am Wed-Fri;
noon-2am Sat. **Main courses** 105kr-295kr.
Credit AmEx, DC, MC, V. **Map** p305 F8.
Yet another Stureplan restaurant overhauled with a
new design and a brasserie concept. With huge windows on to the street, the spacious dining room is
perfect for people-watching. The menu – a mix of
traditional Swedish dishes with international classics – is fairly ambitious, but doesn't always succeed. The stylishly dressed Östermalm matrons who
lunch here after a shopping expedition don't seem to
mind. For a more intimate and reliable experience,
you may want to opt for adjacent Teatergrillen
(Nybrogatan 3, 54 50 36 65), where the room is decorated with old theatre costumes and the menu covers
oysters, champagne and classic French cuisine.

Undici

Sturegatan 22 (661 66 17/www.undici.org). T-bana Östermalmstorg/bus 1, 2, 42, 55, 56. **Open** *Food served* 5-11pm Tue-Sat. *Bar* 5pm-1am Tue-Thur; 5pm-3am Fri, Sat. *Closed July-mid Aug.* **Main courses** 155kr-295kr. **Set menu** 695kr. **Credit** AmEx, DC, MC, V. **Map** p310 E8.

Owner, footballer Tomas Brolin, grew up in the north of Sweden and played professionally in the north of Italy – Undici is a tribute to both regions. The space is bare, almost sterile, but the menu is more welcoming. Plain Swedish classics mingle with Italian dishes and the odd truly luxurious creation like roasted fillet of venison with artichoke, *gnocchi di potata* and truffle stock. A lounge and bar keep things hopping until the early hours of the morning.

Vassa Eggen

Birger Jarlsgatan 29 (21 61 69/www.vassaeggen. com). T-bana Östermalmstorg/bus 1, 2, 55, 56. **Open** *Restaurant* 11.30am-2pm, 5-10pm Mon; 11.30am-2pm, 5-11pm Tue-Fri; 5-11pm Sat. *Bar* 11.30am-10pm Mon; 11.30am-11pm Tue, Wed; 11.30am-2am Thur, Fri; 5pm-2am Sat; 4-10pm Sun. **Main courses** lunch 95kr-200kr; dinner 295kr. **Set menus** 895kr. **Credit** AmEx, DC, MC, V. **Map** p310 E7.

Vassa Eggen is named after Somerset Maugham's 1945 novel, *The Razor's Edge*, the tale of one man's search for enlightenment – and you'll certainly find culinary enlightenment here. Named as Sweden's best restaurant in 2003 by the Swedish *Gourmet* magazine, it produces international modern food with a twist, along the lines of duck liver terrine with figs or a crab and mussel gazpacho. Desserts feel a bit more like home, with entries such as cardamom and apple compôte. Not far from Stureplan, it's the top choice for gourmet dining in the area, high prices aside. The crowd is young and quite informal, many of them consultants from nearby offices. Among the best business lunches in town.

Middle Eastern

Halv Grek plus Turk

Jungfrugatan 30 (665 94 22/www.halvgrekplus turk.com). T-bana Stadion/bus 1, 42, 44, 56, 62. **Open** *Restaurant* 5.30-11pm Mon-Sat; 5.30-10pm Sun. *Bar* 5.30pm-midnight Mon-Sat; 5.30-11pm Sun. **Mezes** 50kr-95kr each. **Credit** AmEx, DC, MC, V. **Map** p310 E9.

It is worth the extra effort to locate this little gem of a restaurant, born of a friendship between Greek and Turkish restaurateurs. Slightly off the beaten track, the entrance is marked by a tiny, easy-to-miss sign. The decor is modern, almost austere Middle Eastern, accented with elegant lounge sofas, bright colours and soft lighting, while the clientele is a mixed urban set. The menu features small meze dishes, and an assortment of cold and hot dishes. A selection of six meze is about right for two hungry people. Aside from the traditional classics (hummus, meatballs, dolmades, baba ghanoush) the menu includes many inspired original dishes like chicken liver terrine

with Metaxa. The spicy chicken wings are a delight, as are the 'Manti' dumplings (yoghurt and spiced lamb). Service is attentive, friendly and efficient.

Phénicia

Storgatan 27 (662 20 00/www.phenicia.se). T-bana Östermalmstorg/bus 1, 44, 55, 56, 62. **Open** *Restaurant* 4-10.30pm Mon-Thur, Sun; 4pm-12.30am Fri, Sat. *Bar* 4-11pm Mon-Thur, Sun; 4pm-1am Fri, Sat. **Main courses** 170kr-259kr. **Set menus** 249kr-350kr. **Credit** AmEx, DC, MC, V. **Map** p306 F9.

One of a crop of Lebanese restaurants sprouting up all over Stockholm, Phénicia is a good, reasonably priced choice in an expensive area. The spacious two-storey restaurant serves up meze and other

Sabai-Soong. *See p128.*

Eat, Drink, Shop

Lebanese delicacies to large crowds of Middle Eastern dinners, as well as stylish Östermalm women and black-clad advertising and media types from around the corner. The food is good value for money, with its generous portions, and the friendly staff take the time to explain each of the 20 dishes that suddenly crowd the table if you've ordered the meze. Finish off with a water pipe, or consider renting a private room, where you can be entertained by your own belly dancer.

Mediterranean

Brasserie Godot

Grev Turegatan 36 (660 06 14/www.godot.se). T-bana Östermalmstorg/bus 1, 42, 55, 56. **Open** *Restaurant* 5-11pm Mon-Sat. *Bar* 5pm-1am Mon-Sat. Closed 3wks July; 2wks from Christmas. **Main courses** 180kr-295kr. **Credit** AmEx, DC, MC, V. **Map** p310 E8.
The bar seems to have overtaken the restaurant in this classy Östermalm establishment, and that's a shame, because the kitchen showed such promise when it was at the forefront of the brasserie trend a few years ago. The diners are crowded into a corner, while the Ralph Lauren shirt crowd at the bar gets progressively louder. The cuisine here can be variable, despite the beautiful presentation, but portions are, however, good value for money. Expect French brasserie classics such as steak frites, moules marinière and caviar mixed in with Swedish fare. For dessert you can't go wrong with a classic Godot crème brûlée. The attentive waiters try to make up for the invasion of the brat pack.

Divino

Karlavägen 28 (611 02 69/12 04/www.divino.se). Bus 1, 42, 44, 55, 56. **Open** 6-11pm Mon-Sat. Closed July. **Main courses** 245kr-275kr. **Set menu** 685kr. **Credit** AmEx, DC, MC, V. **Map** p310 D7.
Considered by many to be Stockholm's best Italian restaurant, this is certainly one of its most elegant and priciest, and the food usually lives up to the restaurant's heavenly name. Try the entrecôte with prosciutto, sage and Marsala wine or the sumptuous risotto, followed by the requisite creamy tiramisù for dessert. Discerning Italian diners keep the chefs and waiters on their toes, while the other well-heeled guests are grateful for a restaurant that makes Italian food in Stockholm less like Pizza Hut.

Sturehof

Stureplan 2 (440 57 30/www.sturehof.com). T-bana Östermalmstorg/bus 1, 2, 55, 56. **Open** *Restaurant* 9am-1am Mon-Fri; noon-1am Sat; 1pm-1am Sun. *Bar* 9am-2am Mon-Fri; noon-2am Sat; 1pm-2am Sun. **Main courses** 105kr-340kr. **Credit** AmEx, DC, MC, V. **Map** p305 F8.
This classic brasserie offers a choice of several different dining environments. Those who want to be seen sip white wine at the outdoor tables, the after-work crew crowd the tiled bar, while the laidback chill out in the upper lounge. For its part, the massive dining room is elegant, with white linen

Tabbouli for mouthwatering meze. *See p132.*

tablecloths, uniformed waiters and nicely designed furniture, but the atmosphere stays lively and cheerful. The long opening hours make it possible to get a meal here almost any time of day. Waiters are attentive, and the lengthy menu follows classic French bistro tradition, with seafood and shellfish a speciality. Among the starters are a few Swedish classics such as smoked Baltic herring and *toast skagen*. After dinner, step into the lively O-baren (*see p142*).

Swedish

Prinsen

Mäster Samuelsgatan 4 (611 13 31/www.restaurang prinsen.se). T-bana Östermalmstorg/bus 2, 55, 56, 62, 69. **Open** 11.30am-11.30pm Mon-Fri; 1-11.30pm Sat; 5-10.30pm Sun. **Main courses** 125kr-295kr. **Credit** AmEx, DC, MC, V. **Map** p305 F8.
This legendary writers' haunt has become something of an institution – in one corner there's a poet dressed in black, in another a patron of the arts holds

court. Artwork crowds Prinsen's walls (many of the works were payment to settle bills), and harks back to its bohemian past. 'The Prince' can be relied upon to offer atmosphere and an excellent range of classic *husmanskost*. The herring platter and *biff rydberg* (beef with fried potatoes and egg) are Swedish classics. But amid the beef and halibut you'll find more contemporary dishes.

Villa Källhagen
Djurgårdsbrunnsvägen 10 (665 03 10/www.kall hagen.se). Bus 69. **Open** 11.30am-2pm, 5-11pm Mon-Fri; noon-11pm Sat; noon-5pm Sun. **Main courses** lunch 135kr-195kr; dinner 165kr-315kr; brunch 210kr. **Set menu** 595kr. **Credit** AmEx, DC, MC, V. **Map** p307 F13.
A dining experience of the first order is to be had here, where typical Swedish dishes, with a European twist, are transformed into works of art. The dining room offers a romantic view of the Djurgårdsbrunn canal. In summer, you can sit outdoors to eat and then stroll along the water. In autumn and winter, there's a fire blazing in the hearth. Not only the menu but the chair upholstery and table linen change with the seasons. The popular brunch blends Asian treats with a typical Swedish *smörgåsbord*. The restaurant closes in July but the bistro is open, serving a more select but satisfying menu at lower prices.

Kungsholmen

Asian

Hong Kong
Kungsbro Strand 23 (653 77 20/www.hongkong. lunchinfo.com). T-bana Rådhuset/bus 1, 40, 59. **Open** 11am-10pm Mon-Fri; 1-10pm Sat, Sun. **Main courses** lunch 106kr-230kr; dinner 165kr-395kr. **Credit** AmEx, DC, MC, V. **Map** p304 G5.
This is one of only a few places in Stockholm serving authentic Chinese food. The decor is fairly standard but the cuisine is excellent. The owner, Sonny Li, delivers spicy Cantonese and Sichuanese dishes from the giant gas stove. Apart from the stir-fry dishes, there's an ambitious array of steam-cooked choices that vary with the season. The speciality is Peking duck – Chinese business folk (and the King no less) all come here for the red-glazed bird, which must be ordered two days in advance.

Roppongi
Hantverkargatan 76 (650 17 72/www.roppongi.se). T-bana Fridhemsplan/bus 3, 4, 40, 52, 62. **Open** 11am-10pm Mon-Fri; 5-10pm Sat; 5-9pm Sun. **Main courses** lunch 70kr-165kr; dinner 118kr-198kr. **Credit** AmEx, DC, MC, V. **Map** p303 G2.
Roppongi serves the best sushi in this part of town, plus decent tempura and *gyoza* (pockets of fried dough stuffed with minced pork or shrimp), among other things. It's always crowded, especially the few tables that appear outside in the summer. You can always order takeaway sushi and walk down to the water at nearby Rålombshovsparken.

Contemporary

Baguz
Norra Agnegatan 43 (653 69 90/www.baguz.se). T-bana Rådhuset/bus 1, 3, 40, 52, 62. **Open** *Restaurant* 5-10pm Mon, Tue; 5-11pm Wed-Sat; 5-10pm Sun. *Bar* 5-11pm Mon, Tue, Sun; 5pm-midnight Wed, Thur; 5pm-1am Fri, Sat. **Main courses** 155kr-195kr. **Set menu** 375kr. **Credit** AmEx, DC, MC, V. **Map** p304 G4.
This friendly neighbourhood restaurant succeeds admirably in living up to its name (meaning 'good life' in Malay). Its mostly Asian-inspired crossover cuisine is full of surprises such as a dish featuring tender ostrich meat in wine sauce matched to a perfectly grilled lobster tail with crunchy roast potatoes and a sesame-flavoured hollandaise. The service is gracious, and the bar is popular. Baguz attracts a loyal clientele of all ages.

Salzer
John Ericssonsgatan 6 (650 30 28/www.salzer.nu). T-bana Rådhuset/bus 3, 40, 52, 62. **Open** *Kitchen* 5-11pm Mon-Sat; noon-4pm Sun. *Bar* 5pm-midnight Mon-Sat; noon-4pm Sun. **Main courses** 109kr-230kr. **Credit** AmEx, DC, MC, V. **Map** p304 H3.
This intimate restaurant in one of Stockholm's most beautiful functionalist houses is just a stone's throw from the waterfront of Norr Mälarstrand. The calm atmosphere makes the buzz of the city seem far away. Swedish dishes are elegantly mixed with French and Italian inspiration in traditional offerings like *isterband* (lard sausage), as well as in the sole and fillet of lamb. Few places offer such a pleasing combination of good Swedish cosiness and good Swedish style. On Sundays, the generous brunch buffet draws the neighbourhood's young families.

Spisa Hos Helena
Scheelegatan 18 (654 49 26/50 26/www.spisahos helena.se). T-bana Rådhuset/bus 1, 3, 40, 52, 62. **Open** *Restaurant* 5-10pm Mon-Thur; 5-11pm Fri, Sat. *Bar* 5-11pm Mon-Thur; 5pm-midnight Fri, Sat. Closed July. **Main courses** lunch 69kr; dinner 119kr-198kr. **Set menus** 255kr; 265kr. **Credit** AmEx, DC, MC, V. **Map** p304 G4.
A home from home for many locals, 'Spis', as it's affectionately called, serves straightforward, delicious modern European cuisine that seeks not to intimidate but simply to tickle the taste buds. The sesame-grilled tuna is lovely, but if you're in the mood for something more basic, there's always a club sandwich or salad on the menu. None of the main courses are more than 200kr, and the red walls make this as cosy and welcoming a place as you're likely to find, especially in winter when the flickering candles make you wish you lived here.

Stockholm Taste
Wargentinsgatan 3 (654 56 10). T-bana Rådhuset/ bus 1, 40, 52, 56. **Open** 11am-8pm Mon-Thur; 11am-6pm Fri. **Main courses** 55kr-59kr. **No credit cards**. **Map** p304 G4.

Eat, Drink, Shop

A stylish yet cosy soup café, this is one of the best-kept secrets on Kungsholmen. Head here for a lunch as tasty and filling as it is inexpensive. The soups are often exotic, using Indian or Asian spices and ingredients, and the fresh bread is delicious. Get here early for one of the few tables or a seat at the counter. The owners couldn't be friendlier and they're happy to wrap up your lunch to take away if you'd rather eat picnic-style at the park around the corner.

Middle Eastern

Tabbouli

Norra Agnegatan 39 (650 25 00/www.tabbouli. lunchinfo.com). T-bana Rådhuset/bus 1, 3, 40, 52, 62. **Open** *Restaurant* 5-10pm Mon-Thur; 5-10.45pm Fri, Sat. *Bar* 5-11pm Mon-Thur; 5pm-midnight Fri, Sat. **Main courses** 145kr-189kr. **Set menus** 235kr; 295kr. **Credit** AmEx, DC, MC, V. **Map** p304 G4.

This Middle Eastern restaurant aspires to an elegance not typical for Lebanese dining, with its harem-like decor, but the low tables in the cosy labyrinth of the cellar dining area ensure that at least part of your meze lands in your lap. Fortunately, the food is so good you don't mind picking up the crumbs. Aside from an expertly prepared meze buffet, the lamb dishes are unusually good (the secret, the owner says, is marinating the meat for two days in oil). The service can be a little rough around the edges, but we hope this is only growing pains.

Traditional Swedish

Mäster Anders

Pipersgatan 1 (654 20 01/www.masteranders.se). T-bana Rådhuset/bus 3, 40, 52, 62. **Open** 5-11pm Mon-Wed, Sun; 5pm-1am Thur, Fri; 1pm-1am Sat. **Main courses** 165kr-340kr. **Credit** AmEx, DC, MC, V. **Map** p304 G4.

For a century Mäster Anders has served beer and traditional Swedish cuisine. Every night there is a different house special, but you are guaranteed well-prepared and honest food. The grill menu is a particularly good deal, as the generous portions are complemented with a couple of side dishes. Mäster Anders also makes one of the best burgers in town. This popular, slightly worn, but cosy restaurant has no pretensions. Prices are as congenial as the service.

Further afield

Contemporary

Edsbacka Krog

Sollentunavägen 220, Sollentuna (96 33 00/40 19/ www.edsbackakrog.se). Commuter train to Sollentuna Centrum then bus 525, 527, 607 to Edsbacka. **Open** 11.30am-2.30pm, 5.30pm-midnight Mon-Fri (Jan-Apr, Aug-Nov closed Mon); 2pm-midnight Sat. Closed July. **Main courses** 295kr-425kr. **Set menus** 750kr; 795kr; 1,175kr. **Credit** AmEx, DC, MC, V.

This temple to the god of food – with a distinctly French bent – is in a charming inn dating back to 1626, and is the only restaurant in Sweden to be awarded two Michelin stars. As it's in Sollentuna, just north of Stockholm, the easiest way to get here is by taxi. It's a small price to pay (compared with what your dinner will cost), and you'll get food of the highest order. The menu is French-meets-Swedish and follows the seasons, with fish, game and vegetables sourced locally. You might come across Swedish duck with sea buckthorn, truffle sauce and ravioli, or desserts such as the airy soufflé of wild strawberries. The interior, surroundings and service are all exquisite, too. Chef Christer Lingström has opened Edsbacka Bistro across the street, serving excellent steaks, and at a considerably lower price than in this stately inn.

Middle Eastern

Cave de Roi

Storgatan 70, Huvudsta Centrum (27 13 54/ www.cavederoi.com). T-bana Huvudsta Centrum/ bus 113, 196, 198, 396. **Open** *Restaurant* 3pm-midnight Mon-Sat. *Bar* 3-11pm Mon, Tue; 3pm-1am Wed, Thur; 3pm-3am Fri, Sat. **Main courses** 109kr-190kr. **Set menus** 250kr-350kr. **Credit** AmEx, DC, MC, V.

When it comes to Lebanese restaurants, this is the real McCoy. It's located in a boring suburban mall above a T-bana station in Solna, outside Stockholm. Sorry, but that's the way it is. Cave de Roi is one of very few restaurants for which the city crowd will leave town. The food is good, but the atmosphere is even better – when they start playing (loud) Middle Eastern hits, Lebanese families dance around the long tables. And so should you. Give yourself enough time for a coffee and the *nargileh* (hookah). You can order à la carte Monday to Wednesday, but it's set menu only the rest of the week. Belly dancers gyrate from Thursday to Saturday.

Swedish

Lux

Primusgatan 116, Lilla Essingen (619 01 90). Bus 1, 49. **Open** 11am-2pm Tue-Fri; 5-11pm Tue-Sat; 1-9pm Sun. **Main courses** 220kr-280kr. **Credit** AmEx, DC, MC, V.

On the small, residential island of Lilla Essingen, just off Kungsholmen, Lux is considered to be one of the city's best restaurants, and we agree. Its stately old building has magnificent views of the Mariebergsfjärden inlet. The interior may feel a bit overly sparse and Scandinavian, but the food more than compensates. The chef and his crew serve thoroughly contemporary, high-quality Swedish food – such as halibut with Karl Johan mushrooms, filet of venison with spiced sausage, beetroot and pickled chanterelles – without making too much of a fuss about it. Lux is a bit off the beaten path, but it's well worth seeking out.

Eat, Drink, Shop

Bars

A night out in Stockholm is more about *krog* than grog.

Akkurat.
See p139.

Egalitarian welfare state? Forget it. When it comes to bars and nightlife, Stockholm is anything but democratic, famous instead for its terrifyingly trendy bars, VIP-membership cards and fickle bouncers. But don't let this put you off. Stockholm's bar scene extends beyond the trend-meets-money epicentre of Stureplan, and is diverse enough to provide everything from minimalism and Martinis to cosy local bars.

The trendiest bars (and clubs) are in the business district around **Stureplan** in Östermalm. Recognisable by their stylish, minimalist interiors (birch wood, white walls, frosted glass), these venues set out to convey an air of luxury. The doormen are notoriously fussy, often rejecting would-be patrons solely on appearance. To enjoy this part of town at the weekend, dress fashionably and arrive before the queues start building at around 10pm. In other parts of town, notably the working class-turned-bohemian district of **Södermalm**, there are plenty of great bars and the doormen are less picky. Although long queues occur in areas other than Stureplan, only the truly inebriated risk being rejected.

Dance clubs and live music venues are an important part of Stockholm nightlife but they do not occupy centre stage. Instead, the scene is based around the *krog* – which is essentially a bar-cum-restaurant. (An explanation for this is that any establishment that serves alcohol must, by law, also serve food.) *Krogar* often take on club elements, with DJs, bouncers at the door and late-night dancing on whatever floor space is available. In fact, many of Stockholm's best bars also house its best clubs (*see pp193-196* **Clubs**).

Although *krogar* come in many shapes and sizes, the distinction between a trendy *krog* and an untrendy one (aka *B-krog*) is usually quite clear. While happy to queue for 30 minutes to get into a popular *krog*, most Stockholm twentysomethings, in their desperation to be seen in only the hippest bar, shun *B-krogar*, unwilling to stop in even for a single beer.

B-krogar are easily recognised by their lack of class or attention to detail. Many have nondescript interiors or are remnants of Stockholm's 1980s faux-Irish/London pub phase. Some offer rowdy fun, along with

Hotellet. *See p142.*

cheap beer, pool tables and jukeboxes. Generally, the clientele is either too young to get into the trendier bars (18 to 20 or younger) or too old to want to (35 and up).

Opening hours can vary greatly, though most bars stay open on Friday and Saturday nights until either 1am or 3am. A small number of places around Stureplan shut at 5am, which is the latest closing time allowed by law. Söder bars close earlier at around 1am.

Stiff taxes make alcohol expensive in Sweden. A large glass of beer generally sets you back between 30kr and 50kr and cocktails start at around 70kr. To counterbalance this, a typical Stockholmer's weekend will start with a few drinks with friends at home. This tradition, called *värma* ('warming'), is particularly common among students. As a result, the bars don't begin to fill until around 9.30pm to 11pm. After that the popular places fill up quickly, though, so arrive before 10.30pm to avoid queuing.

Despite the relatively high prices, the selection of beer on offer is lacklustre. Most Swedes are content to order a *stor stark* ('large strong'), which invariably results in a large glass of bland local lager, such as Pripps, Spendrups or Falcon. If your favourite beer is not on tap, ask for it in a bottle. Mixed drinks have enjoyed increased popularity recently, prompting bartenders to expand their repertoire with the help of a shaker and mixing stick.

Although the drinking age in Sweden is 18, bars are free to set limits higher than that, so limits of 20 or 23 are not unusual. Of course, exceptions are made, particularly for attractive young women. In the listings below we've mentioned age restriction only when it's 20 or over.

Sweden will introduce a ban on smoking in bars and restaurants on 1 June 2005. The law was passed in May 2004, around the same time that a similar ban began in neighbouring Norway. *See p135* **Up in smoke**.

A particular quirk of Stockholm nightlife is the ubiquitous cloakrooms manned by authoritarian attendants who, it seems, will stop at nothing to get you to hand over your coat. Accept this drawback with a smile. Although the 10kr to 15kr fee is annoying, it will at least prevent your jacket from being stolen. Huge, dripping winter coats are to blame for this mildly mercenary culture.

Gamla Stan

In the Old Town, most of the bars are situated around **Kornhamnstorg** or on nearby **Järntorget**. If you're a jazz fan, try the bar at **Stampen Jazzpub** (*see p215*), which is generally pretty lively. *See also p140* **Flyt**.

Engelen

Kornhamnstorg 59 (50 55 60 00/www.wallmans. com). T-bana Gamla Stan/bus 3, 53, 55, 59, 76. **Open** *Bar* 4pm-3am Mon-Sat; 5pm-3am Sun. *Food served* 4-11pm Mon-Sat; 5-11pm Sun. **Minimum age** 23. **Admission** (after 8pm) Mon-Thur, Sun 50kr; Fri, Sat 80kr. **Credit** AmEx, DC, MC, V. **Map** p305 J7.

Posing as a rustic tavern, Engelen (both bar and restaurant) caters firmly to passing tourists and middle-aged locals looking to get down and party. The main room has a stage where bands play covers from 8.30pm to midnight most days. When that's finished, guests move down to the vaulted nightclub in the cellar where Top 40 music is mixed with a selection of popular classics.

Medusa

Kornhamnstorg 61 (21 87 00/www.medusabar.com).
T-bana Gamla Stan/bus 3, 53, 55, 59, 76. **Open**
Bar 2pm-3am daily. *Food served* 2-10pm daily.
Minimum age *Mon-Thur, Sun* women 18, men 20;
Fri, Sat women 21, men 23. **Admission** (after 11pm)
60kr. **Credit** AmEx, MC, V. **Map** p305 J7.

A small bar with a cavernous basement, Medusa is
Gamla Stan's heavy-metal hangout. The upstairs
bar, painted plain orange, plays basic rock music to
a mixed crowd of tourists and local headbangers.
Downstairs in the twisty blue catacombs, the music
is louder and harder. A small bar serves beer to
guests whooping it up on the two tiny dancefloors.
Mind your head.

Norrmalm

Berns Salonger

Berzelii Park (56 63 20 00/www.berns.se). T-bana
Kungsträdgården/bus 2, 47, 55, 69, 76. **Open** *Bar*
Mid Aug-June 11.30am-1am Mon, Tue; 11.30am-3am
Wed, Thur; 11.30am-4am Fri, Sat; 11.30am-midnight
Sun (July-mid Aug from 1pm Sat, Sun). *Food served*
Mid Aug-June 11.30am-3pm Mon; 11.30am-3pm,
5-11pm Tue-Sat; 11.30am-3.30pm Sun (July-mid Aug
5-11pm Tue-Fri; 1-11.30pm Sat). **Minimum age**
23. **Admission** varies. **Credit** AmEx, DC, MC, V.
Map p305 G8.

Built in 1863, Berns was once Stockholm's foremost
venue for exclusive, cabaret-style entertainment.
Since reopening in 1989, the baroque mansion has
once again emerged as the city's number one late-
night party palace. With five bars on three levels,
Berns combines a hip club in the basement with a
ballroom bar and balcony area hideaways. In the
summer, the outside terrace bar is packed. The
queue varies in size through the evening: arrive
before 11pm to avoid the rush (and the entrance fee
that applies Thursday to Sunday). The line starts to
wane around midnight, only to pick up later when
neighbouring bars close. The notoriously picky
bouncers guard not only the front entrance but also
the downstairs club and upstairs terrace. Depending
on their mood, they may or may not demand to see
a membership card.

Up in smoke

With little controversy or upheaval, the
Swedish government voted in May 2004
to join a handful of nations worldwide that
have banned smoking in eating and drinking
establishments. While in other countries
this law has been hugely controversial,
in Sweden it raised little public outcry, and
lawmakers approved it by an overwhelming
vote of 245 to 45. Enforcement of the law
is scheduled to begin on 1 June 2005.

Representatives of the Moderate Party
and the Liberal Party were the only members
to vote against the anti-smoking law. 'This
is a powerful punch into thin air. It is not
possible for us to tax and ban our way to
a better and happier life,' Moderate Party
legislator Carl-Axel Johansson warned
the Swedish news agency TT.

Under the new law, smoking will only
be permitted in designated areas where
consumption of food or drink – even coffee –
is forbidden, and other patrons are not
required to pass through. The law is so
sternly worded that Swedes joke that
they might be arrested for smoking
while eating cough lozenges.

Ireland, Norway and the Netherlands have
all introduced similar smoking bans in recent
years, which are designed to do more than
protect staff from the effects of passive
smoking. They also aim to 'de-normalise'
smoking as a social activity.

As it happens, the Swedes are enthusiastic
users of oral moist snuff tobacco, or *snus*.
Sweden's level of consumption of this product
continues to be one of the highest in the world
– more than 5,000 tonnes of the stuff is sold
here every year. After a similar anti-smoking
law was put into place in Norway, *snus* makers
saw their sales soar. *Snus* is sold in cans
containing tiny pouches of tobacco that are
placed between the user's lip and gum. Those
who use it admit that it looks horrible, tastes
horrible and smells horrible. Due to the long
tradition of *snus* use in Sweden and Norway,
these two countries were even exempted from
the EU ban on *snus* in 1992.

In Sweden, *snus* was once the tobacco
of choice of the working class, favoured by
lumberjacks and truck drivers, but in recent
years it's become increasingly trendy. It's
now something of a fashion accessory
among the partying classes who associate
smoking with low income, low education
and bad health.

In Norway it's estimated that about one in
ten young men in the country now uses *snus*,
according to industry figures, but that's still
well behind Sweden. Norwegians purchase
about 15 million cans of *snus* a year; in
Sweden it's 190 million cans. So, in 2005
smoking may become a thing of the past
in Sweden, but it seems that tobacco will
still be one of the Swedes' favourite things.

Eat, Drink, Shop

Eat and drink your way around the world

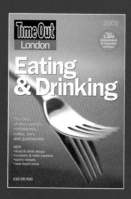

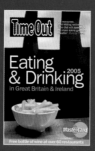

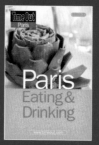

Café Opera

Operahuset, Karl XIIs Torg (676 58 07/www.cafe opera.se). T-bana Kungsträdgården/bus 2, 55, 59, 62, 76. **Open** *Bar* 5pm-3am daily. *Food served* 5pm-2.30am daily. **Minimum age** 23. **Admission** (after 11pm) 100kr. **Credit** AmEx, DC, MC, V. **Map** p305 G7.

In the back of the Stockholm Opera House, Café Opera is one of the most elegant and exclusive venues in town. A restaurant by day, in the evening it's an extravagant party bar with a sizeable dance-floor. The interior is a luxurious mix of Scandinavian chic and remodelled baroque. The crowd ranges from twentysomething trend-followers to scantily clad women and older men in suits.

Fredsgatan 12

Fredsgatan 12 (411 73 48). T-bana Kungsträdgården/ bus 3, 53, 62, 65. **Open** *May-Aug* 9pm-3am Mon-Sat. *Closed Sept-Apr.* **Minimum age** 20. **Credit** AmEx, DC, MC, V. **Map** p305 H7.

In the historic Royal Academy of Arts building, trendy Fredsgatan 12 is best known for its outside terrace, open only in the summer. Hip types groove to the music and take in the view towards Gamla Stan and the Riksdag. Half of the floor space is on the wide steps leading to the entrance, so watch out for the odd broken beer glass rolling down the steps. The restaurant inside is equally stylish (*see p115*).

Icebar

Nordic Sea Hotel, Vasaplan 4 (50 56 30 00/www.nordic hotels.se). T-bana T-Centralen/bus 1, 47, 53, 59, 69. **Open** 3pm-midnight Mon-Sat; 3-9pm Sun. **Admission** 125kr. **Credit** AmEx, DC, MC, V. **Map** p305 G6.

You can be as cool as you like about this slightly gimmicky attraction, designed by the people behind the Icehotel in Jukkasjärvi in the far north of Sweden, but the minute you done your silver high-tech poncho and sip from your ice glass, you will be giggling and snapping photos along with the rest of them. This tiny sub-zero bar, maintained at a chilly -4°C (23°F), is in a corner of the Nordic Sea Hotel (*see p48*) in Norrmalm. With 20 minutes of chilling usually enough for most, the turnover is high, and the chances for socialising therefore slim. Loud music and fine Absolut shooters (one included in the steep entrance fee) keep spirits high in the adverse conditions.

Karlssons & Co

Kungsgatan 56 (54 51 21 40/www.karlsson-co.com). T-bana Hötorget/bus 1, 52, 56. **Open** *Bar* 11am-3am Mon-Fri; noon-3am Sat. *Food served* 11am-11.30pm Mon-Fri; noon-11.30pm Sat. **Admission** (after 9pm) Wed, Fri, Sat 90kr; Thur 40kr. **Minimum age** 27. **Credit** AmEx, DC, MC, V. **Map** p305 F6.

Next door to Kicki's (*see below*), this bar and restaurant caters mainly to a crowd of older party-goers and tourists. Faux mooseheads and nostalgic American signs adorn the walls, and the usual drinks are served up from three bars. Karlssons also has a large dancefloor, blackjack and roulette tables, and five slot machines.

Kicki's

Kungsgatan 54 (10 00 26/www.kickis.nu). T-bana Hötorget/bus 1, 52, 56. **Open** *Bar* 10am-3am Mon-Fri, 11am-3am Sat, noon-3am Sun. *Food served* 10am-9.30pm Mon-Fri; 11am-9.30pm Sat; noon-9.30pm Sun. **Admission** (after 9pm) Fri, Sat 60kr. **Minimum age** women 18, men 20. **Credit** AmEx, DC, MC, V. **Map** p305 F6.

Local party-goers mix with tourists at this camp dive-bar next to the pedestrian shopping street Drottninggatan. Karaoke is on offer every night (10.30pm-1.30am) except Wednesdays, when a cover band takes over and 'model competitions' are held. Fridays feature a soft-core male strip act and Saturdays are foam parties. Kicki's utterly unimpressive interior has three bars, two cramped dance-floors, a blackjack table and dozens of tacky framed posters. Seedy but fun.

The Loft

Regeringsgatan 66 (411 19 91). T-bana Hötorget/ bus 1, 52, 56. **Open** *Bar* 3pm-1am Mon-Thur; 3pm-2am Fri, Sat; 3pm-midnight Sun. *Food served* 3-10.30pm daily. **Minimum age** 23. **Credit** AmEx, MC, V. **Map** p305 F7.

One of the few Irish pubs in Stockholm actually staffed by Irishmen, the Loft bar-restaurant is home-from-home to expats from all corners of the English-speaking world. Although the interior is reminiscent of a medieval tavern, it doesn't try as hard as some of its more commercial competitors. Sports are shown on two TVs and one projector screen. Priority is given to Gaelic football, rugby and hurling.

Vasastaden

Nightlife in Vasastaden is quite spread out, with most of the bars either on cosy **Rörstrandsgatan** or within a few blocks of the busy intersection of **Odengatan** and **Sveavägan**.

The Bagpipers Inn

Rörstrandsgatan 21 (31 18 55). T-bana St Eriksplan/ bus 3, 4, 42, 72. **Open** *Bar* 4pm-midnight Mon; 4pm-1am Tue-Thur; 3pm-1am Fri; 2pm-1am Sat; 2-11pm Sun. *Food served* 4-11pm Mon-Thur; 3-11pm Fri; 2-11pm Sat, Sun. **Minimum age** 23. **Credit** AmEx, MC, V. **Map** p308 D2.

The bartenders wear kilts at this Scottish-themed pub decorated with dark wood, green walls and knick-knacks from the Highlands. The beer is not cheap (46kr-49kr for a pint), but there's a good selection of around a dozen brews on tap, mainly from the UK and Ireland. The crowd is mainly thirtysomethings and out-of-towners drawn by the cosy atmosphere. The Bagpipers Inn is usually packed at the weekends and in the summer, when outside seating is available.

Cliff Barnes

Norrtullsgatan 45 (31 80 70/www.cliff.se). T-bana Odenplan/bus 2, 40, 52, 69. **Open** *Bar* 11am-1am Mon-Fri; 6pm-1am Sat. *Food served* 11am-11pm

Eat, Drink, Shop

Lydmar Hotel. *See p142.*

Mon-Fri; 6-11pm Sat. **Minimum age** 23. **Credit** AmEx, MC, V. **Map** p308 C4.

On the outskirts of town in what was once a home for widows, Cliff Barnes is a down-to-earth party bar/restaurant. The worn wooden floors, high ceilings and large vaulted windows make it ideal for enthusiastic beer drinking and loud conversation. At 11pm on Fridays and Saturdays the lights are turned down and the music (popular classics from the 1960s and '70s) is turned up. Although several large signs clearly forbid it, dancing on the tables is not uncommon. Cliff Barnes takes its name from JR's unlucky arch rival in *Dallas*, and a framed portrait of Ken Kercheval (the actor who portrayed Barnes) decorates the bar's main wall. *See also p123.*

La Habana

Sveavägen 108 (16 64 65). T-bana Rådmansgatan/ bus 2, 42, 52, 53, 72. **Open** *Bar* 5pm-1am daily. *Food served* 5-10pm Mon-Wed, Sun; 5-10.30pm Thur-Sat. **Minimum age** 20. **Credit** AmEx, DC, MC, V. **Map** p309 D6.

As one of only two Cuban bars in Stockholm, La Habana is a refreshing alternative to the otherwise largely mainstream bars in the area. The interior is all dark wood and white walls, but the crowd, the drinks and the music are much more colourful as Latin Americans and Swedes meet and mix. The small basement bar serves great Mojitos, and the floor comes alive with salsa dancing in the late hours.

Musslan Bar

Dalagatan 46 (34 64 10). T-bana Odenplan/bus 4, 40, 47, 53, 72. **Open** *Bar* 8pm-1am Mon; 6pm-1am Tue-Sat. *Food served* 8-11pm Mon; 6-11pm Tue-Sat. **Minimum age** 20. **Credit** AmEx, DC, MC, V. **Map** p308 D4.

Trendy young things frequent this tiny, dimly lit bar. Lush sofas, stainless-steel tables and a blue ceiling with tiny starry lights set Musslan apart from the competition. It's a place to chill out and have a cocktail while the DJ (Wed-Sat) spins soul or techno.

Paus

Rörstrandsgatan 18 (34 44 05). T-bana St Eriksplan/ bus 3, 4, 42, 72. **Open** *Bar* 5pm-1am Mon-Sat. *Food served* 5-11pm Mon-Sat. **Minimum age** 23. **Credit** AmEx, DC, MC, V. **Map** p308 E3.

Well placed on a quiet, residential street of cafés and bars, Paus has a cream-coloured interior with large monochrome paintings and a giant mirror wall. It specialises in quality cocktails but doesn't take itself too seriously, with a laid-back, neighbourhood feel. Shunning the guest DJs of similarly decorated places, the soft music seems to be whatever CDs the bartender brought to work that day.

Storstad

Odengatan 41 (673 38 00). T-bana Rådmansgatan/ bus 2, 4, 42, 53, 72. **Open** *Bar* 5pm-1am Mon, Tue; 5pm-3am Wed, Thur; 4pm-3am Fri; 6pm-3am Sat. *Food served* 5-11pm Mon-Fri; 6-11pm Sat. **Minimum age** 23. **Credit** AmEx, DC, MC, V. **Map** p309 C6.

The hip mix with the suit-and-tie brigade at the hottest bar in Vasastaden. Storstad (literally 'Big Town') has a chic white interior, huge windows and a large L-shaped bar that allows for a great deal of person-to-person interaction. This is a trendy spot and features the usual guest DJs playing all the right tunes, but it is not as reserved as similar venues – some might even call it a classy pick-up bar. For a darker version of the same thing, check out its sister bar, Olssons Skor, next door.

Tranan

Karlbergsvägen 14 (52 72 81 00/www.sturehof gruppen.se). T-bana Odenplan/bus 2, 4, 40, 69, 72. **Open** *Bar* 5pm-1am daily. *Food served* 5-11.45pm daily. **Minimum age** 23. **Credit** AmEx, DC, MC, V. **Map** p309 D5.

Described as a 'modern classic' in the local entertainment guides, Tranan is the quintessential Stockholm bar. In the basement of the well-respected Tranan restaurant (*see p122*), it combines minimalist chic with the cosy feel of a cellar. A DJ spins records as professionals in their late 20s congregate around sturdy wooden tables. Never too surprising, Tranan holds its own as one of the most enduring grade-A bars in Stockholm.

Södermalm

Nightlife hotspots on Söder are **Götgatan** and the area around **Medborgarplatsen**. Several small bars are also scattered south of **Folkungagatan**. The **Hotel Rival** (*see p55*) on Mariatorget has a cosy, art deco cocktail bar, and the **Clarion Hotel** (*see p53*) has two lively bars. *See also p140* **Thaiboat**.

Akkurat

Hornsgatan 18 (644 00 15/www.akkurat.se). T-bana Mariatorget/bus 43, 55, 66, 74. **Open** *Bar* 11am-midnight Mon-Thur; 11am-1am Fri; 3pm-1am Sat; 6pm-1am Sun. *Food served* 11am-11pm Mon-Fri; 3-11pm Sat; 6-11pm Sun. **Minimum age** 23. **Credit** AmEx, DC, MC, V. **Map** p314 K7.

Beer lovers frustrated with Stockholm's lack of good ale should head straight to Akkurat. Don't be put off by the run-of-the-mill pub interior, as this bar offers 28 varieties of beer on tap, from fermented Belgian lambics to British cask-conditioned ale. There are 600 varieties of bottled beer and 400 whiskies. True connoisseurs can book taste tests, starting at 220kr per person. Music every Sunday at 9pm includes anything from cover groups to indie rock.

Fenix

Götgatan 40 (640 45 06/www.fenixbar.nu). T-bana Slussen or Medborgarplatsen/bus 59, 66. **Open** *Bar* 11am-1am Mon-Fri; noon-1am Sat; noon-midnight Sun. *Food served* 5-11pm daily. **Minimum age** 23. **Credit** AmEx, DC, MC, V. **Map** p314 L8.

This gaudy party bar offers a refreshing alternative to the tasteful minimalism of many Stockholm drinking dens. With red walls, crazy artwork and mosaic decorations, it attracts a crowd of twenty- and thirtysomethings dressed for a night out. The cavernous basement has a dancefloor and winding lounge area.

Folkhemmet

Renstiernas Gata 30 (640 55 95). Bus 2, 53, 59, 66, 76. **Open** *Bar* 5pm-1am daily. *Food served* 5-11pm daily. **Credit** AmEx, DC, MC, V. **Map** p315 M9.

One of the most enduring bars in the Nytorget area, Folkhemmet is a favourite watering hole for artists, musicians and media folk. It gets packed at the weekends. The minimalist interior combines a dining area with a bar and DJ. A tiny adjoining bar (closed Mon), decorated in bright red, doubles as a dancefloor. Folkhemmet takes its name from the 1930s political ideal of the 'people's home' or welfare state.

Gondolen

Stadsgården 6 (641 70 90/www.eriks.se). T-bana Slussen/bus 2, 3, 53, 76. **Open** *Bar* July 5.30pm-1am Mon-Sat. Aug-June 11.30am-1am Mon-Fri; 1pm-1am Sat. *Food served* July 5.30-11pm Mon-Sat. Aug-June 11.30am-2.30pm Mon-Fri; 5-11pm Sat. **Credit** AmEx, DC, MC, V. **Map** p314 K8.

At the top of the historic Katarina lift, Gondolen is an ideal place for a tall drink and a wide view of the city. The bar sits under the walkway connecting the lift with Mosebacke (*see p92*), and provides a panoramic view of Djurgården to the east and Riddarfjärden to the west. Drinks are reasonably priced, despite the feeling of international luxury. You can get to the bar either from Mosebacke in the Katarinahissen (5kr) or via the restaurant's lift at Stadsgården 6.

Kvarnen

Tjärhovsgatan 4 (643 03 80/www.kvarnen.com). T-bana Medborgarplatsen/bus 55, 59, 66. **Open** *Kvarnen* 11am-3am Mon-Fri; 5pm-3am Sat, Sun.

H20 5pm-3am Mon-Fri; 7pm-3am Sat. *Eld* 10pm-3am Wed, Thur; 9pm-3am Fri, Sat. *Food served* 11am-11pm Mon-Fri; 5-11pm Sat, Sun. **Minimum age** 23. **Credit** AmEx, MC, V. **Map** p315 L8.

Originally a beer hall, Kvarnen ('the Windmill') has evolved into one of the most popular late-night pubs on Söder. The lofty main room, filled with rows of tables and loud chatter, plays no music and retains the look and feel of a beer hall. It is flanked by two more recent additions: the small Mediterranean-themed H20 bar in what used to be a kitchen, and the flame-inspired Eld ('Hell') bar in the basement. Eld heats up in the wee hours when dancing erupts on the black-and-white chequered floor. Kvarnen is also packed with Hammarby supporters before matches. Show up early at the weekend, preferably before 10pm, to avoid the horrific queue that winds down the block. Bouncers are strict but fair.

Mosebacke Etablissement

Mosebacketorg 3 (55 60 98 90/www.mosebacke.se). T-bana Slussen/bus 2, 3, 53, 76. **Open** *Bar* Mid May-Aug 11am-1am Mon-Thur, Sun; 11am-2am Fri, Sat. Sept-mid May 4pm-1am Mon-Thur, Sun; 4pm-2am Fri, Sat. *Food served* Mid May-Aug 11am-midnight daily. Sept-mid May 4-9pm daily. **Minimum age** varies. **Admission** 60kr-80kr. **Credit** AmEx, DC, MC, V. **Map** p314 K8.

A definite winner among musicians and underground types, Mosebacke is Stockholm's hottest venue for cutting-edge performance acts and live music (*see p216*). The historic building, part of Södra Teatern (*see p215*), features two bars and a dancefloor/stage area – check local papers for details or drop by for a surprise show. In the summer, two additional bars open on the large outdoor terrace, which offers a fantastic view of Stockholm harbour. It also hosts some great clubs; *see p195*.

El Mundo

Erstagatan 21 (743 03 53). Bus 2, 53, 66, 76. **Open** *Bar* 5pm-midnight Mon-Thur, Sat, Sun; 4pm-midnight Fri. **Credit** AmEx, DC, MC, V. **Map** p315 L10.

More continental than Nordic, El Mundo looks a bit like the type of small arty bar you might find in Paris. The furniture appears to be odds and ends from an antique shop, and the red and grey walls are adorned with a mixture of framed photos of jazz greats and kitschy religious objects. There's a cracking cocktail menu, which includes specialities such as Frozen Mango Pisco and Raspberry Rum. On Fridays (4-7pm) the owner, Björn, lowers the prices of drinks and serves up free tapas, while playing his favourite records. The old-fashioned piano in the corner is put to use a few days a month when transvestite Peggy Sands visits El Mundo to sing songs from the 1930s and '40s. The bar is usually packed on Fridays and Saturdays. Outside seating in summer.

Nada

Åsögatan 140 (644 70 20). T-bana Medborgarplatsen/ bus 2, 53, 59, 66, 76. **Open** *Bar* 5pm-1am daily. *Food served* 5-11pm daily. **Credit** AmEx, MC, V. **Map** p314 M9.

Eat, Drink, Shop

Locals congregate at this small two-room bar, known for its tapas menu and gold-adorned ceiling. Situated in the heart of the SoFo district, Nada is low-key on weekdays when patrons can be seen drinking beer and playing board games. DJs are on hand daily with anything from garage to Janis Joplin. On weekends Nada is filled to the brim with local partygoers making their first stop of the night. Outside seating in summer.

O'Learys

Götgatan 11 (644 69 01/www.olearys.se). T-bana Slussen/bus 2, 3, 53, 59, 76. **Open** *Bar* 5-11pm Mon; 5pm-midnight Tue-Thur; 5pm-1am Fri; 1pm-1am Sat; 1-11pm Sun. *Food served* 5-10pm Mon-Fri; 1-10pm Sat, Sun. **Minimum age** 21. **Credit** AmEx, DC, MC, V. **Map** p314 K8.

This Boston-Irish sports bar is popular with Anglophiles, American expats and die-hard sports fans mainly in their 30s and 40s. The green interior is covered with framed sports posters, neon beer signs and, above all, televisions: it's got three big-screen TVs and 35 regular televisions, including one in the toilet. There are 45 beers to choose from, most from England, Ireland and the US. Along with the obligatory slot machines, O'Learys also has a 'pop-a-shot' basketball game. Call in advance to reserve tables during major sporting events.

Other locations: Kungsholmsgatan 31, Kungsholmen (654 52 10).

Pelikan

Blekingegatan 40 (55 60 90 90). T-bana Skanstull/bus 3, 55, 59, 74. **Open** *Bar* 3.30pm-1am Mon-Fri; 1pm-1am Sat, Sun. *Food served* 5-11pm daily. **Credit** AmEx, MC, V. **Map** p315 M8.

This charming beer hall is well away from the action in a mainly residential area in southern Södermalm. The clientele ranges from ageing regulars to young Southside hipsters in designer clothes. Drop in for a beer or visit the adjoining bar, Kristallen, adorned with oriental rugs and ornate chandeliers.

Snaps

Götgatan 48 (640 28 68). T-bana Medborgarplatsen/bus 55, 59, 66. **Open** *Bar* 5pm-1am Mon-Wed; 5pm-3am Thur-Sat. *Food served* 5-11pm Mon-Sat. **Minimum age** 23. **Credit** AmEx, DC, MC, V. **Map** p314 L8.

In the vaulted basement of a 17th-century mansion, Snaps is one of Söder's most popular party bars, second only to Kvarnen and Mosebacke (for both,

Liquid refreshment

Since Stockholm is one of the world's most watery cities, it figures that the city should boast a few bobbing boozers. The following are three of our favourite watery joints. Note that the party boat/bar/restaurant **Patricia** (*see p213*) is also hugely popular.

Flyt

Kornhamnstorg, Gamla Stan (21 37 29/ www.flyt.se). T-bana Gamla Stan/bus 3, 53. **Open** *June-Aug* 3pm-midnight Mon; 3pm-1am Tue-Thur; noon-1am Fri, Sat; noon-midnight Sun. **Credit** AmEx, DC, MC, V. **Map** p305 J7/8.

Not unlike Tvillingarnas (*see below*), Flyt is situated on a pontoon bridge connected to an old steamboat. However, the venue's more central location on the edge of the Old Town gives it a more upbeat feel, accentuated by the pop and rock music flowing from the speakers. Relax with a beer and watch the motor boats line up to wait for the lock (of Slussen) to open.

Thaiboat

Kajplats 300, Södermalm (462 94 83/ www.thaiboat.se). T-bana Skanstull/bus 3, 4, 55, 74. **Open** *May-Sept* 11am-1am daily (food served until 11pm). **Credit** AmEx, DC, MC, V. **Map** p315 O9.

For a less typical bar-on-boat experience head to the Hammarby lock (Hammarbyslussen) where this bar is on a pontoon connected to a faux-Oriental sailing vessel. Once you're on board there's Thai food and an extensive selection of exotic drinks (Mai Thai, Vodka Lippo and so on) served in two small bars. Thatched roofs, fake palm trees and colourful lights give it all a Ko Pha Ngan kind of feel. Best of all, a small section of the pontoon has been turned into a fake beach, complete with sand and tiny deckchairs.

Tvillingarnas

Strandvägskajen 27, Östermalm (660 37 14/ www.tvillingarnas.com). Bus 44, 47, 69, 76. **Open** *Apr-Sept* 8am-1am daily (depending on the weather). **Credit** AmEx, DC, MC, V. **Map** p306 G10.

Located on a pontoon by the bridge connecting Östermalm to Djurgården, Tvillingarnas bar and restaurant is a great place to wind down and watch boats glide by. Don't worry if the weather isn't great – blankets and heat lamps, coupled with soft pop or soul music, provide a cosy atmosphere even on overcast days. Tvillingarnas also rents out boats for short excursions on the nearby Djurgården canal.

see p139). The main room features a dining area, bar and blackjack table. For more action, venture downstairs to the Rangus Tangus club, a dancefloor/lounge in tones of deep red. In summer, you can eat outside in a large courtyard. Show up before 11pm to avoid queuing.

Metro

Götgatan 93 (442 03 30). T-bana Skanstull/bus 3, 4, 55, 74. **Open** *Bar* 4pm-1am Mon-Thur; 4pm-2am Fri, Sat. *Food served* 4-10pm Mon, Sun; 4-11pm Tue-Sat. **Admission** free, unless there's a performance. **Minimum age** 20. **Credit** AmEx, DC, MC, V. **Map** p315 N8.

Originally a cinema, Metro has become one of Södermalm's most popular nightspots. The rows of seats have been replaced with a large, circular bar around which twenty- and thirtysomethings rub elbows, mingle and flirt. Beyond the bar, under a fleet of bulbous lamps, is a sizeable lounge area. Another bar is in a separate room near the entrance. Yet another bar, in the restaurant, is open to non-dining guests from around midnight.

Öst 100

Östgötagatan 100 (55 69 76 70/www.ost100.com). T-bana Skanstull/bus 3, 4, 55, 74. **Open** *June-Aug* 11am-3am daily. *Sept-May* 5pm-1am Mon-Wed; 5pm-3am Thur, Fri; 6pm-3am Sat. **Credit** AmEx, DC, MC, V. **Map** p315 O9.

This spacious and chic restaurant and nightclub in a modern glass office building near the Hammarby Lock (Hammarbyslussen). Frightfully hip when it opened in 2003, Öst 100 has become a premier summer hotspot for Stockholm's young movers and shakers, with long queues after 11pm on weekends. Hang out at the bar or lounge as the DJ plays house and hip hop. Later in the evening furniture is moved aside to make a small dancefloor. In summer there's a large outside seating area along the harbour.

WC

Skånegatan 51 (644 19 81). T-bana Medborgarplatsen/bus 55, 59, 66. **Open** *Bar* 5pm-1am daily. *Food served* 5-11pm daily. *Brunch* 11.30am-3.30pm Sat, Sun. **Minimum age** 20. **Credit** AmEx, MC, V. **Map** p315 M8.

A small, rectangular basement venue, WC is one of the more popular of the many bars on Skånegatan. The colourful interior, funky lighting and bar stools with holes in the seat are self-consciously cool. On the downside, it can get hopelessly crowded on weekend nights. Claustrophobes, beware.

Östermalm

Most bars and nightclubs around **Stureplan** are on or near one of the three main streets intersecting the square: Kungsgatan, Birger Jarlsgatan and Sturegatan. In addition to those listed here, don't miss the myriad bars at glam Stureplan club **Spy Bar** (*see p196*). *See also p140* **Tvillingarnas**.

Öst 100 – hip Hammarby hotspot.

The Dubliner

Smålandsgatan 8 (679 77 07/www.dubliner.se). T-bana Östermalmstorg/bus 2, 43, 47, 62, 65. **Open** *Bar* 4pm-3am Mon-Fri; 1pm-3am Sat; 4pm-1am Sun. *Food served* 4-11pm Mon-Fri, Sun; 1-11pm Sat. **Minimum age** 23. **Credit** AmEx, DC, MC, V. **Map** p305 F8.

One of the few genuine Irish pubs in central Stockholm, the Dubliner is run and staffed by English-speaking expats. Drop in for a pint as the random bands play anything from traditional Irish music to cover songs from the '70s. The Dubliner is also a good place to catch sporting events. There are seven beers on tap including Guinness, Kilkenny and John Smith's, as well as 25 bottled beers.

East

Stureplan 13 (611 49 59/www.east-restaurang.se). T-bana Östermalstorg/bus 1, 2, 55, 56. **Open** *Bar* 11.30am-3am Mon-Sat; 5pm-3am Sun. *Food served* 11.30am-11pm Mon-Sat; 5-11pm Sun. **Minimum age** 23. **Credit** AmEx, DC, MC, V. **Map** p305 F8.

A sushi restaurant by day, East turns into Stockholm's foremost hip hop hangout by night. Two bars serve beer and cocktails while a DJ plays hard-hitting beats for one of the most ethnically diverse crowds in the city. A small section of the first bar doubles as a dancefloor later. It's somewhat difficult to get past the bouncers, so dress to impress and arrive before 10.30pm to avoid the hassle and the wait.

Halv Trappa Plus Gård

Lästmakargatan 3 (611 02 75/www.halvtrappaplus gard.se). T-bana Östermalmstorg/bus 1, 2, 55, 56. **Open** *Bar* 5pm-midnight Mon, Tue; 5pm-1am Wed, Thur; 4pm-3am Fri, Sat. *Food served* 5-11pm Tue-Sat. **Minimum age** 23. **Credit** AmEx, DC, MC, V. **Map** p305 F7.

A few years ago Halv Trappa was the watering hole for trendy professionals in their late 20s looking for a hint of glamour. Since then the place has been remodelled, with an upscale Chinese restaurant on the ground floor, and now it's decidedly less trendy. Still, there's a stylish, minimalistic bar and lounge, and in summer the back patio – complete with a bar, heaters and Chinese lanterns – is a Stureplan fave. The club nights here (*see p194*) are brilliant.

Hotellet

Linnégatan 18 (442 89 00/www.hotellet.info). T-bana Östermalmstorg/bus 1, 42, 44, 55, 56. **Open** *Bar* 5pm-midnight Mon, Tue; 5pm-1am Wed, Thur; 4pm-1am Fri; 6pm-1am Sat. *Food served* 5-11pm Mon-Fri; 6-11pm Sat. **Minimum age** 25. **Credit** AmEx, DC, MC, V. **Map** p310 E8.

Featured in international design magazines such as *Wallpaper**, newly remodelled Hotellet has become the hotspot for young urban professionals. Its two storeys, plus an extra level upstairs, contain a total of four bars. The downstairs lounge heats up at night as the DJ sorts out the hip hop and club music. In summer, Hotellet opens its outside patio, with a finely mowed lawn, tables and white chairs.

Laroy

Birger Jarlsgatan 20 (54 50 37 00). T-bana Östermalmstorg/bus 1, 2, 55, 56. **Open** *Bar* 5pm-1am Tue, Wed; 5pm-2am Thur; 5pm-3am Fri; 7pm-3am Sat. *Food served* 5-10pm Tue-Fri; 7-10pm Sat. **Minimum age** 25. **Credit** AmEx, DC, MC, V. **Map** p305 E8.

Rich kids in designer shirts flash platinum cards and order bottles of champagne at this posh, two-storey bar and restaurant with a view over Stureplan. Although the air is thick with glamour and extravagance – or perhaps because of that – Laroy is popular with hopeful posers, particularly young girls looking for the high life and a few free drinks. Although there's no dancefloor, people let loose on all available floor space as Top 40 music pumps through the speakers. Dress posh and arrive before 10pm to ensure admittance.

Lydmar Hotel

Sturegatan 10 (56 61 13 00/www.lydmar.se). T-bana Östermalmstorg/bus 1, 2, 55, 56. **Open** *Bar* 11.30am-1am Mon-Thur; 11.30am-2am Fri; 1pm-2am Sat; 1pm-1am Sun. *Food served* 11.30am-11pm Mon-Fri; 1-11pm Sat, Sun. **Minimum age** 25. **Credit** AmEx, DC, MC, V. **Map** p305 E8.

As far as hotel bars are concerned, the Lydmar goes beyond the call of duty. The main room is spacious and furnished with linear black leather couches and easy chairs. Popular with the after-work crowd and for late-night cocktails, it also features sporadic live

music a few times a week. The bands are usually lesser-known jazz acts, but reputable underground groups such as The Roots have also been known to make unannounced appearances. Dress fashionably: doormen can be picky when the place is crowded. Guests of the hotel are automatically let in. For a review of the hotel, *see p57*.

O-baren

Stureplan 2 (440 57 30/www.sturehof.com). T-bana Östermalmstorg/bus 1, 2, 55, 56. **Open** 5pm-2am daily. **Minimum age** 23. **Credit** AmEx, DC, MC, V. **Map** p305 F8.

A dark rock, hip hop and soul den in a back room of the exclusive Sturehof restaurant (*see p130*), O-baren has a bar and large dancefloor bounded by bleacher-like seats. Although spontaneous dancing is commonplace, the clientele never loses its cool.

Kungsholmen

The busy **Fridhemsplan** area has plenty of bars in this otherwise mainly residential area.

Dovas

St Eriksgatan 53A (650 80 49). T-bana Fridhemsplan/bus 3, 4, 57, 59. **Open** *Bar* 11am-1am daily. *Food served* 11am-11.30pm daily. **Minimum age** 20. **Credit** AmEx, MC, V. **Map** p303 F3.

Dovas is easily one of the most unsettling dives in Fridhemsplan. Its darkened interior with wooden booths houses a bizarre mix of local drunks and others too young to get into trendier places with a higher minimum age. Tattoos and shaved heads are commonplace, as are random conversations that start with an accusation and end with some inebriated barfly putting his arm round your shoulder. The beer is dirt cheap at 23kr for a half-litre glass.

Johnnys

St Eriksgatan 22 (653 50 50). T-bana Fridhemsplan/bus 3, 4, 40, 57, 62. **Open** *Bar* 4pm-1am daily. *Food served* 4-11pm daily. **Credit** AmEx, MC, V. **Map** p303 G2.

Johnnys has three pool tables, slot machines, table football, blackjack and a jukebox. If you don't mind walls decorated with charity-shop art, the low beer prices (28kr for a 40cl glass) make Johnny's a great place to start the evening. It heats up at the weekends, when youngsters queue outside.

Lokal

Scheelegatan 8 (650 98 09). T-bana Rådhuset/bus 3, 40, 52, 62. **Open** *Bar* 4pm-1am Mon, Tue, Sun; 4pm-2am Wed, Thur; 4pm-3am Fri, Sat. *Food served* 4-11pm daily. **Minimum age** 23. **Credit** AmEx, DC, MC, V. **Map** p304 G4.

When Lokal first opened a few years back, everyone compared it to Storstad (*see p138*) in Vasastaden. Both have similarly stylish white interiors, enormous shopfront windows, L-shaped bars and guest DJs playing soul or house. However, Lokal is (as the name implies) more of a local venue. This means more suit-and-tie yuppies and fewer downtown hipsters.

Cafés

Coffee to go? Coffee to stay, more like, for hours and hours...

Piccolino. *See p146.*

Café culture in Sweden is as rich as the coffee the natives consume by the gallon. As the pub is to the Brits, and the coffee shop to the Americans, so the café is to the Swedes. Coffee is a serious business in Sweden – apart from the Finns, the Swedes drink more coffee per capita than any other nation, on average downing 4.5 cups each per day – and, unlike the take-out cup culture prevalent elsewhere, Swedes like to sit down with a classic white porcelain cup and saucer for their cup of java. And they like it fully leaded – decaf is hard to find, even in the capital, and serving instant coffee at home is a no-no.

This caffeine society started with King Karl XII, who brought coffee to Sweden from Turkey in 1714. It fell from favour under the reign of later monarch King Gustav III, however, as he branded it poison in the latter half of the 18th century and banned its consumption. As part of an attempt to prove the toxic perils of coffee, he devised an experiment using a couple of convicted murderers: one he sentenced to coffee on a daily basis, the other to pint-sized doses of tea. But the experiment fizzled as the killers lived well into old age, with the coffee drinker – or so the story goes – outliving the tea drinker. And both of them outlived Gustav, who was murdered.

Coffee climbed back up the local charts in 1855, when the home-brewing of alcohol was criminalised as the country attempted to curb rampant alcohol abuse. Many Swedes turned to caffeine as a booze replacement. And in the 19th century, when sexuality was a taboo subject and spicy food was thought to arouse the desires of the Devil, coffee and biscuits were one of life's few pleasures.

At the beginning of the 20th century it was considered indecent for a woman to visit a restaurant unless she was accompanied by a man. So instead, women organised coffee parties or met up at cafés; today you will still sometimes hear the term *kaffekärring* ('coffeelady') for a scandalmonger.

Getting a coffee fix, with a little something sweet on the side, is now a firmly established Swedish pastime. They call it *fika*, which loosely translates as 'indulge in coffee and chat at leisure'. For a marathon *fika*, it is wise to find a café offering endless refills (*påtår*) for free or a token charge.

The best Cafés

For hot chocolate extraordinaire
Chokladkoppen (*see p144*).

For coffee with an urban view
Café Panorama (*see p145*).

For romancing
Blå Porten (*see p147*) or Galento (*see p146*).

For SoFo's eponymous hangout
South of Folkungagatan (*see p149*).

For Sweden's answer to Starbucks
Wayne's Coffee (*see p149*).

For taking the kids
The Cookbook Café (*see p149*).

For coffee alfresco
Lasse i Parken (*see p148*).

For retro surroundings
Valand (*see p147*) or Ritorno (*see p147*).

For the best *semla* in town
Thelins (*see p151*).

Eat, Drink, Shop

You can have your *fika* in an old-fashioned *konditori* (a café and bakery) selling traditional cakes, or in Italian-run joints, the best places for espresso. There are trapped-in-time places that haven't changed their decor (or staff) since the 1950s, and chilled-out modern cafés with sleek sofas and spacey sounds. Nowadays even chains like 7-Eleven offer a quick, budget *fika*, but most Swedes still prefer the real thing. American chains such as Starbucks may have invaded the rest of Europe, but they've found it difficult in Sweden – perhaps because they don't really understand the *fika* tradition and how seriously Swedes take their coffee. Still, there are a number of home-grown chains based more or less on the American model, such as Wayne's Coffee (*see p149*), Robert's Coffee and Coffee Cup.

Most cafés offer an extensive range of espresso-based coffee drinks, though at the traditional places you'll sometimes have to settle for plain coffee – although even that is a lot stronger here than in the UK or the US. You'll also find tea (black and fruit teas, not always herbal ones) and biscuits, cakes and sandwiches. Some pastries are seasonal. *Semla* (a bun with whipped cream, sugar and almond paste), sometimes eaten with warm milk, is only served around Easter. And you will only find the Christmas cake *lussekatt* (a saffron bun with raisins) in December. Other popular sweets are gingerbread biscuits and *kanelbulle*, a cinnamon bun. Some places serve full-blown meals.

The system in cafés is generally the same: unless you're being served at a table, drinks should be paid for at the till when you order. If you're at a table, the waiter will bring the bill with your drinks. You may be expected to pay immediately; it is not customary to tip, but you can if you wish. Table prices will almost always be the same as bar prices.

Most importantly, don't worry about overstaying your welcome. As long as you have even a sip of coffee left in your cup, nobody expects you to leave. You're supposed to be there for hours – that's what *fika* is all about.

Gamla Stan

For ice-cream and fresh waffles, stop at **Café Kåkbrinken** (Västerlånggatan 41, 411 61 74), near Sundbergs Konditori (*see below*).

Chokladkoppen

Stortorget 20 (20 31 70/www.chokladkoppen.com). T-bana Gamla Stan/bus 3, 53, 55, 59, 76. **Open** 9am-11pm daily. **No credit cards. Map** p305 J7.
Just how good can a hot chocolate really be? To find out, skip Gamla Stan's tourist traps and head for this place on Stortorget, the charming square at the centre of Gamla Stan. Colourful Chokladkoppen has a trendy feel and loud music – dance and cheesy pop

– and is popular with Stockholm's gay crowd (*see p210*). The laid-back service suffers at weekends when it gets ridiculously busy. In summer, the tables outside are a prime spot. Along with its famous hot chocolate, it serves fantastic cakes and snacks.

Grillska Husets Konditori

Stortorget 3 (787 86 05). T-bana Gamla Stan/bus 3, 53, 55, 59, 76. **Open** 9am-6pm Mon-Fri; 11am-6pm Sat, Sun. **Credit** AmEx, MC, V. **Map** p305 J8.
This café in a corner of Stortorget is run by a charitable group that works with the homeless. Give the downstairs a miss and head for the tranquil first-floor terrace, one of Gamla Stan's best kept secrets. With good-value pastries and friendly service on offer, spend your change here and make a difference.

Kaffekoppen

Stortorget 18 (20 31 70). T-bana Gamla Stan/bus 3, 53, 55, 59, 76. **Open** 8am-11pm Mon-Thur, Sun; 8am-midnight Fri, Sat. **No credit cards. Map** p305 J7.
This sister café to neighbouring Chokladkoppen (*see above*) has rickety old wooden tables and chairs and a tiny 13th-century interior, where it serves homemade delights – the white chocolate cheesecake is fantastic. Sit outside and you could land yourself a ringside seat for a concise history of Stockholm's Old Town, as Stortorget is a customary stop for guides taking their flocks to nearby Nobelmuseet (*see p69*).

Muren

Västerlånggatan 19 (10 80 70). T-bana Gamla Stan/bus 3, 53, 55, 59, 76. **Open** 9am-11pm daily. *Sept-May* 8am-11pm daily. **No credit cards. Map** p305 H7.
Navigate the cobbled stones to this chameleon café, which transforms itself from a trendy café in winter into a popular ice-cream parlour in summer. Remnants of the building's 13th-century wall remain intact (though not visible), hence the name, which means 'the wall'. This gay-friendly establishment serves the usual selection of sandwiches and pastries when in café mode and otherwise it serves one of the largest selections of ice-cream in the capital. The famously huge cones come in four flavours – vanilla, chocolate, cinnamon and saffron – and fill the air with a sweet aroma. Seating is sparse.

Sundbergs Konditori

Järntorget 83 (10 67 35). T-bana Gamla Stan/bus 3, 53, 55, 59, 76. **Open** *June-Aug* 9am-9pm daily. *Sept-May* 9am-10pm Mon-Fri; 10am-10pm Sat, Sun. **Credit** DC, MC, V. **Map** p305 J8.
This place has served hot coffee from a copper samovar for more than 200 years. Believed to be Stockholm's oldest *konditori*, it was founded in 1785 by Johan Ludvig Sundberg. According to local lore, King Gustav III had a secret passageway from the Kungliga Slottet straight to the bakery. Don't expect newfangled frappuccinos and smoothies here: come to Sundbergs for traditional cakes and atmosphere. This is a good starting point for navigating the curiosities and cobbles of nearby Västerlånggatan, Gamla's Stan's busiest street.

Creem. See p146.

Norrmalm

In addition to the following, try old-fashioned **Vete-Katten** (Kungsgatan 55, 20 84 05), a tearoom with classic Swedish pastries.

Atrium

Nationalmuseet, Södra Blasieholmshamnen 2 (611 34 30/www.restaurangatrium.se). T-bana Kungsträdgården/bus 65. **Open** *June-Aug* 11am-8pm Tue; 11am-5pm Wed-Sun. *Sept-May* 11am-8pm Tue, Thur; 11am-5pm Wed, Fri-Sun. **Credit** AmEx, DC, MC, V. **Map** p305 H8.

Many museums have excellent cafés, especially the Dansmuseet (*see p76*) and Aquaria Vattenmuseum (*see p82*), but by far the best is this place. You can *fika* here without forking out the museum entrance fee, so contemplating the works of Carl Larsson isn't obligatory. Though the museum, opposite the Royal Palace, is a bit dark and moody, sitting in the glass-roofed courtyard café is like having coffee in Renaissance Florence. Atrium offers a bit more than your average café – the food, served buffet-style, is as exquisite as the surroundings.

Café Panorama

5th floor, Kulturhuset, Sergels Torg 3 (21 10 35/ www.kulturhuset.stockholm.se).T-bana T-Centralen/ bus 47, 52, 56, 65, 91. **Open** *June-Aug* 11am-6pm Tue-Sat; 11am-5pm Sun. *Sept-May* 11am-7pm Tue-Sat; 11am-6pm Sun. **Credit** DC, MC, V. **Map** p305 G7.

Kulturhuset (*see p234*) is an essential stop for any culturally minded visitor, and this top-floor café has sensational *skorpor* (crisp rolls, usually eaten with jam or cheese) and a good lunch menu. It provides a bird's-eye view over Sergels Torg, but don't come expecting beauty – Stockholm's busiest square has been voted the ugliest part of the city. If it's full, there's a café two floors below and another coffee stop on the lower ground floor.

Piccolino

Kungsträdgården (811 78 08). T-bana Kungsträdgården/bus 2, 47, 55, 59, 62. **Open** *June-Aug* 8am-10pm Mon-Fri; 10am-10pm Sat, Sun. *Sept-May* 10am-9pm daily. **Credit** DC, MC, V. **Map** p305 G8.

What once was a lone glasshouse structure in Kungsträdgården has duplicated five fold into a row of cafés almost spanning the park's length. But Piccolino, Stockholm's first espresso bar, is the original and best. Opposite the winter ice rink and summertime outdoor stage, and popular with Swedish celebs, this small café is good for people-watching. The elms surrounding it are important for many locals: 30 years ago they were saved after a sit-down protest against the decision to build a Tunnelbana station next door to Café Opera.

Tintarella di Luna

Drottninggatan 102 (10 79 55). T-bana Rådmansgatan/bus 2, 4, 42, 52, 72. **Open** 9am-7pm Mon-Fri; 10am-5pm Sat; 11am-5pm Sun. **No credit cards. Map** p309 E6.

Tintarella di Luna is one of the city's more laid-back Italian cafés, but it's very small, so be prepared to wait for a table. The *macchiato* is amazing, although cornetto and *cantuccini* are the only desserts. Don't miss the quotes (in Swedish) of world-famous Swedish author/playwright August Strindberg that fill the pavement outside – if they whet your appetite, the Strindberg Museum (*see p78*) is just across the street.

Vasastaden

Café Levinsky's

Rörstrandsgatan 9 (30 33 33). T-bana St Eriksplan/bus 3, 42, 47, 507. **Open** 9am-10pm Mon-Thur; 9am-8pm Fri; 10am-8pm Sat; 10am-9pm Sun. **Credit** MC, V. **Map** p308 E3.

Whenever you've got a smoothie craving, head to Levinsky's (try the blueberry and banana). Alongside the usual café offerings, Levinsky's has a welcome Mexican twist; the enchiladas come very highly recommended. The only mystery is the collection of Heinz soup cans on display, which, incidentally, don't feature on the menu. For a delicious dessert, pop round the corner to Stockholms Glasshus (Birkagatan 8, 30 32 37, www.glasspasta.com) for home-made ice-cream in flavours you had previously only dreamed about.

Other locations: Vallhallavägen 155, Östermalm (662 65 24); Götgatan 58, Södermalm (644 71 20).

Creem

Karlbergsvägen 23 (32 52 65). T-bana Odenplan/bus 4, 42, 47. **Open** 8am-10pm Mon-Thur; 10am-8pm Fri-Sun. **Credit** DC, MC, V. **Map** p309 D5.

On first impressions this place looks frighteningly trendy, but don't let the designer-look interior put you off, as it is actually one of the city's cosiest cafés. The salami sandwiches are first-class, while the health-conscious can opt for the popular low-fat dishes (*hälsotallrik*). The sofas in the inner room guarantee relaxation.

Other locations: Flemminggatan 22, Kungsholmen (651 53 00); Folkungagatan 57, Södermalm (640 28 38).

Galento

Surbrunnsgatan 31 (612 00 45/www.galento.com). T-bana Rådmansgatan/bus 2, 4, 42, 72, 96. **Open** 10am-7pm Mon-Fri; 10.30am-6pm Sat, Sun. **No credit cards. Map** p309 C6.

At first glance Galento strikes a romantic chord with its dulcet lighting and cavernous feel. But, in fact, it's bursting with Bohemian ensembles and lonely philosophers. The saffron-spiced salmon soup is the biggest catch on the menu, but you can also sample 'O'Boy', the nation's favourite powdered chocolate milkshake. There's a culturally sound magazine collection, and modern jazz on the stereo, although it would ideally be turned down a notch or two.

Gino's Coffee

Odengatan 47 (644 40 33/www.ginoscoffee.com). T-bana Rådmansgatan/bus 2, 4, 42, 72, 96. **Open** 8am-11pm Mon-Sat; 8am-9pm Sun. **Credit** AmEx, DC, MC, V. **Map** p309 C6.

Eponymous owner Gino, a former hairdresser and self-styled entrepreneur, has opened his second café on the busiest street in Vasastaden (the first is on Gamla Stan). It's a cool joint, with discerning music, bringing in the young professionals of Vasastaden. This is one of the most spacious cafés in the area and there is talk of transforming it into a café-nightclub. This is a relatively new venture but, as we went to press, there were plans to take,the brand all over town. Wayne's Coffee had better watch out.

Other locations: Västerlånggatan 54, Gamla Stan (442 22 68).

Kafe Kompott

Karlbergsvägen 52 (31 51 77). T-bana St Eriksplan/bus 3, 42, 47, 507. **Open** 10am-8pm Mon-Fri; 9.30am-6pm Sat, Sun. Closed mid July-mid Aug. **Credit** MC, V. **Map** p309 D4.

Breakfast and brunch buffets are the main attraction at this café, where the British-style fry-up has a continental twist. It's an all-you-can-eat affair, with pancakes and jam for dessert. Despite being a tad pricey, it's hugely popular, especially on the weekends. The double doors make it pushchair-friendly and it's a good spot for a hungry family.

113 50 Café & Deli

Sveavägen 98 (15 74 45). T-bana Rådmansgatan/bus 52. **Open** 9am-9pm Mon-Fri; 11am-5pm Sat; noon-6pm Sun. **No credit cards. Map** p309 D6.

Students and travellers on a budget will love the low-priced, enormous pasta salads and sandwiches served here. Inside it's rather bare and basic but the service is friendly and efficient. Named after its post-code, this is mainly a hangout for students from Handelshögskolan, the nearby school of economics. On Sundays there's a queue out into the street.

Ritorno

Odengatan 80-82 (32 01 06). T-bana Odenplan/bus 4, 40, 53, 69, 72. **Open** 7am-10pm Mon-Thur; 7am-8pm Fri; 8am-6pm Sat; 10am-6pm Sun. Closed July. **Credit** AmEx, DC, MC, V. **Map** p308 D4.

Time stands still at this 1950s café, where beautiful old jukeboxes are still in working order. The regulars voiced a collective outcry when a revamp was recently suggested, so the battered leather sofas and kitsch decor remain. Ritorno offers everything from traditional shrimp sandwiches to calorie-dripping Danish pastries with funny names, such as 'one of those' and 'sumthing sweet'. If you don't drink coffee, try the apple soda Pommac. A local hangout for artists and writers, the café doubles as a gallery and the paintings on show are for sale.

Sosta

Sveavägen 84 (612 13 49). T-bana Rådmansgatan/bus 52. **Open** 8am-6pm Mon-Fri; 10am-5pm Sat. **No credit cards. Map** p309 D6.

This is a standing-room-only espresso bar known all over Sweden for its extraordinary coffee and low prices – although some say it's as famous for the well-dressed *baristas* making the *doppios* and serving cornettos. Try the focaccias or the home-made strawberry sorbet and you'll realise that Sosta is the closest you'll get to Italy in Scandinavia. **Other locations**: Jakobsbergsgatan 7, Norrmalm (611 71 07); Götgatan 30, Södermalm (505 259 70).

Valand

Surbrunnsgatan 48H (30 04 76). T-bana Odenplan or Rådmansgatan/bus 2, 4, 42, 72, 96. **Open** 8am-7pm Mon-Fri; 9am-7pm Sat. **No credit cards.** **Map** p309 C5.

Silence is golden at Valand, one of the city's most peaceful cafés. This *konditori* is a throwback to the '50s; the cranky old couple who run it have refrained from updating the place, hence the original retro look. The service is fairly slow and downbeat, but then again this isn't where you come looking for a quick coffee buzz. You head to Valand's vinyl couches for traditional cakes (try the vanilla and almond bun) and to feel like you're an extra in an old black-and-white movie.

Vurma

Gästrikegatan 2 (30 62 30). T-bana St Eriksplan/bus 3, 42, 47, 507. **Open** 11am-6pm daily. **Credit** DC, MC, V. **Map** p308 D3.

This retro hotspot comes highly recommended; even the staff hang out here on their day off. The lengthy menu adds an exotic twist to the usual sandwiches and snacks, catering imaginatively for both the vegetarian and carnivorous palate. The decor is a '70s kaleidoscope of colour, with swirls of oranges, browns and greens. The service is good, as is the grub, and the soothing tunes tone down the brash interior. If you fancy a grassy retreat after brunch, then Vasaparken is nearby. Vurma's Kungsholmen branch has its own bakery, so rest assured the pastries are fresh.

Other locations: Polhemsgatan 15, Kungsholmen (650 93 50).

Djurgården

In addition to those listed below, many of Djurgården's museums have good cafés. Try the café at the **Aquaria Vattenmuseum** (*see p82*), with its waterfront view; Café Ektorpet, set outside an 18th-century cottage on a hill overlooking the water, at **Prins Eugens Waldemarsudde** (*see p83*); or one of **Skansen's** (*see p85*) numerous cafés and eateries, the best of which is Café Petissan, situated in the Town Quarter in a cosy building from the late 17th century.

Blå Porten

Djurgårdsvägen 64 (663 87 59). Bus 44, 47/tram 7/ferry from Slussen or Nybrokajen. **Open** *May-Aug* 11am-10pm Mon-Fri; 11am-7pm Sat, Sun. *Sept-Apr* 11am-7pm Mon, Wed, Fri-Sun; 11am-9pm Tue, Thur. **Credit** AmEx, MC, V. **Map** p306 H11.

The 'Blue Door' is, without doubt, Stockholm's most romantic café. Neighbouring the prominent art gallery Liljevalchs (*see p203*), this beautiful, piazza-like garden is a secret hideaway in the heart of the island. The interior isn't that exciting, so you should probably choose somewhere else on a rainy day. There's a medieval-style table inside laden with a mouth-watering display of desserts. If you're visiting Vasamuseet, Skansen or Gröna Lund, then Blå Porten is the nearby retreat you may need.

Rosendals Trädgård

Rosendalsterrassen 12 (54 58 12 70/www.rosen dalstradgard.com). Bus 47/tram 7. **Open** *Mid Jan-Mar, Oct-mid Nov* 11am-4pm Tue-Sun. *Apr* 11am-5pm Tue-Sun. *May-Sept* 11am-5pm daily. Closed mid Nov-mid Jan. **Credit** MC, V. **Map** p307 H13.

The green-fingered café in this upmarket, ecologically oriented garden centre offers some of the best cakes and sandwiches in town – all of it organic and grown or baked on the premises. Rosendals Trädgård is well known for its seasonal desserts, and its recipes now fill the pages of bestselling cookbook *Rosendals trädgårdscafé*. In summer, people eat fruit pie at picnic tables or on the grass under the apple trees; in winter they keep warm with a mug of *glögg* (mulled wine) in the greenhouses. There is a small shop selling jam, bread and flowers (which you can pick yourself). To get there, take bus 47 to the last stop at Waldemarsudde then continue a few feet in the same direction and you'll see a sign – it's a little tricky to find, so be prepared to ask for directions.

Eat, Drink, Shop

Blå Porten: a green hideaway in the heart of Djurgården. *See p147.*

Södermalm

Blooms Bageri

St Paulsgatan 24 (640 90 36). T-bana Mariatorget/bus 43, 55, 66. **Open** 8am-6pm Mon-Fri; 10am-5pm Sat, Sun. **No credit cards. Map** p314 L6.
This small café close to Södermalm's beautiful viewpoint, Mariaberget, knows that there's nothing more relaxing than seeing other people work – only a window divides Blooms Bakery from its café. The bread and buns are as fresh as can be – often still warm from the oven. Watch out for the porcelain dog in the middle of the café: to the joy of regulars many newcomers bump into it.

Café dello Sport

Pålsundsgatan 8 (669 23 22). T-bana Hornstull/bus 4, 66. **Open** 9am-5pm daily. **Credit** DC, MC, V. **Map** p313 K3.
Since it's customary at this football-obsessed café to wear the same pair of underpants for as long as Italy is on a winning streak, there's been a lot more laundry for the owners of late. Don't let a full season of Serie A fixtures put you off though, the focaccias, cappuccinos and Italian sodas are worth the trip.

Glasbruket Café & Galleri

Katarinavägen 19 (462 00 17). T-bana Slussen/bus 2, 3, 53, 76, 96. **Open** 11am-5pm Mon-Fri; noon-5pm Sat, Sun. **No credit cards. Map** p315 K8.
Only the sweet-smelling aromas wafting from this café could lure you away from the street with the most breathtaking view of the city. This has to be the best natural vantage point in Stockholm and a

must for keen photographers. Only a stone's throw from the fast-food joints of Slussen, Glasbruket serves healthy breakfast and lunch alternatives. A place to dawdle over a cup of organic coffee and a slice of Greek almond cake.

Lasse i Parken

Högalidsgatan 56 (658 33 95). T-bana Hornstull/bus 4, 66. **Open** *May-Aug* 11am-4.30pm daily. *Sept-Apr* 11am-5pm Sat, Sun. **Credit** MC, V. **Map** p313 K2.
Those who dream of visiting Pippi Longstocking's home, Villa Villerkulla, usually head for the children's theme park, Junibacken (*see p189*). But the closest you'll really get to Astrid Lindgren's creation is here, just above the beaches of gloomy Reimersholme. Café owner Lasse Helgö has kept the original features of this Pippi-style, 18th-century dwelling, where you'll find everything from fresh blueberry pie to cheddar sandwiches. With a well-used outdoor stage, it's a charming oasis of good food, drink and theatre. Take a toilet check before, as the outdoor loos are the kind you normally find at rock festivals. To get there, take bus 4 over Västerbron to Högalidsgatan for an amazing view of Långholmen.

Lisas Café & Hembageri

Skånegatan 68 (640 36 36). T-bana Medborgarplatsen/bus 59. **Open** 6.30am-3am Mon-Fri; 8am-3pm Sat. **No credit cards. Map** p315 M9.
Motherly Lisa has been getting up at 4am every morning for the last 13 years to serve locals. She has around 250 photos of regulars gracing the walls of her café and claims she can tell you a story about each and every one of them. Cinnamon buns (*kanelbulle*)

are the house speciality, but ask for a latte or a frappuccino at your peril, since any coffee with warmed-up milk is barred from her menu – she champions the survival of the plain coffee. Open all hours, and as local as they come, Lisas will continue to weather the storm of competition from trendy new cafés sprouting up in the area.

Puck

Hornsgatan 32 (641 10 30). T-bana Slussen/bus 2, 3, 4, 53, 76, 96. **Open** 10am-6pm daily. **Credit** MC, V. **Map** p314 K7.

A quiet retreat from the nearby hustle of Slussen, this small, cosy café is well-frequented by locals. Puck is known for its good sandwiches and the kind of laid-back charm that people have come to expect from the south side of the city, and the staff are only too willing to chat. Vegetarians are also well catered for, with inventive recipes and not a nut cutlet in sight. Opening hours can vary at weekends depending on the severity of the boss's hangover.

South of Folkungagatan

Skånegatan 71 (702 06 60). T-bana Medborgarplatsen/bus 3, 59, 66. **Open** 9am-7pm Mon-Fri; 11am-6pm Sat, Sun. **Credit** MC,V. **Map** p315 M9.

The area now ambitiously dubbed SoFo, short for South of Folkungagatan, has become something of a hub for independent fashion designers, small record shops and trend-conscious types. From young mums to middle-aged hippies, the eclectic mix of clientele at this café personifies the area's celebrated diversity. South of Folkungagatan is famed for its hot paninis, which are named after local streets – try the Folkungagatan, with cheese, ham, walnuts and honey.

String

Nytorgsgatan 38 (714 85 14). T-bana Medborgarplatsen/bus 3, 59, 66. **Open** 9.30am-8pm Mon-Fri; 10.30am-8pm Sat, Sun. **No credit cards**. **Map** p315 M9.

Once a furniture shop that served coffee to its customers, String is now a café that also sells furniture. Everything from the deckchair you sit on to the plate you eat off is for sale, and this is also the closest you'll get to having your coffee in a shop window. String is as fun and hip as its young fan base, whose favourite hangover cure is the weekend breakfast buffet, and it has started offering live music in the basement on Sunday afternoons.

Wayne's Coffee

Götgatan 31 (644 45 90/www.waynescoffee.se). T-bana Slussen/bus 3, 55, 59, 74. **Open** 8am-8pm Mon-Fri; 10am-7pm Sat; 11am-7pm Sun. **Credit** MC, V. **Map** p314 L8.

No need to look for Wayne, he has a habit of popping up just about everywhere in town. Friendlier and more personal than other US-inspired cafés, Wayne's is deservedly popular among locals. You'll find branches all over the city, but perhaps the most perplexing version is within the SEB Bank at

Sergels Torg. Wayne's caters, unusually in Sweden, for the decaf drinker and the weight-conscious – low-fat milk (*lätt mjölk*) is available on request. Everything on the menu, from the fruit smoothies and chocolate-chip cookies to the pitta bread rolls, is delicious.

Other locations: Drottninggatan 31, Norrmalm (20 17 80); Kungsgatan 14, Kungsholmen (791 00 86); Odengatan 52, Vasastaden (34 56 88); Vasagatan 7, Norrmalm (24 59 70); SEB, Sergels Torg 2, Norrmalm (56 84 95 20); Mäster Samuelsgatan 28 (in Akademibokhandeln), Norrmalm (20 07 90).

Östermalm

Café Restaurant Austria

Strandvägen 1 (667 76 24). T-bana Östermalmstorg or Kungsträdgården/bus 47, 62, 69, 76. **Open** 9am-8pm Mon, Sun; 9am-9pm Tue-Sat. **Credit** AmEx, DC, MC, V. **Map** p305 F8.

Upper class Östermalm ladies meet here to sample *sachertorte* and other Austrian delights. Others are attracted by the view of boats leaving Nybroviken for the archipelago. With the exclusive Swedish design store Svenskt Tenn (*see p175*) a couple of doors away, Café Austria has a plum location on one of Stockholm's most luxurious streets. It is definitely a place for cake lovers but not for those on a tight budget, as prices are impressively high. Though there isn't a formal rule, this is the kind of establishment that can get a bit snobby about a coffee order without a slice on the side.

The Cookbook Café

Birger Jarlsgatan 76 (20 63 08/www.thecook bookcafe.com) T-bana Rådmansgatan or Tekniska Högskolan/bus 2, 43. **Open** 10am-6pm Mon-Fri; 11am-4pm Sat. Closed July. **Credit** MC, V. **Map** p309 D7.

Run by two Swedish-American sisters with a taste for wholesome goodness, the Cookbook Café has become a culinary institution in Stockholm. You might have to negotiate a maze of parked-up prams to get inside – it's like a mothers and toddlers group at times. But if you do find a free seat, everything from the lunch dishes to dessert is delicious. No doubt they are inspired by the enormous collection of cookbooks from around the world in the café, the most bizarre of which has to be *Cooking in the Nude for Golf Lovers*.

Gateau

Sturegallerian, Stureplan (611 75 64/www.gateau. se). T-bana Östermalmstorg/bus 1, 2, 55, 56, 91. **Open** 8am-7pm Mon-Fri; 9am-5.30pm Sat; 11am-5pm Sun. **Credit** AmEx, DC, MC, V. **Map** p305 F8.

Hold on to your purse strings – sweet-toothed tourists could blow their holiday budget at Gateau, purveyor of amazingly good cakes and pastries. Spaciously spread out on the first floor of luxurious shopping centre Sturegallerian, Gateau has several award-winning chefs on board. Prices are deservedly high but the afternoon tea special (warm scones,

Eat, Drink, Shop

jam, marmalade and tea) won't break the bank. Gateau also has a small shop in the mall, on the floor below, selling cakes and bread.

Saturnus

Eriksbergsgatan 6 (611 77 00). T-bana Östermalmstorg/bus 2, 42, 44. **Open** 8am-9pm Mon-Fri; 10am-midnight Sat, Sun. **Credit** AmEx, DC, MC, V. **Map** p309 E7.

Sweden's Crown Princess Victoria has been known to frequent this place, although the famous cinnamon buns hardly need the royal seal of approval; these gigantic pastries are out of this world and are big enough to feed a small family. You might have problems finding this Saturnus, though – there isn't a proper sign, just a model of the planet hanging above the entrance. It's close to independent cinema Zita (*see p200*), so it's packed with cineastes during evenings and weekends.

Sturekatten

Riddargatan 4 (611 16 12). T-bana Östermalmstorg/ bus 2, 55, 91. **Open** *May-Aug* 9am-6pm Mon-Fri; 10am-5pm Sat. *Sept-Apr* 8am-8pm Mon-Fri; 10am-6pm Sat, Sun. **No credit cards. Map** p305 F8.

If it ever stops serving fine coffee and cakes, Sturekatten should be delicately preserved forever. With two storeys of lace and antiques it's like an 18th-century doll's house. The speciality is apple pie with meringue but it also serves delicious *semlor* (whipped cream and almond paste buns). The waitresses don old-style black and whites and, though it may sound like a pensioner's pleasure dome, it's actually just as popular with teenagers. Free tables don't come easy, so if the queue is too long, try sister café Vete-Katten (Kungsgatan 55, 20 84 05) in nearby Norrmalm for a similar taste of old-fashioned hospitality.

Wienerkonditoriet

Biblioteksgatan 6-8 (611 21 16). T-bana Östermalmstorg/bus 2, 55, 91, 96. **Open** 7am-10pm Mon-Thur; 7am-11pm Fri; 8am-11pm Sat; 10am-10pm Sun. **Credit** AmEx, DC, MC, V. **Map** p305 F8.

This is an open-all-hours establishment for the local breakfast club and late-night *fika* fanatics. Located on one of Stockholm's most fashionable shopping streets, this is a good hangout for Ab Fab types. The main attractions are the shrimp sandwiches and the wide variety of fine pastries, but you will have to fight for the good seats.

Kungsholmen

Bagel Deli

St Göransgatan 67 (716 11 40). T-bana Fridhemsplan/ bus 3, 40, 52, 62, 74. **Open** 7am-9pm Mon-Fri; 10am-9pm Sat, Sun. **Credit** AmEx, MC, V. **Map** p303 F2.

This school of bagel wizardry wouldn't be out of place on New York's Upper West Side. They are keen on cream cheese here, but there's a feast of fillings on the menu and you can't fail to pick a winner. Otherwise, the salads are stomach-stuffing – piled high with the best bits, you'll have to hunt for the

boring lettuce leaves. There's always something typically Swedish and seasonal on the menu, and the lattes are some of the best in town. No wonder this place is packed at weekends.

Café Julia

St Eriksgatan 15 (651 45 15). T-bana Fridhemsplan/ bus 3, 52, 94. **Open** 10am-9pm Mon-Fri; 11am-7pm Sat, Sun. **Credit** AmEx, DC, MC, V. **Map** p303 G2.

This haven for home-made soft cheese started out in a one-room apartment with a young couple making cheese in their bathtub (keep reading). Now the bathroom has expanded to become one of Kungsholmen's most popular cafés. The soft cheese is churned in six flavours (try the horseradish), and any questions about the recipes are regarded as industrial espionage. The home-made cheesecake is, needless to say, the most popular dessert. Julia also sells picnic baskets filled with goodies.

Ett Litet Kök

Alströmergatan 20 (660 71 09/www.ettlitetkok.se). T-bana Fridhemsplan/bus 3, 4, 94. **Open** *June-Aug* 10.30am-5pm Mon-Fri; 11am-4pm Sat. *Sept-May* 10am-6pm Mon-Fri; 10am-5pm Sat, Sun. **Credit** AmEx, DC, MC, V. **Map** p303 F2.

Adjoining trendy interior design store R.O.O.M (*see p175*), this café-cum-restaurant isn't the best advert for the furnishings on sale. Simple in style but verging on the barren, it doesn't quite live up to its comfy name 'the little kitchen'. It's a shame, however, because the fodder on offer is superb. Aside from the daily lunch menu, the range of sandwiches and buns is plentiful and delicious. The café is particularly good fun if you're the kind of person who finds it amusing to watch couples and newly-weds argue over the colour of lampshades.

Muffin Bakery

Fridhemsgatan 3 (651 88 00/www.muffin bakery.se). T-bana Fridhemsplan/bus 49, 52, 57, 74. **Open** 9am-8pm Mon-Fri; 9am-6pm Sat, Sun. **Credit**, MC, V. **Map** p303 G2.

The Muffin Bakery's American-style, super-sized muffins are so famous that they even have their own cookbook. The café itself is a bit drab, so opt to sit outside on the grassy hideaway instead. It's so popular with young parents on their way to the playgrounds and beaches of Rålambshovsparken, that it can be hard to find a seat. Stick to the sweet options, as the savoury muffins can be a bit too cheesy. Anyway, who needs to consider the other options when there are chocolate cheesecake muffins?

På Hörnet

Pilgatan 28 (651 00 31). T-bana Rådhuset/bus 40, 52. **Open** 9am-9pm Mon; 7am-3pm Tue-Fri. **Credit** AmEx, DC, MC, V. **Map** p304 G3.

You can't help but feel you're in someone's home kitchen in this quaint corner-house café. Close to the local police station, it's brimming with contented cops here for the plentiful, easy-on-the-pocket lunchtime menu. The dessert trolley, though, could be piled a little higher.

Primo Ciao Ciao

Hantverkargatan 76A (653 90 23/www.primociao ciao.nu). T-bana Fridhemsplan/bus 3, 40, 62.
Open 11am-10pm Mon-Sat; noon-10pm Sun.
Credit AmEx, DC, MC, V. **Map** p303 G2.
Worthy of a visit for the macchiato alone, this place is a pure Italian job, sleek and suave. It prides itself on serving up authentic food and drink, and the Sicilian pizza chef could well tempt your tastebuds with 35 varieties on the menu. The service is exceptionally good and prices are very reasonable. This is not a quiet spot, though – the next-door neighbour is a fire station.
Other locations: Bondegatan 44, Södermalm (640 01 10).

Thelins

St Eriksgatan 43 (651 19 00/www.thelins konditori.se). T-bana Fridhemsplan/bus 3, 4, 57, 59.
Open 7.30am-7pm Mon-Fri; 9am-6pm Sat, Sun.
Credit MC, V. **Map** p303 F2.
A traditional *konditori* and the place to sample the finest sweet Swedish delicacies, Thelins has more than 100 years of experience in this business. A home from home for the silver-haired brigade, it's not exactly at the cutting edge of the city's café scene, but it does house the very best *semla* in Stockholm. Pick up a numbered ticket on your way in – it's a rather impersonal touch but at peak times it's the only way to control the rush. Don't be afraid to ask the staff for some advice on what to order – they might look bored but they are passionate about their cakes.
Other locations: Erikdalbergsallén 4, Östermalm (663 62 89).

Laid-back lunches at friendly **Puck** on Södermalm. *See p149.*

Shops & Services

Bag yourself some Swedish classics.

The elegant **NK** department store is a national treasure. *See p153.*

Although Sweden gave the world two of its most ubiquitous megastores – H&M and IKEA – the Stockholm shopping experience is, in fact, much more about smaller shops with high standards of quality and customer service.

To describe Stockholm's shopping districts in their simplest terms: **Östermalm** is the upper crust; **Norrmalm** represents the mainstream; **Södermalm** caters to alternative shoppers; **Gamla Stan** is touristy with a scattering of quirky shops; and **Kungsholmen** is best described as up-and-coming, and is particularly good for second-hand records.

For any visitor new to town, the best place to start is NK. This glamorous department store is a Stockholm institution and places you in the heart of the main shopping area in **Norrmalm**, where you'll be surrounded by the usual multinational chains, plus a few home-grown alternatives. From NK it's a short walk to a variety of malls and departments stores; elegant Sturegallerian on Stureplan, the huge Åhléns next to Sergels Torg, or the more downmarket Gallerian across the street on Hamngatan. For discount clothing, head

towards **Sergels Torg** and then brace yourself before battling the crowds on boxy **Drottninggatan**, the city's busiest shopping street. Pedestrianised from the water all the way to Radmansgatan, Drottninggatan is a long and not particularly interesting line of chain stores, including the likes of Debenhams, H&M and Top Shop.

For luxury labels head to **Östermalm**. On and around Birger Jarlsgatan and Stureplan you'll find Louis Vuitton, Versace, Mulberry, MaxMara, Emporio Armani, Gucci, Cerrutti and Georg Jensen. This is also the quarter for exquisite interior decor stores, especially along Sibyllegatan and Strandvägen.

Over on **Södermalm**, **Götgatan** has emerged as one of the city's trendiest shopping strips, with boutiques like 10 Swedish Designers, Lush, Filippa K, DesignTorget and c/o Stockholm among others. **Gamla Stan** is undoubtedly a tourist trap – wise Stockholmers steer well clear of its main shopping street Västerlånggatan on summer days – but there are some lovely, quirky small shops squeezed in between the tacky souvenir sellers.

Kungsholmen's ongoing revival was sparked by the moderately trendy Västermalmsgallerian, while neighbouring **Vasastaden** is good for antiques (on Upplandsgatan) and second-hand records and CDs (around St Eriksgatan). Beware that in the more residential areas, the distances between shops can be uncomfortably far, so it's best to know where you are heading.

It's unlikely that Stockholm will ever become known as the place to snap up a bargain, but standards are high and it can be good value. Highly developed consumer protection rights allow purchasing on a sale-or-return basis (keep the receipt) and lengthy guarantees.

OPENING HOURS AND TAX REFUNDS

Small retailers are usually open 10am to 6pm on weekdays, 11am to 2pm on Saturdays and closed on Sundays. Some aren't even open on Saturdays. Only bigger, more tourist-oriented shops tend to open on Sundays. Department stores are usually open from 10am to 7pm on weekdays and 10am or 11am to 5pm or 6pm at the weekend.

In many shops, non-EU residents can ask for a Tax-Free Cheque when purchasing items costing more than 200kr (not including taxes). The cheque can be cashed at customs when leaving the country (with a refund of 10 to 12 per cent). Look for the 'Tax-Free Shopping' sticker on shop doors, and be sure to get only one cheque for all your purchases in the department stores. For further information, call Global Refund on 0410 48 450 or visit www.globalrefund.com. Note that taxes are always included in the listed price in Sweden.

One-stop

Homesick Brits may want to visit **Debenhams** on Drottninggatan (No.53, 50 57 40 00). If you happen to find yourself in eastern Östermalm, you may want to pop by **Fältöversten** (Karlaplan 13, 52 80 01 45, www.falto versten.se), a recently remodelled shopping centre housing 60 chain stores.

Department stores

Åhléns

Klarabergsgatan 50, Norrmalm (767 60 00/www. ahlens.se). T-bana T-Centralen/bus 47, 52, 56, 59, 65. **Open** 10am-8pm Mon-Fri; 10am-7pm Sat; 11am-6pm Sun. **Credit** AmEx, DC, MC, V. **Map** p305 G6.
You can't get much more central than Åhléns, located in a massive brick building next to Sergels Torg. It's an excellent mid-range department store with a good cosmetics and perfume section, a well-stocked homewares department and a large CD shop. The clothing department stocks threads by

Swedish designers and international labels. You can get a luxurious facial in the Stockholm Day Spa and there's a huge supermarket in the basement.

NK

Hamngatan 18-20, Norrmalm (762 80 00/www.nk.se). T-bana Kungsträdgården or Östermalmstorg/bus 2, 43, 47, 55, 59, 62, 69, 76. **Open** 10am-7pm Mon-Fri; 10am-6pm Sat; noon-5pm Sun (*June, July* noon-4pm Sun). **Credit** AmEx, DC, MC, V. **Map** p305 F7.
Eternally elegant, Nordiska Kompaniet is one of the city's most treasured institutions. The famous revolving clock on the roof – formed from the letters NK – is visible from all over town. A sort of Swedish Selfridges, it's a first-class store, particularly good for clothes, Swedish souvenirs (crafts and glassware in the basement) and gourmet food. You can get your photos developed while you have a coffee in Café Entrée, one of several great eateries. NK's iconic status made the fatal stabbing here of foreign minister Anna Lindh in 2003 all the more shocking.

Shopping centres

Bruno Götgatsbacken

Götgatan 36, Södermalm (757 76 00). T-bana Slussen or Medborgarplatsen/bus 2, 3, 43, 53, 55, 59, 66, 76. **Open** *Shops* 10am-7pm Mon-Fri; 10am-5pm Sat; noon-4pm Sun. *Cafés & restaurants* call for details. **Credit** varies. **Map** p314 L8.
Sometimes called Galleria Bruno, this micro-mall, opened in 2004, consolidates Götgatan's status as one of Stockholm's hippest shopping streets. There's a café in the atrium, a cool new restaurant (Ljunggren; *see p125*) and several typically Swedish stores, including Filippa K, WE/JL, H&M and interiors shop David Design.

Gallerian

Hamngatan 37, Norrmalm (www.gallerian.se). T-bana Kungsträdgården/bus 2, 47, 55, 59, 69. **Open** 10am-7pm Mon-Fri; 10am-6pm Sat; 11am-4pm Sun. **Credit** varies. **Map** p305 G7.
Located just down from Sergels Torg and just up from NK, Stockholm's first shopping mall is the place for everyday items rather than luxury goods. Among its 60 shops and cafés you'll find Foot Locker, BR-Leksaker for toys, Levi's and the Swedish DIY specialist Clas Ohlson. Though a recent renovation expanded its top and bottom floors, Gallerian still doesn't quite live up to its potential and is dwarfed in size by nearby NK.

PUB

Hötorget 13-15, Norrmalm (402 16 15/www.pub.se). T-bana Hötorget/bus 1, 52, 56. **Open** 10am-7pm Mon-Fri; 10am-5pm Sat; noon-5pm Sun. **Credit** AmEx, DC, MC, V. **Map** p305 F6.
Facing the bustling outdoor fruit and veg market at Hötorget, PUB is more of a mall than a department store, and a pretty boring one at that. Greta Garbo once worked in the millinery department and modelled hats for the store's catalogue.

Sturegallerian

Entrances at Grev Turegatan 9 & Stureplan,
Östermalm (www.sturegallerian.se). T-bana
Östermalmstorg/bus 1, 2, 55, 56, 62. **Open** 10am-
7pm Mon-Fri; 10am-5pm Sat; noon-5pm Sun *(June,*
July noon-4pm Sun). **Credit** varies. **Map** p305 F8.

If Sergels Torg is the people's centre of Stockholm,
Sturegallerian and its environs are the centre for the
jet set. As the city's most glamorous mall it has
plenty of upmarket boutiques for picky customers, as
well as super-spa Sturebadet (*see p172*), and the kind
of ambience that comes only with a glass roof and
marble floors. Café Pluto and Tures are excellent
hangouts for post-retail refreshments, or there's the
elegant Sturehof (*see p130*) if you want to push the
boat out. The bookshop Hedengrens (*see below*) has
a good collection of books in English about Stockholm.

Västermalmsgallerian

St Eriksgatan & Fleminggatan, Kungsholmen
(737 20 00/www.vastermalmsgallerian.com).
T-bana Fridhemsplan/bus 1, 3, 4, 57, 59. **Open**
10am-7pm Mon-Fri; 10am-5pm Sat; 11am-5pm Sun.
Credit varies. **Map** p303 F2.

This pleasant shopping mall connected to the
Fridhemsplan T-bana station kickstarted the
revitalisation of Kungsholmen when it opened its
doors a few years back. Shops include an ICA
supermarket, Björn Borg, H&M, Face Stockholm,
Granit, DesignTorget and many others. Café W is
busy all day long.

Auctions

As well as the auctioneers listed below, the
world-famous auction houses of **Christie's**
(Sturegatan 26, 662 01 31, www.christies.com)
and **Sotheby's** (Arsenalsgatan 6, 679 54 78,
www.sothebys.com) have offices in Stockholm
that are open for valuations and advice.

Bukowskis

Arsenalsgatan 4, Norrmalm (614 08 00/
www.bukowskis.se). T-bana Kungsträdgården or
Östermalmstorg/bus 2, 47, 55, 59, 76. **Open** 9am-
5pm Mon-Fri. **Credit** AmEx, MC, V. **Map** p305 G8.
Bukowskis is probably Scandinavia's biggest and
best auction house specialising in art and design.
Four times a year it holds auctions of rare pieces of
art, furniture, porcelain and jewellery dating from
the 16th to the 19th centuries. Alternatively, try the
Auktionskompaniet auctions of second-hand bargains, held every other week on Sundays at noon.
Other locations: Auktionskompaniet,
Regeringsgatan 47, Norrmalm (23 57 00/
www.auktionskompaniet.se).

Books

The book section at department store **NK**
(*see p153*) has a good selection of fiction titles
in English, as well as a decent range of
guidebooks and maps.

Akademibokhandeln

Mäster Samuelsgatan 32, Norrmalm (613 61 00/
www.akademibokhandeln.se). T-bana T-Centralen or
Hötorget/bus 43, 47, 52, 59, 69. **Open** 10am-7pm
Mon-Fri; 10am-5pm Sat; noon-4pm Sun. **Credit**
AmEx, DC, MC, V. **Map** p305 F7.

Akademibokhandeln has seven branches in the city
and offers the best range of English paperbacks in
Stockholm. This recently expanded flagship store
now has an excellent paperback department, which
has a wine bar looking out over the street.
Other locations: throughout the city.

Alfa Antikvariat

Drottninggatan 71A, Norrmalm (21 42 75).
T-bana Hötorget. **Open** 10am-6pm Mon-Fri; 10am-
4pm Sat. **Credit** AmEx, DC, MC, V. **Map** p305 F6.

This used bookshop on Drottninggatan has a good
English department in the basement and lots of
English paperbacks on the ground floor. This is the
place to grab some holiday reading or to find a classic old orange Penguin.

Hedengrens

Sturegallerian, Stureplan 4, Östermalm (611 51 28/
www.hedengrens.se). T-bana Östermalmstorg/bus 1,
2, 55, 56. **Open** 10am-8pm Mon-Fri; 10am-5pm Sat;
noon-5pm Sun *(June, July* noon-4pm Sun). **Credit**
AmEx, DC, MC, V. **Map** p305 F8.

Opened in 1898, Hedengrens is one of Stockholm's
most famous bookshops. It specialises in novels and
the arts, and half the stock is in English. Check out
the English translations of Swedish authors such as
Selma Lagerlöf, Torgny Lindgren and Astrid
Lindgren. The fiction section also includes titles in
Spanish, Italian, German, French, Danish and
Norwegian. Ideal for browsing.

Pocketshop

Central Station main floor, Norrmalm (24 27 05/
www.pocket shop.se). T-bana T-Centralen/bus 47, 53,
69. **Open** 5.40am-10pm Mon-Fri; 7am-8pm Sat; 9am-
10pm Sun. **Credit** AmEx, DC, MC, V. **Map** p305 G6.

Pocketshop has around 400 contemporary fiction
titles in English. The two branches in the Central
Station (one in the main hall, the other downstairs
by the commuter trains) are a great place to pick up
a book for a long train ride.
Other locations: Götgatan 40, Södermalm (640 94
05); Kulturhuset, Sergels Torg, Norrmalm (22 05 15);
Gallerian, Hamngatan 37, Norrmalm (406 08 18);
Västermalmsgallerian, Kungsholmen (654 83 00).

Sweden Bookshop

Slottsbacken 10, Gamla Stan (453 78 00/www.sweden
bookshop.com). **Open** *Oct-July* 10am-6pm Mon-Fri.
Aug-Sept 10am-6pm Mon-Fri; 11am-4pm Sat.
Credit AmEx, DC, MC, V. **Map** p305 H8.

The Swedish Institute bookshop, just down the street
from the Royal Palace, is the best place to find books
about Sweden in more than 30 languages. These
range from Astrid Lindgren's children's books to
Henning Mankell's thrillers, as well as publications
on Swedish food, history, culture and language.

Famous **Hedengrens** bookshop – the perfect place for a rainy afternoon. *See p154.*

Specialist

For newsstands specialising in international newspapers and magazines, *see p283.*

Alvglans

Folkungagatan 84, Södermalm (642 69 98/ www.alvglans.se). T-bana Medborgarplatsen/bus 2, 53, 59, 66. **Open** 10am-6pm Mon-Fri; 10am-4pm Sat. **Credit** MC, V. **Map** p315 L9.
The *Spawn* action figures alone are worth the trip to Södermalm and the comics heaven of Alvglans. The shop stocks bestsellers such as *X-Men* and *Spider-man,* as well as rare animé movies and manga DVDs.

Kartcentrum

Vasagatan 16, Norrmalm (411 16 97/www.kart centrum.se). T-bana T-Centralen/bus 2, 3, 53, 62, 69. **Open** 9.30am-6pm Mon-Fri; 9.30am-4pm Sat. **Credit** AmEx, DC, MC, V. **Map** p305 G6.
Conveniently located opposite Central Station, this travel specialist has a good range of maps, guidebooks and atlases, as well as CD-Rom maps and marine charts for the more intrepid traveller.

Konst-ig

Basement, Kulturhuset, Sergels Torg, Norrmalm (50 83 15 18/www.konstig.se). T-bana T-Centralen/ bus 47, 52, 56, 59, 65. **Open** 11am-7pm Mon; 10am-7pm Tue-Fri; 10am-5pm Sat; noon-4pm Sun. **Credit** AmEx, MC, V. **Map** p305 G7.
Stockholm's leading art bookshop, covering design, art, architecture, photography, fashion and more. Located in the basement of Kulthurhuset, next to DesignTorget (*see p169*).

Rönnells Antikvariat

Birger Jarlsgatan 32, Östermalm (545 05 60). T-bana Östermalmstorg/bus 1, 2, 55, 56. **Open** 10am-6pm Mon-Fri; 11am-3pm Sat. **Credit** AmEx, DC, MC, V. **Map** p310 E7.
This three-storey antiquarian bookshop offers tons of titles in English. Rönnells is also a publishing company specialising in Swedish experimental art and poetry from the 1960s.

Electronic goods & photo developing

Fotoquick

Sergels Torg 12, Norrmalm (21 30 40/www. fotoquick.se). T-bana T-Centralen/bus 47, 52, 53, 56, 69. **Open** 9am-6.30pm Mon-Fri; 10am-4pm Sat; 11am-3pm Sun. **Credit** AmEx, MC, V. **Map** p305 G5.
The cost of film developing in Stockholm can vary a great deal, sometimes by as much as 100kr per film. Fotoquick is a cheap option, developing a 36-print colour film in one hour for 169kr.
Other locations: Central Station, Norrmalm (21 29 55); Hamngatan 16, Norrmalm (21 40 42); Ringens Köpcentrum, Götgatan 100, Södermalm (640 98 10).

OnOff

Kungsgatan 29, Norrmalm (701 07 10/www.onoff. se). T-bana Hötorget/bus 1, 43, 52, 55, 56. **Open** 10am-7pm Mon-Fri; 10am-4pm Sat; noon-4pm Sun. **Credit** AmEx, MC, V. **Map** p305 F7.
Sweden's biggest retailer of electronic goods, including computers, cameras, audio-visual equipment and mobile phones. While the prices are certainly

Head to super Swede **H&M** for cost-cutting chic.

friendly, the only 'but' is that they are understaffed, so save valuable queuing time by calling in advance to check what you're looking for is in stock.
Other locations: Sveavägen 13-15, Norrmalm (54 51 12 00); Fältöversten, Karlavägen 19, Östermalm (701 06 20).

Fashion

Budget

Dressmann
Drottninggatan 30, Norrmalm (21 89 20/www.dress mann.com). T-bana T-Centralen/bus 47, 52, 56, 59, 65. **Open** 10am-7pm Mon-Fri; 10am-5pm Sat; noon-5pm Sun. **Credit** AmEx, DC, MC, V. **Map** p305 F6.
Dressmann is the place to find a great suit for next to nothing, but be prepared to spend hours looking through the racks of ill-fitting trousers and poor-quality shirts before finding it. Unfortunately staff are too busy to be very helpful.
Other locations: throughout the city.

H&M
Hamngatan 22, Norrmalm (796 54 32/www.hm.com). T-bana Kungsträdgården or T-Centralen/bus 2, 43, 47, 59, 65. **Open** 10am-7pm Mon-Fri; 10am-5pm Sat; noon-5pm Sun. **Credit** AmEx, DC, MC, V. **Map** p305 F7.
International megastore H&M needs little introduction. By quickly designing copies of each new season's catwalk fashions, H&M has made itself almost as well known worldwide as IKEA. The clothes are both trendy and cheap. There are branches all over

Stockholm but Hamngatan is the large flagship store, whose selection is well worth a few hours of your browsing time.
Other locations: throughout the city.

Indiska Magasinet
Drottninggatan 53, Norrmalm (10 91 93/www. indiska.se). T-bana T-Centralen/bus 47, 52, 56, 59, 65. **Open** 10am-7pm Mon-Fri; 10am-6pm Sat; 11am-5pm Sun. **Credit** AmEx, DC, MC, V. **Map** p305 F6.
Once upon a time Indiska was associated with poor quality and design, dressing only backpackers coming home from eight months in Asia and missing the tie-dye scarves from those blurry nights in Goa. But these days it sells fashionable but still orientally influenced clothes, bags, scarves and even furniture, all at nearly Asian prices.
Other locations: throughout the city.

Lindex
Kungsgatan 48, Norrmalm (21 77 80/www. lindex.se). T-bana Hötorget/bus 1, 52, 56. **Open** 10am-7pm Mon-Fri; 10am-4pm Sat; noon-4pm Sun. **Credit** AmEx, DC, MC, V. **Map** p305 F7.
A very reasonably priced Swedish chain for women and children. Despite its rather middle-aged image, Lindex is great for stylish underwear and swimwear.
Other locations: Sergels Torg 14, Norrmalm (54 51 77 10); Gallerian, Hamngatan 37, Norrmalm (21 59 20); PK-Huset, Hamngatan 10-14, Norrmalm (54 52 42 30); Ringen, Götgatan/Ringvägen, Södermalm (642 33 32).

VeroModa
Hamngatan 37, Norrmalm (14 10 41/www. veromoda.com). T-bana Kungsträdgården or T-Centralen/bus 2, 43, 47, 59, 62. **Open** 10am-7pm

Mon-Fri; 10am-6pm Sat; 11am-4pm Sun. **Credit** AmEx, DC, MC, V. **Map** p305 G7.

VeroModa is the only chain of clothes shops that can compete with H&M when it comes to cheap but trendy items. The designs are slightly more basic than H&M's, though, and the selection is smaller. Womenswear only.

Other locations: Drottninggatan 66, Norrmalm (21 52 20); Adam & Eva, Drottninggatan 68, Norrmalm (21 48 11).

Mid-range

Diesel has a spacious shop on Kungsgatan 3 (678 07 09) and you can find **Oasis** on Grev Turegatan 12 (611 21 15), both near Stureplan.

Boutique Sportif

Renstiernas Gata 26, Södermalm (411 12 13). *Bus 2, 53, 59, 66, 76.* **Open** 11am-7pm Mon-Fri; 11am-5pm Sat. **Credit** AmEx, MC, V. **Map** p315 M9.

Boutique Sportif has its own take on streetwear, with logo sweatpants, funky tees for her or baggy pants for him. The shop is best known for its tops with different parts of the city printed in capital letters on the front. Do get your own hooded jacket with 'SoFo', 'Vasastan' or simply 'Stockholm' across the chest, but don't worry about the grumpy looking staff – they won't bite.

Brothers

Drottninggatan 53, Norrmalm (411 12 01/www. *brothers.se).* *T-bana T-Centralen/bus 47, 52, 56, 59, 65.* **Open** 10am-7pm Mon-Fri; 10am-5pm Sat; noon-4pm Sun. **Credit** AmEx, DC, MC, V. **Map** p305 F6.

This nationwide chain provides Swedish men with everything from suits to socks. The shop is spacious and the staff are friendly and happy to sort you out with own label Riley or something slightly more costly from Swedish designer J Lindeberg.

Other locations: Fältöversten, Karlavägen 13, Östermalm (664 71 60); Ringen, Götgatan/Ringvägen, Södermalm (642 41 61).

Cali

Brunnsgatan 9, Norrmalm (56 74 99 08/www. *caliroots.se).* *T-bana Östermalmstorg/bus 1, 2, 55, 59.* **Open** noon-6.30pm Mon-Fri; noon-5pm Sat. **Credit** MC, V. **Map** p305 E7.

Cali has a great selection of streetwear for men and women: sneakers from Vans, baggy pants from Fresh Jive, handbags from Sophia Coppola's Milk Fed.

Champagne

PK-Huset, Hamngatan 10-14, Norrmalm (10 75 64). *T-bana Kungsträdgården or Östermalmstorg/bus 2, 43, 47, 55, 59, 62, 76.* **Open** 10am-7pm Mon-Fri; 10am-5pm Sat; noon-4pm Sun. **Credit** AmEx, DC, MC, V. **Map** p305 F7.

At this two-floor shop women can find everything from mid-range label Replay to exclusive designers such as Dolce & Gabbana, plus cleverly put see-through tops, comfy T-shirts from Juicy Couture or a fancy dress. Don't miss out on own label Do Rose,

the low-cut trousers in basic colours or the chic shoe selection. The fitting rooms are small with rather unflattering lighting.

Companys

Biblioteksgatan 1, Östermalm (545 018 55). *T-bana Östermalmstorg/bus 2, 47, 55, 59, 62, 76.* **Open** 10am-7pm Mon-Fri; 10am-5pm Sat; noon-4pm Sun. **Credit** AmEx, DC, MC, V. **Map** p305 F8.

Danish chain Companys' large shop in Stockholm's fashion district gives the impression of expensive exclusivity but actually, apart from a few Marc Jacobs Mary Janes, prices are reasonable. Go for own label Designer's Remix – pick out a grass-green stretch top or an orange shirt with printed, sparkling rocking horses. Women's clothing only.

Other locations: NK, Hamngatan 18-20, Norrmalm (762 83 88).

Hugo Kläder

St Eriksgatan 39, Kungsholmen (652 49 90/ *www.hugo-sthlm.com).* *T-bana Fridhemsplan/bus 1, 3, 4, 40, 62.* **Open** 10.30am-7pm Mon-Fri; 11am-4pm Sat; noon-4pm Sun. **Credit** AmEx, DC, MC, V. **Map** p303 F2.

Fashion-conscious men who don't worry about paying a little extra to look a little extra get everything from underwear to suits at Hugo Kläder. Staff handpick a few garments from different international labels every season, so this is the place to find something exclusive. Tiger and Filippa K are sold here.

Peak Performance

Biblioteksgatan 18, Östermalm (611 34 00/www. *peakperformance.com).* *T-bana Östermalmstorg/* *bus 1, 2, 55, 59.* **Open** 10am-7pm Mon-Fri; 10am-5pm Sat; noon-4pm Sun. **Credit** AmEx, DC, MC, V. **Map** p305 F8.

Originally designed for hikers, climbers, skiers and other people preferring fresh air to smoky bars, Peak Performance has now turned more mainstream.

Plagg

Odengatan 75, Vasastaden (31 90 04/www.plagg.se). *T-bana Odenplan/bus 2, 4, 40, 53, 72.* **Open** 10am-6.30pm Mon-Fri; 10am-5pm Sat; noon-4pm Sun. **Credit** AmEx, DC, MC, V. **Map** p309 D5.

At Plagg, the smart-looking 21st-century woman gets classy clothing from designers such as Denmark's DAY/Birger et Mikkelsen or Sweden's hugely successful Tiger. The selection is larger than you think when you see the size of the shop.

Other locations: St Eriksgatan 37, Kungsholmen (650 31 58); Rörstrandsgatan 8, Vasastaden (30 58 01); Götgatan 31, Södermalm (442 00 55); Sturegallerian, Östermalm (679 95 00).

Solo

Smålandsgatan 20, Östermalm (611 64 41/www. *solo.se).* *T-bana Östermalmstorg/bus 2, 47, 55, 59, 62, 76.* **Open** 10am-7pm Mon-Fri; 10am-5pm Sat; noon-5pm Sun. **Credit** AmEx, DC, MC, V. **Map** p305 F8.

Solo has one of the best selections of jeans in Stockholm. The friendly and persuasive staff know how to flatter both you and your bottom. Look out

Eat, Drink, Shop

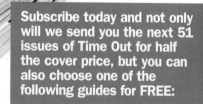

for Swedish jeans specialists Acne and Nudie. Apart from the jeans, keep an eye out for Swedish designer Rodebjer and her less expensive label Stitches. **Other locations**: Västermalmsgallerian, Kungsholmen (653 38 20).

Svea

Birger Jarlsgatan 7, Östermalm (679 60 13/ www.sveasvea.se). T-bana Östermalmstorg/bus 2, 47, 55, 62, 65. **Credit** AmEx, DC, MC, V. **Map** p305 F8.
This quirky Swedish label Svea mixes girly pink tutus with sporty sweats. Best known for the print of a yellow crown on comfy hooded jackets and cute cotton underwear.

Designer

Most of the designer shops are clustered around hot spot **Stureplan**: on the lower end of Birger Jarlsgatan and along swanky Biblioteksgatan. On Birger Jarlsgatan you'll find plenty of top-end international designers, including **Gucci** (No.1, 54 50 05 44), **Cerruti** (No.5, 678 45 00), **Hugo Boss** (No.6, 611 42 40), **Max Mara** (No.12, 611 14 66) and **Versace** (Nos.21-23, 611 91 90, 678 14 00). **Emporio Armani**'s newly redesigned flagship store can be found at Biblioteksgatan 3 (678 79 80).

Götgatsbacken (the northern part of Gotgatan) on Söder had a facelift about ten years ago and now houses various fashion boutiques, including **Filippa K** (*see below*). The area on Södermalm newly dubbed as **SoFo** (*see p94* **SoFo**), south of Folkungagatan, has a high concentration of independent fashion designers. The department stores **NK** and **Åhléns** (for both, *see p153*) also have a good designer collection.

Acne

Hamngatan 10-14, Östermalm (20 34 54). T-bana Östermalmstorg/bus 2, 47, 55, 59, 62, 76. **Open** 10am-7pm Mon-Fri; 10am-5pm Sat; noon-5pm Sun. **Credit** AmEx, DC, MC, V. **Map** p305 F7.
The not-so-glamorously named Acne started out as an advertising agency, became a jeans manufacturer and is now an all-round designer. It's still best at denim but also makes clothes for hip media kids in other fabrics.

Anna Holtblad

Grev Turegatan 13, Östermalm (54 50 22 20/ www.annaholtblad.se). T-bana Östermalmstorg/ bus 1, 2, 55, 56. **Open** 10.30am-6.30pm Mon-Fri; 10.30am-4pm Sat. **Credit** AmEx, DC, MC, V. **Map** p305 F8.
Anna Holtblad is one of Sweden's top designers, dressing the trendy and financially stable 30-plus woman in classic clothing. The choice of fabrics and designs is exquisite. If you want to pick up a few staples for your 'capsule wardrobe', let Holtblad sort you out. Get the perfect black turtleneck or an ever-so-soft white T-shirt. The high quality means her clothes last longer than most.

Filippa K

Götgatan 23, Södermalm (55 69 85 85/www.filippak. com). T-bana Slussen/bus 2, 3, 43, 53, 55, 59, 76. **Open** 11am-7pm Mon-Fri; 10am-4pm Sat; noon-4pm Sun. **Credit** AmEx, DC, MC, V. **Map** p314 L8.
With clean Scandinavian lines and not overly imaginative designs, Filippa K has created the uniform for Swedish men and women wanting to dress like everybody else. The label favours colours without colour, such as beige, chocolate, navy and black. **Other locations**: Grev Turegatan 18, Östermalm (54 58 88 88); Biblioteksgatan 2, Östermalm (611 88 03).

J Lindeberg

Grev Turegatan 9, Östermalm (678 61 65/www. jlindeberg.com). T-bana Östermalmstorg/bus 1, 2, 55, 56. **Open** 10am-7pm Mon-Fri; 10am-5pm Sat; noon-5pm Sun. **Credit** AmEx, DC, MC, V. **Map** p305 F8.
With his clean designs and flamboyant twist, Johan Lindeberg has become a household name for the capital's media, fashion and PR types. The staff are playful but professional, the designs impeccable.

Maria Westerlind

Drottninggatan 81A, Norrmalm (23 45 45/www. westerlind.com). T-bana Hötorget or Rådmansgatan/ bus 52, 69. **Open** 11am-6pm Mon-Fri; 11am-3pm Sat. **Credit** AmEx, DC, MC, V. **Map** p309 E6.
Traditional lines, mild colours and simple fabrics are what make Maria Westerlind one of Sweden's up-and-coming young designers. The twentysomething women who get their striped dresses and floral skirts here are aware of style and quality, but prefer not to be too eye-catching.

Mrs H Stockholm

Drottninggatan 110, Vasastaden (30 01 02/www. mrsh.se). T-bana Hötorget or Rådmansgatan/bus 52, 69. **Open** 11am-6.30pm Mon-Fri; 11am-4pm Sat. **Credit** AmEx, DC, MC, V. **Map** p309 E6.
Mrs H stocks bags, shoes, clothes and make-up for the true fashionista. Here you will find designs from Swedish award-winning duo Dedicated Follower of Fashion, comfy Ugg boots, Rykiel rah-rah skirts, Danish Ole Henriksen cosmetics and Hollywood's favourite jeans – Paper. Quite expensive.

Le Shop

Nytorgsgatan 23, Södermalm (644 91 55). T-bana Medborgarplatsen/bus 2, 53, 59, 66, 76. **Open** noon-7pm Mon-Fri; noon-5pm Sat. **Credit** AmEx, MC, V. **Map** p315 L9.
Modest as this venue might seem, the edgy designs for men and women are most certainly not. Le Shop is the place to find something no one else will be wearing, as there's just one sample in each size. Both Swedish and international designers, such as Lisa Dixell, Rosetta or Surface to Air, feature.

Tiger Dam

Jakobsbergsgatan 8, Norrmalm (440 30 60/ www.tigerofsweden.com). T-bana Östermalmstorg/ bus 2, 43, 59. **Open** 10.30am-6.30pm Mon-Fri; 11am-4.30pm Sat; noon-4pm Sun. **Credit** AmEx, DC, MC, V. **Map** p305 F8.

(vertical tab) **Eat, Drink, Shop**

Tiger first became known for sponsoring Swedish pop phenomenon Kent with suits, and suddenly he was dressing a whole generation of young males. Suits are still its trademark, but now Tiger also makes clothes for women and is constantly first with the very latest designs. The look is classic but fashionable. Also sells quality shoes and accessories. **Other locations**: PK-Huset, Hamngatan 10-14, Norrmalm (20 20 55).

Tjallamalla
Bondegatan 46, Södermalm (640 78 47/www. tjallamalla.com). Bus 2, 53, 59, 66, 76. **Open** noon-6pm Mon-Fri; noon-4pm Sat. **Credit** AmEx, MC, V. **Map** p315 M9.

Situated in Bohemian, latte-drinking Söder, Tjallamalla sells young Swedish fashion to young Swedish fashionistas. Clicking away in their straight-out-of-*Elle* shoes, the customers are more NYC than Sarah Jessica Parker herself. Tjallamalla stocks a total of 150 local designers, such as Rodebjer, Åsa Westlund and jeans specialist Nudie.

Children

H&M (*see p156*) is the most successful clothes shop for both parents and teenagers in Sweden. You'll find kids' clothes at the larger H&M stores, such as Hamngatan 22 (796 54 34),

Pure glass

Mix sand with a bit of lime, potash and red lead, and you'll get one of Sweden's biggest claims to fame when it comes to design. King Gustav Vasa founded the first glassworks in Stockholm in the mid 16th century, but the large amounts of fuel needed for the furnaces could only be found in the extensive forests in the south-east, in Småland, where the country's glass industry has been centred for hundreds of years.

Though glass art is a very Swedish tradition, its two largest crystal glass companies – **Orrefors** and **Kosta Boda** – are now Danish-owned. The Danish takeover has steadied a glass market that was on the verge of shattering. Glassware sales have gone down – for today's homemakers it is just not as important as it used to be to have a complete series of umpteen glasses in a display case. Collectors have also been more cautious about investing in art glass, but the market seems to have stabilised now, judging by a rise in the second-hand value of collectables.

An uncertain glass market, though, hasn't stopped Sweden's most innovative designers from experimenting. One of the most prominent artists on the contemporary design and art glass scene is **Per B Sundberg**, who has been with Orrefors for a decade. Sundberg is well known for his professional playfulness and has revitalised glass design by working with it in new, irreverent ways.

In a project entitled 'SPACE', several designers have gone about combining fibre optics with glass. 'Glass and light belong together,' explains designer **Erika Lagerbielke**, who has created a cascade of spiralled drips, with fibre optics enclosed in

the crystal. **Olle Brozén**, **Malin Lindahl** and **Erika Höglund** are other fresh names making waves, behind more established talents such as **Ulrika Hydman-Vallien**, **Ingegerd Råman** and **Bertil Vallien**. Hydman-Vallien is still one of the biggest commercial successes of Swedish art glass.

During 2005, which the Swedish government has designated an official 'Year of Design' (www.merdesign.se), there will be various art glass events around town, including an autumn exhibition entitled 'Art Glass from the Antique to Today' at the **Medelhavsmuseet** (Museum of Mediterranean Antiquities; *see p76*) in Norrmalm. For a full programme of events visit the 'Year of Design' website.

WHERE TO BUY IT
In addition to the following specialist outfits, department stores **NK** and **Åhléns** (for both, *see p153*) also have well-chosen selections of Swedish crystal and glassware. To see how glass is made, visit the glassworks at **Skansen** (*see p85*).

Blås och Knåda
Hornsgatan 26, Södermalm (642 77 67/ www.blas-knada.com). T-bana Mariatorget/ bus 3, 43, 55, 59, 66. **Open** 11am-6pm Mon-Fri; 11am-4pm Sat; noon-4pm Sun. **Credit** MC, V. **Map** p314 K7.
Gallery-cum-shop Blås och Knåda (blow and knead) specialises in contemporary glass and china. The extremely varied range covers everything from kitschy floral coffee mugs to sublime high-class glass art. Expensive.

Crystal Art Centre
Tegelbacken 4, Norrmalm (21 71 69/ www.cac.se). T-bana T-Centralen/bus 3,

Sergelgatan 1 (796 54 41) and Drottninggatan 56 (796 54 57), all situated in Norrmalm. The **NK** (*see p153*) kids' department deals in designer babies' and children's clothing and shoes.

Kalikå

Österlånggatan 18, Gamla Stan (20 52 19/www. kalika.se). T-bana Gamla Stan/bus 2, 43, 55, 59, 76. **Open** 10am-6pm Mon-Fri; 10am-4pm Sat; 11am-3pm Sun. **Credit** AmEx, DC, MC, V. **Map** p305 J8.
Only the absence of incense reveals that this is not a time machine with the dial set to the 1970s. With clothes, hats, finger puppets and stuffed toys all in brightly coloured velour, you can reincarnate your

youngster as a hippie kid. Alternatively, get the decade's back-to-the-roots feeling by buying a DIY kit and putting the clothes and products together yourself in the famous Swedish/IKEA way.

Polarn o Pyret

Hamngatan 10, Norrmalm (411 41 40/www.polarno pyret.se). T-bana Östermalmstorg/bus 2, 47, 55, 59, 62, 69. **Open** 10am-7pm Mon-Fri; 10am-6pm Sat; 11am-4pm Sun. **Credit** AmEx, DC, MC, V. **Map** p305 F8.
Polarn o Pyret (the Pal & the Tot) became famous in the 1970s when its striped, long-sleeved T-shirt dressed a whole generation of kids. With a retro revival in the new millennium, today grown-ups

53, 62, 65. **Open** 9am-6pm Mon-Fri; 9am-2pm Sat (*May-Sept* noon-4pm Sun). **Credit** AmEx, DC, MC, V. **Map** p305 H6.
Specialists in handmade crystal and Swedish design since 1977.

Nordiska Kristall

Kungsgatan 9, Norrmalm (10 43 72/www. nordiskakristall.com). T-bana Östermalmstorg or Hötorget/bus 1, 2, 52, 55, 56. **Open** 10am-6.30pm Mon-Fri; 10am-5pm Sat; noon-4pm Sun. **Credit** AmEx, DC, MC, V. **Map** p305 F7.
Nordiska Kristall stocks crystal from all the good Swedish glass brands and also from Italian Venini. The shop is run by the Kjellander family, which has worked with glass for eight generations. Downstairs you will find a gallery, and the shop also

arranges various courses and seminars to learn more about glass.
Other locations: Österlånggatan 1, Gamla Stan (10 77 18).

Orrefors & Kosta Boda

Birger Jarlsgatan 15, Östermalm (611 21 20/ www.orrefors.com/www.kostaboda.com). T-bana Östermalmstorg/bus 1, 2, 47, 55, 56, 62, 69, 76. **Open** 10am-6pm Mon-Fri; 10am-4pm Sat; (*May-Aug* noon-4pm Sun). **Credit** AmEx, DC, MC, V. **Map** p305 F8.
This shop is worth a visit to get a very good overview of what's hot and what's not from Orrefors and Kosta Boda, the two largest companies in the Swedish glass industry. Check out the showroom, where you will find works from some of the country's most prominent designers.

Eat, Drink, Shop

Tiger Dam. *See p159.*

and children alike can be seen sporting Polarn o Pyret's characteristic soft fabrics and simple styles. And, of course, stripes.

Other locations: Gallerian, Hamngatan 37, Norrmalm (411 22 47); Sveavägen 9, Norrmalm (23 34 00); Fältöversten, Karlavägen 13, Östermalm (660 62 75); Ringen, Götgatan/ Ringvägen, Södermalm (642 03 62).

Fetish

Those looking for the latest in fetish, punk or Goth fashions should check out the range of shops along the two intersecting streets of Gamla Brogatan and Klara Norra Kyrokgata, just west of Hötorget in Norrmalm. *See also p178* **Secrets.**

Blue Fox

Gamla Brogatan 27, Norrmalm (20 32 41/www. bluefox.nu). T-bana T-Centralen/bus 1, 47, 53, 69. **Open** 11am-6pm Mon-Fri; 10am-4pm Sat. **Credit** MC, V. **Map** p305 F6.

Feel like dying your hair the same shade of green as Kermit the frog? Is your nose feeling empty without an iron ring that makes you look like Disney's Ferdinand the Bull? Would a little black latex number take Saturday night to wuthering heights for you and your significant other? Blue Fox specialises in tattoos, piercings, and heavy metal and Goth clothing. Get everything from glossy trousers, kick-ass boots and Sid Vicious-style tartan trousers to jewellery with lots of attitude.

Cum

Klara Norra Kyrkogata 21, Norrmalm (10 40 18/ www.cum-clubwear.nu). T-bana T-Centralen/bus 47, 53, 69. **Open** *noon-6pm Mon-Fri; noon-4pm Sat.* **Credit** AmEx, MC, V. **Map** p305 F6.
All the furry, see-through, neon-coloured clothes you can imagine, and a wide selection of glittery killer heels. The clubwear is fetish-influenced.

Eve Collection

St Eriksgatan 19, Kungsholmen (650 92 15/www. evecollection.nu). T-bana Fridhemsplan/bus 3, 4, 40, 62. **Open** *11am-6pm Mon-Wed, Fri; 11am-8pm Thur; noon-4pm Sat.* **Credit** MC, V. **Map** p303 G2.
A selection of love toys and great underwear in PVC and latex, plus high-heeled shoes and boots up to size 46 for those who don't put comfort first and can afford to take a taxi to the party.

Larger sizes

Big and Trendy

Jakobsbergsgatan 6N, Norrmalm (611 23 23/www. bigandtrendy.aos.se). T-bana Östermalmstorg/ bus 42, 47, 56, 59. **Open** *10am-6.30pm Mon-Fri; 10am-5pm Sat; noon-4pm Sun.* **Credit** AmEx, DC, MC, V. **Map** p305 F8.
Selling Swedish labels Almia and the slightly more casual Proforma, Big and Trendy stocks all sorts of well-designed gear in sizes 42 (UK 16/US 14) to 54. **Other locations**: Almia, PUB, Hötorget 13-15, Norrmalm (21 39 93).

Lingerie & underwear

Also try **Lindex** (*see p156*) and the new **H&M Beautybox** in the Gallerian mall (*see p153*).

Björn Borg

Sturegallerian, Stureplan, Östermalm (678 20 40/ www.bjornborg.net). T-bana Östermalmstorg/bus 1, 2, 55, 56. **Open** *10am-7pm Mon-Fri; 10am-5pm Sat; noon-5pm Sun (June, July noon-4pm Sun).* **Credit** AmEx, DC, MC, V. **Map** p305 F8.
Björn Borg, once the king of tennis, is now the king of Swedish underwear. The collection, from under-wear to bags and shoes, is ace.
Other locations: Västermalmsgallerian, St Eriksgatan 45, Kungsholmen (652 12 40).

Gustaf Mellbin

Västerlånggatan 47, Gamla Stan (20 21 93). T-bana Gamla Stan/bus 3, 43, 53, 55, 76. **Open** *10.30am-6pm Mon-Fri; 10.30am-2pm Sat.* **Credit** AmEx, DC, MC, V. **Map** p305 J7.
The shop assistants at stylish lingerie shop Gustaf Mellbin could become your new best friends if you're looking for good service and cups up to F, G and even H. Expensive but worth it.

NK Damunderkläder

1st floor, NK, Hamngatan 18-20, Norrmalm (762 80 00/www.nk.se). T-bana Kungsträdgården or Östermalmstorg/bus 2, 43, 47, 55, 59, 62, 69, 76. **Open** *10am-7pm Mon-Fri; 10am-6pm Sun; noon-5pm Sun (June, July noon-4pm Sun).* **Credit** AmEx, DC, MC, V. **Map** p305 F8.
NK is the best place to buy women's underwear in Stockholm. You'll find expensive, colourful designer lingerie from the likes of DKNY and Calvin Klein, as well as NK's own label of less eye-catching stuff. The fitting rooms are spacious, with flattering light-ing, and include a sitting area for accompanying friends and family. The men's section stocks almost as large a variety of high-quality undies.

Second-hand & vintage

59 Vintage Store

Hantverkargatan 59, Kungsholmen (652 37 27/ www.59vintagestore.com). T-bana Rådhuset/bus 3, 40, 52, 62. **Open** *11.30am-6pm Mon-Fri; 11am-3pm Sat.* **Credit** AmEx, DC, MC, V. **Map** p304 G3.
'Retro with a feeling of now' is how shop owner Anette defines the clothes she packs into her small shop. Her carefully selected dresses, jackets, skirts, trousers and tops from the 1960s, 1970s and 1980s are definitely worth a detour.

Lisa Larssons Second Hand

Bondegatan 48, Södermalm (643 61 53). Bus 2, 53, 59, 66, 76. **Open** *1-6pm Tue-Fri; 11am-3pm Sat.* **No credit cards. Map** p315 M9.
If you want to find the perfect little leather jacket, this is the place. In the crammed and crowded shop, Lisa keeps an entire wall full of second-hand leather jackets and coats. There are also more dressy items for men and women, but be ready to fight for what you want as this is a popular Saturday excursion for Stockholm's trendy young things.

Mormors Skattkista

Bondegatan 56, Södermalm (643 61 09). Bus 2, 53, 59, 66, 76. **Open** *1-6pm Mon-Fri.* **No credit cards. Map** p315 M9.
Vintage clothes, bags and jewellery from as far back as the 1920s. The quality is good, since the owner has pre-selected the stock, not letting just any old thing into her shop. For the man in your life, how about buying a pair of 1960s cufflinks or an Yves St Laurent coat? Don't wear a backpack, though: the shop is tiny.

Myrorna

Götgatan 79, Södermalm (55 60 33 68/www. myrorna.se). T-bana Skanstull/bus 3, 4, 55, 74. **Open** *10am-6pm Mon-Fri; 10am-4pm Sat.* **Credit** AmEx, DC, MC, V. **Map** p315 N8.
The Swedish Salvation Army's charity shops were originally just charity shops, but have now become the place for teenagers to get everything from cos-tume party outfits to a pair of slightly worn denims. Furniture and household items too.

Eat, Drink, Shop

Other locations: Adolf Fredriks Kyrkogata 5-7, Norrmalm (54 52 08 91); Tomtebogatan 5, Vasastaden (54 54 36 66); Hornsgatan 96, Södermalm (55 60 59 82).

Små Smulor

Skånegatan 75, Södermalm (642 53 34/www.stads missionen.se). Bus 2, 59, 66, 76. **Open** 10am-6pm Mon-Fri; 10am-4pm Sat. **Credit** MC, V. **Map** p315 M9.
With its location next to trendy Nytorget, you would think that this charity shop would be a) exclusively stocked and b) very expensive. But Små Smulor is neither. Discover a dress Farrah Fawcett could have worn in *Charlie's Angels*, as well as 1970s crockery in vibrant colours.
Other locations: Hantverkargatan 78, Kungsholmen (652 74 75); Bondegatan 46, Södermalm (642 19 41); Hornsgatan 58, Södermalm (642 93 35); Stortorget 5, Gamla Stan (787 86 61).

Fashion accessories

Bags, gloves & hats

Mrs H Stockholm (*see p159*) is a fine stop for bags and shoes, and **Accessorize** has a shop on Biblioteksgata 5 (611 04 05), near Norrmalmstorg.

Östermalms Handskaffär

St Eriksgatan 31, Kungsholmen (650 06 02). T-bana Fridhemsplan/bus 1, 3, 4, 40, 62. **Open** 11am-6pm Mon-Fri; 11am-3pm Sat. **Credit** AmEx, DC, MC, V. **Map** p303 F2.
Even if the shop looks pretty empty from the outside, Östermalms Handskaffär is most definitely not. In a few square metres, you can find the most

feminine jewellery from Holmquist & Co, pink suede or traditional black leather gloves, and colourful bags from Danish label Friis & Co. With its mid-range prices, this shop is a must. There's also a small stock of women's clothes upstairs.
Other locations: Karlavägen 61, Östermalm (661 30 78).

Wedins Accent

PUB, Hötorget 13-15, Norrmalm (54 52 31 83). T-bana Hötorget/bus 1, 52, 56. **Open** 10am-7pm Mon-Fri; 10am-5pm Sat; noon-5pm Sun. **Credit** AmEx, MC, V. **Map** p305 F6.
Looking for soft suede gloves, large bags, a silk scarf or a new leather wallet? Wedins accent has it all, with price tags more suited to the hippie than the yuppie.
Other locations: Drottninggatan 66, Norrmalm (54 52 32 63); Sergelgatan 11-15, Norrmalm (54 51 79 53); Kungsgatan 48, Norrmalm (21 30 06).

Jewellery

Antikt, Gammalt & Nytt

Mäster Samuelsgatan 11, Norrmalm (678 35 30). T-bana Östermalmstorg/bus 1, 2, 47, 59, 69. **Open** 11am-6pm Mon-Fri; 11am-4pm Sat. **Credit** AmEx, DC, MC, V. **Map** p305 F8.
The place to go when you need an antique rhinestone tiara or a glass brooch in any colour, size or price range. The shop was dreamed up by Tore and Mats Grundström when they discovered a warehouse full of long-forgotten 1940s gear. Be warned: you will have to fight over all the best pieces with stylists and other dedicated followers of fashion. The shop assistants (and owners) are not too interested in assisting, and quality isn't top of the agenda. Great fun, though.

Cheap glam at **Glitter**.

Efva Attlings Studio

Hornsgatan 42, Södermalm (642 99 49/www.
efvaattlingstockholm.com). T-bana Mariatorget/
bus 43, 55, 59, 66. **Open** 10am-6pm Mon-Fri;
11am-3pm Sat. **Credit** AmEx, DC, MC, V.
Map p314 K6.
Efva Attling is the glamorous lady silversmith who
first made it as an Eileen Ford model and pop star
(with the band X-models), and then hit the headlines
for marrying the gorgeous female musician Eva
Dahlgren. She makes simply beautiful silver and
gold jewellery with names such as 'Homo Sapiens'
and 'Divorced with Children'. Popular with celebs
and frightfully expensive.
Other locations: Birger Jarlsgatan 9, Östermalm
(611 90 80).

Glitter

Gallerian, Hamngatan 37, Norrmalm (411 27 40).
T-bana Kungsträdgården or T-Centralen/bus 43,
47, 59. **Open** 10am-7pm Mon-Fri; 10am-6pm Sat;
11am-4pm Sun. **Credit** AmEx, MC, V. **Map** p305 G7.
Glitter is a countrywide chain of budget jewellery
shops, but this is the only one in Stockholm. It is
the place to pick up a pair of dirt cheap plastic earrings or a beautiful bracelet of faux pearls. The
prices somehow manage to compete with H&M,
which is saying something.

Guldfynd

Ringen, Götgatan/Ringvägen, Södermalm (642 88
10/www.guldfynd.se). T-bana Skanstull/bus 3, 4, 55,
74. **Open** 10am-7pm Mon-Fri; 10am-5pm Sat; noon-
4pm Sun. **Credit** AmEx, DC, MC, V. **Map** p315 N8.
Guldfynd is the largest jewellery retailer in Sweden,
selling a wide selection of basic jewellery in gold and
silver, as well as watches and the like.

Other locations: Adam & Eva, Drottninggatan 68,
Norrmalm (54 51 01 10); Gallerian, Hamngatan 37,
Norrmalm (21 49 43); Sergelgatan 11-15, Norrmalm (54
51 04 88); St Eriksgatan 34, Kungsholmen (650 11 36).

WA Bolin

Stureplan 5, Östermalm (611 40 05). T-bana
Östermalmstorg/bus 1, 2, 55, 56. **Open** *Sept-mid*
June 10am-6pm Mon-Fri; 11am-3pm Sat. *Mid June-*
Aug 10am-6pm Mon-Fri. **Credit** AmEx, DC, MC, V.
Map p305 F8.
Bolin provides the royal family with antique jew-
ellery and most of the objects are rather expensive.
But it is possible to find pieces at lower prices.

Zanzlöza Zmycken

Jakobsbergsgatan 9, Norrmalm (678 40 55/www.
zanzlozazmycken.se). T-bana Östermalmstorg/bus 2,
55, 56. **Open** 11am-6.15pm Mon-Fri; 11am-5pm Sat.
Credit AmEx, DC, MC, V. **Map** p305 F8.
Situated off swanky Biblioteksgatan, you expect to
be robbed at Zanzlöza Zmycken. But look carefully
between the heavy Dior designs and you can find a
less expensive but still glamorous selection of neck-
laces, rings and earrings.
Other locations: Storkyrkobrinken 8, Gamla Stan
(411 36 65).

Shoes

Din Sko

Drottninggatan 53, Norrmalm (24 77 22).
T-bana T-Centralen/bus 47, 52, 56, 59, 65.
Open 10am-7pm Mon-Fri; 10am-5pm Sat; noon-4pm
Sun. **Credit** AmEx, DC, MC, V. **Map** p305 F6.
Swedish shoe chain Din Sko makes a real effort to
keep up with fashion without raising prices, and it

TimeOut
Online

vw.timeout.cc

ver 50 of the world
greatest cities.
On one great site.

succeeds. You can find the latest designs at very low prices – cheaper than any other shoe shop in town. **Other locations**: Sergelarkaden 1, Norrmalm (21 03 93); Drottninggatan 50-52, Norrmalm (545 178 90).

Don & Donna

Biblioteksgatan 9, Östermalm (611 01 32). T-bana Östermalm/bus 1, 2, 55, 56. **Open** 10am-6.30pm Mon-Fri; 10am-5pm Sat; noon-4pm Sun. **Credit** AmEx, DC, MC, V. **Map** p305 F8.
Don & Donna's handsome, expensive footwear is a favourite with Stockholm's twentysomethings.

Jerns Skor

Nybrogatan 9, Östermalm (611 20 32). T-bana Östermalmstorg/bus 2, 47, 62, 69, 76. **Open** 10am-6pm Mon-Fri; 10am-3pm Sat. **Credit** AmEx, DC, MC, V. **Map** p305 F8.
Chain store Jerns puts the emphasis on elegance when it comes to footwear, although you can still find a pair of beaded thongs. It's the place for bigfoots to find smart designs in larger sizes. Unfortunately, the shop assistants are also rather stressed.
Other locations: Sveavägen 44, Norrmalm (10 15 33); Drottninggatan 37 (women's shoes only), Norrmalm (40 20 72 09); Drottninggatan 33 (men's shoes only), Norrmalm (402 07 21); Gallerian, Hamngatan 37, Norrmalm (20 97 50).

Nilson Skobutik

Biblioteksgatan 3, Östermalm (611 94 56). T-bana Östermalmstorg/bus 45, 55, 59, 62, 69, 76. **Open** 10am-6.30pm Mon-Fri; 10am-5pm Sat; noon-4pm Sun. **Credit** AmEx, DC, MC, V. **Map** p305 F8.
Upmarket chain store Nilson can fit you out with a pair of high-quality leather boots, high-heeled slingbacks or smart loafers. Trendy styles at good prices.
Other locations: Kungsgatan 7, Norrmalm (20 62 25); Gallerian, Hamngatan 37 (men's shoes only), Norrmalm (411 71 75); Sergelgatan 27, Norrmalm (406 04 40); Sergelarkaden 1, Norrmalm (24 99 80).

Rizzo

Biblioteksgatan 10, Östermalm (611 28 08/www. rizzo.se). T-bana Östermalmstorg/bus 1, 2, 55, 56. **Open** 10am-6.30pm Mon-Fri; 10am-5pm Sat; noon-4pm Sun. **Credit** AmEx, DC, MC, V. **Map** p305 F8.
A few years ago Rizzo made mostly sensible shoes. Now heels and strappy sandals are taking over the collection. The men's section includes cool labels such as Debut, Paul Smith and Boss.
Other locations: Kungsgatan 26 (women's shoes only), Norrmalm (781 04 96); Gallerian, Hamngatan 37, Norrmalm (21 85 21).

SkoUno

Gamla Brogatan 34, Norrmalm (20 64 58). T-bana Hötorget or T-Centralen/bus 1, 47, 52, 53, 69. **Open** 10am-6pm Mon-Fri; 10am-4pm Sat. **Credit** AmEx, MC, V. **Map** p305 F6.
With its selection of Dr Martens and Spice Girls-style platform Buffalos, SkoUno is definitely one of Stockholm's most vibrant boutiques.
Other locations: Drottninggatan 70, Norrmalm (21 98 89); Gamla Brogatan 23, Norrmalm (21 34 61).

Sneakersnstuff

Åsögatan 124, Södermalm (743 03 22/www. sneakersnstuff.com). T-bana Medborgarplatsen/bus 59, 66. **Open** 11am-6pm Mon-Fri; noon-5pm Sat. **Credit** AmEx, MC, V. **Map** p315 M8.
A great variety of sneakers and trainers that you would usually only manage to find in New York, Paris or London. Aimed at the clubgoer rather than the marathon man, twentysomethings come here to pick up the latest release from Nike or a pair from US basketball label And 1. Streetwear also available.

Florists

You'll find excellent flower stalls in the city's open spaces, such as **Östermalmstorg**, **Norrmalmstorg**, **Hötorget**, **Odenplan**, **Medborgarplatsen** and **Södermalmstorg**. For more exotic blooms, visit the flower shop in the entrance of **NK** (*see p153*).

Christoffers Blommor

Kåkbrinken 10, Gamla Stan (24 00 75). T-bana Gamla Stan/bus 3, 53. **Open** noon-6pm Mon-Fri; 11am-6pm Sat, Sun. **Credit** MC, V. **Map** p305 J7.
Christoffer is charming and his small florist shop on one of the narrower streets in Gamla Stan is a good place to grab some fashionable flowers.

Melanders Blommor

Hamngatan 2, Norrmalm (611 28 59/www. melandersblommor.se). T-bana Östermalstorg/bus 2, 47, 62, 69, 76. **Open** 9am-6pm Mon-Fri; 10am-4pm Sat. **Credit** AmEx, DC, MC, V. **Map** p305 F8.
Established in 1894, this small shop is probably the poshest – and certainly the oldest – florist in Stockholm, supplier to the king and various other well-heeled Swedes.

Food & drink

For information on Sweden's idiosyncratic attitude to the purchase of booze and on how to buy alcohol, *see p177* **Booze rules**.

Bakeries & pâtisseries

Riddarbageriet

Riddargatan 15, Östermalm (660 33 75). T-bana Östermalmstorg/bus 2, 47, 62, 69, 76. **Open** 8am-6pm Mon-Fri; 8am-3pm Sat. **Credit** MC, V. **Map** p306 F9.
The best bread in Stockholm. The cakes are outstanding too, but it's Johan Sörberg's sourdough loaves that the locals love. There are a handful of small tables inside and it's one of the few places in town that gives you tea in a pot. Sister property to the bakery at the Hotel Rival (*see p55*).

Vete-Katten

Kungsgatan 55, Norrmalm (20 84 05/www.vete katten.se). T-bana Hötorget or T-Centralen/bus 1, 47, 53, 69. **Open** 7.30am-8pm Mon-Fri; 9.30am-5pm Sat. **Credit** AmEx, DC, MC, V. **Map** p305 F6.

The old-fashioned Vete-Katten tearoom, established in 1928, serves classic Swedish pâtisseries such as *prinsesstårta* ('princess tart' – a cream-filled cake topped with green marzipan), but it's the marvellous mousse gâteaux and fruitcakes that really stand out. You can also buy biscuits, bread, cinnamon, vanilla and cardamom rolls, plus home-made ice-cream in mandarin, rhubarb and passionfruit flavours.

Chocolate

Ejes Chokladfabrik

Erik Dahlbergsgatan 25, Gärdet (664 27 09/www.ejeschoklad.se). T-bana Karlaplan/bus 1, 4, 62, 72. **Open** *Late Aug-late July* 10am-6pm Mon-Fri; 10am-3pm Sat. Closed late July-late Aug. **Credit** MC, V. **Map** p310 D10.

The mocha nougat and Irish coffee truffles alone are worth the trip to this traditional chocolate maker, which was established in 1923. Everything is made by hand without preservatives. Just going into the shop, crammed with chocolates, is an experience. Call 664 27 09 to book a chocolate tasting.

Coffee & tea

Sibyllans Kaffe & Tehandel

Sibyllegatan 35, Östermalm (662 06 63/www.sibyllanskaffetehandel.com). T-bana Östermalmstorg/bus 1, 42, 44, 56, 62. **Open** 9.30am-6pm Mon-Fri. **No credit cards. Map** p306 F9.

When the wind comes from the south you can smell the heady fragrance of Sibyllans ten blocks away. This family-run shop dates back to World War I and the interior, with its old-fashioned tea and coffee jars, hasn't changed since. There's a vast range of teas from all over the world. Sibyllans' own blend, Sir Williams, is a mix of Chinese green teas.

Delicatessens

Androuët Ostaffär

Sibyllegatan 19, Östermalm (660 58 33/www.androuet.nu). T-bana Östermalmstorg/bus 1, 47, 62, 69, 76. **Open** 10.30am-6pm Mon-Fri; 10.30am-3pm Sat. **Credit** AmEx, DC, MC, V. **Map** p306 F9.

In 1909 Henri Androuët set up his first cheese store in Paris; in 1997 the Stockholm shop opened. You'll find more than 100 different cheeses available from all over France. Many of them are fairly obscure, but most are unmissable.

Cajsa Warg

Renstiernas Gata 20, Södermalm (642 23 50/www.cajsawarg.se). Bus 2, 3, 55, 66, 76. **Open** 11am-9pm Mon-Fri; 10am-9pm Sat, Sun. **Credit** AmEx, DC, MC, V. **Map** p315 L9.

A famous Swedish chef at the beginning of the 20th century, Cajsa Warg was known for her creative cooking. This shop, which has a large takeaway menu, uses her name to sell everyday groceries and deli items (Swedish, Mediterranean and Asian).

Health food

Stockholm is blessed with many small health food shops, and most of the major supermarkets have sections devoted to various nut-free, gluten-free and fat-free foods. **Skanstulls Hälsokost** (Ringvägen 106, Södermalm, 641 52 79) sells everything from organic vegetables to aromatherapy oils and vitamin pills.

International

The English Shop

Söderhallarna 134, Södermalm (640 44 04/www.englishshop.se). T-bana Medborgarplatsen/bus 55, 59, 66. **Open** 10am-7pm Mon-Wed; 10am-7pm Thur, Fri; 10am-4pm Sat. **Credit** AmEx, DC, MC, V. **Map** p314 L8.

All the tea (Tetley, Twinings, Typhoo), biscuits (Ginger Snaps, Digestives, Jaffa Cakes) and other British treats you could ever want. Decent prices, and handily located inside Söderhallarna (*see p175*). **Other locations**: Farsta Centrum (605 49 00).

Hong Kong Trading

Kungsgatan 74, Norrmalm (21 79 76). T-bana T-Centralen/bus 1, 47, 53, 59, 69. **Open** 10am-6.30pm Mon-Fri; 10am-3.30pm Sat. **Credit** AmEx, MC, V. **Map** p304 F5.

There are quite a few Asian food shops nearby and friendly Hong Kong Trading is one of the biggest. It has a well-assorted stock of noodles and herbs and a great range of fresh Asian vegetables and fruits. Staff are helpful.

Rinkeby Orientlivs

Hinderstorpsgränd 24, Rinkeby (761 36 61). T-bana Rinkeby. **Open** 9am-7pm Mon-Fri; 10am-6pm Sat, Sun. **Credit** MC, V.

Rinkeby Orientlivs, just outside Stockholm, stocks food from all over the world, including Middle Eastern baklava, South American *mate*, Greek olives, African coffee, large trunks of exotic nuts and all sorts of canned foods. The shop also has a good butcher, and for fresh and really cheap vegetables there's a great outdoor market just outside the door.

Taj Mahal Livs

Kammakargatan 40, Norrmalm (21 22 81). T-bana Rådmansgatan/bus 43, 46, 52. **Open** 10am-6pm Mon-Fri; 10am-4pm Sat. **No credit cards. Map** p309 E6.

Asian, Indian and African foodstuffs are sold in this kitschy shop. There's everything from huge sacks of rice and lentils to shelves stacked with African hairstyling products and Asian herbs and spices. It's a family-run place and sometimes closes for family events and holidays.

Supermarkets

Food is expensive in Sweden, particularly in Stockholm. **ICA** and **Konsum** are probably the biggest supermarket chains, but **Konsum** has a

Brightly coloured stationery, **Ordning & Reda**'s trademark.

'greener' profile, with organic alternatives in most categories. Go to **Prisxtra City** or **Vivo Daglivs Klippet** for cheap bargains and more family sizes. In the fancy area of Östermalm (around Östermalmstorg) you will find more delicatessen-style supermarkets. Both **NK** and **Åhléns** (for both, *see p153*) have excellent, though pricey, supermarkets in their basements.

Gifts & stationery

Bookbinders
Norrlandsgatan 20, Norrmalm (611 18 80/www. bookbindersdesign.com). T-bana Östermalmstorg/ bus 1, 2, 55, 56. **Open** 10am-7pm Mon-Fri; 10am-5pm Sat; noon-4pm Sun. **Credit** AmEx, DC, MC, V. **Map** p305 F8.
Originally opened in 1927, Bookbinders sells some of the best stationery in Stockholm. Prices are high, but so is the quality of the vividly coloured paper, books, linen-covered boxes and folders.
Other locations: NK, Hamngatan 18-20, Norrmalm (762 88 81); Åhléns, Klarabergsgatan 50, Norrmalm (676 60 00).

Bungalow Porslin
Kungsholmsgatan 15, Kungsholmen (654 48 40/ www.bungalow.se). T-bana Rådhuset/bus 1, 40, 52, 59. **Open** noon-6pm Mon-Fri; 10am-3pm Sat. **Credit** MC, V. **Map** p304 4G.
Bungalow specialises in 20th-century Swedish ceramics and has masses of stuff from major companies such as Gustavsberg piled high on the shelves. It's far from precious – this is the sort of stuff that was

considered unfashionable until just a few years ago – and the store is a good place to find affordable, distinctive plates, cups, saucers and bowls.

Coctail & Coctail Deluxe
Coctail: Skånegatan 71, Södermalm (642 07 40/ www.coctail.nu). Coctail Deluxe: Bondegatan 34 (642 07 41). Bus 2, 53, 59, 66, 76. **Open** *Both* 11am-6pm Mon-Fri; 11am-4pm Sat. **Credit** MC, V. **Map** p315 M9.
A pair of colourful kitsch emporia selling all the funky furniture, unusual jewellery, colourful housewares and retro clothing you could ever want, not to mention garden gnomes and Elvis bead curtains.

DesignTorget
Kulturhuset, Sergels Torg, Norrmalm (50 83 15 20/ www.designtorget.se). T-bana T-Centralen/bus 47, 52, 56, 59, 65. **Open** 10am-7pm Mon-Fri; 10am-5pm Sat; 11am-5pm Sun. **Credit** AmEx, MC, V. **Map** p305 G7.
The concept of DesignTorget is that promising new designers can sell their work on a commission basis alongside established companies. You'll find an assortment of jewellery, household goods, ceramics, textiles and furniture, as well as some original gifts and amusing gadgets. The stock changes regularly.
Other locations: Götgatan 31, Södermalm (462 35 20); Birger Jarlsgatan 18, Östermalm (611 53 03); Västermalmsgallerian, St Eriksgatan 45, Kungsholmen (33 11 53).

Ordning & Reda
Götgatan 32, Södermalm (714 96 01/www.ordning-reda.com). T-bana Medborgarplatsen or Slussen/bus 2, 3, 43, 53, 55, 59, 66, 76. **Open** 10am-6pm Mon-Fri; 11am-4pm Sat; noon-4pm Sun. **Credit** AmEx, DC, MC, V. **Map** p314 L8.

Heaven for stationery addicts. Ordning & Reda was established by the same family that owns Bookbinders, and sells all sorts of fun and brightly coloured stationery.
Other locations: Drottninggatan 82, Norrmalm (10 84 96); NK, Hamngatan 18-20, Norrmalm (762 84 62); Åhléns, Klarabergsgatan 50, Norrmalm (676 60 00); Sturegallerian, Stureplan, Östermalm (611 12 00); Fältöversten, Karlaplan 13, Östermalm (667 84 40).

10 Swedish Designers

Götgatan 25, Södermalm (643 25 04/www. tiogruppen.com). T-bana Slussen/bus 2, 3, 43, 53, 55, 59, 66, 76. **Open** 10am-6pm Mon-Fri; 11am-4pm Sat; noon-4pm Sun. **Credit** MC, V. **Map** p314 L8.
Tiogruppen was set up by ten young textile artists in 1970 and their creations have become design classics. The colourful, bold geometric designs – available as bags, cushions, oven gloves, trays, ironing board covers or just fabric – are a must-have.

Health & beauty

Complementary health

Inspira Handelsbod

Rörstrandsgatan 42, Vasastaden (34 54 23/ www.inspira.cc). T-bana St Eriksplan/bus 3, 4, 47, 72. **Open** noon-6.30pm Mon-Fri. Closed 4wks in summer. **No credit cards. Map** p308 D2.
Fresh herbs, natural cough mixtures and other handmade herbal medicines and hygiene products are sold in Inspira. You can browse through the books or why not try some 'heart wine' or 'nerve cookies'?

Cosmetics & perfume

As well as the following shops, try the cosmetics counters of the department stores (*see p153*).

c/o Stockholm

Götgatan 30, Södermalm (50 52 59 51/ www.costockholm.se). T-bana Medborgarplatsen or Slussen/bus 2, 3, 43, 53, 55, 59, 66, 76. **Open** 10.30am-7pm Mon-Fri; 10.30am-5pm Sat. **Credit** AmEx, DC, MC, V. **Map** p314 L8.
A spacious temple of beauty, with its own hair salon and espresso bar. There's a vast array of cosmetics, underwear, scented candles, sunglasses and other fashionable bits and pieces. The bulk of the products are for women, though one corner is given over to men's stuff.
Other locations: NK, Regeringsgatan 38, Östermalm (762 80 00).

Cow Parfymeri

Mäster Samuelsgatan 9, Östermalm (611 15 04). T-bana Östermalmstorg/bus 2, 43, 55, 59, 62, 69. **Open** 11am-6pm Mon-Fri; 11am-3.30pm Sat. **Credit** AmEx, DC, MC, V. **Map** p305 F8.
This small boutique sells top-line cosmetics, such as Commes des Garçons, Philosophy and Vincent Longo. The staff are professional make-up artists and although it's all a bit elitist, the products and service are well worth the extra pennies.

Face Stockholm

Biblioteksgatan 1, Östermalm (611 00 74/ www.facestockholm.com). T-bana Östermalmstorg/ bus 2, 55, 59, 62, 69. **Open** 10am-7pm Mon-Fri;

10 Swedish Designers.

Hair & Face

Gamla Brogatan 21 & 25, Norrmalm (406 07 07/ 20 42 22/www.hair-facestockholm.se). T-bana Hötorget or T-Centralen/bus 1, 47, 52, 53, 56, 65. **Open** 10am-7pm Mon-Fri; 10am-5pm Sat. **Credit** MC, V. **Map** p305 F6.

These two small, pleasant Hair & Face salons near T-Centralen are good places to pop into if you want a trendy Swedish hairdo at a fair price.
Other locations: Regerinsgatan 27, Norrmalm (677 00 33); PUB, Hörtorget, Norrmalm (21 88 81).

Klippoteket

Riddargatan 6, Östermalm (679 56 50). T-bana Östermalmstorg/bus 2, 47, 62, 69, 76. **Open** 8am-8pm Mon-Wed; 8am-7pm Thur, Fri; 9am-3pm Sat. **Credit** AmEx, DC, MC, V. **Map** p305 F8.

Young, friendly staff offer trendy, as well as classic, cuts (400kr-450kr). It's usually possible to get an appointment with a few days' notice.
Other locations: Riddargatan 3, Östermalm (611 40 66).

Pharmacies

Access to medication is strictly controlled in Sweden and in most cases you need a doctor's prescription (only prescriptions from Nordic countries are allowed). However, you can buy painkillers and other simple medicines in state-run pharmacies all over town (look out for the green *apotek* sign). For more information on prescription medicines, call **Läkemedelsupplysningen** (medicine information office) toll-free on 020 66 77 66.

Apoteket CW Scheele

Klarabergsgatan 64, Norrmalm (454 81 30/ www.apoteket.se). T-bana T-Centralen/bus 47, 52, 56, 59, 69. **Open** 24hrs daily. **Credit** AmEx, MC, V. **Map** p305 G6.

Apotek Enhörningen

Krukmakargatan 13, Södermalm (0771 45 04 50). T-bana Mariatorget/bus 43, 55, 66, 74. **Open** 8.30am-10pm daily. **Credit** AmEx, MC, V. **Map** p314 L6.

Spas

In addition to those listed below, the **Stockholm Day Spa** on the fourth floor of Åhléns (*see p153*) offers massages, hydrotherapy and facial treatments.

Centralbadet

Drottninggatan 88, Norrmalm (24 24 02/www. centralbadet.se). T-bana Hötorget/bus 1, 47, 52, 53. **Open** 6am-9pm Mon-Fri; 8am-9pm Sat, Sun (changing rooms close 10pm daily). **Admission** 90kr-130kr. **Minimum age** *women* 18; *men* 23. **Credit** AmEx, DC, MC, V. **Map** p305 F6.

In 1904 Jugendstil architect Wilhelm Klemming realised a dream about an 'open window to nature' when he designed Centralbadet. Set back from the

10am-5pm Sat; noon-4pm Sun. **Credit** AmEx, DC, MC, V. **Map** p305 F8.

A combination of high-quality, no-nonsense cosmetics, streamlined packaging, clean interiors and impeccable service have resulted in the Swedish success story that is Face Stockholm. Mother-and-daughter team Gun Nowak and Martina Arfwidson have now exported the concept to Ireland, Norway and New York, but there's nothing like visiting the original. There are 12 branches in the city, including two on Drottninggatan.
Other locations: throughout the city.

Hair salons

Stockholm has plenty of hairdressers. In the simpler drop-in salons, prices for a haircut vary from about 150kr to 300kr. **Toni & Guy** (Götgatan 10, Södermalm (714 56 56/www.toni andguy.se) has its largest European branch in Stockholm.

Björn Axén

Norrlandsgatan 7, Norrmalm (54 52 73 50/ www.axens.se). T-bana Östermalmstorg/bus 2, 47, 55, 59, 62, 76. **Open** 9am-6pm Mon, Tue, Fri; 9am-8pm Wed, Thur; 9am-2.30pm Sat. **Credit** AmEx, DC, MC, V. **Map** p305 F8.

Queen Sylvia is among the customers at Stockholm's most chic hair salon. A cut costs around 610kr, but it's half that if you're willing to let a trainee loose on your locks.
Other locations: Åhléns City, Klarabergsgatan 50, Norrmalm (54 52 73 50).

Eat, Drink, Shop

street in a pretty garden, it has beautiful art nouveau interiors and a fairly inexpensive café. Take a dip in the pool or jacuzzi, experience different types of sauna, have a massage (one-hour Swedish massage costs 550kr) or a treatment (herbal bath costs 300kr). Friendly staff and a delightful air of faded grandeur make it more appealing than fashionable Sturebadet (*see below*).

Hasseludden Yasuragi

Hamndalsvägen 6, Saltsjö-boo (747 61 00/www. hasseludden.com). Bus 417 to Hamndalsvägen then 10mins walk/Vaxholmsbolaget boat from Strömkajen. **Open** 8am-10pm daily. **Admission** *8am-4pm Mon-Thur* 750kr; *4-10pm Mon-Thur* from 950kr; *Fri-Sun* 1,000kr-1,200kr. **Credit** AmEx, DC, MC, V.

The renovation of the run-down 1970s premises of Hasseludden into a Japanese spa hotel, including a pool, outdoor hot bath, sauna and restaurant, was a masterstroke. Massages and beauty treatments are also available. Located on the edge of the Stockholm archipelago, it makes for a brilliant day trip. Best to book in advance. For a review of the Hasseludden hotel, *see p58*.

Sturebadet

Sturegallerian, Stureplan, Östermalm (54 50 15 00/www.sturebadet.se). T-bana Östermalmstorg/ bus 1, 2, 55, 56, 62. **Open** 6.30am-10pm Mon-Fri; 9am-7pm Sat, Sun. *July, Aug* 6.30am-9pm Mon-Fri; 9am-6pm Sat, Sun. **Admission** annual membership 16,700kr; day membership 295kr. **Minimum age** 18. **Credit** AmEx, DC, MC, V. **Map** p305 F8.

Dating from 1885, swanky Sturebadet is the traditional upper-class and celeb favourite, next to the hub of their universe, Stureplan. It offers a gym with ten personal trainers, assorted massages, treatments and cures, a beautiful art nouveau pool, plus an extraordinary Turkish bath that can be rented for meetings with up to 20 people (3,500kr for two hours). Naturally, this doesn't come cheap: the Breakfast Club deal, which includes breakfast each weekday, costs 13,950kr a year.

Interiors

What is it about Nordic countries and interior design? As with Helsinki and Copenhagen, Stockholm is extraordinarily rich in furnishings and fabric, and you'll find everything from second-hand goods in charity shops to elegant boutiques specialising in 20th-century classics and interior design shops packed with the best in Scandinavian design. For more on Swedish design, *see pp36-40*.

Antiques & second-hand

Stockholm has several good second-hand shops run by charitable organisations, including **Emmaus** (Götgatan 14, Södermalm, 644 85 86), **Myrorna** (*see p163*) and **Små Smulor** (*see*

p164). There is also a huge flea market in the **Skärholmen centre** (710 00 60, www.loppmarknaden.se), which is about 20 minutes south-west of central Stockholm on the T-bana, though this location may be changing after May 2005 (check on the website for more news).

There are several branches of **Stadsmissionen** (www.stads missionen.se), a not-for-profit organisation that sells people's cast-off clothing, books and household items to raise money for the homeless and other needy Swedes. They can be found at Stortorget 5, Gamla Stan (787 86 61); Bondegatan 46, Södermalm (642 19 41); and Hantverkargatan 78, Kungsholmen (652 74 75).

For antiques, there's a terrific cluster of shops on Upplandsgatan in Vasastaden, near the Odenplan T-bana station. These include **Domino Antik** (Upplandsgatan 25, 33 78 58), for 20th-century furniture and lights; **Old Touch** (Upplandsgatan 43, 34 90 05) for lace and crystal; **Jerner Antik** (Upplandsgatan 36, 30 92 40) for rustic pieces; **Carléns** (Upplandsgatan 40, 31 34 01) for glass pieces; **Bacchus** (Upplandsgatan 46, 30 54 80) for china and 20th-century pieces. Around the corner is the self-explanatory **Deco Design** (Odengatan 80, 31 44 04).

Jacksons

Tyska Brinken 20, Gamla Stan (411 33 30/ www.jacksons.se). T-bana Gamla Stan/bus 3, 53, 55, 59, 76. **Open** noon-6pm Mon-Fri; noon-3pm Sat. **Credit** AmEx, DC, MC, V. **Map** p305 J7.

An extensive range of exclusive international and Scandinavian design and decorative arts from the 1880s to the 1980s. Well worth a visit.

Other locations: Sibyllegatan 53, Östermalm (665 33 50).

Kurt Ribbhagen

Birger Jarlsgatan 13, Östermalm (679 82 36). T-bana Östermalmstorg/bus 1, 2, 55, 56. **Open** 9am-6pm Mon-Fri. **Credit** AmEx, DC, MC, V. **Map** p305 F8.

Kurt Ribbhagen is the best antique silver shop in the whole of Stockholm. It's also handily located next door to Georg Jensen, where you can buy modern Danish silver.

Modernity

Sibyllegatan 6, Östermalm (20 80 25/www. modernity.se). T-bana Östermalmstorg/bus 2, 47, 62, 69, 76. **Open** noon-6pm Mon-Fri; 11am-3pm Sat. **Credit** AmEx, DC, MC, V. **Map** p306 F9.

Scotsman Andrew Duncanson set up Modernity in Gamla Stan before moving to larger premises in Östermalm. He specialises in Scandinavian 20th-century design, including furniture, ceramics, glass and jewellery. If you're a fan of the likes of Alvar Aalto and Arne Jacobsen, then this place is an absolute must.

Clean lines and creative cosmetics at **Face Stockholm**. *See p170.*

Furniture & home accessories

Stockholm is heaving with shops devoted to interior design. Check out **DesignTorget** (*see p169*) and **10 Swedish Designers** (*see p170*).

Apparat

Nytorgsgatan 36, Södermalm (653 66 33). T-bana Medborgarplatsen/bus 2, 53, 59, 66, 76. **Open** 11.30am-6.30pm Mon-Fri; 11.30am-4pm Sat; noon-3pm Sun. **Credit** AmEx, DC, MC, V. **Map** p315 M9.
Apparat sells well-designed objects for the home, including notepads, storage boxes, tea cups, coffee tables and a slew of books to put on them.

Asplund

Sibyllegatan 31, Östermalm (662 52 84/www. asplund.org). T-bana Östermalmstorg/bus 1, 44, 55, 56, 62. **Open** 11am-6pm Mon-Fri; 11am-4pm Sat. **Credit** AmEx, MC, V. **Map** p306 F9.
The airy Asplund showroom is a good source of newly produced design classics, including furniture, rugs, glasswares and lighting, by Scandinavian and international designers.

Carl Malmsten Inredning

Strandvägen 5B, Östermalm (23 33 80/www. c.malmsten.se). T-bana Östermalmstorg/bus 47, 55, 62, 69, 76. **Open** 10am-6pm Mon-Fri; 10am-4pm Sat. **Credit** MC, V. **Map** p306 G9.
High-quality furniture, textiles and light fittings by the talented Swedish designer Carl Malmsten (*see pp36-40* **Design**). The shop, which is now run by his grandson Jerk Malmsten, sells classics from the 1950s and 1960s, as well as rugs and books.

David Design

Götgatan 36, Södermalm (694 75 75/www.david.se). T-bana Slussen/bus 2, 3, 43, 55, 59, 76. **Open** 10am-7pm Mon-Fri; 10am-5pm Sat; noon-4pm Sun. **Credit** AmEx, MC, V. **Map** p305 F8.
The latest in contemporary Swedish (and international) design, from the likes of Mats Theselius. Clean lines and bright colours characterise the products, from sofas, chairs and tables to mirrors.

Elviras Värld

Renstiernas Gata 24, Södermalm (640 09 00/ www.elvirasvarld.com). Bus 2, 3, 53, 66, 76. **Open** *Mid Aug-June* 11am-6pm Mon-Fri; 11am-3pm Sat; noon-3pm Sun. *July-mid Aug* noon-6pm Mon-Fri; noon-3pm Sat. **Credit** AmEx, DC, MC, V. **Map** p315 L9.
Elviras Värld has both new furniture and restored antiques. Much of the furniture is beautiful and well selected, and the textiles are particularly handsome.

Formtanke

Döbelnsgatan 23, Norrmalm (411 44 38/www. formtanke.com). T-bana Rådmansgatan/bus 2, 4, 42, 43, 52. **Open** varies; call first. **Credit** AmEx, MC, V. **Map** p309 E6.
High-quality, well-designed Scandinavian home accessories, made in a wide range of materials, including wood, silver, bronze and brass.

Granit

Götgatan 31, Södermalm (642 10 68/www.granit. com). T-bana Medborgarplatsen or Slussen/bus 43, 55, 59, 66. **Open** 10am-7pm Mon-Fri; 10am-5pm Sat; noon-4pm Sun. **Credit** AmEx, DC, MC, V. **Map** p314 L8.

Granit. *See p173.*

Granit is almost like a Gap for the home – it sells lots of simple things at low prices: storage boxes, unadorned glassware and crockery, spices, coffee, notebooks and photo albums, plus hundreds of other plain but pleasant items. Be warned: it's almost impossible to go into Granit without finding something you want to buy.

Other locations: Kungsgatan 42, Norrmalm (21 92 85); Västermalmsgallerien, St Eriksgatan 45, Kungsholmen (650 73 25).

Iittala Butiken

Norrlandsgatan 18, Norrmalm (678 07 75/www. iittala.fi). T-bana Östermalmstorg/bus 1, 2, 55, 56. **Open** 11am-6pm Mon-Fri; 11am-4pm Sat. **Credit** AmEx, DC, MC, V. **Map** p305 F8.

Finnish housewares giant Iittala's Stockholm shop is a fabulous source of things for the kitchen or dining room. Particularly good buys include Alvar Aalto's curvaceous 'Savoy' vase, Alfredo Haberli's stripey crockery, and mugs decorated with Moomins.

Other locations: NK, Hamngatan 18-20, Norrmalm (762 80 40).

IKEA

Kungens Kurva, Skärholmen (020 43 90 50/ www.ikea.se). Bus 173, 707, 710, 748/free IKEA bus from Regeringsgatan 13 on the hr 11am-5pm daily and from IKEA on the half-hr 11.30am-5.30pm daily. **Open** 10am-8pm Mon-Fri; 10am-6pm Sat, Sun. **Credit** AmEx, DC, MC, V.

In Sweden IKEA is more than just a furniture store, it's a way of life. Recently renovated and expanded, this is now the world's largest IKEA store and well worth visiting even if you're not after any furniture, just to see how the Swedes spend their weekends. There are dozens of mocked-up rooms to stroll through, and the on-site restaurant sells excellent meatballs with lingonberries.

Other locations: Barkarby, Barkarby Handelsplats, Järfälla (020 43 90 50).

Klara

Nytorgsgatan 36, Södermalm (694 92 40). Bus 3, 46, 59, 66, 76. **Open** 11am-6pm Mon-Fri; 11am-4pm Sat. **Credit** AmEx, DC, MC, V. **Map** p315 M9.

A shop that's all about Scandinavian minimalism, free from knick-knacks and unnecessary decoration. You'll find a small but well-selected range of furniture, cutlery and kitchenware. Good for gifts.

Other locations: Birger Jarlsgatan 34, Östermalm (611 52 52).

Lagerhaus

Drottninggatan 31-37, Norrmalm (23 72 00/www. lagerhaus.se). T-bana T-Centralen/bus 47, 52, 56, 59, 69. **Open** 10am-7pm Mon-Fri; 10am-5pm Sat; noon-4pm Sun. **Credit** AmEx, MC, V. **Map** p305 G7.

Huge smelly candles, absurd kitchen implements, cheap minimalist porcelain and paperback fiction – all under the same roof. It's a bit chaotic, but if you're lucky you might find something that looks more expensive than it really is.

Other locations: Birger Jarlsgatan 18, Östermalm (611 80 40).

Nordiska Galleriet

Nybrogatan 11, Östermalm (442 83 60/www. nordiskagalleriet.se). T-bana Östermalmstorg/bus 2, 47, 55, 62, 69, 76. **Open** 10am-6pm Mon-Fri; 10am-4pm Sat; noon-4pm Sun. **Credit** AmEx, DC, MC, V. **Map** p305 F8.

In its large, fashionable home on Nybrogatan, Nordiska Galleriet sells furniture, lights and gifts from Nordic and international designers. Both past masters (Alvar Aalto, Arne Jacobsen) and contemporary names (Philippe Starck, Jonas Bohlin) feature.

Norrgavel

Birger Jarlsgatan 27, Östermalm (545 220 50/ www.norrgavel.se). T-bana Östermalmstorg/bus 2, 3, 43, 55, 56. **Open** 10am-6pm Mon-Fri; 10am-4pm Sat; noon-4pm Sun (closed Sun May-Aug). **Credit** AmEx, DC, MC, V. **Map** p310 E8.

Functionalist furniture – with truly elegant beds, chairs and shelves – and a wealth of home accessories, inspired both by Japanese minimalism and 1950s Scandinavian design.

R.O.O.M.

Alströmergatan 20, Kungsholmen (692 50 00/www. room.se). T-bana Fridhemsplan/bus 1, 3, 4, 57, 59. **Open** *June-Aug* 10am-6pm Mon-Fri; 10am-4pm Sat. *Sept-May* 10am-6.30pm Mon-Fri; 10am-5pm Sat; 11am-5pm Sun. **Credit** AmEx, DC, MC, V. **Map** p303 F2.

R.O.O.M. sells beautiful, expensive furniture and furnishings, all so perfectly displayed that it's a good source of ideas even if you don't buy anything. It also sells lots of tablewares, books and small giftsized items. It's particularly popular for a weekend browse followed by a *fika* in the adjoining café.

Svenskt Tenn

Strandvägen 5, Östermalm (670 16 28/www.svenskt tenn.se). T-bana Östermalmstorg/bus 47, 55, 62, 69, 76. **Open** 10am-6pm Mon-Fri; 10am-4pm Sat. **Credit** AmEx, DC, MC, V. **Map** p306 G9.

A Stockholm classic. Founded by artist and designer Estrid Ericson in 1924, Svenskt Tenn is best known for the furniture and textiles created by Josef Frank, who worked for the company for 30 years after joining in 1934. His designs are still the mainstay of the shop's products, which are not cheap. *See also pp36-40* **Design**.

Launderettes

Tvättomaten

Västmannagatan 61, Vasastaden (34 64 80/www. tvattomaten.com). T-bana Odenplan/bus 2, 4, 40, 47, 53, 69. **Open** *Aug-June* 8.30am-6.30pm Mon-Fri; 9.30am-3pm Sat. *July* 8.30am-6.30pm Mon-Fri. **No credit cards**. **Map** p308 D4.

Because all apartment buildings have their own *tvättstuga* (laundry room), launderettes are something of a rarity in Stockholm. This is the only one in the city centre. A one-hour self-service wash costs about 70kr. Alternatively you can let the staff deal with your dirties (160kr same day service; 90kr next day service). Dry-cleaning service.

Markets

Food

If you think the following are a bit overpriced, head for the suburban outdoor markets of **Skärhomen**, **Tensta** and **Rinkeby** for great produce at low prices.

Hötorgshallen

Hötorget, Norrmalm (www.hotorgshallen.se). T-bana Hötorget/bus 1, 52, 56. **Open** *Indoor market* May-Aug 10am-6pm Mon-Fri; 10am-3pm Sat. Sept-Apr 10am-6pm Mon-Thur; 10am-6.30pm Fri; 10am-4pm Sat. *Outdoor market* usually 10am-7pm Mon-Fri; 10am-5pm Sat; noon-5pm Sun. **Map** p305 F6.

A visit to Hötorgshallen, located below the Filmstaden multiplex, is a culinary trip around the world. Built in the 1950s, the hall was renovated in the 1990s and its international character has grown along with immigration to Stockholm. You can buy everything from Middle Eastern falafel to Indian spices, as well as fantastic fish and meat, and there are several good places to grab lunch. Outside there's a bustling fruit, vegetable and flower market on Hötorget, which first opened as a market back in the 1640s.

Östermalms Saluhall

Östermalmstorg, Östermalm (www.ostermalms hallen.se). T-bana Östermalmstorg/bus 1, 55, 56, 62. **Open** 9.30am-6pm Mon-Thur; 9.30am-6.30pm Fri; 9.30am-4pm (*June-Aug* 9.30am-2pm) Sat. **Map** p305 F8.

The flagship of market halls in Stockholm, this gastronomic temple has been serving the city's gourmets since 1888. Designed by Isak Gustav Clason, the 28m-high (93ft) ceiling and beautifully crafted interior is magnificent. Get tempted by a wide variety of fresh bread from Amandas Brödbod, delicious chocolate from Betsy Sandbergs Choklad, excellent fish and seafood from Melanders Fisk, vegetables from Lisa Janssons and ready-to-eat foods from Depå Sushi or Tysta Mari. The numerous well-reputed restaurants and cafés are filled with well-heeled Östermalm ladies who lunch. The square outside has a handsome flower stall and an open-air café, Lisapåtorget, which is a sibling to Lisa Elmqvist's excellent fish restaurant inside the hall. Expensive but worth it.

Söderhallarna

Medborgarplatsen 3, Södermalm (714 09 84/ 442 09 80/www.soderhallarna.com). T-bana Medborgarplatsen/bus 55, 59, 66. **Open** 10am-6pm Mon-Wed; 10am-7pm Thur, Fri; 10am-4pm Sat. **Map** p314 L8.

Söderhallarna, which is a rather unsightly glass-and-concrete construction, is Stockholm's newest indoor market. It's handy for a great selection of fresh produce – if you can endure its soulless, mall-like atmosphere.

Eat, Drink, Shop

Other

Also try the flea market in the **Skärholmen centre** (*see p171*).

Street

Hornstulls Strand 4, Södermalm (no phone/www. streetinstockholm.se). T-bana Hornstull/bus 4, 40, 66, 74. **Open** 11am-5pm Sat, Sun. **Map** p313 M3.
Street opened in August 2004 as a weekend-only outdoor market on the western shore of Södermalm but it is expected to be open daily by the beginning of 2005. Street's declared aim is to be Stockholm's answer to London's Camden market – a place where people come to browse stalls selling trendy clothing, artwork and accessories. As this guidebook went to press the market was outdoor-only but a large indoor space, with a restaurant, was being prepared for the winter.

Music

Bashment

Bondegatan 6, Södermalm (640 05 84/info@ bashment.com). T-bana Medborgarplatsen/bus 2, 55, 59, 66, 76. **Open** 10am-8pm Mon-Fri; 11am-8pm Sat; noon-5pm Sun. **Credit** MC, V. **Map** p315 M8.
Bashment sells Jamaican reggae and dancehall in a laid-back manner. This is one of the few shops in Stockholm for obscure Afro-Caribbean music, and a good source of gig tickets too.

Mega Skivakademien

Sergels Torg, Norrmalm (56 61 57 00/www.mega.se). T-bana T-Centralen/bus 47, 52, 56, 59, 65. **Open** 10am-7pm Mon-Fri; noon-4pm Sun. **Credit** AmEx, DC, MC, V. **Map** p305 G7.
Welcome to northern Europe's biggest record store. It's on three floors: the basement is chart-oriented, and there's a good selection of classical and jazz on the ground floor. There are also videos, DVDs and magazines. Despite its size, it's not particularly cheap.

Multi Kulti

St Paulsgatan 3, Södermalm (643 61 29/www.multi kulti.se). T-bana Slussen/bus 2, 3, 43, 53, 55, 59, 76. **Open** 11am-6.30pm Mon, Tue; 11am-7pm Wed-Fri; 11am-4pm Sat. **Credit** MC, V. **Map** p314 K7.
The smell of incense fills this tiny, classic shop which has just about every style of world music you could possibly imagine. It also stocks a small range of books and videos. Staff are both committed and knowledgeable.

Nitty Gritty Records

St Eriksgatan 98, Vasastaden (33 32 80/ http://w1.833.telia.com/~u83303555). T-bana St Eriksplan/bus 3, 4, 42, 47, 72. **Open** 11am-6pm Mon-Wed, Fri; 11am-7pm Thur; 11am-3pm Sat. **Credit** AmEx, DC, MC, V. **Map** p308 D3.
A sweet little shop run by club promoter Robert Baum. You'll find an excellent selection of soul, R&B, funk, Latin and rare groove – mainly new, but some second-hand stuff too.

Pet Sounds

Skånegatan 53, Södermalm (702 97 98/www.pet sounds.se). T-bana Medborgarplatsen/bus 2, 55, 59, 66, 76. **Open** 11am-7pm Mon-Fri; 11am-4pm Sat; noon-4pm Sun. **Credit** AmEx, MC, V. **Map** p315 M8.
Pet Sounds is the oldest and still the best indie shop in Stockholm. There's a lot of 1960s music and soundtracks, plus a decent range of soul music.

Pitch DJ Store

Gamla Brogatan 27, Norrmalm (22 56 40/www. pitch.nu). T-bana T-Centralen/bus 47, 52, 53, 59, 69. **Open** 11am-7pm Mon-Fri; 11am-4pm Sat. **Credit** AmEx, MC, V. **Map** p305 F6.
The Pitch DJ Store is where Stockholm's hip hop DJs hang out.

Snickars Records

Repslagargatan 11, Södermalm (643 13 44). T-bana Slussen/bus 3, 43, 55, 56, 59. **Open** noon-7pm Mon-Fri; noon-5pm Sat. **Credit** MC, V. **Map** p314 K7.
DJ and music producer Mika Snickars' shop is the best place for vinyl when it comes to new and retro house, garage and disco.

Second-hand

St Eriksgatan in Kungsholmen is *the* street for second-hand music in Stockholm. As well as the most wide-ranging shop, **Skivbörsen** (No.71, 32 03 17), there are plenty of other options, including **Record Palace** (No.56, 650 19 90), **The Beat Goes On** (No.67, 31 27 17), **Record Hunter** (No.70, 32 20 23), **Golden Oldies Shop** (No.96, 32 22 40), **Nitty Gritty Records** (*see p176*), **Masen's Rock Center** (No.100, 34 32 00) and nearby **Atlas** (Torsgatan 31, 34 06 17).

Mickes Serier, CD & Vinyl

Långholmsgatan 13, Södermalm (668 20 22). T-bana Hornstull/bus 4, 40, 66, 74. **Open** 11am-usually 9pm daily. **Credit** AmEx, MC, V. **Map** p313 L3.
Mickes Serler, CD & Vinyl has everything from second-hand ABBA albums to rarities that are not even for sale. Expect a cosy atmosphere and a lot of small talk.
Other locations: Långholmsgatan 20 (668 10 23).

Musical instruments

Halkan's Rockhouse

Noe Arksgränden 2, Södermalm (641 49 70/ www.halkans.com). T-bana Medborgarplatsen/ bus 55, 59, 66. **Open** noon-6pm Mon-Fri; noon-3pm Sat. **Credit** (over 100kr only) AmEx, MC, V. **Map** p314 K8.
Just off Götgatan, Halkan's is the place to head if you're looking for old guitars or professional repairs. Other good instrument shops nearby include Vintage Guitars (Götgatan 28, 643 10 83) and Estrad (Folkungagatan 54, 640 12 60) for keyboards and assorted studio equipment.

Eat, Drink, Shop

Booze rules

Sweden has long had a troubled relationship with alcohol. Alcohol abuse reached unprecedented (and still unsurpassed) heights in the mid 19th century, when it was estimated that Swedes were consuming a staggering average of 50 litres of *aquavit* per person per year. Society responded with a widespread temperance movement, followed by strong governmental restrictions on the sale of alcohol. Citizens were given ration books – a practice not abolished until 1955 – and suspected alcoholics were blacklisted from alcohol retailers.

Even today, Sweden has some of Europe's most stringent laws on alcohol sales, designed to promote a 'healthy drinking culture' (though many would still identify Sweden as a binge-drinking nation, at least at weekends). All forms of strong alcohol may only be purchased at the state-owned alcohol-retailing monopoly **Systembolaget**. It wasn't until 2001 that its stores were allowed to open on Saturdays. Prior to the late 1990s, customers also had to request their purchases over the counter – much like at a pharmacy. Today, however, many of these shops have been converted, and the government – generously – now lets you handle the bottles yourself.

Sweden's entrance into the EU in 1995 has, however, rocked the boat considerably. The Swedish government's tight control over the sale of alcohol – through high taxes, limited opening hours of its retail monopoly and heavy customs duties on alcohol – is rapidly slipping away. The amount of alcohol Swedes are now allowed to bring with them into the country increased substantially in 2004 when the country was forced to comply with EU regulations. Consequently, Swedes are buying more alcohol abroad (courtesy of ferryboat rides to Finland and Estonia and bridge-crossings to Denmark, where prices are cheaper), and are apparently drinking more.

In addition, though the EU has allowed Sweden to continue its retail monopoly, it sued the country in 2004 – unresolved at the time we went to press – over its prohibition of the private import of alcohol. Decreases in sales at the Systembolaget and a bribery scandal in November 2003, in which store managers were caught taking bribes to give certain distributors preferential treatment, certainly did not help the government's cause.

Whether or not you approve of the Swedish way, you'll find there are some advantages to the Systembolaget's monopoly. The shops are spotless, the staff professional and ready to give advice, and there's an impressive selection of both Swedish and imported brands (some 2,500 in total) – a far cry from your average off-licence. There are fine wines from around the world, unusual beers, a huge range of spirits from brännvin to tequila – and you can always order items not in stock when you visit. Systembolaget stocks beer containing 3.5 to 4.5 per cent alcohol by volume (*mellanöl*) and over 4.5 per cent (*starköl*). Weaker beer, called *lättöl* (under 2.5 per cent) or *folköl* (2.25 to 3.5 per cent), is sold in supermarkets. As proof of Sweden's obsession with alcohol, Stockholm has two museums entirely dedicated to the subject: **Vin & Sprithistoriska Museet** (*see p80*) and **Systembolagets Museet** (*see p79*).

Systembolaget

Klarabergsgatan 62, Norrmalm (21 47 44/ www.systembolaget.se). T-bana T-Centralen/ bus 47, 52, 56, 59, 65. **Open** 10am-8pm Mon-Fri; 10am-3pm Sat. **Credit** AmEx, MC, V. **Map** p305 G6.

This is the largest Systembolaget shop in Stockholm; it also has longer opening hours than most shops. The branch at Grev Turegatan 3 specialises in wine. You'll find a complete listing of all shops in the back of the Systembolaget catalogue.

Other locations: throughout the city.

Eat, Drink, Shop

Opticians & eyewear

Stureoptikern

Grev Turegatan 9, Östermalm (611 55 00/www. stureoptikern.se). T-bana Östermalmstorg/bus 1, 2, 55, 56, 62. **Open** 10am-7pm Mon-Fri; 10am-5pm Sat; noon-4pm Sun. **Credit** AmEx, DC, MC, V. **Map** p305 F8.

Stureoptikern has a large selection of sunglasses, including Armani, Gucci, Helmut Lang and Hugo Boss. It also offers eye tests and consultations, contact lenses and glasses repairs.
Other locations: Götgatan 71, Södermalm (640 61 91).

Synsam

Norrlandsgatan 10, Norrmalm (679 85 15/ www.synsam.se). T-bana Kungsträdgården or Östermalmstorg/bus 1, 2, 47, 55, 59, 62, 69, 76. **Open** 9am-6pm Mon-Fri; 10am-3pm Sat. **Credit** AmEx, DC, MC, V. **Map** p305 F8.

Scandinavia's largest group of opticians has around a dozen branches in Stockholm, and it's usually possible to get an appointment fairly quickly. A good place to buy sunglasses, contact lens supplies or, if you want to look totally Scandic, a pair of Danish Lindberg spectacles.
Other locations: throughout the city.

Sex shops

Lovestore (641 71 66, Bondegatan 6, www.lovestore.nu), near **Secrets** (*see below*), is a female-run store selling toys, lubricants and erotic clothing.

Secrets

Katarina Bangata 17, Södermalm (640 92 10/www. afroditesapotek.com). T-bana Medborgarplatsen or Skanstull/bus 55, 59, 66. **Open** noon-6.30pm Mon-Fri; noon-4pm Sat. **Credit** AmEx, MC, V. **Map** p315 M8.

Shop owner Ylva Franzén is a well-known sex counsellor in Sweden, most famous for her crash courses in orgasm techniques (only a few a year, so make sure you book early!). Despite the very graphic display of sex toys, the atmosphere is feminine and friendly, and Ylwa and her staff are happy to give advice on lubricants. There's also a selection of seductive underwear.

Souvenirs & crafts

The small shop inside the **tourist office** (*see p289*) sells lots of typical Swedish souvenirs, including *Pippi Longstocking* books, the painted Dala horses that you see everywhere, assorted elks and mini Midsummer poles. The basement at department store **NK** (*see p153*) has a better selection, especially of Swedish glassware. For more information on Swedish glass, *see p160* **Pure glass**.

Konsthantverkarna

Mäster Samuelsgatan 2, Östermalm (611 03 70/www. konsthantverkarna.a.se). T-bana Östermalmstorg/bus 2, 47, 55, 69, 76. **Open** Sept-May 11am-6pm Mon-Fri; 11am-4pm Sat. June, July 11am-6pm Mon-Fri; 11am-3pm Sat, Sun. **Credit** AmEx, MC, V. **Map** p305 F8.

Founded 50 years ago, this co-operative of Swedish craftsmen has developed from a simple shop stocking handicrafts to a modern art gallery-cum-shop. Most materials are represented – ceramics, glass, wood, silver, leather, textiles – plus a range of clothes. Artists from the co-operative and invited guests put on shows eight times a year.

125 Kvadrat

Kocksgatan 17, Södermalm (640 97 77/www. 125kvadrat.com). T-bana Medborgarplatsen/ bus 59, 66. **Open** 11am-6pm Mon-Fri; 11am-4pm Sat, Sun. **Credit** AmEx, MC, V. **Map** p315 M8.

A gallery and boutique devoted to new Swedish crafts and design pieces, stocked with high-quality ceramics, glass and fabrics. The artists and artisans who make the pieces take turns at staffing the shop.

Skansen Butik

Djurgårdsslätten 49-51, Djurgården (442 82 68/ www.skansen.se). Bus 44, 47/ferry from Slussen or Nybrokajen/tram 7. **Open** Jan, Feb 11am-4pm daily. Mar, Apr, Sept-Dec 11am-5pm daily. June-Aug 11am-7pm daily. **Credit** AmEx, DC, MC, V. **Map** p307 J11.

You don't have to pay the entrance fee if you just want to visit the shop at Skansen's front gate. As you might expect, it's got a fine array of traditional arts and crafts – wooden items, textiles, glassware and ceramics – as well as more modern designed products, specialist books and folk music CDs. If you visit the town quarter inside Skansen, you can have the satisfaction of buying items direct from the potter or glassblower, as well as watching them being made.

Svensk Slöjd

Nybrogatan 23, Östermalm (663 66 50/www. svenskslojd.se). T-bana Östermalmstorg/bus 2, 47, 55, 59, 62. **Open** Sept-May 11am-6pm Mon-Fri; 11am-4pm Sat. June-Aug 11am-6pm Mon-Fri; 11am-3pm Sat. **Credit** AmEx, DC, MC, V. **Map** p305 F8.

With its aim of broadening the audience for Swedish traditional crafts, the Association of Swedish Handicraft was founded in the late 19th century. Visit its shop on Nybrogatan to see work by 160 artisans, including glass, pottery, textiles, baskets, clothing and wooden objects, and Sami craft from the far north of the country. It's expensive, but worth a look for a tour of characteristic Swedish craftsmanship. Bestsellers are traditional cardigans from Skåne in the south of Sweden, candle-holders and scarves.

Sport

You can rent bikes all along Strandvägen; it will cost about 150kr a day for a mountain bike in fairly good shape. For specific shops, *see p223* **Cycling & rollerblading**.

Fiskarnas Redskapshandel

St Paulsgatan 2, Södermalm (55 60 96 50/www.
abfiskarnas.se). T-bana Slussen/bus 2, 3, 43, 53, 55,
59, 76. **Open** 9am-6pm Mon-Fri; 10am-2pm Sat.
Credit AmEx, DC, MC, V. **Map** p314 K7.
You can fish in the middle of the city (popular spots
include the bridges by the parliament building and
the eastern side of the Royal Palace). From angling
to professional fly-fishing gear, Fiskarnas has the lot.

Friluftsbolaget

Sveavägen 62, Norrmalm (24 30 02/www.frilufts
bolaget.se). T-bana Rådmansgatan/bus 43, 52.
Open 10am-6pm Mon-Fri; 10am-5pm Sat.
Credit DC, MC, V. **Map** p309 E6.
Everything you need for that outdoors or camping
weekend. Friluftsbolaget specialises in the Swedish
brand Fjällräven, famous both for its outstanding
quality and timeless 1970s cut.
Other locations: Kungsgatan 26 (24 19 96).

Tickets

You can also book tickets for major events
through **Biljett Direkt** (077 170 70 70, www.
ticnet.se) and the **tourist office** (*see p289*).

Box Office

Norrmalmstorg, Norrmalm (10 88 00/www.
boxoffice.se). T-bana Östermalmstorg or
Kungsträdgården/bus 2, 47, 55, 59, 62, 69, 76.
Open *June-mid Sept* 10am-6pm Mon-Fri. *Mid Sept-*
May 10am-6pm Mon-Fri; 10am-4pm Sat. **Credit**
AmEx, DC, MC, V. **Map** p305 F8.
Tickets for opera and major theatre shows, concerts
and sporting events in both Stockholm and abroad.
You have to visit the shop in person to buy tickets
for Stockholm venues. Expect to incur 5% commis-
sion if you pay with a foreign credit card.

Toys

Kalikå (*see p160*) sells colourful finger puppets
and plenty of artistic and learning-oriented toys.
For the usual branded plastic toys, there's a huge
branch of **Toys'R'Us** (Tangentvägen 3, 710 39
00) in Kungens Kurva, near IKEA.

BR-Leksaker

Gallerian, Hamngatan 37, Norrmalm (54 51 54 40/
www.br-leksaker.se). T-bana Kungsträdgården or
T-Centralen/bus 43, 47, 55, 62, 65. **Open** 10am-
7pm Mon-Fri; 10am-6pm Sat; 11am-4pm Sun. **Credit**
AmEx, DC, MC, V. **Map** p305 G7.
Swedish toy brand Brio's concept is that children
learn while they play. In the Gallerian mall, opposite
NK, you'll find Brio's brilliant wooden toys and train
sets, plus Barbie and other well-known brands.

Bulleribock

Sveavägen 104, Vasastaden (673 61 21). T-bana
Rådmansgatan/bus 2, 4, 42, 43, 52, 72. **Open**
11am-6pm Mon-Fri; 11am-3pm Sat. **Credit** AmEx,
MC, V. **Map** p309 D6.

It's no wonder that Swedish children seem content
– and clever – when they spend their pocket money
at places like Bulleribock, which specialises in
colourful, traditional toys.

Krabat & Co

Folkungagatan 79, Södermalm (640 32 48/www.
krabat.se). T-bana Medborgarplatsen/bus 2, 3, 53,
59, 66, 76. **Open** 10am-6pm Mon-Fri; 10am-3pm
Sat. **Credit** AmEx, MC, V. **Map** p315 L9.
Who do you want to be? Krabat has great dressing-
up outfits for wannabe knights, fairies, Indian chiefs,
pirates, clowns and Robin Hoods. There are also
authentic mini tools and kitchen equipment.
Other locations: Kungsgatan 53, Norrmalm
(24 94 20).

Travel

On Sveavägen, between Kungsgatan and
Sergels Torg, there is a crowd of travel
agencies, including **STS**, **Reservaruhuset**,
Apollo, **Flygvaruhuset**, **Ticket**, **Ving**,
Resia, **Always** and **Fritidsresor**.

Kilroy Travels

Kungsgatan 4, Norrmalm (0771 54 57 69/
www.kilroytravels.com). T-bana Östermalmstorg or
Hötorget/bus 1, 2, 43, 55, 56. **Open** *Shop* 10am-6pm
Mon-Fri. *Phone enquiries* 9am-6pm Mon-Fri.
Credit MC, V. **Map** p305 F7.
There are 33 Kilroy branches in six countries.
Originally focusing on cheap tickets for students
and young people, they now offer tickets for all ages.
Be prepared to queue.
Other locations: Allhuset, Stockholm University,
Frescati (0771 54 57 69).

Video rentals

To rent videos in Sweden you have to show ID
and provide a local address and phone number
(giving a hotel address is OK).

Buylando

St Eriksgatan 34, Kungsholmen (654 28 20/www.
buylando.se). T-bana Fridhemsplan/bus 1, 3, 4, 57,
59. **Open** 10am-11pm Mon-Sat; noon-11pm Sun.
Credit AmEx, DC, MC, V. **Map** p303 F2.
There are four Buylandos in town. Each has a large
collection of DVDs and VHS tapes for sale or rental.
Other locations: Valhallavägen 163, Gärdet (666 98
53); Östermalmstorg 2, Östermalm (660 06 05); St
Eriksplan 15, Vasastaden (33 38 88).

Casablanca

Sveavägen 88, Vasastaden (673 50 50). T-bana
Rådmansgatan/bus 2, 4, 43, 52, 72. **Open** 11am-
midnight Mon-Fri; noon-midnight Sat, Sun.
Credit AmEx, DC, MC, V. **Map** p309 D6.
From Ingmar Bergman to the newest blockbuster,
Casablanca has it all. Renting a video costs 19kr-
40kr depending on how new the film is. For non-res-
idents a deposit of 60kr-100kr is required.

Eat, Drink, Shop

Taking time off?
Take Time Out.

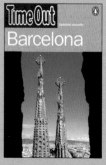  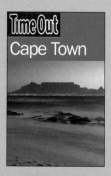

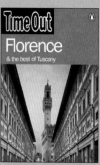  

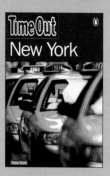  

Arts & Entertainment

Festivals & Events

Four seasons of fun.

Stockholm Jazz Festival. *See p185*.

In Sweden the seasons are celebrated wholeheartedly, something that must be due in large part to the harshness of its winters – on the shortest day of the year in Stockholm the sun rises at 8.44am and disappears at just 2.49pm – and the relief that spring and summer bring. The coming of spring amounts to something of a national obsession: Swedes feverishly await the first flowers and the cleaning up of street gravel, while weather reports show a line across the country indicating which parts of the country spring has already reached.

Sweden also carefully nurtures its traditions, so the calendar is dotted with long-celebrated, quintessentially Swedish events such as **Valborgsmässoafton** (Walpurgis Night; *see below*) and **Luciadagen** (Lucia Day; *see p187*); these are surefire winners for visitors. The calendar isn't all tradition, though; there are plenty of newer events with a more contemporary flavour – for example the **Pride** celebrations (*see p186*), **Restaurangernas Dag** (*see p183*) and **Re:Orientfestivalen** (*see p184*) – and the festival scene in Stockholm continues to diversify each year.

For general information on seasonal events and festivals, contact the **tourist office** (*see p288*). For information on the seasons and weather in Sweden, and the dates of public holidays, *see pp278-90* **Resources**.

Spring

Påsk (Easter)

Date Mar/Apr.

For most Swedes, Easter's greatest significance is getting four days off, just in time to overhaul the boat, shake the cobwebs off the summer cottage or tidy up the garden. Still, the painting and eating of eggs is a hallowed tradition at the Easter smörgåsbord, along with salmon and pickled herring prepared in endlessly creative ways. On Maundy Thursday or Easter Saturday, young girls dress up and paint themselves as Easter witches, and then go around begging sweets from generous neighbours, giving hand-drawn Easter cards in exchange. This custom recalls the old Swedish superstition that Easter was the time when witches flew to see the devil on the Blåkulla (Blue Mountain).

Valborgsmässoafton (Walpurgis Night)

Throughout the city. **Date** 30 Apr.

Ancient pagan custom dictates that Swedes light bonfires on the last night of April to protect themselves against witches gathering to worship the devil. Today the celebration marks the end of winter and the coming of spring, and the bonfire usually accompanied by choral singing. Walpurgis Night is celebrated all over Stockholm (and Sweden, for that matter), but for visitors the place to be is either the open-air Skansen museum (*see p85*), where fireworks add extra sparkle to the evening's festivities, or Evert Taubes Terras on Riddarholmen.

Första Maj (May Day)

Date 1 May.

If you happen to be in Stockholm on May Day, you'll probably run into marchers waving banners in Sergels Torg and other large squares throughout the city. The first of May has been celebrated in various forms since 1890. In the early 19th century, May Day was a hugely popular festival in Djurgården park and featured a royal procession. By the late 19th century, however, it had turned into a rally of industrial workers. It's a lot more low-key these days, but it's still an important event for left-wing Stockholmers. You may see schoolchildren selling plastic mayflowers for charity; having one of these pinned on your lapel shows your solidarity. Due to the cold climate, there's no maypole dancing – that is saved for Midsummer (*see p184*).

Tjejtrampet

Around Gärdet (450 2610/www.tjejtrampet.com). **Map** p311. **Date** May.

Given that Stockholm is such a bicycle-friendly city, it makes sense that it should host the world's largest women-only bicycle race. Since the race first started in 1990, some 80,000 women have cycled the 42km (26-mile) course. It is open to cyclists of all levels. Teenage girls and grandmothers pedal side-by-side in a show of female unity and in the spirit of friendly competition.

Stockholmska Spektakel (Stockholm Spectacle)

Gamla Stan, Kungsträdgården & other parts of the city (661 30 91/www.stockholmskaspektakel.se). **Date** late May.

The Old Town's 18th-century history comes alive during Stockholm Spectacle, when history buffs dress in historical costume and parade through the cobblestone squares of Gamla Stan to sing, dance and perform burlesque comedy. There's a handicrafts fair, folk dance lessons on Slottsbacken and a costume ball in the Great Hall of the Nordiska Museet (*see p83*).

Restaurangernas Dag – Smaka på Stockholm (A Taste of Stockholm)

Kungsträdgården (070 41 56 40/073 92 12 40/ www.restaurangernasdag.se). **Map** p305 G7/8. **Date** 10 days in late May.

Held over the course of ten days, this food fest gives you the chance to get a real taste of Stockholm. More than 30 restaurants, including some of the city's finest, set up shop in Kungsträdgården, offering samples of their wares at a fraction of the usual price.

You can watch duelling chefs from the esteemed Franska Matsalen (*see p115*) and Operakällaren (*see p117*) outdo each other in producing fast food, something you're not likely to see in their elegant dining rooms. Bands play on two open stages and one or two restaurants even bring their own DJ.

Summer

Parkteatern (Park Theatre)

Parks throughout the city (506 20 284/www.stads teatern.stockholm.se). **Date** June-Aug daily.

There's been free outdoor theatre in Stockholm's parks since 1942, and many performances can be enjoyed by non-Swedish speakers, such as circus shows, music concerts, modern and classical dance. There are workshops on everything from playing steel drums to klezmer or Swedish folk dance. A schedule can be found on the website. *See also p232.*

Stockholm Early Music Festival

Tyska Brinken 13, Gamla Stan (070 460 03 90/ www.semf.se). **Map** p305 J7. **Date** 1st wk in June.

This four-day event attracts an impressive roster of established and new artistic talent from Sweden and Europe performing a programme of music from the Middle Ages, Renaissance and baroque periods. It's not always what you might expect – baroque music can come with a gypsy swing, early Irish songs are sometimes accompanied by a gold-stringed harp and in 2004 the festival added theatrical performances to the programme. The festival takes place in the Old Town (Gamla Stan) and consists of three concert series: evening concerts in the Tyska Kyrkan (German Church; *see p70*), afternoon concerts in the Finska Kyrkan (Finnish Church; *see p69*) and lunchtime concerts in the Kungliga Myntkabinettet (Royal Coin Cabinet; *see p63*).

Stockholm Marathon

Start point: Lidingövägen, Hjorthagen. Finish point: Stockholms Stadion, Hjorthagen (54 56 64 40/www. marathon.se). **Map** p310 C9. **Date** Sat in early June.

Few cities can match the beauty of this marathon route, which takes runners along waterside Strandvägen, Norrmälarstränd and Skeppsbron. Head for Lidingövägen to watch the runners take off, or if you want to be ready to glimpse the winner at the finish line, position yourself at Stockholms Stadion on Vallhallavägen. Much of the inner city is closed to vehicular traffic during the race, so you'll have to make your way by foot or public transport, weaving your way through the crowds.

Skärgårdsbåtens Dag (Archipelago Boat Day)

Strömkajen, Norrmalm (662 89 02). **Date** 1st Wed in June. **Map** p305 G8/H8.

If the idea of travelling on one of Stockholm's old-fashioned steamboats appeals, there's no better day to do it than Archipelago Boat Day. A parade of steam-driven vessels, whistles blowing, make their way from Strömkajen to Vaxholm in the early

Arts & Entertainment

evening. For those who don't catch a ride, good places to view the boats are Strömkajen, Skeppsholmen, Kastellholmen and Fåfängen. The boats arriving in Vaxholm are greeted by live music and an outdoor market; visitors have a couple of hours to explore Vaxholm before returning to Stockholm.

Nationaldag (National Day)
Date 6 June.

The Swedish flag flies from every official building and many private homes on this day, which celebrates Gustav Vasa's election as King of Sweden on 6 June 1523 and the adoption of a new constitution on the same date in 1809. If you want a glimpse of the royal family in their traditional blue-and-yellow folk costumes, visit the open-air Skansen museum (*see p85*), where, since 1916, the King of Sweden has presented flags on this day to representatives of various organisations and charities. Unlike neighbouring Norway, where the National Day is an enthusiastic celebration of national pride, in politically correct Sweden it is a working day. There has, however, been recent talk of making it into a public holiday.

Ulriksdals Flower Show
Ulriksdals Slottspark, Stora Skuggansv 22 (402 61 30/ www.ulriksdalsflowershow.se). T-bana Bergshamra, then bus 503. **Date** 2nd wk in June.

Modelled on London's Chelsea and Hampton Court Palace shows, the three-day Ulriksdals Flower Show started in 2004, reflecting the Swedes' fervent interest in gardens. The show couldn't have found a more beautiful setting than the verdant lawns of this palace outside Stockholm, and many make a day of it, bringing along a picnic. The gardens on display, however, are vastly outnumbered by commercial stalls selling everything from seeds and plants to vases and garden furniture. The emphasis on sell rather than show is particularly galling considering the 130kr entrance fee.

Re:Orientfestivalen
Södra Teatern, Mosebacketorg 1-3, Södermalm (702 15 99/www.reorient.se). **Map** p314 K8.
Date 2nd wk in June.

Stockholm takes on an multicultural flavour during this annual festival, bringing together artists from the Middle East, northern Africa, India and Europe to perform at Södra Teatern (*see p216*) on Södermalm. During the four-day festival, there's a bazaar selling crafts, clothes and food and, in the evenings, festival-goers can sit back and smoke a Turkish water pipe at the Oum bar or dance to at the Re:Orient Club. A lecture series on topics such as the future of the Middle East, the clash of civilisations or post-colonialism add some intellectual weight to this laid-back festival.

Mayo Boules Festival
Kungsträdgården, Norrmalm (714 04 20/ www.mayo.se). **Map** p305 G8. **Date** mid June.
Boules, or pétanques as aficionados call it, has a long tradition in Sweden, particularly with upper-class

Midsummer

Midsummer (the Friday and Saturday closest to 24 June) is the Swedes' big summer festival, when they make the most of the long hours of daylight (even as far south as Stockholm it doesn't get completely dark). It's most likely that it has descended from a prehistoric summer solstice festival of light and fertility.

Many Stockholmers leave for the archipelago for the weekend, and the city pretty much closes down – shops, restaurants and museums are shut – but if you'd like to see some traditional celebrations, head for open-air folk museum **Skansen** (*see p85*). On both days there's dancing around the maypole, traditional games and folk dance displays. Sweden's Midsummer celebrations differ from those elsewhere in Europe: instead of a bonfire (which would seem pointless in the land of the midnight sun), the Swedes dance around the maypole, since it is too cold to do so in May. The Midsummer festival wouldn't be complete without new potatoes boiled in dill, served with *matjes* herring, and the first crop of native strawberries.

seniors, but a group of boules-crazy folk breathed new life into the sport by launching northern Europe's largest boules festival in 1994. The name, La Mayonnaise (or Mayo for short), is a jibe at the world's largest boules festival, La Marseillaise, in France. But there's nothing stuffy about this crowd-pleasing festival, which organises friendly competitions for work colleagues, seniors and rookies, as well as more serious contests between the official international teams.

Drottningholms Slottsteater

Drottningholms Slottsteater (556 93 100/box office 660 82 25/www.drottningholmsslottsteater). T-bana Brommaplan, then bus 301-323/theatre boat from Klara Mälarstrand-City Hall jetty (Stadshusbron). **Box office** *Mar-Aug* 11am-noon, 2-3pm Mon-Fri. Closed Sept-May. **Tickets** 165kr-600kr. **Credit** AmEx, DC, MC, V. **Map** p241. **Date** mid June-mid Aug.

This season of concerts, opera and dance takes place every spring and summer at this 18th-century court theatre, designed by architect Carl Fredrik Adelcrantz at the request of Queen Lovisa Ulrika. This annual festival has taken place since 1922, and has earned a growing international reputation, with its performances of works by Haydn, Handel, Gluck and Mozart. The music is played on authentic instruments, and the ballets are reconstructed from the 18th century. Theatregoers often take a pre-concert picnic on the lawns outside the theatre.

Music på Slottet (Music at the Royal Palace)

Royal Palace, Gamla Stan (10 88 00/ www.royalfestivals.se). **Map** p305 H7/H8. **Date** mid June-early Sept.

Classical music, jazz and folk come together during more than 25 evening concerts held in the beautiful rooms of the Kungliga Slottet (Royal Palace; *see p63*). Established artists and ensembles, as well as up-and-coming stars, make an appearance at this festival, which includes orchestral concerts by the Royal Swedish Chamber Orchestra and the Royal Stockholm Ensemble. Concerts are held in the Hall of State, the Royal Chapel and Gustav III's Antikmuseum.

Stockholm Jazz Festival

Skeppsholmen (55 61 45 64/55 69 24 40/ tickets 07 71 70 70 70/www.stockholmjazz.com). *Bus 65.* **Tickets** 40kr-300kr. **Map** p306 H9. **Date** 1wk mid July.

The Stockholm Jazz Festival in July is one of Sweden's premier live music festivals, pulling in some top-rate international artists (Stevie Wonder in 2004). The main site on the island of Skeppsholmen couldn't be more picturesque; other venues include Konserthus (*see p220*), and stages in Kungsträdgården, Mosebacke Etablissement (*see p216*) and Fasching (*see p215*). Some 30,000 spectators come to listen to more than 40 concerts featuring jazz, soul, blues, latin and more. Skeppsholmen becomes one huge jazz party, with eateries overflowing and, unavoidably, peddlers hawking festival merchandise.

Walpurgis Night. *See p182.*

Stockholm Pride Week

Tantolunden, Södermalm (www.stockholm pride.org). T-bana Zinkensdamm or Hornstull/ bus 74, 94, 190, 191. **Map** p313 M4. **Date** 1wk in July/Aug.

Since its birth in 1998, Stockholm Pride Week has grown into one of the city's largest festivals, and the biggest gay Pride celebration in Scandinavia, with five days of partying, plus debates and entertainment. The heart of the action is the large open space of Tantolunden park on the quickly trendifying island of Södermalm. The festival includes art exhibitions, debates, films, parties and, on the Saturday, the big parade. *See also p208.*

Midnattsloppet (Midnight Race)

Start: Ringvägen. Finish: Hornsgatan (649 71 71/ www.midnattsloppet.com). **Map** *Start & finish* p313 L5. **Date** mid Aug.

This popular night-time race, which has been going for over 23 years, could only be possible in the land of the midnight sun. More than 16,000 runners of all ages navigate a 10km (6.2-mile) course around Södermalm. But it's much more than a race – and some 200,000 spectators don't hesitate to get in on the act with loud cheering, asphalt-pounding enthusiasm, music and partying. To catch the starting gun, position yourself at Ringvägen, just south of the Zinkensdamm athletics field, at 10pm and then wait for the first runners to cross the finish line at Hornsgatan, not far from the starting point.

Autumn

Stockholm Beer & Whisky Festival

Factory, Nacka Strand (662 94 94/www.stockholm beer.se). **Tickets** 160kr-180kr. **Minimum age** 20. **Date** 3 days in Sept.

This festival has earned a hallowed place among the four best beer fests in the world – alongside the Great British Beer Festival in London, the Great American Beer Festival in Denver, USA, and Uur Van Het Bier in Antwerp. It welcomes thousands of beer, cider and whisky lovers each year to sample the wares, and experts are on hand to teach you the right way to enjoy the beverages.

Lidingöloppet

Around Lidingö (765 26 15/www.lidingoloppet.se). **Date** weekend in late Sept-early Oct.

The world's biggest cross-country race has become a tradition for Swedes and runners from all over the world, drawn to the beautiful scenery and the challenging course. The first Lidingöloppet was held in 1965, and every year thousands of runners from some 30 different countries pass the finish line each year on Grönsta Gärde. The categories are 30km (19 miles) for men and 10km (six miles) for women, but there are categories for all ages and distances. Races are held over the course of one weekend in early autumn.

Stockholm Open

Kungliga Tennishallen, Lidingövägen 75, Norra Djurgården (450 26 25/www.stockholmopen.se). **Tickets** 120kr-400kr adult; 40kr-55kr concessions. **Map** p311 B11. **Date** last wk in Oct.

This prestigious tennis tournament was the brain-child of the veteran tennis star Sven Davidson. In 1969 he received a letter from American colleagues asking him to arrange a competition in Sweden with tennis pros and amateurs from all over the world. The event, which recently marked its 32nd year, was televised from the start, thus drawing a huge world-wide audience, along with 40,000 spectators each year), and has earned accolades as one of the best organised tournaments in Europe.

Stockholm International Film Festival

Various venues around Stockholm (677 50 00/ www.filmfestivalen.se). **Date** mid Nov.

As the leading competitive film festival in northern Europe, the ten-day Stockholm Film Festival is aimed at launching young filmmakers and broadening the forum for innovative high-quality films in Scandinavia. Films at the ten-year-old festival include up-and-coming American independents, visions from the Nordic and Baltic countries, and works from Asia. The focus remains on first-time filmmakers, but there are also retrospectives of past masters. It might not be Cannes, but the festival attracts some big names: past guests have included Dennis Hopper, Quentin Tarantino, the Coen brothers and Lars von Trier.

Winter

Stockholm International Horse Show

Globen, Arenavägen, Johanneshov (077 131 00 00/ www.stockholmhorseshow.com). T-bana Globen/bus 4, 150, 164. **Tickets** 95kr-275kr. **Date** late Nov.

Stortorget twinkles for the **Christmas market**. *See p187.*

This international three-day event features everything from dressage to a steeplechase with Shetland ponies, and attracts around 70,000 people. There are special children's performances, as well as a Christmas show.

Advent

Date Dec.

You can tell Christmas is approaching when you start to spot the Advent candles or Advent stars (made of straw, wood shavings or metal) hanging in the windows of homes, shops and offices. Every home has its Advent candlestick, usually a little box with four candle-holders nestled in moss and lingonberry sprigs. The first candle is lit on the First Sunday of Advent and allowed to burn down only one quarter, so that it won't burn out before the fourth candle is lit. The smell of baking Swedish gingersnaps (*pepparkakor*) also sweetens the long wait for Christmas.

Christmas markets

Date early-end Dec.

Skansen's Christmas market – one of the biggest in Sweden and dating back to 1903 – is held at weekends throughout December until Christmas Eve (the only day Skansen is closed). Look out for Swedish craft products, traditional Christmas ornaments made of straw, hand-dipped candles, sweets (including *polkagris*, oversized red and white striped sticks) and Christmas fare such as smoked sausage, eel, salmon, *pepparkakor* (gingersnaps), *glögg* (mulled wine) and saffron buns. Stortorget in Gamla Stan also holds a Christmas market, as does Rosendals Trädgård on Djurgården, with many tasty treats from its own gardens, such as lingonberry jam.

Nobeldagen (Nobel Day)

Konserthuset, Hötorget, Norrmalm & Stadshuset, Hantverkargatan 1, Kungsholmen (Nobel Foundation 663 09 20/www.nobel.se). **Date** 10 Dec.

The year's Nobel Prize laureates are honoured in a ceremony at Konserthus (Concert Hall; *see p220*). In the evening, the royal family attends a banquet at Stadshuset (City Hall; *see p104*). Tickets for this glittering affair are coveted by Stockholmers, but they are usually only granted to a powerful and privileged few. The rest have to be content with watching the proceedings on television and sighing over the fabulous menu, prepared by a top Stockholm chef. Nobel Prizes in Physics, Chemistry, Physiology or Medicine, Literature and Peace have been awarded since the late 1920s, based on the will of Swedish businessman Alfred Nobel (*see p104* **Peace man?**).

Luciadagen (Lucia Day)

Date 13 Dec.

Among the best-known of Sweden's festivals, Lucia is celebrated in mid-December, in the heart of the winter darkness. The Lutheran Swedes adopted the Sicilian St Lucia because Lucia is connected with *lux*, the Latin for light. All over Sweden, girls dressed in white, full-length chemises with red ribbons around their waists are led by a woman dressed as Lucia,

with a crown of lit candles on her head (although these days the lighting is often artificial).

Jul (Christmas Day)

Date 24-26 Dec.

Sweden may have an unwavering reverence for many past traditions, but Christmas is the most important. The main celebration is at home, held on Christmas Eve (though restaurants all over the city will be offering the traditional, overflowing *Julbord* or *smörgåsbord*). A traditional *Julbord* ('Christmas table') is typically eaten in three stages. You start with various types of herring and salmon, then move on to the meats (meatballs, sausages and ham), accompanied by 'Jansson's Temptation' – an anchovy, potato and cream casserole. You polish it all off with a sweet berry-filled pastry. Later in the evening, rice porridge is eaten. Tradition has it that finding the hidden almond in the porridge means you're destined to marry within the year. A family member disguised as Father Christmas, or what the Swedes call *jultomten* (Christmas elf), also comes bearing gifts. Christmas Day itself is usually a quiet day, reserved for recovering from the previous day's excesses and visiting relatives and friends.

Nyårsafton (New Year's Eve)

Date 31 Dec.

The New Year's Eve celebration in Sweden is a public and raucous contrast to the quiet and private Christmas festivities. Visitors can join the crowds at Skansen (*see p85*), where New Year's Eve has been celebrated every year since 1895. At the stroke of midnight, a well-known Swede reads Tennyson's 'Ring Out, Wild Bells,' which is as much an institution as watching the ball drop in Times Square in New York. Throughout the city, crowds fill the streets, feasting on seafood at various restaurants and moving from one club or bar to another. At the stroke of midnight, streamers and party trumpets accompany the sound of fireworks set off over the water.

Stockholm Furniture Fair

Sollentunamässan, Mässvägen 1, Älvsjö (www.stockholmfurniturefair.com). Pendeltåg train to Älvsjö. **Date** 2nd wk in Feb.

It's not surprising that a city obsessed with design should be the home of Scandinavia's premier interiors event. It's primarily a trade affair, but the general public are welcome on the last day. The city's hotels tend to be booked solid during the week of the fair, so book ahead.

Stockholm Art Fair

Sollentunamässan, Sollentuna (www.sthlmartfair. massan.com). Pendeltåg train to Sollentuna. **Date** 4 days in early Apr.

At the beginning of April, the Swedish art industry gets together for four intense days. Everyone's there – art students, artists, gallery owners, dealers, curators, critics and visitors – and events include seminars, talks and meetings, as well as the opportunity just to enjoy the art.

Arts & Entertainment

Children

Probably the most child- (and parent-) friendly city in the world.

Gröna Lund: all the fun of the fair. *See p189*.

In the 2003 *Mother's Index* – Save the Children's annual report ranking the well-being of mothers and children around the world – Sweden topped a list of nearly 120 countries. A healthy attitude towards children and a sturdy welfare state mean the young are generally taken care of and respected by society. Visiting families will also find themselves well catered for and, in light of the current baby boom, in good company.

Thanks to its large public sector, Sweden's much-admired social welfare policy includes a childcare system that is highly developed and heavily subsidised. All children from 18 months to school age are given a daycare spot if their parents work or study, and parents are supported by paid maternity and paternity leave totalling more than a year.

Stockholm is convenient for parents and fun for children. You'll notice many parents pushing their prams around the city, and new mums sitting at cafés or restaurants openly breast-feeding. Getting around the city is easy, since Stockholm has an excellent public transport system, with lifts and ramps for prams in almost every Tunnelbana station. Under-sevens travel free on public buses, the Tunnelbana and commuter trains, and bus travel is also free for one adult with a child in a pram or stroller.

If your family likes to spend time outdoors, as the Swedes do, Stockholm offers wide pavements, plenty of open green spaces and a beautiful location on the water. In winter, when the lakes are frozen over, you'll see parents skating across the ice pushing prams. If you're not that adventurous, there are plenty of indoor activities to keep young ones amused. For restless, sightseeing-weary kids, most museums and other attractions have children's sections, usually with toys, hands-on displays or other special activities.

The best place for children in Stockholm is the island of **Djurgården**. As well as acres of grass to run around on, it contains most of the city's best kids' attractions; it's also mainly traffic-free (cars of non-residents are banned at weekends) and there are ample opportunities for exploring on foot or by bike, bus or tram. One of the most popular family destinations on Djurgården is **Junibacken** (*see p189*), imaginary home of Pippi Longstocking and other characters created by Sweden's most famous and beloved children's author, Astrid Lindgren (1907-2002).

There are no restaurants specifically aimed at kids, largely because kids are so well catered for in general – most Stockholm restaurants offer high chairs, children's menus and help with warming baby food. If you want to avoid the American-inspired (yet very child-friendly) haunts such as Hard Rock Café or Fridays, your best bet is to eat in a museum restaurant. Otherwise, the trendy **Kafe Kompott** (*see p146*) is a good option (though heed the sign outside stating how many prams are allowed in at one time); there's a rocking horse at the back.

INFORMATION AND PRICES

For a list in English of museums, festivals and other events, pick up a copy of *What's On Stockholm* from the **tourist office** (*see p288*), or visit its website at www.stockholmtown.com. Visit **www.parentnetsweden.com** for information in English, covering everything from doctors to sightseeing.

Attractions

The **Aquaria Vattenmuseum** (*see p84*), a small but interesting aquarium on Djurgården, is worth a visit.

Fjärilshuset

Haga Trädgård, Hagaparken (730 39 81/www. fjarilshuset.se). T-bana Odenplan then bus 515. **Open** *Apr-Sept* 10am-4pm Tue-Fri; 11am-5.30pm Sat, Sun. *Oct-Mar* 10am-3pm Tue-Fri; 11am-4.30pm Sat, Sun. **Admission** 70kr; 60kr concessions; 30kr 4-16s; free under-4s. **Free with SC**. **Credit** MC, V.

In a beautiful setting at the northern end of historic Hagaparken (*see p106*), the fantastic Butterfly House – all 8,530sq m (3,050sq ft) of it – is a miniature tropical rainforest in the midst of an English park. Mingle with free-flying exotic butterflies and birds, or check out the pond full of koi carp and the Asian garden. There's also a very child-friendly café in the adjacent greenhouse, which offers an extensive children's menu, as well as indoor and outdoor areas for packed lunches.

Gröna Lund

Allmänna Gränd, Djurgården (58 75 01 00/www. gronalund.com). Bus 44, 47/tram 7/ferry from Slussen or Nybroplan. **Open** *May-early June, late Aug-mid Sept* days & times vary; call for details. *Early June-late Aug* noon-11pm Mon-Thur; noon-midnight Fri, Sat; noon-8pm/10pm Sun. Closed mid Sept-end Apr. **Admission** 50kr; free under-7s; multi-ride booklets 150kr-220kr. **Free with SC**. **Credit** AmEx, DC, MC, V. **Map** p306 J11.

Gröna Lund, Sweden's oldest amusement park, is a children's paradise on Djurgården's western shore, with gentle rides for young children, including carousels, Ferris wheels (of different sizes), a fun house, the ghost train, bumper cars, as well as some

more hair-raising rollercoasters and Europe's highest freefall 'power tower'. Worried parents will find the park highly safety-conscious: leaflets in English provide detailed descriptions of each ride, and any age or height restrictions are clearly signposted. The park is a baby-friendly place, with pram ramps on all the stairs and a Happy Baby Centre – a secluded nursery for soothing tots. The park also hosts concerts and children's theatre performances (in Swedish) throughout the year. You can buy multi-ride booklets or pay for each ride separately. Gröna Lund presents magic shows and plays for children on its Lilla Scenen (Little Stage), including plays based on Swedish children's books. Note that on concert nights it costs more to get in. *See also p84.*

Junibacken

Galärvarvsvägen, Djurgården (58 72 30 00/www. junibacken.se). Bus 44, 47/tram 7/ferry from Slussen or Nybroplan. **Open** *June-Aug* 10am-5pm (End June-mid Aug 10am-8pm) daily. *Sept-May* 10am-5pm Mon-Fri; 9am-6pm Sat, Sun. **Admission** 95kr; 85kr concessions, 3-15s; free under-3s. **Free with SC**. **Credit** AmEx, DC, MC, V. **Map** p306 G10.

No child will want to miss Junibacken, a mini indoor theme park dedicated to Pippi Longstocking and other characters created by author Astrid Lindgren. Lindgren had enormous popular appeal and was an important public figure in Sweden. Her heroine Pippi is fiercely independent, boisterous and rebellious, always challenging the status quo. A true humanitarian, Pippi saves children from danger and speaks up for the powerless and oppressed, and in her own way reveals the flaws in society. Like Pippi, Lindgren herself was an outspoken activist, fighting for environmental causes, animal rights and non-violence, as well as a more child-centred educational system.

At Junibacken, take a train ride (ask for narration in English) that crosses miniature fictional landscapes, flies over rooftops and passes through quaint Swedish houses. In Pippi's house, Villa Villekulla, kids are welcome to dress up like Pippi, wreak havoc inside and slide down the roof. Stories by other writers feature too, and activities include face painting, storytelling and visits from some of the storybook characters. Adults seeking relaxation can take in the lovely views of the water and shipyards. There's also a very good book/gift shop that carries many of the better-known children's books in translation.

Skansen & Skansen Akvariet

Djurgårdsslätten 49-51, Djurgården. Bus 44, 47/tram 7/ferry from Slussen or Nybroplan. **Map** p307 H12-J12. *Skansen (442 80 00/www.skansen.se).* **Open** *Jan-Apr, Oct-Dec* 10am-4pm daily. *May* 10am-8pm daily. *June-Aug* 10am-10pm daily. *Sept* 10am-5pm daily. **Admission** 30kr-80kr; free-30kr 6-15s; free under-6s. **Free with SC**. **Credit** AmEx, DC, MC, V. *Skansen Akvariet (660 10 82/www.skansen-akvariet. se).* **Open** *May* 10am-5pm Mon-Fri; 10am-6pm Sat, Sun. *1st 3 wks June* 10am-6pm Mon-Fri; 10am-7pm Sat, Sun. *Midsummer-end July* 10am-8pm daily. *1st 2 wks Aug* 10am-7pm daily. *Last 2 wks Aug* 10am-6pm Mon-Fri; 10am-7pm Sat, Sun. *Sept-Apr* 10am-4pm Mon-Fri;

Arts & Entertainment

10am-5pm Sat, Sun. **Admission** 65kr; 35kr 6-15s; free under-6s. **Free with SC**. **Credit** AmEx, MC, V.

Skansen is really a zoo, aquarium, amusement park, theatre and museum rolled into one. Young children might find the old buildings a bit dull, but the animals are always a hit. The regular zoo (feeding time 2pm daily) specialises in Nordic animals, among them brown bears and wolves, while the children's petting zoo, Lill-Skansen, houses farm animals. In the small aquarium (Akvariet; separate entrance fee), kids can pet a snake or a ray, and see pygmy marmosets and tamarins. For a completely un-Disneylike experience, the charming Galejan amusement park has rides dating back to the 19th century; there are even carousels of differing sizes to cater for all ages. Other diversions include guided pony rides, horse and carriage rides, and events for youngsters almost every day of the year. Some sights are only open in summer. *See also p85.*

Museums

The **Vasamuseet** (*see p86*) on Djurgården is a surefire hit for children over six who like (very) big boats. Another good option for older kids who are interested in the natural world is the **Naturhistoriska Riksmuseet** (*see p109*), just north of Stockholm. Kids who love anything on wheels can take a trip through the transportation of yore at the **Spårvägsmuseet** (Transport Museum; *see p92*) on Södermalm, which will house a temporary exhibition containing some of the toys from the closed Leksaksmuseet (Toy Museum) until it settles on a new home. If you think your kids would find a postal museum incredibly dull, think again; in the 17th-century vaulted cellar of Gamla Stan's **Postmuseum** (*see p70*), kids can create, stamp and post their own postcards, load a postal van with packages and deliver letters (to a talking postbox).

Musikmuseet

Sibyllegatan 2, Östermalm (51 95 54 90/www. stockholm.music.museum). T-bana Östermalmstorg/ bus 2, 47, 55, 62, 69, 76. **Open** *June, July* 10am-7pm Tue; 10am-4pm Wed-Sun. *Aug-May* 11am-7pm Tue; 11am-4pm Wed-Sun. **Admission** 50kr; 25kr concessions; free under-7s. **Free with SC.** **Credit** MC, V. **Map** p305 F8.

A large part of the Music Museum is dedicated to fostering a love of music in children through song, play and dance. The Klåjnk room (loosely translated as 'Boing!') contains amazing instruments all painstakingly made for small fingers to manage, such as a pint-sized harp and an organ where you pull rather than press the keys. In the new interactive Lirum room, which was created with the disabled in mind (though all kids will enjoy it), sensors and high-tech synthesisers help make sound for you. On Fridays (Jan-May, Oct-early Dec 11am-noon), informal music classes are offered on a drop-in basis. Trained musicians lead other activities (in Swedish) throughout

the school year. You can bring your own food to the museum or visit the spacious Café Mix next door for lunch. *See also p99.*

Nordiska Museet

Djurgårdsvägen 6-16, Djurgården (51 95 60 00/457 06 60/www.nordiskamuseet.se). Bus 44, 47/tram 7/ ferry from Slussen or Nybroplan. **Open** *July, Aug* 10am-5pm daily. *Sept-June* 10am-5pm Tue-Sun. **Admission** 60kr; free under-18s. **Free with SC**. **Credit** AmEx, MC. **Map** p306 G11.

In the Lekstugan ('Playhouse') at Sweden's museum of cultural history, you can travel back in time to 1895 in a vivid re-creation of life in the Swedish countryside. Kids can try their hand at different occupations at the farm cottage, mill, stable and general store. They can touch and use all the exhibits – even objects that are 100 years old. Children must be accompanied by an adult; other rules are clearly signposted in Swedish and English. *See also p84.*

Tekniska Museet

Museivägen 7, Gärdet (450 56 00/www.tekniska museet.se). Bus 69. **Open** 10am-5pm Mon, Tue, Thur, Fri; 10am-8pm Wed; 11am-5pm Sat, Sun. **Tours** *Engine Hall* adults 1pm Sat, Sun. *Mine* children 1pm Sat, Sun. *Miniature Railway* 3pm Mon-Fri; noon, 3pm Sat, Sun. **Admission** (incl Telemuseum) 60kr; 40kr concessions; 30kr 6-19s; 120kr family; free under-6s. Free 5-8pm Wed. **Free with SC**. **Credit** MC, V. **Map** p307 G14.

The interactive Museum of Science and Technology is one of Sweden's largest science museums, but don't let the name fool you – although it is highly pedagogical, the museum is more like a fun house, and a great place for kids of all ages. The Minirama room will have babies cooing with special mirrors, blocks and assorted toys; in the Teknorama area, small kids can discover how machines work by using their own bodies (such as running inside a huge wheel to generate electricity). For older children the main hall has aeroplanes suspended from the ceiling, steam-driven cars and a 1927 Harley-Davidson. *See also p101.*

Junibacken. *See p189.*

Outdoors

The green island of Djurgården is always a good option if you have children in tow. Much of its western side is taken up by the open-air **Skansen** museum (*see p85*). The waterside café **Djurgårdsbrons Sjöcafé** (*see p223*), just across the bridge on Djurgården, doubles as a boat and bike rental company. You can hire paddleboats, rowing boats, canoes, kayaks, bicycles or rollerblades for a practical and fun way to explore the island and its waterways. The bikes come in different sizes, and some have child seats. Further into the island, at **Rosendals Trädgård**, you'll find a small but charming playground built from logs and natural materials. You can eat at the outdoor café (*see p147*) or bring along a picnic.

The playground at **Humlegården** in Östermalm is graffiti-free, disabled-accessible, completely fenced in and has separate sections for different age groups, all of which make it one of the city centre's most attractive and safest play areas. It contains a caretaker's building with toilets, changing tables and coffee or juice is on sale. Tricycles, wagons and sandbox toys are also provided. Further afield, there's glorious **Hagaparken** (*see p106*) – delights include the colourful butterflies and birds at **Fjärilshuset** (*see p189*).

If you want to experience the archipelago but don't have time to explore it properly, tiny **Fjäderholmarna** island (*see chapter* **Central Archipelago**) is just a 20-minute boat ride away. Kids can visit an aquarium, explore a wooden playground in the form of a ship, pet bunnies in the Trädgården garden and choose from extensive ice-cream options. You can also borrow life jackets for your kids if they want to play on the rocky shores.

Boats to Fjäderholmarna are operated by **Strömma Kanal** (58 71 40 00/ www.strommakanalbolaget.com) from Nybrokajen, and **Stockholms Ström** (21 55 00/www.rss.a.se) from Slussen.

In winter (usually between November and February), head for the outdoor small **ice skating rinks** (skates for hire) at Kungsträdgården and Medborgarplatsen.

Swimming

If you're visiting Stockholm during an especially warm summer, you won't need a swimming pool – you can dive straight into the water around the city. *See p226* for the best spots. If that sounds too chilly, the beautiful Jugendstil bath house **Centralbadet** (*see p171*) offers an alternative. A special baby pool is kept at a pleasantly warm 31°C (89°F), and older kids can use the rather small adult pool under supervision. For other indoor swimming options, *see pp226-7*.

Vilda Vanadis

Sveavägen 142, Vasastaden (34 33 00/www. vanadisbadet.se). Bus 2, 40, 52, 515, 595. **Open** *May-Sept* 10am-6pm daily. Closed Oct-Apr. **Admission** 55kr; free kids under 80cm/31.5in. **No credit cards. Map** p309 B5.
This outdoor adventure pool has water slides, tube slides and a toddlers' pool. There's a new hotel (*see p53*) attached, and a restaurant overlooking the pool.

Theatre, film & music

Children's theatre is a pretty popular activity in Stockholm. There are performances (mostly in Swedish) at **Dramaten, Stockholms Stadsteatern, Intiman, Dockteatern Tittut, Marionetteatern** (for all, *see* *pp232-38* **Theatre & Dance**) and the **Spårvägsmuseet** (*see p92*). **Teater Pero** (612 99 00, www.pero.se) and **Pygméteatern** (31 03 21, www.pygme teatern.com) are also worth a visit.

If you're planning a trip to the cinema, remember that children's films are sometimes dubbed (unlike films for adults, which are rarely dubbed) – check the newspaper film listings. There's also an **IMAX** (*see p200*), where you get earphones for an English translation of the films (mainly documentaries); under-fives are not admitted.

The **Konserthuset** (*see p220*), one of Stockholm's main venues for classical music, features a 'Family Saturday' series during the school year when Stockholm's Royal Philharmonic plays to a boisterous crowd of toddlers and kids. Expect a mix of classical favourites, popular Swedish music, singalongs and guest appearances by clowns, magicians and other characters.

Babybio

Sture, Birger Jarlsgatan 41, Östermalm (678 85 48/ www.biosture.se). T-bana Östermalmstorg/bus 1, 2, 55, 56. **Open** *Jan-June, Sept-Dec* 11am every other Fri. Closed July, Aug. **Tickets** 60kr; babies free. **Credit** MC, V. **Map** p309 E7.

The innovative concept of a 'baby cinema' was specially created for breastfeeding mothers and new parents who thought they'd never go to the movies again. Lock your pram outside and carry your baby in with you (babies get their own seats inside).

Dimmed lighting and sound, changing tables in the foyer and in the theatre itself, free nappies, microwaves for warming baby food and an intermission where you can buy coffee and cakes all make for a unique breastfeeding/movie-watching experience. Films, which are presented in their original language, are shown every other Friday.

Resources & activities

Hemfrid i Sverige

(02 00 11 45 50/www.hemfrid.se). **Open** 8am-5pm Mon-Fri. **No credit cards.**

This outfit offers an array of services for busy parents, including babysitting, house cleaning, laundry and cooking. Rates vary.

Rum för Barn

4th floor, Kulturhuset, Sergels Torg (switchboard 50 83 15 08/library 50 83 14 16/www.kulturhuset. stockholm.se). T-bana T-Centralen/bus 43, 47, 56, 59, 65. **Open** *Library* 11am-5pm Mon, Sat, Sun; 10am-6pm Tue-Fri. *Workshop* noon-4pm Mon, Sat, Sun; 1-4.30pm Tue-Fri. **Admission** library free; workshop 10kr. **No credit cards. Map** p305 G7.

The fourth floor of Kulturhuset (*see p234*), the city's main cultural centre, is dedicated to activities for children aged up to 12. There's an arts and crafts workshop, a children's library containing books in English and other languages, and internet access just for kids. Daily events (in Swedish), such as film screenings, storytelling and poetry readings, are tailored to different age groups. Teens addicted to surfing can visit the Access IT cybercafé in the basement.

Skansen.
See p189.

Clubs

Feel the beat of the tambourine? Well, you will…

When you look at the excessive nightlife guides in the Friday newspapers in Stockholm, you can easily get the feeling that the city's clubland is as big as London's or Barcelona's. And that would be a mistake. The key difference is that in Sweden, a 'club' isn't really a proper big and glitzy nightclub, with lightshows, foam parties and pricey cocktails, but usually a party in a bar or restaurant hosted by promotors and DJs. This arrangement has, like so many other things in Swedish life, to do with the country's strict rules and regulations (before there can be dancing you must get dance permission, and in order to get that, you need drinking permission, and in order to get that, you needs a certain type of kitchen, and so on and so forth).

The result is a strange bar-restaurant-club hybrid utterly unfamiliar to non-Swedes. Restaurants are more suited to eating than partying, after all, and the whole thing can seem a bit amateurish. Still, it's not all bad news: the crowds tend to be docile and friendly, and the atmosphere is much more intimate than in most European and US superclubs. The club scene is still relatively young in Stockholm, and so too is its fan base; many of the trendiest clubs are dominated by twentysomethings, while a slightly more mature crowd can be expected at the city's DJ bars (see below).

Stockholm's nightlife concentrates in the inner city, split between **Stureplan**, the hub of the town's more glamorous VIP world of limos and neon, and **Södermalm**, the hip district where the former working-class inhabitants have been pushed out to make room for designers, DJs and musicians, with Norrmalm in the middle for immortals. By contrast, Vasastaden and Kungsholmen have mostly bars and cafés, while nightlife in Gamla Stan is a combination of the touristy and the gay scene.

Since Stockholm isn't very big and public transportation is very good, it's quite easy to travel between different parts of town in one night. In Söder the bars tend to close around 1pm and clubs at 3am, while around Stureplan things shut down at 5am, making the after-midnight hours the busiest.

The best club nights tend to be slightly secretive one-offs, but you can find out what, when and where in the Friday editions of *Aftonbladet, Expressen, Dagens Nyheter, Metro* or *City*. Or you can check out the monthly *Nöjesguiden, Rodeo* or *Paus*, or visit www.alltomstockholm.se or www.yosthlm.com. Another good way to learn about the hottest nights is to pick up flyers in the clothing shops and cafés around Stureplan or on Södermalm.

The high price of alcohol, an integral part of the city's nightlife, means that people tend to go out pretty late, first having a *förfest* (pre-party) at someone's house. Once they're out on the town, if Swedes happen to dance (they must be drunk first, of course, although drugs are strictly forbidden) they prefer to do it to pop music with sing-a-long-choruses (see *p212* **Schlager, schlager, schlager**). In short, Sweden does not have a tradition of serious club dancing or ritualistic decadence, and its club culture reflects this.

DJ BARS

With dance music but no dancing, Stockholm's DJ bars are a contradictory concept. A result of Sweden's byzantine laws regulating nightclubs, these bar/club hybrids are where many people start the night before they head for a club (although plenty end up going no further). Of course, most bars play music, especially in Södermalm, but the following are the best and the most clubby (and, as it

---

The best **Clubs**

For partying alfresco
Halv trappa plus gård (see p194) or Trädgården (see p196). Summer only.

For reggae
Club Studio One at **Fasching** (see p194).

For A-C-list celebrity spotting
Spy Bar (see p196).

For a Latin party
La Isla (see p196).

For a little something of everything
Mondo (see p195) or **Daily News Café** (see p194).

happens, they all serve excellent food as well): **Fredsgatan 12** (*see p137*), **Lydmar** (*see p142*), **Metro** (*see p141*) and **Tranan** (*see p138*). For others, *see pp133-42* **Bars**.

Gamla Stan

Källaren Diana
Brunnsgränd 2 (10 73 11/www.kallarendiana.com). *T-bana Gamla Stan/bus 3, 53, 55, 56, 59, 76.* **Open** Thur-Sun; opening hours vary. **Minimum age** 18-20. **Admission** free-80kr. **Credit** AmEx, DC, MC, V. **Map** p305 J8.
In the heart of the old town lies this old cavernous restaurant, with history dating back to Carl Michael Bellman's day. Not a troubadour in sight, these days you'll find punk, rock and ska and reggae on Thursday at 'Social Flogging' and techno on Friday at 'State'. Sunday varies in its party theme but admission is always free.

Riddarkällaren
Södra Riddareholmshamn 19 (411 68 76). *T-bana Gamla Stan/bus 3, 53, 55, 56, 59, 76.* **Open** 9pm-3am Fri; 10pm-4am Sat. **Minimum age** 20. **Admission** 60kr-100kr. **Credit** AmEx, MC, V. **Map** p305 J6.
On a small, virtually uninhabited islet, this old restaurant is home to two extremely popular clubs: indie Metropolis on Friday, and *schlager* gay heaven Lino (*see p213*) on Saturday.

Norrmalm

Berns Salonger
Berzelii Park (56 63 20 00/www.berns.se). *T-bana Kungsträdgården/bus 2, 47, 55, 69, 76.* **Open** 11.30am-1am Mon, Tue; 11.30am-3am Wed, Thur; 11.30am-4am Fri, Sat; 11.30am-midnight Sun. (*July-Aug* from 1pm Sat, Sun). **Minimum age** 23. **Admission** varies; call for details. **Credit** AmEx, DC, MC, V. **Map** p305 G8.
Under the guidance of Sir Terence Conran, Berns has been redesigned as a mega entertainment palace on several floors. Since the historic interior had to stay intact, the decor is an unlikely marriage of 19th-century elegance and modern style. It has the most beautiful ballroom in town, with a 20m- (66ft-) ceiling, cut-glass chandeliers, red velvet carpets outside and beautiful people inside dancing to new house and R&B from top DJs. There's a VIP room in the basement for Stockholm's hippest faces.

Café Opera
Kungliga Operan, Karl XIIs Torg (676 58 07/ www.cafeopera.se). T-bana Kungsträdgården/ bus 2, 47, 55, 69, 76. **Open** 5pm-3am daily. **Minimum age** 23. **Admission** from 11pm 100kr. **Credit** AmEx, DC, MC, V. **Map** p305 G8.
After a decade in the shadow of the places around Stureplan, Café Opera has started to take back the crown and mantle as the party king of Stockholm. The businessmen with ties round their foreheads

Kharma. *See p196.*

and the young girls in miniscule dresses are now outnumbered once more by celebs, hipsters, media folk and even royalty.

Daily News Café
Kungsträdgården (21 56 55) T-bana Kungsträdgården/bus 2, 47, 55, 59, 62. **Open** 10pm-3am Mon, Wed; 5pm-3am Thur; 9pm-3am Fri, Sat. **Minimum age** 20. **Admission** 80kr-100kr. **Credit** AmEx, DC, MC, V. **Map** p305 G8.
Daily's was hot in the 1980s, but after Stureplan took over from Kungsträdgården as the centre of the Stockholm universe, it – like the others – had some tough years. Nowadays it's back on track, but the clientele isn't as cool as before. It's a large place, and is good for a group of friends with different musical tastes, and everyone from drag queens to club kids to office types will enjoy themselves.

Fasching
Kungsgatan 63 (21 62 67/www.fasching.se). *T-bana T-centralen/bus 1, 47, 53, 69.* **Open** 7pm-1am Mon-Thur; 7pm-4am Fri, Sat. **Minimum age** 20. **Admission** call for details. **Credit** AmEx, DC, MC, V. **Map** p304 F6.
There are gigs and jam sessions at this legendary jazz club six nights a week, but it's the club nights at the weekend that really lift the roof. On Friday, it's the classic reggae and soca bash, Club Studio One, with Micke Goulous and friends at the decks. On Saturday it's Soul!, a clubbing institution that packs the dancefloor with the best in funk, northern soul and disco for a mixture of top mods, jazz cats and party animals. There's a new club night on Thursdays called Fasching Expansions, which celebrates the crossover between jazz and club music.

Halv trappa plus gård
Lästmakargatan 3 (611 02 75) T-bana Östermalmstorg/bus 1, 2, 43, 55, 56. **Open** 5pm-

Berns Salonger.
See p194.

1am Mon, Tue; 5pm-3am Wed-Sat. **Minimum age** 23. **Admission** varies; call for details. **Credit** AmEx, DC, MC, V. **Map** p305 F7.
Come summer this fairly fashionable bar (*see also p142*) has one of the most popular courtyards in town. In 2003, the people behind music and club culture website www.bomben.se took over the musical direction, resulting in some of the city's best club nights (including Thursday's Smet, with leftfield disco, pop and house, and Tuesday's electronica-based Kilotin). The dancefloor is far from ideal, however.

Stacy

Regeringsgatan 61 (411 59 00). T-bana Hötorget/bus 1, 43, 56, 59. **Open** 6pm-midnight Mon, Tue; 6pm-3am Wed-Sat. **Minimum age** Mon-Thur usually 20; Fri, Sat 25. **Admission** after 11.45pm Fri, Sat, club nights 100kr. **Credit** AmEx, DC, MC, V. **Map** p305 F7.
Former Euro-reggae star Dr Alban owns this enormous restaurant and stylish nightclub, where the music leans toward dancehall, R&B and hip hop. This place is popular with ghetto-fabulous, Cristal-sipping types wearing Fubu and expensive running shoes.

Södermalm

Bonden

Bondegatan 1 (641 86 79). T-bana Medborgarplatsen/bus 55, 59, 66. **Open** 5pm-midnight Mon-Fri; 1-11pm Sat, Sun. **Minimum age** 20. **Admission** varies. **Credit** AmEx, MC, V. **Map** p314 M8.
This small and sweaty club with a hysteric dancefloor is open nightly in the heart of east Söder. The theme changes each night – anything from slick R&B (Fridays) to riot girl punk (Wednesdays) – and there's often no admission charge. It attracts a young and generally smart SoFo crowd.

Debaser

Karl Johans Torg 1 (462 98 60/www.debaser.se). T-bana Slussen/bus 2, 3, 53, 76. **Open** 8pm-3am daily. **Minimum age** Mon-Thur 18; Fri-Sun 20. **Admission** varies. **No credit cards. Map** p305 J8.
This is the archetypal rock club – stylishly grim and raw, and located under a bridge in an old distillery. It's open seven nights a week with live acts and DJs, as well as a wild dancefloor. Come early (before 11pm) if you don't want to queue for hours. The music favours pop on Friday and rock on Saturday. Among its theme nights, Wednesday's Club Killers is the monthly ska and rock steady night for the coolest cats.

Mondo

Medborgarplatsen 8 (673 10 32/www.mondo stockholm.com). T-bana Medborgarplatsen/bus 55, 59, 66. **Open** hrs vary. **Admission** varies. **Minimum age** varies. **Credit** AmEx, DC, MC, V. **Map** p314 L8.
This huge cultural centre is always worth a visit. With three stages, four dancefloors, five bars, a restaurant, a gallery and a cinema, there's always something going on. At least one club takes place nightly, and sometimes there are two or three taking place simultaneously on different floors, with music ranging from rock to disco. Saturday's Go Bang! is very popular, featuring underground disco, house and garage from guest DJs. *See also p216.*

Mosebacke Etablissement

Mosebacke Torg 3 (55 60 98 90/www.mosebacke.se). T-bana Slussen/bus 2, 3, 53, 76. **Open** 4pm-1am Mon-Thur, Sun; 4pm-2am Fri, Sat. **Minimum age** varies. **Admission** 60kr-80kr. **Credit** AmEx, DC, MC, V. **Map** p314 K8.
Some of the best club nights in town are held at this classic jazz joint (*see p216*). Friday is Blacknuss, which even after ten years still keeps the vibe going

Arts & Entertainment

with an irresistible combination of soul, disco and hip hop, and bands often play here until the wee hours. Every other Saturday is Raw Fusion, with the freshest sounds of underground hip hop and house mixed with Latin, Brazilian and jazz flavours for an initiated crowd. International DJs play regularly, and many beg to come back to play again, and for free. The outdoor terrace is popular in summer (*see p139*).

Södra Teatern

Mosebacke Torg 1-3 (55 69 72 30/www.sodra teatern.com). T-bana Slussen/bus 2, 3, 53, 76. **Open** 8pm-1am daily. **Minimum age** 18-20. **Admission** 50kr-70kr. **Credit** AmEx, DC, MC, V. **Map** p314 K8.
In the foyer, bar and basement of this ever-popular cultural centre are clubs you won't find anywhere else in town: Kurdish, Balkan or Indo-Asian, sometimes a combination of the three, with bands, poetry readings and spoken-word performances. The crowd is as mixed as the acts.

Östermalm

Chiaro

Birger Jarlsgatan 24 (678 00 09). T-bana Östermalmstorg/bus 1, 2, 55, 56, 91. **Open** 11.30am-1am Mon-Wed; 11.30am-3am Thur; 11.30am-5am Fri; 7pm-5am Sat. **Minimum age** 25. **Admission** 120kr after 11pm Fri, Sat. **Credit** AmEx, DC, MC, V. **Map** p305 E8.
The basement club at Chiaro, Sinners, features trendy sounds played by good local DJs, while the main floor is more a traditional nightclub, filled with kids in pink shirts, Prada loafers and a Rolex on each wrist ordering iced buckets of booze for 1,500kr. Still, never underestimate the entertainment value of watching people spend a month's salary in one night.

Kharma

Sturegatan 10 (662 04 65/www.kharma.se). T-bana Östermalmstorg/bus 1, 2, 55, 56, 91. **Open** 10pm-3am Thur-Sat. **Minimum age** 23. **Admission** varies. **Credit** AmEx, DC, MC, V. **Map** p305 F8.
Smaller and a bit more secretive than the rest of the Stureplan scene, this place is no less excessive, with a good mix of club kids and media types who are, perhaps, a bit more music-conscious than the rest of the Stureplan crowd. It's at its best on Thursday, Friday and Saturday, when you should book a table to be sure to get in.

Spy Bar

Birger Jarlsgatan 20 (54 50 37 01/www.thespybar. com). T-bana Östermalmstorg/bus 1, 2, 55, 56, 91. **Open** 10pm-5am Wed-Sat. **Minimum age** 25. **Admission** 120kr. **Credit** AmEx, DC, MC, V. **Map** p305 E8.
A favourite of current and former celebrities, this is *the* most glamorous and extravagant club in Stockholm. Nicknamed 'Spyan' ('the puke') by detractors, Spy is frequently mentioned in the national tabloids *Expressen* and *Aftonbladet* and an initiate gossip magazines – usually in connection with some minor celebrity scandal. Upstairs is a veritable labyrinth of bars and VIP rooms with plush carpets and chandeliers. To help keep its place in society, the club publishes a glossy magazine, and distributes coveted VIP passes to the rich and famous. The rest are forced to stand in a circular horde and hope that the head bouncer (a celebrity in his own right) will let them in. If catching a glimpse of a Swedish ex-football star or would-be pop singer is your idea of a perfect evening, this is the place for you.

Sturecompagniet

Sturegatan 4 (611 78 00/www.sturecompagniet.se). T-bana Östermalmstorg/bus 1, 2, 55, 56, 91. **Open** 10pm-5am Wed-Sat. **Minimum age** 23. **Admission** 120kr after 10pm Fri, Sat. **Credit** AmEx, DC, MC, V. **Map** p305 F8.
At the weekend this beautiful, three-storey, five-dancefloor party palace with an elaborate interior of marble, roses and purple is Stockholm's most fashionable spot. This is where people who care about such things want to be seen sipping a Cosmo in their new Margiela outfit, or dancing to DJ Viet-Naam's mix of hip hop and R&B. Only the prettiest things will make it through the enormous queue, however.

Kungsholmen

La Isla

Flemminggatan 48 (654 60 43/www.isla.se). T-bana Fridhemsplan/bus 3, 4, 57, 59. **Open** 8pm-1am Wed; 8pm-3am Fri, Sat. **Minimum age** 18. **Admission** 70kr after 1pm. **Credit** AmEx, DC, MC, V. **Map** p303 F3.
The largest and longest-running Latin disco or 'salsoteque', Isla is open three nights a week playing Afro-Caribbean sounds for a predominantly Latin crowd from the northern suburbs. There are salsa courses and an excellent restaurant.

Trädgården

Flemminggatan 2-4 (50 82 67 09/www.tradgarden. com). T-bana Rådhuset/bus 1, 3, 40, 52, 62. **Open** June-Aug Mon-Sat. Closed Sept-May. **Minimum age** call for details. **Admission** varies. **Credit** call for details. **Map** p304 F4/G4.
Trädgården means 'the garden', and that's pretty much what this is: an outdoor yard where you hang out playing games, sipping a cold beer or a long drink, grabbing some barbecue food before dancing under the stars (or the ceiling, if it rains). Needless to say, this is a summer place, when there are clubs six nights a week.

The Viper Room

Eriksgatan 46 (650 11 83/www.viperroom.se). T-bana Fridhemsplan/bus 3, 4, 57, 59. **Open** 9pm-3am Fri, Sat. **Minimum age** 18. **Admission** 60kr after 10pm. **Credit** AmEx, DC, MC, V. **Map** p303 F3.
If you can't afford the ticket to the Greek islands for a hedonistic party week, try the Viper Rooms instead. As with most places around residential Fridhemsplan, the crowd is made up of ordinary people whose main goal is to get very drunk and find someone to take home.

Film

Rich pickings from Swedish filmmakers. And it's not *all* serious either.

The Swedes are a nation of keen cineastes, with a healthy home-grown market, a long and varied filmmaking history and one of the highest densities of cinemas per capita in Europe (over nine cinemas per 100,000 inhabitants, compared to approximately 1.2 in the UK and the Netherlands).

In the 1920s, during the silent film era, Sweden was among the world's leading filmmaking nations. Directors such as Victor Sjöström and Mauritz Stiller made an impact with films that were widely regarded as masterpieces at the time, and which are now considered classics. Several of these were based on books by Selma Lagerlöf (Nobel Prize laureate, 1909), including *The Phantom Carriage* (1921) and *The Treasure of Arne* (1919) by Sjöström, and *The Story of Gösta Berling* (1924) by Stiller (the film that catapulted Greta Garbo to fame). These films were ground-breaking, as they were shot on location using nature as a key element, at a time when most films were still shot in studios.

The golden age of Swedish film was, however, brief, as some of the film industry's biggest stars were lured abroad – Sjöström, Stiller and Garbo all emigrated to Hollywood. The 1930s and '40s were characterised by rather provincial and burlesque comedies, and it was not until the early '50s that Swedish film

again attracted the world's attention. Alf Sjöberg's version of Strindberg's play *Miss Julie* (1951) and Arne Mattsson's *One Summer of Happiness* (1952) stunned audiences in Venice and Berlin. At Cannes in 1956, Ingmar Bergman won international fame with *Smiles of a Summer Night*, and he remained in the spotlight throughout his filmmaking career.

The most successful Swedish filmmaker of all time, **Ingmar Bergman** has made more than 40 films, among which the most renowned are *Summer With Monika* (1953), *The Seventh Seal* (1956), *Wild Strawberries* (1957) and, of course, *Fanny and Alexander* (1982) – which Bergman said at the time would be his last film. He kept that promise for 20 years, then made *Saraband* (2003), a follow-up to his internationally successful TV series *Scenes from a Marriage*. Outside Sweden, Bergman is best known for his film work, but he has also been an honoured theatre director, often working at Stockholm's famous Kungliga Dramatiska Teatern (*see p234*).

With the exception of Bergman, Swedish film wasn't very fertile until the late '60s, when government funding helped a new generation of filmmakers to emerge. Driectors such as Jan Troell, Bo Widerberg and Viglot Sjöman became big names in an increasingly politicised era of filmmaking.

Mikael Håfström's *Evil. See p198.*

Swedish film has a reputation for being deeply serious, largely due to Bergman's work. Sweden also has the largely undeserved reputation of being the birthplace of pornographic film. Titles often referred to are: *Do You Believe in Angels?* (1961), *Dear John* (1964) and *I Am Curious: Yellow* (1967). These films were considered extremely daring in their time, but by today's standards they are far from pornographic. Paradoxically, along with being the first makers of 'porn', the Swedes have the oldest system of film censorship in the world, established in 1911.

These days Swedish film is less serious, fairly wordy and not sensationally erotic, and comedies, satires and farces almost always generate the most reliable audiences and the highest income. That said, an exciting new era in Swedish filmmaking began with Lukas Moodysson's excellent *Fucking Åmål* (1998). He was the first in a line of directors to challenge the norm by making a very different film, one that took teenagers seriously. Moreover, Moodysson showed that such filmmaking was possible on quite a small budget, paving the way for more diverse filmmaking and a new kind of talent. In the new millennium, a wave of young immigrant filmmakers are gaining international recognition for movies such as

Reza Parsa's *Before the Storm* (2000) and Josef Fares' *Jalla! Jalla!* (2000). Other recent films worth seeing are Mikael Håfström's drama *Evil* (2003), which was nominated for an Oscar, Teresa Fabik's *Hip Hip Whore* (2004) and Tomas Alfredson's black comedy *Four Shades of Brown* (2004). Swedish actors with international careers include Stellan Skarsgård (*Breaking the Waves*, 1996; *King Arthur*, 2004), Peter Stormare (*Fargo*, 1996; *The Brothers Grimm*, 2004), Pernilla August (the *Star Wars* prequels) and Lena Olin (*The Unbearable Lightness of Being*, 1987; *The Swedish Job*, 2004).

For more Swedish films of note, see *p292-94*.

THE INDUSTRY

Two companies, **SF** (Svensk Filmindustri, www.sf.se) and **Sandrews Metronome** (www.sandrew.se), completely dominate the film market in Sweden. These huge integrated chains cover production, distribution and exhibition, and take about 70 per cent of the total box office sales in Sweden. In Stockholm, SF and Sandrews together run 18 of the 24 cinemas. SF is the bigger of the two, but Sandrews is the more creative when it comes to film choice – although both are pretty mainstream. In 2004, SF announced plans to

Skandia. *See p200.*

purchase Sandrews, a move that would give it a virtual monopoly on the market. As this book went to press, the planned purchase awaited the (unlikely) approval by the Swedish Competition Authority. Behind the two big players are Folkets Hus and Våra Gårdar, with more than 200 cinemas up and down the country.

Until ten years ago, most film production took place in Stockholm and was usually controlled by SF or Sandrews. Recently though, under new funding initiatives, a large portion of the work moved to regional production centres spread around the country, but especially to **Film i Väst** outside Gothenburg. Virtually every recent successful film was produced at Film i Väst, now Scandinavia's major regional film organisation. The number of films made per year has been showing a clear upward trend in recent years, but the national funding system currently in place ends in 2005, so the future of the Swedish film industry is once again uncertain.

TIMES AND TICKETS

Cinemas open one hour before the first screening (usually around 11am or 5pm). All films are shown in their original language with Swedish subtitles. Only children's films are dubbed, but it's quite common to find an original language version too. Tickets usually cost between 75kr and 85kr, with discounts for children, pensioners and matinées. Listings and information can be found in the daily papers.

As in most cities, cinemas are busiest at the weekend, and you should book in advance on those days. For cinema chains (SF and Sandrews), you can buy tickets for any film in any of that company's other cinemas. Commercials generally start five minutes before the listed start time, and films generally start five to ten minutes later. Films are classified as being suitable for 7-, 11- or 15-year-olds.

FESTIVALS

The most important film festival in Scandinavia is the **Gothenburg Film Festival** (www.goteborg.filmfestival.org) in February. Stockholm's **International Film Festival** (www.filmfestivalen.se) takes place in November and, although not as renowned as Gothenburg's, shows a fine array of feature films, documentaries and retrospectives. Uppsala – 80 kilometres (50 miles) north of Stockholm – holds an **International Short Film Festival** (www.shortfilmfestival.com) in October.

Cinemas

Astoria

Nybrogatan 15, Östermalm (660 00 25/ www.sandrews.se). T-bana Östermalmstorg/bus 2, 47, 62, 69, 76. **Credit** AmEx, MC, V. **Map** p305 F8.

A modern, THX-classified single-screener, this is Stockholm's leading first-run cinema. Built in the late 1920s, the cinema has been restored several times but maintains a '50s flavour. Blockbusters only.

Filmhuset

Borgvägen 1-5, Gärdet (665 11 00/www.sfi.se). T-bana Karlaplan/bus 56, 72, 76. **No credit cards**. **Map** p311 E12.

The Film House, one of the city's largest cinemas, is located just on the border of Gärdet, in eastern Stockholm. A late 1960s concrete colossus designed by Peter Celsing (who designed the Kulturhuset, *see p234*), the building resembles a film camera and is full of witty architectural details referencing filmmaking. The Swedish Film Institute is housed here, as well as the Department for Film Studies of the University of Stockholm. In addition, there are two cinemas that host the Film Institute's Cinemateket screenings (weekdays, August-May). The shop selling books and DVDs has been refurbished and, although it's compact, it has a superb collection for film enthusiasts. At the time of writing, Filmhuset was undergoing extensive redesign: a multi-level glass atrium will house the library, due to be completed by autumn 2005.

Grand

Sveavägen 45, Norrmalm (660 00 25/www.sand rews.se). T-bana Rådmansgatan/bus 43, 52. **Credit** AmEx, MC, V. **Map** p309 E6.

Like the Victoria and the Saga (for both, *see p200*), the Grand shows slightly unusual films. It has four nice auditoriums and doors adorned with film stars in intarsia. This is the cinema Olof Palme visited just before he was shot.

Kvartersbion

Hornstulls Strand 3, Södermalm (669 19 95). T-bana Hornstull/bus 4, 40, 66. **No credit cards**. **Map** p313 L2.

Cinemas in Stockholm tend to be either downtown or around Medborgarplatsen. Kvartersbion is an exception, located in Hornstull in eastern Söder. It distinguishes itself from other cinemas by being completely free from luxury and modernity (it looks about the same as it did in the '40s) and is run by just one person. The programme is rather limited, mostly reruns from Zita or Sture, but locals are devoted to their cinema, which will hopefully pull Kvartersbion through hard times – rent increases were proving threatening in 2004.

Rival

Hotel Rival, Mariatorget 3, Södermalm (56 26 00 00/ www.rival.se). T-bana Mariatorget/bus 2, 55, 191, 192. **Credit** AmEx, MC, V. **Map** p314 K6.

This classic, late 1930s cinema on pretty Mariatorget has been reinvented. The 700-seat art deco cinema has been lovingly preserved, its restored pillars, sconces and seats now combined with state-of-the-art technology. Films, mainly first-runs, are shown at weekends only (Friday to Sunday), when viewers can enjoy the film undisturbed by the rustling of popcorn (it is banned), followed by a drink in the art deco cocktail bar or a meal upstairs in the restaurant (*see p125*). Loyal to the original concept of putting several facets under one roof, this entertainment centre houses a bar, bakery and a boutique hotel (*see p55*). Trivia fans, take note: the Rival complex is co-owned by Benny Andersson, of ABBA fame.

Röda Kvarn

Biblioteksgatan 5, Östermalm (56 26 00 00/ www.sf.se). T-bana Östermalmstorg/bus 2, 47, 55, 59, 62. **Credit** AmEx, MC, V. **Map** p305 F8.
A two-screen downtown cinema showing commercial and sometimes less commercial films. With its classic cinema stylings (red velvet, hardwood details), and its dark and cosy atmosphere, screenings in the beautiful Röda Kvarn (the name translates to 'Moulin Rouge') are a pleasure. The smaller auditorium, Lilla Kvarn, is nice too – but try to avoid the front row, as the seats are too close to the screen.

Saga

Kungsgatan 24, Norrmalm (56 26 00 00/www.sf.se). T-bana Hötorget/bus 1, 2, 46, 52, 56. **Credit** AmEx, MC, V. **Map** p305 F7.
A cinema comparable to the Victoria (*see below*) when it comes to the selection of films – but in a different area of the city, and with a much more glamorous look, with mirrors, chandeliers and columns.

Skandia

Drottninggatan 82, Norrmalm (56 26 00 00/ www.sf.se). T-bana Hötorget/bus 1, 47, 52, 53, 69. **Credit** AmEx, MC, V. **Map** p305 F6.
This eccentric and internationally known cinema opened in 1923. Most interiors, designed by the architect Gunnar Asplund, are still intact. Over the past few decades Skandia has lived under the constant threat of being shut down and rebuilt, since, as a single-screener, it struggles to run at a profit; thus far the council has protected it because of its unique architecture. Daily screenings ceased in 1996 and today it's open only for 'singalongs' and short runs. If the cinema is open during your visit, don't miss it – the inner foyer is quite overwhelming, with its red velvet, statues and golden ornaments.

Sture

Birger Jarlsgatan 41, Östermalm (678 85 48/ www.biosture.se). T-bana Östermalmstorg/bus 1, 2, 55, 56. **Credit** MC, V. **Map** p309 E7.
This three-screen cinema shows art house films, as well as more commercial fare – always carefully chosen. There are Cinemateket screenings twice a day and Filmögat (for young audiences) on Saturday afternoons. The curtain in Cinema 1 – made by Ernst Billgren, one of Sweden's most famous contemporary artists – is a huge painting containing, among other things, a pike, a flounder and a squirrel; Billgren says it is based on the notion that, 'It's easier for a squirrel to catch a flounder in the sea, than for a film consumer to find a cinema not showing Hollywood films.'

Victoria

Götgatan 67, Södermalm (660 00 25/ www.sandrews.se). T-bana Medborgarplatsen/ bus 59, 66. **Credit** AmEx, MC, V. **Map** p314 M8.
A modest five-screen cinema on Södermalm, showing the critics' favourites. There are rather odd Neptune fountains outside the toilets.

Zita

Birger Jarlsgatan 37, Östermalm (23 20 20/ www.zita.se). T-bana Östermalmstorg/bus 1, 2, 55, 56. **No credit cards**. **Map** p309 E7.
The only cinema in town with a bar, Zita shows films from all over the world. Run by pure idealists, it's owned by the not-for-profit association Folkets Bio, and Zita is its flagship in Sweden. It must certainly be the only cinema playing 1970s-style 'elevator music' in the toilets. Zita frequently shows documentaries, and every day during the summer months it screens short films (10-20 minutes) free of charge, often the work of film students. Children's films take place every Saturday and Sunday daytime, except during summer.

Multiplexes

Other multiplexes in the city centre are **Biopalatset** (644 31 00, www.sandrews.se) and **Filmstaden Söder** (56 26 00 00, www.sf.se), both located at Medborgarplatsen on Södermalm.

Filmstaden Sergel

Hötorget, Norrmalm (56 26 00 00/www.sf.se). T-bana Hötorget/bus 1, 52, 56. **Credit** AmEx, MC, V. **Map** p305 F6.
At lively Hötorget, this is the place to go to imbibe a bustling multiplex atmosphere. Its 14 screens and an average visitor age of 15 imply a rather nasty and noisy milieu, but actually Filmstaden works quite well for the kind of films shown here. As most visitors cross this square at least once a day, it's easy to pop in and buy tickets in advance.

IMAX

Cosmonova

Naturhistorska Riksmuseet, Frescativägen 40, Northern Frescati (51 95 51 30/www.nrm.se/ cosmonova). T-bana Universitet/bus 40, 540.
No under-5s admitted. **Credit** AmEx, MC, V.
Located in the Museum of Natural History (Naturhistoriska Riksmuseet; *see p107*), this IMAX cinema is paradise for families, but also worth a visit for any cinema buff. Films shown on its 11m-high (36ft) dome-shaped screen are usually nature-based, and worth seeing. A few tips for your visit: during the summer and school holidays, book in advance and be prepared to queue. Unusually, the website, the spoken information in the cinema and the screenings are in Swedish only, so don't forget to buy an earphone for translation when buying your tickets.

Cradle of Swedish film

Anyone wanting to experience a slice of Swedish filmmaking history first-hand should visit **Råsunda**, north-west of the city in Solna, where there's a historic film town – Sweden's equivalent to Hollywood – dating back to the 1920s. During the 1910s, filmmaking in Stockholm took place on the island of Lidingö, north-east of the city centre. However, to the annoyance of directors, trains had a tendency to stop when shooting was in progress for passengers to get a glimpse of movie stars. Svensk Filmindustri, the production company, needed to move further away from the city and the eyes of unwanted spectators. A defunct ostrich farm in Råsunda was the chosen location and, in 1920, Filmstaden, then one of the largest and most modern studios in the world, was born. This self-contained little town behind walls housed not only studios, but also a film laboratory, vaults, dressing rooms (with an oriel window for Greta Garbo), editing rooms and a directors' pavilion.

More than 350 films were produced here during its glory days (1920-1960). Almost every Swedish film star and director from that period has worked in Filmstaden, including, of course, Ingmar Bergman, who even had his own cinema for close scrutiny of the day's shoot – now fully restored to its original 1950s appearance and sometimes open for tours and screenings. His classic films *Wild Strawberries* and *The Seventh Seal* were both filmed here, as well as the distinctly non-Bergman *Pippi Longstocking*.

By 1969 productivity at the studios had slackened and Svensk Filmindustri moved out. In the '90s, however, when the construction companies HSB and Skanska purchased Filmstaden, big plans were launched for the revitalisation of the area. The redevelopment of the 58,000-square-metre (624,000-square-foot) complex has involved a commercial-cultural compromise; the old studios became a modern SF multiplex cinema (Filmstaden Råsunda; 56 26 00 00), and many of the surrounding buildings are being remodelled into 600 upmarket apartments, due to be completed in 2006. The directors' pavilion, which also features a black and white photos of early Swedish film stars, is now a lovely open-air café-restaurant with beautiful gardens. The former gatekeeper's cottage is now home to Filmstadens Kultur, dedicated to the area's cultural preservation. Stop here for information, to book guided tours (call ahead for English) and to check out its temporary exhibits.

The guided tours are rich with anecdotes, such as the story of the rotating floor that 1920s director Mauritz Stiller insisted upon to maximise natural sunlight. This carousel, concealed beneath the present floor, was a complicated and expensive construction that proved useless as the designers forgot to take into account the sun's changing altitude throughout the year. It was used only once.

Filmstadens Kultur

Greta Garbos väg 3, Råsunda, Solna (827 00 10/www.filmstadenskultur.se). T-bana Näckrosen. **Open** *Cinema* Mon-Fri 5-10pm; 11am-10pm Sat, Sun. *Restaurants* 11am-11pm daily. *Culture House* 9am-5pm Mon-Fri; noon-4pm Sat, Sun. **Admission** call for details.

Galleries

Local and international artists paint an interesting picture.

The Stockholm art scene has been undergoing a transformation over the last couple of years. Though left somewhat in the shadow of the many young and talented Swedish artists moving into continental Europe, the local gallery scene is becoming increasingly vibrant, and is arguably more interesting now than it has been for a long time.

The change was hard to spot at first – artist-driven spaces opened and closed, information spread by word of mouth, and new art magazines appeared and disappeared in a flash. But the local movement was strong-willed enough to survive and small galleries have continued to appear, creating a solid platform for Swedish and international artists. Meanwhile, the **Moderna Museet** (Modern Art Museum; *see p89*), on Skeppsholmen, reopened in 2004 livelier than ever, helping to create a buzz around modern art in Stockholm.

There is a rich variety of art spaces in Stockholm, and an increasing number in the suburbs. In traditional **Östermalm** – where the major galleries settled in the early 1980s when the art-trading business was good – younger and trendier galleries have also begun to emerge, revitalising art in the area. Meanwhile, the avant-garde pack tends to stick to **Södermalm** and the suburbs. The eastern part of Södermalm around Hornstull, in particular, is emerging as a key area for cutting-edge, artist-run spaces, as well as for art magazines and other art outfits, such as the digital media workshop **CRAC** (Creative Room for Art and Computing; www.crac.org). Several times a year, a selection of galleries, spaces and art magazines on Söder – including CRAC, ID:I Galleri, Candyland and Fylkingen – take part in an 'open house' event called **Southern Comfort**. To find out the dates, contact the participating organisations.

The free brochure *Konstguiden*, available at all major art spaces and galleries, provides comprehensive gallery listings; it's published twice a year, in autumn and spring. Also worth a look is **www.konsten.net** (Swedish only) for up-to-date reviews, or **www.come.to/ artinsweden** and **www.artistfinder.com** for information about Swedish artists and links to galleries. For information on the **Stockholm Art Fair**, held in the the spring, *see p187*.

Note that many galleries open from noon onwards and most are closed on Mondays. During the summer most of them are closed from mid June to mid August. Admission is free unless otherwise stated.

Norrmalm

Wetterling Gallery
Kungsträdgården 3 (10 10 09/www.wetterling gallery.com). T-bana Kungsträdgården or T-Centralen/bus 2, 55, 59, 62, 76. **Open** 11am-5.30pm Tue-Fri; 1-4pm Sat. Closed early June-Aug. **Credit** AmEx, MC, V. **Map** p305 G8.
Situated in the popular Kungsträdgården park, in the city centre, this large gallery exhibits mainly young American and British artists, such as Diti Almog, Karen Davie, Gavin Turk and Julian Opie. It also hosts graduate shows from Swedish art schools.

Vasastaden

Andréhn-Schiptjenko
Markvardsgatan 2 (612 00 75/www.andrehn-schiptjenko.com). T-bana Rådmansgatan/bus 2, 4, 42, 43, 53. **Open** 11am-5pm Tue-Fri; noon-5pm Sat. Closed Midsummer-end Aug. **No credit cards.** Map p309 C6.
Opened in 1991, Andréhn-Schiptjenko is one of Stockholm's leading contemporary art galleries. Its portfolio includes international artists (Xavier Veilhan, Uta Barth and Abigail Lane), as well as new and well-established Swedish artists (Annika Larsson, Palle Torsson, Anna Kleberg and Tobias Bernstrup). Internationally active, the gallery takes part in several important fairs around the world, successfully presenting what some art critics in the 1990s referred to as the 'Swedish miracle' – the flow of gifted, young Swedish artists into continental Europe.

Brändström & Stene
Hudiksvallsgatan 6 (660 41 53/www.brandstrom stene.se). T-bana St Eriksplan/bus 3, 4, 70, 73, 77. **Open** noon-6pm Thur, Fri; noon-4pm Sat, Sun. **No credit cards. Map** p308 C3.
Brändström & Stene has moved back to the city centre from the suburb of Liljeholmen, but has kept its stimulating blend of established and emerging artists firmly intact. A frequent participant in art fairs, this gallery has an international reputation and is one of Stockholm's most significant galleries. It represents well-known artists such as Elin Wikström and Annica Karlsson Rixon, plus emerging stars such as Dejan Antonijevic and Jordan Wolfson.

Milliken.

Knäpper + Baumgarten

*Tegnérgatan 4 (54 59 31 19/www.knapper
baumgarten.com). T-bana Rådmansgatan/bus 2,
42, 43, 44, 52.* **Open** 11am-6pm Tue-Fri; noon-4pm
Sat. Closed Midsummer-Aug. **Credit** AmEx, MC, V.
Map p309 D7.

Formerly with Galleri Lars Bohman (*see p206*),
Ebba von Baumgarten opened this gallery together
with Angelika Knäpper in 2003. Their exhibitions
tend to feature emerging Scandinavian and international artists.

Milliken

*Luntmakargatan 78 (673 70 10/www.milliken
gallery.com). T-bana Rådmansgatan/bus 2, 42, 43,
44, 52.* **Open** noon-5pm Wed-Sat. Closed July.
No credit cards. Map p309 D6.

Housed in old factory premises, this space has an
industrial air – unusual for a gallery right in the city
centre – which lends it a cool New York feel. The
gallery's three high-ceilinged rooms provide great
conditions for exhibiting. Milliken focuses on an
international blend of artists, from emerging youngsters to big stars: you'll find the Swedish duo
Bigert & Bergström, Olav Westphalen, Madeleine
Berkhemer and Tony Cragg, among others.

Djurgården

Liljevalchs Konsthall

*Djurgårdsvägen 43 (50 83 13 30/www.liljevalchs.
com). Bus 44, 47/ferry from Slussen or Nybroviken.*
Open *June-Aug* 11am-5pm Tue-Sun. *Sept-May*
11am-8pm Tue, Thur; 11am-5pm Wed, Fri-Sun.
Admission 50kr; 30kr concessions; free under-18s.
Free with SC. Credit DC, MC, V. **Map** p306 H11.

This beautiful 1916 building next to the aquarium
is a fine example of Swedish neo-classicism and is
owned by the City of Stockholm. Originally built
from a donation by the businessman Carl Fredrik
Liljevalch, it attracts a wide audience to its 12 exhibition rooms, where you can view themed and solo
shows (which change every three months) by

Swedish and international artists. A very popular
event is the annual open exhibition, Vårsalongen, in
which a jury selects works by both established
artists and amateurs, resulting in a vivid blend of
high art and kitsch. Also look out for the year-round
talks and discussions, entitled 'Nyfiken på'. Next to
the building, connected by a pretty garden, is the
lovely restaurant-café Blå Porten (*see p147*).
Altogether, Liljevalchs Konsthall is a unique place
where contemporary art and architecture blend in
an unusually successful way. *See also p81.*

Södermalm

Candyland

*Gotlandsgatan 76 (www.glimp.se/candyland). T-bana
Skanstull.* **Open** 1-7pm Sat, Sun. **No credit cards.
Map** p315 M9.

At this art collective, formed in 2004, ten artists
exhibit their own work, as well as the work of other
artists, presented in a rich variety of media – from
installations and painting to video and photography
– in an exciting, creatively interactive venue.

ID:I Galleri

*Tjärhovsgatan 19 (mobile 073 705 20 67/www.idi
galleri.org). T-bana Medborgarplatsen/bus 59, 66.*
Open 4-8pm Thur, Fri; noon-4pm Sat, Sun. **No
credit cards. Map** p315 L9.

One of the newer non-commercial venues in the city,
ID:I is run by 19 artists who are each in charge of the
space for three weeks a year, during which time they
are free to exhibit or invite others. United by the belief
that government backing creates artistic restraints,
they run the space with their own funds – and provide a meaningful input to the Stockholm art scene.

Index

*St Paulsgatan 3 (640 94 92/www.indexfoundation.nu).
T-bana Slussen/bus 59.* **Open** noon-4pm Tue-Sun.
Closed June-Aug. **No credit cards. Map** p314 K7.

The Swedish Contemporary Art Foundation started
out as a photography gallery, but has widened its

A developing scene

Photographers and artists rave about the Nordic light, but photography has traditionally taken a back seat on Stockholm's gallery scene. But now there are at least three galleries in the capital specialising in photography – one of them, the newly opened **Fotografins Hus** on Skeppsholmen, is entirely dedicated to the medium. The two others are **Galleri Kontrast** and **CFF**, both in Södermalm.

The quality of artistic photography in Stockholm has improved dramatically in recent years, with audience and curators demanding not only interesting ideas, but also the craftsmanship of good filmmaking and photography.

Although Swedish photography is still something of a specialist interest, even mainstream audiences have heard of **Elisabeth Ohlson Wallin** (www.ohlson.se), whose *Ecce Homo* series – depicting Jesus Christ in the company of homosexuals – made her the most talked-about Swedish photographer to come out of the 1990s. In 2004 she published book/calendar H.O.M.O in which homosexuals portray saints (*pictured*). 'Swedish galleries used to be a bit uncertain about the artistic value and

Elizabeth Ohlson's **H.O.M.O.**

exhibition practice to include video and installations. This deceptively small space opens up once you get inside. Next to the desk of director Mats Stjernstedt is a small reading corner, where you can watch tapes from the gallery's 'videoteque'. Index presents Nordic newcomers and established international artists not previously shown in Sweden.

Konstakuten

Nackagatan 11 (641 77 90/www.konstakuten.com). Bus 2. **Open** (during exhibitions) 4-8pm Thur; noon-4pm Sat, Sun. **No credit cards. Map** p315 M11.
The Art Emergency Room is one of the most important artist-run spaces to have emerged in Stockholm in recent years. Situated in Hammarby harbour in the south-eastern part of the city, it is a vital part of

an area that is becoming increasingly significant for the contemporary, avant-garde art scene. Showing mostly young newcomers from Nordic countries and elsewhere in Europe, Konstakuten is sure to give you a sampler of cutting-edge art.

Östermalm

ALP Galleri Peter Bergman

Riddargatan 35 (661 61 10/www.alpgallery.com). T-bana Karlaplan/bus 47, 69, 76. **Open** noon-5pm Tue-Sat. Closed July, Aug. **No credit cards. Map** p306 G9.
Since opening in 2000, this gallery has become a important part of the Swedish art scene. With his portfolio of young Nordic artists, gallery owner Peter

message of photographs. It has improved, but Sweden still lags behind,' says Ohlson Wallin, who tends to shun galleries as she prefers to 'create her own rooms'.

Since it opened in 2004, **Candyland** (*see p203*) – a ten-strong collective of artists and photographers in Södermalm – has been a creative force behind Stockholm's photography scene. Outside the collective, Nadja Ekman has, in collaboration with photographer Eva Stackelberg, invented a new method whereby photographs are developed on to glass, giving them a translucent look.

Even the established highbrow galleries in Östermalm exhibit photography, but you won't always see the word 'photography' in their adverts; browse the websites when you plan your gallery visits. Photography is often exhibited at the following galleries: **Konstakuten** (*see p204*) in Södermalm; **Natalia Goldin Gallery** (*see p206*) on Kungsholmen; **Andréhn-Schiptjenko** (*see p202*) in Vasastaden; and **ALP Galleri Peter Bergman** (*see p204*), **Galleri Charlotte Lund** (*see p205*) and **Galleri Lars Bohman** (*see p206*) in Östermalm.

If you visit Stockholm during September, don't miss the biennial month-long photographic festival **xpoSeptember** (www.xposeptember.se). It is organised by Kulturhuset (*see p234*) and hosted at around 50 venues in the city.

Centrum för fotografi (CFF)

Tjärhovsgatan 44 (640 20 95/ www.centrumforfotografi.se). T-bana Medborgarplatsen/bus 2, 3, 53, 55, 66. **Open** noon-4pm Tue-Sun. Closed July, Aug. **No credit cards. Map** p315 L9.

CFF is an interest group actively working to spread the word about photography and photographers. Its website has a digital gallery, where original photographs by the group's members are sold and distributed. It also runs a gallery space, recently moved here from nearby Kungsholmen, which is used by members and invited international and Swedish artists. There are also talks, seminars, research and discussions on contemporary photography.

Fotografins Hus

Slupskjulsvägen 26A, Skeppsholmen (611 69 69/www.fotografinshus.se). T-bana Kungsträdgården/bus 65. **Open** noon-7pm Tue, Wed; noon-5pm Thur-Sun. **Admission** 40kr. **No credit cards. Map** p306 H9.
Located near the Moderna Museet (*see p89*), the recently opened Fotografins Hus has more than 300sq m (400sq yards) of spanking new exhibition space to play with. Privately run, it shows the full breadth of photography by exhibiting artistic, documentary and commercial work. Workshops, debates and seminars on various aspects of the medium are arranged on a regular basis.

Galleri Kontrast

Hornsgatan 8, Södermalm (641 49 99/ www.gallerikontrast.se). T-bana Slussen/ bus 2, 3, 43, 53, 55, 59. **Open** noon-6pm Wed-Fri; noon-4pm Sat, Sun. Closed 20 June-1 July. **Credit** AmEx, MC, V. **Map** p314 K7.
Galleri Kontrast is run by the Press Photographers' Club, so the focus is on documentary work. Every year there are about 20 exhibitions, one of which is 'Picture of the Year'.

Bergman shows an instinctive feeling for high-quality art, and the gallery participates in international art fairs such as Art Basel and Art Cologne.

Galleri Charlotte Lund

Skeppargatan 70 (663 09 79/www.galleri charlottelund.com). T-bana Karlaplan/bus 1, 42, 44. **Open** noon-6pm Tue-Fri; noon-5pm Sat. **No credit cards. Map** p310 E10.
Situated in the heart of Östermalm on Skeppargatan, where many of the city's galleries are located, this is one of the more reliable and interesting venues for high-quality art. The gallery's three rooms are in a first-floor apartment. You'll find both established and up-and-coming Swedish and international artists working in a variety of media.

Galleri Flach

Skeppargatan 27 (661 13 99/www.galleriflach.com). T-bana Östermalmstorg/bus 56, 62. **Open** 1-5.30pm Tue-Fri; noon-4pm Sat. Closed July, Aug, Christmas-mid Jan. **No credit cards. Map** p306 F9.
James Flach and wife Eva-Lotta Holm Flach run this three-roomed space featuring both Swedish and international artists, including Frank Darius, Björn Wessman, Twan Janssen, Maria Hedlund and Andreas Eriksson.

Galleri Göran Engström

Karlaplan 9A (660 29 29/www.galleryengstroem.se). T-bana Karlaplan/bus 42, 44. **Open** noon-5pm Tue-Fri; noon-4pm Sat. Closed July. **No credit cards. Map** p310 E10.

Arts & Entertainment

The area around Karlaplan and along Karlavägen – one of the city's more chic neighbourhoods – is one of the most important gallery districts in Stockholm. Göran Engström's gallery, among the oldest art spaces in town, opened in the early 1970s and exhibits Swedish artists working with traditional techniques within painting or sculpture. His stable includes several of the most renowned contemporary Swedish artists including Max Book, Ola Billgren (who died in 2001) and Martin Wickström. The gallery has also expanded its portfolio to include younger artists such as Helena Mutanen, Sophi Vejrich and Martin Ålund.

Galleri IngerMolin
Kommendörsgatan 24 (52 80 08 30). T-bana Stadion/bus 44, 56, 62. **Open** noon-6pm Tue-Thur; noon-4pm Fri, Sat; 1-4pm Sun. Closed mid June-Sept. **No credit cards. Map** p310 E9.
For a long time Inger Molin has been working towards eliminating the line between 'art' and 'crafts'. Her gallery, which opened in 1998, shows crafts-oriented work – such as ceramics, textiles and glass – and is definitely worth a visit.

Galleri Lars Bohman
Karlavägen 16 (20 78 07/www.gallerilars bohman.com). T-bana Rådmansgatan/bus 42. **Open** 11am-5.30pm Tue-Fri; noon-4pm Sat, Sun. Closed Midsummer-Aug, mid Dec-mid Jan. **No credit cards. Map** p309 D7.
As one of the city's most prominent galleries, Lars Bohman represents a rich range of contemporary artists, both Swedish and foreign, working with all kinds of media. The newly expanded space now has five rooms in all. Recent shows have included artists such as Donald Baechler, Domenico Bianchi, Ernst Billgren, Lena Cronqvist, Sabine Hornig, Bjarne Melgaard and Dan Wolgers.

Galleri Magnus Karlsson
Riddargatan 29 (660 43 53/www.gallerimagnus karlsson.com). T-bana Karlaplan or Östermalmstorg/ bus 47, 69, 76. **Open** noon-5pm Tue-Fri; noon-4pm Sat. Closed July, Aug. **No credit cards. Map** p306 F9.
Magnus Karlsson works with some of Sweden's most important painters, including Mamma Andersson – who represented Sweden at the Venice Biennale in 2003 – and Jockum Nordström. The gallery also presents up-and-coming sculptors and painters, and is internationally active.

Galleri Nordenhake
Nybrogatan 25B (21 18 92/www.nordenhake.com). T-bana Östermalmstorg/bus 1, 2, 55, 56, 62, 65. **Open** noon-5.30pm Tue-Fri; noon-4pm Sat. Closed July, Aug. **No credit cards. Map** p305 F8.
Well-known gallery owner Claes Nordenhake moved his space from Stockholm to Berlin in the 1990s. Now he's back in Sweden with this small venue in the capital. Like in his main space in Berlin, internationally acclaimed artists are displayed alongside younger emerging talents. Definitely worth a visit.

Roger Björkholmen Galleri
Karlavägen 24 (611 26 30/www.rogerbjork holmen.com). T-bana Karlaplan/bus 42, 44. **Open** noon-5pm Tue-Fri; noon-4pm Sat. Closed mid June-mid Aug. **No credit cards. Map** p309 D7.
This small street-front gallery, which opened in 1992, shows important Swedish and international artists. You'll find photographic and video work, sculpture and painting. There's only room for a few pieces of art, which gives it an intimate atmosphere. Owner Roger Björkholmen was one of the main organisers behind Stockholm's alternative art fair, the Stockholm Smart Show, from 1994 to 1997.

Mia Sundberg Galleri
Skeppargatan 39 (660 96 20/www.miasund berggalleri.se). T-bana Östermalmstorg/bus 1, 44, 55, 56, 62. **Open** noon-5pm Tue-Fri; noon-4pm Sat. Closed July, Aug. **No credit cards. Map** p306 F9.
An excellent gallery where you'll find a mix of artists from Sweden and abroad. Keep an eye out for work by recently graduated artists, as the gallery maintains an interest in new faces.

Gärdet

Magasin 3 Stockholm Konsthall
Frihamnen (545 680 40/www.magasin3.com). Bus 1, 76. **Open** noon-7pm Thur; noon-6pm Fri-Sun. Closed June-Aug; 2wks over Christmas. **Admission** 25kr; free under-15s. **Credit** MC, V.
Magasin 3 opened in 1987 and is housed in an old warehouse (*magasin*) in the port area. Whereas other institutions suffer from a lack of funds, Magasin 3 is one of the most busily expanding privately funded art spaces in Sweden. Showing six to eight exhibitions a year, it focuses on young, established international and Swedish artists, with all media represented. Previous shows have included Philip-Lorca DiCorcia, Juan Muñoz, Mona Hatoum, Katharina Grosse, Henry Darger and Jan Larsson. Exhibitions showing parts of the permanent collection are held continuously, making impressive use of this huge space.

Magasin 3 Projekt
Djurgårdsbrunnsvägen 68 (54 56 80 40/ www.magasin3.com/projekt). Bus 69. **Open** noon-7pm Thur; noon-6pm Fri-Sun. Closed late Oct-late May. **Credit** MC, V.
In 2002 innovative Magasin 3 opened this summer gallery just north of Djurgården; it's an experimental and site-specific space, where invited artists, architects and designers work in close relation with the surroundings in an ongoing process. Film and video programmes run all summer.

Kungsholmen

Natalia Goldin Gallery
Svarvargatan 2 (651 43 43/www.nataliagoldin.com). T-bana Fridhemsplan/bus 1, 4. **Open** noon-5pm Thur-Sat; also by appointment. **No credit cards. Map** p303 E2.

This recently opened gallery has proved to be an exciting venue. Concentrating on young and emerging Swedish artists – several of them doing their first solo exhibition at the gallery – owner Natalia Goldin has shown a sharp eye for what's fresh.

Further afield

There is a growing art scene in Stockholm's suburbs. In addition to those listed below, the following galleries are worth visiting: **Millesgården** (*see p110*) in Lidingö; **Botkyrka Konsthall** (Tumba Torg 105, Tumba, 530 612 25, www.botkyrka.se), in one of the city's rougher suburbs, which has succeeded in attracting a wider audience to modern art; local gallery **Norrtälje Konsthall** (Lilla Brogatan 2, Norrtälje, www.norrtalje.se); **Marabouparken** (Allén 9, Sundbyberg, 29 45 90, www.marabou parken.se), with its impressive modernistic sculptures; and **Skulpturens Hus** (Vinterviksvägen 60, Aspudden, 19 62 00, www.skulpturenshus.se), once a base for Nobel's dynamite production in the early 20th century.

Färgfabriken
Lövholmsbrinken 1, Liljeholmen (645 07 07/www. fargfabriken.se). T-bana Liljeholmen/bus 133, 152. **Open** usually noon-6pm Thur-Sun; call to check. **Admission** 40kr; 30kr concessions; free under-18s. **Credit** AmEx, DC, MC, V. **Map** p313 L1.
The Centre for Contemporary Art and Architecture, in the southern suburb of Liljeholmen, occupies an important position on the Stockholm art scene. Founded in 1995, it is housed in an old factory, with one main exhibition space, plus three smaller rooms. A variety of projects – exhibitions, installations, talks and performances – are facilitated by the bar-café and reception on the ground floor. Recent projects have included an installation by filmmaker David Lynch and an exhibition by German artist Carsten Höller.

Konst2
Skärholmstorget 3, Skärholmen (710 33 66/www. konst2.com). T-bana Skärholmen. **Open** noon-5pm Thur-Sat. **No credit cards.**
This not-for-profit space plays a leading role in the process-oriented art that began to emerge in Stockholm during the late 1990s and is really taking off right now. Exploring the boundaries between art, music, design, fashion and text, this experimental space opened its gates in autumn 2003. Konst2 invites Swedish and international guests to create or participate in seminars, workshops, exhibitions and talks.

Tensta Konsthall
Taxingegränd 10, Tensta Centrum (36 07 63/www. tenstakonsthall.com). T-bana Tensta. **Open** noon-5pm Tue, Thur-Sun; noon-7pm Wed. **Admission** 20kr; 10kr 12-18s. **No credit cards.**
Tensta Konsthall has been around since the mid 1990s but, after changing management in spring 2004, is now run by the successful trio of Jelena Rundqvist, Ylva Ogland and Rodrigo Mallea Lira – founders of Konst2 (*see above*). Despite being so far out, Tensta is well worth a visit – not only for the exhibition hall but also for the great food markets in the area.

Magasin 3 Projekt. *See p206*

Gay & Lesbian

Welcome to the world's prettiest and politest gay scene.

Stockholmers taking **Pride**.

In the Swedish capital, being gay is emphatically no big deal. Most Swedes have a thoroughly enlightened view of homosexuality and discrimination is uncommon. If, however, you are discriminated against, Sweden even has a 'homo-ombudsman' to help you make your case. Same-sex couples can register their relationship and receive the same rights as married couples and, since 2002, can also adopt children.

A side effect of such an admirably free-thinking city is that the gay scene is relatively small and very mixed. It's not uncommon to see primary school groups having hot chocolate at a gay café, or straight couples on a date at a gay bar that's known for good food. In addition, there's no real gay quarter in Stockholm. While Södermalm has the most alternative vibe and has hosted the annual Pride celebrations (*see below*) for some years, Gamla Stan is increasingly emerging as a hub of gay life. Still, in reality, there are gay hotspots all over the city.

What Stockholm's gay scene lacks in size, sophistication and definition, it makes up with

sheer exuberance: its gay bars, restaurants and cafés are fun, the people are friendly and there's an absence of the cooler-than-thou attitude you find on the gay scene in many larger cities.

You may notice a certain similarity between some gay-oriented locales, and that's not a coincidence. Mälarpaviljongen (*see p209*) Chokladkoppen, Torget, Djurgårdsterrassen and (for all, *see p210*) were all created by two entrepreneurs, a Swede and a Finn, whose partnership has transformed the gay scene here in recent years. Their formula of creating stylish venues that serve great food and drink in prime locations has worked miracles, making Stockholm gay life cooler and far more cosmopolitan now than ever before.

TAKING PRIDE

Stockholm's annual **Pride** celebration (*see p186*) is the largest in Scandinavia and usually takes place in late July or early August. The focus of activity is Pride Park, an enclosure set up in one of Stockholm's parks (most recently in

Tantolunden in Södermalm, map p313 M4/5). Inside will be a number of stalls set up by gay cafés and bars, plus a stage for performances by pop stars. Other highlights of the event include a gay film festival at the Zita cinema (see p200), the always-popular coronation of the new Mr Gay Sweden and a parade through Stockholm (usually peaceful and festive, although in 2003 it was marred when some marchers were attacked in Gamla Stan by an anti-gay gang). For a full programme of events, see www.stockholmpride.org.

INFORMATION

To find out what's happening in town pick up a copy of *QX*, the excellent, free gay newspaper that chronicles all that's happening in the city. It's in Swedish but is easy to follow and its website, www.qx.se, has a guide to the city in English. *QX* produces an invaluable map of gay Stockholm, which is widely available at gay and gay-friendly bars and cafés, and you can listen to Radio QX online. Other gay websites include **Corky** (www.corky.se) and **Sylvia** (www.sylvia.se) for women, and **Sylvester** (www.sylvester.se) for men. All three are in Swedish, but with easy-to-follow listings. Tune into **Stockholm Gay Radio** (95.3FM, or www.gayradion.nu) to catch the latest edition of the English-language magazine programme *Leaping Lesbians* and other shows. For gay and lesbian healthcare and helplines, see pp278-90.

Where to stay

Two men or two women checking in together at a hotel in Stockholm won't cause so much as a raised eyebrow. There are, however, a handful of hotels that actively court gay visitors. These include the **Lord Nelson**, **Lady Hamilton** and **Victory** hotels (for all, see p44), a trio of upscale properties with a historic maritime theme in Gamla Stan, and the three locations of **Pensionat Oden** (www.pensionat.nu, doubles 699kr-1,095kr) in Södermalm (Hornsgatan 66B), Vasastaden (Odengatan 38) and Norrmalm (Kammakargatan 62), which have low prices but small rooms. There's also the pleasant **Zinkensdamm** hostel and hotel (see p56) located right in Tantolunden park. In the city centre, by Central Station, the extremely stylish **Nordic Light Hotel** (see p47) is the official sponsor of Stockholm Pride.

Bars & restaurants

Mälarpaviljongen
Norr Mälarstrand 62, at Polhemsgatan (650 87 01/www.malarpaviljongen.se). T-bana Rådhuset or Fridhemsplan/bus 3, 52.

Open *Summer* 9am-midnight daily. Closed Winter. **Credit** AmEx, MC, V. **Map** p304 H3.
This wonderful alfresco bistro-bar on the island of Kungsholmen opened in 2004 and was an instant hit, albeit only on days when the sun shone. The setting is ideal: a short walk from Stadshuset (see p104) on a stretch of the waterfront popular for sunbathing and strolling. Views over to Södermalm are lovely and there's even a glassed-in gazebo jutting out over the water – the best place to sit on cooler evenings. The clientele is mixed by day, but gets increasingly gay as the evening wears on. Open all day for bistro-style food, its only drawback is the often interminably slow service. Closed in winter.

Mandus
Österlånggatan 7, Gamla Stan (20 60 55). T-bana Gamla Stan/bus 43, 46, 55, 59, 76.

Open *Bar* 5pm-midnight daily. *Food served* 5-11pm daily. **Credit** AmEx, DC, MC, V. **Map** p305 H8.
Hidden away down one of Gamla Stan's quieter cobbled streets, Mandus is a small bar-restaurant, with flamboyant decor in the form of a mirror ball, gold lamé curtains and copious amounts of glitter. It's usually packed (which isn't that strange considering its diminutive size), always very welcoming and often good fun, even if the food is unremarkable. The real draws here are the atmosphere and its handy Old Town location. From here, consider moving on to Chokladkoppen (see p210) for dessert, before heading down to Torget (see p210).

Roxy
Nytorget 6, Södermalm (640 96 55/www.roxy sofo.se). T-bana Medborgarplatsen or Skanstull/ bus 59. **Open** 5-11pm Mon; 5pm-midnight Tue-Thur; 5pm-1am Fri, Sat; 5-11pm Sun. **Credit** AmEx, DC, MC, V. **Map** p315 M9.
Roxy opened on Valentine's Day 2004 and many Stockholmers quickly fell in love with its trendy, lounge-like interior, good food and cool clientele, which includes a large contingent of chic lesbians. Its slightly out-of-the-way location on a pretty green square in Södermalm enhances its status as somewhere a little bit different. Roxy is a welcome addition to the city.

Side Track
Wollmar Yxkullsgatan 7, Södermalm (641 16 88/ www.sidetrack.nu). T-bana Mariatorget/bus 43, 55, 66. **Open** 6pm-1am Tue-Sat. **Credit** AmEx, MC, V. **Map** p314 L7.
A narrow, subterranean bar and restaurant popular with the T-shirt-and-jeans set, Side Track is not in the slightest bit fashionable, and that suits the all-male crowd just fine. Along with SLM (see p213) and the Muscle Academy (see p213), it forms something of an unofficial Butch Triangle on Södermalm. Side Track isn't for the claustrophobic, but if you're ready to elbow your way up to the bar and order a *stor stark* (a 'big, strong' beer) you're sure to enjoy yourself.

Arts & Entertainment

No sex please – we're Swedish

All around the world it's the same story. The international image of Swedes is that of saucy blond creatures just waiting for the slightest excuse to fling off their clothes and romp naked in the woods. We don't know how that happened, except that... well, it's true. Swedes are not at all shy about nudity. They're unashamed of their bodies and like to be naked, indoors or out.

But that's where it ends. It's a big national tease. There are no open-air orgies on the streets of Stockholm. The woods are not full of well-built men longing for you to walk by so that they can leap out and have their wicked, blue-eyed way with you. Oh, grow up! Nudity isn't always sexual, you know.

Swedes are, in fact, quite modest. Compared with gay bars in many other countries, you may find a noticeable lack of flirting in Swedish gay bars (at least until the booze kicks in).

Still, if all you want to do is look, you can certainly get an eyeful. There are several spots around Stockholm where gay Swedes gather to fling off all of their clothing, soak in the sun and eye each other up. That's *all* they do there though. So keep your hands to yourself.

● **Frescati**: Take the T-bana to Universitetet, then turn left under the bridge. Walk towards the water and follow the lakeside path until you suddently notice that it's an almost all-male crowd lying on the rocks and the cliffs above.

● **Långholmen**: Take the T-bana to Hornstull, cross the bridge on to Långholmen and head west towards the cliffs, where there are amazing water views.

● **Kärsön**: Take the T-bana to Brommaplan, and then take a bus towards Drottningholm and get off at Brostugan. Walk around the field, then through the forest.

Torget

Mälartorget 13, Gamla Stan (20 55 60).
T-bana Gamla Stan/bus 3, 53. **Open** *Bar* 4pm-1am Mon-Thur; 3pm-1am Fri; 1pm-1am Sat, Sun. *Food* served 11am-11pm daily. **Credit** AmEx, DC, MC, V. **Map** p305 J7.

Torget is, by far, Stockholm's coolest gay bar. It's got the lot – a great location close to the Gamla Stan T-bana station, friendly staff, stylish decor (topped off with sparkly rotating chandeliers), a good mixture of locals and visitors, and extraordinarily good food. You'll find something going on here every night of the week, whether it's *Barbarella* or some other camp classic sequence projected on to the walls or DJ Edward af Sillén playing Swedish *schlager* music (*see p212* **Schlager, schlager, schlager**). The atmosphere can be anything from relaxed, on weekday lunches, to frenetic on weekend evenings.

Cafés

Anna på Kungsholmen

Drottningholmsvägen 9, Kungsholmen (652 11 19). T-bana Fridhemsplan/bus 3, 4, 40, 57, 62. **Open** 9am-8pm Mon-Fri; 11am-6pm Sat, Sun. **No credit cards. Map** p303 G2.

Tiny, cosy, friendly and colourful, Anna's café on Kungsholmen used to be attract a predominantly lesbian crowd but is now frequented by a mixed clientele. Particularly good at lunchtime for delicious home-made food, Anna's features fantastic, freshly made baked goods, as well as tasty salads and lasagne. There is some outdoor seating for sunny days.

Chokladkoppen

Stortorget 20, Gamla Stan (20 31 70/www.choklad koppen.com). T-bana Gamla Stan/bus 3, 53, 55, 59, 76. **Open** 9am-11pm daily. **No credit cards. Map** p305 J7.

There's something wonderful about the fact that the world's best gay hot chocolate café (a narrow field, admittedly) is housed in one of Stockholm's most photographed buildings, just across from the Nobel Museum (*see p69*) in the heart of Gamla Stan. As well as the rich, dark hot chocolate, there's also superb chocolate cake, white chocolate cheesecake and huge sandwiches. Unfortunately, the staff aren't always particularly friendly and, on weekends, it can take ages to get served.

Copacabana Café

Hornstulls strand 1, Södermalm (669 29 39). T-bana Hornstull/bus 4. **Open** 10am-9pm Mon-Thur; 10am-7pm Fri; 11am-7pm Sat, Sun. **No credit cards. Map** p313 M3.

This is a pleasant lesbian café with a Brazilian air about it on a quiet side street on Södermalm. You'll find the best mango-lime smoothies in Stockholm here, as well as nice staff, good grub and lots of old magazines to browse. On sunny days sit outside and watch the boats go by on the canal.

Djurgårdsterrassen

Sirishovsvägen 3, Djurgården (662 62 09/ www.djurgardsterrassen.se). Bus 44, 47/ tram 7/ferry from Slussen or Nybrokajen. **Open** *Bar* 11am-late daily (depending on weather). *Food* served 11am-10pm daily. Closed early Sept-late May. **Credit** AmEx, DC, MC, V. **Map** p307 H13.

Arts & Entertainment

This beautiful, open-air café-bar-restaurant is perfect for a glass of wine on a summer evening or a *fika* – coffee and a small cake – to punctuate a weekend stroll on the greenest of Stockholm's islands. It's also notable as the first gay establishment visited by the king and queen of Sweden.

Populära Sibirien

Roslagsgatan 9, Vasastaden (16 56 59). T-bana Rådmansgatan/bus 4. **Open** 11.30am-10pm Mon-Fri; noon-10pm Sat; 2-7pm Sun. **Credit** AmEx, DC, MC, V. **Map** p309 C6.

This café's odd name, which translates as Popular Siberia, refers to the nickname used for this part of town, just north of the city centre. It's run by two blonde former airline stewards and, just as you would expect, they're very good at welcoming you, seating you and providing you with excellent tea and coffee. Attracts a loyal crowd of regulars.

Clubs

Since Stockholm's gay clubbing scene is quite small, the clubs are in constant competition. Lately it seems that **Lino** has captured the male crowd on Saturday nights, while **TipTop** has the women, **Connection** and TipTop are battling it out for Friday nights, while **Bysis** has lost many of its lesbian patrons to **Roxy** and TipTop. That said, however, all of this is likely to change at the drop of a tight, Calvin Klein vest, so the best way to know what's the hottest place on any given night is to ask around.

Bysis

Hornsgatan 82, Södermalm (84 59 10). T-bana Mariatorget or Zinkensdamm/bus 4, 43, 55, 66, 74. **Open** *Bar* 4-10pm Tue-Sat. *Club* 7pm-1am Wed, Fri. *Food served* 11am-3.30pm, 4pm-10pm Tue-Sat. **Admission** free. **Credit** AmEx, DC, MC, V. **Map** p314 K5.

This rustic tavern (formerly known as Häcktet) in the middle of the main street of Hornsgatan on Södermalm used to be especially popular with lesbians but is now quite mixed. Regulars love its courtyard, which is open until 10pm, and the fact that the DJ plays unapologetic pop instead of *schlager* (*see p212*) or dance music. It doesn't attract the glamorous crowd but, as a result, Bysis is a good place to find a warm atmosphere, and people of all ages having fun.

Connection

Storkyrkobrinken 9, Gamla Stan (20 18 18/www.clubconnection.nu). T-bana Gamla Stan/ bus 3, 53. **Open** 10pm-3am Fri-Sat. **Admission** free. **Credit** AmEx, DC, MC, V. **Map** p305 H7.

Every Friday and Saturday night, Cattellins, a very traditional restaurant in the heart of the Old Town, transforms itself into Connection, a popular club with several bars, including an outdoor bar in summer months. There's something charming about seeing its very old-fashioned interior packed with a mixed crowd of fashionable men and women. The music policy tends toward happy-go-lucky Europop.

Lash

Wollmar Yxkullsgatan 18, Södermalm (moible 07 08 79 17 09/www.welcome.to/clublash). T-bana Mariatorget/bus 43, 55, 66. **Open** 9.30pm-late usually the last Thur of mth. **Admission** varies. **Credit** MC, V. **Map** p314 L6.

Housed in the same underground club as SLM (*see p213*), Lash is a women-only club with a dresscode that runs the gamut from leather-and-latex to kinky-in-corsets. This Södermalm club has many different theme nights, though, and admission and opening times vary considerably, so be sure to check the website before you set out.

Malarpaviljongen. *See p209.*

Schlager, schlager, schlager

More than 30 years after they won the Eurovision Song Contest in Brighton with 'Waterloo', the footprints left by Abba's sequined platform boots are – for better or worse – still stamped all over Swedish music. The musical *Mama Mia!* is due to open (in Swedish) at the Cirkus theatre (*see p234*) early in 2005, but perhaps ABBA's most obvious legacy right now is *schlager*. This is the music that can be heard – nay, cannot be avoided – at bars and nightclubs across Stockholm. Deeply unfashionable a few years ago, *schlager* is suddenly booming.

To the uninitiated, *schlager* can sound just like any other uptempo euro-pop. But, as any fan will tell you, it is, in fact, a very particular type of uptempo euro-pop. Songs are always exuberant, often a bit camp and usually exactly three minutes long.

Generally speaking, *schlager* songs get to the chorus very quickly, to make them all the easier to sing along to, and they may well involve an unsubtle key change, after which the first half of the song is more or less repeated.

Every year Stockholm holds a competition (called a Melodifestival) to choose its entry for the annual Eurovision Song Contest. This is where you'll find *schlager* in its purest form. ABBA are the original *schlager* band, but current stars include Shirley Clamp (Melodifestival runner-up, 2004), Charlotte Nilsson (Eurovision winner, 1999) and Carola (Eurovision winner, 1991). As a guideline, if a song comes on that makes you roll your eyes but also causes you to unconsciously tap your feet, it's *schlager*.

The breeding ground for this virulent strain of music was Stockholm's gay scene, but *schlager* subsequently escaped and went on to take over the rest of Sweden. Now even the ferries to Finland proudly advertise their *schlager* bars.

To hear *schlager* at its best, try to catch Stockholm's best *schlager* DJ, Edward af Sillén, on Thursdays at **Torget** (*see p210*) and Saturdays at **Lino** (*see p213*).

Edward af Silléns plays **Club Lino**.

Lino

Restaurang Scorpio, Södra Riddarholmshamnen 19,
Riddarholmen (411 69 76). T-bana Gamla Stan/bus
3, 53. **Open** 10pm-4am daily. **Admission** 100kr.
Credit (bar only) AmEx, MC, V. **Map** p305 J6.
Saturdays at Lino are dependably good fun, with two
dancefloors (one playing *schlager*, one playing dance
music), three bars and a mostly-male crowd that's
more grown-up than the one at the TipTop (*see below*).
Inside it's the kind of familiar club that could be anywhere in the world, but there's an outdoor bar where
you can enjoy a beer while gazing up at the ancient
buildings of Riddarholmen, the tiny island next to
Gamla Stan. Walking out at 3am to find it bright and
sunny and promptly going for a swim off Norr
Mälarstrand is one of summer's treats.

Patricia

Stadsgårdskajen 152, Södermalm (743 05 70/
www.patricia.st). T-bana Slussen/bus 2, 3, 53, 76.
Open 5pm-1am Wed, Thur; 6pm-5am Fri, Sat;
6pm-3am Sun. **Admission** free; 90kr after 10pm.
Credit AmEx, DC, MC, V. **Map** p315 K8.
The *Patricia* was built in Middlesbrough, England,
and once served a stint as the royal yacht of Queen
Elizabeth, the Queen Mother, but now it's established as one of the crown jewels of gay life in
Stockholm. Every Sunday for the past ten years
gays and lesbians have gathered here to eat, drink
and dance on this three-level party boat moored at
Slussen. Sunday is half-price food night, so book
ahead to enjoy a delicious dinner that constitutes
one of the best deals in town. The mood, food and
crowd are excellent; the views from the decks are
the icing on the cake.

SLM

Wollmar Yxkullsgatan 18, Södermalm (643 31 00/
www.slm.a.se). T-bana Mariatorget/bus 43, 55,
66. **Open** 10pm-2am Wed, Fri, Sat. **Admission**
membership 300kr per yr; non-members pay 50kr
after 11pm Sat. **Credit** MC, V. **Map** p314 L6.
Scandinavian Leather Men (SLM – get it?) is a little
corner of Berlin in Sweden in the form of a basement
leather bar. A heavy door and an iron stairway
lead down to a labyrinth of darkrooms, bars and a
dancefloor. To get in you'll have to respect the international dress code of skinhead, military, leather,
denim or construction style. Expect a cool, raw
atmosphere – not for the limp of wrist or the faint
of heart. Men only.

TipTop

Sveavägen 57, Vasastaden (32 98 00). T-bana
Rådmansgatan/bus 1, 43, 52, 56. **Open** 4pm-2am
Mon, Tue; 4pm-3am Wed-Sat. **Admission** free.
Credit AmEx, DC, MC, V. **Map** p309 D6.
TipTop is the longest-running gay disco in town,
though it's beginning to show its age. There are two
dancefloors, four bars and a lesbian lounge called
the Ladies Room. Weekday evenings can be very
sleepy but weekends are packed, although this is
also the time when the 'Oh-we're-so-crazy-we're-
going-to-a-gay-club' crowd is on the prowl.

Sunday's gay night on party boat **Patricia**.

Other

In the mid 1980s Stockholm's gay saunas
were shut down to prevent the spread of AIDS,
but under new legislation they were allowed to
reopen in 2004. Stockholm has seen nothing of
the projected surge of sauna openings, though.
Check *QX* for any new developments.

Stockholm also has several video clubs of
the sort where Bergman films are the last thing
you're likely to find. The biggest are **Basement**
in Södermalm (Bondegatan 1, 643 79 10, open
noon-6am Mon-Thur, Sun; noon-8am Fri, Sat),
US Video in Norrmalm (Regeringsgatan 76,
545 158 30, www.us video.nu, open 24 hours),
and **H56** in Vasastaden (Hagagatan 56, 33 55
44, www.haga video.nu, open 11am-6am daily).

T.M.A. The Muscle Academy

Björngårdsgatan 1B, Södermalm (642 63 06).
T-bana Mariatorget/bus 43, 55, 56, 59, 66.
Open 11am-10.30pm Mon-Fri; 1-7.30pm Sat, Sun.
Day membership 100kr. **Credit** AmEx , MC, V.
Map p314 L7.
Stockholm's only exclusively gay gym is for serious
training, not cruising. This is a friendly, no-frills
place for men who want weights – and lots of them
– plus a liberal sprinkling of Tom of Finland prints.

Arts & Entertainment

Music

Meet your new favourite bands.

Nalen. See p215.

Rock, Pop & Jazz

After a decade of Swedes going out to listen to DJs spinning records, while reminiscing about the good old days when they wore a bleached Stone Roses T-shirt to gigs, the Stockholm live music scene has, quite suddenly, started to take off again.

The old venues are packed out again, and several new places have opened, not only for the Bruce Springsteens of the world, but also for up-and-coming acts. Maybe it's got something to do with the end of the IT boom and the subsequent fall in the city's commercial rents, or maybe it's because pop and rock have begun to feel exciting again. Then again, maybe – and this is most likely – it's just because some idealistic fools were lucky enough to find suitable venues with no grumpy neighbours living upstairs complaining about the noise (which happens regularly on the nightclub scene, forcing clubs to lower the volume after 10pm, or to simply close altogether and open a sushi takeaway instead).

Whatever the cause, the good news is that everybody's going out to hear bands again.

There's generally something on every night of the week, either local bands playing at the smaller venues or touring groups promoting new albums in the larger venues.

FESTIVALS

Sweden's short summers offer a limited window for music festivals. The season starts at the end of May with two festivals on the University campus: **Pop Dakar** (www.popdakar.nu), which has grown from a small indie thing to a considerably bigger indie thing that also features the best of Swedish pop, followed by **Popaganda** (www.popaganda.nu), now one of Sweden's biggest and best festivals for national and international pop, rock and electronica. Best of all – both are free.

In July there's **Accelerator: the Big One** (www.luger.se/accelerator/english.asp) at Münchenbryggeriet (*see p216*) on Södermalm, a popular one-day festival that features mainly Swedish, British and US acts, with plenty of big names. A couple of weeks later is the **Stockholm Jazz Festival** (*see p185*), which features old and young giants in soul, jazz and funk. At the beginning of August there's the annual **Pride** festival (*see p185*), which has much more varied music offerings than just euro pop these days.

Taking advantage of the long summer days, alfresco concerts take place on various stages around the city. Among the larger outdoor concert venues are waterside **Sjöhistoriska Museet** (*see p101*), **Stadion** (*see p229*), the Solliden stage at **Skansen** (*see p85*) and Alfred Nobel's old factory at **Skulpturens Hus** (Vinterviksvägen 60, 19 62 00, www.skulpturens hus.se) in Vinterviken; smaller, under-the-stars gigs take place at **Trädgården** (*see p196*), **Gröna Lund** (*see p189*) and on the terrace at **Kulturhuset** (*see p234*).

INFORMATION AND TICKETS

Check the listings in the Friday editions of *Expressen, Aftonbladet, Dagens Nyheter, Metro* or *City* to find out what's on, and look out for posters around town. For tickets to major concerts try www.ticnet.se, or stop by the record store **Mega Skivakademien** at Sergels Torg. Flyers for small pop and rock concerts can be found at record shops like **Pet Sounds** and **Record Hunter**; visit **Bashment** and **Ablaze** (Östgötagatan 20) on Söder for reggae and hip hop flyers. For all music shops, *see p176*.

Most venues serve alcohol and, therefore, usually have an age limit of at least 18. Venues without a bar usually admit all ages.

Gamla Stan

Stampen

Stora Nygatan 5 (20 57 93/www.stampen.se). T-bana Gamla Stan/bus 2, 3, 53, 55, 59, 76. **Open** 8pm-1am Mon-Thur; 8pm-2am Fri, Sat. **Admission** 100kr-120kr. **Credit** AmEx, DC, MC, V. **Map** p305 H7.

Once a pawn shop, tiny Stampen is Stockholm's best known jazz pub. It might have passed its heyday, but interesting live acts still appear every night (9pm-12.30am), playing swing, dixie, trad jazz, blues, rockabilly and country. The crowd is more mature (and touristy) these days; younger cats prefer the somewhat hipper basement dancefloor.

Norrmalm

Fasching

Kungsgatan 63 (tickets 1-5pm Mon-Fri 53 48 29 60/club & restaurant 53 48 29 60/ www.fasching.se). T-bana T-Centralen/bus 1, 47, 53, 69. **Open** 7pm-1am Mon-Thur; 7pm-4am Fri, Sat. **Admission** varies. **Credit** AmEx, DC, MC, V. **Map** p304 F6.

As the fading photos on the walls attest, many of the greats have performed at this classic jazz club (capacity 600). Gigs and jam sessions are held nightly, and you'll hear all forms of jazz, as well as

Latin and Afro sounds and even some hip hop. The crowd is a happy mix of all ages and nationalities. All in all, a cool and bohemian Manhattan-style joint. Don't overlook the good restaurant.

Glenn Miller Café

Brunnsgatan 21A (10 03 22/www.glennmiller cafe.com). T-bana Hötorget/bus 1, 43, 52, 56. **Open** 5pm-1am Mon-Thur; 5pm-2am Fri, Sat. **Admission** free. **Credit** MC, V. **Map** p305 E7.

This simple, cosy jazz pub has live music several nights a week. It's often packed with a mix of older fans and twentysomethings who are mates with the band. If you love trad jazz, and are not claustrophobic, this is your place. Good, reasonably priced food is served (*see p119*).

Nalen

Regeringsgatan 74, Norrmalm (50 52 92 00/ www.nalen.com). T-bana Hötorget/bus 1, 2, 43, 56. **Box office** 1hr before concert. **Tickets** free-420kr. **Credit** MC, V. **Map** p305 E7.

Since this legendary dance palace reopened in 1998, it has become the sort of wide-reaching venue that Stockholm always lacked. Built in 1888, Nalen was famous as a jazz mecca from the 1930s until the end of the '60s, when a church took over and got rid of all that sinful noise. Thoroughly but sensitively renovated, Nalen now caters for all kinds of music. There are two auditoriums – Stora Salen (capacity 400) and Harlem (capacity 80) – plus a restaurant, a bar and a club room, Alcazar.

Djurgården

Cirkus

Djurgårdsslätten 43-45 (box office 660 10 207/ www.cirkus.se). Bus 47/tram 7/ferry from Nybroplan or Slussen. **Box office** 11am-6pm Mon-Fri & 2hrs before a show. **Tickets** 250kr-650kr. **Credit** AmEx, DC, MC, V. **Map** p307 J11.

In royal park Djurgården, next to Skansen's zoo and opposite Gröna Lund amusement park, Cirkus is a cylindrical wooden building built in 1892 for circus troupes. It's got seating for 1,700, as well as a bar and a restaurant. Cirkus is an atmospheric place, but the fact that it's all-seated can be a drawback (especially if you're 16 and Robbie Williams is in town).

Södermalm

Debaser

Karl Johans Torg 1 (462 98 60/www.debaser.nu). T-bana Slussen or Gamla Stan/bus 2, 3, 43, 53, 55, 59, 76. **Open** 8pm-3am Mon-Sat. **Admission** varies. **Credit** MC, V. **Map** p305 K8.

Debaser quickly became one of the leading live rock venues in the city when it opened up in 2002. Appropriately rough around the edges and located under a bridge in an old distillery, Debaser is every inch the rock club. Bands play here seven nights a week, and there's DJ action on club nights (*see p195*). Arrive before 11pm to avoid the (often long) line.

Fylkingen

*Munchenbryggeriet, Torkel Knutssonsgatan 1
(84 54 43/www.fylkingen.se). T-bana Mariatorget/
bus 43, 55, 56.* **Open & admission** varies;
call for details. **Admission** usually 80kr.
Credit *Bar* MC, V. **Map** p314 L6.

This converted brewery is the best place to hear
alternative, DIY and experimental music (*see also
p221*). There is always has something interesting
going on – intermedia art or electro-acoustic impro-
visation, say – though the music might not be to
everyone's tastes. Plenty of arty parties gather here,
and they all nod meaningfully when someone is
screaming on stage in a plastic bra.

Göta Källare

*Folkungagatan 45 (57 86 79 00/www.gotakallare.
com). T-bana Medborgarplatsen/bus 55, 59, 66.*
Open *Club* 9pm-3am Fri, Sat. *Concerts* call for
details. **Tickets** 100kr-250kr. **Credit** AmEx, DC,
MC, V. **Map** p314 L8.

Renovated in 2004, with new VIP booths and a
podium for go-go dancers, this is a stylised, medium-
sized venue. Göta Källare recently launched 'Vive le
Rock', a night featuring three blues-based rock
bands on the first Sunday of the month. For those
favouring more old-fashioned beats, there are weekday performances by Swedish 'dance-bands' (oom-
pah bands with men in golden suits playing for five
hours straight). International pop and rock bands,
as well as hip hop acts, also play here for alternative
Södermalm types, who head to Mondo (*see below*)
immediately after the concert. (Note that the entrance
is by the steps leading down to the T-bana station.)

Kafe 44

*Tjärhovsgatan 44 (644 53 12/www.kafe44.com).
T-bana Medborgarplatsen/bus 55, 59, 66.* **Open**
concerts twice a wk; call for details. **Tickets** 40kr-
100kr. **No credit cards**. **Map** p315 L9.

This hangout for Södermalm's anarchists hosts a lot
of punk and rock concerts, as well as an alternative,
righteous brand of hip hop. There's no minimum age
and no alcohol is served, but with the sort of bands
that play here, you won't need a drink to get a kick.
Even though this previously grungy café is newly
painted, try not to look too well groomed if you don't
want to stand out from the crowd.

Mondo

*Medborgarplatsen 8 (673 10 32/www.mondo
stockholm.com). T-bana Medborgarplatsen/bus 55,
59, 66.* **Open & admission** varies; call for details.
Map p314 L8.

After a shaky start – a delayed opening in 2003
and initial financial problems – Mondo, on Söder's
busy Medborgarplatsen, has quickly established
itself as an integral part of Stockholm nightlife.
With more than ten concerts a week (country, pop,
rock, hip hop and reggae) in three spaces (the
largest holds 1,200), as well as five bars, four dancefloors, a cinema, a gallery and a decent restaurant,
nobody can remember what they used to do before
Mondo existed. *See also p195*.

Mosebacke Etablissement

*Mosebacketorg 3 (information 55 60 98 90/
www.mosebacke.se). T-bana Slussen/bus 2, 3, 43, 53,
55, 59, 76.* **Box office** 11am-4pm Mon-Fri.
Summer 11am-1am Mon-Thur, Sun; 11am-2am Fri,
Sat. *Winter* 4pm-1am Mon-Thur, Sun; 4pm-2am Fri,
Sat. **Tickets** 90kr-250kr. **Credit** AmEx, DC, MC, V.
Map p314 K8.

Many of Sweden's finest jazz artists have appeared
on Mosebacke's two stages – Stora Salen and the
more intimate Cornelisrummet. A lot of jazz is still
performed, but the programme is more varied now
– there's also pop, rock, salsa and reggae. Mosebacke
has been a well-known address since the 18th century, when troubadour Carl Bellman used to played
here; playwright August Strindberg also hung out
here a century later. There are also some popular
bars (*see p138*) and great club nights (*see p195*) here.
It is next door to Södra Teatern (*see below*).

Münchenbryggeriet

*Torkel Knutssonsgatan 1 (84 54 43/www.fylkingen.
se). T-bana Mariatorget/bus 43, 55, 56.* **Open**
varies. **Tickets** 80kr-420kr. **Credit** AmEx, DC,
MC, V. **Map** p305 K6.

This old brewery is now a popular medium-sized
concert hall used by acts of all kinds. One night the
audience is packed with rastas praising Jah and raising their lighters to dancehall missionary Capleton,
another you might find bespectacled types lined up
for Belle & Sebastian. In summer, there are gigs on
the stage in the open-air courtyard. Also home to
Fasching (*see p215*) and Fylkingen (*see above*).

Södra Teatern

*Mosebacketorg 1-3 (55 69 72 30/www.sodra
teatern.com). T-bana Slussen/bus 2, 3, 43, 53, 55,
59, 76.* **Box office** noon-6pm Mon-Fri; noon-4pm
Sat. **Tickets** 100-240kr. **Credit** AmEx, DC, MC, V.
Map p314 K8.

This cultural centre has always got something of
interest going on. Built in 1859, the main auditorium,
Stora Scenen (capacity 400), has red-velvet chairs for
low-key pop and folk concerts, while the basement,
Kägelbanan (capacity 700), hosts more singalong and
danceable pop. Otherwise, there's world music, as
well as poetry readings and spoken-word performances. The crowd is as mixed as the acts. Touring
theatre companies also perform here on occasions.

Tantogården

*Ringvägen 24 (668 22 71/www.tantogarden.se).
T-bana Zinkensdamm/bus 66.* **Open** varies;
call for details. **Admission** varies; call for details.
Credit AmEx, DC, MC ,V. **Map** p313 L5.

This arena (one indoor stage, one outdoor) was *the*
place for indie rock in the 1990s, but it was forced to
shut down for years due to complaints from its neighbours. Now open under new owners, the venue has
lost its dominant position. Still, its location on the
south-east corner of beautiful Tantolunden park (*see
p90*) almost makes you feel like you are out in the
countryside, and if you're into obscure punk and rock,
and the occasional reggae act, it can be a fun night.

Thank you for the music

The Hives.

Ask most people what they think of when they think of Sweden and they'll most likely say, 'blondes', 'IKEA' or 'pickled herring'. And, you know, fair enough. But the Swedes would really much rather they said 'pop music'.

The Swedes *love* pop music. They first properly embraced it in the '70s in the form of ABBA, they hugged it tight in the '80s with Roxette and in the '90s with Army of Lovers, Ace of Base and Dr Alban. Now they're squeezing the life out of it via rock groups like the Hives, the Concretes, Sahara Hotnights and the Hellacopters; pop groups like the Cardigans, Soundtrack of Our Lives, the Ark and Eskobar; arty stars like Stina Nordenstam, Stakka Bo, Jay-Jay Johanson; and Swedish chart-toppers such as Robyn, Meja, A-Teens and Deniz Pop. Swedish producer Max Martin, meanwhile, is busy fine-tuning the music of global stars such as Britney Spears and the Backstreet Boys at his legendary Cheiron Studios. It's such an embarrassment of pop riches – Sweden is, after all, the third biggest exporter of music in the world – that they've come to call it the 'Swedish Pop Wonder', marvelling at their own ability to produce so many pop stars out of such a small population.

The combination of government support, widespread affluence and the Swedes' avid admiration for US and British culture probably has something to do with it. Anyone who wants to can attend a local Kommunala Musikskolan (Public Music School), and every

town offers free or low-cost music courses and rehearsal facilities to children and young adults. By way of further encouragement, in 1998 the Swedish government created the Music Export Prize, awarded to artists considered to be 'ambassadors for Sweden on the international music arena'.

All of the hit Swedish bands sing their lyrics in English – a maximum potential Swedish-language audience of nine million is pretty small, after all – but the catchy, simple melodies behind the words are a very Swedish thing. Swedes think their love of melody can be traced back to the need for cheerful songs in the long, dark winters and its strong tradition of folk music. This heritage is inherent in almost all Swedish music – even streetwise hip hop acts sample old troubadours, and many cover Carl Michael Bellman or Evert Taube classics. In addition, bands are happy to perform them on the ever-popular TV show *Sing-a-long at Skansen* (*Allsång på Skansen* in Swedish).

So, don't be fooled by all the shiny leather jackets and degenerate looks, it's only what they learned at the school of rock (you really can get a degree in pop here). In reality, it's all very innocent. As crooner Jens Lekman, the latest small-town Swede on the brink of world fame, puts it: 'When people think of Sweden they get the wrong idea, like Cliff Richard who thought it was all porn and gonorrhoea'. Er, Cliff, you were supposed to think of *blondes*.

Debaser. See p215.

Östermalm

Lydmar Hotel

Sturegatan 10 (56 61 13 00/www.lydmar.se). T-bana Östermalmstorg/bus 1, 2, 55, 56. **Open** 11.30am-1am Mon-Thur; 11.30am-2am Fri; 1pm-2am Sat; 1pm-1am Sun. **Admission** free. **Credit** AmEx, DC, MC, V. **Map** p310 E8.

The stylish bar in this music-friendly hotel (*see p57*) hosts live gigs, plus a small festival in October. The usual offerings include lots of acid jazz, funk and rare groove, but also hip hop and organic house music. World stars (Billy Bragg, Beverly Knight, Jungle Brothers) have all stepped on to the small, sweaty stage, but they're easy to miss as they're often a word-of-mouth affair. DJs also play here regularly.

Further afield

Allhuset

Universitetsvägen 10, Frescati (16 20 00/www.su.se). T-bana Universitetet/bus 40. **Open** 11am-1am Mon-Thur; 11am-3am Fri. **Tickets** 60kr-240kr. **Credit** MC, V.

At this modern venue (capacity 500) on Stockholm University campus, students wearing T-shirts adorned with their favourite band's name talk about music and drink cheap beer in a relaxed atmosphere. There are gigs from interesting Swedish and international acts, and plenty of up-and-coming bands.

Dieselverkstaden

Markusplatsen 17, Sickla (718 82 90/www.diesel verkstaden.se). Bus 150, 401, 403, 404-422, 491, 492, 496, 497/train from Slussen to Sickla Strand. **Open, admission & credit** vary; call for details.

Just south-east of Södermalm, in what used to be an old factory for assembling ship engines, the people who ran the Tantogården (*see p216*) ten years ago have opened this cultural centre. Along with a good concert hall, there's also a restaurant, café, cinema, library and theatre.

Globen

Arenavägen, Johanneshov (box office 07 71 31 00/ www.globen.se). T-bana Globen. **Box office** *In person* 9am-6pm Mon-Fri; 10am-3pm Sat and 2hrs before concerts. *By phone* 9am-7pm Mon-Fri; 10am-4pm Sat; 10am-3pm Sun. **Tickets** 120kr-600kr. **Credit** AmEx, DC, MC, V.

Like it or not (and many don't), you can't deny that Globen – the world's largest spherical building – is Stockholm's most recognisable structure. It's also an arena for everything from sports events to gala parties and, of course, concerts. It holds up to 16,000 people, so caters well for big-name acts like David Bowie and Destiny's Child. If you're seated up high, you should probably bring binoculars or watch the giant TV screens instead. The atmosphere, as ever with large stadiums, is practically non-existent.

Klubben

Fryshuset, Hammarby Fabriksväg 13 (www.frys huset.se). T-bana Gullmarsplan and then bus 150 or bus 74. **Open** varies; call for details. **Tickets** 220kr-320kr. **No credit cards**.

Just a bit south of Södermalm, in the Fryshuset youth centre (where lots of bands rehearse), lies Klubben, a key venue for hardcore, heavy metal and hip hop. Expect a young crowd, lots of headbanging and stage-diving and, since there's no bar and no age restrictions, lots of drinking in the bushes outside.

Classical Music & Opera

If you are looking for value for money, Stockholm is the place to be when it comes to classical music and opera. The city may be light years away from, say, Vienna as a musical city, but it certainly shines when it comes to the sheer number of mid-range concerts. Big surprises, edginess and glamour are rare, but Stockholm offers high artistic quality and dozens of concerts every month. Likewise, only a few of the biggest touring stars stop by, but that's not all bad in this agent-ruled era in which artists' fees have skyrocketed and you pay more for the name than the music.

The main reason for this musical smörgåsbord, not to mention the diversity of the audiences, is a praiseworthy social democratic cultural policy in Sweden. The aim of this policy is to subsidise musical diversity and it seems to be working, as there are 300 free concerts every year. Otherwise, tickets cost around 100kr or even less for students and under-20s. Consequently, around 80 per cent of the revenues of the symphony orchestras come from government subsidies.

The policy has also resulted in Stockholm having far more ensembles and venues than most cities its size. The city has two full-sized symphony orchestras that can compete with the best in Europe, two permanent opera houses and a healthy chamber music scene. The most prominent institutions are the **Kungliga Operan** (the Royal Opera), the **Swedish Radio Symphony Orchestra** and the **Royal Stockholm Philharmonic Orchestra**. As with most established orchestras in the world, these offer a traditional repertoire, though all have been modernising in recent years.

One of the main instigators of Stockholm's impressive classical music scene was King Gustav III (1746-92), who built the first opera house, the **Kungliga Operan** (*see p221*), in 1782. Unfortunately for him, he was later assassinated at a masked ball there – an event that inspired Verdi to write his opera *Un Ballo in Maschera* (A Masked Ball). The current opera house at Gustav Adolfs Torg is still the centre of the Swedish opera scene. Its orchestra, the famous **Kungliga Hovkapellet** (Royal Court Orchestra), was founded in the 16th century and is said to be the oldest continuously active orchestra in the world.

Whereas Denmark has Nielsen, Norway Grieg and Finland Sibelius, Sweden has never had one of its composers enthroned in the Classical Music Hall of Fame, but music by Swedish composers is frequently played in Stockholm. There are performances of works by such composers as Wilhelm Stenhammar, Franz Berwald, Wilhelm Peterson-Berger, Hugo Alfvén, Allan Pettersson and Hilding Rosenberg. Frequently played contemporary composers include Anders Hillborg, Jan Sandström, Sven-David Sandström, Anders Eliasson and Daniel Börtz. Contemporary musicians to look out for include trumpet player Håkan Hardenberger, clarinet player Martin

Fröst, trombonist Christian Lindberg and his brother, lutist Jacob Lindberg. Violinist Cecilia Zilliacus is one of the brightest instrumentalists of the new generation, and don't ever pass up the chance of a concert with Swedish classical music's biggest name, mezzo soprano Anne Sofie von Otter.

THE SEASON

The music calendar is strictly seasonal, running from August to June, with concerts held primarily on weekdays. In the summer, the focus of activity moves to the court theatres and parks around town. One exception is the **Stockholm Konserthuset** (*see p220*), which, from 2004, stays open in July for a four-week summer festival. Another important date is the **Baltic Sea Festival** (www.sr.se/berwaldhallen), which started in 2003; for more information contact organisers Berwaldhallen (*see below*). The opera season runs from September to May.

INFORMATION AND TICKETS

Venues and websites are usually the most reliable source of information. The monthly English-language tourist magazine *What's On Stockholm* lists the main concerts, although the Friday entertainment section (*På Stan*) of daily *Dagens Nyheter* provides better listings. Also check out the free daily papers *Metro* and *Stockholm City*. On www.konsertguiden.nu you can search by genre and location for concerts all over the country – but you'd better brush up your Swedish language skills before attempting.

You can buy tickets by phone or online from most venues. For the major venues, tickets are also sold by **Biljett Direkt** (077 170 70 70, www.ticnet.se); the website is in English.

Main venues & ensembles

Berwaldhallen

Dag Hammarskjöldsväg 3, Östermalm (box office 784 18 00/www.berwaldhallen.se). Bus 56, 76, 69. **Box office** noon-6pm Mon-Fri & 2hrs before a concert (or contact Biljett Direkt or www.ticnet.se). Closed July. **Tickets** 75kr-370kr. **Credit** AmEx, DC, MC, V. **Map** p307 F11.

The Berwaldhallen was built in 1979 for the Sveriges Radio Symfoniorkester (Swedish Radio Symphony Orchestra) and the Radiokören (Radio Choir). The acclaimed modernist hall is built mainly underground. The Symfoniorkester, established in 1967, enjoyed a particularly successful period under the direction of Finnish Esa-Pekka Salonen (now with the Los Angeles Philharmonic) during the second half of the 1980s. The current conductor, Austrian Manfred Honeck, joined in 2000. The orchestra has a more contemporary touch than other Swedish orchestras, commissioning a significant amount of new music from Swedish and international composers.

The Radiokören is considered to be one of the best choirs in the world and has recorded with the Berliner Philharmonic and Claudio Abbado. The current principal conductor of the choir is Stefan Parkman. Berwaldhallen also produces the Baltic Sea Festival every August.

Konserthuset

Hötorget, Norrmalm (box office 50 66 77 88/ www.konserthuset.se). T-bana Hötorget/bus 1, 43, 52, 59. **Box office** 11am-6pm Mon-Fri; 11am-3pm Sat & 2hrs before concerts. Closed 1mth from Midsummer. **Tickets** 70kr-420kr. **Credit** AmEx, DC, MC, V. **Map** p305 F7.

Konserthuset has been the home of the Kungliga Filharmonikerna (Royal Stockholm Philharmonic Orchestra) since its inauguration in 1926. Architect Ivar Tengbom wanted to 'raise a musical temple not far from the Arctic Circle', and the bright blue structure is one of the foremost examples of early 20th-century Swedish neo-classical design. With its 1,800 seats, the Main Hall is used for major concerts, while the beautiful chamber music hall, the Grünewald Hall (capacity 460), entirely decorated by painter Isaac Grünewald, handles smaller events.

The Kungliga Filharmonikerna, which celebrated its centenary in 2002, performs here regularly. It acquired an international reputation under the leadership of Antal Dorati and later with Gennady Rozhdestvensky and Paavo Berglund. Under its current chief conductor and artistic adviser, American Alan Gilbert, it has entered a new phase of development, hoping for a place among Europe's top orchestras. Konserthuset's repertoire is based in the classical and romantic periods, but it also hosts the internationally renowned annual Composer Festival in the autumn, focusing on living composers.

Nybrokajen 11

Nybrokajen 11, Norrmalm (box office 407 17 00/ www.nybrokajen11.rikskonserter.se). T-bana Kungsträdgården or Östermalmstorg/bus 2, 47, 55, 59, 62, 69. **Box office** *End Aug-mid May* 11am-5pm Mon-Fri. *Mid May-end Aug* 11am-4pm Mon-Fri. Also 2hrs before concerts. **Tickets** 100kr-200kr. **Credit** MC, V. **Map** p305 G8.

The newest venue on the Stockholm classical music scene is Nybrokajen 11, named after its address opposite the Kungliga Dramatiska Teatern. The elegant former home of the Royal Academy of Music was nicely transformed into a permanent stage for the Rikskonserter (Swedish Concert Institute). The main hall (capacity 600) hosts mainly chamber music from all periods, with Swedish and international artists. Stallet, a converted stable, is an intimate venue especially for world music.

Other ensembles

Kroumata

(54 54 15 80/www.kroumata.rikskonserter.se).
Kroumata was formed in 1978 and has since developed something of a cult status. It commissions and

performs works by Swedish and international composers, and has toured more than 35 countries. Since 1997 Kroumata has had its own venue, Capitol (St Eriksgatan 82), a converted theatre that serves as both rehearsal studio and intimate concert hall for a few performances a year. Check the website for details of what's on.

Stockholm Sinfonietta

Riddarhuset, Riddarhustorget 10, Gamla Stan (www.sinfonietta.a.se). T-bana Gamla Stan/bus 3, 53. **Tickets** around 180kr. **Map** p305 H7.

The members of the Stockholm Sinfonietta came first from the Kungliga Filharmonikerna. It has worked with a host of venerable names, including conductors Sixten Ehrling and Okko Kamu, with soloists such as Catalan soprano Montserrat Caballé and Swedish cellist Frans Helmerson. The repertoire stretches all the way from baroque to contemporary and the Stockholm Sinfonietta has the sole right to perform at the marvellous Riddarhuset; check its website or local newspapers for details of forthcoming concerts.

Stockholms Nya Kammarorkester (SNYKO)

Check press for concert details.

Formed by former members of the Sveriges Radio Symfoniorkester, the Stockholm Chamber Music Orchestra, mostly known by its abbreviation SNYKO, is today one of the most sought-after Scandinavian ensembles, with an international reputation for both its classical and contemporary repertoire. The orchestra performs regularly in Stockholm and tours extensively, often with artistic advisor Esa-Pekka Salonen.

Churches & other venues

Those who love classical music in unique surroundings shouldn't overlook the city's church music. Music programming in Stockholm's central churches is rich and ambitious. One of the finest organs is to be found in the **Gustav Vasa Kyrka** excellent organ concert series. Other musical churches are **Storkyrkan** (on Gamla Stan, *see p69*); **Riddarholmskyrkan** (on Riddarholmen, *see p71*); **Katarina Kyrka** (on Södermalm, *see p91*); **St Jakobs Kyrka** (Norrmalm, *see p78*); **Engelbrektskyrkan** (Östermalmsgatan 20, Östermalm, 406 98 00); **Hedvig Eleonora Kyrka** (Storgatan 2, Östermalm, 663 04 30); and **Tyska Kyrkan** (on Gamla Stan, *see p70*).

Check local papers to find out what's on, or visit the tourist centre at **St Clara Kyrka** in Norrmalm (*see p78*), which provides listings of church concerts. Particularly around Christmas, you're likely to have more ecclesiastic musical options than you can handle.

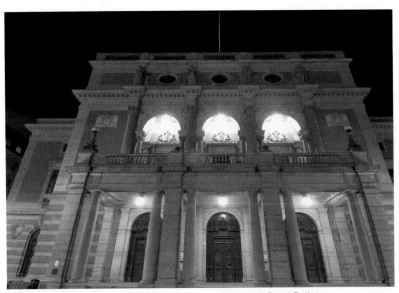

Kungliga Operan – prestigious home of the Royal Opera and Royal Ballet.

Since classic dance hall **Nalen** (*see p215*) reopened in 1998, its stages, bars and restaurants have hosted a diverse programme of music, including rock, troubadours, salsa, electronica. It also hosts a classical chamber music series on Sundays, promoted by the Swedish Artists' and Musicians' Interest Organisation (SAMI).

Contemporary & experimental

EMS (55 60 88 51, www.ems.rikskonserter.se) is the centre for electro-acoustic music in Sweden; it works closely with **Fylkingen** (*see p216*), located in the same building, providing studios for musicians and promoting concerts and festivals. Fylkingen, on Södermalm, has been the the main forum for Swedish experimental music since 1933.

Opera

Folkoperan

Hornsgatan 72, Södermalm (box office 616 07 50/ www.folkoperan.se). T-bana Mariatorget/bus 4, 43, 55, 56, 74. **Box office** *June-Aug* noon-6pm Wed-Fri. *Sept-May* noon-7pm Wed-Sat. **Tickets** 250kr-375kr. **Credit** AmEx, DC, MC, V. **Map** p314 K6.
Folkoperan has been a healthy rival to Kungliga Operan (*see below*) since its founding in 1976. Its modern stagings of classic operas sung in Swedish, its unconventional and often controversial productions and the intimacy of the auditorium are among Folkoperan's distinctive features. It has toured Europe and the US with *Don Carlos, Carmen* and recently written Swedish opera *Marie Antoinette*, by Daniel Börtz. Folkoperan's *Wagner Ring Cycle* runs through 2005. Its main season runs from September to May, when there are performances most nights of the week. Its bar-restaurant, called Folkoperan Bar & Kök (*see p125*), is popular with a trendy young crowd.

Kungliga Operan

Gustav Adolfs Torg, Norrmalm (box office 24 82 40/ www.operan.se). T-bana Kungsträdgården/bus 2, 43, 55, 59, 62, 76. **Box office** noon-6pm Mon-Fri; noon-3pm Sat. **Tickets** 40kr-560kr. **Credit** AmEx, DC, MC, V. **Map** p305 G7.
When it opened in 1782, this opera house was considered one of the most modern in operation. Only 100 years later it was demolished to make way for the current opera house, which was completed in 1898. The Royal Opera has sent a string of great singers on to the international stage – among them Jenny Lind, Jussi Björling, Birgit Nilsson and Elisabeth Söderström – but, as is the case with Swedish footballers and hockey players, the most talented leave the country at a young age and rarely return to the Kungliga. The building itself is impressive, with a golden foyer and a red and gold auditorium that can seat as many as 1,100. It's also the home of the Swedish Royal Ballet (*see p238*).

Arts & Entertainment

Sport & Fitness

Sport for all and all for sport in democratic Sweden.

Swimming by
Stadshuset. *See p226*.

Sweden boasts very high levels of participation in sport throughout the country, thanks mainly to a strong democratic tradition, which means that sport is highly organised (about as far as you can get from the street football of Latin America) and available to all. Generous government support, together with plentiful outdoor space – lakes, a long coastline and ubiquitous forest (covering half the country) – create fantastic conditions for many sports and outdoor activities. In addition, the Swedish law known as *allemansrätten* encourages free access to the countryside.

You can get as hands-on as you want while you're in Stockholm. Jog around Djurgården on a sunny spring day, take on the locals at badminton (which is virtually the national sport), try your skates on a city rink (or catch the pros at an ice hockey game at Globen in autumn), or head out on a long-distance skating adventure on the frozen sea in the dead of winter.

As in most of Europe, the main year-round obsession is football (*fotboll*). It's played in the summer, and watched and gambled on in the winter when the other European leagues are in action. Although Sweden has produced many great tennis players, interest in the sport has sadly diminished enormously and the city's plentiful courts are often empty. The new game in town is golf, which has boomed in the past decade, with stars such as Annika Sörenstam drawing a lot of international attention; there are dozens of decent golf courses within an hour's drive of Stockholm.

There are plenty of big annual sporting events, such as the **Vasaloppet** in March (a 90-kilometre/56-mile cross-country skiing race; www.vasaloppet.se), **Vätternrundan** (a 300-kilometre/186-mile bike race around Lake Vättern in southern Sweden) and the **Stockholm Marathon** in early June (*see p183*). Another spectacular is the long-distance skating race **Vikingarännet** (*see p226* **Skating on the edge**).

For more information on the sports listed here, or any others, contact the **Swedish Sports Confederation** (699 60 00, www.svenskidrott.se) or the **tourist office** (*see p288*).

Participation sports/fitness

Badminton

Badmintonstadion
*Hammarby Slussvägen 4, Södermalm (642 70 02/
www.badmintonstadion.se). T-bana Skanstull/bus 3, 4,
55, 74.* **Open** 6am-11pm Mon-Thur; 6am-8.30pm Fri;
9am-5.30pm Sat; 9am-9.30pm Sun. **Rates** *Per court*
100kr-130kr/hr; 80kr concessions. **Credit** MC, V.
Map p315 O8.
Badminton is one of the most popular recreational
sports in Sweden, and this is the city's largest hall.

Frescatihallen
*Svante Arrhenius Vägen 4, Norra Djurgården
(15 27 00/www.frescatihallen.com). T-bana
Universitetet/bus 40.* **Open** *2nd wk Aug-mid June*
7am-11pm Mon-Thur; 7am-9pm Fri; 8am-7pm Sat;
8am-10pm Sun. *Mid June-1st wk Aug* 2-10pm Mon-
Thur; 2-9pm Fri; 8am-7pm Sat; 8am-10pm Sun.
Rates *Per court* 110kr-120kr/hr; 60kr-95kr
concessions. **Credit** AmEx, DC, MC, V.

Sundbybergs Rackethall
*Örsvängen 10, Sundbyberg (628 20 29). T-bana
Hallonbergen.* **Open** *Mid Aug-mid June* 7am-10pm
Mon-Thur; 7am-9pm Fri; 8am-9pm Sat, Sun. *Mid
June-end June, 1st 2wks Aug* 7am-10pm Mon-Thur;
7am-7pm Fri; 8am-7pm Sat, Sun. Closed July.
Rates *Per court* 60kr-90kr/hr. **Credit** MC, V.

Billiards, snooker & pool

There are billiards clubs, which may have a bar,
and then there are bars with pool or snooker
tables. Almost all the options in the Stockholm
region are in the latter category, but here are
two clean billiards clubs with professional staff.

Jolo & Co
*Västmannagatan 50, Vasastaden (31 50 60/www.
jolo.se). T-bana Odenplan/bus 2, 4, 40, 53, 69, 72.*
Open *Mid Aug-Midsummer* 11am-midnight Mon-
Thur; 11am-1am Fri; 2pm-1am Sat. **Rates** *per person*
44kr/hr; *per table* 132kr/hr (1 person per table must
be a member; membership costs 100kr per year,
which includes 2hrs of play time for 1 person).
Credit AmEx, MC, V. **Map** p308 D4.

Stockholms Biljardsalong
*Gyldéngatan 2, Vasastaden (31 32 50/www.
stockholmsbiljardsalong.nu). T-bana Odenplan/bus 2,
4, 40, 53, 69, 72.* **Open** 4pm-2am Tue-Fri; 3pm-2am
Sat; 4pm-midnight Sun. **Rates** *Per person* 38kr/hr.
Per table 114kr/hr (1 person per table must be a
member; membership costs 100kr per year, which
includes 2hrs of play time for 1 person). **Credit**
AmEx, MC, V. **Map** p309 D5.

Climbing

The most popular outdoor rock climbing is
found at **Häggsta**, 35 kilometres (22 miles)
south of Stockholm outside Huddinge, where
there are options for most ability levels. For
more information check with the **Stockholm
Climbing Club** (www.utsidan.se/skk) or the
Swedish Climbing Association (618 82 70).
Alternatively, try one of the following indoor
climbing centres. There is also a climbing wall
at SATS Sports Club (*see p224*).

Karbin
*Västberga Allé 60, Hägersten (744 38 40/www.
karbin.com). Bus 143, 165 from T-bana Liljeholmen
or 144 from Gullmarsplan.* **Open** *Mid Aug-end June*
noon-10pm Mon-Fri; noon-8pm Sat, Sun. *End June-
mid Aug* 4-10pm daily. **Rates** 80kr; 60kr under-17s
(excl equipment). **Credit** AmEx, DC, MC, V.
Situated a few miles south of the city, this place has
700sq m (2,300sq ft) of indoor wall.

Klätterverket
*Markusplatsen 17, Sickla (641 10 48/www.
klatterverket.se). Bus 150, 401, 403, 404-422, 491,
492, 496, 497 from Slussen/saltsjöbanan from
Slussen to Sickla station.* **Open** *Mid Aug-end June*
noon-10pm Mon-Fri; 10am-8pm Sat, Sun. *End June-
mid Aug* 3-9pm daily. **Rates** 80kr (excl equipment).
Credit AmEx, DC, MC, V.
This is Sweden's biggest indoor climbing centre,
with 1,000sq m (3,280sq ft) of wall.

Cycling & rollerblading

Stockholm's compact size makes it ideal for
rollerblading or cycling. There are plenty of
cycle paths, some of which have very beautiful
stretches. The island of **Djurgården** is a good
place for cycling – lots of green space and few
cars at weekends – or try the circuit around the
bay of **Riddarfjärden** (across the demanding
Västerbron bridge, along Söder Mälarstrand,
Centralbron and Norr Mälarstrand).

Cykel och Mopeduthyrningen
*Strandvägen, Kajplats 24, Östermalm (660 79 59).
Bus 47, 69, 76.* **Open** *Apr-Sept* 9am-9pm daily;
call for opening hours in winter. **Rates** *Bikes*
60kr/hr; 200kr/day. **Credit** MC, V. **Map** p306 G10.
Offers mopeds in addition to bikes and inline skates.

Djurgårdsbrons Sjöcafé
*Galärvarvsvägen 2, Djurgården (660 57 57). Bus 44,
47, 69, 76.* **Open** *Mar/Apr-Sept/Oct* 9am-9pm daily.
Rates *Inline skates* 60kr/hr. *Bikes* 65kr/hr. **Credit**
AmEx, DC, MC, V. **Map** p306 G10.
This is a handy place for renting inline skates and
bikes, just over the bridge on Djurgården. It's also
got a pleasant waterside café.

Servicedepån
*Scheelegatan 15, Kungsholmen (651 00 66). T-bana
Rådhuset/bus 1, 3, 40, 52, 59, 62.* **Open** 10am-6pm
Mon-Fri. **Rates** *Bikes* 125kr/day. **Credit** MC, V.
Map p304 G4.
Rents out regular bikes and tandems.

The city is a jogger's delight. See p225.

Fitness clubs

The number of fitness clubs in Stockholm continues to grow apace. The two most popular, with plentiful branches, are listed below, but for non-members these are rather expensive. Alternatively, visit one of the many public swimming pools (see p226), some of which have gyms. There are also plenty of small gyms: ask at your hotel or look in the Yellow Pages.

Friskis & Svettis

Mäster Samuelsgatan 20, Norrmalm (429 70 00/ www.sthlm.friskissvettis.se). T-bana Hötorget/bus 43, 47, 59. **Open** 6.30am-9pm Mon-Thur; 6.30am-7.30pm Fri; 9am-1pm Sat; 3-6.30pm Sun. **Rates** 80kr non-members. **Credit** AmEx, DC, MC, V. **Map** p305 F7.
Less geared to the good-looking body than SATS (*see below*), this place focuses more on general health and the average age is 45 rather than 30. The telephone number is the same for all branches.
Other locations: Långholmsgatan 38, Södermalm; Ringvägen 111, Södermalm; St Eriksgatan 54, Kungsholmen; Tegeluddsvägen 31, Gärdet; Sveavägen 63, Vasastaden.

SATS Sports Club

Regeringsgatan 47, Norrmalm (50 32 80 00/ www.satssportsclub.com). T-bana Hötorget/bus 43, 47, 59, 69. **Open** 6.30am-10pm Mon-Thur; 6.30am-9pm Fri; 10am-6pm Sat, Sun. **Rates** 200kr non-members. **Credit** AmEx, DC, MC, V. **Map** p305 F7.
SATS has a dozen locations in Stockholm – we've listed the most central branches here. All are well equipped and clean, with plenty of good classes. You will sweat alongside a real mix of Stockholmers. The Regeringsgatan branch has a climbing wall.
Other locations: Kocksgatan 12-14 (556 093 60); St Eriksgatan 34 (545 531 40); Birger Jarlsgatan 6C (54 50 14 60).

Golf

Golf enthusiasts hardly have a shortage of facilities – there are some 50 courses within an hour's drive of Stockholm – but the game's increasing popularity has led to rocketing green fees, usually around 450kr-600kr, and a need to reserve tee times. You are allowed to play at any of the courses, despite what some of the more snooty members may think. Websites **www.golf.se** and **www.golfdigest.se** provide extensive information on golfing options (Swedish only).
For really great golf you should head north out of Stockholm to **Ullna** (51 44 12 30, www.ullnagolf.se) or **Kungsängen** (58 45 07 30, www.kungsangensgc.se). Alternatively, the Värmdö courses **Fågelbro** (57 14 18 00, www.fagelbrogolf.se) and **Wermdö** (57 46 07 20, www.wgcc.nu) are both a half-hour drive south of the city. Also in the south is **Saltsjöbaden Golfklubb** (717 01 25, www.saltsjobadengk.se), which has steadily improved in recent years.
Several 'pay and play' courses suitable for beginners can be found around the city. One is **Årsta Golf**, located just south of Södermalm (81 30 00/www.arstagolf.se).

Ice skating

Given that Stockholm is surrounded by frozen water for much of the year, it's not surprising that skating choices are numerous: indoor and outdoor rinks, lakes and even the frozen waters of the archipelago.
The most central outdoor skating rinks are in **Kungsträdgården** in Norrmalm and at **Medborgarplatsen** on Söder, where you can rent skates for a small fee and squeeze yourself on to the small rinks. Popular with families, they're usually open from November to February. There are also plentiful ice hockey rinks, such as **Zinkensdamm**, open to the public for a few hours every day. Call the tourist office for a full list and information.
Skating in the city cannot compete, however, with the lakes or archipelago. Long-distance skating (*långfärdsskridskoåkning*) is a popular sport, and Sweden has some of the best conditions in the world for it. See *p226* **Skating on the edge**.

Östermalms Idrottsplats

Fiskartorpsvägen 2, Hjorthagen (50 82 83 51). T-bana Stadion/bus 55, 77, 291, 293. **Open** varies; call for details. **Admission** free. **Map** p310 B/C9.
This place usually has an ice rink/lane from December to the end of February, and is open to the public when there are no matches on. It's ideal for practising long-distance skating.

Zinkensdamms Idrottsplats

*Ringvägen 16, Södermalm (668 93 31). T-bana
Zinkensdamm/bus 4, 66, 76.* **Open** *Nov-Feb* 8am-
2pm Tue-Thur; 8am-11pm Sat; 1-4pm Sun.
Admission free. **Map** p313 L5.

Next to the rink is a bandy field, which is also open
to the public. Bring your hockey (or bandy) stick and
ask if you can join one of the games that are usually
in progress.

Jogging & running

When the sun is out, Stockholm seems to have
endless beautiful jogging routes. Some of the
best spots are **Riddarfjärden, Långholmen,
Djurgården, Hagaparken** and the south
side of **Södermalm**. If you're into a little
competition, try the **Stockholm Marathon**
(*see p183*) in June, attracting top-class runners
and enthusiastic amateurs, who mingle in a
festive atmosphere. Exclusively for women, and
very popular, is **Tjejmilen** ('Girls' Run'), in late
August or early September, a ten-kilometre (six-
mile) street race on Djurgården (54 56 64 40,
www.tjejmilen.se). Another street race, this time
on Södermalm, is the carnival-like ten-kilometre
(six-mile) **Midnattsloppet** (Midnight Race;
see p184), which takes place in August.

Kayaking & canoeing

Djurgårdsbrons Sjöcafé (*see p223*) rents
kayaks and canoes, as well as pedal boats and
rowing boats. Reliable canoeing outfits include
Svima Sport in Solna (Ekelundsvägen 26, 730
22 10, www.svima.se) and **Brunnsvikens
Kanotcentral** by Brunnsviken lake (Frescati
Hagväg 5, 15 50 60, www.bkk.se).

For trips in the archipelago or around
Lake Mälaren, contact the **tourist office**
(*see p288*) or the following kayaking agencies:
Kajakboden Aquarius in Tyresö (Varvsvägen
9, Tyresö Strand, 770 09 50, www.kajak
boden.com); **Kayak Support** in Bromma
(Nockeby backe 20, 87 73 77, www.kayak.se);
Archipelago Ljusterö Kajakcenter on the
island of Ljusterö (mobile 070 768 94 47), or
Skärgårdsgumman on Utö (50 15 76 68).

Sailing & boats

Most outfits focus on corporate sailing tours,
other companies (including Tvillingarnas
Båtuthyrning; *see below*) offer smaller boats
that can be rented without a skipper for a few
thousand kronor per day. Rates vary depending
on the type of boat you want. For nautical
charts, books and other equipment, try well-
stocked **Nautiska Magasinet** in Gamla Stan
(Slussplan 5, 677 00 00).

Tvillingarnas Båtuthyrning

*Strandvägskajen 27, Östermalm (660 37 14/
www.tvillingarnas.com). Bus 44, 47, 69, 76.* **Open**
Apr-Sept 8am-1am daily. Closed Oct-Mar. **Credit**
AmEx, DC, MC, V. **Map** p306 G10.

This central rental agency, located just before the
bridge over to Djurgården, has a popular restaurant
and hires out sailing boats and motorboats.

Skiing

Skiing is one of Sweden's most popular sports.
Stockholm is relatively close to good downhill
skiing, such as at places like **Flottsbro**
(53 53 27 00, www.flottsbro.com), which is
40 kilometres (25 miles) south of the city. It's
excellent for a day trip, but not very demanding
for experts. About 20 kilometres (13 miles)
to the north of Stockholm is **Väsjöbacken** in
Sollentuna (35 31 85, www.vasjobacken.com),
which offers good conditions for cross-country
skiing. Another good spot for cross-country
skiing is just south of the city at **Lida** (778
43 80, www.botkyrka.se/lida).

A six-hour drive 400 kilometres (249 miles)
west of the city takes you to some proper ski
slopes at **Sälen** (0280 187 00, www.salen.se
or 0280 880 00, www.skistar.com/salen), in the
region of Dalarna. The best downhill skiing in
the country can be found at Sweden's biggest
resort, **Åre** (0647 177 00, www.skistar.com/are),
north-west of Stockholm, which is close enough
by plane for a long weekend trip.

Cheaper alternatives are the numerous skiing
day trips on offer. These start around 7am, and
after three hours in a bus you get six hours of
skiing, for an all-in price of around 300kr.

Hire a **kayak** and get paddling.

Skating on the edge

Few experiences measure up to the feeling of sailing smoothly across mirror-like ice atop two sharp blades, and there is no better natural skating environment than the frozen waterways around Stockholm in winter. Out on the ice, seasoned skaters can easily cover up to 150 kilometres (93 miles) a day.

The skating season starts as early as November when small lakes begin to freeze, but the main season is usually from December to March. It should be pointed out that long-distance skating on lake or sea ice requires caution and good preparation. You should have proper equipment, including ice prods (small, sharp devices used to drag yourself up from the water should the ice break), a whistle (to signal for help), an ice pike (designed to measure the quality of the ice) and a set of dry clothes (preferably stored in a plastic bag in your backpack to keep them dry and also to serve as a flotation device). Before you set out, always make sure you have up-to-date information on ice quality and weather forecasts.

The golden rule is never to skate alone: it's best to join a group with a guide. The **Stockholm Ice Skate Sailing & Touring Club** (768 23 78, www.sssk.se) is the largest skating organisation outside the Netherlands with about 11,000 members and is famed for its excursions. Before becoming a member, though, you have to pass a beginner's course; contact the club for more details. (The website **www.isplanket.com** has information in English).

Skating equipment can be rented in the city centre at **Slipspecialisten** (St Eriksgatan 15, 650 60 14). Alternatively, head out to Norrviken lake in Sollentuna (96 58 79), where equipment can be rented and there are ploughed courses of three to 14 kilometres (1.8 to 8.7 miles).

For a real challenge, try the 80-kilometre (50-mile) **Vikingarännet** race (Viking Run; 55 63 12 45, www.vikingarannet.com), from Uppsala to Stockholm. The race is only held when there's enough ice, usually in February.

Romme (0243 23 53 00, www.rommealpin.se) is best for slalom, and **Kungsberget** (0290 622 10, www.kungsberget.se) has a big half-pipe for snowboarders. The website **www.skiinfo.se** offers all the information you'll need (in various languages), including snow reports and accommodation options.

Swimming

Stockholm's swimming pools vary from modern versions with everything you could hope for and more, to beautiful Roman-inspired bathing temples. The latter category includes **Centralbadet** (*see p171*) and **Sturebadet** (*see p172*). Both have weights and machines and, for a little extra, you can get a massage. If you're into serious swimming, try **Eriksdalsbadet** or **Forsgrenska Badet**, both of which also have weights and machines. In summer, kids will love the outdoor pool **Vilda Vanadis** (*see p191*).

Of course, in summer you could just take a dip in the waters around the city. Thanks to a successful purification treatment in the 1960s, the waters are clean for swimming. Although you can swim almost everywhere, avoid dirty Karlbergskanalen (between Kungsholmen and Vasastaden) and leave the waves and the strong currents in Strömmen (east of Gamla Stan) to the fishermen. On Djurgården, try the small spit

Waldemarsudde (get off bus 47 or tram 7 at Ryssviken and follow the path south to the water's edge) on the southern shore, which is ideal for bathing. Green Långholmen has numerous bathing spots, such as the western side of the island or the crowded little beach near the former prison (now a youth hostel/hotel). On Kungsholmen, try the southern side at **Smedsuddsbadet** opposite Långholmen, which has a sandy beach that is very popular with families, or the south-western tip at **Fredhäll**, where you can climb down from Snoilskyvägen or Atterbomsvägen on to the rocks. **Stadshuset** (*see p104*), though not a designated spot, is also good for jumping in.

Eriksdalsbadet

Hammarby Slussväg 20, Södermalm (50 84 02 50/ www.eriksdalsbadet.com). T-bana Skanstull/bus 3, 4, 55, 74. **Open** *End Aug-end May* 6.30am-9pm Mon-Fri; 9am-5pm Sat; 9am-6pm Sun. *End May-end Aug* 6.30am-8pm Mon-Fri. **Admission** 65kr; 45kr concessions; 30kr 4-17s; free under-4s. **Credit** AmEx, DC, MC, V. **Map** p315 O8.
Recently rebuilt, this is the main arena for Swedish swimming competitions. It also has adventure pools for children and an outdoor pool.

Forsgrenska Badet

Medborgarplatsen 6, Södermalm (50 84 03 20). T-bana Medborgarplatsen/bus 59, 66. **Open** *Sept-*

May noon-9pm Mon; 6.30am-9pm Tue, Thur; 6.30am-6pm Wed; 6.30am-7pm Fri; 9am-4pm Sat; 10am-5pm Sun. Closed June-Aug. **Admission** 50kr; 30kr concessions; 15kr 7-17s; free under-7s. **Credit** MC, V. **Map** p314 L8.
Relaxed, 25-metre (82-foot) pool, open since 1939.

Liljeholmsbadet

Bergsunds Strand 2, Södermalm (668 67 80). T-bana Hornstull/bus 4, 40. **Open** *Sept-mid June* 7am-7pm Mon, Fri; 7am-4pm Tue, Wed; 7am-5pm Thur; 8am-2pm Sat. Closed June-Aug. **Admission** 50kr; 30kr concessions; 15kr 7-19s; free under-7s. **No credit cards. Map** p313 K2.
This old-style bohemian swimming pool is situated on a pontoon moored in western Södermalm. Monday is women only; Friday is men only.

Vanadisbadet

Sveavägen 142, Vasastaden (34 33 00/www. vanadisbadet.se). Bus 2, 40, 52, 515, 595. **Open** *May-Sept* 10am-6pm daily. **Admission** 55kr; free children under 80cm/31.5in. **No credit cards.**
An outdoor adventure pool with several water slides and other family-friendly stuff. A new hotel (*see p53*) and restaurant have been built.

Tennis

Eriksdal

Hammarby Slussväg 8, Södermalm (640 78 64/ www.hellas.se/tennis/eriksdal). T-bana Skanstull/bus 3, 4, 55, 74. **Open** *Courts* 7am-11pm Mon-Thur; 7am-9pm Fri; 9am-6pm Sat; 9am-11pm Sun. *Reception* 9am-4pm Mon-Fri. **Rates** 110kr-160kr/hr. **No credit cards. Map** p315 O8.

Outdoor courts in southern Södermalm, which are covered during winter.

Kungliga Tennishallen

Lidingövägen 75, Hjorthagen (459 15 00/www.kungl. tennishallen.com). Bus 73. **Open** 7am-11pm Mon-Thur; 7am-9pm Fri; 8am-8pm Sat; 8am-10pm Sun. **Rates** 235kr-255kr/hr. **Credit** AmEx, DC, MC, V.
The Stockholm Open tournament is played at this facility, which is also open to the public.

Tennisstadion

Fiskartorpsvägen 20, Hjorthagen (545 252 54/www. tennisstadion.se). T-bana Stadion/bus 55, 73. **Open** *Mid Aug-end June* 7am-11pm Mon-Thur; 7am-10pm Fri; 8am-8pm Sat; 8am-10pm Sun. *End June-mid Aug* 8am-9pm Mon-Thur; 8am-7pm Fri; 9am-5pm Sat, Sun. **Rates** *Indoors* 220kr-240kr/hr; 130kr students. *Outdoors* 100kr/hr. **Credit** MC, V.
A good place for both indoor and outdoor tennis.

Ten-pin bowling

Birka Bowling

Birkagatan 16, Vasastaden (30 50 10/www.birka bowling.com). T-bana St Eriksplan/bus 3, 4, 72. **Open** 11am-11pm Mon-Sat; 11am-10pm Sun. **Rates** *per lane* 220kr-320kr/hr. **Credit** AmEx, MC, V. **Map** p308 D3.

Kungsholmens Bowling

St Göransgatan 64, Kungsholmen (651 55 16/www. kungsholmensbowling.se). T-bana Fridhemsplan/bus 1, 3, 4, 59. **Open** noon-11pm Mon-Fri; 11am-11pm Sat; noon-8pm Sun. Limited opening hrs June-Aug; call for details. **Rates** *Per lane* 200kr-230kr/hr. **Credit** MC, V. **Map** p303 F2.

There's plenty of **skiing** on Stockholm's doorstep. *See p225.*

The big three

It rarely gets hotter in Stockholm than when local sports clubs clash. Three teams – **Hammarby**, **Djurgården** and **AIK** – dominate virtually all the professional sports in the capital, and they combine to make Stockholm a force in most major Swedish sports, including men's and women's football, ice hockey, handball and floorball.

The teams' traditional affiliations to certain neighbourhoods still stand. Hammarby is strongly connected to Södermalm (known as 'Bajenland', a reference to Hammarby's nickname, Bajen), where both people and pubs are decorated in its green and white colours. A 'sacred' place for hardcore Hammarby fans is the statue of legendary player Lennart 'Nacka' Skoglund at Katarina Bangata 24 (T-bana Skanstull), and a group of fans gather there to celebrate their hero each Christmas Eve.

AIK's fans mostly come from north-western Stockholm and their home stadium, Råsunda, is in Solna, north-west of Vasastaden. AIK's colours are black and yellow, and AIK fans are often referred to as 'the rats' by opposing fans. The reason for this connection is long forgotten, though one theory is that the black jerseys the team wore in the 1920s were so faded and grey that the players resembled rodents.

Djurgården supporters are generally from the wealthy northern suburbs and classy Östermalm. They normally play at the 1912 Olympic stadium, Stadion, but due to a dispute with the city council they have temporarily moved to Råsunda. The direct translation of the word 'Djurgården' is 'animal farm', which produces a predictable slew of insults from opposing fans.

Although there have been riots between AIK and Djurgården fans over the years, most conform to the 'ice-cold Swede' stereotype when it comes to discussing the latest results – keen, but keeping their voices down. Intra-city matches (or derbies) are always party-like affairs, with a great atmosphere and much prestige at stake. Football derbies are played at **Råsunda** (*see p230*), the national stadium and AIK's home ground; ice hockey derbies are played at **Globen** (*see p230*).

All three teams are among the country's best in football. AIK won the championship (*Allsvenskan*) in 1998, Hammarby won in 2001 and Djurgården took back-to-back titles in 2002 and 2003. In ice hockey, Hammarby has won eight championships (*Elitserien*) in its existence, but the last one was 50 years ago and, despite big efforts in recent years, the team now plays in the second division. Djurgården won the ice hockey title in 1999. Sadly, severe financial difficulties mean that the future of the AIK ice hockey team is in doubt. Hammarby and Djurgården also play in the premier handball league, while Hammarby has one of Sweden's most successful men's bandy teams, while AIK dominates the women's league.

AIK

(735 96 00/www.aik.se).
Founded 1891.
Colours black and yellow.
Stadiums *Football* Råsunda. *Ice hockey* Hovet. *Floorball* Solnahallen.
Famous players Börje Salming (ice hockey, Toronto Maple Leafs); Johan Mjällby (football, Celtic); Anders Limpar (football, ex-Arsenal).
Supporters' pubs *Football* East (Solnavägen 104, T-bana Solna Centrum), 1891 (run by the supporters at Råsunda Stadion) and Dick Turpin (Solnavägen 55, T-bana Solna

Södra Bowlinghallen

Hornsgatan 54, Södermalm (642 25 00/ www.bowlinghallen.com). T-bana Mariatorget/ bus 4, 43, 53, 66. **Open** noon-midnight daily. Limited opening hrs June-Aug; call for details. **Rates** *per lane* 190kr-270kr/hr. **Credit** AmEx, DC, MC, V. **Map** p314 K6.

Svea Bowlinghall

Sveavägen 118, Vasastaden (441 85 50/www. sveabowlinghall.se). T-bana Odenplan/bus 2, 4, 40, 42, 52, 72. **Open** noon-midnight Mon-Sat; noon-7pm Sun. **Rates** *per lane* 250kr-440kr/hr. **Credit** AmEx, DC, MC, V. **Map** p309 C5.

Spectator sports

All the daily newspapers provide decent listings (in Swedish) of the day's events and TV coverage, usually concentrating on football and hockey, but covering other sports too. Ticket brokers (booking fee 5kr-30kr) are a good source of information. The biggest ticket broker in Stockholm is **Biljett Direkt** (077 170 70 70, www.ticnet.se). Alternatively, you could try **Derbybutiken** (Mäster Samuelsgatan 46, 21 03 03) or

Centrum). *Ice hockey* Röda Kvarn (Arenavägen 33, T-bana Globen).

The only Swedish club to have won titles in bandy, football, ice hockey, floorball and handball. These days it has strong teams in football, floorball and women's bandy.

Djurgården

Football (545 158 00/www.dif.se). Ice hockey (556 108 00/www.difhockey.se). Handball (07 36 43 32 60/www.difhandboll.se).
Founded 1891.
Colours light and dark blue.
Stadiums *Football* Råsunda (Stadion is Djurgården's original home ground but they have temporarily moved their games to Råsunda stadium). *Ice hockey* Globen. *Handball* Eriksdalshallen.
Famous players Mats Sundin (ice hockey, Toronto Maple Leafs); Gösta 'Knivsta' Sandberg (represented the Swedish national team in football, bandy and ice hockey).
Supporters' pubs *Football* Esplanad (Karlavägen 36, T-bana Stadion), Läwenbräu (Fridhemsplan 2, T-bana Fridhemsplan). *Football/ice hockey* Östra Station/ Järnvägsrestaurangen (Valhallavägen 77, T-bana Tekniska Högskolan).

Djurgården has been strongest in ice hockey during the past decade, last winning the championship in 1999, but nowadays the football team is even stronger with titles in 2002 and 2003.

Hammarby

(462 88 25/462 88 10/www.hammarby-if.se/www.hammarbyfotboll.se).
Founded 1897.
Colours white and green.
Stadiums *Football* Söderstadion. *Bandy* Zinkensdamm. *Ice hockey* Hovet. *Handball* Eriksdalshallen.

Famous players Ronnie Hellström (football, ex-Kaiserslautern); Lennart 'Nacka' Skoglund (football, ex-Inter Milan).
Supporters' pubs *All sports* almost anywhere you can think of in Södermalm, but the most traditional spot is undoubtedly Kvarnen (Tjärhovsgatan 4, T-bana Medborgarplatsen, *see p139*). *Bandy* Zinkens krog (Ringvägen 14, T-bana Zinkensdamm/bus 4).

Hammarby is involved in pretty much everything – from boxing and athletics to bandy, speedway and floorball – although the focus is on football, especially after the rather unexpected championship title win in 2001. Bohemian Hammarby is traditionally famous for its cavalier playing style, and its fans' preference for a beer and a chat rather than a scrap has made the club very popular in recent years.

the box office at **Globen** (Globentorget 2, 077 131 00 00, www.globearenas.se).

Major stadiums

Globen

Arenavägen, Johanneshov (600 34 00/725 10 00/ box office 077 131 00 00/www.globearenas.se). T-bana Globen. **Box office** *In person* Mid Aug-mid May 9am-6pm Mon-Fri; 9am-4pm Sat. *Mid May-mid Aug* 9am-6pm Mon; 9am-4pm Tue-Fri. *By phone* (tickets to be collected from a Globen distributor; ask for nearest) 9am-7pm Mon-Fri;

10am-4pm Sat; 10am-3pm Sun. **Credit** (in person only) AmEx, DC, MC, V.

The most famous sports hall in Stockholm is the futuristic Globen – the huge white sphere south of Söder that can be seen from all over the city. It hosts major competitions in tennis, ice hockey, handball, showjumping and floorball (Sweden's fastest-growing sport), as well as concerts and other big events. With a capacity of just under 14,000, it is also the home arena of the Djurgården ice hockey team. Next door is **Söderstadion**, Hammarby football team's home ground, and **Hovet**, the home arena of ice hockey teams AIK and Hammarby.

Råsunda Stadion

Solnavägen 51, Solna (box office 735 09 35). T-bana Solna Centrum/bus 505. **Box office** 9am-4.30pm Mon-Thur; 9am-3pm Fri. **Credit** MC, V.

A short T-bana ride from the city centre, this is the national football stadium and home ground to AIK and (temporarily) Djurgården. Built in 1937, it has a capacity of just over 37,000. You can buy tickets for most Råsunda events at Globen (*see p229*).

Stockholms Stadion

Lidingövägen 1, Hjorthagen (50 82 83 62). T-bana Stadion/bus 4, 72, 73. **Map** p310 C8/C9.

The historic Stockholm Olympic Stadium, often known simply as Stadion, was built for the 1912 Olympic Games and is usually the home ground of Djurgården IF's football team (although they have temporarily moved their games to Råsunda Stadion). Architecturally, it's well preserved, but the old-fashioned facilities result in some practical difficulties. For tickets, contact Biljett Direkt (*see p228*) or other ticket outlets.

Bandy

Little known outside Scandinavia and Russia (although it originated in Britain), bandy (*innebandy* in Swedish) has re-established itself in Stockholm in the late 1990s when Hammarby IF became one of the nation's best teams. It is now Sweden's third largest sport (after ice hockey and football). To understand bandy, look first at ice hockey, then increase the number of players on each team from six to 11, remove most of the bulky pads, get rid of much of the violence, replace the puck with an orange, vinyl-covered sphere slightly larger than a racquetball and spread the players out on an outdoor rink roughly the size of a football field. Add an enthusiastic crowd carrying 'bandy briefcases', usually an old brown bag with a thermos filled with *kaffekask* (a mix of spirits and coffee), and you have bandy, a Swedish classic.

The home rink of Hammarby IF is **Zinkensdamms Idrottsplats** (*see p224*). The bandy season runs here from November through to March.

Football

Stockholm has three teams in Sweden's premier Allsvenskan league – Hammarby, Djurgården and AIK. Both Hammarby and Djurgården also have excellent women's teams. Hammarby's stadium, **Söderstadion** at (Globen; *see p229*), isn't huge (capacity 16,000), but the fans create a fantastic atmosphere. Djurgården and AIK play their home matches at a bigger arena, **Råsunda** (*see above*), which is seldom sold out so you can buy tickets on the spot. An exception are derby matches, which are always played at Råsunda. The season runs from April to November. For more on the city's teams, *see p228* **The big three**.

Handball

Handball arouses enormous interest in Sweden because of the success of the national team. Since Hammarby and Djurgården joined the premier league in 2002, interest in handball in the capital has increased markedly. Both city teams play in **Eriksdalshallen** in southern Söder (Ringvägen 68-70, 50 84 64 90), except when they play each other – on those occasions they play in the much bigger **Hovet** (*see p229* **Globen**). The handball season runs from September to April.

Eriksdalsbadet. *See p226.*

Spotlight on Sven

As we went to press in early autumn of 2004, Sven-Göran Eriksson's future as the manager of England's national football team was hanging in the balance. Sweden's most famous name in international sport had weathered a stormy summer of scandalous revelations and all eyes were on the 2006 World Cup qualifiers.

Known affectionately as 'Svennis' in his homeland, the smalltown boy from Torsby who had failed to fulfil his own ambitions to become a star player, instead rose through the managerial ranks. He tasted success managing clubs like IFK Gothenburg, Benfica, Sampdoria, Roma and Lazio, but became a Swedish national hero when he was crowned England's manager in 2001, following Kevin Keegan's resignation after England lost their opening World Cup 2002 qualifier against Germany at Wembley.

Eriksson won the next four qualifiers, including the historic 5-1 demolition of Germany in Munich, and England came back from the depths of despair to win the group and book their ticket to Japan. But after an inspired victory over old rivals Argentina, Sven's star began to wane as England lost in the quarter-finals to Brazil.

Taking England to the last eight wasn't enough for a wildly expectant public and critics soon began to fill as many column inches with Sven's off-the-field antics as his prowess on the sidelines. As the first non-English manager to claim the post, the mild-mannered Swede was always going to arouse the curiosity of English fans, and the British press dug through his past relentlessly.

Reports of an affair with fellow Swede Ulrika Jonsson did wonders for his smooth-talking image but dented his upright reputation. And super Sven was seen as a traitor when he flirtatiously talked shop with Chelsea. But all was forgiven when he signed a new £4 million per year contract in 2004 that locked him in with the England team until 2008.

After that, things seemed to go downhill again. The outcome to Euro 2004 was disappointingly mediocre. Eriksson and his players reached the final eight but were under fire on their return from Portugal. Another storm was also brewing: claims emerged that Sven had cheated again on his long-term partner with a secretary at the Football Association. Moreover, he was accused of lying about it to his employers. But in the end it was the FA that suffered – it emerged that they had offered to dish the dirt on Eriksson's affair to the *News of the World* if the paper covered up chief executive Mark Palios' relationship with the same woman. The story ripped through the tabloids and hit the FA right where it hurt.

Following an enquiry, Eriksson was cleared of misconduct and he set out on the road to his second World Cup with England. After a rocky start, the highlight of the 2006 sporting calendar could well be Sven's desire to prove that he is the man to bring victory back to English football.

Horse racing & showjumping

The **Stockholm International Horse Show** (*see p186*) in November/December is a three-day show featuring dressage, four-in-hand driving and showjumping. For trotting (*trav* in Swedish), in which horses pull a small two-wheeled vehicle and driver, go to **Solvalla** in Sundbyberg (635 90 00, www.solvalla.se). Solvalla also hosts the prestigious two-million-kronor **Elitloppet** race during the last weekend in May.

For horse racing, **Täby Galopp** (756 02 30, www.tabygalopp.se), 20 kilometres (12 miles) north of Stockholm, is Scandinavia's premier track. Racing takes place throughout the year in a variety of events, from dirt racing in May to the top flat and jump races in summer and autumn.

Ice hockey

Ishockey is the most popular sport in winter, with elite teams **Djurgården** and **AIK** drawing big crowds to the Globen (*see p229*) for their matches. As with football, the derbies are the biggest games of the year. The season runs from September to April.

Tennis

The flagship event is the **Stockholm Open** (*see p186*) at the beginning of October, although the event was much more popular 15 years ago when Stefan Edberg and Mats Wilander were attracting huge crowds. It takes place at **Kungliga Tennishallen** (*see p226*) and is easy to get tickets for.

Arts & Entertainment

Theatre & Dance

A home-spun theatre scene but cutting-edge dance.

Theatre

Stockholm is the heart of Swedish theatre: the number of theatres in relation to the city's population is well above the European average and there's no shortage of high-quality productions putting them to good use. What the theatre scene lacks, though, is an international outlook – unfortunately, there are few guest performances from foreign groups or actors. In addition, Swedish theatre rests heavily on a naturalistic tradition, and you will really have to look hard for daring, innovative styles.

Kungliga Dramatiska Teatern (*see p234*), or Dramaten, is Sweden's national theatre, established in 1788. Over the years it has boasted a large number of superb actors and directors – the master of them being, of course, Ingmar Bergman. Although he has retired from Dramaten (one can never be too sure, though, he has retired before), his spirit pervades the decorative Jugendstil building at Nybroplan. Dramaten has several stages for its productions, ranging from safe, traditional plays to modern drama.

The city's other key theatre, **Stockholms Stadsteatern** (*see p234*), located in Kulturhuset, also has numerous stages, but it has a wider repertoire than Dramaten. Lately, Stadsteatern has been hosting more risk-taking theatre. Sweden has an excellent track record for theatre for children, and Stadsteatern has an ambitious children's programme.

The heroes of Swedish theatre are Ingmar Bergman and August Strindberg (*see also p236* **Anarchy in August**), Sweden's national author. Strindberg started his own theatre in the 1900s (Strindbergs Intima Teatern; *see p237*) and his plays are still performed regularly in the capital. A more recent central figure in Swedish theatre is the prolific and often controversial playwright **Lars Norén**, whose major work is the trilogy *The Death of Classes*, of which the third part hasn't yet been completed.

There are also numerous smaller groups and stages all over the city. Quality varies but there are certainly gems worth seeking out, particularly in Vasastaden and Södermalm, where more experimental shows can be found.

Musicals are immensely popular; you'll find classic English originals translated and produced in Swedish, as well as home-grown

fare. Private producers dominate this commercial genre. In February 2005 the curtain goes up for *Mamma Mia* at Cirkus.

Many theatres close their doors during some or all of the summer months. However, Dramaten has a summer programme, which in 2004 included a very successful version of *King Lear*, followed by *Chanson Suicide*, a one-man cabaret by Rikard Wolff.

THEATRE IN SUMMER

In summer, the performance scene transforms as many venues close and new ones open, often outdoors. The biggest is **Parkteatern**, which presents home-grown and international theatre and dance in parks all over the city, including Djurgården and Humlegården. It is organised by Stadsteatern (*see p234*) and the standard is high – and, best of all, it's free. In addition to the theatrical repertoire, the city's parks also play host to contemporary circus, dance and children's performances. Find a programme at www.stadsteatern.stockholm.se/parkteatern. Bring a blanket and a picnic and head for the park in good time, as hundreds of people turn out.

Outside theatre can also be found at **Lasse i parken** (*see p148*), a lovely old café in Södermalm mostly presenting comedies in the *Shirley Valentine* mould. On rainy days a shelter is erected and blankets are loaned out.

Don't miss the summer-only season of theatre, opera and dance at **Drottningholms Slottsteater** (box office 660 82 25, www.drottningholmsslottsteater.dtm.se). The 18th-century theatre next to the royal castle offers top-quality performances. There are only a few dates, so advance booking is essential. The lush park surroundings of the royal castle are exceptional and worth a trip in themselves (*see p244*).

OTHER LANGUAGES

For the majority of casual visitors, though, all this is likely to be of little interest, since almost all theatre is performed in Swedish. Sometimes it is, of course, possible to enjoy a well-acted or well-known play without getting the words. Alternatively, Teater Pero (*see p237*) has a long tradition of mime theatre.

For English speakers there is the **English Theatre Company** (*see p234*), which stages very conventional productions. Spanish-speaking **Aliasteatern** (*see p234*) has gradually moved towards Hispanic works translated into Swedish, though there are still occasional Spanish-language performances. Touring productions in various languages appear quite regularly.

Stockholm is also home to one of the world's most interesting nouveau cirque groups, **Cirkus Cirkör** (53 19 98 30, www.cirkor.se), which has a large production centre and school in the southern suburb of Norsborg. Co-productions have included *Romeo and Juliet* (with Dramaten), *Trix* (with Orionteatern) and, most recently, *Hjälp!* (with Parkteatern).

INFORMATION AND TICKETS

'På stan', the weekly Friday supplement of newspaper *Dagens Nyheter* (www.dn.se/pastan) and website www.alltomstockholm.se both have up-to-date theatre listings (in Swedish). Most venues have an up-to-date website, and some have information in English. The major tourist office is located in Kungsträdgården.

Tickets are usually sold at the venue (or via their website). For major venues and productions, you can also book at **Box Office** (*see p178*) or via **Biljett Direkt** (077 170 70 70, www.ticnet.se, MC, V accepted). Most theatres are closed on Mondays.

Major venues

The largest commercial theatre, showing large-scale musicals and comedies (in Swedish), is **Oscarsteatern** (Kungsgatan 63, box office 20 50 00). Other commercial theatres include **Göta Lejon** (Götgatan 55, box office 643 67 00), **Maximteatern** (Karlaplan 4, box office 643 40

Kungliga Dramatiska Teatern.
See p234.

23), **Intiman** (Odengatan 81, box office 30 12 50) and **China Teatern** (Berzelii park 9, box office 56 63 23 50). **Cirkus** (Djurgårdsslätten 43-45, next to Skansen, box office 660 10 20, www.cirkus.se) also presents large-scale shows.

Södra Teatern (*see p215*) is mainly a music venue, but it occasionally hosts good theatre shows.

Kulturhuset

Sergels Torg, Norrmalm (box office 50 62 02 00/ www.kulturhuset.stockholm.se). T-bana T-Centralen/ bus 47, 52, 56, 59, 69. **Box office** *Winter* noon-7pm Tue-Fri; noon-6pm Sat; noon-4pm Sun. *Summer* noon-3pm Tue-Sat. **Tickets** 100kr-190kr. **Credit** AmEx, DC, MC, V. **Map** p305 G7.

Kulturhuset, or the House of Culture, turns 30 in 2004 and is one of the most prominent modern buildings in Stockholm, designed by architect Peter Celsing. The building certainly lives up to its name: there are three galleries, a library (with a wide selection of foreign newspapers), activities for children, cafés and a terrace with a formidable city view. There are two stages in the building – Kilen and Hörsalen – showing a wide spectrum of theatre, dance and music, with Kilen showing the more experimental work. The International Writers' Stage has hosted productions of works by Isabel Allende, Julia Kristeva and Umberto Eco. The building also houses the Stockholms Stadsteatern (*see below*), with its six stages.

Kungliga Dramatiska Teatern

Nybroplan, Östermalm (box office 667 06 80/ www.dramaten.se). T-bana Östermalmstorg or Kungsträdgården/bus 47, 55, 62, 69, 76. **Box office** *Sept-July* noon-7pm Mon-Sat; noon-4pm Sun. Closed Aug. **Tickets** 120kr-280kr. **Credit** AmEx, DC, MC, V. **Map** p305 F8.

The Royal Dramatic Theatre, known as Dramaten, is Sweden's number one theatre, and some of the country's finest actors tread its boards. Ingmar Bergman has now retired but he has been the driving force behind Dramaten since the early 1960s, directing a colossal number of productions. The main stage mounts the classics of Shakespeare and Strindberg, mixed with avant-garde dramatic works. The interior is glorious, and spending the intermission in the mirror hall or on the balcony is a real treat. When the bulbs outside show a red light, it means that the main stage is sold out. Dramaten's other stage, Elverket (Linnégatan 69) – a converted power station – has a younger profile, producing interesting modern drama, often with dance or nouveau cirque elements.

Stockholms Stadsteatern

Sergels Torg, Norrmalm (box office 50 62 02 00/ www.stadsteatern.stockholm.se). T-bana T-Centralen/ bus 47, 52, 56, 59. **Box office** *Winter* noon-7pm Tue-Fri; noon-6pm Sat; noon-4pm Sun. *Summer* noon-3pm Tue-Sat. **Tickets** 45kr-210kr. **Credit** AmEx, DC, MC, V. **Map** p305 G7.

With six stages in all, plus its successful summer Parkteatern programme (*see p232*), Stadsteatern is one of Scandinavia's largest theatrical institutions. Like Dramaten, it has a largely conventional repertoire. There are exceptions, though, such as the hugely successful *Det allra viktigaste*, an extraordinary four-hour play with a gay theme, directed by Suzanne Osten. The smaller stages, Backstage/Lilla Scenen and Unga Klara, offer more experimental drama which is aimed at a younger audience. The Marionetteatern puppet theatre, created in the 1950s by puppet master Michael Meschke, has recently found its home at Stadsteatern. The shows are aimed mainly, but by no means only, at children. The adjacent puppet museum, Marionettmuseet, contains more than 4,000 puppets from all over the world.

Smaller venues & groups

Aliasteatern

Hälsingegatan 3, Vasastaden (box office 32 82 90/ www.aliasteatern.com). T-bana St Eriksplan or Odenplan/bus 4, 47, 72. **Box office** *Aug-June* noon-6pm Mon-Fri. Closed July. **Tickets** 60kr-250kr. **No credit cards. Map** p308 D4.

This small theatre has been Stockholm's link to Spanish-language drama from Spain and Latin America since 1978. In the past decade, however, it has mainly (but not exclusively) performed the works of Spanish-speaking dramatists in Swedish. The programme also includes music and children's plays.

Dockteatern Tittut

Lundagatan 33, Södermalm (box office 720 75 99/ www.dockteatern-tittut.com). T-bana Zinkensdamm/ bus 4, 66. **Box office** *Sept-May* 9am-5pm Mon-Fri. Closed June-Aug. **Tickets** 60kr. **No credit cards. Map** p313 K4.

This puppet theatre in Söder has been making high-quality shows for children (aged from two) for over 25 years, combining puppet and shadow play. Performances are held in the daytime.

The English Theatre Company

(662 41 33 or 660 11 59/www.englishtheatre.se). **Tickets** 220kr-300kr. **Credit** varies.

This is Stockholm's only theatre group presenting theatre in English; there is an annual production of *A Christmas Carol*. Check out the website (in English) for a current schedule.

Fria Teatern

Önskehemsgatan 15, Högdalsplan, Högdalen (box office 99 22 60/www.friateatern.se). T-bana Högdalen/bus 143, 165, 744, 745, 746. **Box office** 10am-4pm Mon-Fri; 10am-7pm on performance days. **Tickets** 70kr-200kr.

This suburban theatre has been threatened by financial crisis ever since it opened in 1968, but it always manages to survive, keeping its political edge and showing high-quality theatre for adults and children. A smaller affiliated stage, Lilla Scenen, at Bergsgatan 11 on Kungsholmen, opened in 2002.

Parkteatern's free summer theatre – just bring a blanket and a picnic. *See p232.*

Fylkingen

*Münchenbryggeriet, Torkel Knutsonsgatan 2,
Södermalm (84 54 43/www.fylkingen.se). T-bana
Mariatorget/bus 4, 43, 55, 66.* **Box office** 10am-
5pm Mon-Fri. **Tickets** free-80kr. **No credit cards.**
Map p304 K6.

Founded way back in 1933, Fylkingen is the place
to be if you're into new music (*see p216*) and intermedia art. It's always been committed to new and
experimental forms: 'happenings', musical theatre
and text-sound compositions were prominent in the
1960s. In recent years, more and more performance
art and dance have been presented. Fylkingen holds
several ambitious festivals every year.

Intercult

*Offices: Nytorgsgatan 15, Södermalm (box office
644 10 23/www.intercult.se).* **Box office** 9am-5pm
Mon-Fri. **Tickets** 100kr-220kr. **Credit** varies,
depending on where performance is held.

Intercult is more of a production group than a conventional theatre, with a strong international focus.
It's a highly political forum – with the spotlight
mainly trained on the Balkans and the Baltic region
– and it holds a wide range of cultural gatherings and
guest performances.

Judiska Teatern

*Djurgårdsbrunnsvägen 59, Gärdet (box office 667 90
13/information 660 02 71/www.judiskateatern.org).
Bus 69.* **Box office** *Oct-May* 6-7pm Wed, Thur;
2-7pm Fri; 5-6pm Sat; 3-4pm Sun. Closed June-Sept.
Tickets 90kr-180kr. **Credit** AmEx, MC, V.

The Jewish Theatre is not as focused on religion
as the name might suggest. The actors perform

finely crafted poetic theatre, mainly new work, in a
beautiful old building with a super-modern interior.
Well worth a visit.

Moment

*Gubbängstorget 117, Gubbängen (box office 50 85
01 28/www.moment.org.se). T-bana Gubbängen.*
Tickets 160kr. **No credit cards.**

This cultural centre, a converted 1940s cinema in the
suburb of Gubbägen, is run by a group of young
artists and directors. The programme includes interesting new drama, music, art exhibitions and cinema.
It's 20 minutes by T-bana from the city centre.

Orionteatern

*Katarina Bangata 77, Södermalm (information
640 29 70/box office 643 88 80/643 37 16/
www.orionteatern.se). T-bana Skanstull/bus 3, 59,
76.* **Box office** *Sept-Midsummer* 2-6pm Tue, Wed;
2-7pm Thur, Fri; noon-7pm Sat; noon-4pm Sun.
Closed Midsummer-Aug. **Tickets** 100kr-230kr.
Credit DC, MC, V. **Map** p315 N10.

The Orion Theatre, Stockholm's largest avant-garde
theatre company, was formed in 1983 and is one of
the most interesting groups in Stockholm. It has
collaborated with the likes of Peking Opera from
Shanghai and Theatre de Complicité from London.
The building, once a huge factory, is an unusual and
effective theatre space, holding almost 500 people.

Strindbergs Intima Teater

*Barnhusgatan 20, Norrmalm (box office 20 08 43/
www.strindbergsintimateater.se). T-bana T-Centralen
or Hötorget/bus 1, 47, 53, 65.* **Box office** open 2hrs
before play starts. **No credit cards.** **Map** p304 F5.

Anarchy in August

The prolific dramatist, author, poet and sometime painter and photographer August Strindberg managed to provoke controversy and outrage throughout his life, and long after his death. His ideas were so ahead of their time that his works were alternately censored, banned and panned. Perhaps not surprising for a man who wanted to 'blow up the entire bastion of culture'.

Born in Stockholm in 1849, Strindberg was the son of a shipping merchant, Carl Oscar Strindberg, and his former servant, Ulrika Norling. Strindberg wrote later about his unhappy childhood – his authoritarian father and his mother's early death, both of which cast a long shadow over his life and work. He studied at Uppsala University but left without gaining a degree, and then found work as a librarian, teacher, journalist and critic. At the time Scandinavia was at the forefront of world culture, with the widespread fame of Ibsen in theatre and Munch in painting, both of whom deeply influenced the young Strindberg. In 1872 he wrote his first major play, *Master Olof*, a historical drama that defied the period's social and theatrical conventions.

In 1877 Strindberg married Baroness Siri von Essen, and together they had three children. His breakthrough as a novelist came two years later with *The Red Room*, referring to one of the private dining rooms in **Berns Salonger** (*see p114*). Using a then unknown colloquial style, he laid bare contemporary society.

In 1883, feeling unappreciated in Sweden, Strindberg moved abroad. He was to wander fairly aimlessly through bohemian Europe for the next 15 years, often longing for and writing about his homeland. During this time he wrote some of the works that were to gain him not only fame but also his perhaps undeserved reputation as a misogynist, such as *Miss Julie* and *The Father*, exploring – well ahead of their time – the psychology of gender roles.

In 1888 he wrote in a letter, 'If I had to define my present standpoint it would be: Atheist, Christ hater, Anarchist... PS. Woman, being small and foolish and therefore evil, should be suppressed.' With friends like Zola and Nietzsche, it's hardly surprising that he felt that way.

However, Strindberg had a penchant for unconventional relationships with independent young women. After his divorce in 1892, he had a brief and unhappy marriage to Austrian

journalist Frieda Uhl, and later married actress Harriet Bosse, whom he divorced in 1904. In the 1890s Strindberg also began to gain the international success that he longed for.

In 1894 the onset of his famous 'inferno period' was to gain him the reputation, again perhaps rather unfairly, of a madman. Influenced by 18th-century Swedish mystic Emanuel Swedenborg, he became fascinated by the occult and alchemy. At the same time he was also very involved in painting and photography, experimenting with symbolism and even prefiguring the surrealists. The largest collection of his paintings can be found at the **Nordiska Museet** (*see p84*).

In 1897 Strindberg returned to Stockholm, where he was to stay until his death. His flirtation with the occult had caused a creative sea change, and he began to write dozens of expressionistic plays – works that no one knew how to stage, let alone understand. Dramas such as *A Dream Play* were to inspire the later development of absurdist theatre. In 1907 he founded his own theatre, the **Intima** (*see p235*), no doubt in an attempt to have his plays presented sensitively. In 1908 he moved to what was to be his last home, 'the Blue Tower', at Drottninggatan 85, now the **Strindbergsmuseet** (*see p79*). A statue of him stands in nearby Tegnérlunden park.

On his last birthday, in 1912, Strindberg was finally hailed as a writer of the people when he was awarded the Anti-Nobel Prize with money raised by national subscription to compensate him for not winning the Nobel Prize itself. He died later that year on 14 May.

Founded by August Strindberg in 1907, this small theatre used to show the dramatist's plays exclusively. Nowadays the programme, coordinated by Strindbergsmuseet (*see p79*), is more varied and includes guest performances and theatre for children. For more about Strindberg's life, *see p236* **Anarchy in August**.

Teater Brunnsgatan Fyra

Brunnsgatan 4, Norrmalm (box office 10 70 50/ www.brunnsgatanfyra.nu). T-bana Östermalmstorg/ bus 1, 2, 55, 56. **Box office** *Sept-June* 5-7pm Tue-Sat; 2-4pm Sun. Closed July, Aug. **Tickets** 180kr-220kr. **No credit cards. Map** p305 E7.

Kristina Lugn – one of Sweden's best, and best-known, poets and dramatists – took over this small theatre when its creator, actor Allan Edwall, died. Its modest appearance is not to be mistaken for modest material; some of Sweden's most prominent actors and dramatists can be found working in this stone cellar, among them Erland Josephson, Lena Nyman and Staffan Westerberg. Often sold out.

Teater Galeasen

Slupskjulsvägen 32, Skeppsholmen (box office 611 00 30/611 09 20/www.galeasen.se). Bus 65. **Box office** *Mid Jan-June, Aug-mid Dec* 10am-4pm (10am-8pm on performance nights). Closed July, mid Dec-mid Jan. **Tickets** 150kr-200kr. **Credit** MC, V. **Map** p306 H9.

In the 1980s and early 1990s this was the hip spot for theatregoers, and gallons of red wine were consumed in the name of art. Nowadays, things have changed and actors of that generation are now household names. But Galeasen has continued to be a nursery for young actors and directors, and the work on show here is still high-quality.

Teater Giljotin

Torsgatan 41, Vasastaden (box office 30 30 00/ www.teatergiljotin.com). T-bana St Eriksplan/bus 3, 4, 72, 77. **Box office** 1hr before play. **Tickets** 160kr-220kr. **No credit cards. Map** p308 D3.

Virpi Pahkinen.
See p238.

Led by director Kia Berglund and musician Richard Borggård, this outfit produces well-directed and often new Nordic plays.

Teater Pero

Sveavägen 114, Vasastaden (box office 612 99 00/ www.pero.se). T-bana Rådmansgatan/bus 2, 4, 42, 52, 53, 72. **Box office** 11am-2pm Sat; 1hr before play. **No credit cards. Map** p309 C6.

Teater Pero has a strong tradition of mime, and has been producing shows for children and adults for over 20 years. When the company is on tour, the stage is let to guest performers.

Teater Scenario

Odengatan 62, Vasastaden (box office 643 71 82/ www.teaterscenario.com). T-bana Odenplan/bus 2, 4, 40, 42, 53, 72. **Box office** 1hr before play. Closed mid June-mid Aug. **Tickets** 80kr-150kr. **No credit cards. Map** p309 D5.

A small theatre company featuring a new generation of exciting dramatists, notably Daniela Kullman and Dennis Magnusson.

Teater Tribunalen

Hornsgatan 92, Södermalm (box office 84 94 33/ www.tribunalen.com). T-bana Zinkensdamm or Mariatorget/bus 4, 43, 55, 66. **Box office** *Early Aug-May* 1hr before performance. Closed June-early Aug. **Tickets** 100kr-160kr. **No credit cards. Map** p314 K5.

Angry, political, radical theatre with an ideological inheritance from the 1970s, and often loved by the critics. Brecht and Fassbinder are the house gods.

Dance

The Stockholm dance scene is a lot more vibrant and international in outlook than the city's theatrical output, at least outside the larger, more traditional institutions. Plus, for non-Swedish speakers, dance constitutes a considerably more appealing option than Swedish theatre.

Stockholm has a prestigious dance history. The **Kungliga Balett** (Royal Ballet), located at the Kungliga Operan (*see p238*), is one of the world's oldest ballet companies, founded in 1733. The dance repertoire at Operan is dominated by conventional classics. For an edgier style, consider **Stockholm 59 North** (www.stockholm59north.com), a small group of dancers from the Royal Ballet, who stage their own more modern productions, mainly performed outside the Operan. The **Cullberg Balett** (www.cullbergbaletten.com), a truly international company with a solid reputation, is also based in Stockholm. Mats Ek, founder Birgit Cullberg's son, no longer leads the company, but he is still active as a freelance choreographer.

Stockholm's dance audience has grown steadily during the last decade, thanks largely to **Dansens Hus** (House of Dance; *see p238*), which opened in 1990. Its extensive programme includes visiting companies from around the world, and the quality is consistently high. The award-winning Finnish-Swede choreographer Kenneth Kvarnström took over the helm in 2004. Dansens Hus hosts some of the most interesting and creative local choreographers around, including Cristina Caprioli, Örjan Andersson, Virpi Pahkinen and Helena Franzén; watch out also for young Malin Hellkvist Sellén. **Moderna Dansteatern** (*see below*) is smaller, but has been the home for freelance groups of dancers and choreographers for over 20 years.

Dance theatre also has a strong position in Sweden – award-winning Birgitta Egerbladh with her Pina Bausch-inspired, humorous choreography now has her base at Stockholms Stadsteatern (*see p234*). For one week in August, outdoor festival **Parkteatern** (*see p232*) is devoted to dance.

For dance listings, check the Swedish-language magazine *Danstidningen* (www.danstidningen.se) or 'På Stan', the Friday supplement of *Dagens Nyheter*.

Venues

Dansens Hus

12-14 Barnhusgatan, Norrmalm (box office 50 89 90 90/www.dansenshus.se). T-bana Hötorget or T-Centralen/bus 1, 47, 53, 69. **Box office** *Mid Aug-Midsummer* noon-6pm Mon-Fri; Sat, Sun when there is a performance. Closed Midsummer-mid Aug. **Tickets** 160kr-270kr. **Credit** AmEx, DC, MC, V. **Map** p305 E6.

The House of Dance is the major venue for Swedish dance. This is where you'll find the Cullberg Ballet when they're in town, and the international guest list might include the likes of Anna Teresa de Keersmaeker's company Rosas, Nederlands Dans Theater and Akram Khan. The Swedish dance group Bounce! has also been a huge success here, with its funny, street dance-inspired shows, drawing a large and not necessarily habituated audience.

Kungliga Operan

Gustav Adolfs Torg, Norrmalm (box office 24 82 40/ www.operan.se). T-bana Kungsträdgården/bus 2, 43, 55, 59, 62, 76. **Box office** *Sept-May* noon-6pm Mon-Fri; noon-3pm Sat. Closed June-Aug. **Tickets** 40kr-560kr. **Credit** AmEx, DC, MC, V. **Map** p305 G7. The Royal Opera is home to Sweden's finest classical company, the Royal Ballet. The dancers are outstanding and, though the repertoire is usually traditional, there is occasionally some modern work shown. For example, eminent choreographer Birgitta Egerbladh has visited, flexing the feet of some astonished classical dancers. The interior is completely over the top – the chandelier weighs two tons and the Golden Room is beautiful. *See also p220*.

Moderna Dansteatern

Slupskjulsvägen 32, Skeppsholmen (box office 611 32 33/www.mdt.a.se). Bus 65. **Box office** opens 30mins before performance. **Tickets** 150kr. **No credit cards. Map** p306 H9.

The small Modern Dance Theatre was founded by Margaretha Åsberg, the grande dame of Swedish dance, and has single-handedly provided a space for postmodern dance in Stockholm. More recently, performance art has also found a refuge here.

Dansens Hus.

Trips Out of Town

Trips Out of Town

Gulf of Bothnia

Björkö (p267)
Arholma (p263)

Väddö

Hallstavik

Erken

Norrtälje

Rimbo

Blidö

Yxlan

Norra Ljusterö

Söara Ljusterö

Finnhamn (p259)

Svartsö

Stora Kalholmen (p2nn)

E18

Åkersberga

Vallentuna

Arlanda Airport

Upplands Väsby

Storvreta

Björklinge

Uppsala (p250)

E4

Märsta

Sigtuna (p249)

Steninge Slott (p246)

Rosersbergs Slott (p246)

E18

Kungsängen

Skoklosters Slott (p246)

Bålsta

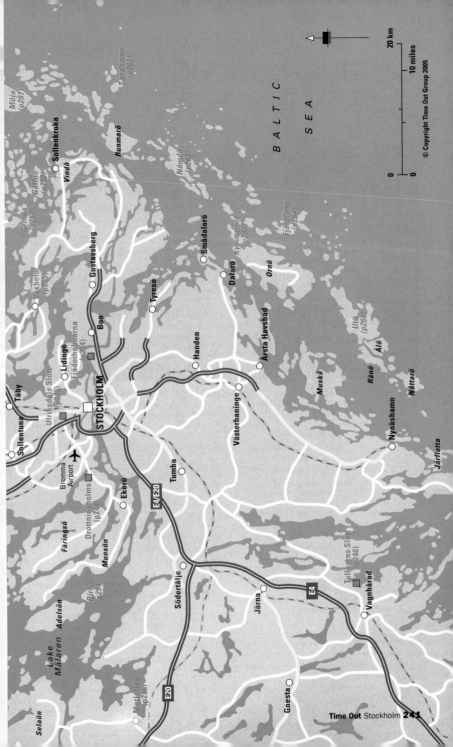

BALTIC SEA

© Copyright Time Out Group 2005

20 km
10 miles

Möja (p261)
Sandhamn (p262)
Sollenkroka
Vindö
Runmarö
Gällnö (p258)
Grinda (p257)
Vaxholm (p255)
Nämdö (p263)
Gustavsberg
Boo
Fjäderholmarna (p264)
Lidingö
Ulriksdals Slott (p246)
Täby
Sollentuna
STOCKHOLM
Bromma Airport
Drottningholm (p240)
Ekerö
Färingsö
Munsön
Birka (p251)
Adelsön
Selaön
Lake Mälaren
Mariefred (p246)
E20
Södertälje
Tumba
E4/E20
Tyresö
Handen
Västerhaninge
Ärsta Havsbad
Dalarö
Smådalarö
Kymmendö (p261)
Ornö
Fjärdlång (p261)
Muskö
Utö (p265)
Ranö
Älö
Nåttarö
Järna
Tullgarns Slott (p246)
Vagnhärad
E4
Nynäshamn
Järflotta
Gnesta

Getting Started

Get ready to set sail.

With a beautiful archipelago (*skärgård*) made up of tens of thousands of pine-covered islands, rocks and skerries, and a bounty of historical castles and palaces on its doorstep, Stockholm is tailor-made for weekend getaways.

To the west of Stockholm, you'll find an area rich in history, and dotted with castles and palaces, the grandest being the royal family's home of **Drottningholm**, an hour's trip by boat from the city. **Mariefred** boasts Gustav Vasa's fortress of **Grippsholms Slott**, while other palaces occupy scenic positions along the shores of Lake Mälaren. North of Stockholm lies the former Viking stronghold of **Sigtuna**, one of the oldest towns in Sweden, and beyond that is historic **Uppsala**, dominated by its university and cathedral. You can also explore Viking remains on the island of **Birka**. For all, *see pp244-253* **Day Trips**.

The Stockholm archipelago begins just a few miles east of the capital, covering about 140 kilometres (90 miles) from north to south. Only 150 of the islands are inhabited, but many Stockholmers have summerhouses in the archipelago and visitor numbers swell in the warmer months, especially July. The landscape varies tremendously, from the more populated, thickly wooded inner archipelago to the bare,

flat rocks of the central and outer islands. We've highlighted certain islands within three sections: the **Central Archipelago** (nearest to Stockholm, and best if you have only a spare day or so), and the remoter **Southern Archipelago** and **Northern Archipelago**.

Further into the Baltic lie other attractions, notably the large island of **Gotland** to the south, one of Sweden's most popular summer destinations with the beautiful medieval city of Visby. On the other side of the Baltic Sea are Finland and the Baltic states; if you have time, take a weekend ferry to **Helsinki** or **Tallinn**.

WHEN TO VISIT

The archipelago is best visited from mid June to mid August – during the rest of the year many hotels, restaurants and other facilities are closed, ferries are few and far between, and some islands pretty much shut down to visitors. But don't let that put you off. Some islands are open all year round and the archipelago during the autumn and winter is considerably calmer. However, don't forget to call and book in advance as some of the year-round places only open if there is a booking.

During the summer the archipelago often gets more sunshine than the mainland, but it's still a good idea to pack a raincoat and sweater.

Sunscreen and mosquito repellent are also recommended, and ticks like the archipelago so don't forget tweezers. Shops and restaurants can be a rarity in the smaller and remoter places, so you might need to take your own food supply with you, and cashpoints are also few and very far between.

INFORMATION

The tourist office (*see p288*) produces a useful free brochure to accommodation in the archipelago, covering hotels, B&Bs, youth hostels and camping. **Skärgårdsstiftelsen** (Archipelago Foundation, 440 56 00, www.skargardsstiftelsen.se), set up in 1959, offers plenty of information via its website; other useful sites are www.dess.se and www.skargardshandlarna.com (both Swedish only).

RIGHT TO ROAM

Sweden has a long tradition of allowing public access to state and privately owned land. These rights are collectively known as *allemansrätten*. The rules can get complicated but if you follow the basic guidelines of 'do not disturb or destroy', and the following tips, you should be OK.

● You can walk or cycle where you like, as long as you don't damage nature, cross cultivated fields or come too close to people's homes.

● You can camp on private property at a reasonable distance from buildings for 24 hours, without asking permission. In nature reserves you can camp for 48 hours on the same spot, after which you need permission.

● Campfires are allowed, except during very dry spells. Don't cut limbs from living trees and avoid lighting fires on flat rocks, since this can crack them. Always put out any fire before you leave.

● You can swim or boat where you like – but not from private docks. Fishing with a rod and reel is allowed from the shore, but not with nets or from boats.

Getting there

The easiest way to get around is by ferry – we've listed the main companies below. If you want to visit a lot of islands, Waxholmsbolaget's 16-day **Båtluffarkortet** (Archipelago Pass; 490kr) allows unlimited travel on its ferries (and travel for 20kr per trip on Strömma Kanalbolaget and Cinderellabåtarna boats). It's available from the Stockholm tourist office (*see p288*) and Waxholmsbolaget's terminals.

Cinderellabåtarna

58 71 40 00/www.cinderellabatarna.com. **Leave from** Strandvägen, Östermalm. **Map** p306 G9. Cinderella's three boats travel to many of the most popular archipelago islands, including Vaxholm, Grinda, Finnhamn and Möja.

Strömma Kanalbolaget

58 71 40 00/www.strommakanalbolaget.com. **Leave from** Strandvägen, Östermalm. **Map** p306 G9. These ferries serve the key islands in the archipelago and many destinations around Lake Mälaren, also offering dinner and lunch cruises.

Waxholmsbolaget

Timetables and tour information 679 58 30/www.waxholmsbolaget.se. **Leave from** opposite the Grand Hôtel, Strömkajen, Norrmalm. **Map** p305 G-H8. In operation since 1896, Waxholmsbolaget services the whole archipelago. It has three classic steamers, eight new fast ferries and seven year-round vessels.

Island dreams

As well as being a summer playground for Stockholmers, the archipelago is home to 12,000 people year round. Yet only 30 years ago, the number of people living on the islands was looking perilously low.

The expansion of Stockholm in the 1950s meant that many new jobs were created in the city, while rural jobs in the archipelago were disappearing fast. In addition, large-scale industrial fishing was forcing the archipelago's fishermen out of business. The population shrank from 12,000 after World War II to an ageing population of 6,000 by the mid 1960s.

It was during the same period that mainlanders began to rediscover the islands, and the archipelago changed from an agricultural area to become primarily a tourist attraction. Many cottages were bought by wealthy city dwellers as summer retreats, making the islands' populations boom in the summer months. A summer house on the archipelago became the dream of the average 'Svensson'.

In response to the problems of depopulation in the archipelago, the local authorities in Stockholm established the **Skärgårdsstiftelsen** (Archipelago Foundation; *see above*) to protect the islands' culture and natural surroundings. The organisation, which owns 15 per cent of all land in the archipelago, also supports local businesses, and the islands now buzz with small enterprises.

The latest big thing to hit the archipelago is mobile phone reception and the internet. Stockholmers are beginning to discover that they can live an idyllic island life and still be in touch with the office. Suddenly, it is no longer seen as just a holiday resort.

Trips Out of Town

Day Trips

Viking cities and royal retreats.

Drottningholm.

Drottningholm

The grand palatial estate of Drottningholm – the permanent residence of the Swedish royal family since 1981 – attracts more than 100,000 visitors annually. Located ten kilometres (six miles) west of central Stockholm, on the sparsely populated island of Lovön, it is an essential excursion from the city. The well-preserved grounds – with 300-year-old trees framing the statues and fountains of the French garden behind the palace – and excellent examples of 17th- and 18th-century architecture, including a functioning theatre from 1766 and exotic Kina Slott at the western end, led UNESCO to add the entire site to its World Heritage List in 1991.

Constructed at the height of Sweden's power in Europe during the mid 17th century, **Drottningholms Slott** was built to impress – and it still does. Wealthy dowager Queen Hedvig Eleonora financed the initial construction of the palace, which lasted from 1662 to 1686. The royal architect Nicodemus Tessin the Elder modelled the waterfront residence on the Palace of Versailles. Highlights include the monumental staircase, Ehrenstrahl

drawing room and Hedvig Eleonora's state bedchamber. After Tessin's death in 1681, his son, Tessin the Younger, took over the project; Karl XI's gallery dates from this period.

The palace's second period of growth began after Lovisa Ulrika married Crown Prince Adolf Fredrik in 1744. She added a second storey above the wings and decorated its rooms with rococo furnishings and paintings. Her extensive library of books and natural specimens were visited by the famous botanist Carl von Linné (also known as Linnaeus) and other leading scientists of the 18th century.

Lovisa Ulrika was also a great lover of the arts and she commissioned architect Carl Fredrik Adelcrantz to build **Drottningholms Slottsteater**. The theatre still has its original stage sets and hand-driven machinery in place, and is the world's oldest working theatre – concerts, ballets and operas are held here in the summer (see p232). Simple sound effects include a wooden box filled with stones to create thunder. The tour of the theatre also includes the **Teatermuseum**, which focuses on 18th-century theatre, with displays of drawings, paintings, costumes and stage models. In the gift shop you can buy, among other things, books, miniature models of Swedish chairs and apple juice fresh from the Drottningholm orchards.

Armed soldiers dressed in camouflage guard the palace to ensure that the royal family's residence in the southern wing isn't accessed by members of the public. Crown Princess Victoria has a separate house on the estate. Different regiments around the country take turns to guard the palace. The family attends Christmas mass in the Palace Chapel, housed beneath the dome of the northern wing.

Behind the palace is the long rectangular **French baroque garden**, laid out in five stages separated by lateral paths. Its bronze statues are copies of early 17th-century works by the Dutch sculptor Adriaen de Vries. The originals were moved across the street to the **Museum de Vries**, which opened in 2001. The statues – spoils of war from Denmark's Fredriksborg Palace and Prague – are arranged in the former royal stable in the same pattern as those in the garden.

North of the baroque garden is the beautiful, lake-studded extensive **English Park**, so named because it followed the English style of naturalistic landscaping and planting that was fashionable at the time. It was added by Gustav III after he took over the palace in 1777. He also thoughtfully planned a memorial for himself – never finished – on one of the islands in the lakes north of the theatre.

Kina Slott stands near the end of the garden down a tree-lined avenue. As a surprise for Lovisa Ulrika's 33rd birthday in 1753, Adolf Fredrik had a Chinese-inspired wooden pavilion built here. Ten years later it was replaced by this rococo pleasure palace, also designed by CF Adelcrantz. Little was known about China at the time and the country was considered an exotic paradise. Wall paintings inside the pavilion's two curved wings show Chinese people playing cards and relaxing under trees. The royal family used to come here during the day to escape work, read books and take naps. The palace, which was carefully and extensively renovated between 1989 and 1996, has been repainted in its original red colour with yellow trim and light-green roofs; guided tours are available.

Adelcrantz also designed the nearby **Vakttältet**, a Turkish tent-style structure painted with blue and white stripes. Built as a barracks for Gustav III's dragoons, it's now a musty-smelling exhibition that shows the guards' kitchen and waiting area. Across from Kina Slott is the small **Confidencen** pavilion. When the family wanted to dine in private, they sat in the top room and servants hoisted up a fully set table from below. Down the road behind the palace is the former studio of the

20th-century Swedish artist **Evert Lundqvist** (402 62 70, open for guided tours in Swedish 4pm Sun May-Aug, 50kr).

The rest of Lovön is dotted with private homes and old red barns. The waterworks on its western shore produces 40 per cent of Stockholm's drinking water, direct from Lake Mälaren. Kärsön, the island across the bridge from Drottningholm, has an 18-hole Frisbee golf course and a swimming area out on its northern tip.

Drottningholms Slott

402 62 80/www.royalcourt.se. **Open** *May-Aug* 10am-4.30pm daily. *Sept* noon-3.30pm daily. *Oct-Apr* noon-3.30pm Sat, Sun. Closed mid Dec-early Jan. Guided tours in English daily mid June-Apr; weekends May-mid June. **Admission** 60kr. **Credit** AmEx, MC, V. **Free with SC**.
A combined ticket to Kina Slott and Drottningholms Slott costs 90kr, and includes a discount on tickets to the theatre.

Kina Slott

402 62 70. **Open** *May-Aug* 11am-4.30pm daily. *Sept* noon-3.30pm daily. Closed Oct-Apr. Guided tours wkends May-mid June; daily mid June-Sept. **Admission** 50kr.

Museum de Vries

402 62 80. **Open** by guided tour only (call for times). Closed Sept-mid May. **Admission** 50kr.

Slottsteater

Administrative office May-Sept 759 04 06/Oct-Apr 55 69 31 07/www.drottningholmsslottsteater.dtm.se. **Open** (guided tours only) *May* noon-5pm daily. *June-Aug* 11am-5pm daily. *Sept* 1-4pm daily. Closed Oct-Apr. **Admission** 60kr.

Vakttältet

402 62 70. **Open** *Mid June-mid Aug* noon-4pm daily. Closed mid Aug-mid June. **Admission** free.

Where to eat

First-class restaurant **Drottningholms Wärdshus** (759 03 08/81, www.drottningholms wardshus.se, main courses 210kr-270kr, closed dinner Sept-May, Jan, Easter, Christmas) occupies an 1850s building across the street from the estate, near the jetty. There's also a bar, conference facilities and tables outside in the garden in summer.

Drottningholmspaviljongen (759 04 25, www.drottningholmspaviljongen.com, main courses 100kr-185kr, weekends only Oct-Dec, closed Jan) offers daily lunch specials, including Swedish *husmanskost*, sandwiches, steak, wiener schnitzel and salmon; there's also a children's menu. Located in an early 20th-century villa near the palace's waterfront, it has outdoor seating in summer.

Trips Out of Town

Drottningholm's only café, **Kina Slotts Servering** (759 03 96, closed dinner & Nov-Mar), is located in an old building with an open fireplace and slanted roof near Kina Slott. It sells waffles, assorted pastries and sandwiches. Prices at these eateries are quite high, so you may want to opt for a picnic on the lawns.

Getting there

By metro/bus
T-bana to Brommaplan, then bus 177, 178, 301-323.

By boat
The nicest way to get to Drottningholm by far. Between May and early Sept you can travel by steamboat from Stadshusbron near the Stadshuset on Kungsholmen (80kr single, 110kr return); the journey takes 1hr. The most frequent service is between early June-mid Aug. Contact **Strömma**

Kanalbolaget (58 71 40 00/www.stromma kanalbolaget.com) for more information.

By car
From Kungsholmen take Drottningholmsvägen west towards Vällingby, then at Brommaplan follow the signs to Drottningholm. It's about a 15-minute drive.

By bicycle
There is a well-signposted cycle path from outside the Stadshuset in Stockholm to Drottningholm; the ride takes about 50mins.

Mariefred

The most scenic way to travel to Mariefred, 70 kilometres (43 miles) south-west of Stockholm, is by boat; as you near the small town you get a magnificent view of its main attraction, **Gripsholms Slott** (*see p248*). The castle was built as a fortress for King Gustav Vasa in 1537.

How the other half lived

Most visitors' first stop on the palace trail is Drottningholm (*see p244*), and rightly so. But there are several other palaces around Lake Mälaren worth visiting. During Sweden's century-long Age of Greatness, beginning in the early 17th century, many of the nobility, generals and businessmen growing wealthy from the country's wars built palatial estates in the countryside around Stockholm, especially along the shores of Lake Mälaren. Today, many of these palaces are open to the public – usually only in summer – offering guided tours of their stately, antique-laden interiors and magnificent gardens. Since sailing on Lake Mälaren and the Baltic Sea was the main means of transport, most of the grand entrances to these show-off homes face the water.

The closest to Stockholm is **Ulriksdals Slott**, about seven kilometres (four miles) north of the city centre on the shore of Edsviken, an inlet of the Baltic Sea. The palace was built in 1640 for Jacob de la Gardie, who led the Swedish forces that captured Moscow in 1610. Summertime performances are given at **Confidencen** (*see p245*), the country's oldest rococo theatre, and the palace's Orangery Museum exhibits Swedish sculptures from the 18th and 19th centuries.

Rosersbergs Slott stands 20 kilometres (13 miles) north of Stockholm between Upplands Väsby and Sigtuna, and is best reached by car. This white baroque palace was built in the 1630s on a small hill above

Lake Mälaren. King Karl XIV Johan spent summer holidays here in the early 1800s, and the palace still has many well-preserved furnishings from the period.

A few kilometres north along the shore is the much livelier **Steninge Slott**. Royal architect Nicodemus Tessin the Younger designed this bright yellow palace and its two wings in 1680. The cultural centre, in the former stables behind the palace, has a large selection of glassware, a gallery (exhibitions summer only) and a café.

An even grander palace, **Skoklosters Slott**, lies 15 kilometres (nine miles) north-west across the same inlet. The four round corner towers of this palace, with a white-plastered stone façade, are a perfect backdrop for the jousting tournaments held in July. Count Carl Gustav Wrangel, the governor of Swedish-occupied northern Germany who commissioned the palace in 1654, only spent two weeks of his life here. A guided tour shows the ornately decorated rooms, a 17th-century armoury and scaffolding left standing in the incomplete ballroom after the count's death in 1676. A church from 1225 is located nearby, along with old racing cars and automobile oddities in the Skokloster Motormuseum.

About 45 kilometres (28 miles) south of Stockholm, on the Baltic Sea, is the early 18th-century **Tullgarns Slott**. Gustav III's youngest brother lived here in the 1770s, although most of the interior decor was changed a century

The town itself is charming, with two-storey wooden buildings in pastel colours laid out according to a late 17th-century streetplan, but it can get crowded in summer. Mariefred, meaning 'Marie's Peace', comes from the name of the monastery that once stood where the church is today.

Gripsholms Slott is a few hundred metres south of the town on an island just big enough for its four round brick towers and two courtyards. It's named after Lord High Chancellor Bo Jonsson Grip, who built the first fortress on the site in the 1380s. King Erik XIV, Gustav Vasa's son, used the castle to imprison his brother Johan and his wife for six years. In the 17th century, Queen Hedvig Eleonora was sent here after her husband's death to prevent her from meddling in the country's politics. Gustav III finally took some pride in the castle

in the late 18th century and built a theatre in one of the towers; today it's one of the most well-preserved theatres from that era in Europe. The castle's three floors are full of furniture and art from the last 400 years. The Swedish national collection of portraits is also displayed here, including famous paintings of Gustav Vasa and the present royal family.

The **tourist office** (*see p248*) in the Rådhuset on the town square provides a free leaflet describing a short walking tour of the town's historic buildings. **Mariefreds Kyrka**, a white church with a tall black spire not far from the tourist office, was built in 1624 and restored in 1697 after a fire. At **Callanderska Gården** (Klostergatan 5, open 1-4pm daily in summer), next to the church, a turn-of-the-20th-century house has been preserved with its original furnishings and decor. The ground-

later when Crown Prince Gustav began using the palace as a summer residence. An English-style park and ponds surround the estate, which also contains a design gift shop, café and restaurant. In summer, you can feast on wild hogs cooked over an open fire or watch outdoor performances.

For more information on these and other palaces in the region, visit www.royalcourt.se or www.malarslott.nu.

Rosersbergs Slott

59 03 50 39/www.royalcourt.se. Pendeltåg commuter train to Rosersberg then 2km (1.2 mile) walk. **Open** (guided tours only, by advance booking) mid May-Aug. Closed Sept-Apr. **Admission** 50kr.

Skoklosters Slott

018 38 60 77/www.skoklostersslott.se. Ferry Kung Carl Gustav (mid May-Aug only) from Uppsala/train to Bålsta, then bus 894. **Open** (guided tours only) Apr Sat, Sun. May-early Nov daily. Early Nov-Mar group bookings only. **Admission** 65kr.

Steninge Slott

59 25 95 00/www.steningeslott.com. Train to Märsta then bus 580 to Tellusgatan and 2km (1.2 mile) walk; see website for directions. **Open** Palace (guided tours only) end June-early Aug daily; early Aug-end June weekends. Cultural Centre 10am-5pm Mon-Sat; 11am-5pm Sun. **Admission** Castle 60kr. Gallery 50kr.

Tullgarns Slott

55 17 20 11/www.royalcourt.se. Train to Södertälje Hamn then bus 702 and 2km (1.2 mile) walk. **Open** (guided tours only) Mid May-Aug 11am-4pm daily. Sept noon-3pm Sat, Sun. Closed Oct-mid May. **Admission** 50kr.

Ulriksdals Slott

402 61 30/www.royalcourt.se. Train to Ulriksdal then bus 503. **Open** (guided tours) June-Aug noon-4pm Tue-Sun. Closed Sept-May. **Admission** Palace 50kr. Orangery 40kr.

floor shops along pedestrianised **Storgatan**, which leads down to the water, sell fabrics, glassware, linen clothes and local handicrafts.

Other sights include **Grafikens Hus** (0159 231 60, www.grafikenshus.se, closed Mon Aug-May, admission 60kr), located down the road from the castle in the former Royal Barn, which sells artwork; you might also see artists using its printmaking workshop. The art is of a high quality but not necessarily worth the admission fee, unless you're planning on buying.

Rides on a 100-year-old steam train are offered by **Museijärnvägen** (0159 210 00, www.oslj.nu), situated in the yellow railway station near the main road into town. You can also use this train to get to Mariefred from Läggesta station (*see below*).

Gripsholms Slott

0159 101 94/www.royalcourt.se. **Open** *Mid May-mid Sept* 10am-4pm daily. *Mid Sept-mid May* noon-3pm Sat, Sun. Closed mid Dec-early Jan. Guided tour in English 1pm daily mid May-mid Sept. **Admission** 60kr. **Free with SC**. Credit AmEx, DC, MC, V. **Map** p241.

Where to eat

The formal dining room and veranda of **Gripsholms Värdshus & Hotel** (*see below*; main courses 200kr-250kr, closed Christmas & 1st wk Jan) offers fine dining with splendid views from its two restaurants.

Strandrestaurangen (0159 133 88, www.strandrestaurangen.com, main courses 65kr-195kr, closed dinner Mon-Fri, Sun & Oct 2004-Apr 2005), located at the end of Storgatan, serves traditional Swedish fare in an old house overlooking the water. **Konditori Fredman** (0159 121 10), the café and bakery across from the Rådhuset, serves lunch specials of pies, pizzas and lighter dishes. In summer, there are plenty of kiosks selling hot dogs and ice-cream.

If you're driving from Stockholm, you may want to stop off at **Taxinge Slottscafé** (0159 701 14, www.taxingeslott.se, open weekends Oct-Apr), located a few kilometres east of Mariefred. It claims to have the largest dessert table in northern Europe, with 50 kinds of cakes, cookies and pastries – hence its nickname, Kakslottet ('cookie castle'). During weekends in July you can catch a boat from Mariefred to Taxinge, eat lots of cake and then take the old steam train to Läggesta station, or the other way round (tickets 100kr).

Where to stay

Mariefred is really a daytrip destination, but if you want to stay overnight the nicest accommodation is at Sweden's oldest inn,

Gripsholms Värdshus & Hotel

(Kyrkogatan 1, 0159 347 52, www.gripsholms-vardshus.se, doubles 1,250kr-2,190kr). Established in 1609, this was Mariefred's first inn, built after the inhabitants protested about having to lodge and feed King Karl XI's entourage when he was in town. The foundations of Mariefred's 15th-century monastery were discovered during renovations to the inn in 1987; timbers and other artefacts found were used to decorate the beautiful two-storey hotel. Many of the 45 rooms have views of the water and castle.

Along waterside Strandvägen is the charming little B&B **In My Garden** (0159 133 53, www.inmygarden.se, doubles from 900kr). It has two rooms, a small shop selling ceramics, bags and accessories, plus, of course, a large garden with water views.

Enquire at the **tourist office** (*see below*) for hostels, camping and cottages.

Tourist information

Mariefred Turistbyrå

Rådhuset, Rådhustorget (0159 296 99/www.imariefred.nu). **Open** *May-Aug* 9.30am-6.30pm daily. *Sept-Apr* 9am-5pm Mon-Fri.

Getting there

By train/bus

You can catch a regional train from Central Station in Stockholm to Läggesta station, where you continue to Mariefred by bus or vintage steam train. The steam train runs daily end June-mid Aug, weekends May-Sept. The **Museijärnvägen** (*see above*) offers a round-trip package (express train, steam train, steamboat) during high season, and costs around 250kr. Alternatively you can take bus 304 from Läggesta to Mariefred and get off at Mariefred School, which is near Gripsholms Slott.

By boat

Gripsholms-Mariefreds Ångfartygs (669 88 50, www.magasin1.net/mariefred) runs a steamboat service (180kr round trip) to and from Mariefred on the *Mariefred*, which was built in 1903 and has travelled the same route for 100 years. It departs from Klara Mälarstrand near the Stadshuset at 10am, arriving in Mariefred at 1.30pm; the return boat leaves at 4.30pm, arriving in Stockholm at 8pm. The steamboat runs weekends mid May-mid Sept and Tue-Sun early June-end Aug. There's no service for the rest of the year.

By car

Head south from Stockholm on the E4/E20 to Södertälje, then follow the E20 west towards Göteborg. After about 30km (19 miles) exit on to highway 223 towards Mariefred and follow the signs to the town centre and castle. The whole trip takes 40mins.

Sigtuna – from Viking trading port to archaeological hotspot in the space of 1,000 years.

Sigtuna

A thousand years ago this small town by Lake Mälaren was the most important in Sweden. Founded around 980 by King Erik Segersäll, who built a royal hall in the middle of the town where the first Swedish coins were minted (originally intended as gifts with the king's head on rather than for trading), Sigtuna was a major trading port during Viking times.

Later the town became the centre of activity for Christian missionaries. After the founding of Stockholm in the mid 13th century, and King Gustav Vasa's later Reformation when he demolished many churches and monasteries, Sigtuna fell into ruin. Virtually all that is left from its great period are the remains of three 12th-century granite churches (from an original seven) bordering the town centre, and a large collection of artefacts in the Sigtuna Museum.

Sigtuna's main street, **Stora Gatan**, is an archaeological hotspot. The street today stands exactly where it did 1,000 years ago, although it's three metres (ten feet) higher. A centuries-old practice of throwing rubbish on the main street, then covering the rubbish with boards, has, over the years, resulted in layer upon layer of exciting discoveries. Today you will find shops selling handicrafts, antiques and clothes, and restaurants with lovely views of the water.

Many of the buildings date back to the 18th and 19th centuries. The **Rådhus**, in the central square, was built in 1744 and is the smallest town hall in Sweden. The **Sigtuna Museum** (*see below*) is built on the site of a former king's residence and has an excellent exhibition on the Vikings. It also runs the Rådhus and **Lundströmska Gården**, a middle-class house where a merchant lived with his family. Stop by the tourist office (*see p250*) on Stora Gatan – the building with a carved dragon's head over the door – to book a tour of the town.

Off the main street, you can take a rather melancholy stroll through the church ruins and cemeteries of **St Lars**, **St Per** and **St Olof**. The red brick church of **St Maria**, which happens to look quite new compared to the others, was actually built by the Dominicans in the 13th century and is one of the oldest brick buildings in Sweden. It was originally part of a monastery consisting of four buildings, which Gustav Vasa had torn down in 1530 during the Reformation.

Down by the water, you can rent canoes and bicycles, take in the view from a café or stroll along the path. Summer is the ideal time to visit Sigtuna, but seeing frozen Lake Mälaren during winter is breathtaking. On your way to or from the town, you may want to visit the palaces of **Rosersberg** and **Steninge** (*see p246* **How the other half lived**).

Sigtuna Museum

Stora Gatan 55 (59 78 38 70/www.sigtuna.se/museer). **Open** *June-Aug* noon-4pm daily. *Sept-May* noon-4pm Tue-Sat. **Admission** 30kr. *Lundströmska Gården,*

The charming university town of **Uppsala**.

Stora Gatan 39. **Open** *June-Aug* noon-4pm daily.
Admission 10kr. *Rådhus* **Open** *June-Aug* noon-4pm
daily. **Admission** free. **Credit** AmEx, DC, MC, V.

Where to eat

For a good meal in a charming 18th-century
pub, head two blocks west of the town square to
Amandas Krog (Långgränd 7, 59 25 00 24,
main courses 125kr-200kr). You can order a
lunch special of fish, meat or pasta, or
something fancier such as crayfish soup or
grilled venison. The **Båthuset Krog & Bar**
(59 25 67 80, main courses 180kr-260kr, closed
Mon, dinner only) is located out on the water
from Ångbåtsbryggan; a wooden dock leads to
the restaurant, which serves hearty portions of
fresh mussels and cod. For one of the best
waterfront views, visit the terrace at the **Sigtuna
Stadshotell**'s top-notch restaurant (mains
165kr-295kr, *see below*), serving traditional
Swedish food with an international touch.

If you've got a sweet tooth, duck into **Tant
Bruns Kaffestuga** (Laurentii Gränd 3, 59 25
09 34). This low-ceilinged café named after a
character in a popular children's book is famous
for its desserts and its life-size doll out front.
Also worth a visit is **RC Chocolat** (Stora
Gatan 49, 59 48 03 85, closed Mon) for delicious
pralines, homemade hot chocolate and ice-cream.

Farbror Blå Cafe & Kök (Stora Torget 4,
59 25 60 50, main courses 89kr-145kr), by
Rådhuset, offers basic dishes such as salads
and pasta, and has a good outdoor dining area
in summer.

Where to stay

Founded in 1909, the **Sigtuna Stadshotell**
(Stora Nygatan 3, 59 25 01 00, www.sigtuna
stadshotell.se, doubles 1,690kr-2,590kr, closed
4wks July, Aug), near the western end of the
town's main pedestrian street, is one of Sweden's
best small hotels and the only hotel outside
Stockholm or Gothenburg to earn five stars. Its
26 smart rooms are immaculately furnished and
extraordinarily comfortable. Sigtuna's proximity
to Arlanda Airport has made it a popular location
for conference hotels, including **Stora Brännbo
Konferens & Hotell** (Stora Brännbovägen 2-6,
59 25 75 00, www.storabrannbo.se, doubles
700kr-1,400kr, closed weekends Sept-May). This
environmentally friendly hotel north-west of the
town square has 100 plainly furnished rooms
and a large dining hall.

Sigtuna Camping (59 25 27 00, 4-bed
cabins 450kr/day, tent 25kr/day), situated
in Rävsta east of the city centre, is open all
year round.

Tourist information

Sigtuna Turism

Stora Gatan 33 (59 48 06 52/www.sigtuna.se/turism).
Open *June-Aug* 10am-6pm Mon-Sat; 11am-5pm Sun.
Sept-May 10am-5pm Mon-Fri; noon-4pm Sat, Sun.
Closed Christmas.

Getting there

By train/bus

Take the Pendeltåg commuter train (www.sl.se) or
the Uppsala train (www.tim-trafik.se) to Märsta. The
Uppsala train is faster, but make sure it goes via
Märsta and not Arlanda. From Märsta, take bus 570
or 575 to Sigtuna bus station, near the town centre.
From Stockholm Central Station the trip takes 1hr.

By car

Head north on the E4 for about 30km (18 miles) then
exit on the 263 and follow the signs to Sigtuna. Drive
about 10km (six miles) west until you come to a
roundabout, where you turn towards Sigtuna
Centrum. The entire journey takes about 50mins.

Uppsala

The historic city of Uppsala, Sweden's answer
to Cambridge or Oxford, is home to the oldest
university in Scandinavia – dating back to 1477
– and some 30,000 students. It's a bustling,

charming city, situated at the northern tip of Lake Mälaren, about 70km (40 miles) north of Stockholm, with ancient buildings, plenty of cafés and beautiful parks.

The city's magnificent Domkyrkan, Scandinavia's largest cathedral, stands on a ridge to the west of the downtown area beside a 16th-century brick castle. The small Fyrisån river runs along a man-made stone channel through the centre of town. One block to the east is a pedestrian shopping street and the busy main square of **Stora Torget**. The former home and garden of the famous botanist Carl Linnaeus (whose face adorns the 100kr note) are located nearby, along with several other university museums.

Uppsala was founded slightly to the north of its present location; it moved southwards in the 13th century as construction began on the **Domkyrkan** (*see p252*), today the city's most striking landmark by far. This red brick Gothic cathedral, completed in 1435, was built on a cross plan. The building is as tall as it is long, with two western towers rising up a neck-craning 118.7 metres (389 feet); more than half a million people visit each year. Inside there's an enormous vaulted ceiling, a floor covered with gravestones and Sweden's largest baroque pulpit, designed by Tessin the Younger. It's also the last resting place of some famous Swedes. Linnaeus and the philosopher Emanuel Swedenborg are buried here, and Gustav Vasa is entombed beneath a monument depicting him and his two queens. The **Skattkammaren** (Treasury) is situated in the northern tower; it displays medieval tapestries and treasures, along with the bloodied clothes of members of the Sture family who were murdered by King Erik XIV in 1567.

The buildings of Uppsala University are scattered throughout the city. Across from the cathedral stands the **Gustavianum** (*see p253*), formerly the university's main building, now a museum. Beneath its copper onion dome are exhibits on the history of science and the university, an old anatomical theatre, some Nordic, classical and Egyptian antiquities, and the curiosities of the Augsburg Art Cabinet.

At the top of the main street, Drottninggatan, the striking early 19th-century university library, **Carolina Rediviva** (Dag Hammarskjöldsväg 1, 018 471 39 00), looks down on the town centre. The library contains five million volumes and

Viking visit

If you liked the Viking collection at the **Historiska Museet** (*see p98*), then you might want to visit the excavated ruins of the real Viking city from which many of the artefacts originated. Located 25 kilometres (15 miles) west of central Stockholm on the green island of Björkö, **Birka** was founded around AD 700, making it one of Sweden's oldest settlements. Archaeological evidence from Birka has revealed that the Vikings were not the barbarians of popular conception, but rather had a strong hierarchical class system and a wealth of carefully crafted products. A king who lived on the nearby island of Adelsön governed the city's roughly 1,000 permanent inhabitants, mainly farmers, craftsmen and professional soldiers. Arabic coins and east European pearls found among the ruins testify to the international importance of Birka's harbour and the nautical skills of the Vikings. For unknown reasons – perhaps due to the spread of Christianity or the development of nearby **Sigtuna** (*see p249*) – the Vikings abandoned Birka around AD 960.

Stepping off the steamboats that bring visitors to Birka in summer, you'll see little evidence of the former city, aside from the fields dotted with hundreds of burial mounds. But the **Birkamuseet** (56 05 14 45, www. raa.se/birka, open daily May-3rd wk Sept, 50kr), located next to the dock on the western shore, contains magnificent finds from the excavations plus detailed models of how the city once looked.

The best way to travel to Birka is by steamboat with **Strömma Kanalbolaget** (*see p243*, 9.30am daily May-mid Sept, 245kr), which leaves from Stadshubron near the Stadshuset. Or take the 1880 steamer *Edjern* with **Museiföreningen Ångfartyget Ejdern** (55 01 88 99, www.ejdern.org, 200kr), which runs every few days from mid May to mid September from Borgmästaruddena near Central Station. The price of the museum is included with both companies. The only food on Birka is at **Restaurang Särimner** near the museum (56 05 10 31, closed Sept-Apr, main courses 65kr-130kr), serving lunch specials, sandwiches and meat pies.

If Birka piques your curiosity, two very entertaining novels about the Vikings are Michael Crichton's *Eaters of the Dead* (based on an actual travel log from AD 922) and Frans G Bengtsson's Swedish classic *The Long Ships*.

Trips Out of Town

the famous Silver Bible, written in silver and gold letters around AD 520 (bible viewings 9am-8pm Mon-Fri, 10am-5pm Sat). Extensive construction work is being carried out on the library until 2006, but this should not affect the display of the Bible. For science enthusiasts, the university also has museums on biology, evolution, medicine and psychiatry.

The **Upplandsmuseet** (St Eriks Torg 10, 018 16 91 00, www.uppmus.se, closed Mon, admission 30kr), one of the city's few non-university museums, is housed in a former watermill near the river, and its artefacts date from Viking to modern times.

Up the hill from the cathedral is the huge, earth-red **Uppsala Slott** (*see p253*), built by Gustav Vasa in the late 1540s as a fortress. His sons later added to the building, although much of it was destroyed in the city fire of 1702. It houses an art gallery and the county governor's residence, **Vasaborgen** (*see p253*), but is not as spectacular as you might expect. A guided tour goes through its apartments and grand ballroom, helping you sort out the rivalries within the Vasa family, and wax models portray scenes from the 16th century. The castle's freestanding bell tower, Gunillaklockan, has become a symbol of Uppsala; it strikes at 6am and 9pm.

The university's grand **Botaniska Trädgården** (Villavägen 8, 018 471 28 38, www.botan.uu.se), west of the castle, includes a tropical greenhouse, baroque formal garden and 11,000 species of plants. To see where the university's first botanical garden stood, visit **Linnéträdgården** (*see p253*), situated one block north of pedestrianised Gågatan. Carl Linnaeus (1707-78), also known as Carl von Linné in Sweden, restored the garden in 1741 soon after becoming a professor at the university. One of Sweden's most famous scientists, Linnaeus developed a method of classifying and naming plants that was adopted by botanists around the world. His attempts at growing coffee, cacao and bananas here – to make Sweden more economically independent – were unsurprisingly thwarted by the Swedish winter. He lived in the small house on the corner of the property, now the **Linnémuseet** (*see p253*). It has a permanent exhibition on his life and work (much of which was carried out in the house), and you can see the original furnishings, his writing room and doctor's medical kit.

Linnaeus also had a country residence ten kilometres (six miles) south-east of the city at **Hammarby** (018 32 60 94, www.hammarby. uu.se, park closed Oct-Apr, museum & café closed Mon & Oct-Apr, bus 886 or 807 from central Uppsala, then 2km walk), where he stored his extensive collections and cultivated an idyllic meadow. Linnaeus Week takes place in early August every year, when 18th-century costumed characters roam the streets, and there are lectures and botanical walks.

When you get tired of sightseeing, the city's six-block pedestrian shopping street, Gågatan, has two indoor malls and several restaurants and pubs. The huge window of the pool at **Centralbadet** (St Persgatan 4, 018 10 16 60, admission 35kr) looks out across the river to the two towers of the cathedral. For a bit more splash, head for the adventure pool and slides at **Fyrishov** (Idrottsgatan 2, 018 727 49 50, www.fyrishov.se, admission 90kr). You can also stay the night here (*see p253*).

Gamla Uppsala (Old Uppsala), two kilometres (1.2 miles) to the north of Uppsala, is the site of the original settlement. Between AD 500 and 1000 Sweden's pagan kings ruled from this site, which was also a busy marketplace and point of departure for expeditions. They gathered here every nine years to sacrifice humans and animals over a period of nine days. Visiting the area today, you'll see the grass-covered, sixth-century burial mounds of three kings and a stone church built on the site of a heathen temple. The **Gamla Uppsala** museum (*see below*) opened in 2000, with exhibits about Viking history and myths.

If you're going to be in the area for a few days, a couple of castles outside the city are also well worth a visit. The 15th-century fortress of **Wiks Slott** (018 56 10 00, www.wiksslott.com), 20 kilometres (12.5 miles) to the south-west, is recommended. It's one of Sweden's best-preserved medieval fortresses. Guided tours (2pm daily, 60kr) are offered from Midsummer to mid August (book ahead for English). In summer there is a boat from Uppsala to Wiks Slott, passing Skokloster (*see p246* **How the other half lived**). A 45-minute drive to the north of Uppsala are **Örbyhus Slott** (0295 614 00, guided tours mid May-early Sept, closed Mon, admission 50kr), where Erik XIV was poisoned with pea soup, and the old iron-mining villages of Uppland County.

Domkyrkan

Domkyrkoplan (018 18 71 73/www.uppsaladom kyrkoforsamling.se). **Open** *Cathedral* 8am-6pm daily. *Treasury* May-Sept 10am-5pm Mon-Sat; 12.30-5pm Sun. Oct-Apr 11am-3pm Tue-Sat; 12.30-3pm Sun. **Admission** *Cathedral* free. *Treasury* 30kr.

Gamla Uppsala

Disavägen (018 23 93 00/group bookings when closed 018 23 93 12/www.raa.se/gamlaupppsala). *Bus 2 or 110 from central Uppsala.* **Open** *May-Aug* 11am-5pm daily. *Sept-Apr* noon-3pm Sun. Closed 3wks from mid Dec. **Admission** 50kr; 30kr concessions; 7-18s; free under-7s.

Gustavianum

*Akademigatan 3 (018 471 75 71/www.gustavianum.
uu.se).* **Open** 11am-4/5pm Tue-Sun. **Admission**
40kr; 30kr concessions; free under-12s.

Linnéträdgården & Linnémuseet

*Svarbäcksgatan 27 (museum 018 13 65 40/
www.linnaeus.uu.se).* **Open** *Garden* May-Sept 9am-
7/9pm daily. Closed Oct-Apr. *Museum* May-mid Sept
noon-4pm Tue-Sun. Group bookings all year.
Admission *Garden* 20kr. *Museum* 25kr.

Uppsala Slott

018 727 24 85. **Open** *Castle* (guided tours only)
June-Aug Swedish 12.15pm, 2pm daily; English 1pm,
3pm daily. Closed Sept-May. *Art gallery* noon-4pm
Tue-Fri; 11am-5pm Sat, Sun; noon-8pm 1st Wed
every month. **Admission** 80kr.

Vasaborgen

018 50 77 72/www.vasaborgen.se. **Open** *May-Aug*
11am-5pm daily. Closed Sept-Apr. **Admission** 40kr.

Where to eat

The city's finest dining can be found at
Domtrappkällaren (St Eriksgränd 15, 018 13
09 55, www.domtrappkallaren.se, main courses
90kr-290kr, closed lunch Sat & all day Sun),
which serves Swedish and French cuisine in a
13th-century vault near the cathedral steps. If
you want the same atmosphere at a cheaper
price, try the pub lunch. One block east is
Hambergs Fisk (Fyristorg 8, 018 71 21 50,
main courses 85kr-260kr, closed Mon, Sun &
July), specialising in seafood.

To watch the pedestrian traffic at Stora
Torget, visit **Restaurang Rådhussalongen**
(Nos.6-8, 018 69 50 70, main courses 89kr-
192kr). It occupies part of the old town hall, and
is also a popular bar-nightclub in the evenings.

For an excellent vegetarian lunch, try **Fröjas
Sal Vegetarisk Restaurang** (Bäverns Gränd
24, 018 10 13 10, set menus 65kr-80kr, closed Sat
June-Aug, Sun) opposite the bus station. One of
Uppsala's most famous old-fashioned cafés is
Ofvandahls Hovkonditori (Sysslomansgatan
5, 018 13 42 04, closed Sun July), founded in the
late 19th century. You can also fill up on pastries
and marzipan sweets at the **Güntherska
Hovkonditoriet** (Östra Ågatan 31, 018 13 07
57), located by the river near the main square.

In Gamla Uppsala, **Restaurang Odinsborg**
(018 32 35 25, www.odinsborg.com, buffet 150kr,
closed Mon-Fri Oct, Nov) serves a popular buffet
in a late 19th-century rustic-style building.

Where to stay

Since Uppsala is located less than a 30-minute
drive from Arlanda Airport, there are several
accommodation options. The **Radisson SAS**

Hotel Gillet (Dragarbrunnsgatan 23, 018 68
18 00, www.radissonsas.com, doubles from
990kr) is one block east of Uppsala's main
shopping street in a recently renovated 19th-
century building with 160 rooms, swimming
pool, sauna and gym.

Most of the rooms at the **First Hotel Linné**
(Skolgatan 45, 018 10 20 00, www.firsthotels.se,
doubles from 845kr, closed 2wks Dec-Jan) have
views of Linnaeus's botanical garden next door.
The hotel has a cosy restaurant and wine bar,
plus a sauna, solarium and herb garden.

Three blocks south-west of the train station,
the scenically located **Grand Hotell Hörnan**
(Bangårdsgatan 1, 018 13 93 80, www.grand
hotellhornan.com, doubles 900kr-1,482kr) has
been renovated in its original early 20th-century
style. The 37 spacious, high-ceilinged rooms
have nice views overlooking the Fyrisån river,
the cathedral and Uppsala Slott.

Cheaper options include youth hostel
Vandraren STF (Vattholmavägen 16C, 018
10 43 00, www.vandraren.com, from 255kr per
person, closed mid Aug-mid June), a short
walk or bus ride north of downtown, or you
can rent a bike at the hostel. All the rooms have
bathrooms. If you prefer sleeping outdoors, a
15-minute walk north-west of the town centre
brings you to the year-round **Fyrishovs
Camping** (Idrottsgatan 2, 018 727 49 60,
www.fyrishov.se, tent 115kr-130kr, caravan
135kr-195kr). It has tent sites and cottages,
as well as a mini golf course and canoe rental.

Tourist information

Uppsala Tourism

*Fyristorg 8 (018 727 48 00/fax 018 13 28 95/
www.uppland.nu).* **Open** 10am-6pm Mon-Fri;
10am-3pm Sat.

Getting there

By train

Several trains a day leave for Uppsala from
Stockholm's Central Station; see www.sj.se or call
0771 75 75 75 for times. Once in Uppsala, you can
walk to most of the major sites but there is also an
excellent bus system.

By bus

Swebus Express's (www.swebusexpress.se) bus 899
departs several times a day from Stockholm's City
terminal (Cityterminalen). The journey takes about
1hr and costs 60kr one way.

By car

Follow the E4 north from Stockholm for about
50mins. The highway passes through the eastern
half of Uppsala, from where you follow the signs to
Uppsala Centrum to the west.

Central Archipelago

A small hop from Stockholm, but a big change from city life.

The islands that make up the Central Archipelago (Mellersta Skärgården) are all easily accessible from Stockholm and ideal for a day, or even half-day, trip. The nearest islands to the city are **Fjäderholmarna**, less then 30 minutes from the city; **Vaxholm**, one of the most visited islands in the archipelago and with the largest year-round population; and **Grinda**, offering excellent swimming spots and fine dining. Further out are the quiet retreats of **Gällnö** for a back-to-nature experience, plus historic **Möja** and the popular island group of **Finnhamn**.

Fjäderholmarna

The four small islands that make up Fjäderholmarna are the closest archipelago islands to Stockholm – a mere six kilometres (four miles) east of downtown. They are the perfect place to get a glimpse of the archipelago without having to take a long boat ride or spend the night. They're also well set up for kids.

Ferries drop visitors off at the main island of **Stora Fjäderholmen** (which is often what people mean when they say Fjäderholmarna). A paved walking path circles the island, passing

the restaurants, small museums and handicraft boutiques on the northern and eastern shores, and the forested area and flat rocks to the west. About a dozen people live on **Ängsholmen** and Stora Fjäderholmen. The smaller islands of **Libertas** and **Rövarns Holme** provide sanctuary for birds, but there's no way to get to them unless you have your own boat.

If you do have a boat, you can spend the night in Stora Fjäderholmen's guest harbour (716 39 10, closed Oct-Apr, 120kr per night), which is run by the Shell petrol station. There is no other accommodation on any of the islands, and camping is not allowed. Generally most of the island's venues open in time for the first boat at 10.30am. The handicraft shops and boat museum usually close around 5-5.30pm, while the restaurants are often open until midnight, leaving time to catch the last boat back to Stockholm. The island is open from early May to early September and most venues are open every day during the season. After September boats are few and far between.

The islands have a long and winding history. Sailors and archipelago residents regularly visited as early as the 1600s. The first tavern

Fjäderholmarna's **Boat Museum**. See p255.

was built on Stora Fjärderholmen around 1700, and sailors stopped to eat, drink or play cards before heading on to Stockholm. In the 1800s the tavern was turned into a restaurant, and a new boathouse tavern was added on the southern shore. In the mid 1850s Ångsholmen had a run of bad luck: it was first used by the city as a sewage dump, then as a place to quarantine sick immigrants. The Swedish military occupied the islands from World War I to the mid 1980s, and burned down most of the historic buildings. Once the islands were reopened to the public, they became a popular tourist destination and are now part of Ekoparken, the National City Park.

When the weather is good, the northern cliffs of Stora Fjärderholmen are flooded with sunbathing Stockholmers and tourists, and the place can feel a bit cramped. Swimming options are limited, with no easily accessible beaches. The ferries from Stockholm dock on the northern shore next to the guest harbour and the **Östersjöakvariet** aquarium (718 40 55, closed Oct-Apr). Housed in a cave dug out by the military to store ammunition, it features Baltic Sea fish in large tanks illustrating different areas of the archipelago. The shop also doubles as the tourist office.

The **Spiritum Museum** (Vodka Museum; 55 60 15 60, www.spiritum.se, guided tours 50kr) opened in 2002 in the cave next door to the aquarium and focuses on the island's 'Vodka War' of the 1880s. When the city authorities wouldn't let Lars Olsson Smith sell his distilled vodka, made using a new technique, he arranged for a partner to distribute it at the island's tavern. Free rides were offered from Stockholm and customers brought the largest containers they could find. The venture was an enormous success – until the city refused to renew the firm's liquor licence. Smith's distillation method is still used by Sweden's famous Absolut Vodka company.

Further along the path, rowing boats of all kinds are exhibited in the **Allmogebåtar Museum** (Boat Museum; 070 477 98 51, admission free) on the eastern side of the island, as well as everything from oars to engines.

Following the path, you come across the **outdoor theatre**, which puts on plays every summer against the beautiful backdrop of boats. Just by the theatre is a playground resembling a ship sunk into the sand. Further round, on the southern shore, a small street contains an **art gallery** and studios where artists make (and sell) pottery, linen goods and wooden handicrafts. At **Åtta Glas** (716 11 24) you can watch glass being blown and then buy the finished article in the little shop next door.

At the top of the hill in the middle of the island is an informal garden (open 11am-5pm daily) where you can eat a picnic, enjoy a game of boules or just sit with a coffee.

Guided 45-minute tours of Stora Fjärderholmen take place daily in July, weather permitting, with **WeFix Event Fjäderholmarna** (715 80 65, www.wefix.nu, booking essential), taking you through some light archipelago history along the way.

Where to eat

As you step off the ferry, the **Rökeriet** (716 50 88, www.rokeriet.nu, main courses 50kr-235kr) is on your left along the water's edge. At the café counter you can order smoked salmon, shrimps or a glass of wine. The indoor restaurant, adorned with fishing nets, has a beautiful view over the neighbouring islands. **Fjäderholmarnas Krog** (718 33 55, www. fjaderholmarna.com, main courses 165kr-295kr), on a nearby eastern spur, sports a more modern look; the veranda overlooks the guest harbour and the menu offers fancy dishes at fancy prices. For dessert, try **Systrarna Degens Glasstuga** (716 78 01, closed Oct-Apr), which specialises in ice-cream and smoothies. **Fjäderholmarnas Magasin** (718 08 50, www.fjaderholmarna.com, closed Oct-Apr, main courses 49kr-135kr), located on the southern shore, serves typical Swedish lunch specials and salads, and the patio has a view of Nacka Strand.

Tourist information

The island doesn't have a tourist office, but info is available from the **Östersjöakvariet** (718 40 55; *see above*). You can usually pick up a free brochure with a map on the ferry or try www.fjaderholmarna.nu (Swedish only).

Getting there

By boat

Strömma Kanalbolaget (*see p243*) ferries leave from Nybroplan (every 30mins 10am-8.30pm mid May-end Aug; every hr 10am-11.30pm early May-mid May; every hr 10am-8pm, then 9.30pm, 10.30pm, 11.30pm end Aug-early Sept; 6 times each afternoon early-end Sept, return 80kr). **Fjäderholmslinjen** boats (21 55 00, www.rss.a.se/fjaderholmslinjen) depart every hour from Slussen 10am-10pm daily May-early Sept; return 80kr.

Vaxholm

The island of Vaxholm, just 3.5 kilometres (two miles) long, is by far the most populated and easily accessible island in the archipelago. It is located about 17 kilometres (11 miles) north-east of Stockholm and is connected to the mainland by highway 274. The place is overrun in summer, when roughly a million visitors come for Vaxholm's waterfront restaurants, handicraft shops and art galleries. Ferries from Stockholm dock at Vaxholm's historic downtown, located on the island's south-east corner. The town has a lively, beach-side feel and frequent outdoor events in the summer, and booths selling everything from used books to wooden figurines line the wharf. On the main street of Hamngatan, to the north, you'll find all the conveniences of a small town, including an early 20th-century cinema.

Gustav Vasa founded the city of Vaxholm in the 1540s after winning Sweden's war with Denmark. The city supplied food and water to the newly constructed fortress and tower located on the small island to the east. Several additions were made to the fortress in the 1800s, and today it contains the **Vaxholms Fästnings Museum** (541 721 57, open 11am-5pm daily July, Aug, guided tours only Sept-June, in English 3pm, admission 50kr). Exhibits focus on the defensive history of Stockholm during the last 500 years, the castle's former role as a prison and the nearby Ytterby mine. The museum reopened in 2003 after extensive renovations and is easily reached by a two-minute boat trip (40kr return) from Vaxholm wharf; boats leave every 15 minutes (noon-5pm June, Aug, 11am-5pm July). The fortress also hosts a summer café serving lunch, plus a B&B with 59 beds in the former officers' mess.

People began building summerhouses on Vaxholm in the 1850s when a daily steamboat service from Stockholm started running. Many of these small wooden homes, painted yellow and red, are tucked into the town's narrow streets and along the north-eastern shore. A 19th-century fisherman's house in the Norrhamn area, north of downtown, has been preserved at the **Hembygdsgården Museum** (Trädgårdsgatan 19, 541 317 20, closed Sept-June & July, Aug Mon-Fri, admission 10kr). You see how the family might have lived, as well as objects relating to fishing, hunting and boating. The museum's outdoor café (closed mid Sept-Apr) has an enviable location on a grassy peninsula next to a popular swimming spot.

West of Hamngatan is the neo-classical **Vaxholm Kyrka**, designed in the 1760s by Carl Fredrik Adelcrantz, who also built several churches in Stockholm. It took more than 40 years to build because of an embezzlement scandal on the church board. It hosts evening concerts in the summer. The city's old **Rådhuset** (Town Hall) is now home to the tourist office, and the cobbled square outside has a small ice-cream

bar and stalls selling handicrafts in summer. Every year Vaxholm harbour hosts a steamboat festival, **Skärgårdsbåtens Dag** (*see p183*), on the second Wednesday in June.

If you have a bike or car you may want to visit **Eriksö Friluftsområde** (541 301 01), on the island's western tip, which has a park, swimming area, mini golf course and campsite. Further to the south-west, on the mainland, stands the 17th-century castle of **Bogesunds Slott** (contact youth hostel on 541 322 40), which has a cosy café. The castle was abandoned in 1910 , taken over by the state in 1946 and opened to the public in 2003 (guided tours 2pm, 3pm Wed-Sun July). The castle was built by Per Brahe the Younger, who fought with Gustav Vasa and founded the Swedish city of Gränna.

In summer there is **outdoor theatre** in Vaxholm. There are plans for performances at the fortress in 2005 and at the castle in 2006.

Where to eat

There's a good choice of restaurants to choose from along the wharf, including seafood, Italian and Chinese. For fine dining and water views, try **Waxholms Hotell** (*see below*; main courses 119kr-300kr, closed dinner Sun), serving dishes such as turbot stuffed with truffles and lobster. In the summer you can enjoy the harbour life from the outdoor veranda of the hotel's Kabyssen restaurant (main courses 115kr-200kr); and there's a nightclub on Friday and Saturday evenings. For more down-to-earth fare, take a seat on the outdoor patio of the popular restaurant and pub **Hamnkrogen** (Söderhamnen 10, 541 320 39, main courses 80kr-180kr). You will also find pizzas and hamburgers in abundance.

On the same street as Hembygdsmuseet you'll find **Strömingslådan**, a small, red kiosk in a garden selling herring prepared in every way possible and plenty of local specialities for takeaway (Trädgårdsgatan 12, 541 302 47, closed Sept-May).

Where to stay

Since Vaxholm is generally a destination for day-trippers, there aren't many places to stay. The sole hotel, **Waxholms Hotell** (Hamngatan 2, 541 301 50, www.waxholms hotell.se, doubles 1,025kr-1,600kr), built in 1901, has light, tastefully decorated rooms and satellite TV. The **Fortress** B&B (541 751 10, www.kastelletbnb.com, closed Christmas-mid Jan, rates from 750kr) offers 59 beds, some facing the water. It is a historic house and most of the rooms still have tile stoves.

Alternatively, you can book B&Bs (around 250kr per person per night) through the Vaxholm tourist office (*see below*). **Vaxholms Strand & Camping** (541 301 01, closed Oct-Apr) is located at the western end of the island and its sandy beach is a good spot for families. The **Bogesunds Vandrarhem** youth hostel (541 322 40, www.bogesundsvandrarhem.se, 210kr per person per night) is next to Bogesunds Slott on the mainland, to the south-east.

Tourist information

Vaxholms Turistbyrå & VisitVaxholm AB

Rådhuset (541 314 80/www.visitvaxholm.se). **Open** *June-Aug* 10am-6pm Mon-Fri; 10am-2pm Sat, Sun. *Sept-May* 10am-3pm Mon-Fri; 10am-2pm Sat, Sun. Stop by the tourist office for maps, fishing licences and an events schedule. Website **www.vaxholm.se** gives general information on facilities and attractions.

Getting there

By metro & bus

T-bana Tekniska Högskolan, then bus 670 to Vaxholm. The whole journey takes about 1hr.

By boat

Waxholmsbolaget boats (*see p243*) from Strömkajen are the best option; they run several times a day all year (single 65kr). **Cinderellabåtarna** boats (*see p243*) from Strandvägen are less frequent, running up to three times a day mid June-end Aug (60-90mins, single 90kr).

By car

Head north on the E18 for 15km (9 miles) then exit at the Arninge Trafikplats on to highway 274. Follow signs to Vaxholm, which will lead you through Stockholmsvägen and Kungsgatan to downtown.

Grinda

Grinda, just over an hour away by boat from Stockholm and accessible year round, is one of the archipelago's most popular islands. Visitors come for the peaceful surroundings, excellent swimming, good restaurant dining and pine forests. Boats stop at the north and south piers, and wooden signs guide you along the 15-minute walk to the middle of the island, where you'll find the inn, guest harbour, shop and restaurant.

The island's first inhabitants can be traced back to the Middle Ages. In 1906 Henrik Santesson, the first director of the Nobel Foundation, bought the island. Summerhouses in the archipelago were fashionable at the time and Santesson commissioned architect Ernst Stenhammar to design a summer residence. The result was a beautiful art nouveau stone house, the present-day **Grinda Wärdshus** (*see p258*). When Henrik died in 1912, his wife Alfhild took over and brought war children to stay on the island during the summer. The large house was used as a girls' camp, summer camp and treatment facility until 1995. In 1998 Skärgårdsstiftelsen bought Grinda, and today it is a nature reserve, covered in pine forests and rocks flattened by the last Ice Age. **Grinda Gård** is the starting point for a three-kilometre (1.8 miles) path that takes you through the forest to Grinda's highest point, Klubbudden, 35 metres (115 feet) above sea level.

Grinda has plenty of good swimming spots; Källviken, along the path to the guest harbour and the inn, has a shallow sandy beach, ideal for children. There are some popular spots between Källviken and the guest harbour, and by the northern and southern piers. The tall cliffs on the eastern shore make bathing difficult.

Vaxholm. See p255.

Islands at war

For most Stockholmers, the archipelago conjures up images of Midsummer holidays and natural beauty. Yet the hundreds of islands that lie off Sweden's eastern coast are also Stockholm's last line of defence from invasion.

This was demonstrated most clearly in the summer of 1719. Sweden was at war with Russia, and Peter the Great sent his fleet across the Baltic Sea to raid the Swedish coast in the hope of forcing the Swedes to sign a peace treaty. Some 26,000 Russians, sailing in a fleet of several hundred ships, attacked the coast from Norrtälje to Nyköping. Towns, villages and farms on the mainland and in the archipelago were burned to the ground, and 20,000 people were made homeless.

By August 1719 the Russians had set their sights on Stockholm. In the city, the sound of cannons and the smell of smoke coming from burning buildings on the outskirts was already making the inhabitants panic. Many people left the capital, but the queen stoically remained in the palace, and even sent ladies from her court to attend a reception at the British Embassy.

The Swedish navy managed to head off the Russian fleet at Vaxholm, but the invading ships found a southern route into the inner archipelago. It was at the narrow channel at Baggenstäket, just 15 kilometres (9.3 miles) from the city centre, that Swedish forces managed to beat back the Russians. Six thousand enemy troops landed, to be met by ill-equipped Swedish 'home guard' regiments numbering about 700. Still, under the leadership of Rutger Fuchs, the Swedes lost only 30 men, whereas 500 Russians were killed and the remainder retreated. Fuchs was showered with honours and went down in history as 'Stockholm's saviour'.

The power and proximity of Russia continued to make Swedes nervous through the ages. A memorial to the battle at Baggestäket was erected on Skogsö in 1905, at a time when the 'Russification' of Finland was in full swing and Sweden was looking carefully over its shoulder.

More recently, the Stockholm archipelago was the backdrop for scare stories about Soviet submarine incursions. During the early 1980s, a period of heightened Cold War tension, Swedish forces claimed to have sighted a number of Soviet craft and chased them out of the archipelago. One of the most famous submarine chases was at Hårsfjärden in 1982, an episode that caused a crisis in Swedish relations with communist Russia. Although doubt was later cast on the claims that the sightings were, in fact, submarines, a Russian sub had already run aground in 1981 outside the southern city of Karlskrona.

In 2004, however, any past ill feelings between the two countries seemed to finally have been set aside when Stockholm hosted a submarine expo that featured a Russian U-137 sub – the same type that got stranded off the Stockholm archipelago in 1981, making front-page news.

Where to eat

Award-winning **Grinda Wärdshus** (*see below*; mains 95kr-245kr, booking essential) is open year round and is the island's best restaurant; try speciality poached catfish. **Framfickan** (same number as above, closed Aug-mid June, mains 75kr-130kr), by the guest harbour, offers lighter pasta dishes, and has an outdoor veranda.

Where to stay

Grinda Wärdshus (54 24 94 91, www.grinda wardshus.se, 775kr-1,325kr per person per night) has 30 double rooms in the red wooden houses, built in 2003, beside the restaurant. The rooms have no telephone or TV, but are light and stylish. **Grinda Stugby & Vandrarhem** (54 24 90 72, www.grinda.nu, closed Nov-Apr, cottages 500kr-900kr, hostel 215kr, campsite 60kr per person per night) runs 31 basic cottages, a hostel with 44 beds and the campsite. Camping is only allowed in the designated area.

Getting there

Cinderella boats depart twice a day from Strandvägen (mid June-end Aug, single 90kr-110kr) and stop at the south pier. **Waxholmsbolaget** boats run all year (single 80kr) to both piers. There are several crossings a day during the summer.

Gällnö

For more than 500 years people have farmed and fished on the X-shaped island of Gällnö, which is located three kilometres (1.9 miles) south-east of Grinda. The well-preserved village of **Gällnöby** stands near Hemfladen harbour on the western shore, surrounded by woods and fields. Along the curved peninsula to the north there's a youth hostel, camping spots and beaches. Few summerhouses have been built on Gällnö, and pine forests and two working farms cover most of the island. A 10,000-year-old cave, carved out by glaciers, is located in the north, below the Torsviken inlet.

The island's early farmers struggled with meagre harvests and suffered invasions by both the Danes and Russians. The Danes stopped at Gällnö in 1612 on their way to plunder Vaxholm; the Russians made a more thorough job of it in 1719, burning down a farm and destroying all the island's crops. The oven they built to bake coarse bread can still be found halfway between Gällnöby and **Gällnönäs**, a smaller village on the eastern side. In 1977, Skärgårdsstiftelsen (*see p243*) bought parts of the island to avoid private exploitation.

Ferries dock at two points along the island's elongated southern shore, first at **Gällnö** on the south-western shore, then at Gällnönäs to the east. From the Gällnö dock, visitors can walk about one kilometre north to Gällnöby, where most of the island's 30 permanent residents live. There is a shop, freshwater pump, public telephone and post office.

If you want to explore the neighbouring island of **Karklö**, you can hire a rowing boat on the northern Brännholmen peninsula. After rowing across to Karklö, you must attach two boats together then row back over to Brännholmen, leave one boat and row over to Karklö again. This rather complicated (and tiring) method means that there are always boats on both shores.

Where to eat

The waterfront store, **Gällnö Handelsbod** (571 663 10, closed end Aug-mid May), sells basic supplies and fresh bread, and rents out rowing boats. It also has a café. No other food is available on the island, except wild blueberries.

Where to stay

You'll find **Gällnö Vandrarhem** (571 661 17, rates 165kr, closed Oct-Apr) in the middle of a field, a short walk north of Gällnöby. Opened in 1981 in a former schoolhouse, the youth hostel also acts as the island's tourist information centre (*see below*). The hostel has 34 beds, most of them in two- to four-bed cottages. There is a sauna, but no TV, breakfast or restaurant and you need to book well in advance and bring your own supplies. Gällnö's **campsite** is about 1.5 kilometres (one mile) north of the hostel, by a sandy beach on Torsviken. Call **Gällnö Vandrarhem** for B&Bs.

Tourist information

There's no tourist office as such, but **Gällnö Vandrarhem** (*see above*) provides information on cottage rentals, B&Bs and local events. They will also help you find a guide or arrange a boat taxi.

Värmdö Turistbyrå

Odelbergs Väg 11, Gustavsberg, Värmdö (570 345 67/www.varmdo.se/turism). **Open** *June-Aug* 10am-5pm Mon-Fri; 11am-4pm Sat, Sun. Closed Sept-May. If the youth hostel on Gällnö is closed, the closest tourist office is on the nearby island of Värmdö.

Getting there

By boat

Waxholmsbolaget boats (*see p243*) run year-round from Strömkajen to Gällnö's two docks. The journey takes 2hrs and costs 100kr. **Cinderellabåtarna** boats (*see p243*) leave Strandvägen twice a day mid June-end Aug, taking 90mins and costing 130kr.

By car/bus & boat

Drive east on highway 222, or take bus 434 from Slussen, to Sollenkroka on the island of Vindö (80mins). From there you can board one of the **Waxholmsbolaget** boats (*see p243*).

Finnhamn

The island group of Finnhamn, 45 kilometres (28 miles) north-east of central Stockholm and just under five kilometres (three miles) north-west of Möja, comprises **Stora Jolpan, Lilla Jolpan, Idholmen** and several smaller islands. With as many as 200,000 visitors each year, it's one of the most visited areas in the archipelago. The ferry docks on the northern tip of Stora Jolpan, a stone's throw from the island's only restaurant and grocery store. Further south, on a hill, is the youth hostel. A land bridge connects Stora Jolpan to Idholmen, which has cottages for rent, meadows dotted with wildflowers in the spring and an organic farm. The islands have plenty of good spots for swimming. There are small beaches with flat rocks on Stora Jolpan and Idholmen.

The islands got their name after Finnish ships stopped on them during the 19th century on their way to and from Stockholm. The city of Stockholm bought the islands in the mid 1940s and they became the first recreational area in the archipelago – the cottages in **Stugbyn** and **Sjölängorna** were built in the 1950s to give poorer families from Stockholm the opportunity to spend time in the archipelago at a reasonable price. Skärgårdsstiftelsen (*see p243*) took control of Finnhamn in 1998 and it became a nature reserve in 2000.

Trips Out of Town

At the youth hostel you can rent rowing boats or book the sauna on the dock near the north-west corner of Stora Jolpan. The large farm on Idholmen shut down in the 1940s, but a recently opened organic farm sells eggs, vegetables and preserves. If you want to explore the smaller islands there's a boat you can borrow moored on Idholmen's shore.

For getting away from it all, you may want to visit the secluded island of **Stora Kalholmen** to the south, where you pump your own water outside the youth hostel and read by kerosene lamp at night.

Where to eat

The **Café-Krogen** bar-restaurant on Stora Jolpan (542 464 04, main courses 89kr-249kr, closed Nov-Easter) has a splendid view of the water and offers fish, pasta and several grilled alternatives. The **Sommarbutik** (542 462 07, open daily June-Aug), behind the restaurant, stocks just about everything you might need, including charcoal for the barbecuing areas around the island. Groups of 50 or more can rent the **Sliphuset** building with catered food from the youth hostel. It's got wooden benches, a gravel floor and kerosene lamps.

Where to stay

The 89-bed youth hostel, **Vandrarhemmet Utsikten** (542 462 12, www.finnhamn.se, 275kr per person per night), has a spectacular view of the water and basic rooms with bunk beds. The nearby **Sommargården** (closed Nov-Mar, groups only Apr-1st wk June, Aug-Oct), part of the youth hostel, was used as a kids' holiday camp until 1995. There are four basic houses sleeping one to six.

You can also book **cottages** by the week on Idholmen during the summer via the youth hostel. The **reception** in the youth hostel sells basic necessities, and lends games. The hostel also has a TV room and a 60kr breakfast buffet. **Camping** is only allowed at the designated spot on Stora Jolpan; pay the 60kr nightly fee at the youth hostel reception.

Getting there

By boat

Cinderellabåtarna boats (*see p243*) leave twice a day mid June-end Aug from Strandvägen, reaching Finnhamn in about 2hrs (single 120kr). The older **Waxholmsbolaget** boats (*see p243*) can take as long as 3hrs. Boats run less frequently out of season.

Finnhamn. *See p259.*

Möja

Archaeological remains indicate that people came to **Möja**, located three kilometres (two miles) south-east of Stora Kalholmen, at some point during the Viking age. Then, during the 13th century Finnish and Estonian fishermen began using it as a base for their spring and autumn fishing. The island was badly hit by the Russians in 1719, who burned down every house except the chapel. As on Gällnö, the Russians built ovens which can still be found around the western harbour of **Hamn**.

Fishing was for a long time the main source of income on the island, and when the water froze in winter fishermen would use a horse and sleigh to take their catch to Stockholm. A new chapter in the island's history started in the 1900s when Waxholmsbolaget started running its boat service. As Stockholmers began building summerhouses on the island, it became known for its strawberries. The climate and landscape allowed the strawberries to ripen slowly, and by the 1940s there were as many as 500,000 strawberry plants growing here. These days, tourism is the main industry.

Möja, 45 kilometres (28 miles) east of Stockholm, has a year-round population of about 300 but that figure triples in the summer. The island's services and businesses are centred on the village of **Berg**, where the ferries make one of their stops. Here you'll find a restaurant, bakery, grocery store and post office, as well as a very small museum.

Also in Berg you'll find **Möja Kyrka**, a white-steepled church built in 1768. For more secular entertainment, visit the **Dansbanan**, north-west of the village, home to occasional discos, a cinema and a beer tent.

A great view of the island and the archipelago can be had from the hill to the north-east of the village. At the top you'll find a reconstructed beacon of the kind once used to signal between islands. In 1719, when the Russians destroyed pretty much everything on their way through the archipelago, this beacon was used to warn islands closer to Stockholm of the danger.

Halfway up the road to the north of Berg lies the small village of **Ramsmora**, which boasts the very popular Wikströms Fisk restaurant (see below) and its shop. **Långvik** village is on the island's north-west corner and its **Skärgårdsgalleriet** sells handicrafts.

The western side of Möja is less developed, with pine forests often running right down to the water. Bicycles can be rented near the harbour in Berg, on the southern tip, or at the youth hostel (see below) in Långvik. There are few cars on the island and the best way to get around is on foot or by bicycle, although locals seem to prefer mopeds. Swimming is tricky as plant life and buildings block access to most of the shoreline, but you can join the bathing boat (contact the tourist information, 150kr), which takes you out to one of the many islands in the Möja nature reserve and picks you up again a few hours later. One of the islands' few sandy beaches can be found at Saltvik on the western shore. Hiking and cycling trails criss-cross the pine forests and beautiful meadows.

Where to eat

Möja Krog (Bergs Brygga, 571 641 85, main courses 78kr-250kr) sits near the ferry harbour in Berg. Located in an old yellow house, it's known for its beautiful view, grilled fish and live music in the summer. It's often closed out of season (mid Aug-mid June), so phone ahead to check the opening hours. **Wikströms Fisk** (571 641 70, www.wikstromsfisk.nu, main courses 75kr-180kr, booking essential), in Ramsmora, is run by one of the few full-time fishermen still on the island. The Wikström family serve up fresh fish such as salmon and herring on the patio or in the tavern behind.

Grocery chain **Konsum** runs two shops on the island, in Berg and Långvik (Berg 571 640 13, Långvik 571 64 007, open daily all year, but fewer hours during low season). The shop in Berg is the larger one and you can order alcohol from Systembolaget. It is also a pharmacy agent and runs the petrol station. There's also a **bakery** in Berg for those with a sweet tooth.

Where to stay

There are several cottages and rooms for rent on the islands from 200kr-300kr per night per person; call the tourist office. There are no campsites on the island, so when you set up your tent obey the public access laws (see p243).

Tourist information

Contact the Möja (571 640 53, www.moja.nu) or the Värmdö tourist offices (see p259).

Getting there

By boat

By far the best way to get to Möja is by ferry with **Waxholmsbolaget** (see p243) from Strömkäjen or **Cinderellabåtarna** (see p243) from Strandvägen. Boats depart twice a day and take 2-3hrs.

By car/bus & boat

Take bus 434 from Slussen or drive east on highway 222 to Sollenkroka on the island of Vindö (1hr 20mins). From there you can board one of the ferries to Möja. It's about 25mins from Sollenkroka to Möja.

Southern Archipelago

From sailing to Strindberg on Stockholm's summer isles.

Sandhamn.

A few large islands dominate the Southern Archipelago (Södra Skärgården), including **Utö**, which is open all year round, the sailing mecca of **Sandhamn**, and the nature reserves of **Nämdö** and **Fjärdlång**. Tiny **Kymmendö** gave inspiration to writer August Strindberg.

Sandhamn

For archipelago beauty without total isolation, opt for Sandhamn. The island (officially named Sandön, but known as Sandhamn) boasts a hotel and conference centre, various restaurants and bars, bustling nightlife and a long, sandy beach. Sandhamn is situated 48 kilometres (30 miles) east of Stockholm and is the sailing capital of the east coast – Sweden's most famous sailing race, Gotland Runt (Round Gotland), starts and finishes at Sandhamn at the end of June. The **Kungliga Svenska Segel Sällskapet** (Royal Swedish Yacht Club; www.ksss.se) was established here a century ago and the beautiful old clubhouse is home to one of the island's best restaurants, **Seglarrestaurangen** (*see p263*). Pine forests cover most of the island, but the village dates back to the 1600s and has a few shops, a post office and a small museum.

Unlike other islands in the archipelago that relied on fishing and agriculture, Sandhamn developed as a toll and pilot station. The early buildings in the village centred on these services, such as **Sandhamns Värdshus**, a restaurant (*see p263*) built in 1672 by the boat pilots. When the Russians briefly occupied the island in 1719, many of its original structures were destroyed. In the late 1800s, steamboats travelling to the island brought summer visitors who built many of the small, red cottages still seen today on the village's narrow streets. The island receives more than 100,000 visitors each year, but there is a permanent population of just 120.

Many of the island's points of interest are near the ferry dock. The **Hembygdsmuseum** (closed Sept-Midsummer) stands by the water in a small, red 18th-century storehouse, containing equipment from the toll station and an exhibit on alcohol smuggling. The **Tullhuset** (Toll House) is nearby; it operated until 1965 but is now leased out to private residents. In the 1870s August Strindberg lived with his wife in a building, now called **Strindbergsgården**, situated along the walkway overlooking the harbour.

There are beaches at **Fläskberget**, to the west of the village, and at **Dansberget** to the east, but you should really take the 20-minute walk through the forest to the beautiful sandy beach at **Trouville** in the south. Bikes can be rented at the **Viamare Sea Club** (57 45 04 00, www.viamareseaclub.com), which also has an outdoor pool (open daily June-Aug), bar and café.

Where to eat

With an additional 2,400 residents during the summer to feed, Sandhamn has enough restaurants to satisfy most tastes and budgets. An upmarket choice is **Seglarrestaurangen**, at the Sandhamn Hotell & Konferens (*see below*), with its veranda and views of the harbour. The historic **Sandhamns Värdshus** (57 15 30 51, www.sandhamns-vardshus.se, main courses 95kr-250kr) serves fish and wild game in a cosy environment, and also has a pub. An even livelier time can be had at **Dykarbaren** (57 15 35 54, www.dykarbaren.se), a popular bar with a restaurant upstairs. Sandhamn also has a bakery and two groceries. The **Sands Hotell** (*see below*) also has a restaurant.

Where to stay

The **Sandhamn Hotell & Konferens** (57 45 04 21, www.sandhamn.com, doubles from 1,250kr), overlooking the guest harbour, was rebuilt in 1999 as a conference centre with 81 luxurious rooms, pool, fitness centre and sauna. In 1890, Theodor Sand opened a hotel named after himself, which was later closed and the building torn down. Today there is a new **Sands Hotell** (57 15 30 20, www.sands hotell.se, doubles 1,500kr) on the same spot, with splendid views. The interior is sleek and airy, with whitewashed wooden floors. For B&Bs, contact **Sandhamns Turistinformation** on 57 15 30 00.

Getting there

By boat

Boats operated by **Sandhamnspilen** (765 04 70, www.sandhamn.com) run boats from Strandvägen to Sandhamn (2hrs, single 120kr). The other option is to catch bus 434 from Slussen to Stavsnäs (1hr), which arrives in time for the ferry to Sandhamn (25mins, single 65kr). **Waxholmsbolaget** (*see p243*) and **Cinderellabåtarna** boats (*see p243*) depart several times a day from Stockholm during the summer.

Nämdö

The Nämdö archipelago, south-west of Sandhamn, consists of hundreds of islands – from Aspö in the north to Mörtö in the south.

The main island of Nämdö, 38 kilometres (27 miles) east of Stockholm, is eight kilometres (five miles) long and two kilometres (1.25 miles) wide, and has 40 permanent residents.

The main reason to visit Nämdö is to enjoy nature; there are some good swimming spots and two small lakes dot each end of the island. The highest point is **Nämdöböte** in the north-east corner, 42 metres (138 feet) above sea level, from where you can see as far as Stockholm's Globen arena on a good day. Most of Nämdö's houses can be found on the eastern side, as can the main village of **Sand**. The middle of the island is covered with pine forests, while the hilly western half is home to elk, deer and foxes.

The village of Sand, one of the island's ferry stops, is home to the **Hembygdsmuseum** (57 15 90 47, open noon-3pm daily July, weekends to mid Aug); located in a 19th-century schoolhouse, it displays handicrafts, art and old photos. The annual **Nämdödagen** (Nämdö Day) celebrations on the last Saturday in July take place in Sand.

The village of **Solvik**, further north, has a popular restaurant, its own ferry dock and year-round grocery store **ICA Guns Livs** (*see below*), which also rents out bikes. **Skärgårdsstiftelsen** (*see p243*) runs an organic farm, **Östanviks Gård** (*see below*). You can take a guided tour of the farm, which is also the starting point for a six-kilometre (four-mile) nature trail. The farm also acts as Nämdö's tourist information centre. Some of the island's oldest structures stand around the village of **Gamla Östanvik** north of Solvik. This area was rebuilt after Russians destroyed most of Nämdö's buildings in 1719.

Where to eat

In Solvik, **Nämdö Hamnkrog** (57 15 61 57, www.namdohamnkrog.se, closed Oct-Apr, closed Mon-Fri May-mid June, mid Aug-mid Sept) serves cocktails, beer and hot meals. The restaurant seats 130 outside and there's live music on Saturdays. **ICA Guns Livs** (57 15 60 17) offers a wide range of food for picnics, and customers can also order alcohol or pick up pharmacy items. **Kerstins Bryggcafé**, on the pier, sells sandwiches and ice-cream.

Further north, **Östanviks Gård** (57 15 64 18, www.ostanviksgard.se) sells eggs, vegetables and meat. It has a garden café in summer.

Where to stay

ICA Guns Livs (*see above*) rents cottages with ovens, fridges and running water (closed Dec-Mar). Some are located on grass lawns near the shore and others in meadows or surrounded by trees. The year-round cottages at **Östanviks Gård** (*see above*) have similar facilities.

Trips Out of Town

Kymmendö.

Camping is allowed, as long as tents are away from buildings and cultivated fields. Two good spots are near the dock at Östanviks Gård and on the eastern beach of Långvik harbour.

Tourist information

ICA Guns Livs and **Östanviks Gård** (for both, *see p263*) provide information for visitors.

Getting there

By train/bus/car & boat

Waxholmsbolaget boats (*see p243*) leave from Strömkajen in spring and summer; the journey takes 2-2.5hrs. Boats also leave year-round from Saltsjöbaden (single 80kr) and Stavsnäs (65kr); the trip takes 1-1.5hrs. To get to Saltsjöbaden, take the train from Slussen or drive via highway 222 through Nacka, then follow the exit towards Saltsjöbaden. To get to Stavsnäs, catch bus 434 from Slussen, or drive east on highway 222 for about 1hr.

Fjärdlång

This three-and-a-half-kilometre (two-mile) long island is a nature reserve, known for its many species of birds and great kayaking. Although there are no real beaches, the island has plenty of smooth rocks from which to swim. Trails wind up through the lush pine and deciduous forests, leading to the highest point near **Mörkviken** harbour. Here you are 36 metres (120 feet) above sea level and you get a spectacular view of the archipelago. In the south-west, by the ferry dock, the youth hostel (*see below*) rents out kayaks and boats.

At the beginning of the 20th century, archipelago farmers began selling their land to well-off businessmen from Stockholm. One such man was the wealthy financier Ernest Thiel, who built a large summerhouse on Fjärdlång in 1917,

today the youth hostel. After a series of bad speculations, he was forced to sell his home on Djurgården to the state (now the Thielska Galleriet, *see p86*), as well as parts of the island.

The nearby island of **Kymmendö** became famous in 1887 when August Strindberg (*see p236* **Anarchy in August**) wrote a very thinly disguised novel about its residents entitled *Hemsöborna* (The People of Hemsö). The people of Kymmendö were not happy. Strindberg said that he had found paradise the first time he set foot on Kymmendö, but he was never allowed back after *Hemsöborna* was published. The island is only open to day-trippers and the season runs from May to September. The main attraction is Strindberg's small cottage. Visitors arrive on the south-west shore, where the restaurant **Carlssons Backficka** and other facilities are located, all operated by Kymmendö Service (50 15 42 65).

Where to eat

There is no restaurant on the island, but the hostel (*see below*) does run a kiosk (closed end Sept-Apr) with a strictly limited range of food. You should make sure you have enough supplies before you arrive on the island.

Where to stay

The grand **Fjärdlångs Vandrarhem** (50 15 60 92, doubles 125kr-170kr, closed mid Oct-May) offers hostel accommodation in a red-painted, two-storey building set on a round stone hill. The hostel offers four-bed cottages and rooms with four to six beds in the main building, with a shared kitchen in the hostel. Cottages are usually rented out by the week. The hostel also runs the guest harbour and campsite (50kr per night, pay at the reception in the harbour).

Tourist information

During the summer, the **youth hostel** (*see p264*) can help with most queries. **Haninge Kommun** (606 82 58, www.haninge.se, call 9am-noon), may be able to help out of season.

Getting there

By boat/bus/car

Waxholmsbolaget boats (*see p243*) run from Strömkajen mid June-end Aug (2.5hrs, single 120kr). Waxholmsbolaget also runs boats from Dalarö year round (1hr, single 65kr). **Dalarö Kustfart** (single 80kr) runs a service from Dalarö during the summer.
  In summer, you can get to Kymmendö from Stockholm with **Waxholmsbolaget** (*see p243*) or **Strömma Kanalbolaget** (*see p243*); the trip takes 2-3hrs. Alternatively, take the train to Haninge Centrum and switch to bus 839 to Dalarö, or drive south on highway 73 to Handen, then take highway 227 east. From Dalarö, Kymmendö is a short boat ride with **Waxholmsbolaget** (*see p243*) or **Dalarö Kustfart** (50 15 07 00, www.dalarokustfart.se). Boat taxis are available from **Kymmendö Service** (*see p264*).

Utö

Utö is one of the largest islands in the archipelago, and over the summer it receives about 300,000 visitors. The main harbour is **Gruvbryggan**, where ferries from Stockholm arrive and most of the island's facilities can be found, including the tourist office, the only hotel, restaurants, shops and the guest harbour. Ferries also stop midway along the island at **Spränga**, and at the southern tip of the adjoining island of **Ålö**, which is connected to Utö by road. Utö is busiest in summer, when Stockholmers flock to their holiday homes and boats bustle about the marina, but it never seems to get too crowded.

Utö has been inhabited since pre-Viking times and ancient burial grounds have been found at Skogsby on the southern half of the island. Utö is also well known for its 700-year-old mining history; Sweden's oldest iron ore mine can be found here. The geological uniqueness of Utö is what drew early prospectors – it's one of the very few places in the world to contain the iron mineral holmquistite – and mining continued uninterrupted until 1879.

When mining was no longer profitable, Utö was bought by industrial magnate 'Plank Anders' Andersson, who set up a timber yard and sawmill, which is still intact today and offers the best view of the island. At the end of the 19th century, merchant EW Lewin bought the island from 'Plank Anders' for 140,000kr, and promoted it as a fashionable summer resort for the Stockholm elite. The locals were not made so welcome, however. Lewin needed accommodation for his visitors, so the former miners were forced to vacate their homes in **Lurgatan** (built during the 1700s and today used as holiday cottages).

Today, about 230 people live on Utö year-round, mainly in the centre of the island at **Spränga**, where a school and many of the island's summerhouses can be found. The village is also home to an impressive stone church, which was built in 1850 and contains the oldest working church organ in Sweden.

Behind **Utö Värdshus** (*see below*) are the **old mine pits**, now filled with water and rocks (the latter were thrown in by the Russian army in 1719 in an attempt to destroy the mine). The pits are still an impressive sight.

The small **Gruvmuseet** (Mining Museum; closed mid Aug-mid June, admission 10kr) is housed in an old wooden barn (the former fire station) beside the hotel. At the top of the nearby hill is the wooden **Kvarnen** (windmill; closed mid Aug-mid June), which was built in 1791 and in operation until 1927. The old machinery is still inside and there's a fantastic view from the top.

Utö is ideal for swimming and some of the best beaches can be found on the southern shore. **Stora Sand** and **Storsand** both offer lovely sandy stretches. It's a 15-kilometre (nine-mile) cycle ride to Storsand on Ålö, but check with tourist information first so you don't end up in the middle of a shoot-out (southern Utö contains a military firing range).

Families should head for **Barnesbad**, a child-friendly beach 1.5 kilometres (one mile) north of Gruvbryggan harbour. At the harbour you can also play tennis, beach volleyball, miniature golf, football and boules. The best way to get around Utö is by bike, which you can rent at Gruvbryggan during high season (get there early as it's popular). The tourist office also rents out bikes and these can be booked in advance. Alternatively, hire a kayak or rowing boat to explore the coast; tuition is available.

Where to eat

Gourmet cooking is served up at the beautiful **Utö Värdshus** restaurant (50 42 03 00, www.uto-vardshus.se, main courses 112kr-228kr), which is frequently voted the best restaurant in the archipelago. It's renowned for its fish (shrimp and pike sausages, perch, halibut and salmon), much of it caught locally. A short stroll after dinner will bring you to **Bakfickan** (closed mid Aug-May), a popular cellar bar.

In summer, you can eat at **Seglarbaren** (50 42 03 00, closed mid Aug-mid June, main courses 70kr-150kr), a restaurant on the waterfront by the main harbour. The island's bakery, **Utö Bageri** (50 15 70 79, closed Sept-May), near the harbour, sells great pastries, sandwiches and coffee, as well as its own special sailors' bread, Utölimpa, which stays fresh for three weeks if stored in a cool, dark place. The adjoining restaurant, **Dannekrogen** (same phone), is a homely place. Pick up picnic supplies at the shop opposite.

Other summer-only eating options include pizza parlour **Pizzastugan** at Spränga (50 15 73 50, closed mid Aug-mid June) and **Båtshaket** (50 15 74 63, closed Sept-mid June, main courses 50kr-180kr), which serves up excellent fresh fish next to the landing stage on Ålö.

Where to stay

A five-minute walk uphill from Gruvbryggan is **Utö Värdshus** (*see p265*), the island's only hotel. The main building, housed in the 18th-century mine office, contains the reception, bar and a fine restaurant. It offers a variety of accommodation in scattered historic buildings, including four-person **wooden cottages** with shower, WC and a small outdoor area; the 18th-century **Stenhotellet** (with double rooms and bunk beds); and the **Kvarnvillan**, below the windmill, with en suite doubles and views across the harbour. It's busy year-round, so book ahead.

Utö Värdshus also runs the **STF Youth Hostel** (50 42 03 15, 325kr per person per night, closed Oct-Apr), with 64 beds. You can also rent basic cottages through the tourist office (*see below*) – most are around Spränga. Camping is available near the harbour (contact the marina office).

Tourist information

Utö Turistbyrå

Gruvbryggan (50 15 74 10/www.utoturist byra.se). **Open** usually 10am-4/5pm daily.

Getting there

By boat

Waxholmsbolaget boats (*see p243*) run from Strömkajen several times a day May-Aug (2.5-3hrs, single 120kr). Boats also stop at the next-door island of Ålö, so if you phone ahead you can arrange for a bike to be waiting there and cycle north to Utö.

By train, bus & boat

From Central Station take a pendeltåg train to Västerhaninge (about 35mins), then bus 846 to Årsta Havsbad (SL passes valid on the train and bus), then a boat (single 55kr) to Utö. The journey takes about 1.5hrs to Gruvbryggan; another 15mins to Spränga.

Utö. *See p265.*

Northern Archipelago

Northern delights.

Björkö

The northernmost island in the archipelago, large and lively Björkö (meaning 'island of birches') is connected to the mainland by a small strip of road in its north-west corner. Pine forests interspersed with fields dominate the landscape, with narrow harbours cutting its jagged shoreline. It is one of the few active farming communities in the archipelago, and cattle and horses can be seen grazing almost everywhere. Two inlets from the north and south nearly divide the 13-kilometre (eight-mile) long island in half. Most of Björkö's amenities, such as its early 20th-century church, seafaring museum and youth hostel, lie on or east of this divide. The ferries from Stockholm and Arholma arrive in **Simpnäs**, on the eastern shore.

Björkö's shipbuilding industry grew in the 18th century as trade increased with Stockholm. The Crimean and Franco-Prussian Wars during the 19th century were boom years for the island, and almost every tree was cut down to make ships. As motors replaced sails, production declined and tourism became the new moneyspinner. The men made rich by the island's small shipping companies built themselves grand homes on farms around the island. A few of these residences still stand, at **Kulla**, **Blekunge** and Simpnäs; the house at Skeppsmyra on the southern shore is now the hostel **Lyckhem Vandrarhem** (*see below*). You can learn more about the island's shipping history at the **Sjömannaförenings Museum** in Simpnäs (0176 910 05, closed mid Aug-Midsummer & Midsummer-mid Aug Mon-Fri, admission free).

On top of a hill in the middle of the island is **Björkö-Arholma Kyrka** (0176 524 10, www.svenskakyrkan.se/vaddo). This wooden church, decorated with paintings by artist Harald Lindberg, was built in 1914 after residents complained of having to row several kilometres to Sunday services on Vätö island.

Hikers can explore the beautiful flora and fauna of the island by walking the trail that follows the eastern shore. For something a little faster, you could rent a bike (45kr per day) or a canoe or boat (150kr per day) from **Skeppsmyra Lyckhem Vandrarhem** (*see below*). Rowing boats and canoes are also available from the **Björkögården** hostel

(*see below*) on the western shore. In **Bofjärden**, the harbour north-west of Simpnäs, there are smooth, flat rocks from which you can swim.

Where to eat

Aside from the pub, café and shop at the **Skeppsmyra Lyckhem Vandrarhem** (*see below*), which open only when the hostel has bookings, there is only one place to eat on the island: the summer-only **Simpnäs Hamncafé** (0176 917 98) by the harbour in Simpnäs. It serves pastries and sandwiches, and has exhibitions and evening concerts during the summer.

Where to stay

The **Skeppsmyra Lyckhem Vandrarhem** (0176 940 27, www.lyckhemhb.se, 225kr per person per night, closed mid June-mid Aug), on the southern shore, is a two-storey yellow house built in the 1850s. Situated on an expansive green lawn, the hostel has 80 beds, a sauna, washing machines, a TV room and conference facilities, plus a sauna, café, small shop and pub. Cottages are also available for rent (from 450kr per night), some with TV, shower and microwave, and others with more basic facilities. There's also campsite **Skeppsmyra Camping** (0176 940 27, 100kr-125kr per tent per night).

On the western shore, **Björkögården** (0176 910 55, www.kgh.nu, 170kr per person per night, closed Nov-end Apr) has 129 beds and a great swimming spot. This is a private hostel with cottages, run by a Christian organisation with 'a restrictive attitude towards alcohol'.

Arholma

The island of Arholma is located less than a kilometre east of Björkö and is the last outpost in the Stockholm archipelago before the Finnish island of Åland. A large portion of Arholma, which is just five kilometres (three miles) long, has been designated a nature reserve. The ferries dock on the western shore, next to a grocery shop, dancehall, lovely church and windmill. Skärgårdsstiftelsen (Archipelago Foundation; *see p243*) owns a quarter of the island and manages two old farms and a guest harbour. As on many other archipelago islands, Arholma is at its liveliest during summer.

Arholma. *See p267.*

The hostel, shop and church are open all year, but other places on the island are only open from Midsummer to mid August.

Before the 18th century, hunting, fishing and agriculture were the mainstays of the island's economy. But as on Björkö, the people of Arholma learned to become skilled shipbuilders, and in the 19th century several farmers became comparatively wealthy from the trade. Many of the splendid homes these men built were turned into boarding houses at the start of the 20th century. Around the harbour of **Österhamn**, on the eastern side of the island, stand several old boathouses. Another reminder of the island's seafaring past is **Arholma Båk** (0176 561 67, closed early Aug-Midsummer & Fri Midsummer-early Aug), standing on a hill south of the ferry dock.

This red and white circular tower, built in 1768 to signal to ships, now exhibits local artwork and handicrafts.

Near the ferry dock, the charming dancehall **Arholma Dansbana** (0176 560 87) was built in the 1940s and has live music on Saturdays in July, as well as occasional dance courses. The nearby **Arholma Handel** shop (*see below*) also acts as a post office and petrol station.

Where to eat

Your best bet is the organic dishes at **Café Sol & Vind** (0176 560 87, closed mid Aug-Midsummer) at the Arholma Dansbana (*see above*). At **Arholma Handel** (0176 560 12, open all year), by the ferry dock, you can buy groceries and order alcohol.

Where to stay

Arholma Vandrarhem (0176 560 18, www.
algonet.se, call 9-10am, 6-7pm daily, 165kr per
person per night) is just south of the church.
The hostel has 34 beds. There's also a campsite
at the island's north-west corner.

Tourist information

Visit Arholma's website (Swedish only) –
www.algonet.se/~arholma1.

Norrtälje Turistbyrå

*Danskes Gränd 4-6, Norrtälje (0176 719 90/
www.roslagen.nu/engelska/index.html).* **Open** *May-
Aug* 10am-7pm Mon-Fri; 10am-5pm Sat; 11am-5pm
Sun. *Sept-May* 10am-6pm Mon-Sat.

Getting there

By boat

Waxholmsbolaget ferries (*see p243*) from
Strömkajen run to Björkö and Arholma once
daily mid June-mid Aug, taking approximately
3hrs 45mins. **Passbåt** ferries (0176 561 16, www.
algonet.se/~arholma1) make the 20-minute trip
between Arholma and Björkö several times a day.

By car & bus

You can reach Björkö by both car and bus. Catch
bus 676 from Stockholm's Tekniska Högskolan
T-bana station to Norrtälje, then bus 636 to Björkö.
Or head north on the E18 for about 55km (34 miles)
until you reach Norrtälje. From there, head north
on highway 283 to Väddö, from where you follow
the signs south-east to Björkö. There are frequent
boats between Björkö and Arholma.

Way up north

Sweden is divided into three regions: Götaland in the south, Svealand in the middle and Norrland in the north. The latter, meaning literally 'north land', is by far the largest, comprising 58 per cent of Sweden's total land. Sparsely populated by 1.3 million people, most of whom live in cities along the Baltic Sea, Norrland is often described as 'the last wilderness of Europe'. With thousands of acres of pine forests, beautiful national parks, pristine lakes and snow-covered mountains to the north-west, including Sweden's highest, Mount Kebnekaise at 2,111 metres (6,926 feet), the area is irresistibly romantic.

The variations in the region's landscape are so extreme, from the rugged tundra in the north, to the high coast in the east, to the hilly and lake-dotted counties above the southern border of the Dalälven river, that many inhabitants of northern Norrland do not regard people from, say, Gävle or Bollnäs, as true *norrlänningar* (northerners). To earn this title, one must live in the top one seventh of Sweden, which lies within the Arctic Circle. Here the sun shines continuously for two months in the summer and not at all for two months in the winter – perfect for midnight potato growing or gazing at the Aurora Borealis (the Northern Lights). Swedes from all over take advantage of the area's high latitude and natural beauty, with ski trips in the winter and spring, and hiking and camping excursions in the mountains in summer, where the only company they find is of the buzzing, blood-sucking variety.

Norrland is not all about recreation, however, and its exports, including timber, paper, iron ore and hydro power, account for 60 billion kronor of Sweden's net export value. In addition, the areas of northern Norway, Sweden, Finland and Russia constitute what is commonly known as Lapland, the home of Scandinavia's indigenous people, who prefer to be called the Sami rather than Lapps or Laplanders. The origins of the Sami are unknown, although their languages derive from the Finno-Ugric family, as do Finnish, Estonian and Hungarian. Sami are most famously known as nomadic reindeer herders, though there are also groups who fish, hunt and gather. Of the 17,000 Sami living in Sweden today, some still follow the reindeer, now on snow scooters rather than sleds, but many others live like any other Swede.

Just north of Sweden's northernmost city, Kiruna, lies the famous Ice Hotel (www.ice hotel.com), which is rebuilt every year from huge slabs of ice cut from the water. For those not wishing to make a trip so far north, a taster of the hotel's icy offerings can be had at Stockholm's **Icebar** (*see p137*) and **Ice Gallery** (*see p68*). The **Nordiska Museet** (*see p84*) also has an excellent exhibition on the Sami. If you just want the night sun, Stockholm – if you are lucky with the weather – can offer that too. During June, a beautiful twilight illuminates the capital city's night skies, as the sun swings below the horizon for only a few hours.

Trips Out of Town

Baltic & Beyond

From medieval Gotland to hip Helsinki.

Gotland

With 800,000 visitors a year, the island of
Gotland is Sweden's most popular summer
resort. It is located in the middle of the Baltic
Sea, 160 kilometres (100 miles) south-east of
Stockholm, and its largest city, Visby, has a
place on UNESCO's World Heritage list. Gotland
stretches 176 kilometres (110 miles) from north
to south and is 50 kilometres (30 miles) at its
widest point. The island is as famous for its
summer nightlife, focused on Visby, as its
spectacular scenery – a barren landscape of
cliffs and stones in the north and thickly wooded
forests in the south. With a car you can reach
anywhere on Gotland from Visby in under two
hours. Driving or cycling around the island
you'll see unusual rock formations, fields of wild
roses, medieval church ruins and lots of sheep.

People first lived on Gotland about 8,000
years ago, relying on fishing and hunting.
Hundreds of Bronze Age grave sites are dotted
around the island. At the time of the Roman
Empire, Gotlanders started sailing around the
Baltic, trading fur, weapons and slaves. In the
ninth century Gotland Vikings plundered the
fortunes of Russia, the Black Sea and the
Mediterranean. By the 1200s, the island – then
an autonomous republic – was the largest and
richest trading post in the region; gold and
silver treasure from this period has been found
buried all over the island. Civil war broke out
in 1288 between Visby, heavily populated by

Germans, and the rest of the island; Visby
emerged victorious. When Denmark attacked
in the year 1361, the newly independent
residents of Visby sat safely behind the
city walls as the farmers outside were killed.
Danish occupation marked the end of Gotland's
greatness. Ownership of the island alternated
between Denmark and Sweden for years before
it finally became part of Sweden in 1679.

Visby, Gotland's largest city, is on the north-
western shore and is one of the best-preserved
medieval cities in Europe. Its narrow streets
lined with 13th- and 14th-century buildings
are still protected by the defensive 13th-century
wall, which is 3.5 kilometres (two miles) long
and has 50 towers.

The excellent **Gotlands Fornsal**
(Strandgatan 14, 0498 29 27 00, mid Sept-mid
May closed Mon, admission 60kr) is located a
few blocks east of the docks. It contains silver
Viking hoards, re-created interiors from different
periods and the Fenomenalen science centre for
kids. The **Gotlands Naturmuseum** (Museum
of Natural History) is in the same building.
Nearby is **Gotlands Konstmuseum** (Museum
of Art; St Hansgatan 21, closed Mon mid Sept-
mid May, admission 40kr), which displays the
work of some of the island's best artists.

The ruins of a dozen medieval churches stand
around the city, the most impressive being
St Nicolai (St Nicolaigränd). Built in 1230 by
Dominican monks, the church and convent were
burned down in an attack from Lübeck in 1525.

Visby.

The magnificent **Visby St Maria Domkyrka** (Västra Kyrkogatan 5, www.visbydomkyrko forsamling.nu), one of almost 100 medieval churches on Gotland, was built in 1225 for visiting German merchants. It is the only one still in use (the others are in ruins).

Tucked up against the city wall in the north-west corner of Visby is the beautiful **Botaniska Trädgård** (Botanical Garden; St Nikolaigatan 11, www.dbw.nu, admission free), opened in 1855. **Kapitelhusgården** (St Drottensgatan 8, 0498 24 76 37, www.lansmuseetgotland.se, closed mid Aug-mid June) is a courtyard in the centre of town with a café and a herb garden where you can try medieval handicrafts. The streets of Visby are packed for a week in August for the **Medeltidsveckan** (Medieval Week; www.medeltidsveckan.com), with markets, pageants, jousting and medieval costumes.

Three kilometres (1.8 miles) south of Visby is **Kneippbyn** (Kneippbyn 15, 0498 29 61 50, www.kneippbyn.se, open early May-early Sept, admission 85kr-125kr), a popular adventure park, with a rollercoaster, 15 waterslides and a house used in the 1960s Pippi Longstocking films. The park offers various levels of accommodation, from camping to hotels. Buses leave for Kneippbyn from Visby's inner harbour.

The flat countryside outside Visby is perfect for bike riding, or you could rent a car (ask at the tourist office; *see p272*). Some 13 kilometres (eight miles) north of Visby along route 149 are the **Lummelundagrottan** caves (0498 27 30 50/90, May-mid Sept open daily, mid Sept-Apr bookings only, admission 70kr) were created by underground currents. They were first explored in 1948 when three young boys crawled along a 20-metre (65-foot) corridor before stumbling on a great hall, today called Mountain King's Hall.

In July, the island – and Visby especially – is transformed into something of a Swedish Ibiza, with hip Stureplan club nights flying in DJs for guest appearances. Booking is essential for ferries and accommodation during the summer. After August many places outside Visby shut down, but the city still has plenty to offer.

To the south of Gotland are the two small islands of **Stora Karlsö** (www.storakarlso.se, closed mid Sept-May, ferries run until end Aug, then group bookings only) and **Lilla Karlsö** (www.snf.se/lillakarlso, ferries mid May-Sept); the former is a nature reserve, the latter a bird sanctuary. There's a restaurant and hostel (0498 24 05 00) on Stora Karlsö, and its rocky shores and trails are popular with nature fans. The boat timings make day trips possible.

Off the north-east corner of Gotland is **Fårö**, which has camping, great beaches – of which the best is Sudersand – and ancient ruins. It also has one of Gotland's largest tourist attractions,

Hoburgsgubben, a sea-stack formation in the shape of a man. Before you catch the ferry (free), visit open-air museum **Bungemuseet** (0498 22 10 32, www.guteinfo.com/bungemuseet, closed Sept-mid May, admission 60kr) in Fårösund. A bit like a mini Skansen, it's got buildings dating from the Middle Ages to the 1800s and costumed employees demonstrating traditional handicrafts. From Fårösund you can also take a two-hour ferry trip, leaving three times a week, to the isolated island of **Gotska Sandön** (www.gotskasandon.com), which has sandy beaches and small cottages for rent.

Where to eat & drink

You'll find the island's best restaurants and bars in the city of Visby. For coffee and delicious pancakes head to cosy **Rosas Café** (St Hansgatan 22, 0498 21 35 14, closed mid Sept-Nov, Jan-mid Apr). A more Stockholm-style coffee shop is **Vinäger Café** (Hästgatan 3, 0498 21 11 60), with a minimalist interior, great sandwiches and a garden.

One of Visby's more esteemed restaurants is **Friheten** (Strandgatan 6, 0498 24 99 07, main courses 70kr-250kr), with its rustic interior, extensive wine list and knowledgeable staff. **Värdshuset Lindgården** (Strandgatan 26, 0498 21 87 00, main courses 140kr-275kr) is also known for its fine dining, beautiful garden and Gotland specialities, such as boiled, breaded lamb with mustard. Dotted around Stora Torget (the main square) are several pizza and pasta joints, as well as one of Gotland's best seafood restaurants, **Bakfickan** (Stora Torget 1, 0498 27 18 07, main courses 70kr-200kr).

Decent watering holes include **Munkkällaren** (0498 27 14 00) and **Gutekällaren** (0498 21 00 43), which stand side by side on Stora Torget, and **Burmeister** (Strandgatan 9, 0498 21 03 73).

Where to stay

The small and cosy **St Hans Hostel** (St Hansgatan 51, 0498 21 93 16, www.bokahela gotland.nu, doubles 300kr-900kr) in Visby is a self-catering hostel with double rooms. Breakfast in the back garden is a great way to start the day. The owners also run an **apartment hotel** (Tunnbindargatan 17, 0498 21 93 16, closed Oct-May, rates from 1,200kr per night) with two-room flats, and rent out **camper vans** (7,000kr per week) for people who want to tour the island.

The classic **Wisby Hotell** (Strandgatan 6, 0498 25 75 00, www.wisbyhotell.se, doubles 1,280kr-1,930kr) offers first-class accommodation in 134 rooms. Parts of the hotel date back to the 1200s and, after a renovation in the 1990s, today it is an elegant mix of medieval and modern.

Trips Out of Town

Strand Hotel (Strandgatan 34, 0498 25 88 00, www.strandhotel.net, doubles 1,430kr-1,760kr) has an excellent location in the middle of town. Some suites have private saunas; for everyone else there is a pool and sauna room.

Camping and cabins are available a 15-minute walk north of the city along the sea at **Norderstrands Camping** (0498 21 21 57, www. norderstrandscamping.se, cabins 450kr-1000kr, camping 100kr-265kr, closed mid Sept-mid Apr).

Tourist information

Visit http://gotland.net and www.gotlands turistservice.com, both available in English.

Gotlands Turistförening

Hamngatan 4, Visby (0498 20 17 00/www.gotland. info). **Open** daily May-Oct; Mon-Fri Oct-May.

Getting there

By boat

Destination Gotland (0771 22 33 00/www. destinationgotland.se) runs ferries (3-5hrs) between Visby and Nynäshamn, which is 40km (25 miles) south of Stockholm at the end of the commuter train lines. The same company also runs ferries (2.5-4hrs) between Gotland and Oskarshamn, a town 320km (200 miles) south of Stockholm. Visby's harbour is within walking distance of the city centre.

By air

Flights (40mins) to Visby leave several times a day from Arlanda, Bromma and Norrköping airports. Contact **Gotlandsflyg** (0498 22 22 22/www.gotlands flyg.se) or **Skyways** (0771 95 95 95/www.sky ways.se) for schedules and rates.

Beyond Sweden

If you like to pack as many countries as possible into your holidays, consider taking the short cruise from Stockholm to **Helsinki** or **Tallinn**. Ships generally leave Stockholm in the evening and arrive the next morning. During the boat trip, passengers can shop at the tax-free stores, dine in the restaurants and tour the bars and discos – it's almost a rite of passage for young Swedes. When you arrive you get a full day to explore the city before the ship leaves again that evening. In the off-season a package deal, including a round-trip ticket and buffet dinner, can cost as little as 300kr.

The red and white **Viking Line** boats (452 40 00, www.vikingline.se) are known for their drunken youths and live entertainment by C-list pop stars, particularly on the weekends. The classier and pricier **Silja Line** (22 21 40, www. silja.se) is more popular with young families and people who have already sown most of their wild oats. Long shopping promenades with high glass ceilings run down the centre of the ship, and the entertainment is more family-oriented. The **Tallink** ships (666 60 01, www.tallink.se), which travel directly to Tallinn, have pubs with live music, a few tax-free shops and a show by Estonian dancers, followed by a disco.

Helsinki, the capital of Finland, is one of the trendiest cities in northern Europe; don't miss the Museum of Contemporary Art (KIASMA). Tallinn is the capital of Estonia and boasts a fortified medieval old town and several museums. For more information on what to do when you land, contact the **Helsinki Tourist Office** (+358 9 169 37 57, www.hel.fi) or the **Tallinn Tourist Information Centre** (+372 645 7777, www.tourismtallinn.ee).

Prices vary depending on the size of the cabin, how many people share it and where it's located on the boat. To get the cheapest price, you will probably end up below the car deck sharing with three strangers, while the sounds of the engine make sleep virtually impossible. Cabins above the water are quiet and don't cost much more.

Silja and Viking Line ships depart every day, and Tallink every other day. Silja's terminal is at Värtahamnen, just north of Ladugårdsgärdet, and Viking Line's is on the northern shore of Södermalm, and Tallink's is at Frihamnen, just south of Värtahamnen. *See also p275.*

Visby St Maria Domkyrka. *See p271.*

Directory

Features

Directory

Getting There & Around

Stockholm is a compact city and much of it can be easily explored on foot – in fact, walking is often the best way to get around. There's also an efficient **Tunnelbana** (metro) system and a comprehensive network of buses. Cyclists are well catered for with lots of bike lanes. A car is usually a liability: parking is limited and expensive – and the public transport system will get you to most places outside the city.

Arriving & leaving

By air

Four airports serve Stockholm: Arlanda, Bromma, Skavsta and Västerås.

Arlanda Airport
Flight information 797 61 00/other enquiries 797 60 00/www.lfv.se.
Stockholm's main airport, the largest in Scandinavia, is 42km (27 miles) north of the city centre and serves over 15 million passengers a year. International flights arrive and depart from terminals 2 and 5. Domestic flights depart from terminals 3 and 4.

It's a light, spacious, well-designed place, and the facilities are good. For currency exchange there is Forex (terminal 2), X-Change (terminal 5) and SEB exchange (terminal 5), as well as Handelsbanken and SEB banks in Sky City shopping and eating area (which connects terminal 5 with 3 and 4). There are ATMs at terminal 2, 4, 5 and Sky City. All terminals have cafés and bars (open 10am-10pm Mon-Fri, Sun; 10am-6pm Sat), but head to Sky City for more serious eating. There are shops throughout the airport selling glassware and souvenirs, books and newspapers and the usual travel items (open 7am-7.30pm Mon-Fri; 8am-6pm Sat; 8am-7.30pm Sun). You'll also find a branch of the state-run alcohol shop Systembolaget (open 10am-8pm Mon-Fri; 10am-2pm Sat) and a pharmacy (open 7am-7.30pm Mon-Fri; 6am-8.30pm Sat,

8am-7.30 pm Sun). Conference and business facilities are available, along with a hair salon, dry-cleaner, luggage storage, playgrounds, a chapel, a photo booth and internet access (in Sky City, terminals 2, 4 and 5).

The fastest way to get into Stockholm is on the bright yellow **Arlanda Express** train service (020 22 22 24, www.arlandaexpress.com), which arrives at its own terminal next to Central Station (the main station for trains and the Tunnelbana). Trains depart 4-6 times an hour, from Arlanda 5.05am-12.35am daily, and from Central Station 4.35am-12.05am daily. Journey time is 20mins; single fare is 180kr (80kr under-18s; four under-18s free with each full-price passenger). Buy tickets from the yellow automatic ticket booths at Arlanda or Central Station, from the ticket booth or on the train (for 50kr extra). The booths take all major credit cards.

Alternatively, **Flygbussarna airport buses** (600 10 00, www.flygbussarna.se) leave about every 10mins from all terminals to Cityterminalen (the main bus station next to Central Station, *see p275*). Buses run from Arlanda 6.40am-11.45pm daily, and from Cityterminalen 4am-10pm daily. The journey takes around 40mins. A single fare is 89kr (four under-18s free with each full-price passenger). There are also **taxis** – the usual fixed rate to the city is 400kr, but make sure you ask the driver first since there are many taxi firms that set their own prices.

Bromma Airport
797 68 74/www.lfv.se
Stockholm city airport, Bromma, is 8km (5 miles) west of the city centre. Its location makes it popular, but only seven airlines operate from it. The airport has a simple café and restaurant (open 6.30am-8.30pm Mon-Fri; 8.30am-7pm Sat; noon-8pm Sun), as well as a kiosk and flight shop.

You can get into the city centre on **Flygbussarna airport buses**, but their schedules change according to flight times. Single fare is 60kr; the journey takes about 15mins to Cityterminalen. A taxi into town costs around 170kr.

Skavsta Airport
0155 28 04 00/www.skavsta-air.se.
Skavsta serves Stockholm even though it's 100km (62 miles) to the south. It's the airport of choice for budget airlines. Airport facilities include a Forex exchange bureau, restaurant, café, bar, playground and tax-free shops. **Flygbussarna airport buses** (single 130kr) take 60mins to reach the centre of Stockholm, and leave Skavsta 20mins after each arriving flight and Cityterminalen about 90mins before a departing flight. If you can't find a taxi at the airport, you can order one, but the trip to Stockholm will set you back about 1,220kr.

Västerås Airport
021 80 56 10/www.vasterasflygplats.se.
Ryanair flies into Västerås, located 110km (68 miles) north-west of Stockholm. Facilities include a café (open 6am-6pm daily), bar, tax-free shop and car hire. The **airport bus** (single 130kr, journey 75mins) leaves 20mins after an arriving flight for Cityterminalen in Stockholm; it returns about 2hrs before departing flights. There are trains every hour to the city (but you'll have to take a bus or taxi to the train station first). A taxi ride to Stockholm will cost around 1,300kr.

Airlines

Air France 51 99 99 90/
www.airfrance.com
Austrian Airlines 665 64 80/
www.aua.com
British Airways 0200 77 00 98/
www.britishairways.com
Finnair 020 78 11 00/
www.finnair.com
Flynordic 52 80 68 20/
www.flynordic.com
KLM 58 79 97 57/
www.klm.com
Lufthansa 0770 72 77 27/
www.lufthansa.com
Malmö Aviation 020 55 00 10/
www.malmoaviation.se
Ryanair 0900 20 20 240/
www.ryanair.com
SAS 0770 72 77 27/0771 66 10 00/
www.sas.se
Spanair 020 72 75 55/
www.spanair.com
Sterling 58 76 91 48/
www.sterlingticket.com

By train

The major rail travel company in Sweden is **SJ** (www.sj.se). International, domestic and commuter trains arrive and depart from Stockholm's main train station, Central Station. Just below the station, and linked to it, is T-Centralen, the main station for the Tunnelbana system, and there is always a long line of taxis outside.

SJ

Central Station, Vasagatan, Norrmalm (0771 75 75 75). T-bana T-Centralen/bus 3, 47, 53, 62, 65. **Open** *Domestic tickets 6am-10pm Mon-Fri; 8am-10pm Sat, Sun. International tickets 9am-6pm Mon-Fri.* **Map** p305 G6.
To book tickets from abroad, call +46 771 75 75 75 or visit www.swedenbooking.com.
All tickets must be picked up in Sweden.

By bus

Most long-distance coaches (national and international) stop at **Cityterminalen**, Stockholm's main bus station, next to Central Station. This is also where airport buses arrive and depart. T-Centralen is an escalator ride away, and there are always plenty of taxis outside.

Eurolines

Klarabergsviadukten 72, Norrmalm (762 59 60/timetable service from abroad +46 362 90 80 00/www. eurolines.se). T-bana T-Centralen/ bus 3, 47, 53, 62, 65. **Open** *9am-5.30pm Mon-Fri.* **Map** p305 G6.
Operates buses to most major European cities.

Swebus Express

Cityterminalen, Klarabergsgatan, Norrmalm (0200 21 82 18/ www.swebusexpress.se). T-bana T-Centralen/bus 3, 47, 53, 59, 62, 65. **Open** *8am-8pm Mon-Fri; 9am-6pm Sat, Sun.* **Map** p305 G6.
One of the larger Swedish bus companies, Swebus Express covers Sweden's major cities, along with Oslo and Copenhagen. Tickets can be purchased at Cityterminalen or on the bus; it doesn't accept reservations because it always guarantees its passengers a seat.

By car

Stockholm's highway links with Europe have been made easier thanks to the Öresund toll (275kr) bridge between Sweden and Denmark, which opened in 2000 and is crossed by more than 10,000 cars daily. It's 615 kilometres (382 miles) from Stockholm to Malmö; 475 kilometres (295 miles) to Göteborg. Driving in Sweden is relatively safe – Swedish roads are in great condition and there are no other tolls.

By sea

If you arrive in Stockholm by boat, then you have most likely come from Finland or Estonia. These are the main companies:

Birka Cruises

Södermalmstorg 2, Södermalm (702 72 30/www.birka.se). T-bana Slussen/bus 2, 53, 76, 96. **Open** *10am-6pm Mon-Fri; 10am-9am Sat; 10am-2pm Sun.* **Map** p305 K8.
Daily cruises in summer to Gotland, Finland, Tallinn, Riga and Poland. The boat terminal, Stadsgårdskajen, is right next to Slussen.

Silja Line

Kungsgatan 2, Norrmalm (22 21 40/ www.silja.se). T-bana Östermalmstorg/ bus 1, 2, 55, 56, 91. **Open** *9am-6pm Mon-Fri; 11am-3pm Sat.* **Map** p305 F8.
Ferries to/from Finland. Boats dock at Värtahamnen just north-east of the city centre. The terminal has parking, luggage lockers, an ATM, a kiosk and a café. There are taxis at the terminal and Silja Line has its own bus connection to Cityterminalen (single 20kr). Signs tell you how to walk the 5-10mins to the nearest T-bana station, Gärdet (as well as from Gärdet to the terminal).

Tallink

Frihamnen, Ladugårdsgärdet (666 60 01/www.tallink.net/www.tallink.se). Bus 1, 72, 76. **Open** *8am-8pm Mon-Fri; 9am-3.30pm Sat, Sun.*
Ferries go to and from Estonia. Boats dock at the Frihamnen terminal, to the north-east of the city centre. It is served by taxis and has its own bus service between the terminal and Cityterminalen (single 20kr).

Viking Line

Cityterminalen, Klarabergsgatan, Norrmalm (452 40 00/452 40 75/ www.vikingline.se). T-bana

T-Centralen/bus 3, 47, 53, 59, 62, 65. **Open** *8am-7pm Mon-Sat; noon-7pm Sun.* **Map** p305 G6.
Ferries go to/from Finland, and from Helsinki to Tallinn. Boats dock at Vikingterminalen on Södermalm. The terminal has parking, luggage lockers, a café and kiosk. There are plenty of taxis at the terminal but many prefer to walk the 10mins to Slussen. Viking Line also has its own direct bus link to Slussen and Cityterminalen (single 30kr).

Public transport

The **Tunnelbana** (abbreviated to **T-bana**) metro system is the quickest, cheapest and most convenient way of getting around the city. There is also an efficient and comprehensive bus network that operates around the clock and covers areas not reached by the metro or the commuter trains. Both the Tunnelbana and city buses are run by **Statens Lokaltrafik**, or **SL** (600 10 00, www.sl.se).

SL Center

Central Station, T-Centralen, Norrmalm. T-bana T-Centralen/bus 3, 47, 53, 59, 62, 65. **Open** *6.30am-11.15pm Mon-Sat; 7am-11.15pm Sun.* **Map** p305 G7.
This information centre can answer any questions you might have about public transport. It is located on the floor below the main concourse at Central Station. You can pick up maps and timetables here. Another branch will open in summer 2006 at Sergels Torg.
Other locations: Slussen, by Saltsjöbanan (open 7am-6pm Mon-Fri; 10am-5pm Sat); Fridhemsplan (open 7am-6.30pm Mon-Fri; 10am-5pm Sat); Tekniska Högskolan (open 7am-6.30pm Mon-Fri; 10am-5pm Sat).

Fares & tickets

Single tickets on the bus or T-bana cost 30kr-90kr depending on how far you're travelling, and are valid for 1hr from when the trip starts. It is cheaper to buy multi-ticket coupons or travel cards, available from Pressbyrån kiosks and SL Centers. Coupons are available in sets of ten (80kr) or 20 (110kr); ask for *remsa*, Swedish for coupon strip. A 24hr pass with unlimited travel costs 95kr; a 72hr pass is 180kr. A 30-day unlimited travel pass is 600kr. A weekend pass, which allows unlimited travel over four consecutive weekends, is 265kr. There is also the **Stockholm Card**, which includes unlimited travel on public transport, admission to over 70 museums and sights, sightseeing by boat and more (for more details, see p60).

Tunnelbana

The three metro lines are identified by colour – red, green or blue – on maps and station signs. All three lines intersect at T-Centralen.

At interchanges, lines are indicated by the names of the stations at the end of the line, so you should know in which direction you're heading when changing between lines.

The T-bana runs from around 5am-midnight Mon-Thur, Sun; 5.30am-3am Fri, Sat.

Buses

Bus stops are easy to spot and often have see-through shelters to protect waiting passengers from the weather. The city has many one-way streets, so buses often do not follow exactly the same route in both directions, but run along parallel streets.

Most bus routes operate from 5am to midnight daily. You board at the front, and get off through the middle or rear doors. Only single tickets can be bought on board; if you have a pre-paid ticket, get it stamped by the driver. Travel passes should also be shown to the driver.

Night buses

There are plenty of night bus routes serving the city centre as well as the suburbs. Most night buses run from midnight until 5am, when the regular buses take over. The main stations are Slussen, T-Centralen, Odenplan, Fridhemsplan and Gullmarsplan.

Ferries

Many ferry companies operate on Stockholm's waterways. Some routes are used daily by people commuting to work, while others are designed for sightseeing or excursions into the archipelago. These are

separate from public transport, so SL travel passes are not valid on the archipelago ferries.

Cinderella Båtarna

58 71 40 00/www.cinderellabatarna. com. **Credit** AmEx, DC, MC, V. Ferries to Vaxholm, Grinda, Möja, Sandhamn and more. Boats depart from Nybrokajen on Strandvägen. Tickets can be purchased on board.

Djurgårdsfärjan

Year-round ferry service operated by Waxholmsbolaget (*see below*) within Stockholm harbour. It goes to/from Slussen to Djurgården (stopping at Allmänna Gränd, next to Gröna Lund), Skeppsholmen and Nybroplan. From May to August the ferry also stops at the Vasamuseet. Buy tickets in ticket booths before boarding; single 25kr. SL travel passes are valid.

Strömma Kanalbolaget

58 71 40 00/www.strommakanal bolaget.com. **Credit** MC, V. Departs from Stadshusbron (next to the Stadshuset) to Birka and Drottningholm, and from Strandvägen to Fjäderholmarna, Vaxholm and Sandhamn. Tickets can be purchased on the boat (cash only) or in the ticket booths next to the departure points.

Waxholmsbolaget

679 58 30/www.waxholmsbolaget.se. **Credit** MC, V. Covers the whole archipelago, from Arholma in the north to Landsort in the south. Boats depart from Strömkajen outside the Grand Hôtel, opposite the Royal Palace. Tickets can be purchased on the boat. The useful website (in English) includes timetables that you can download.

Local trains

For trips into the suburbs and surrounding towns, there are commuter trains run by SL (as well as buses). The same tickets may be used on these trains as on the T-bana. The main commuter train station is Central Station, and trains will take you to as far north as Bålsta and Kungsängen and as far south as Södertälje, Nynäshamn and Gnesta.

Maps

Stockholm street maps are included at the back of this guide, starting on p303; there's also a Tunnelbana map on

p320. The tourist office has good free street maps, which marks museums and sights; a free map is also available from the round information kiosk on the concourse of Central Station. Bus and Tunnelbana timetables (with maps at the back) can be picked up for free at SL Centers (*see p275*) and ticket booths (although don't expect the booths to have all the timetables to hand). SL Centers also have free transport maps. T-bana maps are also clearly displayed on the platforms and inside carriages.

Taxis

Taxis are easy to find in Stockholm. They can be ordered by phone, online or hailed on the street. There are taxi ranks by main squares and railway and bus stations. There are usually plenty of cabs outside nightclubs and concert venues at closing time, and at ferry terminals when a ferry arrives. Taxis can be hailed on the street when the light on the roof is lit. Cab companies are required by law to have some baby/child seats, but it's best to call the company first to request one, since not all cabs carry them. Taxi services offered in private, unmarked cars are illegal in Sweden and should be avoided.

Fares

Taxi fares (starting at around 30kr) are quite steep; current rates and supplements should be displayed inside each cab. Rates are lower on weekdays and higher on weekends and in the evening, but there's more traffic during the day so the ride will take longer. Rates for the different cab companies can be found on their websites. All the larger taxi firms take credit cards. Don't expect drivers to carry a lot of change.

Taxi companies

The firms listed below take bookings 24hrs a day. All operators speak English, but make sure you have a specific street address, or the name of a bar or restaurant where you can wait, or they will not send a taxi.

Flygtaxi (airport taxis)
020 97 97 97/www.flygtaxi.se
Taxi Kurir 30 00 00/
www.taxikurir.se
Taxi Stockholm 15 00 00/
www.taxistockholm.se
Top Cab 33 33 33/www.topcab.com

Driving

Driving in Stockholm can be a
hassle. There's a lot of traffic
during office hours, free parking
is difficult to find and fuel is
expensive. A car is rarely a
time-efficient form of transport
in town, and it's only out in
the country that it becomes an
asset. If you do choose to drive,
remember the following:

● Tourists can drive in Sweden with
a valid licence from most other
countries. An international driving
licence or EU photo licence can be
useful as a translation/credibility aid.
● Keep your driving licence, vehicle
registration and insurance
documents with you at all times.
● It is compulsory to wear seat belts
in the front and back seats, and to
carry warning triangles, spares (tyre,
bulbs, fanbelt) and tools to fit them.
● Third party motor insurance is
compulsory.
● Children have to sit in special
car seats until around the age of four
(depending on the child's height), and
on booster seats until the age of seven.
● The speed limit is 50kmph
(31mph) in towns, 90kmph (56mph)
on most highways and 110kmph
(68mph) on motorways. Swedes
keep to speed limits more than
most Europeans.
● The legal alcohol limit for drivers
is low at 0.02 per cent. Penalties for
exceeding the limit are severe.
● You must use dipped headlights
during the day.
● You must stop for pedestrians at
designated pedestrian crossings that
do not have traffic lights and don't be
surprised if pedestrians just step out
on the street expecting you to stop.
● You must stop at traffic lights
when the light turns yellow.

Breakdown services

If your car breaks down, look
up *Bilreparationer* in the
Yellow Pages. If it's a rental
car, contact the rental firm.

Motormännens Riksförbund

Problems 020 21 11 11. **Open** 9am-
4pm Mon-Fri. **Office** *Sveavägen*

*159, Norrmalm (690 38 00/www.
motormannen.se).* Bus 40, 46, 52,
515, 595. **Open** 8.30am-5pm Mon-
Fri. **Map** p309 B5.
The Swedish equivalent to the British
AA, with reciprocal arrangements
with most European motoring
organisations. Call the toll-free
number if you have a problem.

Fuel

Petrol stations (*bensinstation*)
sell unleaded fuel (*blyfri* 95 or
98), leaded (just called 96 or 98)
and diesel (*diesel*). Unleaded
petrol pumps are green, leaded
is red and diesel black.

Jet

*Norra Stationsgatan 59-61,
Vasastaden.* **Open** 24hrs daily.
Map p308 B4.
Lower prices than most.

OKQ8

*Katarinavägen 16, Södermalm
(668 01 80/www.okq8.se).* **Open**
24hrs daily. **Map** p315 K8.

Preem

*Norr Mälarstrand 32, Kungsholmen
(652 68 60/www.preem.se).* **Open**
24hrs daily. **Map** p304 H4.

Statoil

*Birger Jarlsgatan 120, Norrmalm
(15 51 71/www.statoil.se).* **Open**
7am-midnight Mon-Fri; 8am-
midnight Sat, Sun. **Map** p309 B6.

Parking

Parking is not easy in the
city centre. If you have parked
illegally or not paid the right
fee, you'll get a hefty fine
from parking attendants or
the police. Parking is allowed
on most streets but you'll pay
for the privilege, at least on
weekdays. *Parkering
Förbjuden* means 'parking
prohibited', and it's illegal to
park closer than ten metres (33
feet) to a pedestrian crossing. Car
parks (*parkering*), indicated by a
white 'P' on a blue sign, charge
20kr-50kr per hour.

If you park illegally, you're
likely to get a fat fine. Your car
will be towed only if it is left in
a spot that hinders traffic or is
dangerous. If your car is
towed, call 508 287 84. You'll

have to pick it up at
Finspångsgatan 1, Lunda, in
Spånga (about 18 kilometres/
11 miles north-west of the city
centre) and pay a fine of 770kr,
plus 25kr per day that they
hold it for you.

Vehicle rental

Car hire is relatively pricey,
but it's a competitive market
so shop around. You have to be
25 years of age to rent a car in
Sweden, and you will need a
credit card. When choosing a
rental agency, check what's
included in the price: ideally,
you want unlimited mileage,
tax and full insurance. Larger
companies often advertise
special offers on their websites;
ask about weekend deals, from
Friday to Monday morning.

Avis

*Vasagatan 10B, Norrmalm (20 20
60/020 78 82 00/www.avis.se).*
*T-bana T-Centralen/bus 3, 47, 53,
59, 62, 65.* **Open** 6am-7pm Mon-Fri;
9am-4pm Sat, Sun. **Credit** AmEx,
DC, MC, V. **Map** p305 G6.
Other locations: Ringvägen 90,
Södermalm (644 99 80); Arlanda
Airport (797 99 70); Bromma
Airport (28 87 00).

Europcar

*Vasaplan 1, Norrmalm (53 48 03
80/020 78 11 80/www.europcar.se).*
*T-bana T-Centralen/bus 3, 47, 53,
59, 62, 65.* **Open** 6am-8pm Mon-
Fri; 10am-4pm Sat; noon-10pm
Sun. **Credit** AmEx, DC, MC, V.
Map p305 H6.
Other locations: Fiskartorpsvägen,
Östermalm (20 44 63); Arlanda
Airport (55 59 84 00); Bromma
Airport (80 08 07).

Hertz

*Vasagatan 26, Norrmalm (454 62
50/020 21 12 11/www.hertz.nu).*
*T-bana T-Centralen/bus 3, 47, 53,
59, 62, 65.* **Open** 7am-6pm Mon-Fri;
9am-3pm Sat, Sun. **Credit** AmEx,
DC, MC, V. **Map** p305 G6.
Other locations: Arlanda
Airport (797 99 00); Bromma
Airport (797 99 14).

Cycling

Stockholm is very bike-friendly.
For good places to cycle and
bike rental places, *see p223*.

Directory

Resources A-Z

Addresses

In Sweden, addresses are written with the building number after the street name. Also, as in the UK, but not the US, the first floor is the floor above street level. The floor at street level is *bottenvåning*, often abbreviated to 'BV'.

Age restrictions

The legal drinking age is 18 to drink in a bar or to buy low-alcohol beer in a grocery store, but you must be 20 years old to buy alcohol at the state-owned monopolistic off-licence **Systembolaget** (*see also* p177 **Booze rules**).

You can smoke or drive at 18. At 15 teens become *byxmyndig*, which, loosely translated, means they are 'in charge of their pants'. In other words, they can legally have sex.

Business services

Stockholm is a great city for doing business – except in July, when most people take a month's vacation and it's hard to find anything but voicemail to take your calls. The city is widely recognised as being receptive and sophisticated and is often used as a test market for new products.

Plenty of conventions take place in Stockholm, so many hotels cater mainly to business travellers (hence higher rates Sunday to Friday) and many venues can be hired for conferences and meetings.

Conventions & conferences

There are two main trade fair/conference centres just on the edge of Stockholm: **Stockholmsmässan**, Mässvägen 1, Älvsjö (749

41 00, www.stofair.se), and **Sollentunamässan**, Box 174, Sollentuna (50 66 50 00, www.massan.com). The website www.fairlink.se provides useful information.

Many bureaux can help with events in the city – look under *Konferensarrangörer* (conference organisers) or *Konferenslokaler* (conference venues) in the Yellow Pages.

Amica (02 01 12 22 22, www.amica.se) organises conferences of any size, while **Svenska Kursgårdar** (07 71 50 55 00/fax 59 41 11 88, www.svenska-kursgardar.se) has 80 conference locations.

Hotels are often booked up during the biggest fairs and conferences. Below we give dates, where available, for major events in 2005; the dates in subsequent years are likely to be similar:

Stockholm International Antiques Fair 27-30 Jan
Stockholm Furniture Fair 9-13 Feb
Lighting 2005 9-13 Feb
Health Fair 18-20 Feb
Stockholm International Boat Show 5-13 Mar
Stockholm Art Fair 7-10 Apr

Nordic Gardens 7-10 Apr
Wilderness Fair 15-17 Apr
Home Improvement Fair 4 days end Sept-early Oct
Food & Beverage 3 days mid Nov
Scandinavian Sail & Motorboat Show 4 days mid Nov
Travel Fair 3 days mid Nov

Couriers

Look in the Yellow Pages under *Budservice* for a list of couriers. Prices vary but a small package sent within Stockholm on the same day costs around 200kr with the following international companies:

DHL
543 450 00/toll-free customer service 0771 34 53 45/www.dhl.se. **Open** 24hrs daily. **Credit** AmEx, DC, MC, V.

TNT
625 58 00/toll-free 020 960 960/www.tnt.com. **Open** 8am-6pm Mon-Fri. **Credit** AmEx, MC, V.

UPS
Toll free 020 120 22 55/020 788 799/ www.ups.com. **Open** 8am-7pm Mon-Fri; 9am-1pm Sat. **Credit** AmEx, MC, V.

Travel advice

For up-to-date information on travel to a specific country – including the latest news on safety and security, health issues, local laws and customs – contact your home country government's department of foreign affairs. Most have websites packed with useful advice for would-be travellers.

Australia
www.dfat.gov.au/travel

Canada
www.voyage.gc.ca

New Zealand
www.mft.govt.nz/travel

Republic of Ireland
www.irlgov.ie/iveagh

UK
www.fco.gov.uk/travel

USA
www.state.gov/travel

Directory

Office & computer services

Megabyte System Svenska

Drottninggatan 94, Norrmalm (55 51 11 11/www.megabyte.se). T-bana Hötorget/bus 1, 47, 52, 53, 69. **Open** 10am-6pm Mon-Fri. **Credit** AmEx, MC, V. **Map** p309 E6.
The latest products from Hewlett-Packard for sale, as well as software, components and servicing.

Mycom

Drottninggatan 63, Norrmalm (55 54 12 22/www.mycom.se). T-bana Hötorget/bus 1, 47, 53, 69. **Open** 10am-7pm Mon-Fri; 10am-5pm Sat; noon-5pm Sun. **Credit** AmEx, MC, V. **Map** p305 F6.
An excellent shop with all kinds of computer equipment for sale: laptops, scanners and software.

New Sec

Regeringsgatan 65, Norrmalm (454 40 00/www.newsec.se). T-bana Hötorget/bus 1, 43, 56. **Open** 8.15am-noon, 1-4.15pm Mon-Thur; 8.15am-noon, 1-4pm Fri. **Map** p305 F7.
A leading commercial property estate agent with offices for lease.

Office Space

Byängsgränd 14, Årsta (681 00 04/fax 681 04 45/www.officespace.se). T-bana Enskede Gård. **Open** 8.30am-4.30pm Mon-Fri.
Offices available at quite low rents in the city for small or medium-sized businesses.

Translation services

Abcom

Stureplan 4A (50 62 09 80/www.abcom.se). T-bana Östermalmstorg/bus 1, 2, 55, 56. **Open** 8am-5pm Mon-Fri. **No credit cards. Map** p305 E5.
A language services provider that translates documents quickly and professionally.

SpråkCentrum

Stureplan 4A, Östermalm (50 62 09 50/www.sprakcentrum.se). T-bana Östermalmstorg/bus 1, 2, 55, 56. **Open** 8.30am-5pm Mon-Thur; 8.30am-4pm Fri. **No credit cards** (bank transfers only). **Map** p305 F8.
This is one of Sweden's oldest translation agencies. The staff translate to and from a huge number of languages and within every field, for both companies and individuals.

Useful organisations

Ministry of Foreign Affairs

405 10 00/www.utrikes.regeringen.se.

National Institute of Economic Research

453 59 00/www.konj.se.

National Tax Board

0771 56 75 67/www.rsv.se.

Statistics Sweden

50 69 48 01/www.scb.se.

Stockholm Migration Board

011 15 60 00/ www.migrationsverket.se
Handles all issues related to immigration, including work visas.

Sveriges Riksbank

787 00 00/www.riksbank.com.
Economic and financial data.

Swedish Stock Exchange

405 60 00/www.stockholmsborsen.se.

Customs

You must be at least 18 years old in order to bring in tobacco products, and 20 to bring in alcohol. Visitors arriving from the EU can bring in alcohol and cigarettes without incurring customs duty for private use. The cut-off points between private and commercial use are as follows:

● 400 cigarettes or 200 small cigars or 100 cigars or 550 grams (19.4 ounces) of loose tobacco.
● 10 litres of spirits (over 22 per cent alcohol), 20 litres of fortified wine or alcoholic drinks containing less than 22 per cent alcohol, 90 litres of wine (maximum 60 litres of sparkling wine) and up to 110 litres of beer.

Visitors arriving from non-EU countries may bring in the following (up to a maximum total of 1,700kr for alcohol):

● 200 cigarettes or 100 small cigars or 50 cigars or 250 grams (8.82 ounces) of tobacco.

● 1 litre of spirits (over 22 per cent alcohol) or 2 litres of any other alcoholic drink with less than 22 per cent alcohol.
● 2 litres of fortified wine or sparkling wine.
● 2 litres of wine.
● Any quantity of beer up to the value of 1,700kr.
● 50 grams (1.76 ounces) of perfume.

Check **Swedish Customs** website www.tullverket.se for more detailed information.

Disabled visitors

Recent legislation demands that all public buildings must be accessible for the disabled and visually impaired; the goal for completion of the required renovations is 2005. However, facilities in Stockholm are already very good compared to many other European cities, so it is not usually a problem for most disabled visitors to get around the capital.

The streets are in good condition and have wide pavements, and curbs have ramps for wheelchairs. Wheelchair-adapted toilets are common in larger restaurants, shopping centres, department stores and in some public and private buildings. Many hotels even have allergy-free rooms.

The public transport system is quite wheelchair-accessible, especially the Tunnelbana, which has plenty of elevators, and most buses can 'kneel' at bus stops – although wide gaps between trains and platforms remain a common complaint.

Most taxis are large enough to take wheelchairs, but do check when you order a cab. Try **Taxi Stockholm** (15 00 00).

De Handikappades Riksförbund

Katrinebergsvägen 6, Liljeholmen (685 80 00/www.dhr.se). T-bana Liljeholmen/bus 77, 133, 143, 152. **Open** Aug-June 8.30am-noon, 1-4pm Mon-Fri. Closed July. **Map** p313 M2.
Supplies information on facilities for the mobility-impaired. The website has an English version.

Directory

Drugs

Drugs, including cannabis, are nowhere near as widely accepted in Sweden as in some parts of Europe. Possession of any drug, including medicine for which you do not have a prescription, is illegal and you can be fined for even the very smallest amount.

The number of party-drug users has increased in the past ten years, and an undercover police squad pursues drug users at nightclubs and parties. All the nightclubs and bars work together with the police against drug use. Their staff are now trained to spot drug users and deny them entry, as well as tip them off to the police.

Electricity

Sweden, along with most of Europe, has 220-volt AC, 50Hz current and uses two-pin continental plugs. The 220V current works fine with British-bought 240V products with a plug adaptor (available at the airport and some stores). With US 110V equipment you will need a current transformer.

Embassies & consulates

Many foreign embassies – including those of the UK, US, Japan and Norway – are clustered in Diplomatstaden, an enclave of villas on the edge of Ladugårdsgärdet (map p311). There's a full list of embassies in the phone book under *Ambassader*. A list of embassy locations is on the tourist office website (www.stockholmtown.com). There is no New Zealand consulate or embassy in Stockholm: a representative in the Hague (+ 31 703 658 037) oversees Sweden.

Australian Embassy
Sergels Torg 12, Norrmalm (613 29 00/www.austemb.se). T-bana

T-Centralen/bus 47, 52, 56, 59, 65. Open 8.30am-12.30pm, 1.30-4.30pm Mon-Fri. Map p305 G7.

British Embassy
Skarpögatan 6-8, Östermalm (671 30 00/www.britishembassy.com). Bus 69. Open *Information* 10am-noon Mon, Wed, Fri. *Visas* 9.30am-noon Mon-Fri. *Consulate* 9.30am-noon, 2-4pm Mon-Fri. Map p307 F12.

Canadian Embassy
Tegelbacken 4, Norrmalm (453 30 00/information 453 30 44/ www.canadaemb.se). T-bana T-Centralen/bus 3, 53, 59, 62, 65. Open 8.30am-noon, 1-5pm Mon-Fri. Map p305 H6.

Irish Embassy
Östermalmsgatan 97, Östermalm (661 80 05/irish.embassy@swipnet.se). T-bana Karlaplan/bus 4, 42, 44, 72. Open 10am-noon, 2.30-4pm Mon-Fri. Map p310 E10.

US Embassy
Dag Hammarskjöldsväg 31, Östermalm (783 53 00/www.usemb.se). Bus 56, 69, 76. Open 9-11am Mon-Fri. *Phone hours* 1-3pm Mon-Fri. Map p307 F12.

Emergencies

To contact the police, ambulance or fire service in an emergency call **112** (free of charge, including from public pay phones). For emergency rooms at hospitals, *see p281* **Accident & emergency**. For central police stations, *see p286* **Police & security**.

Gay & lesbian

Organisations

Gaystudenterna
Universitetet, Nobelhuset, Frescati (674 62 31/16 55 03/www.sus.su.se/ gaystudenterna). T-bana Universitetet. This group of gay activist students (non-students also welcome) works for gay awareness in education, as well as having fun outside the classroom. They arrange parties, film screenings, seminars, debates and pub nights on the first Wednesday of the month at Café Bojan (T-bana Universitetet; there's a sign right outside the T-bana exit). Times vary, so call first or look at the website.

RFSL
Sveavägen 57-9, Vasastaden (457 13 00/www.rfsl.se). T-bana

Rådmansgatan/bus 43, 52. Open *Phone enquiries* 9am-4pm Mon-Fri. Map p309 D6.
The National Association for Sexual Equality, Sweden's gay, lesbian and trans rights group, has its main office here. Hundreds of sub-minority groups – foreigners, disabled, bisexuals, teenagers, seniors, parents of homosexuals, homosexual parents and so on – share the space with counsellors, the monthly *Kom ut!* magazine's editorial staff, a radio station and a library. The website provides reams of information if you speak Swedish.

Healthcare

For an HIV-positive support group, *see p281* **AIDS/HIV**.

Lesbisk Hälsomottagning
Södersjukhuset, Ringvägen 52, Södermalm (616 11 44). Bus 3, 4, 55, 74. Open *Phone enquiries* 10-11am Tue; 3-4pm Thur. Map p314 N6.
Free gynaecological healthcare for lesbians only. Call first to make an appointment.

Venhälsan
Södersjukhuset, Ringvägen 52, Södermalm (616 25 00/www.hiv.nu). Bus 3, 4, 55, 74. Open 5.30-8.30pm Tue-Thur. Map p314 N6.
Free healthcare for both bi- and homosexual men. Located on the fifth floor; take elevator D.

Health

Don't go straight to an emergency room unless you really have an acute emergency. For advice on minor illnesses or prescription drugs, call the 24-hour **Healthcare Information Service** (52 85 28 00, 32 01 00, www.telefonakuten.se); stay on the line if the automatic answering service kicks in and you will be connected to a nurse, who can provide information (in English) about hospitals, doctors and general advice about illnesses.

For advice related to prescription medicine call the **Läkemedelsupplysningen** (medicine information office) toll-free on 020 66 77 66, and press 2. It's open 24 hours daily and staff speak English.

Accident & emergency

The following hospitals have 24-hour emergency rooms:

St Görans Sjukhus
Sanktgöransplan 1, Kungsholmen (58 70 10 00). T-bana Fridhemsplan/ bus 57, 59, 74.

Södersjukhuset
Ringvägen 52, Södermalm (616 10 00). Bus 3, 4, 55, 74. **Map** p314 N6.

AIDS/HIV

The spread of HIV/AIDS has been slow in Sweden, but about 30 new cases per month are still reported. The **AIDS Helpline** (020 78 44 40) can direct you to the closest hospital for tests, treatment and information.

Noaks Ark
Eriksbergsgatan 46, Östermalm (700 46 00/www.noaksark.redcross.se). T-bana Östermalmstorg/bus 1, 2, 55, 56. **Open** *June-Sept* 9am-4pm Mon-Fri. *Oct-May* 9am-5pm Mon-Fri. **Map** p309 F6.
The Red Cross's HIV and AIDS organisation arranges parties and happenings, and runs the Life Gallery exhibition space (Kammakargatan 33, 10 15 60, www.life-foundation.org) in Norrmalm and a café. There's an English version of the website.

Posithiva Gruppen
Magnus Ladulåsgatan 8, Södermalm (720 19 60/www.posithivagruppen.se). Bus 3, 4, 43, 55, 74. **Open** 6pm-midnight Mon-Thur; 6pm-2am Fri; 8pm-2am Sat. **Map** p314 M6.
Support group for HIV-positive bi- and homosexual men. Soup nights, theme nights, relatives' night, pub nights and parties.

Alternative medicine

Alternative medicine, especially massage, is very common in Sweden – who hasn't heard of Swedish massage? The use of other complementary treatments, such as homeopathy and acupuncture, is also rapidly increasing. Acupuncture is even practised on women in labour at the hospitals.

AAA Kliniken Norr
Odengatan 62, Vasastaden (31 21 00). T-bana Odenplan/bus 2, 4, 40, 42, 53, 72. **Open** *Phone enquiries* 8am-8pm Mon-Fri. **No credit cards**. **Map** p309 D5.
A clinic offering acupuncture, massage and chiropractic treatments. Appointments required in advance. **Other locations**: AAA Kliniken Söder, Folkungagatan 50, Södermalm (640 27 50).

Family planning

You can buy condoms in grocery stores, pharmacies, *Pressbyrån*, 7-Elevens and in vending machines at some bars and clubs. You'll need a prescription to get the Pill, though. Abortions are legal until week 18; after that there must be a serious medical reason – non-residents may have difficulty getting abortions at any time.

Mama Mia
Karlavägen 58-60, Östermalm (50 64 90 00/www.mamamia.se). T-bana Stadion/bus 42, 44, 55, 56, 62. **Phone hours** 8am-5pm Mon-Thur; 8am-3pm Fri. **Map** p310 E9.
Family planning and postnatal care. Call in advance for an appointment. **Other locations**: Götgatan 83E, Södermalm (55 69 37 70). *Phone hours* 8am-4pm Mon-Thur; 8am-12pm Fri.

Dentists

Dentists can be found in the Yellow Pages under *Tandläkare*. No appointment is needed for emergency dental care. Try the **Emergency Dental Clinic** at St Eriks Sjukhus, Polhemsgatan 46, Kungsholmen (54 55 12 20/28), open 7.45am-8.30pm daily. Rates vary greatly depending on the treatment you're having, but start at 490kr; if you arrive after 7pm, prices increase by 50 per cent. No appointment needed.

Afta Akuttandvård
Sergels Torg 12, Norrmalm (20 20 25). T-bana T-Centralen/bus 47, 52, 56, 59, 65. **Open** *Drop-in patients* 8am-6pm Mon-Fri; 9am-3pm Sat, Sun. **Map** p305 G7.

Akut tandvården i Stockholm
Kungsgatan 29, Norrmalm (10 92 93). T-bana Hötorget/bus 1, 43, 52, 56. **Open** 8am-11pm daily. **Map** p305 F7.

Doctors

Call beforehand to set up an appointment with these general practitioners. A visit to a doctor costs 140kr with an E111 form, about 500kr without.

Dr Akut
Strandvägen 7B, Östermalm (660 73 44/50 68 61 10/www.doctorakut.se). T-bana Östermalmstorg/bus 47, 62, 69, 76.

Husläkarjouren
Sabbatsbergs Sjukhus, Olivecronas Väg 2, Vasastaden (672 39 90). T-bana Odenplan/bus 4, 40, 47, 53, 72. **Open** *Phone enquiries* 4.30-10pm Mon-Fri; 8am-8pm Sat, Sun. **Map** p308 E4.
Overnight GP. Call first to make an appointment.

Sturehälsan
Birger Jarlsgatan 43, Östermalm (20 37 00/info@sturehalsan.com). T-bana Rådmansgatan/bus 2, 42, 43, 44.

Insurance

EU nationals are entitled to free medical and hospital treatment in Sweden if they have a filled-in E111 form and passport or some other form of identification. Not all treatment is covered, though, so it's advisable to also take out medical insurance.

Non-EU nationals should take out insurance as a matter of course.

Opticians

See p178.

Pharmacies

Pharmacies (*apotek*), identified by a green and white J-shaped sign, can be found all over the city. Most are open 10am-6pm Mon-Fri, and closed at the weekend. For two pharmacies with extended opening hours, *see p171.*

Directory

Helplines

Alcoholics Anonymous

720 38 42. **Open** 11am-1pm, 6-8pm daily.

Children's Helpline (BRIS)

0200 230 230. **Open** 24hrs daily.

Narcotics Anonymous

Helpline 411 44 18/toll free 0771 13 80 00/answering service with information in English 411 44 18 (press 2 for English).

Poison & Medications Hotline

33 12 31. **Open** 24hrs daily.

ID

Swedes have national identity cards, but most people use their driver's licence as ID. It is a good idea to carry some form of identification when you go to bars and clubs if you're under 25 or look like you could be – bartenders and bouncers will often ask for proof of age. Also, ID will be needed if you want to pay the lower price sometimes offered at museums for people under 25 or over 65.

Internet

Stockholm is a world-leader in e-commerce, new media and software development, and has the highest internet use per capita in the world. For websites relating to Stockholm, *see p294*.

Internet service providers

The best solution for a short-term visitor is to find an internet café, as setting up an internet subscription can be too time-consuming for anything less than a stay of several months.

If you're staying for a long time and your business hasn't set you up with internet access,

try the main phone company **Telia** (90 200, www.telia.com in English, or www.telia.se in Swedish).

Internet cafés

There are quite a few cybercafés in the city centre. You can also surf the net at libraries and many hotels and hostels. **Sidewalk Express** (www.sidewalkexpress.se) has various computer terminals offering access around the city, including at Central Station, Cityterminalen; they all cost 19kr per hour.

Café Access

Basement, Kulturhuset, Sergels Torg, Norrmalm (50 83 14 89/ www.kulturhuset.stockholm.se). *T-bana T-Centralen/bus 47, 52, 59, 65.* **Open** 11am-7pm Mon; 10am-7pm Tue-Fri; 10am-5pm Sat; 11am-5pm Sun. Closed Sun in July, Aug. **No credit cards. Map** p305 G7. Has 27 computers, and costs 20kr per half-hour.

Café Zenit

Sveavägen 20, Norrmalm (698 57 40). *T-bana Hötorget/bus 1, 43, 52, 56.* **Open** *Sept-May* 8.30am-6pm Mon-Fri; noon-5pm Sat, Sun. *June, Aug* 10am-6pm daily. Closed July. **No credit cards. Map** p305 F7. If you eat at the café, you can use one of the four computers for free as well as borrow magazines and guides.

Internet Café

3rd floor, PUB, Hötorget 13-15, Norrmalm (24 57 59). *T-bana Hötorget/bus 1, 52, 56.* **Open** 10am-7pm Mon-Fri; 10am-5pm Sat; noon-5pm Sun. **No credit cards. Map** p305 F6. Ten computers at 30kr per half-hour.

M@trix

Hötorget T-bana station, Norrmalm (20 02 93/www.matrix-se.com). *T-bana Hötorget/bus 1, 43, 52, 56.* **Open** 10am-midnight Mon-Thur, Sun; 10am-3am Fri, Sat. **Credit** AmEx, DC, MC, V. **Map** p305 F7. Forty terminals at 60kr per hour for non-members/30kr per hour members, with a minimum cost of 10kr. Membership costs 100kr, but that includes three hours of internet use.

Nine

Sveavägen 122, Vasastaden (612 67 97). *T-bana Rådmansgatan/bus 4, 42, 53, 72.* **Open** 10am-1am Mon-

Fri; 11am-1am Sat, Sun. **No credit cards. Map** p309 C6. Large new internet café with computers at 0.75kr per minute.

Smart Internet Café

Bergsundsgatan 26, Södermalm (641 67 38). *T-bana Hornstull/bus 4, 40, 66, 74.* **Open** 8am-10pm Mon-Fri; 9am-9pm Sat, Sun. **No credit cards. Map** p313 L2. Internet access costs 20kr per hour.

Left luggage

There are left-luggage lockers available in Arlanda Airport, and also at the bus, train and ferry terminals.

Arlanda Airport

See p274. Lockers **Rates** 20kr-30kr per 24hrs. *Manual left luggage storage* **Open** 6am-10pm Mon-Fri; 6am-6pm Sat, Sun. **Rates** 280kr per wk for a suitcase.

Central Station

See p275. **Open** 5am-12.30am. **Rates** 25kr-35kr per 24hrs.

Silja Line Terminal

See p275. **Open** 8am-8.15pm daily.

Viking Line Terminal

See p275. **Open** 6.15am-8.15pm daily. Lockers can be used for a maximum of 24hrs.

Legal help

Information about legal help can be got from the police, trade unions or legal advisers. Lawyers' offices are found in the Yellow Pages under *Advokater.* They are not obliged to help you but most will at least make recommendations.

Libraries

Stockholm's libraries are open to anyone for reference, but if you want to take a book out, you will need ID and an address in Sweden (a hotel address will not do).

Kungliga Biblioteket

Humlegården, Östermalm (463 40 00/www.kb.se). *T-bana Östermalmstorg/bus 2, 42, 44, 55, 56.* **Open** 9am-6pm Mon-Thur; 9am-5pm Fri; 11am-3pm Sat. **Map** p310 E8.

The national library is mainly for research. All publications are published in Sweden.

Stockholms Stadsbiblioteket

Sveavägen 73, Vasastaden (50 83 11 00/www.ssb.stockholm.se). T-bana Odenplan/bus 2, 4, 40, 42, 52, 53, 69, 72. **Open** 10am-8.30pm Mon-Thur; 10am-6pm Fri; noon-4pm Sat, Sun. **Map** p309 D5.

The main library is known to most Stockholmers for its architecture, but it also has books in many languages. Newspapers, magazines and computer terminals are next door in the Annexet.

Utrikespolitiska Biblioteket

Lilla Nygatan 23, Gamla Stan (696 05 27/www.ui.se). T-bana Gamla Stan/bus 3, 53. **Open** 10am-4.30pm Mon-Thur; 10am-4pm Fri. **Map** p305 J7.

Specialises in international politics.

Lost property

Both of the Stockholm's two main public transport companies have lost-and-found centres.

SL

Klara Östra Kyrkogata 4, Norrmalm (412 69 60). T-bana T-Centralen/bus 3, 47, 53, 59, 62, 65. **Open** noon-7pm Mon-Fri; noon-4pm Sat. **Map** p305 G6.

For objects lost on the Tunnelbana, city buses and commuter trains.

SJ

Central Station, Vasagatan, Norrmalm (762 25 50). T-bana T-Centralen/bus 3, 47, 53, 59, 62, 65. **Open** 10am-6pm Mon-Fri. **Map** p305 G6.

For long-distance trains.

Media

International newsstands

Copies of most of the major foreign newspapers and magazines, especially English-language ones, can be found in the city.

Interpress

NK department store, Hamngatan 18-20, Norrmalm (762 87 80). T-bana Kungsträdgården or Östermalmstorg/bus 43, 47, 55, 59, 69. **Open** 10am-7pm Mon-Fri;

10am-5pm Sat; noon-5pm Sun (June, July noon-4pm Sun). **Credit** AmEx, DC, MC, V. **Map** p305 F7.

Press Stop

Götgatan 31, Södermalm (644 35 10/www.press-stop.se). T-bana Medborgarplatsen or Slussen/bus 43, 55, 59, 66. **Open** 10am-6.30pm Mon-Fri; 10am-5pm Sat; 11am-5pm Sun. **Credit** AmEx, MC, V. **Map** p314 L8.

This branch of Press Stop – in the same complex as **DesignTorget** (*see p169*) and a popular branch of **Wayne's Coffee** (*see p149*) – sells magazines specialising in art, architecture and design. Among the 2,500 titles, there's a decent selection of international magazines and newspapers.

Other locations: Gallerian, Hamngatan 37, Norrmalm (723 01 91); Västermalmsgallerian, St Eriksgatan 45, Kungsholmen (21 91 13).

Pressbyrån

www.pressbyran.se.

This chain expects to have 400 kiosks throughout Sweden in a couple of years. It sells international magazines and newspapers as well as sweets, cigarettes, batteries and the like. Kiosks can be found at most Tunnelbana and train stations.

Magazines

For the latest in lifestyle trends and fashion, buy the English-language glossy *Stockholm New* (www.stockholmnew.com) or the new English-language version of trendy art and fashion magazine *Bon* (www.bon magazine.com). For insight into Scandinavian culture, buy the quarterly *Nordic Reach* (subscribe online at www.nordicreach.com). House-proud Swedes choose from several magazines on interior design, of which *Sköna Hem*, *Elle Interiör* and *Lantliv* are the most popular. *Cosmopolitan* arrived on the scene a few years ago but *Amelia, Damernas Värld* and *Vecko-Revyn* are the main contenders for female readership. Men's magazines *Café* and *Slitz* focus on music, fashion and celebrity interviews. *Sonic* and *Groove* have the lowdown on the music scene, and *ETC* offers

left-wing political criticism. *Situation Sthlm*, about the city's street life and politics, is typically sold in T-bana stations by homeless people.

Architecture and design magazines include *Forum*, *Arkitektur* and *FORM*. Sweden's biggest art magazine is glossy *Konstperspektiv* (www.konstperspektiv.nu), while the magazine *Paletten* (www.natverkstan.net/paletten) takes a theoretical approach to contemporary art.

Newspapers

The two main daily papers are *Dagens Nyheter* (738 10 00, www.dn.se), and the right-leaning *Svenska Dagbladet* (13 50 00, www.svd.se). On public transport, you're likely to see people reading *Metro* (402 20 30, www.metro.se/metro), or *Stockholm City* (50 65 63 98, www.stockholmcity.se), both of which are free daily papers distributed at T-bana stations. *Aftonbladet* (725 20 00, www.aftonbladet.se) and *Expressen* (738 30 00, www.expressen.se) are popular evening tabloids with the latest scandals and gossip, as well as weekly TV guides.

On Fridays *Aftonbladet* publishes *Puls*, with weekly entertainment listings; DN's equivalent is *På Stan* (*On the Town*). You can pick both up for free on Fridays at the tourist office (*see p288*). If you can navigate the Swedish, DN's På Stan website has an excellent search engine and calendar. Expressen has recently come out with its pocket-format *Guiden* (*The Guide*), available at the weekend. The monthly publication *Nöjesguiden* (www.nojesguiden.se) features stories about the Stockholm scene and events listings. It's available free from shops, cafés and newsstands.

For Swedish news in English, **SR Radio Sweden**

International lists brief summaries on its website (www.sr.se/rs/red/ind_eng. html). Alternatively, there is a relatively new Swedish news website, **The Local** (www. thelocal.se), which provides a round-up of Swedish-related news in English.

Radio

E-FM
107.5 Mhz
Soul and dance classics from the 1970s and '80s.

Lugna Favoriter
104.7 Mhz
Old and new slow songs.

Mix Megapol
104.3 Mhz
Old and new pop and rock hits.

NRJ
105.1 Mhz
The latest hits.

Radio Sweden
89.6 Mhz
Check the schedule (www.sr.se/rs) for English programming, generally including sport and political topics.

Rockklassiker
106.7 Mhz
Rock classics.

Sveriges Radio P2
93.8/96.2 Mhz
Classical, jazz and opera.

Vinyl
107 Mhz
Golden oldies.

Television

The state channels of **SVT 1** and **SVT 2** were the first to broadcast in Sweden and still earn the highest ratings. Their commercial-free programmes are varied to appeal to all ages.

Deregulation during the mid 1980s ended the state's television broadcasting monopoly and allowed for the creation of several private channels. The most successful of these is the terrestrial **TV4**, with news, soap operas, sitcoms and game shows. Similar programming can be found on **TV3** and **Kanal 5**, both of which are broadcast from abroad and – much to the chagrin of the government – do not always obey Swedish broadcasting regulations.

Hip youths with carefully dishevelled hair present the entertainment programming at popular **ZTV**.

Foreign-made programmes and films are shown in their original language with Swedish subtitles.

Money

The Swedish *krona* (plural *kronor*, abbreviated to kr or SEK) is divided into 100 *öre*. It comes in coins of 50 *öre*, 1kr, 5kr and 10kr, and notes of 20kr, 50kr, 100kr, 500kr and 1,000kr. At the time of going to press: £1 = 13.4kr, $1 (US) = 7.5kr, €1 = 9.1kr.

In 2003 Sweden voted against joining the European Monetary Union (EMU). However, euros are accepted in many shops, restaurants and hotels, at least in areas popular with tourists.

ATMs/cash machines

There are two types of ATM: **Bankomat** (the joint system of the business banks) and **Uttag** (which belongs to FöreningsSparbanken). With major credit cards you can withdraw cash from most ATMs, which usually provide instructions in different languages at the push of a button. Don't forget that banks tend to charge commission. You'll find ATMs all over the city, in department stores, shopping centres and at banks.

Banks & bureaux de change

You can change money in the city at banks, many hotels and specialist bureaux de change, such as **Forex** and **X-change**; the latter tend to be best because they often provide a more favourable exchange rate and have numerous offices in the city centre. There are exchange offices in the tourist office, Central Station (inside the main entrance hall and on the underground train level) and at Arlanda Airport (Terminals 2 and 5).

Banks are usually open 9am-3.30pm Mon-Fri, and some stay open until 6pm at least once a week. All banks are closed at weekends and on public holidays, as well as the day before a public holiday.

Forex
NK, Hamngatan 18-20, Norrmalm (762 83 40/www.forex.se). T-bana Kungsträdgården/bus 47, 55, 59, 62, 76. **Open** 10am-7pm Mon-Fri; 10am-6pm Sat; noon-4pm Sun. **Map** p305 G7.
Other locations: Kungsgatan 2, Östermalm (611 51 10); Central Station, Norrmalm (411 67 34); Cityterminalen, Norrmalm (21 42 80); Vasagatan 14, Norrmalm (10 49 90); Arlanda Airport, Terminal 2 (59 36 22 71).

X-change
Kungsgatan 30, Norrmalm (50 61 07 00/www.x-change.se). T-bana Hötorget/bus 1, 52, 56. **Open** 8am-7pm Mon-Fri; 9am-4pm Sat. **Map** p305 F7.
Other locations: PUB, Hötorget 13-15, Norrmalm (10 30 00); Arlanda Airport, Arrivals Hall, Terminal 5 (797 85 57); Central Stationen, Norrmalm (54 52 30 30).

Credit cards

Major credit and debit cards are widely accepted by hotels, shops, restaurants and many other services (including Tunnelbana ticket machines, and pay-and-display parking machines). If you pay by credit card in a shop, you may be asked for photo ID. Banks will advance cash against a credit card, but prefer you to use an ATM.

For lost or stolen credit cards, phone one of the following 24-hour numbers:
American Express 429 56 00/ 429 54 29.
Diners Club 14 68 78.
MasterCard 020 79 13 24.
Visa 020 79 31 46.

Directory

Money transfers

Local banks don't do money transfers unless you are a customer of the bank. **Forex** (*see p285*; fee from US$20) and **Western Union** are your best bets for money transfers to and from Sweden, and have branches all over Stockholm.

Western Union

020 74 17 42 press 9 for English/ www.westernunion.com. **Open** 8am-8pm Mon-Fri; 8am-5pm Sat; 10am-4pm Sun.
Call the toll-free number to find your nearest branch.

Tax

The sales tax for most commodities is 25 per cent. There is a 12 per cent sales tax on food and hotel bills, and six per cent sales tax on books, movie and concert tickets and transport (taxis, flights, trains). The sales tax is always listed separately on the bill but is included in the displayed price.

Non-EU residents can reclaim tax on purchases above 200kr in shops displaying a 'Tax-Free Shopping' sticker. All you have to do is ask for a tax-free receipt when paying for an item. When you leave the EU, show your purchases, receipts and passport to customs officials and have your Global Refund cheques stamped. The refund can be collected from any Global Refund office or credited to your own bank account. Call **Global Refund** (020 74 17 41, 54 52 84 40, www.globalrefund.com).

Travellers' cheques

Travellers' cheques are accepted as payment in the more touristy areas, but do not expect to be able to use them in smaller shops or restaurants. It's generally better to exchange your travellers' cheques at a bank since they exchange any currency and usually offer the best rates. All major travellers' cheques are accepted these days, except for Eurocheques.

Opening hours

Normal opening hours for shops are 10am-6pm Mon-Fri; 10am-5pm Sat; noon-4pm Sun. Some smaller shops close earlier on Saturdays and do not open on Sundays. All shops are closed on public holidays (*see p289* **When to go**), except some grocery stores that are open every day of the year.

Restaurant opening hours vary greatly. They are usually open by 11am if they serve lunch; otherwise they'll open some time in the afternoon (usually 4 or 5pm). Closing time is around midnight unless the restaurant has a bar, in which case they may stay open until 1am or even later. Note that many restaurants close in July.

Office hours are generally 8.30am-5pm Mon-Fri. For bank opening hours, *see p285* **Banks & bureaux de change**. For post office opening hours, *see below* **Postal services**.

Police & security

The police are not that common a sight in Stockholm, but can always be spotted at concerts or any special events. They speak English and are known to be friendly and helpful. If you are the victim of a crime, call the police on 112. But Stockholm is considered a very safe city, so the chance of that happening is small. Still, it's wise to take the usual city precautions: don't openly flaunt money or jewellery, keep a close eye on your surroundings and be careful in dark areas late at night.

Pickpocketing does occur in crowded places. Muggings are rare and there are no particular areas considered dangerous, but it's best not to walk in dimly lit areas such as parks at night (an increasing number of muggings have taken place in Humlegården, Berzelii Park and Kungsträdgården).

Police HQ

Norra Agnegatan 33-7, Kungsholmen (401 00 00). T-bana Rådhuset/bus 3, 40, 52, 62. **Map** p304 G4.
This is the main police station. Sub-stations are at Bryggargatan 19, Tulegatan 4, Central Station and Södermannagatan 5.

Postal services

Most post offices are open 10am-6pm Mon-Fri, 10am-2pm Sat; they have a yellow sign containing a blue crown and horn symbol. You can also buy stamps at tobacco kiosks, Pressbyrån kiosks (*see p283*) and the tourist office (*see p288*).

Letters and postcards weighing up to 20g cost 5kr within Sweden; 8kr to the rest of Europe; 10kr to the rest of the world.

Mail sent to other European countries generally arrives in 2-3 days, and to the US in about 4-5 days. Yellow post boxes are for national and international mail, while blue boxes are for mail within Stockholm only.

For the express delivery of packages, *see p278* **Business services**.

Posten

Central Station, Vasagatan, Norrmalm (020 23 22 21/www.posten.se). T-bana T-Centralen/bus 3, 47, 53, 59, 62, 65. **Open** 7am-10pm Mon-Fri; 10am-7pm Sat, Sun. **Map** p305 G6.
This handy post office inside Central Station has long opening hours.

Poste Restante

Letters sent Poste Restante can be sent to any post office and there is no extra charge. Items will be kept for a month, and you'll need some form of ID to collect. For the nearest post office (*Postkontor*) to you, look under *Posten* in the Yellow Pages.

Queuing

Swedes, like the British, have a highly developed queuing culture. People just love standing in line, and queue-jumpers will be met with angry glares. In many shops you'll find a ticket machine near the door; even if there's no one else in the shop, don't expect to get served instantly – you'll have to take a ticket and wait for your number to come up. And woe betide if you miss your slot: you'll have to get another ticket and start all over again.

Religion

Most Swedes are nominally members of the Church of Sweden, which is Evangelical Lutheran, but less than ten per cent of the population attends church regularly. In January 2000, church and state were officially separated. Many other Christian sects are represented in Stockholm, and around 50,000 Muslims and 10,000 Jews live in or near the city.

The service and opening times listed below often change in summer, so call ahead to double-check.

Immanuelskyrkan (Evangelical)
Kungstensgatan 17, Vasastaden (58 75 03 31). T-bana Rådmansgatan/bus 42, 43, 46, 52. **Services** *English* 11am Sun. **Map** p309 D6.

Katolska Kyrkan (Catholic)
Folkungagatan 46B, Södermalm (640 15 55). T-bana Medborgarplatsen/bus 59, 66. **Open** *Winter* 7.30am-6pm daily. *Summer* 7.30am-noon, 2-6pm daily. **Services** 5pm, 8pm Mon-Fri; 9am, 5pm Sat; 10am, 11am Sun. **Map** p314 M8.

St Jacob (Ecumenical Church of Stockholm)
Västra Trädgårdsgatan 2, Norrmalm (723 30 00). T-bana Kungsträdgården/bus 46, 55, 59, 62, 76. **Open** 24hrs daily. **Services** *English* 6pm Sun. **Map** p305 G7.

Stockholmsmoskén (Muslim)
Kapellgränd, Södermalm (50 91 09 00). T-bana Medborgarplatsen/bus 59, 66. **Open** 10am-6pm daily. **Map** p315 L8.
Stockholm's only mosque, on Söder; *see also p92.*

Stora Synagogan (Jewish)
Wahrendorffsgatan 3, Norrmalm (58 78 58 00). T-bana Kungsträdgården/bus 46, 55, 59, 62, 76. **Tours** 10am, noon, 2pm Mon-Fri, Sun. **Services** 9am-midnight Sat (bring a passport in order to be let in). **Map** p305 G8.
The Great Synagogue is conservative/liberal.

Storkyrkan (Protestant)
Trångsrund 1, Gamla Stan (723 30 16). T-bana Gamla Stan/bus 43, 46, 55, 59, 76. **Services** 11am Sat, Sun. **Map** p305 J8.
Stockholm's 700-year-old cathedral; *see also p70.*

Smoking

Sweden has passed a law to ban smoking in all public places where food or drink is served; the law will be enforced as of 1 June 2005. For more information, *see p135* **Up in smoke**.

The streets are very clean and you'll be frowned upon if you throw your cigarette butt on to the pavement, although you still see quite a lot of people smoking. You can't smoke in most public places, including bus stop cubicles and all Tunnelbana stations.

Study

Many students come from abroad to study in Sweden. To find schools, look up *Utbildning* in the Yellow Pages.

Universities & colleges

Berghs School of Communication
PO Box 1380, 111 93 Stockholm (58 75 50 00/www.berghs.se).
Offers programmes in journalism, media, advertising and PR.

Handelshögskolan
PO Box 6501, 113 83 Stockholm (736 90 00/www.hhs.se).
Stockholm's School of Economics, the city's main business school, was founded in 1909. The school co-operates with business institutions around the globe and has an exchange programme with 155 places each year.

Konstfack
Visiting address: Valhallavägen 191, Östermalm. **Map** p315 E12.
Postal address: PO Box 3601, 126 27 Stockholm (450 41 00/www.konstfack.se).
The University College of Arts, Crafts and Design opened way back in 1844 and has almost 2,000 applicants every year – only 100 are admitted. The school takes part in Erasmus, Socrates and Nordplus exchange programmes and has about 30 exchange students per year.

Kungliga Tekniska Högskolan
Valhallavägen 79, 100 44 Stockholm (790 60 00/international@admin. kth.se/www.kth.se).
The Institute of Technology is nearly 200 years old and has 18,000 students. It provides one third of Sweden's technical research and has established exchanges all over the world through such programmes as Socrates, Erasmus and Nordtech.

Stockholms Filmskola
Hornsgatan 65, 118 49 Stockholm (616 00 35/www.stockholmsfilm skola.com).
A private school offering pre-university foundation courses (lasting two years) in film studies.

Stockholms Musikpedagogiska Institut
PO Box 26164, 100 41 Stockholm (611 05 02/52 61/www.smi.se).
A small, independent college in Östermalm that specialises in music and related arts at undergrad and postgrad levels.

Stockholms Universitet
106 91 Stockholm (switchboard 16 20 00/international office 16 28 45/study@sh.su.se/www.su.se).
Stockholm University – north of the city centre, with its own T-bana stop, Universitetet – has about 35,000 undergraduate students and 2,200 postgraduate students. Opened in 1878, it has an international graduate programme and exchange programmes such as Socrates, Erasmus, Nordplus and Nordlys.

Telephones

International & local dialling codes

To make an international call from Stockholm, dial 00 and then the country code, followed by the area code (omitting the initial 0, if there is one) and the number. The international code for the UK is 44; it's 1 for the US and Canada; 353 for the Irish Republic; 61 for Australia; and 64 for New Zealand.

To call Stockholm from abroad, dial 00, then 46 for Sweden, then 8 for Stockholm, then the number. Stockholm phone numbers vary in the number of digits they contain. The area code for Stockholm (including the archipelago) is 08, but you don't need to dial it if you're within the area. All phone numbers in this guide are given as dialled from within Stockholm.

Swedish mobile phone numbers begin with 07. Numbers beginning 020 are always toll-free lines.

Operator services

All operators in Sweden speak English or will connect you to someone who does.

National directory enquiries
118 118
International directory enquiries
118 119
National and international operator 90 200
Telephone charges/faults helpline 90 200
Telegrams 020 0021
Time 90 510
Wake-up calls 90 180 – or dial *55* and then the time at which you want to be woken, in four figures according to the 24hr clock, then dial #. To delete the command, press #55#.

Public phones

Public phones, operated by partly state-owned phone company Telia, are not as widespread as they used to be because of the rise in the use of mobile phones. They accept either credit cards or pre-paid phonecards (the few coin-operated phones that still exist are at railway stations and airports), which are available in 30, 60 or 100 units and can be bought at most newsagents, tobacconists and Pressbyrån (*see p283*). One unit buys one minute of a local call; long-distance calls cost two units per minute.

Instructions are given in English. You can make reverse-charge (collect) calls from all public phones (key 2 then enter the number you are calling including the area code), and call emergency services (on 112) for free.

Mobile phones

Stockholm, home of telecom giant **Ericsson**, has truly embraced the mobile phone revolution with open arms and almost everyone now owns a mobile phone.

Sweden is on the worldwide GSM network, so compatible mobile phones should work without any problem.

Komab

Norrlandsgatan 15, Norrmalm (412 11 00/www.komab.se). T-bana Östermalmstorg/bus 2, 47, 55, 56, 59, 69. **Open** 9.30am-6pm Mon-Fri; 10am-3pm Sat. **Credit** MC, V. **Map** p305 F8.
Seriously low prices on mobile phones at Komab – cheaper, in fact, than the price of renting one for a week.

Time

Stockholm is one hour ahead of GMT, six hours ahead of US Eastern Standard Time and nine ahead of Pacific Standard Time. So, when it's 6pm in Sweden, it's 5pm in London and noon in New York, and 9am in Los Angeles.

Summer time (an hour later) runs from late March to late October, with the same changeover days as the UK.

Tipping

There are no fixed rules about tipping in Sweden because the service charge is almost always included. In restaurants, most people leave 5-15 per cent, depending on how satisfied they are. Rounding up the bill is usually sufficient when you pay a bartender (at the bar) or a taxi driver. Tip hotel porters 20kr or so if they carry your luggage to or from your room, and give more if they've lugged lots of horrifically heavy bags.

Toilets

Public toilets (*toalett*; often small, green booths) are usually found near or in parks. They cost 5kr and are clean. Handy ones that are always open include: the corner of Humlegårdsgatan and Sturegatan, on the park side (Östermalm); in the Kungsträdgården park (Norrmalm); and the corner of Odengatan and Sigtunagatan, on the park side (Vasastaden).

You can also pop into a restaurant or café and use its facilities as long as a) you ask first, and b) it's not a very touristy area, where toilets tend to be reserved for customers. Non-guests can use toilets in fast-food restaurants, but some charge 5kr – as do department stores. There are public toilets and showers at Central Station and at Sergels Torg by the entrance to the T-Centralen T-bana station (open 7.15am-10.30pm daily, toilets 5kr, shower with towel 20kr).

Tourist information

Stockholm Information Service

Sverigehuset (Sweden House), Hamngatan 27, Norrmalm (50 82 85 08/www.stockholm town.se). T-bana Kungsträdgården/bus 2, 45, 47, 55, 56, 62. **Open** 9am-6pm Mon-Fri; 10am-3pm Sat, Sun. **Map** p305 G7.

This is the main tourist office in Stockholm (due to move from Kulturhuset in February 2005), with huge amounts of useful info, plus free books and maps and the free monthly magazine *What's On Stockholm* (in English). Make this your first stop before you go anywhere else. You can also buy the Stockholm Card (in person or online – *see p60* **Stockholm Card**) and theatre and concert tickets, and there's a small gift shop, a Forex exchange bureau and, upstairs, a highly recommended bookshop, Sverigebokhandeln. The website – in eight different languages – is excellent and well worth scouring before you visit.

Hotellcentralen

Concourse, Central Station, Vasagatan, Norrmalm (789 24 56/90/hotels@svb.stockholm.se). T-bana T-Centralen/bus 3, 47, 53, 59, 62, 65. **Open** *June-Aug* 8am-8pm daily. *Sept-May* 9am-6pm Mon-Sat; noon-4pm Sun. **Map** p305 G6.
The tourist office's hotel booking centre can find and book hotels in all price brackets. If you ring them to arrange a hotel booking, it's free; if you visit, it costs 60kr (25kr for youth hostels). Staff can only make same-day bookings for hostels. There's loads of free information about the city as well.

Swedish Travel & Tourism Council

11 Montagu Place, London W1H 2AL, UK (00800 3080 3080/ www.visit-sweden.com). **Open** *Phone enquiries* 9am-7pm Mon-Fri.
The Swedish tourism council has an excellent website with all the information you could possibly need in a variety of languages, and also tailored for visitors from particular countries. There are plenty of useful links and telephone numbers.
US office: 655 Third Avenue, New York, PO Box 4649, Grand Central Station (+1 212 885 9700).

Visas & passports

Sweden is one of the European Union countries covered by the Schengen agreement, meaning many shared visa regulations and reduced border controls (with the exception of the UK and Ireland, the Schengen zone now takes in the entire EU, and also extends to Norway and Iceland). To travel to Schengen countries, British and Irish citizens need full passports; most EU nationals usually

need only carry their national identity card when travelling between Nordic countries but it is still a good idea to carry a passport as well.

Passports, but not visas, are needed by US, Canadian, Australian and New Zealand citizens for stays of up to three months. Citizens of South Africa and many other countries do need visas, obtainable from Swedish consulates and embassies abroad (or in other Schengen countries that you are planning to visit).

EU citizens intending to work, study or live long-term in Sweden are required to obtain a residency card after arrival; non-EU nationals have a different procedure and should get a special visa in their home country before entering Sweden.

Visa requirements can change, so always check the latest information with your country's Swedish embassy.

Weights & measures

Sweden uses the metric system. Decimal points are indicated by commas, while thousands are defined by full stops. Throughout this guide, we have listed measurements in both metric and imperial.

When to go

You'll have a very different experience of Stockholm depending on whether you arrive in winter or summer, but all seasons have their charms. Most choose to visit between May and September, which is when most sights and attractions have extended opening hours. The time around Midsummer weekend (nearest 24 June) is the big summer holiday weekend, when many people leave town and much of the city is closed.

July, with its very long days and short nights, is the main holiday month for locals, and many restaurants, bars and shops close for some or all of the month. Mosquitoes can be a nuisance outside the city between June and late September, especially at dusk out in the archipelago.

Winter (November-March) brings short days and cold temperatures – some of the waterways freeze over, but snow doesn't usually stay on the ground long. The city looks stunning just after a snowfall, especially on clear crisp sunny days, which are relatively common.

Public holidays

On public holidays, virtually all shops, banks and offices, and many restaurants and bars, are closed. Banks are also closed the day before a public holiday. Public transport runs a limited service on Christmas and New Year's Day.

Annual public holidays are:
Nyårsdagen
(*New Year's Day*) 1 Jan.
Trettondedagsafton
(*Eve of Epiphany*) 5 Jan.
Trettondedag Jul
(*Epiphany*) 6 Jan.
Skärtorsdagen
(*Maundy Thursday*) 24 Mar 2005, 13 Apr 2006.
Långfredagen
(*Good Friday*) 25 Mar 2005, 14 Apr 2006.
Påskdagen
(*Easter Sunday*) 27 Mar 2005, 16 Apr 2006.
Annandag Påsk
(*Easter Monday*) 28 Mar 2005, 17 Apr 2006.
Valborgsmässoafton
(*Walpurgis Night*) 30 Apr.
Första Maj
(*May Day*) 1 May.
Krist Himmelfärds Dag
(*Ascension*) 5 May 2005, 25 May 2006.
Pingstdagen
(*Whit Sunday*) 8 June 2005, 30 May 2006.

Directory

Annandag Pingst
(*Whit Monday*) 15 May 2005,
4 June 2006.
Midsommarafton
(*Midsummer's Eve*)
25 June 2005, 24 June 2006.
**Midsommardagen
(Midsummer's Day)**
26 June 2005, 25 June 2006.
Nationaldagen
(*National Day*) 6 June.
Alla Helgons Dag
(*All Saints' Day*) 5 Nov 2005,
4 Nov 2006.
Julafton
(*Christmas Eve*) 24 Dec.
Juldagen
(*Christmas Day*) 25 Dec.
Annandag Jul
(*Boxing Day*) 26 Dec.

Women

Great measures have been
taken in Sweden to guarantee
equal opportunities for men
and women. Today, women in
Sweden can combine having a
family and working thanks to
the state-sponsored childcare
programme; almost 80 per cent
of all women work and around
75 per cent of children aged
one to six use the state
childcare system. Swedish
women still earn less than
men, however, partly because
of the professions they choose
and the fact that many
mothers work part-time.

It is unlikely that female
visitors will face any kind of
harassment, and Stockholm
is a very safe city to walk
around, although the normal
precautions are always
recommended.

Kvinnoforum (562 288 00,
www.kvinnoforum.se) works to
enhance the empowerment of
women, while **KvinnorKan**
(723 07 07, www.kvinnorkan.se)
demonstrates and encourages
women's knowledge.

Working in Stockholm

The current unemployment
rate in Stockholm is around six
per cent. Most people speak
English very well and a great
number of companies use
English as a working
language. If you want to work
in Stockholm, but you're not
yet in the country, the best
way to find a job is to register
at some of the many online
recruiting companies, such as
Jobfinder (www.jobfinder.se),
Jobline (www.jobline.se),
Stepstone (www.stepstone.se)
and **Topjobs** (www.topjobs.se).
The European Employment
Services network, **EURES**
(http://europa.eu.int/jobs/
eures) provides a database of
job vacancies throughout the

EU and useful information
about working conditions.

If you're already living in
Sweden, you can start looking
for a job by going to the
state employment agency,
Arbetsförmedlingen; it has
a lot of information and offers
free guidance.

Arbetsförmedlingen

*Norrtullsgatan 6, Vasastaden 113 29
Stockholm (50 88 22 00/www.ams.
se). T-bana Odenplan/bus 2, 4, 40,
53, 72.* **Open** *Phone enquiries*
9.30am-3.30pm Mon-Fri. *Office*
9.30am-3.30pm Mon-Fri. *Self-service*
(use of computers) 8am-3.30pm
Mon-Fri. **Map** p309 D6.

Work permits

All EU nationals can obtain
a work permit in Sweden;
non-EU citizens must apply
for a work permit abroad and
hand in the application to a
Swedish embassy or consular
representative. The rules for
obtaining work permits vary
for different jobs.

EU citizens can stay in
Sweden for three months, after
which they must apply for a
residence permit (which can
take a month to process, so it's
best to apply as soon as you
arrive). Non-EU citizens must
apply for a residence permit
from outside Sweden. You'll
need to produce a valid ID or
passport and other documents
depending on your status
(employee, job-seeker, self-
employed, student, etc).
Contact the **National
Immigration Authority**
(Migrationsverket; 011 15 60
00, www.migrationsverket.se).

Useful organisations

The EU has a website (http://
europa.eu.int/citizensrights/)
with information on your
rights, and useful numbers and
addresses. It also has info on
taxes, recognition of diplomas,
access to employment, rights
of residence and social security,
the national education system
and a route map for job
applicants in the EU.

Average climate

Month	Max temp	Min temp	Rainfall
Jan	0°C/32°F	-5°C/22°F	39mm/1.5in
Feb	0°C/32°F	-5°C/22°F	27mm/1.1in
Mar	3°C/38°F	-3°C/26°F	26mm/1in
Apr	8°C/48°F	1°C/33°F	30mm/1.2in
May	15°C/59°F	6°C/44°F	30mm/1.2in
June	21°C/70°F	11°C/52°F	45mm/1.8in
July	22°C/71°F	13°C/56°F	72mm/2.8in
Aug	20°C/68°F	13°C/56°F	66mm/2.6in
Sept	15°C/59°F	9°C/50°F	55mm/2.2in
Oct	10°C/50°F	5°C/43°F	50mm/2in
Nov	4°C/40°F	0°C/32°F	53mm/2.1in
Dec	1°C/33°F	-3°C/26°F	46mm/1.8in

Directory

Vocabulary

It will only take a few minutes in Stockholm to realise that just about everyone speaks strikingly good English and is happy to oblige you by using it. However, as anywhere else, any attempts you make to learn a few basic phrases will be met with pleasure – or hilarity (Swedish is notoriously difficult to pronounce).

Vowels

Swedish vowels include the standard a, e, i, o, u and sometimes y along with three additional vowels: å, ä and ö. Vowels are long when at the end of a word or followed by one consonant, and short when followed by two consonants.

å – as in **tore**
ä – as in **pet**
ö – as in **fur**
y – as in **ewe**
ej – as in **late**

Consonants

g (before e, i, y, ä and ö), **j, lj,dj** and **gj** – as in **yet**
k (before e, i, y, ä and ö), **sj, skj, stj, tj** and **rs** – all more or less like **sh**, with subtle differences
qu – as **kv** (though q is hardly ever used in Swedish)
z – as in **so**

Alphabetical order

Swedish alphabetical order lists å, ä and ö, in that order, after z.

yes *ja* (yah); no *nej* (nay); **please/ thank you** *tack;* **hello** *hej* (hay); **goodbye** *hej då* (hay daw); **excuse me** *ursäkta* (ewr-shekta); **I'm sorry** *förlåt* (furr-lawt); **do you speak English?** *talar du engelska?* (tah-lar dew engelska?); **how are you?** *Hur är det* (hewr eyre day?)

Sightseeing

entrance *ingång* (in-gawng); exit *utgång* (ewt-gawng); open *öppen* (ur-pen); closed *stängd* (staingd); toilet **(women/men)** *toalett* (too-a-let) *(kvinnor/män);* where *var;* when *när* (nair); near *nära* (naira); far *långt* (lawngt); **(city) square** *torg* (tohrj); church *kyrka* (chewr-ka);

art gallery *konstgalleri;* town hall *stadshus;* street/road *gata/väg;* palace *slott;* metro *tunnelbana;* ticket to... *biljett till...* (bill-yet till); **how much is this/that?** *hur mycket kostar den/det?* (hewr mewkeh costar den/det?); **which way to...?** *hur kommer jag till...?* (hewr comer yah til...?)

Accommodation

hotel *hotell;* youth hostel *vandrarhem;* **I have a reservation** *jag har beställt ett rum* (yah har bes-telt ett room); double room *dubbelrum;* single room *enkelrum;* double bed *dubbelsäng;* twin beds *två sängar;* with a bath *med bad;* with a shower *med dusch*

Days of the week

Monday *måndag;* Tuesday *tisdag;* Wednesday *onsdag;* Thursday *torsdag;* Friday *fredag;* Saturday *lördag;* Sunday *söndag*

Numbers

0 *noll;* 1 *ett;* 2 *två* (tvaw); 3 *tre* (trea); 4 *fyra* (few-ra); 5 *fem;* 6 *sex;* 7 *sju* (shew); 8 *åtta* (otta); 9 *nio* (nee-oo); 10 *tio* (tee-oo); 11 *elva;* 12 *tolv;* 13 *tretton;* 14 *fjorton* (fyoor-ton); 15 *femton;* 16 *sexton;* 17 *sjutton* (shew-ton); 18 *arton;* 19 *nitton;* 20 *tjugo* (chew-goo); 21 *tjugoett* (chew-goo-ett); 30 *trettio* (tretti); 40 *fyrtio* (fur-ti); 50 *femtio* (fem-ti); 60 *sextio* (sex-ti); 70 *sjuttio* (shew-ti); 80 *åttio* (otti); 90 *nittio* (nitti); 100 *hundra* (hewndra); 1,000 *tusen* (tews-sen); 1,000,000 *miljon* (milly-oon)

have you got a table for...? *har ni ett bord för...?* (hahr nee ett boord furr...?); bill *notan* (noo-tan); menu *meny* (men-ew); wine list *vinlista* (veen-lista); breakfast *frukost* (frew-cost); lunch *lunch* (lwnch); dinner *middag* (mid-daag); main course *huvudrätt* (hew-vew-dret); starter *förrätt* (fur-et); bottle *flaska;* glass *glas;* restaurant *restaurang;* cake shop *konditori;* bakery *bageri;* bar-restaurant *krog*

Basic foods & extras

ägg egg; bröd bread; gräddfil sour cream; ost cheese; pommes frites chips/fries; potatis potatoes; ris rice; senap mustard; smör butter; smörgås sandwich; socker sugar.

Swedish specialities (*husmanskost*)

ärtsoppa split pea and pork soup; black & white steak and mashed

potato; fisksoppa fish soup; Janssons frestelse gratin of anchovies and potatoes; kåldolmar stuffed cabbage rolls; köttbullar meatballs; lufsa pork dumpling with smoked salmon; potatissallad potato salad; pytt i panna fried meat and potato hash with a fried egg and pickled beetroots; rimmad oxbringa lightly salted brisket of beef; sillbricka an assortment of herring dishes; smörgåsbord typical self-service buffet, starting with herring, followed by cold dishes, then hot dishes, then dessert

Fruit & veg (*frukt & grönsaker*)

apelsin orange; ärtor peas; bönor beans; citron lemon; hallon raspberry; hjortron cloudberry; jordgubbar strawberries; kål cabbage; lingon lingonberry; lök onion; morötter carrots; nötter nuts; persika peach; smultron wild strawberries; svamp mushrooms; vindruvor grapes; vitlök garlic

Meat & game (*kott & vilt*)

älg elk; biff beef; fläsk pork; kalvkött veal; korv sausage; kyckling chicken; lammkött lamb; rådjur roe deer; ren reindeer; skinka ham

Fish (*fisk*)

ål eel; blåmusslor mussels; forell trout; gös pike-perch; hummer lobster; kräftor crayfish; lax salmon; räkor prawns; sjötunga sole; strömming/sill (inlagd/ sotare) herring (pickled/blackened); surströmming fermented Baltic herring; torsk cod

Cakes & desserts (*bakverk & desserter*)

dammsugare confectionery made with green marzipan and chocolate; glass ice cream; kaka/tårta cake (*kaka* can also mean cookie); lussekatt saffron bun with raisins; ostkaka Swedish cheesecake; pepparkakor gingerbread biscuits; plättar miniature pancakes served with jam and cream; semla whipped cream and almond-paste buns

Drinks (*drycker*)

brännvin schnapps; varm choklad hot chocolate; fruktjuice fruit juice; glögg fortified mulled wine; kaffe coffee; mineral-vatten mineral water; mjölk milk; öl beer; punsch sweet arak-like spirit; rödvin red wine; te tea; vitt vin white wine.

Directory

Further Reference

Books

For books about Sweden in English, visit the Swedish Institute's **Sweden Bookshop** (*see p154*) in Gamla Stan, or the book sections in department stores **NK** or **Åhlens** (for both, *see p153*).

Architecture, art & design

Caldenby, Claes & Hultin, Olof *Architecture in Sweden* 1995-9 (2001) With text in both English and Swedish.

Cargill, Katrin *Creating the Look: Swedish Style* (1996) A practical guide to achieving the Swedish interior design look.

Davis, Courtney *A Treasury of Viking Design* (2000) Scandinavian Viking design in ceramics, textiles, woodwork and so on.

Edenheim, Ralph *Skansen: Traditional Swedish Style* (2002) Illustrated presentation of the interiors of Skansen's buildings from a cultural and historical perspective.

Fiell, Charlotte *Scandinavian Design* (2002) In-depth illustrated guide focusing on 200 designers and design companies.

Hakan, Groth & Schulenburg, Fritz van der *Neoclassicism in the North: Swedish Furniture and Interiors 1770-1850* (1999) Excellent photographs trace the evolution of the neo-classical style in Sweden.

Helgeson, Susanne *Swedish Design* (2002) A survey of Swedish designers of all sorts of products, from glass to furniture. Offers insight into Swedish design philosophies.

Hultin, Olof, Johansson, Bengt Oh, Mårtelius, Johan & Waern, Rasmus *The Complete Guide to Architecture in Stockholm* (1999) Written by experts, this guide introduces the reader to 400 of the most notable buildings in the Stockholm area.

Ostergard, Derek E & Stritzler-Levine, Nina *The Brilliance of Swedish Glass 1918-1939* (1997) Illustrated essays that put Swedish glass production into a wider perspective.

Sjöberg, Lars & Ursula *The Swedish Room* (1994) Illustrated guide to interior design through different periods and regions.

Snodin, Michael & Stavenow-Hidemark, Elisabet (eds) *Carl and Karin Larsson: Creators of the Swedish Style* (1998) Numerous essays by experts.

Stoeltie, Barbara, Stoeltie, René & Taschen, Angelika *Country Houses of Sweden* (2001) Coffee-table book with lovely photographs of Swedish country houses from a variety of periods.

Biographies

Linnea, Sharon *Raoul Wallenberg: The Man who Stopped Death* (1993) Biography of the famous Swedish diplomat who saved the lives of 100,000 Hungarian Jews during World War II and then mysteriously disappeared after going into Soviet custody.

Lovejoy, Joe *Sven-Göran Eriksson* (2002) For football lovers only.

Martinus, Eivor *Strindberg and Love* (2001) In-depth biography of the troubled dramatist, focusing on the four most important women in his life.

Palm, Carl Magnus *From ABBA to Mamma Mia: The Official Book* (2000) The first book published with the co-operation of the band, with lots of good photos.

Fiction & autobiograhy

Bengtsson, Frans G *The Long Ships* (1945) A true Swedish classic, this novel enchants its readers with the many adventures of a fictional Viking named Orm.

Bergman, Ingmar *The Magic Lantern: An Autobiography* (1989) Memoirs of the film master's career and childhood.

Boye, Karin *Kallocain* (1940) A bleak vision of a future totalitarian world state.

Johnson, Eyvind *Dreams of Roses and Fire* (1949) Novel by the winner of the 1974 Nobel Prize for Literature.

Lagerlöf, Selma *The Wonderful Adventures of Nils* (1906) One of Sweden's best-loved modern folk tales, written to teach Swedish schoolchildren about the geography of their country. Tiny Nils explores the Swedish landscape on the back of a goose and lives through many hair-raising experiences.

Lindgren, Astrid *Pippi Longstocking* (1945) Fantastic series of children's books about a girl who does exactly as she pleases.

Mankell, Henning Best-selling crime writer best-known for his series of detective stories starring Inspector Kurt Wallander from southern Sweden.

Moberg, Vilhelm *The Emigrants* (1949) Moving story about what it was like to emigrate from Sweden to the US in the 19th century, later made into a film.

Niemi, Mikael *Popular Music* (2004). A witty, compelling coming-of-age story set in northern Sweden in the 1960s.

Strindberg, August *Miss Julie and Other Plays* (1998) Contains some of the dramatist's key plays: *Miss Julie, The Father, A Dream Play, Ghost Sonata* and *The Dance of Death.*

Wollstonecraft, Mary
Letters Written during a Short Residence in Sweden, Norway, and Denmark (2004) Early feminist and mother of *Frankenstein* author Mary Shelley, Wollstonecraft describes her travels through Scandinavia in 1795.

History, politics & society

Berlin, Peter *The Xenophobe's Guide to the Swedes* (1999) A funny book explaining the complex rules that govern Swedish social interaction.
Carr, Lisa Werner & Robinowitz, Christina Johansson *Modern-day Vikings: A Practical Guide to Interacting with the Swedes* (2001) Discussion of the Viking beginnings of the Swedish character.
Daun, Ake *Swedish Mentality* (1996) Focuses on the development of Swedish culture and society.
Erling, Matz *Glorious Vasa: The Magnificent Ship and 17th-century Sweden* (2001) Fascinating book that provides a great insight into what life was like in 17th-century Stockholm.
Gould, Arthur *Developments in Swedish Social Policy* (2001) An exploration of the development of the Swedish welfare state.
Hadenius, Stig *Swedish Politics during the 20th Century* (1999) Authoritative treatment of all the dramatic political changes that took place between 1900 and 1999.
Hargittai, Istvan & Watson, James *The Road to Stockholm: Nobel Prizes, Science and Scientists* (2002) Discusses the selection process for the scientific laureates and the ingredients

for scientific discovery and recognition.
af Malmborg, Mikael *Neutrality and State-building in Sweden* (2001) The history and future of Swedish neutrality.
Nordstrom, Byron J *The History of Sweden* (2002) Swedish history from prehistoric times to the present.
Swahn, Jan Öjvind *Maypoles, Crayfish and Lucia: Swedish Holidays and Traditions* (1997) A guide to Swedish customs and festivals published by the Swedish Institute.

Film

Before the Storm (Reza Parsa, 2000) Excellent thriller with interweaving stories.
The Best Intentions (Bille August, 1992) The story of Ingmar Bergman's parents, written by Bergman himself.
Elvira Madigan (Bo Widerberg, 1967) Beautiful-looking film about a doomed love affair.
The Emigrants (Jan Troell, 1970) First of two films – the second is *The New Land* – dealing movingly with 19th-century Swedish emigrants to America.
Evil (Mikael Håfström, 2004) Oscar-nominated film about a young rebel in a Swedish private school in the late 1950s.
Fanny and Alexander (Ingmar Bergman, 1982) Family saga seen through the eyes of a small boy, revisiting the typical Bergman themes of religious doubt and the apocalypse.
The Father (Alf Sjöberg, 1969) Film version of Strindberg's play about a battle between husband and wife, descending into madness and death.
Four Shades of Brown (Tomas Alfredson, 2004) Black comedy interweaving four lives.
Fucking Åmål (US title *Show Me Love*, Lukas Moodysson, 1998) All-girl twist to the high-

school romance genre, which won multiple awards.
House of Angels (Colin Nutley, 1992) Prejudice and conflict in rural Sweden.
I am Curious: Yellow (Vilgot Sjöman, 1967) Sexually frank but morally involved tale mixing reportage and fiction.
Jalla! Jalla! (Josef Fares, 2000). Culture clash comedy.
Lilja 4-ever (Lukas Moodysson, 2002) Moodysson darker than usual but very popular in Sweden.
My Life as a Dog (Lasse Hallström, 1985) A witty and touching story of a young boy in 1950s rural Sweden.
Persona (Ingmar Bergman, 1966) An actress refuses to speak, perhaps due to the impossibility of true communication, while her nurse chatters away about her sex life.
The Seventh Seal (Ingmar Bergman, 1956) Unforgettably striking medieval allegory, with plague sweeping through an apocalyptic Sweden and Max von Sydow's knight playing a lengthy game of chess with Death.
Songs from the Second Floor (Roy Andersson, 2000) Loosely connected vignettes deal with traffic jams and redundancy in a surreal black comedy.
Together (Lukas Moodysson, 2000) Excellent comedy about life and love in a '70s commune.
The Treasure of Arne (often called *Herr Arnes Pengar*, Mauritz Stiller, 1919) Bravura premonition-laden drama set in Sweden in the 16th century.
Tsatsiki, Mum and the Policeman (Ella Lemhagen, 1999) Engaging story of a young Stockholmer who longs to meet his Greek father.
Under the Sun (Colin Nutley, 1998) Sweet and satisfying film based around an unconventional love story.

Directory

Wild Strawberries (Ingmar Bergman, 1957) Warm story of an academic who relives and rediscovers his youth.

Wings of Glass (Reza Bagher, 2000) Emotionally involving film about a Swedish-Iranian family's conflict between their Muslim roots and Swedish environment.

Music

Classical

Alfvén, Hugo (1872-1960) Composer of the ballet *Bergakungen* ('Mountain King'), five symphonies and numerous songs.

Berwald, Franz (1796-1868) Wrote operas, chamber music and four symphonies.

Börtz, Daniel (born 1943) Composer whose contemporary chamber music and solo pieces reflect earlier periods.

Eliasson, Anders (born 1947) Composer of complex orchestral works, most notably *Canto del Vagabondo*.

Hardenberger, Håkan (born 1961) Internationally renowned trumpeter.

Hillborg, Anders (born 1952) Writes everything from chamber music to film scores; most famous for his *Celestial Mechanics* for solo strings.

Lindberg, Christian (1958) International trombone virtuoso.

Peterson-Berger, Wilhelm (1867-1942) Composer of operas and piano miniatures with a strong folk influence.

Pettersson, Allan (1911-80) Composer most renowned for his *Symphony No.7*.

Rosenberg, Hilding (1892-1985) Wrote numerous string quartets.

Stenhammar, Wilhelm (1871-1927) Composed chamber music, operas and orchestral pieces.

Sandström, Jan (born 1954) Renowned for his *Motorbike Concerto* for trombone and orchestra.

Sandström, Sven-David (born 1942) Composer of complex orchestral works, ballets and percussion pieces.

Sofie von Otter, Anne (born 1955) The world-famous mezzo-soprano.

Pop & rock

ABBA Their phenomenally successful albums include *Waterloo* (1974) and *Super Trouper* (1980).

Ace of Base 1990s dance band responsible for 'All That She Wants'.

The Cardigans Pop band formed in 1992, with *Life* probably their most well-known album.

The Concretes *The Concretes* (2004) Debut album from eccentric Stockholm-based rockers.

Europe Remembered for the terrible 1986 hit 'The Final Countdown'.

The Hellacopters US-tinged Swedish rock, with albums including *Supershitty to the Max*, *By the Grace of God* and *Cream of the Crap Vol.2*.

The Hives Internationally successful fivesome playing, in their words, 'punk rock music avec kaboom'; albums include *Your New Favourite Band*, *Barely Legal* and *Tyrannosaurus Hives*.

Roxette The '80s-style pop duo most famous for 'It Must Have Been Love' and 'Joyride'.

Sahara Hotnights *Kiss and Tell* (2004) Third album from the garage-rock girl band.

Soundtrack of Our Lives *Behind the Music* (2002) Third album from the successful six-piece rock outfit hailing from Gothenburg.

Websites

City of Stockholm
www.stockholm.se Official information on the city's government, services and history, with useful links.

Destination Stockholm
www.destination-stockholm.se Discounted accommodation, plus restaurant reviews, virtual walks and loads of other useful city information. In multiple languages.

Nobel Prizes
www.nobel.se Everything you ever wanted to know about the Nobel Prizes, their history and the winners.

Royal Family
www.ritva.com Unofficial and quite amusing fan site about the Swedish royal family.

Scandinavian Design
www.scandinaviandesign.com The products and personalities of Nordic design, plus information on museums, magazines and design schools.

Scandinavica
www.scandinavica.com An English-language website dedicated to Nordic culture.

Stockholm Guide
www.stockholmtown.com Official tourist office site with good information on events, activities and attractions in the city and archipelago.

Stockholm Map
www.map.stockholm.se/kartago A zoom-in, zoom-out map of the city, with instructions in Swedish.

Sweden
www.sweden.se 'The official gateway to Sweden', with well-written articles and fact-sheets on elements of Swedish culture.

Swedish Institute
www.si.se Essential source of information about Sweden, Swedes and Swedish culture, plus information about studying in Sweden.

Yellow Pages
www.gulasidorna.se Online Swedish Yellow Pages, also plots locations on maps. Swedish only, but easy to follow.

Directory

Index

Advertisers' Index

Please refer to the relevant sections for contact details.

Place of Interest and/or Entertainment	
Railway Station	
Park	
College/Hospital	
Main Shopping Street	
Area Name	GÄRDET
Subway Station	T
Tourist Information	i

Maps

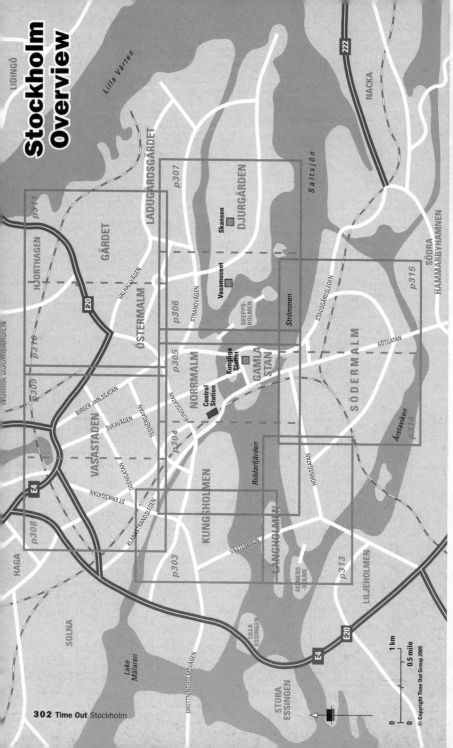

Stockholm Overview

LIDINGÖ

Lilla Värten

LADUGÅRDSGÄRDET

p307

DJURGÅRDEN

Skansen

Vasamuseet

SKEPPS-HOLMEN

Strömmen

Saltsjön

SÖDRA HAMMARBYHAMNEN

p315

p311

GÄRDET

HJORTHAGEN

VALHALLAVÄGEN

ÖSTERMALM

p306

STRANDVÄGEN

p305

NORRMALM

Kungliga Slottet

GAMLA STAN

STADSGÅRDSLEDEN

GÖTGATAN

SÖDERMALM

p310

NORRA DJURGÅRDEN

p309

E20

BIRGER JARLSGATAN

SVEAVÄGEN

TEGNÉRGATAN

Central Station

KUNGSGATAN

p304

VASASTADEN

ODENGATAN

ST ERIKSGATAN

Riddarfjärden

Årstaviken

p314

NACKA

222

HAGA

E4

p308

KLARASTRANDSLEDEN

KUNGSHOLMEN

p303

HORNSGATAN

LÅNGHOLMEN

VÄSTERBRON

REIMERS-HOLME

p313

LILJEHOLMEN

DROTTNINGHOLMSVÄGEN

LILLA ESSINGEM

SOLNA

Lake Mälaren

STORA ESSINGEN

E4

E20

1 km

0.5 mile

0

© Copyright Time Out Group 2005

1

HORNSBERGS STRD

STADSHAGEN

Stadshagen

SANKT GÖRANSGATAN

BARNSLINGAN

AKUTVÄGEN

VÅRDVÄGEN

MAGNETVÄGEN

Sankt Görans Sjukhus

PATIENTVÄGEN

FINSENS VÄG

FRISKVÅRDSVÄGEN

STADSHAGSVÄGEN

STADSHAGENS IDROTTS VÄG

SANKT GÖRANSPLAN

WELANDERS VÄG

BÅBÄRVÄGEN

VIXENVÄGEN

MARIEBERGSGATAN

SANKT GÖRANSGATAN

DROTTNINGHOLMSVÄGEN

LAGERLÖFSGATAN

GJÖRWELLSGATAN

VÄSTERBRONEDFARTEN

RÅLAMBSVÄGEN

MARIEBERG

FYRVERKARBACKEN

Mariebergs -parken

2

KLARASTRANDSLEDEN

Karlbergssjön

IGELDAMMSGATAN

SVARVARGATAN

INDUSTRIGATAN

KUNGSHOLMS STRAND

GJUTARGATAN

Tullmuseet

ALSTRÖMERGATAN

Västermalmsgallerian

FLEMINGGATAN

🚇

ARBETARGATAN

FRIDHEMSGATAN

🚇 🚇

🚇 **Fridhemsplan**

🚇 **Fridhemsplan**

SYSSLOMANSGATAN

FRIDHEMSGATAN

MITISGATAN

NORR MÄLARSTRAND

KARLSVIKSGATAN

ST ERIKSGATAN

TURE NERMANS GRÄND

SVEN RINMANS GATA

BALTZAR VON PLATENS GATA

SMEDSUDDSVÄGEN

Rålambshovsparken

RÅLAMBSHOVSLEDEN

VÄSTERBRON

VÄSTERBRON

Riddarfjärden

Ferries to Drottningholm, Birka & Mariefred

3

RÖRSTRANDSGATAN 🚇

DREJARGATAN

NORRBACKAGATAN

BRÄVALLAGATAN

See p308

ST ERIKSPLAN

🚇 🚇 **St Eriksplan**

VULCANUSGATAN

ATLASGATAN

VÅLUNDSGATAN

ATLASMUREN

E

ST ERIKSGATAN

ST ERIKSBRON

KLARASTRANDSLEDEN

KUNGSHOLMS STRAND

KRONOBERGSGATAN

ÅNGSTRÖMSGATAN

INEDALSGATAN

HALLMANS GATA

GRUBBENS GATA

POLHEMS TVÄRGRÄND

POLHEMSGATAN

FLEMINGGATAN

F

PARKGATAN

KUNGSHOLMEN

KRONOBERGSGATAN

Kronobergsparken

CELSIUSGATAN

See p304 ▶

G

BERGSGATAN

GAMBRINUS-GATAN

HANTVERKARGATAN

JOHN ERICSSONSGATAN

PILGATAN

Pontonjär- parken

PONTONJÄRGATAN

POLHEMSGATAN

NORR MÄLARSTRAND

H

J

0   300 m

0   300 yds

© Copyright Time Out Group 2005

Bellmanmuseet ▢

Långholmsparken

See p313 ▼

LÅNGHOLMEN

KARLSHÄLLSVÄGE

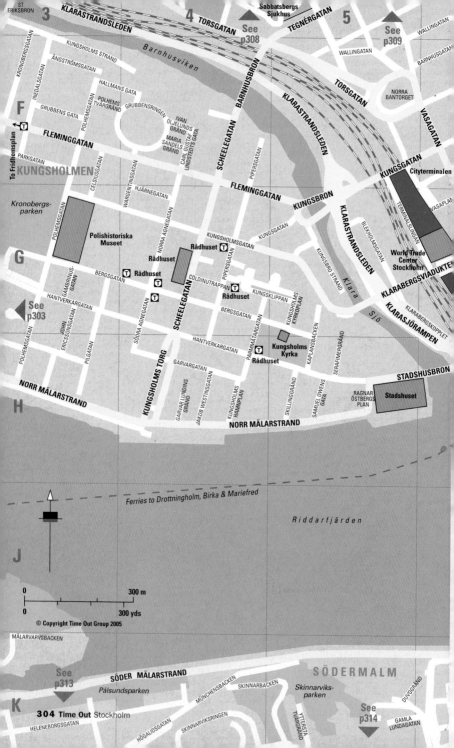

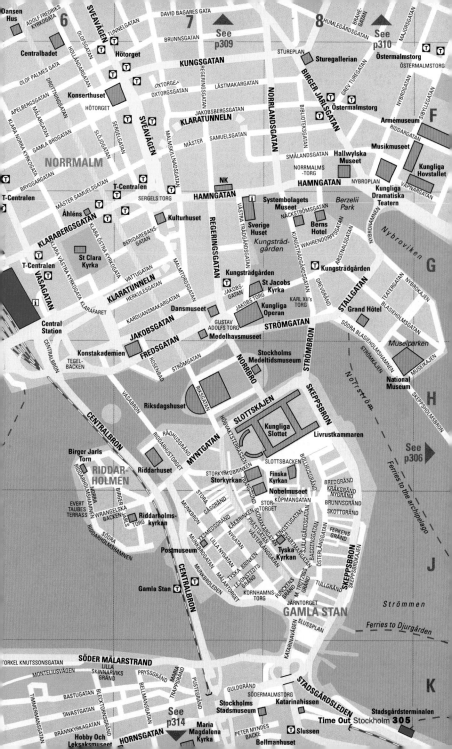

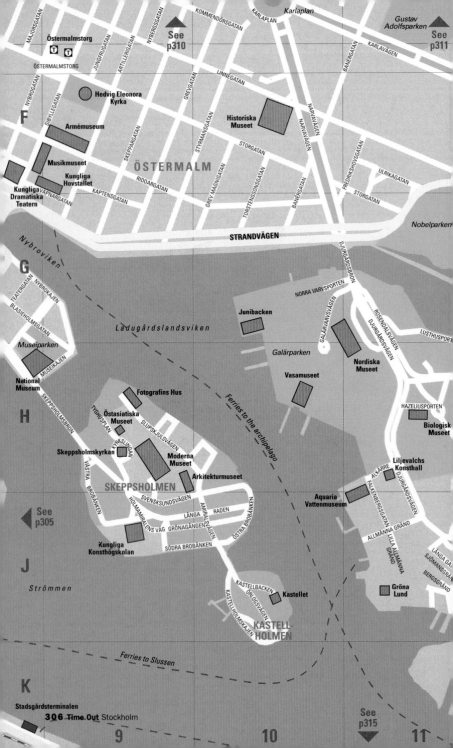

MAJORGATAN

Östermalmstorg
🚇 🚇
ÖSTERMALMSTORG

KOMMENDÖRSGATAN

KARLAPLAN

Karlaplan

Gustav Adolfsparken

See p310

See p311

NYBERGSGATAN
JUNGFRUGATAN
ARTILLERIGATAN
NYBROGATAN
KARLAVÄGEN
BANÉRGATAN

NYBROGATAN
SIBYLLEGATAN

Hedvig Eleonora Kyrka

LINNÉGATAN

GREVGATAN

F

Armémuseum

STYRMANSGATAN

Historiska Museet

NARVAVÄGEN

SKEPPARGATAN

STORGATAN

NARVAVÄGEN

Musikmuseet

ÖSTERMALM

FREDRIKSHOVSGATAN

ULRIKAGATAN

Kungliga Hovstallet

RIDDARGATAN

TORSTENSONSGATAN

STORGATAN

VALHARGATAN

KAPTENSGATAN

GREV MAGNIGATAN

BANÉRGATAN

Kungliga Dramatiska Teatern

STRANDVÄGEN

Nobelparken

Nybroviken

DJURGÅRDSBRON

G

TEATERGATAN
NYBROKAJEN

BLASIEHOLMSGATAN

Ladugårdslandsviken

NORRA VARVSPORTEN

GALÄRVARVSVÄGEN

ROSENDALSVÄGEN
DJURGÅRDSVÄGEN

LUSTHUSPOR

Museiparken

MUSEIKAJEN

Junibacken

Galärparken

Nordiska Museet

National Museum

SKEPPSHOLMSBRON

Fotografins Hus

Vasamuseet

H

TYGHUSPLAN

Östasiatiska Museet

SLUPSKJULSVÄGEN

Ferries to the archipelago

HAZELIUSPORTEN

Biologisk Museet

Skeppsholmskyrkan

KYRKSLINGAN

Moderna Museet

Liljevalchs Konsthall

AKLARRE

VÄSTRA BROBÄNKEN

Arkitekturmuseet

Aquaria Vattenmuseum

DJURGÅRDSVÄGEN

FALKENBERGSGATAN

See p305

SKEPPSHOLMEN

SVENSKSUNDSVÄGEN

AMIRALSVÄGEN

ALLMÄNNA GRÄND

LILLA ALLMÄNNA GRÄND

HOLMAMIRALENS VÄG

LÅNGA

RADEN

ÖSTRA BROBÄNKEN

LÅNGA GA.
SJÖMANSGR.

GRÖNAGÄNGEN

BERGSGRÄND

J

Kungliga Konsthögskolan

SÖDRA BROBÄNKEN

Strömmen

KASTELLBACKEN

ÖRLOGSVÄGEN

Kastellet

Gröna Lund

KASTELLHOLMSKAJEN

KASTELL-HOLMEN

Ferries to Slussen

K

Stadsgårdsterminalen

See p315

9   **10**   **11**

TAPTOGATAN

OXENSTIERNSGATAN

VALHALLAVÄGEN

See
p311

LADUGÅRDSGÄRDET

TV-Huset

Gärdet

0   300 m
0   300 yds
© Copyright Time Out Group 2005

F

To Kaknästornet ↑

GÄRDESGATAN

SKARPÖGATAN

British
Embassy

Radiohuset

US Embassy

DAG HAMMARSKJÖLDS VÄG

DJURGÅRDSBRUNNSVÄGEN

Tekniska
Museet

MUSEIVÄGEN

Berwaldhallen

LABORATORIEGATAN

NOBELGATAN

Sjöhistoriska
Museet

Etnografiska
Museet

Djurgårdsbrunnsviken

G

ROSENDALSVÄGEN

ROSENDALSTERRASSEN

Rosendals
Slott

S k a n s e n

ORANGERIVÄGEN

Rosendals
Trädgård

VALMUNDSVÄGEN

H

DJURGÅRDEN

SIRISHOVSVÄGEN

Cirkus

Skansen
Akvariet

SINGELBACKEN

SOLLIDSBACKEN

DJURGÅRDSVÄGEN

BERGSJÖLUNDSVÄGEN

BECKHOLMSVÄGEN

DJURGÅRDSVÄGEN

RYSSVIKSVÄGEN

PRINS EUGENS VÄG

J

NORDENSKIÖLDS
-GATAN

BECKHOLMSBRON

**BECK-
HOLMEN**

Waldemarsviken

Prins Eugens
Waldemarsudde

K

Time Out Stockholm **307**

12   13   14

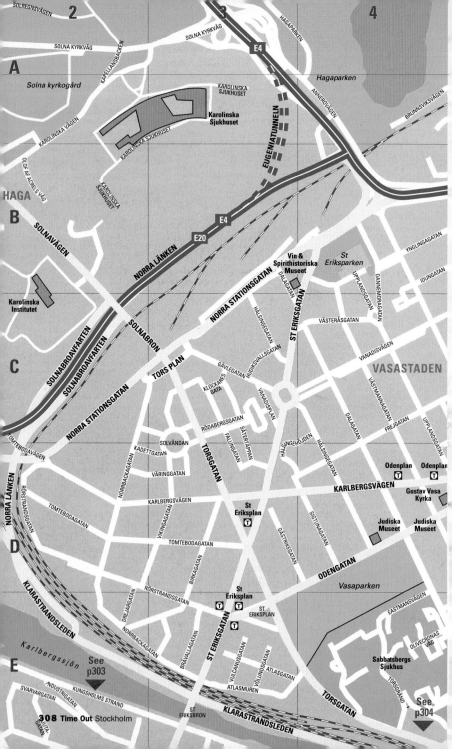

SOLREGNSVÄGEN

SOLNA KYRKVÄG

SOLNA KYRKVÄG

HAGAPARKEN

E4

A

KAPELLANSBACKEN

Solna kyrkogård

KAROLINSKA SJUKHUSET

Karolinska Sjukhuset

Hagaparken

ANNEROVÄGEN

BRUNNSVIKSVÄGEN

KAROLINSKA VÄGEN

KAROLINSKA SJUKHUSET

EUGENIATUNNELN

OLOF ACRELS VÄG

HAGA

SOLNAVÄGEN

KAROLINSKA SJUKHUSET

E4

B

E20

NORRA LÄNKEN

Vin & Spirithistoriska Museet

St Eriksparken

YNGLINGAGATAN

IDUNGATAN

Karolinska Institutet

NORRA STATIONSGATAN

DALAGATAN

ST ERIKSGATAN

UPPLANDSGATAN

DANNEMORAGATAN

VÄSTERÅSGATAN

HÄLSINGEGATAN

SOLNABROAVFARTEN

SOLNABROAVFARTEN

SOLNABRON

C

NORRA STATIONSGATAN

TORS PLAN

GÄVLEGATAN

HUDIKSVALLSGATAN

VANADISVÄGEN

VASASTADEN

VÄSTMANNAGATAN

KLOCKARES GATA

RÖDABERGSGATAN

SÄTERTÄPPAN

VANADISPLAN

DALAGATAN

FREJGATAN

UPPLANDSGATAN

TOMTEBODAVÄGEN

SOLVÄNDAN

KADETTGATAN

FALUNGATAN

HÄLSINGEHÖJDEN

HÄLSINGEGATAN

NORRA LÄNKEN

NORRBACKAGATAN

VÄRINGGATAN

TORSGATAN

Odenplan

Odenplan

RÖRSTRANDSGATAN

KARLBERGSVÄGEN

KARLBERGSVÄGEN

Gustav Vasa Kyrka

TOMTEBODAGATAN

VIKINGAGATAN

St Eriksplan

SIGTUNAGATAN

Judiska Museet

Judiska Museet

D

TOMTEBODAGATAN

BIRKAGATAN

GÄSTRIKEGATAN

ODENGATAN

Vasaparken

KLARASTRANDSLEDEN

RÖRSTRANDSGATAN

DREJARGATAN

NORRBACKAGATAN

St Eriksplan

ST ERIKSPLAN

EASTMANSVÄGEN

OLIVECRONAS VÄG

Karlbergssjön

BRÄVALLAGATAN

VULCANUSGATAN

VÖLUNDSGATAN

ATLASGATAN

E

See p303

KUNGSHOLMS STRAND

ST ERIKSGATAN

ATLASMUREN

Sabbatsbergs Sjukhus

TORSGATAN

TORSGRÄND

See p304

INDUSTRIGATAN

SVARTVARGATAN

NAUTA GATAN

308 Time Out Stockholm

ST ERIKSBRON

KLARASTRANDSLEDEN

TORSGATAN

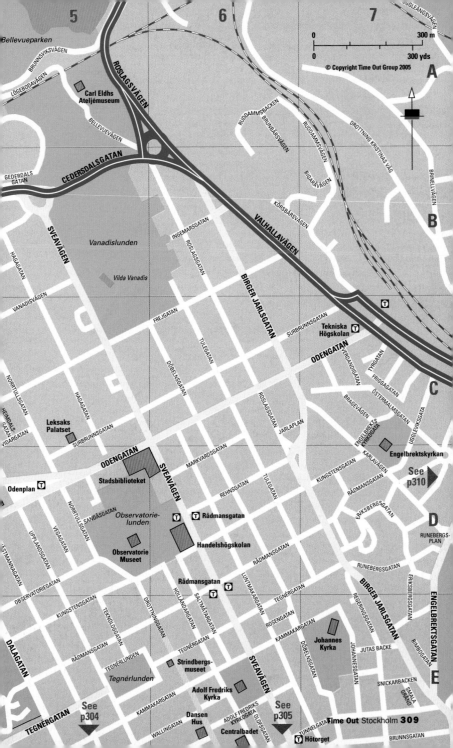

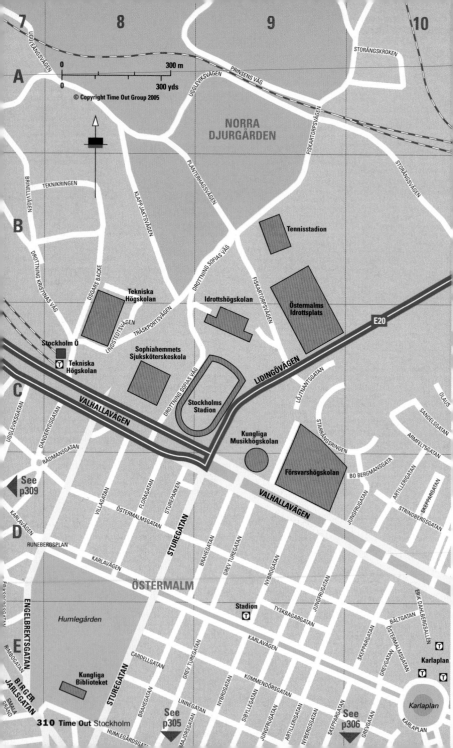

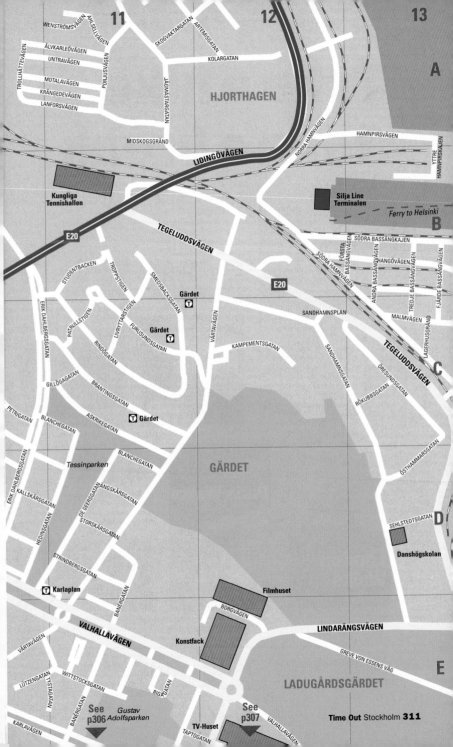

Take a hike...
take a break

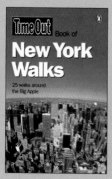

Available from all good bookshops
and at www.timeout.com/shop

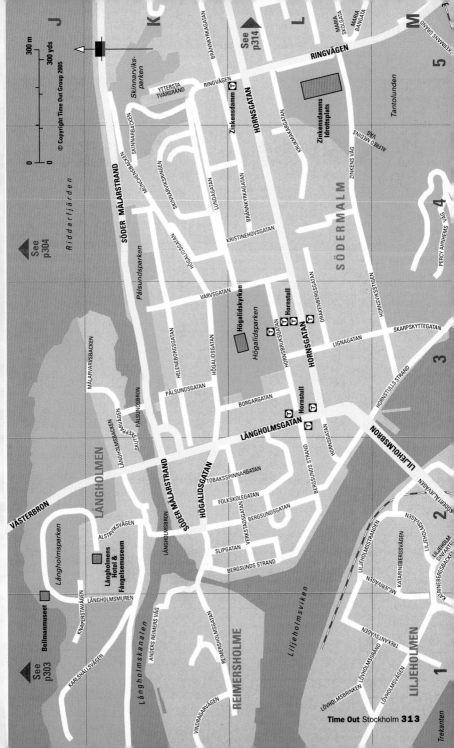

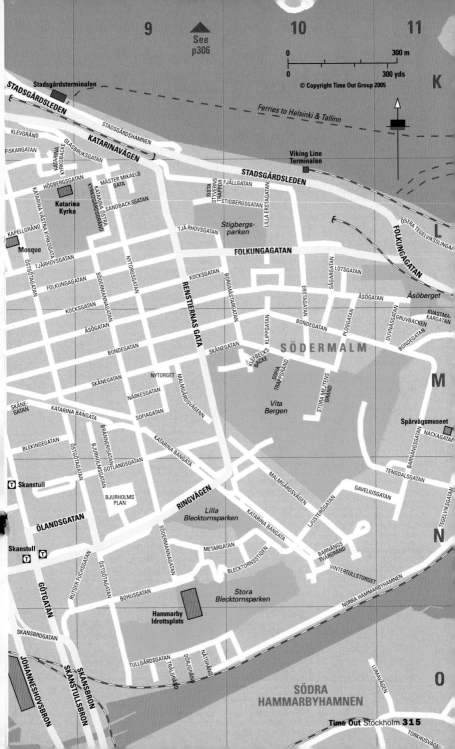

Street Index

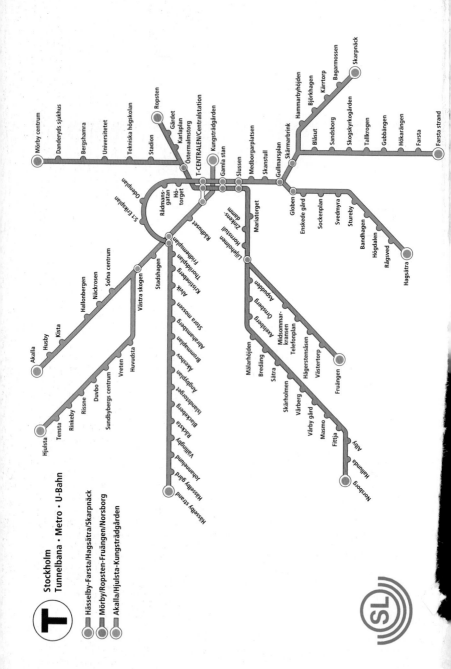

Stockholm
Tunnelbana · Metro · U-Bahn

Hässelby-Farsta/Hagsätra/Skarpnäck
Mörby/Ropsten-Fruängen/Norsborg
Akalla/Hjulsta-Kungsträdgården